Early New Englanders And Kin

A Genealogical Tree of more than 12,000 inter-related individuals with roots in early New England

By Roy Burgess

HERITAGE BOOKS, INC.

Other books by the author include:

Early Missourians and Kin Vol. 1 and 2

Published 1992 By

HERITAGE BOOKS INC.
1540E Pointer Ridge Place, Bowie, Maryland 20716
(301) 390-7709

ISBN 1-55613-644-7

A Complete Catalog Listing Hundreds of Titles on
History, Genealogy & Americana
Free on Request

ACKNOWLEDGEMENTS

I wish to acknowledge with sincere thanks, my gratitude to the many compilers, who have preceded me in building extensive genealogical data about our American ancestors, making it possible for me to add a bit more to this work.

The foundation we have created is quickly diminishing the unknowns about our forebearers. The time may not be far off when researching our relatives will require little personal effort.

I thank Dr. Laird Towle for his encouragement and suggestions during the progress of the work.

And, to Gloria Theen, my thanks and appreciation for her valued help as assistant compiler throughout the entire operation.

C O N T E N T S

INTRODUCTION

The format for this book is especially designed to be a "back-door" approach for genealogical researchers who cannot find public records or published documentations for their individual needs. How fortunate are those who have solved their ancestral and other related lineage problems the easy way, but, they are comparatively few, indeed.

Early New Englanders and Kin provides this new approach, by first laying down a network of inter-related individuals with their ancestors, descendants and date of birth, marriage, and death.

This book contains records of more than 12,000 kin, all related by blood or marriage. This is augmented by a companion book, *Early Missourians and Kin* having more than 14,000 entries. By connecting the links between the two books, the combined kin number is over 26,000 individuals.

This genealogical network provides an opportunity for a researcher to fill in some of the gaps that an individual may find in his lineages, including biographical data.

Evidence warrants an estimate that at least 40 percent of living Americans have New England ancestors. This book has a potential of supplying useful information to these people.

When a person has found one or more persons of his family group in the book index, he has available data about those individuals which include, birth, marriage and death dates, siblings, spouses, and their kin, ancestors, descendants, other blook kin, and kin by marriage.

Many notable persons are found among those in the index. Close and distant kinships to them may be established which include U. S. Presidents, Vice Presidents, Mayflower passengers, American heros, and even Royalty. In fact, the data allows an excellent opportunity to find a common ancestor for two ancestal lines, proving that they are all blood cousins. A pyramiding effect is created with each new linkage, making it easier to find other important kinships.

Familiarity with the book and its available information can create a very interesting new genealogical approach, combining practical genealogy with a new exciting hobby.

INSTRUCTIONS

The research material in this book consists of 4 components:
1.INDEX

	DIVISION
2.SIBLING GROUPS	S
3.ANCESTRAL GROUPS	A
4.DESCENDANT GROUPS	D

INDEX: (Contents)

a.An alphabetical listing of all members
of this network system. Every individual is related to all others either
by blood or marriage.

b."S","A" or "D" under "DIV" to show
which Division is represented.

c.An identification number assigned to
each member. One might have additional
numbers to designate other assignments
For example: He may be identified as
a sibling and also as a spouse or rel-
ative of a spouse; or, simply by ap-
pearing in more than one group. Each
requires a separate entry.

d.Birth, marriage, and death dates when
known.

Symbols used in S and D Divisions.
 Capital letters: Sibling (in "S")
 Lower case suffixes used in both
 "S" and "D" Divisions.
 a: first marriage
 b.c.d. etc.: 2nd,3rd, and
                 4th marriages.
 f: father of a spouse
 m: mother of a spouse
 ff: paternal g. father
 fm: paternal g. mother
 mf: maternal g. father
 mm: maternal g. mother

In some rare occasions additional f and
m suffixes are used to denote additional
generations. (One for each ancestral
generation.)

"S" DIVISION

This type of grouping is normally termed
"Family Group." The term "Sibling Group"
is used here because a group consists of
siblings and spouses, only. Although the
parents are shown heading the list, they
are listed elsewhere in Sibling groups
in which they personally belong.

The Division format is:
Top line: Bracketed number indicating
the number of the Sibling Group. This is
followed by the Group's surname.
Line 2: Father's name and identification
          number.
Line 3: Mother's name and identification
          number.
This is followed by a listing of the
siblings in capital letters. Spouses and
spouses' relatives are shown in lower
case using the symbols shown above.

A bracketed number, i.e. [W26] on the
same line with an individual indicates
where that person's children are found.
If this number is missing, this indicates that descendant data is unknown to
the compiler.

A person is identified in this division
as shown by this example:
                M25Cbmmf
M: An arbitrary component of the Sibling
    Groups

25: A specific Sibling Group
C: The third sibling. Normally the third
   birth if the sequence is known.
b: 2nd marriage
m: mother of spouse
m: maternal g. mother
f: father of maternal g. mother.

A sibling listing may not always be complete, being limited to available
information.

"A" DIVISION
The format is the same as normally used
in ancestral chart compilations.

A person's identification number is
formed by a prefix "A" designating the
"A" Division. This is followed by adding
a number to specify a particular ancestral group. A suffix is then added to
specify a certain person.

This suffix is derived by assigning
number 1 to the person represented by
the chart. His father is #2, twice that
of his child, and his mother twice plus
one, or #3. For each new generation in
ancestry this same principle holds.

A partial chart is shown to illustrate
this procedure:

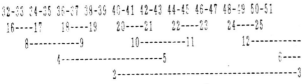

"D" DIVISION

This group consists of singular descent lineages.

Entries are identified as follows:
Prefix "D" to represent the division, followed by a number representing an arbitrary assignment for the group. A suffix is added representing a certain generation, beginning with a high number usually 25, and diminishing one for each generation of descent.

NAME	DIV.	NUMBER	BIRTH	MARRIAGE	DEATH
Abbiatti Michael	S	G59Aa	1945abt	1971Sep 25	
Abbott George	A	A12/180	1605abt		1647
Abbott George Jr	A	A12/90	1631ca	1658 Apr26	1688 Mar22
Abbott Lydia	A	A12/45	1675 Sep31	1695 Nov28	1748 Mar11
Abbott Lydia	S	K35Db	1710ca	1738 Nov30	1754living
Abeel Magdalena	A	A8/75	1657ca	1677 Aug29	1745 Oct20
Abeel Stoffel Janse	A	A8/150	1621	1660	1684
Adair Janet	A	A1/241	1714ca		
Adams Abiel	S	R17D	1685 Dec15	1707 Sep 3	1758
Adams Abraham Jr.	A	A4/452	1676	1703	1763
Adams Alice	S	R17B	1682 Apr 3	1700 Jan 7	1734 Feb19
Adams Bartlett	S	R96C	1738 Mar19		1741 May27
Adams C.	S	N14Db	1765ca		
Adams D.	S	N14Dc	1765abt		
Adams Deborah	S	R96F	1747 Oct17	unm.	1826 Feb23
Adams Edith	S	R16Ba	1688 Jun25	1711ca	1725bef
Adams Elizabeth	S	R17A	1680 Feb23	2 Mar	1766 Dec21
Adams Francis	S	R25Baf	1685abt		
Adams Henry	A	A11/128	~1531ca		1596 Aug12
Adams Henry	A	A11/32	1583 Jan21	1609 Oct19	1646 Oct6
Adams Joanna	S	K39Da	1705 Jan 6	1735ca	1779 Jan10
Adams John	A	A11/64	1555ca	1576ca	1603 Mar
Adams John	A	A11/4	1690 Feb8	1734 Nov23	1761 May25
Adams John Jr.	A	A11/2	1735 Oct19	1764 Oct25	1826 Jul 4
Adams John Quincy	A	A11/1	1767 Jul11	1797 Jul26	1848 Feb23
Adams Joseph	A	A11/16	1626 Feb9	1650 Nov2	1694 Dec6
Adams Joseph	S	K39Daf	1680abt		
Adams Joseph Jr.	A	A11/8	1654 Dec24	1688ca	1736 Feb12
Adams Joshua	S	R96B	1735 Nov21		
Adams Martha	A	A4/125	1730abt	1750 Oct18	
Adams Mary	S	R19Bam	1665abt		
Adams Mary	S	R96E	1744 Sep 3		1764 Feb17
Adams Nathaniel	S	R96D	1740 Nov18		
Adams Peletiah	S	R16Baf	1665abt		
Adams Samuel	A	A19/1502	1650abt		
Adams Samuel	S	R16Bbf	1670abt		
Adams Sarah	S	R96A	1732 Dec 3		
Adams Sarah	A	A4/113	1743 Sept3	1769 Oct12	
Adams Susanna	A	A19/751	1670abt		
Adams Susanna	S	R16Bb	1692 Mar13	1724 Dec 7	1752 Mar17

NAME	DIV.	NUMBER	BIRTH	MARRIAGE	DEATH
Adams Thomas	S	R25Ba	1709 May 5	1731 Dec23	1768 Dec12
Adams William	S	R17C	1683 Dec17		1699
Adams William	A	A4/226	1706 May 8	1729 Apr22	1765ca
Adams William Jr	S	R12Da	1650 May27	1680 Jan29	1685 Jun17
Adams William Sr	S	R12Daf	1625abt		
Adeliza of Clermont	D	D30/35	1100abt		
Adford Mary	A	A19/147	1651	1679	
Adgate Rebecca	S	R117Fam	1680abt		
Adriaens Jannetje	A	A7/131	1620abt li	=A8/131	1663ca
Adriaens Jennetje	A	A8/131	1620abt	=A8/131	1663bef
Ager Ebenezer	S	A19Da	1680ca	1703 Mar 1	1711bef
Ager Ebenezer	S	A42A	1706 Apr23		
Albee Benjamin	A	A2/92	1670ca	1694ca	
Albee James	A	A2/134	1645abt	1671	1717aft
Albee Obadiah	A	A2/46	1705 Oct29		
Albee Rhoda	A	A2/23	1731 Jun 1	1754 May28	1819 Jul19
Alcock Joanna	A	A8/215	1660	1678ca	1746
Alden Elizabeth	S	W19Aam	1635abt		=W19Cam
Alden Elizabeth	S	W19Cam	1635abt		=W19Eam
Alden Elizabeth	S	W28Eam	1635abt		=W19Cam
Alden Elizabeth	S	X13Aam	1635abt		=W19Cam
Alden Elizabeth	S	Q13Fa	1673ca	1733 Dec12	1705 May 8
Alden Hopestill	S	Q13Da	1665ca	1689ca	1753aft
Alden John MF	A	A11/38	1605ca	1624bef	1637Sep12
Alden Joseph	S	Q13Daf	1640abt		
Alden Joseph	S	Q13Faf	1650abt		
Alden Ruth	A	A11/19	1640ca	1657 Feb3	1674 Oct12
Alden Sarah	S	T11Ba	1630ca		1688 Jun13
Aldis Ann	S	C71C	1695		
Aldis Daniel	S	C46Ga	1665ca		
Aldis Daniel	S	C71B	1687		
Aldis Sarah	S	C71A	1686		
Aldis Sarah	S	C71D	1697ca		
Aldrich Jacob	A	A2/222	1677	1699	
Aldrich Mercy	A	A2/111	1700 Jun21	1717 Dec19	
Alexander Elizabeth	S	G54Da	1903 Aug11	1925 Dec25	1981 Aug30
Alexander Anne	S	A32Eam	1690abt		
Alexander Ebem	S	G54Daf	1361 Dec24	1896 Dec17	1935 Mar25
Alexander Mary	S	W28Iam	1670abt		
Alger Daniel	S	Q56B	1727ca		

NAME	DIV.	NUMBER	BIRTH	MARRIAGE	DEATH
Alger Israel	S	Q56A	1725ca		
Alger Israel Jr	S	Q20Ca	1689 Sep 9	1717 Dec25	1762 Nov13
Alger Israel Sr	S	Q20Caf	1665abt		
Alger James	S	Q56C	1728ca		
Alger Nancy	S	C42Ca	1776ca		
Alice of Roucy	D	D30/37	1035abt		
Allen Abigail	A	A6/233	1640	1659ca	1696aft
Allen Abigail	S	R19Eam	1665abt		
Allen Amy	S	W51Aam	1660abt		
Allen Amy	S	W51Dam	1660abt		
Allen Amy	A	A5/39	1663 Aug15	1683 Dec 7	1710Feb 24
Allen Daniel	S	W45Baf	1660abt		
Allen Ebenezer	A	A2/38	1694 Sep25	1719 Jul19	1778 Apr2
Allen Elizabeth	S	W36Aam	1650abt		
Allen George	S	Q11Baf	1600abt		
Allen Hannah	S	W45Ba	1688 Jun 2	1710 Oct 2	1742 aft
Allen James	A	A2/152	1615abt	1637ca	1676
Allen James	A	A5/78	1637ca		1714 Jul25
Allen Jedediah	A	A3/458	1646	1668	1711
Allen Mary	A	A3/229	1681 Nov15	1717ca	
Allen Mary	S	Q13Aa	1718 Jul 9	1741 May13	1790ca
Allen Mary	A	A2/19	1722 Jul22	1745 May17	1790 Aug19
Allen Nathaniel	A	A2/76	1648 Aug29	1677 Apr10	1718
Allen Samuel	S	T11Fbf	1615abt		
Allen Samuel	A	A5/156	1615abt		1663
Allen Samuel	S	Q13Fbf	1640abt		
Allen Sarah	S	T11Fb	1639 Mar30	(2) unk	1690 Sep16
Allen Sarah	S	Q13Fb	1667 Apr14	1705 Oct25	1738living
Allen Susanna	S	C42Ba	1761ca		
Allen William	S	Q11Ba	1627ca	1649 Mar21	1705 Oct 1
Allen William	S	Q19Aaf	1690abt		
Allerton Bartholomew	S	A11A	1612ca	2 mar.	1658
Allerton Dorothy	S	A12C	1640ca		
Allerton Elizabeth	S	A15A	1653 Sep27	2 mar.	1740 Nov17
Allerton Elizabeth	S	A29B	1708ca	1734ca	1747aft
Allerton Frances	S	A15E	1668ca	1685 Jul 1	1698aft
Allerton Gawin	S	A76A	1725abt		
Allerton Isaac	S	A11B	1630ca	2 mar.	1702 Oct
Allerton Isaac	S	A12A	1635ca		
Allerton Isaac	S	A15B	1655 Jun11		

NAME	DIV.	NUMBER	BIRTH	MARRIAGE	DEATH
Allerton Isaac	S	A29A	1702ca	1733ca	1739
Allerton Isaac	S	A76C	1727abt		d. yng
Allerton Isaac Jr	A	A18/22	1627May	1662 Sep 8	1702
Allerton Isaac MF	S	A10A	1586ca	2 mar.	
Allerton Isaac Sr MF	A	A18/44	1585ca	1626ca	=A10A
Allerton John	S	A12D	1642ca		
Allerton Mary	S	W20Dam	1615abt	1636ca	1699Nov 28
Allerton Mary	S	A12B	1637ca		
Allerton Mary	S	A15D	1666ca	1685ca	1700bef
Allerton Mary =P22Aam	S	A11C	1616ca	1636ca	1699 Nov28
Allerton Mary =A11C	A	A8/201	1615	1636ca	1699Nov 28
Allerton Mary=A11C	S	K14Eam	1615ca	1636ca	1699Nov 28
Allerton Mary=W20Dam	S	P22Aam	1615ca	1636ca	1699Nov 28
Allerton Remember	S	A11B	1614ca	1635bef	1655ca
Allerton Sarah	S	P10Aa	1585ca	1611 Nov 4	1633bef
Allerton Sarah	S	A11D	1627ca		d.yng
Allerton Sarah=A15F	A	A18/11	1671ca	1700	1731May 17
Allerton Sarah=A18/11	S	A15F	1670ca	1700ca	1731 May17
Allerton Willoughby	S	A15C	1664ca	3 mar.	1724ca
Allerton Willoughby	S	A76B	1726abt		
Alley Hugh	A	A12/214	1608ca		1674ca
Alley Mary	A	A12/107	1641 Jan 6	1667 Jun 6	1680 Jan 2
Allyn Mary	S	R21Dam	1675abt		
Almy Elizabeth	A	A3/453	1663		1711aft
Almy Katherine	S	K12Eam	1630abt		
Ames Abigail	S	K81D	1705 Feb 9		
Ames Benjamin	S	K81H	1714 Feb24		
Ames Daniel	S	K81G	1712 Oct 7		
Ames Deborah	S	K81F	1710 Apr 1	unm	1755
Ames Elizabeth	S	Q21Aam	1675abt		
Ames Elizabeth	S	K81A	1697 Dec 9		
Ames John	S	K81B	1700 Mar19		
Ames John Jr	S	K22Ka	1672 Apr14	1696 Jan12	1756 Jan 1
Ames John Sr	S	K22Kaf	1650abt		
Ames Jonathan	S	K81E	1707 Jun10		
Ames Joshua	S	K81I	1718 Apr 9		1755Nov 25
Ames Sarah	S	K81C	1702 Jan23		
Amos Mary	S	T25Dam	1680abt		
Amos S.	S	N14Da	1765ca		
Anderson Mary	A	A8/171	1660abt	1682	1717

NAME	DIV.	NUMBER	BIRTH	MARRIAGE	DEATH
Andover Christopher	A	A3/78	1755	1780	1831
Andover Joseph	A	A3/156	1730abt	1751 July1	
Andover Margaret	A	A3/39	1805ca		
Andrews Abigail	A	A12/117	1620ca		1655 Jun24
Andrews Abigail	S	K16Iam	1645abt		
Andrews Ann	A	A2/115	1685ca	1706 Nov 7	
Andrews Henry	S	X23Aaf	1640abt		
Andrews Henry	S	X23Caf	1640abt		
Andrews John Jr.	A	A2/230	1648ca	1685ca	1706abt
Andrews Mary	S	X23Aa	1665ca	1685 Jun26	1737aft
Andrews Mehitable	S	X23Ca	1670ca	1694 Dec20	1704aft
Andrews Robert	A	A12/234	1595abt		1644
Andrus Hannah	S	C31Ha	1720ca		
Andrus Mary	S	C31Da	1710ca		
Angell Daniel	S	C88G	1720		
Angell Daniel Sr	S	C77Ba	1680		
Angell Ezekial	S	C88H	1722		
Angell Job	S	C88F	1718		
Angell John	S	C87Ca	1709		
Angell John	S	C88B	1709		
Angell Joshua	S	C88D	1714		
Angell Mercy	S	C88E	1716		
Angell Nedebiah=C87Ga	S	C88C	1712		
Angell Nedebiah=C88C	S	C87Ga	1712		
Angell Samuel	S	C88A	1707		
Angell Stephen	S	C90Ga	1730abt		
Angell Wait	S	C88I	1724ca		
Angier Edmund	A	A17/114	1580abt		1677
Angier William	A	A17/228	1550ca		1620
Ansel Mary	S	F15Aam	1630abt		
Appell Margaret	D	D33a19	1999 Nov17	1913Sep 3	1988Jan 2
Appleton Jane	A	A17/1a	1806Mar 12		1863Dec 2
Appleton Patricia	A	A19/367	1665abt		
Arey Sarah	S	K30Cbm	1690abt		
Armistead Anthony	A	A14/312	1587ca	1608	
Armistead Anthony	A	A15/48	1640abt		1726Oct26
Armistead Elizabeth	A	A14/39	165abt	1703 Oct 5	1716 Nov16
Armistead Ellyson	A	A15/12	1710abt		1757ca
Armistead John	A	A14/78	1640ca		1688aft
Armistead Mary Marot	A	A15/3	1761ca	1776ca	1797 Apr 5

NAME	DIV.	NUMBER	BIRTH	MARRIAGE	DEATH
Armistead Robert	A	A15/24	1685abt		1742ca
Armistead Robert Booth	A	A15/6	1735abt	1760ca	1767bef
Armistead William	A	A14/156	1610 Aug	1632	1666bef
Armistead William	A	A15/96	1610 Aug	1632	1666bef
Armstrong Elizabeth	A	A3/61	1757 Mar17		1837 Jan15
Armstrong Ephraim	A	A3/122	1730abt	1753ca	1788
Arnold Ann	S	C49Hb	1700ca		
Arnold Catherine	A	A6/25	1690abt	1713 Jan25	
Arnold Elizabeth	S	H27Dbm	1650abt		
Arnold Elizabeth	S	W44Ea	1685ca	1709ca	1730ca
Arnold Seth	S	W44Eaf	1660abt		
Ashley Abigail	A	A8/115	1681 Apr27	1699 Nov25	1723 Apr11
Ashley David	A	A8/230	1642	1663	1718
Ashley Leonard	S	N15Aa	1775ca		
Ashley Mary	A	A12/83	1644 Apr 6	1664 Oct18	
Ashley Robert	A	A12/166	1620ca	1641	1682
Ashton Joshua	S	C93A	1716		
Ashton Mary	D	D29a13	1540abt		
Ashton Rebecca	S	C93D	1720abt		
Ashton Thomas	S	C93C	1720abt		
Ashton William	S	C78Ea	1680		
Ashton William	S	C93B	1718abt		
Aspinwall John	A	A8/20	1735ca	1766 Jun 5	1774 Jul15
Aspinwall John Jr	D	D4a20	1774 Feb10	1803 Nov27	1847 Oct 6
Aspinwall John Jr.	A	A8/10	1774 Feb10	1803 Nov27	1847 Oct 6
Aspinwall John Sr	D	D4af20	1730abt	1766 Jun 5	1774 Jul15
Aspinwall Joseph	A	A8/40	1673 Oct 9	1700 Jul13	1743ca
Aspinwall JosephA08/40	D	D4aff20	1673 Oct 9	1700 Jul13	1743ca
Aspinwall Mary Rebecca	A	A8/5	1809 Dec20	1827 Apr26	1886 Feb24
Aspinwall Mary Rebecca	D	D4/19	1809 Dec20	1827 Apr26	1886 Feb24
Aspinwall Peter	A	A8/80	1612ca	1661 Feb12	1687 Dec 1
Atherold Hannah	A	A10/13	1615ca	1638 Jul 2	1695ca
Atkins Abigail	S	K22Bc	1655ca	1711 Jul24	1732aft
Atkins Experience	S	T15Ha	1706ca	1728 Nov 6	1761living
Atkins Thomas	S	K22Bcf	1630abt		
Atwood Anna	S	H35C	1687 Jan		
Atwood Benjamin	S	H35H	1701 Jun		
Atwood Deborah	S	H35D	1690 Mar		1734 May30
Atwood Ebenezer	S	H35G	1697 Mar		
Atwood Eldad	S	H16Aa	1651 Jul 2	1683 Feb14	1707ca

NAME	DIV.	NUMBER	BIRTH	MARRIAGE	DEATH
Atwood Eldad	S	H35F	1695 Jul 9		
Atwood John	S	H35B	1686 Aug10		
Atwood Mary	S	H35A	1684 Nov		
Atwood Sarah	S	H35E	1692 Apr	1726 May17	
Atwood Stephen	S	H16Aaf	1625abt		
Auchmuty Isabelle	S	P21Na	1720abt	1749 Dec30	1778ca
Auchmuty Robert	S	P21Naf	1685abt		
Auger Henrietta	S	G43Ba	1545abt	1565 Jun11	
Auger Pierre	S	G42Baf	1520abt		
Austem Agnes(Anne)	A	A16/141	1596		1677
Austin Anthony	A	A12/56	1636 Mar	1664 Oct19	1708 Aug22
Austin Daniel	A	A12/14	1720	1749 Dec21	1804 Jun24
Austin Drusilla	A	A12/7	1762 Apr 3	1790 Dec 2	1813 Mar 3
Austin Nathaniel	A	A12/28	1678 May20	1701 Jan27	1760 Dec12
Austin Richard	A	A12/112	1598ca		1638aft
Avery John	S	W32Ga	1685 Feb 4	1710 Nov28	1754 Apr23
Avery Robert	S	W32Gaf	1660abt		
Ayer Adele Augusta	A	A4/7	1867 Dec	1884 Oct 3	
Ayer Daniel	A	A4/112	1743 Jan28	1769 Oct12	1805 Jun 6
Ayer George Manney	A	A4/14	1840 March		1864ca
Ayer James	A	A4/448	1686	1711	1771
Ayer John Varnum	A	A4/28	1912 Jan 3		1877ca
Ayer Samuel	A	A4/56	1777 Dec13	1805 Nov28	1847 Dec12
Ayer William	A	A4/224	1716 Jun18	1741 Jul28	1765living
Ayers Benjamin	S	A28D	1688 Jun19	1713 Apr 9	1753 Sep 1
Ayers Benjamin (Eyres)	S	A75A	1713ca		
Ayers Clemens (Eyres)	S	A75C	1720abt		
Ayers Elizabeth	S	A28E	1691 Oct30		
Ayers Elizabeth(Eyres)	S	A75B	1717 Apr		
Ayers Isaac	S	A28C	1683 Feb23		d.yng
Ayers Lydia	S	A28A	1680 Sep17		
Ayers Simon	S	A15Ab	1652 Aug 6	1679 Jul22	1695
Ayers Simon	S	A28B	1682 Sep 5	unm	1758 Apr 5
Ayers Simon Sr	S	A15Abf	1630abt		
Ayres Ann	S	C21Ja	1780ca		
Babcock Ebenezer	S	B19Aa	1695abt	1722 Oct 9	
Babcock Sarah	S	C14Aa	1710ca		
Backus Elizabeth	S	T27Cam	1685abt		
Backus John	S	R19Daf	1670abt		
Backus Mary	S	R19Da	1692 Nov 8	1712 Dec 3	1770 Oct19

NAME	DIV.	NUMBER	BIRTH	MARRIAGE	DEATH
Bacon Desire	S	W49Aa	1688 Mar15	1709 Mar	1730 Dec29
Bacon Elizabeth	A	A19/181	1695	1715	1761
Bacon James	A	A14/270	1590abt		1649 Nov 9
Bacon James	A	A14/302	1590abt		1649 Nov 9
Bacon John	S	W49Aaf	1660abt		
Bacon John	S	C19Aa	1745ca		
Bacon Martha	A	A14/135	1630abt	1651ca	
Bacon Martha	A	A14/151	1630abt	1651ca	
Bacon Mary	S	W31Cbm	1680abt		
Bacon Mercy	S	WW31Cam	1660abt		
Bagg Eunice	S	N13Ha	1750ca		
Baggs Jonathan	S	B13Caf	1650ca		
Baggs Thomasine	S	B13Ca	1678ca		
Bailey Elizabeth	S	W18Eam	1635abt		
Baille Lucy	A	A13/79	1635abt		
Baillie Ann Elizabeth	A	A7/27	1749 Sep27	1765 Sep	1807 Jul23
Baillie Jean	A	A7/109	1695abt	1718 Dec18	1747ca
Baillie John	A	A7/108	1695abt	1718 Dec18	1747abt
Baillie Kenneth	A	A7/54	1725abt		
Baker Abigail	S	R23D	1693 Dec23	1720 Feb 9	1753 Sep25
Baker Abigail	S	R84I	1746 Sep24		
Baker Alice	S	R23B	1690 Nov 3	1713 Mar 4	1715 Jun14
Baker Alice	S	R83B	1722 Jan26		
Baker Anna	S	R86F	1761 Mar16		
Baker Bethiah	S	R23F	1699 May12	1720 Dec29	1741 Jul13
Baker Bethiah	S	R84C	1733 May11		
Baker Bethiah	S	R85C	1744 Mar30		
Baker Charles	S	R84G	1741 Apr26		
Baker Edward	S	R23J	1705 Oct18	2 Mar	1781 Mar 1
Baker Edward	S	R86A	1748 Mar 6		
Baker Eleanor	S	R23C	1692 Mar31	1716 Jan17	1727 May 6
Baker Eleanor	S	R84A	1727 Sep21		
Baker Elijah	S	R84H	1744 Jul 1		
Baker Elizabeth	S	R83F	1730 Jul29		
Baker Hannah	S	R84B	1729 Feb25		
Baker Hannah	S	R86C	1753 Nov 9		
Baker James	S	R84E	1737 Jan 4		
Baker Jeremiah	S	C20Ea	1753ca		
Baker Jeremiah	S	C22Db	1791		
Baker John	S	R83A	1719 Oct18		

NAME	DIV.	NUMBER	BIRTH	MARRIAGE	DEATH
Baker John	A	A9/30	1797ca		1858 May23
Baker Kenelm	S	R12Ja	1657Mar 23	1687ca	1712ca
Baker Kenelm	S	R23E	1695 Nov 3	1718 Jan22	1771 May22
Baker Kenelm #1	S	R83C	1724		
Baker Kenelm #2	S	R83E	1728 Jul 1		
Baker Keziah	S	R23G	1701 Aug15		1713living
Baker Luceanna	S	W45E	1689 Nov	unmar	1769Jul 11
Baker Lucy	S	R83H	1737 May15		
Baker Lydia	S	W27Aa	1659 Feb18	1681ca	1732abt
Baker Lydia	S	W45Dbm	1660abt		
Baker Mary	S	W28Kam	1660abt		
Baker Mary	A	A9/15	1819ca	1838 Dec25	1860aft
Baker Mehitable	S	R86B	1749 Mar11	unm.	1793 Sep
Baker Priscilla	A	A19/91	1724 Aug 4	1752Dec 9	1812Mar 16
Baker Samuel	S	W27Aaf	1635abt		
Baker Samuel	S	R12Jaf	1635abt		
Baker Samuel	S	R23H	1702 Feb 5	1726 Nov 9	1793 Nov 4
Baker Samuel	S	R84D	1735 Feb26		1759 May
Baker Samuel Jr	S	W42Ea	1678ca	1699	1721 Jan16
Baker Samuel Sr	S	W42Eaf	1650abt		
Baker Sarah	A	A14/161	1600ca	1622	1676
Baker Sarah	S	R23A	1688 Oct28	1712 Mar26	1765living
Baker Sarah	S	R83D	1726 Apr21		
Baker Sarah	S	R85B	1742 Jul 7		
Baker Shute	S	R86D	1756 Nov 7		
Baker Thankful	S	C23Ca	1775ca		
Baker Thomas	S	R84F	1739 Jan24		
Baker Thomas Jr	A	A19/182	1687	1709	1725
Baker William	S	R23I	1705 Oct18	1739 Jan31	1785 Dec10
Baker William	S	R83G	1734 Oct16		
Baker William	S	R85A	1741 Jun13		
Baker William	S	C23Aa	1765ca		
Ballington Agnes	S	G3Aa	1400abt		
Baldwin Grace	A	A12/247	1590ca		1667ca
Baldwin Hannah	A	A3/49	1748 Nov 4	1767 Oct22	1825 Oct20
Baldwin Jerusha	S	G30Aa	1765abt		
Baldwin John III	A	A3/196	1697 Apr10	1719 Apr11	1728
Baldwin John Jr.	A	A3/392	1665abt	1689	1731
Baldwin Joshua	A	A3/98	1721 Nov13	1747 Sep17	1809 May13
Ball Joseph	A	A10/6	1649 May24	1707aft	1711

NAME	DIV.	NUMBER	BIRTH	MARRIAGE	DEATH
Ball Mary	A	A10/3	1708ca	1731 Mar 6	1789 Aug25
Ball William	A	A10/12	1615ca	1638 Jul 2	1680 Nov15
Ballentine Elizabeth	S	P22Ba	1659 Mar 8	1687	1722 Jun12
Ballentine William	S	P22Baf	1630abt		
Ballou Desire	S	C63Ca	1792ca		
Ballou Eliza	A	A6/3	1801 Sep21	1820 Feb 3	1888 Jan21
Ballou James	A	A6/48	1660abt	1683 Jul25	1744after
Ballou James III	A	A6/12	1723 Dec10	1744 June7	1812 Jan21
Ballou James IV	A	A6/6	1761 Apr25	1786 Nov 5	1808 Apr30
Ballou James Jr.	A	A6/24	1684 Nov 1	1713 Jan25	1764 Feb10
Ballou Maturin	A	A6/96	1630abt		1661abt
Bampfield Agnes	D	D30/24	1400abt		
Bampfield John Jr	D	D30/27	1325abt		
Bampfield John Sir Sr	D	D30a28	1290abt		
Bampfield Thomas	D	D30/25	1375abt		
Bangs Elijah Keeler	A	A1/54	1780 Jun 4	1807 Oct29	1856 Sep13
Bangs Hannah	S	H17Eam	1645abt		
Bangs Joseph	A	A1/216	1713 Jan30	1735 Sep18	1757ca
Bangs Lemuel	A	A1/108	1739 Dec31	1774ca	1824 May 9
Bangs Lydia	S	H31Cam	1650abt		
Bangs Mary Ann	A	A1/27	1817 Jun15	1840 Jun 1	
Bangs Rebecca	S	H27Aam	1635abt		=X15Bam
Bangs Rebecca=H27Aam	S	X15Bam	1635abt		
Bangs Samuel	A	A1/432	1680	1703	1750
Bangs Sarah	S	H26Bam	1650abt		
Barker Abigail	S	W45A	1682 Aug 4	1717 April1	1763bef
Barker Alice	S	W11Aam	1635abt		
Barker Alice	S	W45G	1695 Jun 3	1712 Jun 5	1778 Dec14
Barker Ann	S	P12Aa	1643	1663ca	1695aft
Barker Bethiah	S	L15Bb	1715 Sep17		1790 Nov21
Barker Caleb	S	W45C	1685 May24	1709 Jan18	1772 Aug25
Barker Deborah	S	W45D	1686 Nov 7	2 Mar	1734ca
Barker Francis	S	W31Jaf	1660abt		
Barker James	S	W45B	1683 Jan 1	1710 Oct 2	1718 Jul16
Barker John	S	P12Aaf	1620abt		
Barker John	S	P12Caf	1620abt		
Barker John	S	P13Bbf	1620abt		
Barker Lydia	S	W45H	1697 Sep 5	1728 Apr 2	1776 Oct20
Barker Mary	S	C77Ca	1678		
Barker Mary=P12Ca	S	P13Bb	1647ca	1678ca	1711aft

NAME	DIV.	NUMBER	BIRTH	MARRIAGE	DEATH
Barker Mary=P13Bb	S	P12Ca	1647ca	1667ca	1711aft
Barker Rebecca	S	W16Ba	1645abt	1669ca	1711 Apr28
Barker Rebecca =W16Ba	S	W44Bam	1655abt		
Barker Robert	S	W16Fa	1651ca	1681abt	1729 Sep25
Barker Robert	S	W45F	1693 Jul 4	1722 Oct 7	1758ca
Barker Thomas=L15Bbf	S	W31Ja	1684ca	1712 May22	1732ca
Barker Thomas=W31Ja	S	L15Bbf	1684ca	1712 May22	1732ca
Barlow Ebenezer	S	K31Ea	1692 May10	1719 Nov18	1754 May 4
Barlow John	S	T15Aaf	1670abt		
Barlow Mary	S	K121E	1730 Dec20		
Barlow Moses	S	K31Eaf	1670abt		
Barlow Moses #1	S	K121A	1720 Sep 6		d. yng
Barlow Moses #2	S	K121B	1722 May29		d. yng
Barlow Sarah	S	T15Aa	1693 Oct15	17150ct	1733 Jul 2
Barlow Sarah	S	K121D	1727 Jul 7		
Barlow Seth	S	K121C	1725 Mar29		d. yng
Barnaby James	S	W12Ga	1645abt	1670abt	1675abt
Barnaby James Jr	S	W25A	1670	1697ca	1726 Jul5
Barnaby Joanna	S	W15D	1689May 9		
Barnaby Stephen	S	W25B	1674ca	1696 Dec10	1727abt
Barnard Mary	S	C74Ba	1609		
Barnard Rebecca	A	A13/19	1695ca		
Barnard Richard	A	A13/38	1650abt	1678	1698ca
Barnes Benjamin #1	S	R35D	1711 Dec11		d. yng.
Barnes Benjamin #2	S	R35E	1717 Dec20		
Barnes Deborah=X26Aam	S	X26Fam	1665abt		
Barnes Deborah=X26Fam	S	X26Aam	1665abt		
Barnes Elizabeth	S	X15Dam	1645abt		
Barnes Esther	S	W18Fb	1670abt		
Barnes Hannah	S	W22Ba	1660ca	1692ca	1703 Jan17
Barnes Hannah	S	R37D	1718ca		
Barnes Hester	S	K14Dam	1635abt		
Barnes Hester	S	A25Aa	1682 Feb18	1702 Feb23	1770 Nov 1
Barnes Hester	S	R27Cam	1682Feb 18	1702Feb 23	1770 Nov 1
Barnes John	S	W23Ea	1669 Mar6	1693 Jul6	1744 May15
Barnes John	S	W56Gaf	1680abt		
Barnes Jonathan	S	W22Baf	1635abt		
Barnes Jonathan	S	W23Eaf	1640abt		=R15Aaf
Barnes Jonathan	S	W23Gaf	1640abt		=W23eAF
Barnes Jonathan	S	R15Aaf	1640abt		=W23Gaf

NAME	DIV.	NUMBER	BIRTH	MARRIAGE	DEATH
Barnes Jonathan	S	W18Fbf	1640abt		
Barnes Jonathan	S	A25Aaf	1660abt		
Barnes Jonathan	S	W56Ga	1703 Dec16	1726 Sep 8	1748 Oct 2
Barnes Jonathan Jr	S	R15Ca	1684	1708	1737bef
Barnes Jonathan Sr	S	R15Caf	1640abt		=W23Gaf
Barnes Lemuel	S	R35B	1707 Feb16		
Barnes Lydia	S	K29Cam	1680abt		
Barnes Lydia	S	R37C	1714 Jan30		
Barnes Mary	S	K25Fam	1670abt		
Barnes Mercy	S	R35C	1708 Dec19		
Barnes Rebecca	S	R37B	1711 Mar14		
Barnes Sarah	S	W23Ga	1680 Feb28	1702 Oct15	1733aft
Barnes Sarah	S	R37A	1709 Oct 9		
Barnes William	S	R15Aa	1670 Feb14	1704 Nov20	1751 Mar31
Barnes William	S	R35A	1706 Jan 5		1730 Apr16
Barney John	S	C38Da	1728ca		
Barney Joseph	S	C31Ca	1705 abt		
Barney Joseph	S	C38Ea	1732ca		
Barnhill John	A	A7/20	1730abt		1797 Feb27
Barnhill Margaret	A	A7/5	1799 Dec13	1822ca	1861 Jan23
Barnhill Robert	A	A7/40	1700abt		
Barnhill Robert	A	A7/10	1745 Jan31	1778 Sep22	1814 Aug12
Barr Joan	S	A15Dam	1635abt		
Barrett Elizabeth	A	A6/113	1630abt	1667 May26	1718aft
Barrett Lydia	A	A19/217	1659	1678	
Barrett Margaret	A	A5/137	1600abt		
Barron Mary	S	W38Ham	1640abt		
Barrow Mehitable	S	K15Ab	1665ca	1699bef	1744aft
Barrow Robert	S	K15Abf	1635abt		
Barrows Coombs	S	P56B	1704 Dec15		
Barrows Ebenezer	S	P56A	1702 Jul27		
Barrows Elizabeth	S	R26Mam	1710abt		
Barrows Robert	S	P23Baf	1650abt		
Barrows Robert	S	P56C	1709 May17		
Barrows Samuel	S	P23Ba	1672	1701ca	1755 Dec29
Barrows Silvanus	S	P56D	1716 May17		
Barstow Mary	S	W23Dam	1640abt		
Barstow Patience	S	W42Eam	1650abt		
Barstow Sarah	S	W15Da	1645ca	1665ca	1717aft
Bartlett Abigail	S	W58I	1703ca		

NAME	DIV.	NUMBER	BIRTH	MARRIAGE	DEATH
Bartlett Abigail	S	R21Ga	1704 Mar18	1728 Aug30	1776 Aug30
Bartlett Abigail	S	K110I	1745 Nov28		
Bartlett Abigail	S	K114H	1751 Aug21		d.yng
Bartlett Abigail	S	K114M	1762 Nov22		
Bartlett Ann	S	X27Fa	1723 Aug 9	1744 Jun21	1765aft
Bartlett Benjamin	S	W12A	1633abt	1654 Apr 4	1691 Aug
Bartlett Benjamin	S	R12Baf	1640abt		
Bartlett Benjamin	S	W44Caf	1645abt		
Bartlett Benjamin	S	R12Laf	1655abt	1677ca	1724bef
Bartlett Benjamin	S	R14Aaf	1655abt	1677ca	1724bef
Bartlett Benjamin	S	R21Gaf	1655abt	1677ca	1724bef
Bartlett Benjamin	S	W19A	1658ca	1677ca	1724 bef
Bartlett Benjamin	S	W23G	1679ca	1702 Oct15	1717 Mar11
Bartlett Caleb	S	K115J	1755 Feb 8		
Bartlett Charles	S	K110M	1754ca		
Bartlett Chloe #1	S	K114B	1735 Aug26		d.yng
Bartlett Chloe #2	S	K114F	1743 May24		d.yng
Bartlett Daniel	S	X27Faf	1700abt		
Bartlett Deborah	S	W58H	1700ca		
Bartlett Diamond #1	S	K114J	1756 Mar11		d.yng
Bartlett Diamond #2	S	K114L	1759 Oct 9		
Bartlett Ebenezer	S	W19D	1665abt	1725Aug 15	1697abt
Bartlett Ebenezer	S	K30I	1710 Dec 5	2 Mar	1758living
Bartlett Ebenezer	S	K114I	1754 Jan28		1758living
Bartlett Elizabeth	S	W12F	1643ca	1661 Dec26	1712 Feb17
Bartlett Elizabeth	S	K30G	1706 Mar 2	1734 May16	1751bef
Bartlett Elnathan	S	W23C	1666ca	1712 Apr24	1714 Feb7
Bartlett Ephraim	S	K115B	1737 Sep 8		
Bartlett George	S	K110L	1751ca		
Bartlett Hannah	S	W23D	1668ca	1690 Apr	1755abt
Bartlett Hannah	S	K30A	1691 Feb21	1711ca	1757 Sep19
Bartlett Hannah	S	K110C	1727 Dec13		
Bartlett Hannah	S	K112F	1749 Nov30		
Bartlett Ichabod	S	W19F	1672ca	1699Dec 28	1715ca
Bartlett Ichabod=W19F	S	W44Ca	1672abt	1699 Dec28	1715abt
Bartlett Isaac	S	K115D	1742 Sep14		
Bartlett James	S	K30E	1701 Aug 7		1722 Jan13
Bartlett James	S	K114A	1733 Nov 5		
Bartlett James	S	K115G	1749 Aug16		d. yng
Bartlett Jean #1	S	K116D	1752 Apr28		d.yng

NAME	DIV.	NUMBER	BIRTH	MARRIAGE	DEATH
Bartlett Jean #2	S	K116E	1754 Jun28		
Bartlett Jenney	S	K110G	1740 May		d. yng
Bartlett Jerusha	S	K110A	1723 Mar21		d.yng
Bartlett Jerusha	S	K110E	1735 Nov10		
Bartlett John	S	K30C	1696 Apr13	3 Mar	1773 Feb 6
Bartlett John	S	K110F	1737 Feb26		
Bartlett Joseph	S	W12E	1638	1662ca	1711 Feb18
Bartlett Joseph	S	W23B	1665ca	1692 Jun 6	1703 Apr9
Bartlett Joseph	S	K30F	1703 Feb22	1727 Apr 4	1783 May30
Bartlett Joseph	S	K112B	1738 Oct12		
Bartlett Joseph=W12E	S	W19Eaf	1638	1662ca	1711Feb 18
Bartlett Joseph=W12E	S	K14Haf	1638	1662ca	1711 Feb18
Bartlett Joshua	S	K115F	1747 Apr 1		
Bartlett Josiah	S	K112D	1744 Dec 1		d.yng
Bartlett Josiah	S	K115I	1753 Feb 8		
Bartlett Lazarus	S	K115E	1744 Oct25		
Bartlett Lemuel	S	K30K	1715 Dec 9	1742 Nov25	1792 May29
Bartlett Lemuel	S	K116A	1743 Jan29		
Bartlett Lewis	S	K110H	1743 Apr 1		
Bartlett Lydia	S	W12G	1648 Jun8	1670abt	1691 Sep11
Bartlett Lydia	S	W43Bam	1660abt		
Bartlett Malachi	S	K115K	1758 Jun19		
Bartlett Maria	S	K110J	1748 Apr 8		
Bartlett Martha	S	K112E	1746 Feb 4		
Bartlett Mary	S	W12C	1634ca		1692 Sep26
Bartlett Mary	S	W23E	1672ca	1693 Jul6	1726 Feb20
Bartlett Mary	S	W56Gam	1680abt		
Bartlett Mary	S	K110D	1730 Feb21		1748Aug16
Bartlett Mary	S	K116C	1749 Dec 4		
Bartlett Mercy	S	W12H	1650 Mar20	1668 Dec25	
Bartlett Mercy	S	W58E	1694ca		
Bartlett Michael	S	K110K	1750ca		
Bartlett Phebe	S	K114E	1740 Oct 9		
Bartlett Priscilla	S	W58G	1696		
Bartlett Priscilla	S	K110N	1754ca		
Bartlett Rebecca	S	W12B	1634abt	1649 Dec20	1657ca
Bartlett Rebecca	S	W19B	1660ca	(2)1691Aug	1741 Dec14
Bartlett Rebecca	S	R14Aa	1680ca	1701 Nov27	1736 Dec 8
Bartlett Rebecca	S	W58C	1685ca		
Bartlett Rebecca	S	K115C	1739 May20		

NAME	DIV.	NUMBER	BIRTH	MARRIAGE	DEATH
Bartlett Rebecca	S	K116G	1760 Apr14		
Bartlett Rebecca #1	S	K114D	1738 Jun28		d.yng
Bartlett Rebecca #2	S	K114G	1745 May29		
Bartlett Rebecca=W12B	S	A14Ham	1634abt	1649 Dec20	1657ca
Bartlett Rebecca=W12B	S	A14Dam	1634ca	1649 Dec20	1657ca
Bartlett Rebecca=W19B	S	R12Ba	1660ca	1679ca	1741 Dec14
Bartlett Robert	S	K14Ha	1663ca	1687 Dec28	1718 Jan 3
Bartlett Robert	S	W58A	1679 Dec 6		1718bef
Bartlett Robert	S	K30J	1713 Apr30	4 Mar	1791aft
Bartlett Robert	S	K115A	1735 Aug15		
Bartlett Robert Jr	S	W11Aa	1603ca	1629ca	1676ca
Bartlett Robert Sr	S	W11Aaf	1580abt		
Bartlett Robert=K14Ha	S	W56Faf	1670abt		
Bartlett Robert=W19Ea	S	W23A	1663ca	1687 Dec28	1718 Jan3
Bartlett Robert=W23A	S	W19Ea	1663	1687 Dec28	1718 Jan 3
Bartlett Rufus	S	K116H	1762 Aug21		
Bartlett Ruth	S	W58D	1690ca		
Bartlett Samuel	S	W19C	1662ca	1683 Aug2	1713 Dec9
Bartlett Sarah	S	W12D	1635ca	1656 Dec23	1680abt
Bartlett Sarah	S	W23F	1680bef	1695 Sep2	1714 Jul24
Bartlett Sarah	S	W58B	1681ca		
Bartlett Sarah	S	R12La	1681ca	1701 Nov27	1761 Apr 3
Bartlett Sarah	S	K30D	1699 Apr 9	1721 Feb22	1739bef
Bartlett Sarah	S	K110B	1725 Jan20		
Bartlett Sarah	S	K112A	1736 Jan23		
Bartlett Sarah=K30D	S	W56Fa	1699 Apr 9	1721 Feb22	1739bef
Bartlett Sarah=W19E	S	W23Aa	1671bef	1687 Dec28	1718 Jan 3
Bartlett Sarah=W23Aa	S	W19E	1671bef	1687 Dec28	1718 Jan3
Bartlett Stephen	S	K116F	1756 Nov 5		
Bartlett Susannah	S	K115H	1750 Jan16		
Bartlett Thomas	S	K30B	1693 Feb 9	1716 Jan10	1764 Sep28
Bartlett Thomas	S	K114C	1737 Apr11		d.yng
Bartlett Thomas	S	K112C	1742 May31		
Bartlett Thomas	S	K114K	1757 Apr16		1792living
Bartlett William	S	W58F	1695ca		
Bartlett William	S	K30H	1709 Aug 2		d yng
Bartlett William	S	K116B	1746 Oct20		1792living
Barto Wendy	S	G58Ca	1966 Jun22	1987 Apr11	
Barton Mary	A	A2/121	1673ca	1694ca	1736 Oct18
Barton William	A	A2/242	1650abt	1673ca	1700abt

NAME	DIV.	NUMBER	BIRTH	MARRIAGE	DEATH
Bascom Guillaume	S	G40Aaf	1430ca		
Bascom Marie	S	G40Aa	1455ca	1485 Jun 3	
Bass Hannah	A	A11/9	1667 Jun22	1688ca	1705 Oct24
Bass John	A	A11/18	1630 Sep18	1657 Feb3	1716 Sep12
Bass Mary	A	A19/733	1635abt		
Bass Ruth	S	P21Fam	1660abt		
Bass Samuel	A	A11/36	1600abt	1625 Apr25	1694 Dec30
Bass Samuel =A11/36	A	A19/1466	1600abt	1625 Apr25	1694Dec 30
Bassett Elizabeth	S	B11Aa	1630abt	1648 Nov 8	
Bassett Elizabeth	A	A14/9	1730 Dec13	1748ca	1792ca
Bassett Moses	S	R26Naf	1720abt		
Bassett Ruth	S	T13Gbm	1635abt		
Bassett Sarah	S	A23Hb	1676 Dec 6	1719 May30	1732
Bassett Welthea	S	R26Na	1742 Jul 4	1765 Nov 1	1815 Sep25
Bassett William	S	B11Aaf	1600abt		
Bassett William	A	A14/144	1600abt		1646 Dec
Bassett William	S	A23Hbf	1655abt		
Bassett William III	A	A14/36	1671ca	1693 Nov23	1723 Oct11
Bassett William IV	A	A14/18	1709 Jul 8	1729 Jan29	1752aft
Bassett William Jr.	A	A14/72	1645abt	1670ca	1671
Bastian Anne	A	A11/81	1595ca	1613ca	
Bastian Anne	A	A11/101	1595ca	1613ca	1621 May11
Bastian Thomas(Baston)	A	A11/162	1565abt	1588 Nov30	1597ca
Bate --	S	F22Ea	1695abt	1713ca	1716bef
Bate James	S	F22Eaf	1670abt		
Bateman Eleazer	A	A19/250	1660	1686	1751
Bateman Elizabeth	A	A19/125	1688Jul 11	1705 Jul 2	1730aft
Bates Caleb	S	W24Fa	1666 Mar30	1716 Jun10	1747 Aug15
Bates Edward	S	Q16Baf	1670abt		
Bates Elizabeth	S	Q35D	1722 Jan12		1760ca
Bates Joanna	S	Q35A	1718 May28		
Bates Joseph	S	W24Faf	1640abt		
Bates Joseph	S	Q16Ba	1692ca	1716 Apr16	1778 Aug31
Bates Joseph	S	Q35C	1721 Mar18		
Bates Mary	S	R117Eam	1675abt		
Bates Mercy	S	Q35B	1719 Aug 8		
Bates Naomi	S	W46Ea	1695abt	1713 Jan12	
Bates Priscilla	S	Q35F	1726 Jan 6		
Bates Thomas	S	Q35E	1724 Nov 9		
Batt Ann	A	A17/43	1635Apr 7	1653 Jun13	

NAME	DIV.	NUMBER	BIRTH	MARRIAGE	DEATH
Batt Nicholas	A	A17/86	1610ca		1679Dec 6
Batt Richard	A	A17/172	1575abt		1612
Baxter Abigail	A	A11/17	1634 Sep	1650 Nov2	1692 Aug27
Baxter Almira Deborah	S	C52Ea	1802ca		
Baxter Gregory	A	A11/34	1610abt	1630abt	1659 Jun21
Baxter Hannah	S	R117Aam	1670abt		
Bayford Annis	A	A12/177	1603	1625	1682
Bayly Sarah	A	A18/7	1720ca	1752bef	1774
Bazemore William D	S	G56Ba	1933 Aug11	1956 Jun30	
Beacham Elizabeth	A	A2/233	1648ca	1666	
Beaky Joseph	A	A1/52	1785ca		
Beaky Joseph Ambrose	A	A1/26	1818 Jun14	1840 Jun 1	858 Jan27
Beaky Martha Adela	A	A1/13	1841 Jun 1	1862 Dec25	
Beal Martha	S	W39Dam	1645abt		
Beal Nathaniel	S	W29Caf	1640abt		
Beal Susanna	S	W29Ca	1664 Mar3	1686 Dec14	1689 Jun22
Bearse Sarah	S	H24Bbm	1650abt		
Bearse Sarah=H24Bbm	S	X16Bam	1650abt		
Beatrix of Hainault	D	D30/38	1005abt		
Bechi Victor Emanuel	A	A1/104	1755abt		
Bedell Dorothy	A	A14/265	1580ca		1635aft
Bedell Dorothy	A	A14/297	1580ca		1635aft
Bedwell Elizabeth	S	H21Ha	1688ca		1744aft
Beekman Cornelia	A	A1/361	1693	1711	1742
Beekman Gerardus	A	A8/74	1653 Aug	1677 Aug29	1723 Oct10
Beekman Maria	A	A8/37	1704 Jan10	1726 May14	1794ca
Beekman Wilhelmus H.	A	A8/148	1623	1649	1707
Beere Benjamin	S	P17Aa	1674 Jun 6		1714 Jul 3
Beere Charles	S	P33A	1700abt		
Beere Job	S	P33B	1700abt		1745bef
Beere Rachel	S	P33C	1700abt		
Beere Robert	S	P17Aaf	1650abt		
Belcher Abigail	S	R21Ca	1695 Aug23	1720 Apr14	1746 Nov15
Belcher Elizabeth	S	C46Ca	1663		
Belcher Joseph	S	R21Caf	1670abt		
Belcher William	S	G13Aa	1731	1752	1801
Bellinger Ann	A	A7/103	1685abt		1721ca
Bellinger Edmund	A	A7/206	1655abt	1680ca	1700
Bellows Dorcas	S	T26Fb	1722 Oct18	1760 Dec25	1823 Jan19
Bellows Nathaniel	S	T26Fbf	1695abt		

NAME	DIV.	NUMBER	BIRTH	MARRIAGE	DEATH
Beman Ruth	S	G19Aa	1784	1806	1858
Bemas Nancy	S	C52Ba	1790ca		
Benfield Mary	S	P18Bam	1640abt		
Benjamin Mary	S	X26Eam	1680abt		
Bennet Andrew	A	A8/126	1696ca	1719 Dec29	1745 Jul
Bennet Ann	A	A8/125	1694 Nov20	1712 Apr20	1737 Apr13
Bennet Archibald	A	A8/250	1660abt	1682	1712living
Bennet Archibald	A	A8/252	1660abt	1682	1712living
Bennet Barbara	A	A8/63	1724 Nov29	1744 May14	1758 Feb
Bennett Abigail	S	K151A	1723 Jan 5		
Bennett Cornelius	S	P58A	1703 Jul 9		
Bennett Ebenezer	S	P23Da	1678 May19	1702 Aug26	1751 Jan13
Bennett Ebenezer	S	K39Ga	1700ca	1737 Oct25	1751 Aug26
Bennett Ebenezer	S	K155E	1747 Jan31		1778 Nov10
Bennett Esther	S	K155C	1742 Mar26		d.yng
Bennett Hannah	S	K151F	1735 Jan13		
Bennett Jacob	S	K151B	1725 Apr29		
Bennett John	S	P23Daf	1660abt		
Bennett John	S	K155B	1740 May 2		
Bennett John =P23Daf	S	K39Caf	1660abt		
Bennett John=P23Daf	S	K39Gaf	1660abt		
Bennett Joseph	S	Q17Iaf	1685abt		
Bennett Lydia	S	K155D	1743 Jul15		d.yng
Bennett Martha	S	K151E	1733 Dec 8		
Bennett Mary	A	A10/7	1660abt	1707aft	1721ca
Bennett Mary	S	Q17Ia	1708 Nov 5	1736 Jan 6	1765living
Bennett Nehemiah	S	K39Ca	1696ca	1721 May 4	1769 Aug15
Bennett Patience	S	K151D	1730 Jun29		d. yng
Bennett Patience	S	K155A	1738 Sep16	unm	1781 Nov11
Bennett Ruth	S	Q21Fb	1714 Aug24	1746 Jan22	1783 Apr30
Bennett Samuel	S	Q21Fbf	1690abt		
Bennett Sarah	S	P58B	1707 Mar27		
Bennett William	S	K151C	1727 Jul 2		
Benson Joanna	S	Q21Cbm	1680abt		
Benson Robert	A	A8/70	1686 Jan 1	1708 Mar14	1710abt
Benson Samson	A	A8/140	1652	1673	1730
Benson Sarah	S	Q22Fam	1675abt		
Benson Sarah=Q22Fam	S	Q22Dam	1675abt		
Benson Tryntje(Cath.)	A	A8/35	1712 May30	1733 Oct19	1765 Mar31
Bent John III	A	A19/82	1689Nov 29	1711Nov 15	1759

NAME	DIV.	NUMBER	BIRTH	MARRIAGE	DEATH
Bent John Jr	A	A19/164	1636	1688ca	1717
Bent Martha	A	A19/41	1719 Mar 7	1740Mar10	
Beringer Cecile	S	G43Ca	1575abt	1600	
Berryman Benjamin	S	A30Abf	1665abt		
Berryman Elizabeth	S	A30Ab	1690ca	1712ca	1734ca
Bickford Deborah	S	H29Ca	1705 Feb 2	1724 Feb10	1753aft
Bickford Jeremiah	S	H29Caf	1680abt		
Bigelow John	A	A6/132	1617ca	1642	1703ca
Bigelow Joshua	A	A6/66	1655 Nov 5	1676 Oct20	1745 Feb 1
Bigelow Mercy	A	A6/33	1686ca	1706 Jan 2	1744 Feb28
Biggs Sarah	D	D33a23	1770abt		
Bill Ephraim	A	A8/46	1719 Aug15	1746 Apr 3	1802 Nov24
Bill Ephraim=A08/46	D	D4af21	1719 Aug15	1746 Apr 3	1802 Nov24
Bill Lydia	A	A8/23	1753 Jul 7	1772 May26	1838 May 1
Bill Lydia=A08/23	D	D4a21	1753 Jul 7	1772 May26	1838 May 1
Bill Samuel	A	A8/184	1665ca		1729ca
Bill Samuel Jr.	A	A8/92	1690ca		1753 Mar 1
Bill Sarah	A	A8/183	1658	1685	1704
Billings Ebenezer	S	W33Baf	1650abt		
Billings Richard	S	W33Ba	1675 Dec21		1748 Nov20
Billington Eleanor	S	W46Ba	1683ca	1703 Jan26	1755abt
Billington Elizabeth	S	P17Aam	1650abt		
Billington Francis	A	A6/246	1606ca	1634ca	1684ca
Billington Isaac	S	W46Baf	1655abt		
Billington Mercy	A	A6/123	1651 Feb25	1681 Jun27	1718 Sep28
Bingham Abisha	S	R57B	1709 Jan29		
Bingham Achsah	S	T74F	1760 Dec18		
Bingham Alvan	S	T74D	1754 Dec20		
Bingham Anne	S	R57D	1716 Nov		
Bingham Hannah	S	C52Ca	1792ca		
Bingham Jabez	S	T74A	1748 Feb13		
Bingham Jabez Jr	S	T28Aa	1724 Apr12	1746 Dec29	1784
Bingham Jabez Sr	S	T28Aaf	1700abt		
Bingham Jerusha	S	R57A	1708 Feb 2		
Bingham Lemuel	S	R57C	1713 Sep20		
Bingham Lois	S	T74G	1763 Feb18		
Bingham Marah	S	R57E	1720 Feb10		1720 Feb22
Bingham Mary	S	R19Dam	1670abt		
Bingham Mary	S	T74C	1752 Jul 3		
Bingham Mercy	S	T74H	1767 Jun17		

NAME	DIV.	NUMBER	BIRTH	MARRIAGE	DEATH
Bingham Ralph Wheelock	S	T74B	1750 Feb17		1751 Sep15
Bingham Samuel	S	R19Ca	1685 Mar28	1708 Jan 5	1760 Mar 1
Bingham Silas	S	T74E	1758 Jul29		
Bingham Thomas	S	R19Caf	1660abt		
Birchard Sophia	A	A12/3	1792 Apr15	1813 Sep13	1866 Oct30
Bisbee Elisha	S	T22Daf	1700abt		
Bisbee Elisha	S	T18Ca	1710ca		
Bisbee Martha	S	T22Da	1724 Dec 4	1747 Feb10	1754bef
Bishop Eliphalet	S	L23B	1751 Sep23		
Bishop Elizabeth	A	A2/229	1657	1678	
Bishop Elizabeth	S	T16Dam	1670abt		
Bishop Hudson	S	L17Caf	1690abt		
Bishop John	S	Q23Gaf	1685abt		
Bishop Keturah	S	Q23Ga	1708 Apr11	1729 Aug25	1733ca
Bishop Nathaniel	S	L17Ca	1715 Jul	1746 Feb 5	1778aft
Bishop Nathaniel	S	L23A	1747 Oct14		
Bissell Daniel	S	R47D	1724 Feb 2		
Bissell Daniel Jr	S	R117Da	1694 Oct31	1717 Mar18	1770 Nov11
Bissell Daniel Sr	S	R117Daf	1670abt		
Bissell Ebenezer	S	R47E	1736		
Bissell Jabez	S	R47A	1718 Feb16		
Bissell Jerusha	S	R47B	1721 Apr11		1770living
Bissell Margaret	S	R47C	1723 May24		
Bixbee Elizabeth	S	H110C	1731 Dec 3		
Bixbee John	S	H110E	1736 Mar 2		
Bixbee Joseph	S	H30Haf	1680abt		
Bixbee Joseph #1	S	H110A	1725 Jan 1		d yng
Bixbee Joseph #2	S	H110B	1729 Mar23		
Bixbee Moses	S	H30Ha	1704 Jul20	1724 Mar18	1770abt
Bixbee Moses	S	H110H	1740ca		
Bixbee Phebe	S	H110D	1734 Dec21		
Bixbie Joseph	S	X19Dbf	1660abt		
Bixbie Sarah	S	X19Db	1685 Aug 3	1726 Dec12	1774 Dec10
Blackman John	S	W35Baf	1635abt		
Blackman Joseph	S	W35Ba	1661 Jun27	1685 Nov12	1720 May20
Blackman Rebecca	S	W35Da	1668	1693ca	1748
Blackmar Elizabeth	S	C79Da	1682		
Blackmar Mary	S	C79Ba	1674ca		
Blacksoll Mary	A	A17/161	1570abt		1624
Blackwell Alice	S	W47D	1681 May 8	1699ca	1725abt

NAME	DIV.	NUMBER	BIRTH	MARRIAGE	DEATH
Blackwell Alice	S	K138F	1725 May19		
Blackwell Bethia	S	K138E	1722 Dec31		
Blackwell Caleb	S	W47F	1685ca	1708ca	1762 Nov28
Blackwell Caleb=W47F	S	K35Ha	1685ca	1708ca	1762 Nov28
Blackwell Desire	S	W47C	1678 Dec20	1696ca	1773 Jan 2
Blackwell Desire	S	T18Bam	1685abt		
Blackwell Jane	S	W47E	1682 Mar 3	1705ca	1759 Apr24
Blackwell Jane	S	K138A	1710 Feb 7		d.yng
Blackwell John	S	W18Ba	1646ca	1673ca	1688abt
Blackwell John	S	K138C	1717 Mar21		d.yng
Blackwell John =W41Da	S	W47A	1674 Dec26	1701May 7	1741bef
Blackwell John Jr	S	W41Da	1674 Dec26	1701 May 7	1741bef
Blackwell John Sr	S	W41Daf	1646ca	1673ca	=W18Ba
Blackwell John=W18Ba	S	K35Haf	1646ca	1673ca	1688abt
Blackwell Mary	S	K138D	1720 Jun30		
Blackwell Michael	S	W47B	1676		1700abt
Blackwell Nathaniel	S	W47G	1686 Dec27	2 Mar	1757ca
Blackwell Sarah	S	K138B	1715ca		
Blackwell Seth	S	K138G	1729 Nov 1		
Blake Experience	S	Q22Eam	1675abt		
Blake Hannah	S	R21Aam	1660abt		
Blanchard Mehetable	S	R23Ja	1710ca	1742 Dec16	
Blanding Christopher	S	C61Ha	1760ca		
Blanton Hattie Pearl	S	G54Dam	1872 Aug24	1896 Dec17	1922 May10
Blish Joseph	S	F16Gaf	1670ca		1722
Blish Mary	S	F16Ga	1696 April	1718 Jun26	1773aft
Bliss Elizabeth	S	P21Eam	1675abt		
Bliss Rebecca	S	R24Fbm	1680abt		
Blodgett Susannah	S	P15Eam	1645abt		
Bloomer Elizabeth Ann	A	A4/1a	1918 Apr 8	1948 Oct15	
Bloss Myrl Anna	S	C58Da	1908		
Blossom Elizabeth	S	F19Cam	1630abt		
Blossom Elizabeth	A	A1/353	1705	1725	1734
Blossom John	S	B18Ga	1705abt	1727 Apr 6	
Blossom Peter	S	F20Baf	1650abt		
Blossom Thankful	S	F20Ba	1675ca	1700ca	1758ca
Blue Donald	A	A9/26	1799 Jan18	1815 Jan15	1888 Jan14
Blue Jane	A	A9/13	1821 Apr	1841 Nov28	1894 Jun 3
Bobet Deliverance	S	X22Cbm	1665abt		
Bocher George	A	A1/310	1675ca		

NAME	DIV.	NUMBER	BIRTH	MARRIAGE	DEATH
Bocher Susanna	A	A1/155	1703 Jul25	1721ca	1773 Feb11
Bodfish Sarah	S	F20Bam	1650abt		
Bodine Daniel	S	G45Baf	1620ca		
Bodine Maurice	S	G42Ba	1540abt		
Bodine Sarah	S	G45Ba	1655abt	1676 Jun 8	
Bodwell Henry	A	A17/22	1652ca	1681May 4	1745Jun 1
Bodwell Sarah	A	A17/11	1694 Dec 1	1714 Nov15	1737 Feb 4
Bogaert Annatje	D	D8/20	1728 Aug	1746 Dec 4	1773Jul 9
Bogaert Annetje	A	A7/17	1728 Aug	1746 Dec 4	1773 Jul 9
Bogaert Claes Janszen	D	D8a22	1668ca	1695Jun 28	1727Jan 5
Bogaert Claes=D8a22	A	A7/68	1668ca	1695 Jun28	1727 Jan5
Bogaert Jan =D8/21	A	A7/34	1697 May 1	1716 Mar10	1775 Nov 7
Bogaert Jan (John)	D	D8/21	1697May 1	1716Mar 10	=A07/34
Bogaert Jan Louwe	A	A7/136	1630ca		1707aft
Boggs Julia	A	A5/1a	1826 Jan26	1848Aug 22	1902 Dec14
Boles Thankful	S	K31Ha	1705ca	1733 Jan12	
Bolles Samuel (Bouls)	S	W28Faf	1650abt		
Bolling Elizabeth	A	A1/157	1709 Dec17	1727	1754 aft
Bolling Robert Jr	A	A1/314	1682 Jan25	1706 Jan 2	
Bolton Elisabeth	S	K41Da	1714 Sep23	1723 Feb 7	1792 Jun11
Bolton Hannah	S	K41Ba	1721 Jan 9	1740 Mar18	1755 Jul 6
Bolton John	S	K41Baf	1700abt		
Bolton John Jr=K41Baf	S	K41Daf	1700abt		
Bond Anna	A	A2/63	1732 Nov 9	1757 Jan 6	1784ca
Bond John	S	T27Db	1710ca	1759 Aug29	
Bond Jonas	A	A2/252	1664	1688ca	
Bond Josiah	A	A2/126	1695 Jan20	1719 Jan	1781
Bonham Elijah	S	F19F	1669ca		1695 aft
Bonham Elizabeth	S	F19D	1666ca	1684 Jan 9	1704living
Bonham Hannah	S	F19A	1659 Oct 8	1677 Sep19	1689 Aug19
Bonham Hannah	S	F46C	1695 Mar14		
Bonham Hezekiah	S	F19E	1667 May 6	1691	1717living
Bonham Jane	S	F19H	1675 Jan29	unmar	1675 Feb25
Bonham Mary	S	F19B	1661 Oct 4	1681 Jul15	1740abt
Bonham Mary	S	F46A	1691 Oct 4		
Bonham Nicholas	S	F14Aa	1630abt	1658 Jan 1	1684 Jul20
Bonham Pricilla	S	F19I	1677 Nov11	1694 Nov13	
Bonham Samuel	S	F19G	1672 Sept7	unmar	1682 Oct 1
Bonham Samuel	S	F46B	1693 Feb 6		
Bonham Sarah	S	A24Dam	1660abt		

NAME	DIV.	NUMBER	BIRTH	MARRIAGE	DEATH
Bonham Sarah	S	F19C	1664 Feb16	1681 Oct 1	1738 Jan16
Bonham Sarah	S	F46D	1698 Feb14		
Bonney Daniel	S	L17Da	1739 Jul 2	1766 May15	1813 Aug13
Bonney Elisha	S	L17Daf	1715abt		
Bonney Elizabeth	S	T16Da	1694 May	1719 May21	1777 Mar17
Bonney John	S	T16Daf	1670abt		
Bonney Jonathan	S	L24A	1768ca		
Bonney Mary	S	Q17Ga	1704 May 9	1732 Jul20	1736
Bonney William	S	Q17Gaf	1680abt		
Bonum Patience	S	H22Fam	1650abt		
Bonum Patience	S	X14Eam	1650abt		
Bonum Ruth	S	K15Abm	1635abt		
Bonum Ruth	S	P23Bam	1650abt		
Boomer Caleb	S	C31Aa	1705ca		
Boomer Matthew	S	W38Aa	1670abt	1688ca	1744bef
Booth Elizabeth	A	A5/67	1641 Sep10	1658 Oct21	1732 Oct24
Booth John	S	W45Faf	1675abt		
Booth Jonathan	S	N13Ea	1740ca		
Booth Lydia	S	W45Fa	1700 Mar 8	1722 Oct 7	1757living
Booth Richard	A	A5/134	1607ca		1688aft
Booth Robert	A	A15/100	1630abt		1657ca
Booth Robert	A	A15/50	1670abt	1693ca	1695ca
Borden Timothy	S	C72Ea	1705ca		
Bordman Thomas	S	H19Baf	1640abt		
Bortree Esther A	S	N16Aa	1815ca		
Bosworth Benjamin	S	W37Caf	1645abt		
Bosworth David	S	H33Iaf	1765abt		
Bosworth Deborah	S	H120A	1726 Nov19	unm.	1746 Apr21
Bosworth Hannah	S	W56Ham	1675abt		
Bosworth Judith	S	W37Ca	1670abt	1696 Jan 7	1755abt
Bosworth Nehemiah	S	H33Ia	1702 Mar15	1725 Jan27	1762 Dec22
Bosworth Susanna	S	H120B	1728 Sep 8		d. yng
Boteler Margery	D	D29a14	1515abt		
Bouls Joanna (Bolles)	S	W28Fa	1678ca	1701 Jan23	1756abt
Bourn Hannah	A	A1/187	1730 Oct 8	1752 Apr26	
Bourn William Jr	A	A1/374	1704abt	1729	1752 aft
Bourne Elizabeth	S	W51Kam	1680abt		
Bourne Ezra	S	G51Ga	1895abt		
Bourne Hannah	S	W21Ca	1667 Nov18	1690 Jan24	1732aft
Bourne Job	S	W21Caf	1640abt		

NAME	DIV.	NUMBER	BIRTH	MARRIAGE	DEATH
Bourne Martha	S	R11Aa	1614ca	1650	1683bef
Bourne Thomas	S	R11Aaf	1590abt		
Boutwell Betsey	A	A19/39	1723 Mar24	1747ca	
Boutwell John	A	A19/156	1671	1695	1713
Boutwell John Jr	A	A19/78	1702 Apr28	1723Apr 30	
Bowden Mary	S	K22Ja	1670ca	1693 Dec20	1747 Dec18
Bowden Mary=K22Ja	S	Q20Dam	1670ca	1693 Dec20	1747 Dec18
Bowen Abiah	S	Q14Dam	1665abt		
Bowen Abigail	A	A17/13	1700 Jul 5	1721 Sep15	1775 Sep16
Bowen Alice	A	A2/168	1615abt	1636ca	
Bowen Francis	A	A17/208	1575abt		
Bowen Griffith	A	A17104	1600ca	1627ca	1675ca
Bowen Henry	A	A17/52	1633ca	1658 Dec20	1724Mar 13
Bowen John	A	A17/26	1662Sep 1		1696bef
Bowen Joseph	S	C28Ba	1695ca		
Bowen Obadiah	S	C31Fa	1710ca		
Bowen Valentine	S	C31Ka	1725ca		
Bowerman Thankful	S	H19Ba	1668abt	1700 Jun 6	
Bowes-Lyon Claude Jr	D	D28/17	1870abt		
Bowes-Lyon Claude Sr	D	D28a18	1840abt		
Bowker Mary	A	A3/249	1710abt	1736 Sep18	1746aft
Bowker William	A	A3/498	1675abt		1725aft
Bowne John	A	A13/70	1630ca		1684abt
Bowne Sarah	A	A13/35	1669 Nov27		1714ca
Bowne William	A	A13/140	1605ca		1677abt
Bownest Alice	A	A11/121	1575abt		
Boylson Henry	A	A11/160	1570abt		1592 Sep
Boylston Edward	A	A11/80	1590abt	1613ca	1625 Aug20
Boylston Edward=A11/80	A	A11/100	1590abt	1613ca	1625 Aug20
Boylston Peter	A	A11/10	1673ca	1704ca	1743 Sep10
Boylston Sarah	A	A11/25	1642 Sep30	1663ca	1711 Aug8
Boylston Susanna	A	A11/5	1708 Mar5	1734 Nov23	1797 Apr17
Boylston Thomas	A	A11/50	1614 Feb	1639ca	1653
Boylston Thomas Jr.	A	A11/20	1644 Jan26	1665 Dec13	1695ca
Boylston Thomas=A11/50	A	A11/40	1614 Feb	1639ca	1653
Bozworth David	S	K41Aaf	1680abt		
Bozworth David	S	K164D	1735 Nov28		
Bozworth John	S	K164A	1729 Dec29		
Bozworth Nehemiah	S	K41Aa	1702 Mar15	1729 Mar26	1762 Dec22
Bozworth Nehemiah	S	K164B	1731 Apr 3		

NAME	DIV.	NUMBER	BIRTH	MARRIAGE	DEATH
Bozworth Peter	S	K164C	1732 Jan 2		d.yng
Bozworth Sarah	S	K164E	1737 Dec 5		
Bozworth Susanna	S	K164F	1739 Nov 8		
Brackett Hannah	S	K22Gam	1640abt		
Bradford John	S	W53A	1675 Dec29		
Bradford Abigail	S	W53C	1679 Dec10		
Bradford Abigail	S	R14C	1679 Dec10		
Bradford Abigail	S	R26G	1719 Feb28	1740 Oct 4	
Bradford Abigail	S	R73A	1721 May15		
Bradford Abigail	S	R77A	1728 Sep24		
Bradford Abigail	S	R32H	1732 Jun12		
Bradford Abigail	S	R28M	1741 Jun20		1760 Dec17
Bradford Abigail	S	R98E	1744 Aug21		
Bradford Abigail	S	R107E	1765 Jan23		
Bradford Abner	S	R25D	1707 Dec25	1733 Nov 4	1784 Jun18
Bradford Alexander	S	R72B	1713ca		
Bradford Alice	S	R12D	1659ca	(2)1687May	1745 Mar15
Bradford Alice	S	W53B	1677		
Bradford Alice	S	R14B	1677 Jan28	1708 Aug26	1746 Jul14
Bradford Alice	S	R15A	1680 Jan28	1704 Nov20	1775
Bradford Alice	S	R28J	1734 Nov 3	1757 Sep21	1795 Jul 6
Bradford Althea	S	R24D	1704Apr 6		1704Apr
Bradford Althea	S	R24I	1715 Sep19	1740 Feb24	
Bradford Andrew	S	R77J	1745 Jun 2 twin		
Bradford Ann	S	R24A	1699 Jul26	1723 Aug15	1788 Oct 9
Bradford Ann	S	R39F	1726ca		
Bradford Anna	S	R26C	1715 Jul25	1737 Feb23	
Bradford Anna	S	R88B	1732 Jul23		
Bradford Anne	S	R100E	1758 Apr15		
Bradford Asa	S	R107A	1758 Jul 5		1793living
Bradford Azenath	S	R28K	1736 Sep15	3 Mar	1818 Nov15
Bradford Azenath	S	R28K	1736 Sep15	(2)1757ca	1818Nov 15
Bradford Azubah	S	R116B	1765 May21		
Bradford Bathsheba	S	R25B	1703 Nov 8	1731 Dec23	1773 Dec23
Bradford Benjamin	S	R97E	1742 Feb 8		1748 Jul19
Bradford Benjamin	S	R95F	1748 Oct 8		
Bradford Benjamin	S	R99I	1753 May28		
Bradford Benjamin	S	R25C	7705 Oct17	2 Mar	1783
Bradford Betty	S	R106J	1767 Aug22		
Bradford Carpenter	S	R28L	1739abt	1761 Jun18	1823 Jan27

NAME	DIV.	NUMBER	BIRTH	MARRIAGE	DEATH
Bradford Chandler	S	R106G	1761 Aug15		
Bradford Charles	S	R36B	1715 Jan 4		1738living
Bradford Chloe	S	R28N	1743abt		1747 Feb21
Bradford Chloe #1	S	R116A	1762 Jan 4		1770 Mar 4
Bradford Chloe #2	S	R116F	1776 Jan 5		
Bradford Content	S	R280	1745 May21		1745 May22
Bradford Cornelius	S	R99A	1737 Dec10		
Bradford Cynthia	S	R107K	1783ca		1793living
Bradford Daniel	S	R72D	1720ca		
Bradford David	S	R12N	1687bef	1713 Feb23	1729 Mar16
Bradford David	S	R111E	1757 Mar27		
Bradford Deborah	S	R26A	1712 Jun21		1732 Jun10
Bradford Deborah	S	R28I	1732 Nov18	1751 Oct27	1811aft
Bradford Deborah	S	R77F	1738 Aug17		1739 Aug 1
Bradford Deborah	S	R106B	1752 Aug18		
Bradford Deborah	S	R107G	1770ca		1793living
Bradford Deborah	S	R108C	1777ca		
Bradford Eleanor	S	R95G	1750ca		d yng.
Bradford Elijah	S	R26I	1722 Jan23		1740bef
Bradford Elijah	S	R98A	1735 Apr11		
Bradford Eliphalet	S	R34D	1722 Jan20		
Bradford Eliphalet	S	R72J	1728ca		
Bradford Elisha	S	R13B	1669ca	2 Mar	1747 Jun16
Bradford Elisha	S	R25Eaf	1700abt		
Bradford Elisha	S	R25G	1718 Mar25	1761 Jan17	1801 Feb26
Bradford Elisha	S	R28G	1729 Oct 6		1753 Mar
Bradford Elisha	S	R98I	1753 May10		
Bradford Elisha	S	R99J	1755 Oct15		
Bradford Elizabeth	S	R21D	1696 Dec15	1716 Jan10	1777 May10
Bradford Elizabeth	S	X59D	1696 Dec15		
Bradford Elizabeth	S	R38B	1710abt		
Bradford Elizabeth	S	R24H	1712 Oct21	1736 Jun15	1808 Jun27
Bradford Elizabeth	S	R36A	1714 Jan10		1714 Jan21
Bradford Elizabeth	S	R26E	1717 Nov 3	1753 Jul12	
Bradford Elizabeth	S	R73C	1728		
Bradford Elizabeth	S	R36H	1730 Sep15		1730 Oct10
Bradford Elizabeth	S	R88A	1731 Jan17		
Bradford Elizabeth	S	R100B	1747 Jul10		
Bradford Elizabeth	S	R111C	1754 Apr11		
Bradford Emily	S	R116G	1781 Mar 6		

NAME	DIV.	NUMBER	BIRTH	MARRIAGE	DEATH
Bradford Ephraim	S	R12M	1685	1709 Feb13	1746 Oct 6
Bradford Ephraim	S	R26F	1718 Jan 1		1741bef
Bradford Ephraim	S	R106A	1750 Dec13		
Bradford Ephraim	S	R107I	1780		
Bradford Ephraim	S	R108D	1783ca		
Bradford Ezekiel	S	R26L	1728 Mar14	1750 Jul21	1816 Sep
Bradford Ezekiel	S	R106F	1759 Dec15		
Bradford Gamaliel	S	R21G	1704 May18	1728 Aug30	1778 Apr24
Bradford Gamaliel	S	X59G	1704 May18		
Bradford Gamaliel	S	R77C	1731 Sept2		
Bradford George	S	R73F	1732		
Bradford Gershom	S	R21B	1691 Dec21	1716Oct 23	1757 Apr 4
Bradford Gershom	S	X59B	1691 Dec21		
Bradford Gideon	S	R32B	1718 Oct27		
Bradford Hannah	S	R12F	1662 May 9	1682 Nov28	1738 May28
Bradford Hannah	S	R21A	1689 Feb14	1709 Jun16	1772 Jan28
Bradford Hannah	S	X59A	1689 Feb14		
Bradford Hannah	S	R24G	1709 May24	1730 Jan20	1749 May29
Bradford Hannah	S	R25Ea	1720 Apr10	1736 Feb17	1758 May22
Bradford Hannah	S	R28A	1720 Apr10	1736 Feb17	1758 May22
Bradford Hannah	S	R34E	1724 May29		
Bradford Hannah	S	R73B	1724ca		
Bradford Hannah	S	R77G	1740 Jul30		
Bradford Hannah	S	R88F	1740 Mar10		
Bradford Hannah	S	R99G	1748 Mar 9		
Bradford Hannah	S	R98H	1751 Feb28		
Bradford Hannah	S	R116C	1767 Jun28		
Bradford Hannah=R12F	S	R16Bcm	1662May 9	1682Nov 28	1738May 28
Bradford Henry Swift	S	R88D	1736 Aug21		
Bradford Hezekiah	S	R120	1687bef	1714May 21	1760aft
Bradford Hopestill	S	R72E	1721ca		
Bradford Hosea	S	R107D	1763ca		
Bradford Ichabod	S	R25F	1713 Sep22	2 Mar	791 Apr 6
Bradford Ichabod	S	R100A	1744 Aug28		
Bradford Irena	S	R24J	1715 Sep19	1735 Mar18	
Bradford Irene	S	R24E	1704Apr 6		1704Aug 16
Bradford Israel	S	R12L	1677ca	1701 Nov27	1760 Mar26
Bradford Israel	S	R98F	1748 Jul17		1749 Jul
Bradford Israel	S	R100F	1766 Oct28		
Bradford James	S	R19Gb	1689 Mar24	1752 Nov 9	1762 Mar26

NAME	DIV.	NUMBER	BIRTH	MARRIAGE	DEATH
Bradford James	S	R34A	1717 Jul 2		
Bradford James	S	R39H	1733ca		
Bradford James=R19Gb	S	R16B	1689 Mar24	3 Mar	1762 Mar26
Bradford Jeremiah	S	R72I	1727ca		
Bradford Jerusha	S	R16C	1692Nov 26	1716 Nov14	1739 Nov 4
Bradford Jerusha	S	R21E	1699 Mar10	1719 Nov13	1783 Aug19
Bradford Jerusha	S	R39C	1716 Jun27		
Bradford Jerusha	S	R36D	1722 Dec20		
Bradford Jerusha=R21E	S	X59E	1699 Mar10		1783Aug 19
Bradford Jesse	S	R106E	1758 Mar 7		
Bradford Job	S	R72H	1726ca		
Bradford Joel	S	R73E	1730	unm.	1758 Jan23
Bradford Joel	S	R107H	1773 Jan25		
Bradford John	S	R11A	1618ca	1650	1676 Sep21
Bradford John	S	W18Aa	1652 Feb20	1674 Jan6	1736 Dec8
Bradford John	S	R12A	1652 Feb20	1674 Jan 6	1736 Dec 8
Bradford John	D	D9/23	1652ca	1674 Jan 6	=R12A
Bradford John	S	A24Abf	1660abt		
Bradford John	S	R14A	1675 Dec29	1701 Nov27	1724 Mar27
Bradford John	S	R39B	1714 Jan30		1714Jan30
Bradford John	S	R32A	1717 Apr 8		
Bradford John	S	R24K	1717 May20	1736 Dec15	1787 Mar10
Bradford John	S	R73G	1734		
Bradford John	S	R95B	1739 Dec 7		
Bradford Jonathan	S	R27B	1717 Nov13		1740abt
Bradford Jonathan	S	R111B	1752 May15		
Bradford Joseph	S	R11D	1630ca	1664 May25	1715 Jul10
Bradford Joseph	S	R13A	1665 Apr18		
Bradford Joseph	S	R12K	1675 Apr18	2 Mar	1747 Jan17
Bradford Joseph	S	R24B	1702 Apr 9	1730 Mar	1778 Jan 5
Bradford Joseph	S	R28B	1721 Dec 7		1743 Sep 4
Bradford Joseph	S	R73H	1737		
Bradford Joseph	S	R95C	1742 Jun17		
Bradford Joseph	S	R88G	1744 Jan10		
Bradford Joseph	S	R99H	1751 Mar19		
Bradford Joshua	S	R16A	1682 Nov23	1711 Feb17	
Bradford Joshua	S	R25E	1710 Jun23	1736 Feb17	1758 May22
Bradford Joshua	S	R28Aa	1710 Jun23	1736 Feb17	1758 May22
Bradford Joshua	S	R99F	1746 Apr 2		
Bradford Josiah	S	R36E	1724ca		

NAME	DIV.	NUMBER	BIRTH	MARRIAGE	DEATH
Bradford Laurana	S	R28E	1726 Mar27	1745 Nov14	1782living
Bradford Lemuel	S	R27E	1726 Mar 1		1746bef
Bradford Lemuel	S	R97G	1747 Jun16		1748 Jul12
Bradford Lemuel	S	R109B	1750 Feb20		
Bradford Lemuel	S	R100D	1755 Aug22		
Bradford Levi	S	R98B	1737 Oct 1	unm.	1758 Jun
Bradford Levi	S	R98L	1759 Jul 1		
Bradford Lois	S	R28H	1730 Jan30		1752 Oct10
Bradford Lucy	S	R98J	1755 May10		
Bradford Lucy	S	R107C	1762 Oct 2		
Bradford Lusanna	S	R26H	1721 May 3	1752 Apr28	1805 Dec 9
Bradford Lydia	S	R27C	1719 Dec23	(2)1743May	1756 Oct28
Bradford Lydia	S	R97D	1739 Jun22		1748 Jul16
Bradford Lydia	S	R98G	1749 Dec20		
Bradford Lydia	S	R97H	1749 June7		
Bradford Lydia	S	R111A	1750 Jan17		d. yng
Bradford Marcy	S	R97F	1745 Mar13		1745 Aug 9
Bradford Martin	S	R106H	1763 Oct17		
Bradford Mary	S	R12I	1668	1687ca	1720 May 7
Bradford Mary	S	R32D	1722 Oct16		
Bradford Mary	S	R28F	1727 Aug 1		1727 Aug21
Bradford Mary	S	R39G	1728ca		
Bradford Mary	S	R73I	1738ca		1746living
Bradford Mary	S	R98D	1742 Jun13		
Bradford Mary	S	R99D	1744 Mar16		
Bradford Mary	S	R95I	1756 Jan17		
Bradford Mary	A	A3/93	1775ca		
Bradford Mary Gay	S	R116E	1772 Nov 8		
Bradford Melatiah	S	R12G	1664 Nov 1	1689ca	1739 Apr24
Bradford Melatiah	S	R12G	1664 Nov1	(2)1702aft	1739 Apr24
Bradford Melatiah	S	R99E	1744 Mar16		
Bradford Mercy	S	R11C	1627ca	1648 Dec21	1657 May 9
Bradford Mercy	S	R12E	1660 Sep 2	1680 Sep16	1720 Apr 5
Bradford Mercy	S	W53D	1681 Dec20		
Bradford Mercy	S	A24Ab	1681 Dec20	1717 Oct10	1738 Jun27
Bradford Mercy	S	R36G	1728 Jan15		
Bradford Mercy	S	R32G	1731 Apr12		1731 Jun 1
Bradford Mercy=W53C	S	R14D	1681 Dec29	2 Mar	1738 Jun27
Bradford Michael	S	R97B	1735 May16		1735 Oct 2
Bradford Nathan	S	R27D	1722 Apr 3	2 Mar	1787 Oct14

NAME	DIV.	NUMBER	BIRTH	MARRIAGE	DEATH
Bradford Nathaniel	S	R27A	1715 Dec10	1746 Nov24	1751 Mar27
Bradford Nathaniel	S	R109A	1748 Jul26		
Bradford Nehemiah	S	R28D	1724 Jul27		1729living
Bradford Noah	S	R72F	1723ca		
Bradford Peabody	S	R77E	1734 Mar 8		
Bradford Peggy	S	R98K	1757 May 8		
Bradford Perez	S	R21C	1694 Dec28	1720 Apr14	1746 Jun19
Bradford Perez	S	X59C	1694 Dec28		
Bradford Perez	S	R73D	1728ca		
Bradford Perez	S	R97C	1736 Sept3		1748 Jul12
Bradford Perez	S	R95E	1746 Oct10		
Bradford Peter	S	R13C	1676ca		
Bradford Peter	S	R77I	1745 Jun 2 twin		
Bradford Phebe	S	R32I	1735 Mar30		
Bradford Philip	S	R106I	1765 Jun 8		
Bradford Priscilla	S	W53F	1686 Mar10		
Bradford Priscilla	S	R14F	1686 Mar10	1721 Sep17	1732living
Bradford Priscilla	S	R25Cbm	1700abt		
Bradford Priscilla	S	R24C	1702 Apr 9	1724 Jan14	1778 May14
Bradford Priscilla	S	R72C	1717ca		
Bradford Rachel	S	R72G	1725ca		
Bradford Rachel	S	R99C	1741 Jan28		
Bradford Rebecca	S	R29B	1710 Dec14		
Bradford Rebecca	S	R95H	1754 Jan17		
Bradford Rebecca	S	R106D	1756 Sep22		
Bradford Rebecca	S	R107J	1782ca		d. yng
Bradford Rhoda	S	R100C	1751 Jul20		
Bradford Robert	S	R29A	1706 Oct18		
Bradford Robert	S	R88E	1739 Jul21		
Bradford Ruth	S	R25A	1702 Dec11		1702 Feb
Bradford Ruth	S	R26K	1725ca	1749 Aug 3	1767 Aug26
Bradford Ruth	S	R77H	1743 Jul 5		
Bradford Ruth	S	R107F	1768 Jan17		
Bradford Samuel	S	R12H	1667ca	1689 Jul31	1714 Apr11
Bradford Samuel	S	X20Aa	1667ca	1689 Jul31	1714 Apr11
Bradford Samuel	S	W53E	1683 Dec23		
Bradford Samuel	S	R14E	1683 Dec23	1714 Oct21	1740 Mar26
Bradford Samuel	S	R34C	1721 Apr 4		1735 Feb 4
Bradford Samuel	S	R77B	1729 Jan 2		
Bradford Samuel	S	R95A	1736 Jan 4		

NAME	DIV.	NUMBER	BIRTH	MARRIAGE	DEATH
Bradford Samuel	S	R32J	1740 Apr13		
Bradford Sarah	S	R12J	1671	1687ca	1710abt
Bradford Sarah	S	R15C	1686	1708	1718 April1
Bradford Sarah	S	R24F	1706 Sep21	2 Mar	1758living
Bradford Sarah	S	R36C	1718 Dec15		
Bradford Sarah	S	R39E	1720 Aug27		
Bradford Sarah	S	R32E	1725 Apr 4		
Bradford Sarah	S	R99B	1739 Oct16		
Bradford Sarah	S	R95D	1744 Jul27		
Bradford Sarah	S	R108A	1768ca		
Bradford Seth	S	R77D	1733 Sep14		
Bradford Simeon	S	R26M	1729 Aug28	1755 Jan23	1793 Oct 6
Bradford Simeon	S	R107B	1760 Sep 3		
Bradford Simeon	S	R108B	1770ca		
Bradford Solomon	S	R72A	1711ca		
Bradford Susanna	S	R16E	1697ca		d. yng
Bradford Sylvanus	S	R38A	1710abt		
Bradford Sylvanus	S	R28C	1723 Jul 6		1723 Jul12
Bradford Thomas	S	R12C	1658ca	1681ca	1731 Oct 1
Bradford Thomas	S	R39A	1712 Nov14		
Bradford Thomas	S	R97A	1732 Feb 9		1748 Jul 7
Bradford Thomas	S	R111D	1755 Jun18		
Bradford Thomas=R12C	S	R19Gbf	1658cat	1681ca	1731 Oct 1
Bradford Wait	S	R26N	1730abt	1765 Nov 1	1801 Oct20
Bradford Welthea	S	R21F	1702 May15	1723ca	1755 Jun 2
Bradford Welthea	S	X59F	1702 May15		
Bradford William	S	R9A	1565abt		
Bradford William	D	D9/24	1624Jun 17	1650 Jun17	=R11B
Bradford William	S	W19Baf	1624Jun17	=W18Aaf	1702Feb20
Bradford William	D	D27/24	1624Jun17	=R11B	1703Feb20
Bradford William	S	X20Aaf	1624Jun17	=W18Aaf	1703Feb 20
Bradford William	S	W56Baf	1660abt		
Bradford William	S	W53G	1688 Apr15		
Bradford William	S	R14G	1688 Aug15	1714 Dec 9	1728 May 8
Bradford William	S	R16D	1695ca		d. yng
Bradford William	S	R39D	1718 Jul 1		
Bradford William	S	R32C	1720 Dec16		1724 Feb15
Bradford William	S	R34F	1726 Jan25		1753 Dec10
Bradford William	S	R36F	1726 May 9		1726 Jul
Bradford William	S	R32F	1728 Nov 4		

NAME	DIV.	NUMBER	BIRTH	MARRIAGE	DEATH
Bradford William	S	R88C	1734 Apr13		
Bradford William	S	R106C	1754 Mar 9		
Bradford William	S	R116D	1770 Dec15		
Bradford William MF	D	D9/25	1589Mar 19	2 Mar	=R10A
Bradford William MF	D	D27/25	1589ca	2 Mar	1657 May 9
Bradford William=D9/24	S	R11B	1624 Jun17	3 Mar	1703 Feb20
Bradford William=D9/25	S	R10A	1589 Mar19	2 Mar.	1657 May 9
Bradford William=R11B	S	W18Aaf	1624Jun17	1650 Apr23	1703Feb20
Bradford William=R12B	S	W19Ba	1654 Mar11	1678Ca	1687 Jul15
Bradford William=R15B	S	W56Ba	1687bef	1712 Nov18	1729 Mar 9
Bradford William=W19Ba	S	R12B	1654Mar 11	1678ca	1687 Jul 5
Bradford William=W19Ba	S	R15B	1687bef	1712 Nov18	1729 Mar 9
Bradford Winslow	S	R99K	1757		1758 May22
Bradford Zadock	S	R34B	1719 Jul30	unm.	1745 Jan23
Bradford Zenas	S	R98C	1739 Jul 6		1749 Jul
Bradley Martha	A	A19/239	1667	1686	
Brainard Daniel	S	G12Aaf	1670abt		
Brainard Hannah	S	G12Aa	1694		1744
Brainard Martha	S	G26Aa	1740		1796
Brainard Mary	S	G17Aa	1727	1749	1796
Bramhall Joshua	S	W57Iaf	1690abt		
Bramhall Sylvanus	S	W57Ia	1712 Apr30	1762 Jan 7	1779 Mar13
Branch Experience	S	W43Aa	1665ca	1691ca	1697 Nov14
Branch John	S	W43Aaf	1645abt		
Branch P.	S	N13Cd	1740abt		
Bray Ann	A	A15/51	1670abt	1693ca	1692
Bray James	A	A15/102	1645abt		
Breck Abigail	A	A1/151	1732 Jun19	1754 Aug16	1819 Oct28
Breck John	A	A1/302	1705	1727	1761
Breck Sarah	A	A2/239	1665ca		
Breman Jean	S	G41Ba	1485ca		
Brenton Abigail	S	W36Dam	1650abt		
Brewer Christiana	S	N15Ja	1792ca	1814 Jan11	
Brewer Daniel =A1/1074	A	A17/108	1600abt		1646Mar28
Brewer Daniel Jr	A	A17/54	1624ca	1652 Nov 5	1708 Jan 8
Brewer Eliab	A	A19/20	1760 Apr 6	1782 Feb18	1835Sep 24
Brewer Hannah	A	A12/89	1630ca		1717 Oct25
Brewer Hannah	A	A17/27	1665 Jul 5		1706aft
Brewer Israel C	A	A19/10	1797ca		1873
Brewer John Jr	A	A19/160	1642	1668ca	1690

NAME	DIV.	NUMBER	BIRTH	MARRIAGE	DEATH
Brewer Jonathan	A	A19/80	1689Jun 21	1715ca	1753ca
Brewer Samuel	A	A19/40	1716 Nov 4	1740Mar10	
Brewer Sarah Almeda	A	A19/5	1823 Dec17	1844 Mar 3	1906 Jan 2
Brewer William B.	S	N15Jaf	1765abt		
Brewster Abigail	S	R25Cam	1700abt		
Brewster Elizabeth	A	A16/185	1585abt	1611	1666aft
Brewster Elizabeth	S	R12Ma	1690ca	1709 Feb13	1741
Brewster Fear=A10Ab	A	A18/45	1600abt	1626ca	1634bef
Brewster Fear=A18/45	S	A10Ab	1600ca	1626ca	1634bef
Brewster Lydia	S	A21Da	1680 Feb11	1706ca	1749bef
Brewster Sarah	S	R12Bam	1640abt		
Brewster William	S	A21Daf	1655abt		
Brewster William MF	S	A10Abf	1565ca	1590ca	1644Apr 10
Brewster William MF	A	A18/90	1565ca	1590ca	=A10Abf
Brewster Wrestling	S	R12Maf	1670abt		
Bridge Galesha	S	G52Ga	1815ca		
Bridge Prudence	A	A1/269	1664	1684	1723
Bridget Anglier	A	A17/57	1607ca	1644ca	1672 Aug 4
Bridgham Charlotte	S	C61Ia	1763ca		
Briggs Asa	A	A19/46	1755 Jun22	1777Dec 27	1834
Briggs Charles	S	K49E	1711 Feb20		
Briggs Deborah	S	K49A	1693 Mar11		1745living
Briggs Edward	S	K18Ba	1665 Feb19	1692ca	1718 May11
Briggs Esther	S	G32Ca	1770ca	1792	
Briggs Hannah	S	K49B	1698 Dec19		1745living
Briggs John	S	K18Baf	1640abt		
Briggs Josiah	S	K49D	1713 Mar 4		
Briggs Mary	S	W33Ca	1695ca	1714 May10	1729 Jul
Briggs Sally	A	A19/23	1783ca	1799 Oct 7	1869 Jun18
Briggs Seth	A	A19/184	1708	1726	1779aft
Briggs Silas	A	A19/92	1732Apr 17	1754Oct 31	1813 Sep 9
Briggs Susannah	S	K18Ca	1673ca	1695abt	1719 Oct 6
Briggs Thomas	S	K18Caf	1650abt		
Briggs Walter	S	K49C	1701 Feb19		
Brigham Abigail	A	A1/147	1723 Dec31	1742ca	1777Jun12
Brigham John Jr	A	A1/294	1680		1729
Bright Beriah	A	A11/27	1649 Sep22	1671 Nov30	1734 Oct7
Bright Henry	A	A11/108	1560 Sep		1609
Bright Henry	A	A11/54	1602 Dec	1634ca	1686 Oct9
Brimsmead Ebbet	S	R12Iam	1635abt		

NAME	DIV.	NUMBER	BIRTH	MARRIAGE	DEATH
Brinstall Mary	S	C46Ab	1655ca		
Brinton Elizabeth	A	A3/429	1660abt		1708aft
Briswalter Helen	S	G54Ba	1897abt	1917 Jun 7	
Briswalter John	S	G54Baf	1870abt		
Brock Bathsheba	S	R13Bb	1703 May21	1719 Sep	1753living
Brock Bathsheba=R13Bb	S	R25Bam	1703 May21	1717 Sep	1753living
Brock Francis	S	R13Bbf	1680abt		
Brockway Hannah	S	F15Dbm	1670ca		
Brodie Mary	A	A4/25	1782	1805 Feb27	
Brodie Robert	A	A4/50	1735ca		1836 Feb22
Brodie William	A	A4/100	1700abt	1720	
Brodnax Anne	A	A1/79	1730abt	1755 Feb11	1781 abt
Brodnax Edward	A	A1/158	1725abt		1749 abt
Brodnax William	A	A1/316	1675 Feb28	1700 aft	1727 Feb16
Bronson Dorcas	A	A16/57	1633ca	1657bef	1697 May13
Bronson John	A	A16/114	1602ca	1626Nov 19	1680
Brooks Bathsheba	S	X23Gam	1645abt		
Brooks Bathsheba	S	X23Dam	1650abt		
Brooks Henry	S	R16Aaf	1670abt		
Brooks Mary	S	R16Aa	1693 Sep15	1711 Feb17	
Brooks Rebecca	S	C25Ba	1679		
Brooks Robert Jr	S	L11Da	1630ca	1656bef	1669 Sep22
Brooks Robert Sr	S	L11Daf	1585abt		
Broquin Henry	S	G40Ba	1455ca		
Broughton Elizabeth	S	T27Bam	1715abt		
Brown Mary	D	D10am24	1625abt		
Brown Peter	D	D10amf24	1600abt		
Brown Abigail	S	T26Ba	1726 Mar31	1752 Mar31	
Brown Adam	A	A19/88	1721ca	1743Aug 4	1775Jul 20
Brown Adam Jr	A	A19/44	1748ca	1772Dec3	
Brown Alexander	A	A3/92	1773ca		1816 Sept
Brown Anna	S	X26Ha	1715ca	1736 Jan 8	1749 Nov
Brown Benjamin	S	H54I	1720 Jun24		
Brown Bridget	S	R117Ba	1690ca	1712 Sep18	
Brown Deborah	S	C61Aa	1747ca		
Brown Edward	S	R19Ka	1705ca	1744 Sept9	1791 Jul28
Brown Eleazor	S	R117Baf	1670abt		
Brown Esek	S	C84Aa	1679		
Brown George	A	A3/396	1644		1726
Brown George	S	H19Eaf	1650abt		

NAME	DIV.	NUMBER	BIRTH	MARRIAGE	DEATH
Brown George	S	H54G	1716 Dec30		
Brown Hubbard	S	R65A	1745 Dec11		
Brown Isaac	A	A3/46	1771 Apr16	1795 Oct27	1853 Mar 1
Brown Israel Putnam	A	A19/22	1781 Nov 2	1799 Oct 7	1867 Nov 9
Brown Jacob	A	A19/176	1680	1707	1767
Brown James	S	H19Ea	1675ca	1704 Apr13	
Brown James	S	H54F	1715 Jun 4		
Brown Jane	S	H54E	1713 Jun19		
Brown Jane	A	A3/23	1807 Mar16	1825 Jun23	1886 Feb26
Brown Jesse	S	H54B	1706 Jan21		
Brown John	S	T26Baf	1700abt		
Brown Joseph	S	H54A	1704 Feb 5		
Brown Lera	S	G54Bb		1968Jan 20	
Brown Mary	S	K15Cam	1625abt		
Brown Mary	S	Q11A	1626ca	1646ca	1689aft
Brown Mary	A	A1/159	1725abt		
Brown Mary =K15Cam	S	K16Cam	1625abt		
Brown Mercy	A	A3/99	1722 Jan12	1747 Sep17	1784 Jan22
Brown Obadiah	S	C18Da	1755ca		
Brown Peter	S	Q10A	1600bef	2 mar.	1633
Brown Priscilla	S	Q11B	1629ca	1649 Mar21	1697aft
Brown Rebecca	S	Q11C	1631ca	1654ca	1698aft
Brown Rebecca	S	H54H	1718 Apr23		
Brown Ruth	S	H54D	1710 Oct 6		
Brown Sally	A	A19/11	1801 Feb 4		1884
Brown Samuel	A	A3/198	1694 Sep11	1717 Sept5	1769 Oct 3
Brown Zilpha	S	H54C	1708 Oct18		
Brownell Content	S	K62F	1708 Feb11		
Brownell Cynthia	S	C17Ga	1750ca		
Brownell Elizabeth	S	K62B	1700 May13		
Brownell Esther	S	K62E	1706 Feb10		
Brownell Joseph	S	K62A	1699 Feb13		
Brownell Rebecca	S	K62G	1710 Feb28		
Brownell Sarah	S	K62D	1704 Feb20		
Brownell Thomas	S	K20Fa	1674 May25	1698 Nov15	
Brownell Thomas	S	K62C	1702 Feb15		
Brownell William	S	K20Faf	1650abt		
Brownson Roger(Bronson	A	A16/228	1576	1600	1635
Bruce Elizabeth	S	P15Ha	1672 Aug24	1698 Mar 2	1748 Apr20
Bruce George	S	P15Haf	1650abt		

NAME	DIV.	NUMBER	BIRTH	MARRIAGE	DEATH
Bryan Susanna	A	A1/223	1735abt		
Bryant Abigail	S	X17Fbm	1650abt		
Bryant Abigail	S	W56Ea	1703 Jul 5	1722 Dec13	
Bryant Barnabas	S	A62B	1710 Mar 7		d.yng
Bryant Barnabus	S	A62D	1715 Nov18		
Bryant George	S	K40Abf	1710abt		
Bryant Hopestill	S	A62C	1713 Jun23		
Bryant James	S	A24Da	1682 Jul26	1708 Jul 8	
Bryant John	S	X17Fbf	1650abt		
Bryant John	S	A24Daf	1660abt		
Bryant Jonathan	S	X17Fb	1677 Mar23	1726 Nov12	1731bef
Bryant Mercy	S	X17Ba	1670ca	1693 Jun15	1706bef
Bryant Rebeckah #1	S	A62A	1709 May17		d.yng
Bryant Rebeckah #2	S	A62F	1720 Feb 4		
Bryant Samuel	S	W56Eaf	1680abt		
Bryant Sarah	S	T20Fam	1670abt		
Bryant Sarah	S	K40Ab	1731 Oct31	1771 Jan22	1805 Aug20
Bryant Sarah	A	A6/9	1745abt	1769 Aug22	1785after
Bryant Seth	S	A62E	1718 Jul16		
Buck Elizabeth	S	T14Aam	1660abt		
Buck Elizabeth=T14Aam	S	T16Gam	1665abt		
Buck Henry	A	A12/86	1625ca	1660 Oct31	1712 Jul 7
Buck Isaac	S	W37Aaf	1635abt		
Buck James	S	W37Aa	1659 Sep 6		1690bef
Buck James=W37A	S	A25Daf	1666Dec 16	1691May 17	1727May 13
Buck Mary	S	R25Bam	1685abt		
Buck Mary	S	A25Da	1688ca	1710 Jan11	1725 Dec
Buck Ruth	A	A12/43	1681 Dec 4	1699 Mar14	1754bef
Buckley Mary	S	P19Ga	1690abt	1722 May22	
Budd Susan	S	G46Aa	1685abt	1718	
Budd Thomas	S	G46Aaf	1660abt		
Buell Deborah	S	R91D	1738 Sep13		
Buell Elijah	S	R91B	1735 Nov 9		
Buell Hannah	S	R91C	1735 Nov 9		
Buell Ichabod	S	R91E	1741 Feb15		
Buell Joseph	S	R91G	1749 May29		
Buell Oliver	S	R91F	1746 May 6		
Buell Timothy	S	R24Ga	1711 Oct24	1730 Jan20	1794
Buell Timothy	S	R91A	1732 Nov20		
Buell William	S	R24Gaf	1685abt		

NAME	DIV.	NUMBER	BIRTH	MARRIAGE	DEATH
Bulkeley Rebecca	A	A1/293	1681	1701	
Bulloch Archibald	A	A7/24	1729	1764 Oct 9	1777 Feb22
Bulloch James	A	A7/48	1701ca	1729ca	1780 Oct25
Bulloch James	A	A7/12	1765ca	1786 Apr13	1806 Feb 9
Bulloch James Stephens	A	A7/6	1793ca	1831 May 8	1849 Feb18
Bulloch Martha	A	A7/3	1834 July8	1853 Dec22	1884 Feb12
Bullock Squire	S	C31Ea	1710abt		
Bullock Thankful	A	A1/371	1681	1699	1762
Bullock Thankful	S	C25Da	1681	1699	=A1/371
Bump Catherine	S	C63Aa	1785ca		
Bumpas John Jr	S	W21Ea	1673 Sep28	1694ca	1762 Jun22
Bumpas John Sr	S	W21Eaf	1645abt		
Bumpas Samuel	S	W46Fa	1685 Jan	1717 Aug 1	
Bumpas Thomas	S	W46Faf	1660abt		
Bumpfield John II	D	D30/26	1350abt		
Bunker Mary	S	K18Cbm	1675abt		
Burdg Almira Park	A	A3/7	1849 Sep16	1879 Apr16	1943 Jul23
Burdg David	A	A3/448	1660ca	1684	1724bef
Burdg Jacob	A	A3/56	1743 Apr 5	1768	1800abt
Burdg Jacob Jr.	A	A3/28	1783 Jan28	1807 Dec 9	1862 Dec 1
Burdg Jonathan	A	A3/224	1695abt		1765abt
Burdg Oliver	A	A3/14	1821 Sep28	1846 Apr29	1908 Jun11
Burgd Joseph	A	A3/112	1715abt	1739ca	1777living
Burgess Abia	S	B20C	1708 Apr14		
Burgess Abigail	S	B20D	1709 Jun29		
Burgess Albert Carl Sr	S	G54B	1895 Jan 9	2 Mar	1979
Burgess Barbara Ellen	S	G59B	1954 Sep 2	1972 Aug 5	
Burgess Benjamin	S	B15E	1681 May 5		
Burgess Benjamin	S	B16C	1681 May 5		
Burgess Benjamin	S	B18D	1701 May 3		
Burgess Benjamin	S	B21A	1721 Sep27		d yng
Burgess Benjamin	S	B21D	1728 Jul13		
Burgess Clarence Perry	S	G54A	1887 Oct12	2 Mar	1962 Sep
Burgess Clarence Perry	S	N18Ba	1887 Oct12	(1)1907	1962 Sep
Burgess Clyde Cecil	S	G54C	1900 Mar20	(1)1921	1982
Burgess Cora Louise	S	G55C	1924 Apr 8	1948 Feb12	
Burgess David	S	B19H	1713 Aug23		
Burgess Deborah	S	B17B	1694		1779Jul
Burgess Dorothy	S	B16B	1670 Nov12		
Burgess Ebenezer	S	W48Aa	1673 Oct 2	1701 Mar20	1750 May22

NAME	DIV.	NUMBER	BIRTH	MARRIAGE	DEATH
Burgess Ebenezer	S	B15B	1673 Oct 2		1750May 22
Burgess Edward	S	B17A	1692	1720 Jul27	
Burgess Elizabeth	S	B11C	1629ca	1652 Feb12	1717 Sep26
Burgess Elizabeth	S	K19Bam	1645abt		
Burgess Elizabeth	S	B18B	1697 Oct12	1720 Apr 1	
Burgess Esther	S	B17C	1696	1717 Jun20	1764
Burgess Esther	S	B21C	1725 Jul27		
Burgess Esther	S	G55A	1909 Jun22	1933 Aug20	1991 Dec30
Burgess Ethel May	S	G54F	1909 Aug17	1930 Nov 5	
Burgess Ezekial	S	B18F	1705 Aug 9		
Burgess George Milton	S	G57B	1930 Jun 5	1950 May22	1960Mar31
Burgess George W	S	G53Ga	1863 Jan10	1886 Oct11	1935 Jul 5
Burgess Hannah	S	B19C	1701 May 2		
Burgess Ichabod	S	B16D	1684		
Burgess Jacob	S	B11D	1630abt	1670 Jun 1	1719 Mar17
Burgess Jacob	S	W48Aaf	1650abt		
Burgess Jacob	S	B15C	1676 Oct18	1704 Apr27	1769
Burgess Jacob	S	B13E	1680abt		1772Aug15
Burgess Jacob	S	B20F	1715 Nov 9		
Burgess Jacob	S	B17I	1717 Nov11	1739 Sep	1768 Sep18
Burgess Jedidah	S	B20B	1706 Jul29	1729 Dec 4	
Burgess John	S	B11B	1627ca	1657 Sep 8	1701
Burgess John	A	A12/110	1630abt	1657 Sep 8	
Burgess John	S	B13A	1670abt		
Burgess John	S	B17F	1711 Jan10	1740 Apr 3	1795
Burgess John Jr	S	B18H	1710 Oct		
Burgess Joseph	S	B11E	1630abt		1695Aug
Burgess Joseph	S	B13C	1678abt		
Burgess Joseph	S	B18C	1699 Jul 9		
Burgess Joseph	S	B17E	1708 Aug 6	1730 Jan	1789
Burgess Lydia	S	B17D	1700ca		
Burgess Lydia	S	B21F	1734 Feb15	1751	
Burgess Margaret Eliz.	S	G55B	1911 Nov19	(1)1932May	
Burgess Margaret L	S	G57A	1926 Sep27	2 Mar	
Burgess Martha	A	A12/55	1671ca	1700 Oct31	1728 Sep
Burgess Martha	S	B13F	1680abt	1700 Oct31	
Burgess Martha	S	B19D	1703 Feb15		1718Feb 9
Burgess Martha	S	B17L	1727 Apr		
Burgess Mary	S	B13I	1680abt		
Burgess Mary	S	B15F	1685abt		

NAME	DIV.	NUMBER	BIRTH	MARRIAGE	DEATH
Burgess Mary	S	B18A	1695 Dec25	1716 Mar2	
Burgess Mary	S	B19A	1696 Nov27	1722 Oct 9	
Burgess Mary	S	B17G	1712 Sep18		
Burgess Matthias	S	B19H	1711 Mar 4		
Burgess Mercy	S	B13H	1680abt		
Burgess Mercy	S	B17J	1722 Feb22		
Burgess Nathaniel	S	B17M	1729 May17		1893 Jan 1
Burgess Patience	S	B13G	1680abt		
Burgess Ray Elmer	S	G54D	1902 Nov10	2 Mar	
Burgess Rebecca	S	B16A	1667 Jan17		
Burgess Rebecca	S	B17K	1725 Jun		
Burgess Roger Glenn	S	G59A	1951 Jul31	1972 Jul29	
Burgess Roy	S	G54E	1902 Nov10	1929 Jan31	
Burgess Roy =G54E	D	D32a20	1902Nov 10	1929Jan31	
Burgess Samuel	S	B15A	1671 Mar 8		
Burgess Samuel	S	B13D	1680abt		
Burgess Samuel	S	B18E	1703 Feb 3		
Burgess Samuel	S	B20E	1711 Nov 2		
Burgess Sarah	S	B13J	1680abt		
Burgess Sarah	S	B19E	1705 Jan 4		
Burgess Sarah	S	B21E	1730 Oct24	1750	
Burgess Thankful	S	B19F	1707 Jan10	1728 Sep19	
Burgess Thankful	S	B18G	1708 Jun 7	1727Apr 6	
Burgess Thomas	A	A12/220	1620abt		1684
Burgess Thomas	S	B13B	1670abt	1696 Feb26	
Burgess Thomas	S	B15D	1680 Mar29		1757
Burgess Thomas	S	B19B	1698 Aug 8		
Burgess Thomas	S	B17H	1714 May25	1738 Jan	1792 May10
Burgess Thomas	S	B21B	1723 Sep 6		
Burgess Thomas II	S	B12A	1668	1691	1743 Jul 1
Burgess Thomas Jr	S	B11A	1627ca	1648 Nov 8	
Burgess Thomas Sr	S	B10A	1603		1685Feb 13
Burgess Zaccheus	S	B20A	1705 Mar 9		
Burghersh Elizabeth	D	D29a21	1340abt		
Burnam Abigail	S	T280Aam	1675abt		
Burnham Sarah	A	A19/177	1679	1707	1729
Burns John	A	A4/102	1715abt		
Burns Margaret	A	A4/51	1744ca		1789ca
Burr Rebecca	S	R24Kam	1690abt		
Burroughs Elizabeth	S	W40C	1680ca		1699 Aug 7

NAME	DIV.	NUMBER	BIRTH	MARRIAGE	DEATH
Burroughs James	S	W15Ia	1650ca	1674 Dec8	1699aft
Burroughs James	S	W40A	1677ca		1688 Jan 8
Burroughs Mary	S	W40B	1679 Oct30		
Burroughs Thomas	S	W40D	1685 Jul12	1706ca	1722 Dec16
Burrowes Elizabeth	S	Q12Ba	1654 Mar 5	1676bef	1718 Apr 8
Burrowes Jeremiah	S	Q12Baf	1625abt		
Bursley Joanna	S	F18Aam	1645ca		
Bursley Temperance	S	X17Iam	1665abt		
Burson Ann	A	A3/119	1721 Feb 9	1744 Sept	
Burson George	A	A3/476	1660abt	1687	1715
Burson Joseph	A	A3/238	1689 Dec25		1751aft
Burt Abigail	A	A8/45	1718 Mar28	1739 Nov22	1766 Jul22
Burt Abigail=A8/45	D	D4a22	1718 Mar28	1739 Nov22	1766 Jul22
Burt Abigial	S	X21Bb	1676 Jan28	1707bef	1737living
Burt John	A	A8/90	1692 Jan 5	1714 Jun 3	
Burt John =A08/90	D	D4af22	1692 Jan 5	1714 Jun 3	
Burt Richard	S	X21Bbf	1650abt		
Burt William	A	A8/180	1670abt		
Burton Eleanor	S	L17C	1728 May 4	1746 Feb 5	1751 Oct27
Burton Elizabeth	S	L14C	1687after	unm	
Burton Elizabeth	S	L17D	1737 May 9	1766 May15	1807 May17
Burton Hannah	A	A2/251	1655ca	1672ca	
Burton Martha	S	W36Da	1678ca	1702ca	1750 Apr14
Burton Martha	S	L17A	1723 Jun19		1723 Sep15
Burton Penelope	S	L14A	1686 Aug 8		1687 Mar
Burton Penelope	S	L17B	1724 Oct27	1751 Oct23	1788living
Burton Stephen	S	W36Daf	1650abt		
Burton Stephen	S	L12Aa	1660ca	1684 Sept4	1693aftFeb
Burton Stephen Sr	S	L12Aaf	1635abt		
Burton Thomas	S	L14D	1692 Mar19	1722 May10	1779 Oct22
Burwell Edward	A	A14/264	1579 Aug		1626
Burwell Edward	A	A14/296	1579 Aug		1626
Burwell Elizabeth	A	A14/33	1678ca		1734 Dec30
Burwell Joanna	A	A14/37	1675ca	1693 Nov23	1727 Oct 7
Burwell Lewis	A	A14/132	1621 Mar	1646ca	1653 Nov18
Burwell Lewis	A	A14/148	1621 Mar	1646ca	1653 Nov18
Burwell Lewis Jr.	A	A14/66	1647ca		1710 Dec19
Burwell Lewis Jr.	A	A14/74	1647ca		1710 Dec19
Bush George Herbert	A	A1/1	1924 Jun12	1945 Jan 6	
Bush George. U.S.Pres.	D	D2/12	1925 Jun 6	1945 Jan 8	

NAME	DIV.	NUMBER	BIRTH	MARRIAGE	DEATH
Bush J.	S	N15Ka	1790abt		
Bush James Smith	A	A1/8	1825 Jun15	1859 Feb24	1889 Nov11
Bush Obadiah Newcomb	A	A1/16	1797 Jan28	1821 Nov 8	1851ca
Bush Prescott S =A1/3	D	D2/13	1895 May15	1921 Aug 6	1972 Oct 8
Bush Prescott Sheldon	A	A1/2	1895 May15	1921 Aug 6	1972 Oct 8
Bush Samuel P.=A1/4	D	D2a14	1863 Oct 4	1894 Jun20	1948 Feb 8
Bush Samuel Prescott	A	A1/4	1863 Oct 4	1894 Jun20	1948 Feb 8
Bush Timothy	A	A1/64	1740abt	1759 Apr12	1815ca
Bush Timothy Jr	A	A1/32	1766 Apr 1	1791 Jul26	1850 May 4
Busketh Sarah	A	A2/155	1630abt	1656ca	1712
Butler Benjamin	A	A1/176	1727 Dec18	1757 Jan14	1800ca
Butler Courtland P	A	A1/22	1813 Mar 8	1840 Dec16	1891 Aug 9
Butler Courtland=A1/22	D	D2a16	1813 Mar 8	1840 Dec16	1891 Aug 9
Butler Daniel	A	A4/60	1790abt		
Butler George Selden	A	A4/30	1820	1843	1907
Butler Israel	A	A1/352	1696ca	1725	1757 aft
Butler Margaret	A	A10/33	1570abt	1588 Aug3	1652ca
Butler Mary =A16/29	S	R18Gam	1670ca	1691Jan21	1744May 17
Butler Mary =R18Gaf	A	A16/29	.1670ca	1691Jan 21	1744 May17
Butler Mary Elizabeth	A	A1/11	1850 Jul15	1869 Feb24	1897 Jan16
Butler Mary=A1/11	D	D2/15	1850 Jul15	1869 Feb24	1897Jan 16
Butler May Gridley	A	A4/15	1848		
Butler Nathaniel	A	A1/88	1761 Jun14		1829 Sep29
Butler Richard	A	A16/116	1620abt		1684Aug 6
Butler Samuel	A	A16/58	1641		1692 Dec31
Butler Samuel Herrick	A	A1/44	1785 Feb12	1806 Jun26	1851 Dec13
Butler William	A	A10/66	1540abt		
Butterworth Hannah	A	A3/341	1665abt		1735ca
Buxton John	A	A2/234	1644ca	1668	1715ca
Buxton Mary	A	A2/117	1669 Sep 3	1697 Dec25	
Byram Abigail	S	Q13Cam	1640abt		
Byram Deliverance	S	K36Aam	1650abt		
Byram Josiah	S	Q23Ba	1698 May 3	1720 Apr12	1760ca
Byram Mehetabel	S	Q71C	1730 May25		
Byram Nicholas	S	Q23Baf	1675abt		
Byram Rebecca	S	Q71D	1732 Aug26		
Byram Susanna	S	Q71A	1721 Apr27		
Byram Theophilus	S	Q71B	1725 Aug 8		
Cadman Elizabeth	S	K43A	1685ca		
Cadman George	S	K17Ca	1656bef		1718 Nov24

NAME	DIV.	NUMBER	BIRTH	MARRIAGE	DEATH
Cadman William	S	K17Caf	1635abt		
Caldwell A.	S	N13Ca	1735abt		
Caldwell Susana	S	G46Aam	1660abt		
Calkins Hugh	S	T13Ga	1659 Jun	1706 Nov29	1722 Sep15
Calkins John	S	T13Gaf	1635abt		
Campbell Ebenezer Jr	S	Q22Aa	1697 Nov30	1738bef	1764aft
Campbell Ebenezer Sr	S	Q22Aaf	1675abt		
Capen John	A	A19/732	1635abt		
Capen Joseph	A	A19/366	1665abt		
Capen Mary	A	A19/183	1688	1709	
Capen Susanna	A	A5/139	1602	1624	1664
Capet Hugh King France	D	D30/40	950abt	REIGN	987-996
Caplow Mabel	S	G4Aa	1425abt		
Carey Sarah	S	W12Aam	1600abt		
Carman Richard	S	G51Ba	1790abt		
Carpenter Alexander	S	R10Abf	1565abt		
Carpenter Alice	D	D4amm24	1580abt		
Carpenter Alice	S	R10Ab	1590 Aug 3	1623 Aug14	1670 Mar
Carpenter Alice	D	D29a11	1590abt		
Carpenter Alice=R10Ab	D	D27b25	1590 Aug 3	1623 Aug14	1670 Mar
Carpenter Benjamin	A	A6/120	1658 Jan15	1679ca	1727 May22
Carpenter Benjamin	D	D19/25	1658 Jan15	1679ca	=A06/120
Carpenter Elizabeth	S	C78Ba	1670ca		
Carpenter Hannah	S	C25Fa	1685ca		
Carpenter Joseph	A	A6/240	1634ca	1655	1675ca
Carpenter Jotham	D	D19/24	1682 Jun 1	1707 Jul10	1760ca
Carpenter Jotham	A	A6/60	1682 June1	1707 Jul10	1760ca
Carpenter Jotham Jr.	A	A6/30	1708 Aug 1	1728 May11	1777 May10
Carpenter Keiziah	D	D20/25	1697	=A1/379	1763
Carpenter Keziah	A	A1/379	1697	1721	1763
Carpenter Sybill	A	A6/15	1739 Feb26	1761 Dec31	
Carpenter Tabatha	S	C28Ca	1705ca		
Carr Anne	S	W45Ca	1689ca	1709 Jan18	1769 Jul
Carr Caleb	S	C76Ga	1657		
Carr John	S	W45Caf	1660abt		
Carr Mercy	S	C84A	1683		
Carroll Sarah	S	G44Da	1705abt		
Carruthers Elayne	S	G57Ba	1930abt	1950 May20	
Carter Anne	A	A14/17	1702ca	1722ca	1744abt
Carter Catharine	A	A3/393	1665abt	1689	

NAME	DIV.	NUMBER	BIRTH	MARRIAGE	DEATH
Carter John	A	A14/68	1613ca		1669 Jun10
Carter Robert "King"	A	A14/34	1663ca	1701ca	1732 Aug 4
Cartwright Alice	S	P37A	1702 Sep21		
Cartwright Dorcas	S	P37B	1703ca		d yng
Cartwright Edward	S	P19Caf	1655abt		
Cartwright Hazadiah	S	P37D	1707		
Cartwright Phineas	S	P37C	1704ca		d yng
Cartwright Sampson	S	P19Ca	1677 Jan26	1701ca	1741
Cartwright Sarah	A	A7/207	1655abt	1680ca	
Carver Abiezer	S	Q69D	1734 Sep14		1755 Aug31
Carver Benjamin	S	Q69B	1728 Feb28		
Carver Eleazer	S	Q22Eaf	1675abt		
Carver Elizabeth	S	K89A	1717 Feb22		
Carver Elizabeth	S	Q69C	1731 Sep10		
Carver Experience	S	Q69F	1739 May 2		
Carver John	S	K25Faf	1670abt		
Carver Joseph	S	Q22Ea	1700ca	1725 May 4	1778 Sep24
Carver Joseph	S	Q69A	1727 Mar23		
Carver Mary	S	T12Ja	1695 Mar20	1717 Jan20	
Carver Mary	S	K89B	1721 Sep14		
Carver Rebecca	S	Q69H	1744 Sep28		
Carver Robert	S	K25Fa	1694 Sep30	1717 Mar28	1752living
Carver Robert	S	K89C	1723 Aug19		
Carver Robert	S	Q69G	1742 Jun 2		
Carver Sarah	S	Q69E	1736 Feb14		
Carver William	S	T12Jaf	1670abt		
Cary Bridget	A	A14/73	1645abt	1670ca	
Cary Eleazer	S	R19Iaf	1685abt		
Cary Elizabeth	S	T24G	1700 Jul23	1729 Nov10	1742 Aug16
Cary Hannah	S	T24Cam	1660abt		
Cary Hannah	S	T24F	1696 Jul23		1706living
Cary James	S	T13Aa	1652 Mar28	1681 Jan 4	1706 Nov20
Cary James	S	T24E	1692 Oct20	1721 Feb 8	1762 Nov18
Cary John	A	A14/292	1583 Apr		1661 Feb13
Cary John	S	T12Aaf	1625abt		
Cary John	S	T13Caf	1655abt		
Cary Joshua	S	T61B	1725 Feb26	unm.	1748 Jun26
Cary Lydia	S	R19Ia	1706 Feb12	1720 Mar21	1784 Apr 9
Cary Mary	S	T24D	1689 Aug31		1706living
Cary Mehitable	S	T13Ca	1670 Dec24	1700 Dec 5	1724 Jul 8

NAME	DIV.	NUMBER	BIRTH	MARRIAGE	DEATH
Cary Mercy	S	T24C	1686 Jan28	1713 Apr28	1725 Nov18
Cary Miles	A	A14/146	1622 Jan		1667 Jun10
Cary Sarah	S	T61A	1723 Jun10		
Caswell Catherine	S	W29Ja	1681ca	1703 Feb15	1761 Apr 2
Caswell William	S	W29Jaf	1655abt		
Cattell James	A	A3/252	1716	1738 May18	1783
Cattell James Jr	A	A3/126	1743 May16	1763 Jul27	1806
Cattell Jane	A	A3/63	1780 Apr22	1801	1853 Mar29
Cattell Jonas	A	A3/504	1690	1714	1731
Caulkins Elizabeth	S	R24Cam	1670ca		
Caulkins Elizabeth	S	R24Iam	1690abt		
Celine Marie	S	G40E	1455ca		
Chabane Adelaide	S	G40Aam	1430ca		
Chaffee Mary	S	C46Ha	1668ca		
Chamber David	S	G52Aa	1804abt		
Champion Mary	S	F15Db	1693 Jul31	1714ca	1770 Dec12
Champion Rebecca	A	A1/317	1677ca	1700 aft	1723 Dec19
Champion Thomas	S	F15Dbf	1670ca		1705 Apr 4
Champney Mary	S	P15Cam	1630abt		
Chandler Abigail	A	A12/11	1741 Sep11	1761ca	1791 Oct
Chandler Anna	S	R101D	1746 Jun14		
Chandler Benjamin	S	T14Aaf	1660abt		=T16Gaf
Chandler Benjamin	S	T16Gaf	1665abt		=T14Aaf
Chandler Benjamin	S	T44C	1727 May16		
Chandler Betty	S	R26La	1728 Oct21	1750 Jul21	1811 Oct24
Chandler Deborah	S	R105H	1766 Jun		1767Aug 13
Chandler Dorothy	S	Q73F	1738 Mar31		
Chandler Ebenezer	S	R26Ca	1712 Sept8	1737 Feb23	
Chandler Edmund	S	Q23Daf	1675abt		
Chandler Elizabeth	S	Q73D	1736 May18		1766 Nov22
Chandler Ephraim	S	R105A	1750 May18		
Chandler Hannah	A	A8/241	1673	1695	1718
Chandler Hannah	S	R105D	1757 Jun12		1795living
Chandler Henry	A	A12/44	1667 May28	1695 Nov28	1737 Aug27
Chandler Isaac	A	A12/22	1717ca	1740 Feb28	1787 Jun 5
Chandler John	S	Q23Da	1696	1724 May 6	1764 Apr21
Chandler John	S	T44A	1722 Oct25		
Chandler Jonathan	S	Q73B	1731 Sep24		
Chandler Joseph	S	R120af	1670abt		
Chandler Joseph	S	R26Caf	1690abt		

NAME	DIV.	NUMBER	BIRTH	MARRIAGE	DEATH
Chandler Joseph	S	T16Ga	1690ca	1720 Sept8	1774 Sep28
Chandler Judah	S	R101F	1756 Nov14		1772 Apr24
Chandler Judith	S	Q73C	1734 Jul13		
Chandler Keturah	S	T14Aa	1683 May	1703 Jan19	1771 Jan14
Chandler Lucy	S	R105C	1756 Jun 6		1795living
Chandler Lydia	S	X12Dam	1610abt		
Chandler Lydia	S	X12Ham	1610abt		
Chandler Lydia	S	R101A	1740 Mar14		
Chandler Mary	S	R120a	1695abt		
Chandler Mary	S	Q73E	1736 May18		1800living
Chandler Nathan	S	R26Ka	1726 Oct28	1749 Aug 3	1795 Sep21
Chandler Nathaniel	S	R101E	1756 Nov14		1773 Jun14
Chandler Philip	S	R26Kaf	1700abt		
Chandler Philip	S	R26Laf	1700abt		
Chandler Reuben	S	Q73A	1725 May 9		
Chandler Ruth	S	B17Ma	1730abt		
Chandler Ruth	S	R105F	1762 Oct24		
Chandler Sarah	S	R28Kam	1705abt		
Chandler Sarah	S	R105G	1764 Jul23		
Chandler Sceva	S	R101G	1757 Jun12		
Chandler Selah	S	R105B	1756 Jun 6		1773 May21
Chandler Simeon	S	T44B	1724 Jan24		
Chandler Simeon	S	R101C	1744 Jun23		1767 Apr17
Chandler Thomas	A	A12/88	1628ca		1702 Jan15
Chandler William	A	A12/176	1595	1625	1641
Chandler Zilpah	S	R101B	1741 Feb15	unm.	1837 May 7
Chapin Bethiah	A	A2/11	1755 Mar12	1776 May28	1829 Oct6
Chapin Deborah	A	A2/103	1675 Feb12	1693ca	
Chapin John	A	A2/44	1695 May13	1719ca	1770 Aug3
Chapin John	A	A2/22	1730 Oct7	1754 May28	1815 Jul17
Chapin Josiah	A	A2/176	1634ca	1658ca	1726ca
Chapin Josiah=A2/176	A	A2/206	1634ca	1658ca	1726ca
Chapin Seth	A	A2/88	1668 Aug 4		1746 Apr 1
Chapman Avis	S	K16Eam	1615abt		
Chapman Lucille	S	C21Ha	1765ca		
Chase Anne	S	C91Ba	1715ca		
Chase Ezra	A	A4/228	1717 July9	1740 Dec 2	1793 Mar 3
Chase Hannah	S	C37Da	1758ca		
Chase Harold Frank	S	C59Da	1926		
Chase Jacob	A	A4/456	1690abt	1716	1754

NAME	DIV.	NUMBER	BIRTH	MARRIAGE	DEATH
Chase Philadelia	S	C53Ba	1800abt		
Chase Polly	A	A4/57	1784 Aug15	1805 Nov28	1854 Aug
Chase William	A	A4/114	1756 Apr12	1783 Oct 1	1838 Dec 9
Cheever Abigail	A	A8/91	1690 May20	1714 Jun 3	
Cheever Abigail	D	D4am22	1690 May20	1714 Jun 3	
Cheever Mary	A	A8/229	1640	1671	1728
Cheever Thomas	A	A8/182	1658	1685	1749
Cheney Elizabeth	A	A2/17	1707 Sep21	1736 Apr20	1783 Sep21
Cheney Joseph	A	A2/68	1647 Jun 6	1667 Mar12	1704 Sep16
Cheney Josiah	A	A2/34	1685 Jul27	1706ca	1754 Mar16
Cheney Margaret	S	W38Cam	1640abt		
Cheney William	A	A2/136	1604	1626	1667
Chickering Ann	S	C45A	1635		
Chickering Francis	S	C44A	1610abt	=A14/162	1658
Chickering Francis	A	A14/162	1610abt		1658
Chickering Henry	S	C43A	1565		
Chickering Mary	A	A14/81	1648 Apr	1675ca	1720 Mar12
Child Hannah	A	A1/289	1701ca	1721	1788
Child Joseph Jr	S	W38Bb	1658 Jan 7	1705 Jul25	1711 Nov 3
Child Joseph Sr	S	W38Bbf	1630abt		
Child Richard	A	A19/138	1635	1678	1694
Childs Joseph	S	Q15Gaf	1670abt		
Childs Margaret	A	A19/69	1690ca	1701 Dec25	
Childs Priscilla	S	Q15Ga	1693 Nov 5	1718 Dec17	1739 Jul11
Chiles Elizabeth	A	A15/17	1660abt		1702Jan 19
Chiles Walter	A	A15/68	1608abt	1653ca	
Chiles Walter	A	A15/34	1635abt		1672bef
Chillingsworth Mary	S	H27Hbm	1660abt		
Chillingsworth Sarah	S	W42Fam	1660abt		
Chilton Mary	S	T11Dam	1615abt		
Chipman Benjamin	S	R33D	1729 May23		
Chipman Hannah	S	H23Ham	1660abt		
Chipman Hope	D	D2/23	1625abt	1647ca	1683 Jan 8
Chipman John Jr	S	W41Ca	1670 Mar 3	1691ca	1756 Jan 4
Chipman John Sr	D	D2a24	1625ca	1647ca	
Chipman John Sr	S	W41Caf	1645abt		
Chipman Mercy	S	R25Cb	1725 Nov19	1763 Dec 7	1782 Feb13
Chipman Mercy=R25Cb	S	R33C	1725 Nov19	1763Dec 7	1782 Feb13
Chipman Samuel	S	R14Faf	1675abt		
Chipman Seth	S	R14Fa	1697 Feb24	1721 Sep17	1766

NAME	DIV.	NUMBER	BIRTH	MARRIAGE	DEATH
Chipman Seth	S	R25Cbf	1700abt		
Chipman Seth	S	R33B	1724 Nov 1		
Chittenden Alathea	S	W54Ba	1697 Jul	1722 Aug22	1758abt
Chittenden Elizabeth	S	T23Bam	1710abt		
Chittenden Isaac	A	A14/166	1625	1646	1676
Chittenden Joseph	S	W54Baf	1670abt		
Chittenden Nancy	S	C17La	1760ca		
Chittenden Sarah	A	A14/83	1646 Feb25	1666 Jun14	1703 Oct25
Christian Lelitia	A	A15/1a	1790Nov 12	1813Mar 29	1842Sep 10
Chubbuck Alice	S	W39Da	1671 Dec14	1695 Jun24	1745 Jul 9
Chubbuck John	S	W39Daf	1645abt		
Chubbuck Rebecca	S	R14Bbm	1655abt		
Church Abigail	S	W15H	1648 Jun22	1666 Dec19	1677 Dec25
Church Abigail	S	W37A	1666 Dec16	1691 May17	1727 May13
Church Abigail	S	W55Dam	1670abt		
Church Abigail	S	K29Bam	1670abt		
Church Abigail	S	A25Dam	1670abt		
Church Abigail	S	W38F	1675ca		1677 Sep25
Church Abigail	S	W35J	1681ca	1696ca	1720 Jul4
Church Alice	S	W35E	1670 Jun 1		1671
Church Alice	S	W36C	1677ca	1696 Dec18	1732aft
Church Alice	S	W37D	1679 Aug23		
Church Benjamin	S	W15C	1639ca	1667 Dec26	1717 Jan17
Church Benjamin	S	W35F	1671 Jan11		1672
Church Caleb	S	W15G	1646ca		
Church Caleb	S	W38D	1673 Dec16		
Church Caleb	A	A8/52	1728	1751 Sep21	1771ca
Church Charles	S	W15F	1644ca		16590ct 30
Church Charles	S	W36E	1682 May 9	1703 May20	1746 Dec31
Church Charles	S	W37F	1683 Mar	1705Ca	1726 Mar 9
Church Constant	S	W36B	1676 May12	1715ca	1726 Mar 9
Church Deborah	S	W15K	1656 Jan27		
Church Deborah	S	W35I	1676 Mar13	1699 Jul13	1752 Jun 8
Church Deborah	A	A8/13	1783 Mar21	1808 Nov 6	1827 Aug 7
Church Edward	S	W36D	1680	1702ca	1700abt
Church Elizabeth	S	W15A	1636ca	1657 Jan8	1659Feb 3
Church Elizabeth	S	W35B	1663 Jan28	1685 Nov12	1719aft
Church Elizabeth	S	W36F	1684 Mar26	3 Mar	1757 Jul17
Church Hannah	S	W38A	1668 Nov 1	1688ca	
Church Isaac	S	W38G	1678 Jun27	1702 May14	1750abt

NAME	DIV.	NUMBER	BIRTH	MARRIAGE	DEATH
Church John	S	W35D	1668 Jul 5	1693ca	1757 Jan
Church Joseph	S	W15B	1638	1660 Dec13	1710 Mar 5
Church Joseph	S	W35A	1662 Nov 1	1688ca	1715 Mar19
Church Joseph	S	W37E	1681 Mar	1705 Nov 1	1707 Oct
Church Joseph	A	A8/26	1752 Dec14	1777 Apr19	1839ca
Church Joseph Jr.=W35A	A	A8/208	1662 Nov 1	1688ca	1715 Mar19
Church Joshua	S	W38E	1674ca		1690abt
Church Lydia	S	W38C	1671 Jul11	1686 Jan 4	1690 Feb 9
Church Mary	S	W15J	1655ca		1662 Apr30
Church Mary	S	W35C	1666 Mar26	1688ca	1748 Nov11
Church Nathaniel	S	W37C	1670 Feb10	1696 Jan 7	1750abt
Church Nathaniel	S	W36G	1686 Jul1		1687 Feb29
Church Nathaniel	A	A8/104	1693 Feb 8	1717 Mar14	
Church R.	S	N11Fa	1670abt		
Church Rebecca	A	A4/509	1654	1676	1726
Church Rebecca	S	W38H	1678 Jun27	1695ca	1757 Apr 1
Church Richard	S	W11Da	1608ca	1635Mar 14	1668 Dec27
Church Richard	S	W37B	1668 Mar24	1697 Feb 2	1703 Jun17
Church Ruth	S	W38B	1669 Jan12	1689Jun 23	1746 Jan10
Church Sarah	S	W15I	1655abt	1674 Dec8	1690abt
Church Sarah	S	W35G	1673 Sep 3		
Church Sarah	S	W37G	1686 Oct31	1709 Oct 7	1761Sep15
Church Thomas	S	W36A	1674ca	1698 Feb21	1746 Mar12
Church William	S	W35H	1675 Oct10		
Churchill Benjamin	S	Q23Iaf	1695abt		
Churchill Eleazer	S	K109A	1713 Feb26		
Churchill Eleazer Jr	S	K30Aa	1682 Feb23	1711ca	1754 Sep21
Churchill Eleazer Sr	S	K30Aaf	1660abt		
Churchill Elizabeth	A	A12/87	1642 May15	1660 Oct31	
Churchill Elizabeth	A	A14/19	1710ca	1729 Jan29	1779 Apr16
Churchill Henry	A	A14/152	1565	1589	1628
Churchill John	A	A14/76	1591	1626	
Churchill John	S	X28Baf	1680abt		
Churchill Jonathan	S	K109C	1720 Oct19		
Churchill Josiah	A	A12/174	1615ca	1638	1685
Churchill Josiah	S	K109B	1716 Jul20		
Churchill Mary	S	Q23Ia	1720 Apr17	1739 Aug 2	1788 Jul27
Churchill Mary B	S	N16Da	1822ca		
Churchill Priscilla	S	X28Ba	1701 Nov27	1721 Oct31	1740aft
Churchill Richard	A	A14/304	1524		1592

NAME	DIV.	NUMBER	BIRTH	MARRIAGE	DEATH
Churchill William	A	A14/38	1649 Dec	1703 Oct 5	1710ca
Churchman Anna	S	X11Ba	1615ca	1639 Apr16	1665living
Claghorn Andrew Ring	S	H121G	1750ca		d yng
Claghorn Eleazer	S	H121D	1744 Apr 6		1813 Jan22
Claghorn Eliphalett	S	H121E	1746 May16		
Claghorn Elizabeth	S	H121A	1737 Jun23		1746bef
Claghorn Elizabeth	S	H121F	1748ca		1757 Oct12
Claghorn James	S	H121B	1739 Jul30		
Claghorn James Jr	S	H33Ka	1705ca	1736 Jun26	
Claghorn James Sr	S	H33Kaf	1680abt		
Claghorn Sarah	S	H121C	1741 Aug17		
Clap Mary	S	W28Lam	1660abt		
Clapp Hannah	A	A8/237	1646	1668	
Clark Ann	A	A3/199	1695abt	1717 Sept5	
Clark Bethiah	A	A4/461	1697	1718	1727
Clark Diadama	S	G33Db	1800abt		
Clark Elizabeth	A	A4/497	1650abt	1679	1696
Clark Elizabeth	S	P15Ham	1650abt		
Clark Elizabeth	S	X82B	1731		
Clark Eunice	S	Q19Da	1725ca	1746 Jun12	1768living
Clark Faith	S	K14Aam	1615abt		
Clark Faith	S	W29Gam	1670abt		
Clark John	A	A3/398	1670abt		1724 Jun 7
Clark John	S	X26Eaf	1680abt		
Clark Launcelot	S	X26Ea	1703 Dec30	1728 Nov 7	1775living
Clark Margaret	S	G31Aam	1700abt		
Clark Mary	S	X82A	1729		
Clark Mary	S	C21Ga	1760ca		
Clark Sarah	A	A4/499	1663	1685	1722aft
Clark Sarah	S	W32Ba	1678 Jun19	1698 Nov29	1760
Clark Susannah	S	H25Aam	1650abt		
Clark Susannah=H25Aam	S	W41Eam	1650abt		
Clark William	S	W32Baf	1650abt		
Clarke Elizabeth	A	A8/245	1642	1677	1713
Clarke Susanna	S	T20Dbm	1685abt		
Clary Sarah	S	P15Gam	1675abt		
Clavendish-Bentinck N.	D	D28a17	1870abt		
Clayton Mary	A	A3/47	1777 Feb18	1795 Oct27	1822 Jan27
Clayton Thomas Jr.	A	A3/94	1745ca	1772ca	1813
Clement Abiah	A	A4/451	1692	1712	1766

NAME	DIV.	NUMBER	BIRTH	MARRIAGE	DEATH
Clemson James	A	A3/180	1660ca	1698ca	1718 Jul18
Clemson Mary	A	A3/45	1763 Mar 3	1782 Jan10	1817 Jan17
Clemson Thomas	A	A3/90	1710ca	1747 Sep30	1785 Oct30
Clendinnan Ann	S	G50Eam	1730abt		
Cleveland D	S	C51Ia	1710ca		
Cleveland Henry	S	R117Ea	1699 Feb22	1719 Mar19	1770 Nov 8
Cleveland Jabez #1	S	R48D	1736 Nov13		d.yng
Cleveland Jabez #2	S	R48E	1737 Nov 4		
Cleveland Josiah	S	R117Eaf	1675abt		
Cleveland Lucy	S	R48C	1724 Mar 2		
Cleveland Nehemiah	S	R48B	1721 Jul30		
Cleveland William	S	R48A	1719 Jul 7		
Cleverly Sarah	S	P21Gam	1675abt		
Cleves John	A	A14/42	1686ca	1717ca	1750 May25
Cleves Mary	A	A14/21	1720abt	1740ca	1746ca
Clopper Cornelius J.	A	A7/134	1635abt	1657ca	1686aft
Clopper Margaret	A	A7/67	1660 Nov28	1682 Sep 9	1703 May22
Clopton Elizabeth	S	G5Aa	1455abt		
Clopton William	S	G5Aaf	1420abt		
Coates Mercy	S	C14Ba	1715ca		
Coates Sally	S	C60Ea	1800ca		
Cobb Dorothy	S	R27Dam	1710abt		
Cobb Ebenezer	S	Q17Ha	1694 Mar22	1722 Jul28	1801 Dec 8
Cobb Ebenezer	S	Q44A	1723 Mar 4		
Cobb Ebenezer Sr	S	Q17Haf	1675abt		=K30Caf
Cobb Ebenezer=Q17Daf	S	K30Caf	1675abt		
Cobb Ebenezer=Q17Haf	S	Q17Daf	1675abt		
Cobb Elizabeth	S	H24Ea	1680 Oct 6	1701 Feb 4	1714 May16
Cobb Hannah	S	Q17Da	1699 Feb27	1721 Nov16	1725ca
Cobb James	S	H24Eaf	1655abt		
Cobb John	S	K40Daf	1695abt		
Cobb John =T20Baf	S	Q14Caf	1670abt		
Cobb John=Q14Caf	S	T20Baf	1670abt		
Cobb John=Q14Caf	S	Q14Eaf	1670abt		
Cobb Lydia	S	K40Da	1718 Jul 7	1743 Feb23	1809 Aug22
Cobb Martha	S	Q14Ca	1691 Mar23	1708 Jun24	1775 Aug 8
Cobb Patience	S	Q14Ea	1693 Sep23	1717 Feb20	1727 Nov 4
Cobb Rachel	S	T20Ba	1702 Dec 8	1723 Nov23	1769 Jun24
Cobb Rachel	S	K40Gam	1705abt		
Cobb Sarah	S	R14Fam	1675abt		

NAME	DIV.	NUMBER	BIRTH	MARRIAGE	DEATH
Cobb Sarah	S	K30Ca	1702 Apr15	1723 Apr 4	1731 Sep28
Cobham Isabel	D	D30a27	1325abt		
Cobham Josiah	S	X13Acf	1625abt		
Cobham Marah	S	X13Ac	1652 May21	1692aft	1739
Cockayne Judith	D	D28a22	1730abt		
Cocke Anne	A	A1/315	1688ca	1707 Jan 2	
Coe Elizabeth	S	B17Aa	1694 Mar28	1720 Jul27	
Coffin Judith	S	K18Cb	1675abt	1722 Aug31	1760 Dec 2
Coffin Mary	S	K17Fam	1655abt		
Coffin Stephen	S	K18Cbf	1675abt		
Cogsewll Elizabeth	S	A23Ha	1677 Aug 1	1701 Jun16	1718 Jun16
Cogswell Edward	A	A11/184	1570abt		1615
Cogswell Hannah	A	A19/1501	1635abt		
Cogswell John	S	A16Aaf	1650abt		
Cogswell John=A11/92	A	A19/3002	1592ca	1615Sep10	1669 Nov29
Cogswell John=A16Aaf	S	A23Haf	1650abt		
Cogswell John=A19/3002	A	A11/92	1592ca	1615 Sep10	1669 Nov29
Cogswell Margaret	S	A16Aa	1675 Sep 6	1698 May10	1748 Oct19
Cogswell Sarah	S	A17Eam	1645abt		
Cogswell Sarah	S	A17Fam	1645abt		
Cogswell Susanna	A	A11/23	1657 Jan5	1681 Jan21	1701aft
Cogswell William	A	A11/46	1618 Mar	1649ca	1700 Dec15
Cole Daniel	S	H12Iaf	1620abt		
Cole Daniel	S	H13Haf	1630abt		
Cole Daniel	S	H17Abf	1630abt		
Cole Daniel	S	H20Baf	1640abt		
Cole Daniel	S	B19Fa	1705abt	1728 Sep19	
Cole David	S	H59B	1691 Oct 4		
Cole Elisha	S	H59A	1688 Jan26		
Cole Elizabeth	A	A17/33	1610ca	1625 May 6	1688Mar 5
Cole Elizabeth	S	A14Ba	1655ca	1677 Feb10	1681 Jan 4
Cole Elizabeth	S	H79D	1708 Feb10	unm.	
Cole Elizabeth Ryder	S	H19Bam	1670abt		
Cole Ephraim	S	K107A	1718 Oct12		1730
Cole Ephraim Jr	S	K29Ea	1691 Feb 3	1717 May16	1730bef
Cole Ephraim Sr	S	K29Eaf	1670abt		
Cole Gershom	S	H79A	1702 Mar 1		
Cole Hannah	S	R13Ba	1665ca	1702ca	1718 Aug15
Cole Hannah	S	H24D	1675 Mar27	unm.	1729abt
Cole Hannah	S	H127A	1681 Jun28		

NAME	DIV.	NUMBER	BIRTH	MARRIAGE	DEATH
Cole Hannah	S	H59C	1693 Dec15		
Cole Hepsibah	S	X16Dam	1660abt		
Cole Hepzibah	S	H24C	1672 Jun		1725bef
Cole Israel	S	H17Ab	1653 Jun 8	1679 Apr24	1724ca
Cole Israel	S	H127B	1685 Jun28		
Cole James	S	A14EAf	1635abt		
Cole James	S	H78D	1700 Oct23		
Cole James Jr.	A	A8/178	1625ca	1652	1712ca
Cole James=A14Eaf	S	R13Baf	1630abt		
Cole James=A8/178	D	D4af23	1625ca	1652	1712ca
Cole James=H78D	S	X52D	1700 Oct23		
Cole Jane	S	H59D	1695 Jan 4		
Cole Joanne	S	L15Fam	1690abt		
Cole John	S	H24B	1669 Mar 6	2 Mar	1746 Dec13
Cole John	S	K31Daf	1675abt		
Cole John	S	H78B	1696 Oct14		
Cole John Sr=H18Baf	S	H12Ia	1644 Jul15	1666 Dec12	1724 Jan 6
Cole John Jr	S	X18Ba	1669 Mar 6	1694bef	1746 Dec13
Cole John Sr=H12Ia	S	X18Baf	1644 Jul15	1666 Dec12	1724 Jan 6
Cole John=H78B	S	X52B	1696 Oct14		
Cole Jonathan	S	H78A	1694 Oct 4		
Cole Jonathan	S	X52A	1694 Oct 4		
Cole Joseph	S	H24E	1677 Jun11	3 Mar	1766ca
Cole Joseph	S	H78J	1714 Oct13		
Cole Joseph	S	X52I	1714 Oct13		
Cole Joseph	S	H79H	1718 May18		
Cole Joshua	S	H78F	1704 Mar20		
Cole Martha	A	A8/89	1669	1696 Mar 3	1718 Aug11
Cole Martha=A08/89	D	D4a23	1669	1696	1718 Aug11
Cole Mary	S	H13Ha	1658 Mar10	1681 May26	1733 Mar 1
Cole Mary	S	F18Bam	1670ca		
Cole Mary	S	H24F	1679 Oct22	unm.	
Cole Mary	S	H78C	1698 Aug25	1734 Jan30	1751living
Cole Mary	S	X52C	1698 Aug25		
Cole Mary	S	H79I	1721 Apr30		
Cole Mary=K31Da	S	K40Fam	1697ca	1717 Dec19	1766Jan 11
Cole Mary=K40Fam	S	K31Da	1697ca	1717 Dec19	1766 Jan11
Cole Mercy	S	H79G	1716 Sep24		
Cole Moses	S	X52F	1704 Mar20		
Cole Moses	S	H78G	1707 Jul22		1767

NAME	DIV.	NUMBER	BIRTH	MARRIAGE	DEATH
Cole Moses=H78G	S	X52G	1707 Jul22		1767
Cole Nathan	S	H78E	1702 Jan21		
Cole Nathan	S	X52E	1702 Jan21		1743bef
Cole Patience	S	H79C	1706 Dec 8	1728 Dec12	1742bef
Cole Phebe	S	H78H	1709 Oct29		
Cole Phebe	S	X52H	1709 Oct29		
Cole Rebecca	S	K107C	1727 Jun		
Cole Reliance	S	H79F	1713 Aug 2		1724 Aug 2
Cole Rice (Ryce)	A	A17/66	1580abt		1646 May15
Cole Ruth	S	H19Dam	1645abt		
Cole Ruth	S	H20Cam	1645abt		
Cole Ruth	S	H24A	1667 Mar11	1688 Mar21	1727 Mar 4
Cole Ruth	S	H79B	1704 Mar11		
Cole Sarah	S	H24G	1682 Jun10	unm.	
Cole Sarah	S	H79E	1710 Mar 8	1733 Jan31	1759 Feb1
Cole Sarah	S	C37Ga	1766ca		
Cole Sarah #1	S	K107B	1723ca		d.yng
Cole Sarah #2	S	K107D	1730 Jun		
Cole Thankful	S	X52J	1716 Oct19		
Cole Thankful #1	S	H78I	1712 Oct20		d yng
Cole Thankful #2=X52J	S	H78K	1716 Oct19		
Cole William	S	H20Ba	1663 Sep15	1686 Dec 2	1735aft
Coleman Enoch	S	P39E	1725 Mar24		
Coleman Jeremiah	S	P19Ia	1668ca	1714 Jan11	1739
Coleman Jeremiah	S	P39F	1729 Oct19		
Coleman Johannah	S	P39D	1722 Sep19		
Coleman John	S	P19Iaf	1645abt		
Coleman Lydia	S	P39B	1717 Feb17		
Coleman Peter	S	P39A	1716		
Coleman Silvanus	S	P39C	1720 Jun 2		1736
Collack Elizabeth	D	D30a19	1540abt		
Collamore Anthony	A	A14/82	1645abt	1666 Jun14	1693 Dec16
Collamore Elizabeth	A	A14/41	1679 Dec11	1710 Jul31	1758 Jan18
Collier Elizabeth	S	W15Cam	1620abt		
Collier Mary	S	H12Abm	1610abt		
Collingwood Alexander	A	A8/254	1665ca	1691	1745ca
Collingwood Dorothy	A	A8/127	1695ca	1719 Dec29	1736 Jul
Collins Alice	S	R42D	1706 Feb19		1709 Aug25
Collins Alice	S	R42H	1716 Mar14		
Collins Ann	S	R42B	1702 Dec20		

NAME	DIV.	NUMBER	BIRTH	MARRIAGE	DEATH
Collins Edward	A	A12/150	1603		1689
Collins Edward	S	R42G	1713 Nov26		
Collins Elizabeth	S	R24Gam	1690abt		
Collins Elizabeth	A	A4/59	1774 Jan 8	1796 Sept1	1851 Oct27
Collins Hezekiah	A	A4/236	1707 Aug18	1735 Nov 6	1775 Oct10
Collins Hezekiah Jr.	A	A4/118	1739 Dec 1	1765 Dec19	1828ca
Collins Jane	S	X15Fa	1684 Mar 3	1701 Sep30	1739bef
Collins John	S	R42C	1704 Jan 7		
Collins John Jr.	A	A4/472	1679	1703	1755
Collins Joseph	S	X15Faf	1660abt		
Collins Mary	S	R42A	1701 Nov15		1702 Feb17
Collins Nathaniel	S	R42E	1709 Aug17		
Collins Nathaniel Jr	S	R17Ba	1677 Jun13	1700 Jan 7	1756 Dec31
Collins Nathaniel Sr	S	R17Baf	1655abt		
Collins Phebe	A	A12/145	1604		1642
Collins Sybil	A	A12/75	1638ca	1654ca	1672 Jun 3
Collins Sybil=A12/75	S	R17Aam	1638ca	1654ca	1672 Jun 3
Collins William	S	R42F	1711 Jun		
Colson Adam	S	A22Baf	1660abt		
Colson Mary	S	A22Ba	1685ca		1755living
Colston Charles	S	A31Bb	1691 Apr17	1713 May	1724bef
Colston Charles	S	A81B	1715ca		1727 Jan25
Colston Elizabeth	S	A81D	1717ca		1727 Jan
Colston Susannah	S	A81C	1716ca		1726aft
Colston Travers	S	A81A	1714 Jan14		
Colston William	S	A31Bbf	1670abt		
Colston Winifred	S	A81E	1719ca		1727 Jan
Colt Mary	A	A4/489	1675abt	1712	
Colton Ephraim	S	N11Ia	1680ca		
Colwell Robert	S	C87Aa	1702		
Combs James	S	G50Fa	1750abt		
Comstock Abner	A	A4/244	1727ca	1751 Dec12	1811 Mar27
Comstock Anselm	A	A4/122	1762 Aug25	1790 Jan13	1845 Jul28
Comstock Betsey	A	A4/61	1795 Jul13		1857 Apr10
Comstock John Jr.	A	A4/488	1676	1712	1747
Conant Bethiah	S	Q23Gb	1709 Jul26	1733 Oct15	1755aft
Conant Nathaniel	S	Q23Gbf	1685abt		
Cone Daniel Jr	S	G11Ba	1666	1693 Feb14	1725
Cone Daniel Sr	S	G11Baf	1640abt		
Cone Joseph Sr	S	G15A	1711	1734	1804

NAME	DIV.	NUMBER	BIRTH	MARRIAGE	DEATH
Cone Sarah	S	G27Aa	1710abt	1723 Jun13	
Coney Abigail	S	A43A	1712 Jul28		
Coney Anna	S	A43I	1728 Sep23		
Coney Eliza	S	A43C	1716 May15		
Coney John	S	A19Dbf	1655abt		
Coney Joseph	S	A43G	1724 May 8		
Coney Mary	S	A43E	1719 Mar18		
Coney Nathaniel	S	A19Db	1677ca	1711 Sep 6	1742 Nov19
Coney Priscilla	S	A43F	1722 Apr 2	unm	1768 Sep11
Coney Samuel	S	A43D	1718 Apr15		
Coney Thomas	S	A43B	1714 Jul 2	unm	1749 May16
Coney William	S	A43H	1726 Mar29		
Constable Ann	S	A15Fam	1630abt		
Constable Anne	A	A18/21	1620ca	1641ca	1663aft
Contesse Ann	A	A15/5	1710ca		
Contesse Louis	A	A15/10	1685abt		1729 Sep11
Cook Anna	S	R117Ca	1695abt	1718 Mar 5	1735 Jul27
Cook Daniel	A	A6/26	1703 Aug18		1786
Cook Daniel	S	R61G	1732 Aug25		1741bef
Cook Ebenezer	S	H99E	1711 Nov25	1735 Oct 9	1793ca
Cook Ephraim	S	H99F	1712 Sep16		
Cook Hezekiah	S	H99N	1728ca		
Cook Jerusha	S	R61C	1721 Feb20		
Cook John	S	W36Baf	1665abt		
Cook Jonathan	S	H99L	1723ca		
Cook Joshua	S	H99C	1708 Mar23	1730 Oct 8	1801 Mar13
Cook Josiah	S	H99B	1707 Aug30		
Cook Martha	S	H99A	1706 Apr26		
Cook Mary	S	K18Eam	1650abt		
Cook Mary	S	K20Gam	1665abt		
Cook Mary	S	R61D	1723 Aug31		
Cook Mary	S	H99M	1725ca		
Cook Mary	S	R61F	1729 Jul25		
Cook Mercy	S	H99D	1710 Sep		
Cook Moses	S	H99I	1717 May11		
Cook Nicholas	A	A6/52	1659 Feb 9	1684 Nov 4	1730 Dec 7
Cook Patience	S	W36Ba	1680abt	1715ca	1764 Jan17
Cook Phineas	S	R61A	1716 Dec 6		1728 Jan22
Cook Phineas	S	R61I	1736 June7		
Cook Rebecca	S	R61B	1718 Nov26		

NAME	DIV.	NUMBER	BIRTH	MARRIAGE	DEATH
Cook Ruhama #1	S	H99G	1713 Feb18		1721bef
Cook Ruhama #2	S	H99K	1721ca		
Cook Samuel	S	R19Ga	1690 Dec31	1716 Mar14	1745 Aug27
Cook Samuel	S	R61H	1734 Oct 8		
Cook Simeon	S	H99H	1715 Aug24		
Cook Stephen	S	R19Gaf	1670abt		
Cook Tamasin	A	A6/13	1725 Jun16	1744 June7	1804 Apr25
Cook Welthean	S	R61E	1724 Aug20		
Cook Zaccheus	S	H99J	1719ca		
Cooke Aaron III	A	A12/118	1640 Feb	1661 May30	1716 Sep16
Cooke Aaron Jr	A	A12/236	1613	1637bef	1690
Cooke Abigail	S	H97B	1712 Dec22		1715 Nov26
Cooke Abigail	S	H95H	1715 Jun 8		
Cooke Alice	A	A10/89	1545abt		1606 Mar
Cooke Amos	S	K105L	1749 Jan 3		d.yng
Cooke Ann	S	H12Aa	1630ca	1654 Jan18	1656 Jul25
Cooke Ann	S	K91A	1733 Aug14	unm	1768
Cooke Anne	S	K25C	1686 Aug21	1716 Feb 6	1752aft
Cooke Anne	S	H95G	1712 Sep15		
Cooke Asa	S	K95B	1720 Jun12		
Cooke Benjamin	S	H28H	1686 Feb28	1710 Nov23	1727aft
Cooke Benjamin	S	K105B	1729 May18		
Cooke Bethia	S	H22Cam	1645abt		
Cooke Bethia	S	X14Cam	1650abt		
Cooke Bethia	S	K90G	1746ca		
Cooke Caleb	S	H15B	1651 Mar29		
Cooke Caleb	S	K14B	1651 Mar29	1682ca	1721 Feb13
Cooke Caleb	S	H28E	1676 Nov15	1710 Oct18	1736aft
Cooke Caleb	S	K29C	1694ca	1724 Mar 4	1762 Aug19
Cooke Caleb	S	K25G	1697 Apr17	1722 May 6	1724 Mar15
Cooke Caleb	S	H95C	1702 Sep11		
Cooke Caleb	S	K105A	1727 Jul 4		
Cooke Caleb	S	K91C	1736ca		
Cooke Charles	S	K104A	1717 Oct 4		
Cooke Cornelius twin	S	H97D	1719 Jun 2		
Cooke Damaris	S	K26H	1703 May23		1728living
Cooke Daniel	S	K95I	1739 Dec10		
Cooke Deborah	S	H28F	1678 Feb15	1700ca	1745 Apr23
Cooke Deborah	S	H106Aam	1690abt		
Cooke Deborah	S	H94B	1696 Apr12	1718 May29	

NAME	DIV.	NUMBER	BIRTH	MARRIAGE	DEATH
Cooke Deborah	S	H95F	1710 Aug22		
Cooke Desire	S	H94A	1694 Jun14		
Cooke Elijah	S	K90D	1741 Jul24		
Cooke Elisha	S	K92E	1716 Mar10		
Cooke Elizabeth	D	D5/23	1648Jan 18	1667abt	1692
Cooke Elizabeth	S	K25E	1691 Nov30	1715 Oct27	1754ca
Cooke Elizabeth	S	H95D	1704 Nov30		
Cooke Elizabeth	S	H94F	1704ca	1722 Nov 1	
Cooke Elizabeth	S	K29F	1707ca	1734 Jan22	1750 Jun 6
Cooke Elizabeth	S	H97A	1711 Aug 2		1715 Nov17
Cooke Elizabeth #1	S	H28A	1669 Oct12		1670 Apr14
Cooke Elizabeth #2	S	H28D	1674 Jun15	1693 Oct	1727aft
Cooke Elizabeth=D5/23	S	H15A	1648 Jan18	1667abt	1693
Cooke Elizabeth=H15A	S	K14A	1648 Jan18	1667ca	1692
Cooke Elizabeth=K12B	S	W14B	1644abt	1661abt	1715
Cooke Elizabeth=W14B	S	K12B	1644bef	1661abt	1715
Cooke Elknah	S	K105E	1735ca		d.yng
Cooke Ephraim	S	H97F	1722 Jul12		1729Apr 10
Cooke Ephraim	S	K105F	1737 Jun 1		
Cooke Experience	S	H97C	1716ca		
Cooke Fear	S	K105K	1748ca		d.yng
Cooke Francis	S	H15F	1662 Jan 5	1687 Aug 2	1740abt
Cooke Francis	S	K29D	1696ca	1719 Feb 4	1724 May 4
Cooke Francis	S	K104E	1726ca		
Cooke Francis MF	S	K10A	1583aft	1603 Jul 4	1663 Apr 7
Cooke Francis MF=K10A	S	W11Caf	1583aft	1603 Jul 4	1663 Aug 7
Cooke Francis MF=K10A	S	H11Gaf	1583aft	1603 Jul 4	1663 Aug 7
Cooke Francis=H15F	S	K14F	1662 Jan 5	1687 Aug 2	1740abt
Cooke Hannah	A	A2/185	1650abt	1671	
Cooke Hannah	S	H95B	1699 Jan25		
Cooke Hannah	S	K31Ja	1707 Nov 8	1736 Dec 7	1784 Feb25
Cooke Hannah	S	K92A	1707 Nov 8		
Cooke Hannah	S	H94G	1707ca	1724 Nov12	1783 Mar21
Cooke Hannah	S	K90A	1733 Jul22		d.yng
Cooke Hannah	S	K105G	1739 Apr 8		
Cooke Hester	S	K11D	1620bef	1644	1669aft
Cooke Hester	S	Q12Aam	1625abt		
Cooke Hester	S	K12C	1650 Aug16	1667ca	1671ca
Cooke Hester	S	W14C	1659 Aug16		
Cooke Hulda	S	K92C	1712 Aug12		1730 Feb 7

NAME	DIV.	NUMBER	BIRTH	MARRIAGE	DEATH
Cooke Isaac	S	K105D	1732 Mar18		d.yng
Cooke Jacob	S	H11Ga	1618ca	1646 Jun10	1675 Dec
Cooke Jacob	S	K11C	1618ca	2 Mar	1675 Dec
Cooke Jacob	S	H15C	1653 Mar26		
Cooke Jacob	S	K14C	1653 Mar26	1681 Dec29	1747 Apr24
Cooke Jacob	S	K26D	1691 Jun16	3 Mar	1753 Nov20
Cooke Jacob	S	H94H	1708ca		1800 Sept5
Cooke Jacob	S	K95D	1725 Apr19		
Cooke Jacob =H11Ga	D	D5a24	1618abt	1646 Jun	1675 Dec18
Cooke Jacob =H11Ga	S	A14Ebf	1635abt		
Cooke James	S	K25H	1700 Aug19	1731 Feb	1757bef
Cooke James #1	S	K90H	1748ca		d.yng.
Cooke James #2	S	K90I	1749ca		
Cooke Jane	S	K11B	1613bef	1627aft	1650bef
Cooke Jane	S	Q23Ham	1685abt		
Cooke Jane	S	K25D	1688 Mar16	1707 Mar27	1716 Feb 8
Cooke Jesse	S	K95A	1717 Nov 1		
Cooke John	S	K25A	1682 Feb 5	1705Nov 22	1741
Cooke John	S	H94C	1698 Apr 9		
Cooke John	S	K26G	1703 May23	1730 Dec19	1744 Dec 8
Cooke John	S	K95G	1734ca		
Cooke John MF	S	K11A	1607	1634 Mar28	1695 Nov23
Cooke John MF=K11A	S	W11Ca	1607	1634 Mar28	1695 Nov23
Cooke Joseph	S	K25I	1703 Nov28	1732 Jun17	1768aft
Cooke Joseph	S	H100B	1710 May12		
Cooke Joseph	S	K91B	1734ca	unm	1768Jan 26
Cooke Joseph	S	K95H	1735ca		
Cooke Joshua	S	H28G	1682 Feb 4	1705 Feb 7	1740abt
Cooke Joshua	S	H94E	1702ca	1724 Aug 5	
Cooke Joshua	S	X27Ea	1704ca	1755 Dec25	
Cooke Josiah	S	H28B	1670 Nov12		1727
Cooke Josiah	S	K26F	1699 May14	1727 Mar 9	1752bef
Cooke Josiah	S	K97E	1739 Mar17		
Cooke Josiah Jr	S	H13Ea	1645ca	1668 Jul27	1731 Jan31
Cooke Josiah Sr	S	H13Eaf	1610abt		
Cooke Josiah=H13Eaf	S	H12Aaf	1610abt		
Cooke Lucy	S	K90B	1736 Aug29		d.yng
Cooke Lydia	S	K26B	1685 May18	1709 Feb23	1738 Jul 7
Cooke Lydia	S	K92B	1710 Feb 4		
Cooke Lydia	S	R26Nam	1720abt		

NAME	DIV.	NUMBER	BIRTH	MARRIAGE	DEATH
Cooke Lydia	S	K105C	1731 Apr 8		d.yng
Cooke Lydia	S	K97B	1732 Oct23		
Cooke Lydia	S	K105I	1744 Aug21		
Cooke Lydia #1	S	K98A	1732 Jul 7		d.yng
Cooke Lydia #2	S	K98C	1735 Feb17		
Cooke Marcy	S	K25B	1683 Feb21	unm.	1713 Feb11
Cooke Margaret	S	K26E	1695 Nov 3	1716 Apr 5	1742bef
Cooke Margaret	S	K98E	1741 Jul26		
Cooke Maria	S	K90F	1743ca		
Cooke Martha	S	K14E	1659 Mar 6	1682 Mar 2	1722 Sep1?
Cooke Martha	S	H15E	1659 Mar16		
Cooke Martha	S	A14Eb	1659 Mar16	1683 Mar 2	1722 Sep1?
Cooke Mary	A	A12/237	1620ca	1637bef	1645aft
Cooke Mary	S	K11E	1625ca	1645 Dec26	1714 Mar21
Cooke Mary	S	H34Aam	1640abt		
Cooke Mary	S	W14D	1651ca		
Cooke Mary	S	K12D	1651ca	1667ca	1710abt
Cooke Mary	S	H15D	1657 Jan12		
Cooke Mary	S	K14D	1657 Jan12	1678ca	1712 Aug28
Cooke Mary	S	K25F	1694 Aug20	1717 Mar28	1736living
Cooke Mary	S	H94D	1699 Feb 8		
Cooke Mary	S	K95F	1733 Aug20		
Cooke Mary	S	K91D	1738ca		
Cooke Mary twin	S	H97E	1719 Jun 2		
Cooke Mary =D10/25	S	Q12Eam	1625abt		
Cooke Mary =Q12Eam	D	D10/25	1625abt		
Cooke Mary Samson	S	R25Fb	1724 Jan 6	1763 May31	
Cooke Mercy	S	K12E	1656abt	1683ca	1733 Nov22
Cooke Mercy	S	W14E	1656ca		
Cooke Mercy	S	K35Fam	1665abt		
Cooke Mercy	S	K85D	1718 Mar		
Cooke Molly	S	K98F	1743 Oct29		
Cooke Nathaniel	S	H100C	1717 Jul 6		
Cooke Nathaniel	S	K104B	1719 Dec19		
Cooke Paul	S	K85B	1711 May 8		
Cooke Phebe	S	K95C	1722 Aug 5		
Cooke Priscilla	S	K92G	1721 Mar13		
Cooke Rebecca	S	K26C	1688 Nov19	1716 Mar19	1769 Apr14
Cooke Rebeckah	S	K14I	1673ca		d. yng
Cooke Rebeckah	S	K105H	1741 Feb 5		

NAME	DIV.	NUMBER	BIRTH	MARRIAGE	DEATH
Cooke Richard	S	H28C	1672 Sep 1		1754 Apr25
Cooke Richard	S	H100D	1718 Nov23		
Cooke Robert	S	K29B	1691ca	2 Mar	1731 Jan20
Cooke Robert	S	K85C	1714 Jun		
Cooke Robert	S	K104C	1721 Mar12		
Cooke Ruth	S	H15G	1665 Jan17		1675living
Cooke Ruth	S	K14G	1665 Jan17		
Cooke Ruth	S	K106A	1721 Feb 4		
Cooke Ruth	S	K97F	1742 Feb15		
Cooke Samuel	S	K104F	1729 Jul 1		d. yng.
Cooke Sarah	S	B23Aam	1635	1652	=W14A
Cooke Sarah	S	W14A	1635abt	1652ca	
Cooke Sarah	S	K12A	1635ca	1652 Nov20	1712aft
Cooke Sarah	A	A12/59	1662 Jan31	1677 Nov	1739 Apr10
Cooke Sarah	S	K14H	1671	1691 Apr 1	1744 Feb 8
Cooke Sarah	S	W23Ab	1671ca	1691 Apr1	1744 Feb8
Cooke Sarah	S	K29E	1698ca	1717 May16	1730 Oct26
Cooke Sarah	S	H95E	1707 Nov27		
Cooke Sarah	S	K104D	1724 Jun18		
Cooke Sarah	S	K97A	1729 Nov21		
Cooke Sarah	S	K98B	1733 Oct21		
Cooke Sarah	S	K105J	1747 May21		d.yng
Cooke Sarah=K14H	S	W56Fam	1671	1591 Apr 1	1744Feb 8
Cooke Shubael	S	H100A	1711 Apr		
Cooke Silas	S	K85A	1708 Dec 1		
Cooke Simeon	S	K104G	1730 Sep21		
Cooke Solomon	S	H94I	1711		
Cooke Stephen	S	K95E	1729 Mar 7		1749 Dec16
Cooke Submit	S	K97C	1734 Jan20		1753 Jul22
Cooke Susanna	S	K29A	1689ca	1710 Feb15	1769 Oct
Cooke Susanna	S	R25Gam	1700abt		
Cooke Susanna	S	K91E	1740ca		
Cooke Susanna #1	S	K90C	1738 Jan24		d.yng
Cooke Susanna #2	S	K90E	1742ca		
Cooke Susannah	S	K106B	1723 Jul28		
Cooke Sylvanus	S	K98D	1738 May 1	list	
Cooke Tabitha	S	K92F	1719 Jul 8		
Cooke Thankful	S	H95I	1717 Jun12		
Cooke Thomas	S	H95A	1697 Apr27		
Cooke Walter	A	A6/104	1635abt		1695 Jan 5

NAME	DIV.	NUMBER	BIRTH	MARRIAGE	DEATH
Cooke William	S	K26A	1683 Oct 5	1706 Mar18	1740living
Cooke William	S	K31Jaf	1685abt		
Cooke William	S	K92D	1714 Jan15		1731 Apr18
Cooke Zenas	S	K90J	1752ca		
Cooke Zibiah	S	K97D	1737 Jan28		
Coolidge Calvin	A	A19/8	1780Mar 27	1814 Dec 9	1853Apr 30
Coolidge Calvin Pres	A	A19/1	1872 Jul 4	1905 Oct 4	1933 Jan 5
Coolidge Calvin G.	A	A19/4	1815 Sep22	1844 Mar 3	1878Dec 15
Coolidge John	A	A19/16	1756ca	1779 Sep 8	1822Mar 23
Coolidge John Calvin	A	A19/2	1845Mar 31	1868May 6	1926Mar 18
Coolidge Josiah	A	A19/32	1718Jul 17	1742 Apr26	1780 Dec25
Coolidge Obadiah	A	A19/128	1663	1686	1707
Coolidge Obadiah Jr	A	A19/64	1695Aug 27	1717Jul 24	1737aft
Coombs Deborah	S	F16Fa	1673 May	1696bef	1710aft
Coombs Deborah=F16Fa	S	P23A	1673 May	1696bef	1710aft
Coombs Elizabeth	S	P22A	1662 Nov30	1687 Jan12	1723aft
Coombs Elizabeth=P22A	S	A14Ga	1622 Nov30	1687 Jan12	1723aft
Coombs Elizabeth=P22A	A	A8/101	1662 Nov30	1687 Jan12	1723aft
Coombs Frances	S	P23E	1682 Jan6	1712ca	1762living
Coombs Francis	S	P13B	1635ca	2 mar.	1682 Dec
Coombs Francis =P13B	S	F16Faf	1635ca		1682 Dec
Coombs John	S	A14Gaf	1600abt		
Coombs John	S	P11Ba	1615ca	1631ca	1646bef
Coombs John	S	P13A	1632ca	1661 Feb24	1668bef
Coombs John	S	P22B	1664 Jul20	1687	1709ca
Coombs John	S	P53D	1697 Oct 3		
Coombs John Jr.=P13A	A	A8/202	1632ca	1661ca	1668bef
Coombs Lydia	S	P23C	1678 May 8	1701 Feb12	1734 Mar 6
Coombs Mary	S	P22C	1666 Nov28	1689 Dec18	1728 Jul 2
Coombs Mary	S	A21Gam	1670abt		
Coombs Mary	S	P53C	1695 Nov25		
Coombs Mercy	S	P23B	1674 Jan 3	1701ca	1718 Mar25
Coombs Peter	S	P53B	1694 Aug 9		d yng
Coombs Ruth	S	P23D	1681 Mar12	1702 Aug26	1717 Mar11
Coombs Thomas	S	P53A	1692 Sep10		1722bef
Cooper John	A	A19/236	1675	1697	
Cooper Judith	A	A19/59	1736Feb 14	1754 Dec22	1815Sep 2
Cooper Sarah	A	A12/127	1642ca	1659 Oct27	1726 Nov21
Cooper Thomas	A	A12/254	1617ca		1675ca
Cooper Timothy	A	A19/118	1706 Apr 9	1730	

NAME	DIV.	NUMBER	BIRTH	MARRIAGE	DEATH
Coplestone Agnes	D	D30a25	1375abt		
Copley Elizabeth	A	A12/121	1630ca	1650 Sep17	1712 Dec 6
Corbin Ann	S	A29Aa	1709ca	1733ca	1759bef
Corbin Gawin	S	A29Aaf	1685abt		
Corey Abigail	S	C20Ga	1759		
Cornish Joyce	A	A16/237	1580abt	1605	1621
Cornish Mercy	S	K29Aam	1655abt		
Cornish Mercy=K29Aam	S	K33Aam	1655abt		
Cornwall Mary	S	F22Ga	1694 Nov21	1721 May10	1758bef
Cornwall Roger	A	A12/6	1756 Dec25	1790 Dec 2	1805 Aug22
Cornwall William	S	F22Gaf	1670abt		
Corser Fear	S	A21Fa	1685ca	1709 Dec 8	1767 Dec 2
Corses Rebecca	S	C49Ja	1705ca		
Corwin George	S	L11Db	1610 Dec10	1669 Sep10	1684 Jan 3
Corwin Penelope	S	L13A	1670 Aug 7	1684 Feb19	1690 Dec28
Corwin Susanna	S	L13B	1672 Dec10	1694 Nov29	1696 Oct22
Cory Mary	S	K59E	1708ca		
Cory Patience	S	K59D	1706ca		1734living
Cory Philip	S	K59C	1705ca		
Cory Sarah	S	K59F	1710ca		
Cory Thomas	S	K20Ba	1670ca	1693aft	1738bef
Cory Thomas	S	K59B	1704ca		
Cory William	S	K20Baf	1650abt		
Cory William	S	K59A	1703ca		
Cottle Edward	S	H12Ebf	1630ca		
Cottle Mary	S	H12Eb	1653 Nov 1	1701 Apr 9	1706living
Cotymore Elizabeth	A	A11/119	1617ca	1636ca	1645ca
Cotymore Elizabeth	D	D23/24	1617ca	1636ca	=A11/119
Cotymore Rowland	D	D23/25	1590abt		
Coutts Margaret	A	A7/105	1665ca		1710ca
Cowing Israel	S	K41Bbf	1705abt		
Cowing Lydia	S	K41Bb	1726 Mar12	1756 Jan 4	1800 May12
Cox Mary	S	Q16Cam	1675abt		
Crafts Abigail	A	A2/107	1673 Dec 1	1698 May29	1702 Nov 5
Crafts Samuel	A	A2/214	1637	1661	
Craig Daniel	A	A7/42	1750abt	1776abt	
Craig Sarah	A	A7/21	1735ca		
Crampton Dennis	A	A12/70	1635abt	1660 Sep16	1689 Jan31
Crampton Elizabeth	A	A12/35	1662ca	1686ca	
Cranston John	S	C86A	1684		

NAME	DIV.	NUMBER	BIRTH	MARRIAGE	DEATH
Cranston Samuel	S	C85Ba	1660ca		
Crippen Catherine	S	F17Ea	1665ca		1735 Dec 8
Crippen Frances	S	F57B	1710 Jun26		
Crippen Jabez	S	F22Da	1680ca	1707 July9	
Crippen Jabez	S	F57E	1717 Jul14		
Crippen John	S	F57F	1720 Mar20		
Crippen Joseph	S	F57I	1726 Jun 7		
Crippen Lydia	S	F57C	1713 Mar17		
Crippen Mary	S	F17Bb	1668ca	1714	1764 Jun 9
Crippen Mehitable	S	F57G	1722 Jul 6		
Crippen Samuel	S	F57H	1724 Jul 7		
Crippen Susanna	S	F57A	1708 May21		
Crippen Thankful	S	F57J	1728 Apr 2		
Crippen Thomas	S	F22Daf	1650abt		=F17Eaf
Crippen Thomas	S	F57D	1715 May15		
Crippen Thomas=F22Daf	S	F17Eaf	1650abt		
Crisp George	S	X16Daf	1660abt		
Crisp Mercy	S	X16Da	1681 Oct15	1703 Oct13	1746bef
Crispel Antoine	A	A8/138	1635	1680	1707
Crispel Jannetje	A	A8/69	1686 Feb	1704 Dec30	1752 Feb14
Criswell Elizabeth	A	A1/43	1795abt	1816 Sep26	
Croasdale Alice	A	A7/89	1673	1693	1730 Nov16
Croasdale Thomas	A	A7/178	1640abt	1664	1682ca
Crocker Bethia	S	R26Bam	1685abt		
Crocker Eleazer	S	X17Ga	1650 Jul21	1715 Jan26	1723bef
Crocker Hannah	S	F22Ca	1688 Mar26	1708 Dec 7	1751 Mar31
Crocker Hannah=F22Ca	D	D6a22	1688 Mar26	1708 Dec 7	1731Mar31
Crocker James	D	D1/21	1699 Sep 8	1721 Nov21	=G28Aaf
Crocker James =D1/21	S	G28Aaf	1699 Sep 8	1721 Nov21	
Crocker James=D1/21	D	D3a21	1699 Sep 8	1721 Nov21	
Crocker Job	S	W48Bbf	1665abt		
Crocker John	D	D1af22	1637 May 3		1711 May 1
Crocker Jonathan	D	D1a22	1662 Jul15		1744 Aug24
Crocker Jonathan=D1a22	S	F22Caf	1662 Jul15		1744 Aug24
Crocker Jonathan=D1a22	D	D6af22	1662 Jul15		1744 Aug24
Crocker Joseph	S	X17Iaf	1665abt		
Crocker Lydia =G28A	D	D1/20	1735 Jan14	1760 May	1790aft
Crocker Lydia=D1/20	S	G28Aa	1735 Jan14	1760 May	1790aft
Crocker Martha	S	X17Ia	1689 Feb22	1709 Jun30	1747bef
Crocker Mercy	S	X47A	1717ca		

NAME	DIV.	NUMBER	BIRTH	MARRIAGE	DEATH
Crocker Sarah	S	W48Bb	1690 Jan19	1725 May27	1765abt
Crocker William	D	D1aff22	1600abt		
Crocker William	S	X17Gaf	1625abt		
Crois Marie	S	G45Bam	1620ca		
Crooker Abigail	S	T22Fam	1715abt		
Crooker Sarah	S	Q15Dam	1660abt		
Croom Neeltje Janse	A	A8/151	1630ca	1660ca	1681ca
Crosby Elizabeth	S	X16Ia	1693 Sep15	1715 Feb 1	1720ca
Crosby Polly	S	C21Hc	1765ca		
Crosby Simon	S	X16Iaf	1670abt		
Cross Anne	A	A1/279	1651ca	1683ca	1710 aft
Crossman Abigail	S	K39Ja	1715ca	1736 May20	1791 Nov23
Crossman Nathaniel	S	K26Gaf	1690abt		
Crossman Nathaniel	S	K39Jaf	1690abt		
Crossman Phebe	S	K26Ga	1712ca	1730 Dec19	1803 Mar25
Crossman Sarah	S	K34Lam	1695abt		
Crouch E.	S	N13D	1740abt		
Crow R	S	N12Bb	1700abt		
Crowel Lydia	S	W48Cam	1655abt		
Crowell Deliverance	S	H28Ea	1685 Jan11	1710 Oct18	
Crowell John	S	H28Eaf	1660abt		
Cuchman Lydia	S	P52A	1687 Dec13		
Cumning Alanson	S	G33Ba	1790abt		
Curtice Sarah	S	K29Bbm	1680abt		
Curtis Caleb	S	Q39B	1712 Aug15		1729 Nov19
Curtis Ebenezer	S	Q17Ba	1685ca	1709 Jan19	1743living
Curtis Elizabeth	S	Q21Dam	1655abt		
Curtis Elizabeth	S	X17Jbm	1670abt		
Curtis Francis	S	Q17Baf	1660abt		
Curtis Francis Jr	S	W56Haf	1675abt		
Curtis Hannah	S	W56Ha	1712 Jul	1727 Sep28	
Curtis Jacob	S	Q39A	1710 Oct11		
Curtis John	S	H30Faf	1670abt		
Curtis Mary	S	Q39C	1714 Dec21		
Curtis Priscilla	S	H30Fa	1695 Jan27	1724 Oct 1	1772
Curtis Priscilla	S	X26Ia	1720ca	1740 Nov21	
Curtis Sarah	S	Q39D	1717 Aur19		
Cushing Abigail	S	W31Cb	1703 Jan31	1732 Nov29	1778aft
Cushing Hannah #1	S	K99A	1710 Jan 1		d.yng
Cushing Hannah #2	S	K99C	1714 Aug25		

NAME	DIV.	NUMBER	BIRTH	MARRIAGE	DEATH
Cushing Ignatius	S	K27Ba	1689 Sep22	1710 Apr 4	1767bef
Cushing Ignatius	S	K99B	1711 Feb 7		d. yng
Cushing Jeremiah	S	K27Baf	1665abt		
Cushing Joshua	S	W31Cbf	1680abt		
Cushman Abigail	S	A45C	1701 Jul 3		
Cushman Abigail	S	R120D	1722 Dec31		
Cushman Abigail	S	A59I	1722 Dec31		
Cushman Abigail	S	A50G	1727 Nov22		
Cushman Abigail	S	A73G	1743 Oct27		
Cushman Abner	S	A72A	1722 Mar10		
Cushman Alderton	S	A73I	1748 Sep29		
Cushman Alice	S	A59B	1705 Jun26 mar.		no issue
Cushman Alice	S	A66E	1727 Jun		d.yng
Cushman Allerton	S	K28A	1683 Nov21		
Cushman Allerton	S	A25D	1683 Nov21 2 mar.		1730 Jan 9
Cushman Allerton	S	A66A	1712 Dec16		
Cushman Anna	S	A67D	1717 May20		
Cushman Bartholomew	S	A21E	1684ca		1721 Dec21
Cushman Bartholomew	S	A49G	1727ca		d. yng
Cushman Benjamin	S	A21G	1691ca	2 mar.	1770 Oct17
Cushman Benjamin	S	A50E	1722 May25		
Cushman Benjamin	S	A73K	1753 Jun 8		
Cushman Bettee	S	A72G	1735 Sep 3		
Cushman Caleb	S	A50B	1715 May15		
Cushman Charles	S	A70B	1719abt		
Cushman Deborah	S	A72H	1737 Jul 8		
Cushman Desire	S	A21B	1668ca		1762 Feb 8
Cushman Desire	S	A49A	1710 Sep18		
Cushman Ebenezer	S	A71C	1727 Jun 4		
Cushman Elcanah	S	A67F	1721 Sep		
Cushman Eleazer	A	A8/100	1656 Feb20	1687 Jan12	1723aft
Cushman Eleazer	S	A26E	1700abt	1740 Mar 3	1758
Cushman Eleazer	S	P52E	1700ca		
Cushman Eleazer	S	A47D	1710ca		
Cushman Eleazer	S	A70A	1715abt		
Cushman Eleazer	S	A72K	1744 Aug30		
Cushman Eleazer =P22Aa	S	A14G	1656 Feb20	1687 Jan12	1733aft
Cushman Eleazer=A8/100	S	P22Aa	1656 Feb20	1687 Jan12	1723aft
Cushman Elijah	S	A72B	1724 Feb14		d.yng
Cushman Elisha	S	A71H	1737 May20		

NAME	DIV.	NUMBER	BIRTH	MARRIAGE	DEATH
Cushman Elizabeth	S	K28B	1685 Jan17		
Cushman Elizabeth	S	A25E	1685 Jan17	1723 Dec 5	1724 Mar13
Cushman Elizabeth	S	A65A	1703 Dec 5		
Cushman Elizabeth	S	A67H	1728 Sep22	unm	1808 Oct10
Cushman Elizabeth	A	A8/25	1739 Jul29	1764abt	1809 Nov24
Cushman Elizabeth	S	A71I	1739 Jul29		
Cushman Elkanah	S	K14Ea	1651 Jun 1	1682 Mar 2	1727 Sep 4
Cushman Elkanah	S	A14E	1651 Jun 1	1683 Mar 2	1727 Sep 4
Cushman Elkanah	S	R110A	1741 Nov13		
Cushman Elkanah =A65B	S	R27Ca	1706 Jul10	1740 Mar31	1742 Apr26
Cushman Elkanah Jr	S	A65B	1706 Jul10		=R27Ca
Cushman Elkanah Sr	S	R27Caf	1678 Sep15	1702Feb 23	1714 Jan 9
Cushman Elkanah=R27Caf	S	A25A	1678 Sep15	1702 Feb23	1714 Jan 9
Cushman Ephraim	S	A66D	1720 Oct25		
Cushman Experience	S	A63D	1719 Jul12		
Cushman Fear	S	A14F	1653 Jun20		1690bef
Cushman Fear	S	A24F	1689 Mar10	1707 Feb12	1746 Jul13
Cushman Fear	S	R120A	1718 Jul10		
Cushman Fear	S	A59F	1718 Jul10		
Cushman Hannah	S	A45D	1705 Dec25		
Cushman Hannah	S	A65D	1713ca		
Cushman Hannah	S	A73A	1731 Mar19		
Cushman Hannah	S	A72F	1731ca		
Cushman Huldah	S	A50J	1735 Apr 6		
Cushman Huldah	S	A72I	1739 May16		
Cushman Ichabod	S	A24E	1686 Oct30	1712 Nov27	1732 Oct26
Cushman Ichabod	S	A63G	1725 May12		
Cushman Isaac	S	A14D	1648 Feb 8	1675ca	1732 Oct21
Cushman Isaac	S	R120C	1721 Sep29		d yng
Cushman Isaac	S	A59H	1721 Sep29		d.yng
Cushman Isaac	S	A63I	1730 Aug12		
Cushman Isaac	S	A72B	1730 Feb19		
Cushman Isaac Jr	S	W50Da	1676 Nov15	1700 Jan28	1727 Sep18
Cushman Isaac Sr=A14D	S	W50Daf	1648 Feb 8		1732 Oct21
Cushman Isaac=A14D	S	R14Dbf	1648 Feb 9		1732 Oct21
Cushman Isaac=A24A	S	R14Db	1676 Nov15	1717 Oct10	1727 Sep
Cushman Isaac=W50Da	S	A24A	1676 Nov15	2 mar.	1727 Sep
Cushman Isaiah	S	A67I	1730 Feb 2		
Cushman Jabez	S	A25C	1681 Dec28		d.yng
Cushman Jabez	S	A50A	1713 Aug11		

NAME	DIV.	NUMBER	BIRTH	MARRIAGE	DEATH
Cushman Jacob	S	A49E	1719 Mar20		
Cushman James	S	A25B	1679 Oct20		d.yng
Cushman James	S	P52C	1692ca		
Cushman James	S	A65C	1709 Aug29		
Cushman James	S	A66B	1715 May27		
Cushman James	S	A71B	1725 May 4		
Cushman James=A8/50	S	A26C	1692ca	1722 Dec24	1775ca
Cushman James=P52C	A	A8/50	1692ca	1722 Dec24	1775ca
Cushman Jemima	S	A49F	1724 Oct23		d. yng
Cushman Jemima	S	A49H	1729ca		d. yng
Cushman Jerusha	S	A50D	1719 Dec 7		d. yng
Cushman Jerusha	S	A50I	1732 Oct18		
Cushman Joanna	S	A63A	1713 Dec17		
Cushman Job	S	A21D	1680ca	1706ca	1739bef
Cushman Job	S	A48B	1710 Feb20		1729 Nov12
Cushman Job	S	A73F	1741 May16		
Cushman John	S	P52B	1690 Aug13		
Cushman John	S	A26B	1690 Aug13	1715 Jan19	1760living
Cushman John	S	A70C	1722abt		
Cushman Jonathan	S	A45G	1712 Jul28		
Cushman Joseph	S	A49D	1717 Jan 7		d. yng
Cushman Joseph	S	A66F	1729 Feb24		d.yng
Cushman Joseph	S	A73L	1759 Feb23		
Cushman Joshua	S	A45F	1707 Oct14		
Cushman Joshua	S	A73J	1750 Jan27		
Cushman Josiah	S	A25F	1687 Mar21	1709 Dec29	1750 Apr13
Cushman Josiah	S	A67E	1719 Aug12		
Cushman Josiah=A25F	S	K28C	1687 Mar21	1709Dec 29	1750 Apr13
Cushman Lydia	S	W20Da	1662ca	1683ca	1718 Feb11
Cushman Lydia	S	A14H	1662ca	1682ca	1718 Feb11
Cushman Lydia	S	A26A	1687 Dec13	1709 Dec29	1771 Jul 7
Cushman Lydia	S	A47F	1715ca		
Cushman Lydia	S	A48C	1718 Oct31		
Cushman Lydia	S	A71A	1723 Sep 4		
Cushman Lydia	S	A73D	1735 Feb15		
Cushman Maria	S	A48A	1706 Feb16		
Cushman Martha	S	K28D	1691ca		
Cushman Martha	S	A25G	1691ca	1717 Jun 6	1771aft
Cushman Martha	S	A67B	1712 Jan12		
Cushman Mary	S	A14B	1639ca	1676ca	1690bef

NAME	DIV.	NUMBER	BIRTH	MARRIAGE	DEATH
Cushman Mary	S	A24C	1682 Oct12	1702 Mar19	1722 Mar13
Cushman Mary	S	K40Bam	1695abt		
Cushman Mary	S	A66C	1718 Jun 5		
Cushman Mary	S	A63F	1723 Dec22		
Cushman Mary	S	A72C	1725 Sep21		
Cushman Mary	S	A71E	1730 Nov 1		
Cushman Mary	S	A73H	1746 Jul18		
Cushman Mehitable	S	K28E	1693 Oct 8	unm.	1725bef
Cushman Mehitable	S	A25H	1693 Oct 8	unm	1725bef
Cushman Mercy	S	A24G	1692ca		
Cushman Mercy	S	A49B	1712 Feb 8		
Cushman Moses	S	P52D	1693ca		
Cushman Moses	S	A26D	1693ca	1731 Aug22	1766 Aug12
Cushman Moses	S	A72J	1740 Mar22		
Cushman Nathaniel	S	A59E	1712 May28		
Cushman Patience	S	A63E	1721 Apr 8		
Cushman Patience	S	A71K	1744ca		
Cushman Phebe	S	A59A	1702 Mar14		
Cushman Priscilla	S	R120B	1719 Dec12		
Cushman Priscilla	S	A59G	1719 Dec12		
Cushman Rebekah	S	A24B	1676 Nov30	1701 Nov18	1756 Jul 8
Cushman Rebekah	S	A59C	1707 Oct14	mar.	no issue
Cushman Rebekah	S	A63H	1727 Jul11		
Cushman Robert	S	A21A	1664 Oct 4		
Cushman Robert	S	A11Caf	1685abt		
Cushman Robert	S	A45A	1698 Jul 2		
Cushman Ruth	S	A45B	1700 Mar25		
Cushman Ruth	S	A47E	1712ca		
Cushman Samuel	S	A21F	1687ca	1709 Dec 8	1766 Feb19
Cushman Samuel	S	A49C	1715 Jul10		d. yng
Cushman Sarah	S	A14C	1641ca	2 mar.	1695aft
Cushman Sarah	S	A24D	1684 Apr17	1708 Jul 8	1724 Feb 2
Cushman Sarah	S	A59D	1709 Dec 2		
Cushman Sarah	S	A26G	1711ca	1731 Nov23	1755bef
Cushman Sarah	S	A63C	1717 Nov 8		
Cushman Sarah	S	A50F	1725 Sep29		1745 Jan24
Cushman Sarah	S	A72D	1727 Oct20		
Cushman Sarah	S	A73B	1731 Mar19		
Cushman Sarah	S	A71F	1732 Dec 1		
Cushman Seth	S	A71G	1734 Oct16		

NAME	DIV.	NUMBER	BIRTH	MARRIAGE	DEATH
Cushman Solomon	S	A50C	1717 Sep 9		
Cushman Solomon	S	A73C	1733 Feb17		
Cushman Susannah #1	S	A67A	1710 Sep16		d.yng
Cushman Susannah #2	S	A67C	1715 May24		
Cushman Tenperance	S	A71J	1742ca		
Cushman Thomas	S	W20Daf	1607	1636ca	1691
Cushman Thomas	S	A14A	1637ca	2 mar.	1726 Aug23
Cushman Thomas	S	A47B	1705ca		
Cushman Thomas	S	A45E	1706 Feb14		
Cushman Thomas	S	A71D	1728 Jan28		
Cushman Thomas	S	A50H	1730 Oct11		
Cushman Thomas =P22Aaf	S	A11Ca	1607	1636ca	1691
Cushman Thomas=A11Ca	A	A8/200	1607	1636ca	1691
Cushman Thomas=A11Ca	S	K14Eaf	1607	1636ca	1691
Cushman Thomas=A21C	S	K26Faf	1680abt		
Cushman Thomas=K26Faf	S	A21C	1680ca		1726 Jan 9
Cushman Thomas=W20Daf	S	P22Aaf	1607	1636ca	1691
Cushman William	S	A47A	1703ca		
Cushman William	S	A26F	1710 Oct27	1730ca	1777 Dec27
Cushman William	S	A63B	1715 Oct13		
Cushman William	S	A67G	1723 Feb26		
Cushman William	S	A73E	1738 Jun24		
Cushman William=A26F	S	P52F	1710 Oct27		1777 Dec27
Cushman Zibiah	S	K26Fa	1708ca	1727 Mar 9	1743 Nov13
Cushman Zibiah=K26Fa	S	A47C	1708ca	1727 Mar9	1743 Nov13
Cusick Jennie	A	A9/5	1856ca	1878 Feb27	1886 Nov19
Cusick Patrick	A	A9/10	1825ca		1892ca
Dabney Susannah	A	A18/13	1700ca		1752aft
Daggett Susanna	A	A4/473	1685	1703	1753
Dale Elizabeth	A	A19/75	1693Dec 10	1719Nov 18	1737
Dale Robert	A	A19/150	1660ca	1680	1700
Dandridge Martha	A	A10/1a	1731 Jun21	1759 Jan 6	
Dane Hannah	S	A23Gam	1645abt		
Danforth Anna	A	A6/131	1622ca	1643	1704ca
Daniel Chloe	A	A2/27	1745 Sep13	1764 Nov20	1823 May19
Daniel David	A	A2/54	1710 Jul 5	1737 Jan25	1776 May21
Daniel Eleazer	A	A2/108	1681 Mar 9	1709 Jul28	1772 Mar28
Daniel Jean	S	G38Aaf	1385abt		
Daniel Joseph	A	A2/216	1637ca	1665	1715ca
Daniel Joseph=A02/216	D	D21/21	1637ca	1665	1715

NAME	DIV.	NUMBER	BIRTH	MARRIAGE	DEATH
Daniel Phillipa	S	G37Aa	1385ca	1409	
Daniel Phillipa II	S	G38Aa	1410abt		
Daniel Phillippa	S	G41Dam	1475abt		
Daniel Robert	D	D21a22	1610abt		
Daniels Moses	S	N14Ia	1772ca		
Darbe Elizabeth	S	R117Gb	1705ca	1754 Jan14	
Darling Fidelia	S	C67Ba	1775abt		
Dastin Mary	S	A22Bam	1660abt		
Davenport Abigail	S	R13Bam	1640abt		
Davenport Abigail	S	A14Eam	1640abt		=R13Bam
Davenport Anna	A	A2/13	1765 Sept8	1788 Jul20	1842 Aug1
Davenport Hannah	A	A1/261	1686	1710	1769
Davenport John	A	A2/104	1664 Oct20	1694ca	1725 Mar21
Davenport Samuel	A	A2/52	1697 Oct20	1726abt	1773 Jun29
Davenport Seth	A	A2/26	1739 Nov2	1764 Nov20	1813Mar 28
Davenport Thomas	A	A2/208	1620abt	1642ca	1685
Davis Abigail	S	X20Cam	1650abt		
Davis Abigail	S	G52Ca	1810abt		
Davis Charlotte	S	C62Ca	1800ca		
Davis Daniel	A	A19/104	1673Mar 26	1699Apr 27	1740Feb 10
Davis Elizabeth	A	A16/107	1634ca		1702 Jun 3
Davis Esther	A	A3/105	1722ca		1762 Apr18
Davis G	S	G52Ha	1815abt		
Davis Hannah	S	F16Ca	1653 Jan 3	1681 Mar18	1717bef
Davis James	S	G52Ea	1810ca		
Davis Joanna	A	A4/457	1697	1716	1754aft
Davis John	S	F16Caf	1625ca		
Davis John	S	C74Db	1634		
Davis Judith	A	A4/229	1721 Mar21	1740 Dec 2	1808 Feb28
Davis Loyal E	D	D26a17	1885abt		
Davis Mary	S	A22Aam	1665abt		
Davis Mary	S	C49Ba	1685ca		
Davis Mary	A	A19/13	1787Dec 14	1811 Sep 9	
Davis Mary	S	C62Ba	1795ca		
Davis Nathaniel	A	A19/52	1715 Nov 3	1741Apr 16	1802 Jan 5
Davis Nathaniel Jr	A	A19/26	1754Mar 15	1780 Aug14	1835 Jun10
Davis Rachel	A	A19/131	1672	1695	1740
Davis Rebecca	A	A1/51	1775ca	1793 Oct11	
Davis Richard	A	A1/102	1745ca		
Davis Samuel	A	A19/208	1640abt	1665	

NAME	DIV.	NUMBER	BIRTH	MARRIAGE	DEATH
Davis Sarah	S	X19Bam	1660abt		
Davis Thomas	A	A1/204	1710ca	1734 Jan 9	
Davis William	A	A4/458	1675	1700	1753
Davis William	A	A1/408	1685abt		
Dawes Charles Gates	S	G22A	1865 Aug27		1951
Dawes Rufus R	S	G21Aa	1842	1864 Jun18	1899
Dawkins Alice	A	A17/211	1575abt		
Dawson Eliza	A	A1/63	1795ca	1816 May18	
Dawson Henry	A	A1/252	1725abt		
Dawson Samuel	A	A1/126	1795abt		
Day Anthony	A	A16/36	1625ca	1650ca	1707Apr23
Day Dorcas	A	A16/9	1714Feb 2	1735Jun 26	1759Mar 22
Day Elizabeth	A	A3/173	1700abt	1713 Nov19	
Day John	S	F22Haf	1675abt		
Day Lydia	S	F22Ha	1698 Apr11	1722 Dec22	1763 Nov 2
Day Martin	S	N15Da	1780ca		
Day Mary	A	A12/63	1666 Dec15	1687 Feb 4	1723 Apr29
Day Nathaniel	A	A16/18	1665 Apr 9	1689Feb 13	1775 Feb 5
Day Nicholas	A	A3/346	1670abt		1705
Day Robert	A	A12/252	1604ca	1637	1648ca
Day Thomas	A	A12/126	1638ca	1659 Oct27	1711 Dec27
De Beauchamp Eleanor	D	D30/28	1290abt		
De Beauchamp Humphrey	D	D30/29	1260abt		
De Beauchamp Robert	D	D30a30	1235abt		
De Claire Aveline	D	D30/32	1190abt		
De Claire Gilbert	D	D30a35	1100abt		
De Claire Richard	D	D30/34	1130abt		
De Claire Roger	D	D30/33	1160abt		
De Clare Eleanor	D	D29/23	1290abt		
De Clare Gilbert	D	D29a24	1265abt		
De La Montagne Rachel	A	A7/143	1634ca		1664ca
De Lannoy Jean	A	A5/144	1570abt	1596 Jan13	1604
De Meschines Adeliza	D	D30a34	1130abt		
De Mohun Alice	D	D30/30	1235abt		
De Mohun Reynold	D	D30a31	1210abt		
De Ros Margaret	D	D29/18	1415abt		
De Ros William	D	D29a19	1390abt		
De St. Hilaire Maud	D	D30a33	1160abt		
De Veaux Andre	A	A7/100	1685abt		1754aft
De Veaux Mary	A	A7/25	1748	1764 Oct 9	1818 May26

NAME	DIV.	NUMBER	BIRTH	MARRIAGE	DEATH
DeBoogh Catalina	A	A8/149	1625ca	1649	
DeLomagne Jean	S	G39Aam	1400abt		
DeVeaux James	A	A7/50	1710ca	1730ca	1785 Nov23
DeWitt Ines	S	G54Ca	1905abt	1921 Mar 1	
DeWitte Emmerentje C.	A	A8/137	1625abt		
Dean Abigail	S	X22Aa	1680 Nov16	1699 Jan 4	1760bef
Dean Christopher	A	A8/82	1650abt		1689
Dean Elizabeth	S	X12Eam	1620abt		
Dean Elizabeth	S	H24Aam	1640abt		
Dean Hannah	A	A8/41	1675ca	1700 Jul13	
Dean Isaac	S	X22Aaf	1655abt		
Deane Deborah	S	X21Ba	1675ca	1700ca	1702ca
Deane Stephen	S	H12Eaf	1605abt		
Deane Susanna	S	H12Ea	1634bef	1663 Oct28	1701abt
Deane Thomas	S	X21Baf	1650abt		
Delano Abigail	S	T42F	1734 Nov12		
Delano Bethiah	S	W51F	1690 Oct29		1693 Jul19
Delano Betty	S	T42E	1730 Jun30		
Delano Deborah	S	T18Aam	1680abt		
Delano Elisha	S	T42B	1722 Mar25		
Delano Elizabeth	S	T16G	1694ca	1720 Sept8	1727 May16
Delano Ephraim	A	A8/24	1733 Aug25	1764abt	1815 Jul 4
Delano Esther	S	W51J	1698 Apr 4	unmarried	1725abt
Delano Hazadiah	S	T16E	1691ca	1731 Apr 1	1770 Dec 9
Delano Ichabod	S	T42D	1728 Apr 8		
Delano Jabez	S	W51B	1682 Nov 8	2 Mar	1734 Dec23
Delano Jane	S	T16C	1686ca	unm.	1765 Apr 7
Delano Jesse	S	T16H	1698ca		1758 Aug 8
Delano Jethro	S	W51K	1701 Jul31	1727 Oct 9	1777ca
Delano Jonathan	A	A8/96	1648ca	1678 Feb28	1720 Dec23
Delano Jonathan	S	W51A	1680 Jan30	1704 Jun20	1752 Mar25
Delano Jonathan=A5/36	S	W17Ga	1647ca	1677 Feb28	1720 Dec23
Delano Jonathan=A8/96	A	A5/36	1648ca	1678 Feb28	1720 Dec23
Delano Jonathan=W51A	A	A5/18	1680 Jan30	1704 Jun20	1752 Mar25
Delano Joseph	S	T43A	1732 Jun19		
Delano Mary	S	T16F	1691ca	unm.	1771 Mar 7
Delano Mary or (Mercy)	S	W51Ba	1683ca	1709 Feb 8	1716 Apr29
Delano Mercy	S	W51D	1686 Oct27	1712ca	
Delano Nathan	S	W51E	1688 Oct29	1709 Jul 7	
Delano Nathaniel	S	W51I	1695 Oct29	1721 Jan 2	1770 Apr 8

NAME	DIV.	NUMBER	BIRTH	MARRIAGE	DEATH
Delano Philip	A	A5/72	1603 Nov 6	1634 Dec19	1681ca
Delano Philip	S	T12Caf	1635abt		
Delano Philip=A5/72	A	A8/192	1603 Nov 6	1634 Dec19	1681ca
Delano Prince	S	T42C	1725 Apr26		
Delano Priscilla	S	T16B	1686ca	1717ca	1746 Feb 7
Delano Rebecca	S	T16A	1684ca	1715 Aug 4	1774 Sept6
Delano Ruth	S	T42A	1719 Feb25		
Delano Samuel	S	T12Ca	1659ca	1683ca	1728bef
Delano Samuel	S	T16D	1688ca	1719 May21	1739
Delano Sara	A	A8/3	1854 Sep21	1880 Oct 7	1941 Sept7
Delano Sara	D	D4a18	1854 Sep21	1880 Oct 7	1941 Sep 7
Delano Sarah	S	W51C	1684 Jan 9		1690 Feb27
Delano Sarah	S	T16I	1700ca	1728 Apr 4	
Delano Susanna	A	A5/9	1724 Jun23	1746 Nov 5	1806 Aug16
Delano Susannah	S	W51G	1692 Dec 3		1718 Jan20
Delano Thomas=A8/49	S	W51L	1704 May10	1727	
Delano Thomas=W51L	A	A8/48	1704 May10	1727ca	
Delano Warren	A	A8/12	1779 Oct28	1808 Nov 6	1866 Sep25
Delano Warren Jr.	A	A8/6	1809 Jul13	1843 Nov 1	1898 Jan17
Derby Elizabeth	S	X17Aam	1650abt		=A16Cam
Derby Elizabeth=X17Aam	S	X16Cam	1650abt		
Derby Mary	S	H16Bam	1635abt		
Desire Doty	S	T11Bb	1645ca	1688ca	1731 Jan22
Despencer Edward Jr	D	D29/21	1340abt		
Despencer Edward Sir	D	D29/22	1315abt		
Despencer Elizabeth	D	D29/20	1365abt		
Dewey Elizabeth	S	N11Ca	1670ca		
Dewey Hannah	S	N11Da	1670abt		
Dewey Jedediah	S	F22Hbf	1680abt		
Dewey Margaret	S	R117Dam	1670abt		
Dewey Mark	S	N11E	1671ca		
Dewey Zerviah	S	F22Hb	1708Mar1	1766 Jan8	1770aft
Dewsbury Hester(Esther	A	A5/73	1613ca	1634 Dec19	=A8/193
Dewsbury Hester(Esther	A	A8/193	1613ca	1634	
Dexter Mary	S	K31Eam	1670abt		
DiBingo Carmela	S	G54Dbf	1890		
Dibble Abigail	A	A12/33	1666 Jan19		1725after
Dibble Samuel	A	A12/66	1643 Feb19	1666ca	1709 Mar 5
Dibble Thomas	A	A12/132	1613ca		1700ca
Dickens Anne	A	A10/35	1580abt		1637 Apr

NAME	DIV.	NUMBER	BIRTH	MARRIAGE	DEATH
Dickens William	A	A10/70	1550abt	1573Jun 16	1583
Dickens William	D	D11a20	1550abt	1573Jun 16	1583Jan 30
Dickinson Alice	A	A7/91	1675abt		1727aft
Dickinson Daniel	A	A3/356	1674	1698	1709
Dickinson Elizabeth	A	A3/89	1739 Jul13	1759 Apr 5	
Dickinson Joseph	A	A3/178	1706 Dec27	1732 Aug25	1780after
Dickinson Thomas	S	C17Ba	1740ca		
Dighton Frances	S	X13Bcm	1610abt		
Dillingham Elizabeth	S	T15Aam	1670abt		
Dillon Nicholas	A	A3/202	1695abt		1773
Dillon Rebecca	A	A3/101	1725ca	1746 Sep13	
Dilly Patience	S	W43Cb	1675ca	1749 Mar 6	1761after
Dimmick Ann	S	R87A	1724 May23		
Dimmick Dan	S	R87I	1743 May13		
Dimmick Johanna	S	R87D	1730 Aug28		
Dimmick John	S	R24Aaf	1675abt		
Dimmick John	S	R87C	1727 Mar24		
Dimmick Josiah	S	R87E	1732 Mar 2		
Dimmick Oliver	S	R87H	1740 Dec31		
Dimmick Simeon	S	R87F	1735 Sep19		1737 Mar 9
Dimmick Sylvanus	S	R87G	1738 Jun18		
Dimmick Timothy	S	R24Aa	1698 Jul	1723 Aug15	1783 Dec27
Dimmick Timothy	S	R87B	1726 Apr 8		
Dimmock Abigail	S	F38F	1714 Jun30		
Dimmock Bethiah	S	F38B	1702 Feb 3		
Dimmock David	S	F38H	1721 Dec22		
Dimmock Ensign	S	F38D	1709 Mar 8		
Dimmock Ichabod	S	F38E	1711 Mar 8		
Dimmock Joseph	S	F18Aa	1665 Sep17	1669 May17	
Dimmock Mehitable	S	F38C	1707 Mar22		
Dimmock Pharoh	S	F38G	1717 Sept2		
Dimmock Shubael	S	F18Aaf	1640ca		
Dimmock Silence	S	X16Ib	1700ca	1721 Feb 1	1741living
Dimmock Thomas	S	F38A	1699 Jan26		
Dimmon Rebecca	S	K30Ia	1710ca	1732 May11	1749 May11
Dimmon Thomas	S	K30Iaf	1690abt		
Dingley Hannah	S	W43Da	1675 May28	1698 Feb28	1746 Jan14
Dingley Hannah=W43Da	S	R23Ham	1675 May28	1698Feb 28	1746 Jan14
Dingley Jacob	S	W43Daf	1650abt		
Dingley John	S	T11Faf	1610abt		

NAME	DIV.	NUMBER	BIRTH	MARRIAGE	DEATH
Dingley Mary	S	T11Fa	1635ca	1654 Dec19	1655 Jul 1
Dingley Sarah	S	W29Bam	1645abt		
Dixson Rose	A	A3/415	1665abt	1690	
Doane Ann	S	H24Ecm	1660abt		
Doane Daniel	S	H27Daf	1650abt		
Doane Eleazer	A	A3/500	1691	1715	1757
Doane Ephraim	S	H28Gaf	1665abt		
Doane John	S	H17Eaf	1640abt		
Doane John	A	A3/250	1716 Jan11	1739 Dec13	1788aft
Doane Patience	S	H28Ga	1682 Apr	1705 Feb 7	1746aft
Doane Rebecca	S	H27Da	1675ca		
Doane Rebecca	A	A3/125	1754 Apr 5	1771ca	
Doane Rebecca=	S	H17Ea	1668 May12	1685 Jan20	1758 Dec19
Dodson Mary	S	W45Fam	1675abt		
Dodson Sarah	S	W45Ham	1670abt		
Doggett Ebenezer	S	K27Fa	1693 Aug22	1720 Jun 9	
Doggett Ebenezer #1	S	K101A	1722 Jul 5		d.yng
Doggett Ebenezer #2	S	K101C	1726 Jul17		
Doggett John	S	K101B	1723 Feb 6		
Doggett Rebecca	S	W24Ham	1650abt		
Doggett Samuel	S	K27Faf	1670abt		
Doggett Samuel	S	K101D	1728 Jan20		
Doggett Samuel Jr	S	W44Fa	1683 Dec24	1710 Feb20	1745 Sep
Doggett Samuel Sr	S	W44Faf	1660abt		
Doliber Abigail	S	A36C	1685ca		
Doliber Hannah	S	A36G	1695ca		
Doliber John	S	A36F	1695ca		
Doliber Joseph	S	A17Caf	1635abt		
Doliber Joseph	S	A36B	1684ca		
Doliber Margaret	S	A36A	1682ca		
Doliber Peter	S	A17Ca	1660ca	1681ca	1699bef
Doliber Peter #1	S	A36D	1689ca		
Doliber Peter #2	S	A36I	1698ca		
Doliber Samuel	S	A36E	1690ca		
Doliber Thomas	S	A36H	1696ca		
Doolittle Sarah	S	A23Dam	1645abt		
Doors Theis	A	A7/188	1610ca		
Doty Desire	S	H14Bam	1645abt		
Doty Desire	S	T12Eam	1655abt		
Doty Desire	S	H33Cam	1670abt		

NAME	DIV.	NUMBER	BIRTH	MARRIAGE	DEATH
Doty Edward	S	W29Gaf	1620abt		
Doty Edward	S	K24B	1671 Jun28		d.yng
Doty Edward MF	D	D5af23	1600abt		=K14Aaf
Doty Edward 2nd	S	W17Kaf	1640abt		
Doty Edward MF	S	K14Aaf	1600abt		
Doty Elisha	S	K24G	1686 Jul13		
Doty Elizabeth	S	K24D	1675 Feb10		
Doty Isaac	S	K24E	1678 Oct25		
Doty Isaac	S	W57Eaf	1685abt		
Doty Isaac=W57Eaf	S	K30Kaf	1690abt		
Doty Jacob	S	K24C	1673 May27		d.yng
Doty John	S	W29Ga	1642ca	1694 Nov22	1701 May 8
Doty John	S	K24A	1668 Aug24		
Doty John	S	W55Caf	1670abt		
Doty John=W29Ga	D	D5a23	1642	1694 Nov22	1701 May 8
Doty John=W29Ga	S	R23Eaf	1642ca	1694 Nov22	1701 May 8
Doty John=W29Ga	S	K14Aa	1642ca	1694 Nov22	1701 May 8
Doty Josiah	S	K24H	1689 Oct		
Doty Martha	S	K30Fam	1685abt		
Doty Martha	S	K24I	1692 Oct		
Doty Mary	S	Q15Abm	1660abt		
Doty Mary	S	K30Ka	1720 Jan15	1742 Nov25	1810 Nov 5
Doty Mehitable	S	W55Ca	1694 Nov 4	1722 May 4	1769 Feb18
Doty Patience	S	R23Ea	1697 Jul 3	1718 Jan22	1784 Feb18
Doty Rebecca	S	W57Ea	1710 Mar10	1738 Dec14	1766 Jan21
Doty Samuel	S	K24F	1682 Jan31		
Doty Sarah=L15Cam	S	W31Eam	1666 Jun 9	1687 Jun21	1748abt
Doty Sarah=W17Ka	S	L15Cam	1666 Jun9	1687 Jun21	1748abt
Doty Sarah=W31Eam	S	W17Ka	1666 Jun9	1687 Jun21	1748abt
Douglas Euphemia	A	A7/53	1711ca	1733 Jun 7	1766 Dec21
Douglas John	A	A7/212	1640abt	1666	
Douglas John	A	A7/106	1685abt		
Downing Emanuel	A	A11/122	1585 Aug	1622 Apr10	1660ca
Downing Lucy	A	A11/61	1625abt	1649ca	1697 Feb5
Drake Elizabeth	S	F19Eam	1645ca		
Drake Hannah	S	N11Hbm	1655abt		
Drake John Sr.	S	F19Db	1635abt		1740abt
Du Trieux Maria	A	A7/141	1617ca	1650	1670aft
DuFour Galhard	S	G39Aaf	1400abt		
DuFour Jeanne	S	G39Aa	1430abt	1451	

NAME	DIV.	NUMBER	BIRTH	MARRIAGE	DEATH
DuMond Petronella	A	A8/139	1635abt	1680	
DuVergier Desiree	S	G42Bam	1520abt		
Dudley Deborah	A	A4/495	1701 Nov15	1721ca	1800 Mar 8
Dudley Deborah=A4/495	A	A4/255	1701 Nov15	1721ca	1800 Mar 8
Dudley Joseph	A	A4/510	1674ca	1697	1743
Dunbar Peter	S	W39Ba	1668 Sep 6	1691 Mar25	1719 Apr23
Dunbar Robert	S	W39Baf	1640abt		
Duncalf Mary	A	A3/475	1660abt	1685	
Dunham Abigail	S	H16Aam	1625abt		
Dunham Benajah	S	F19Baf	1635ca		
Dunham Benajah	S	F43A	1684 Aug13		
Dunham Calvin	S	N14Aa	1750ca		
Dunham Edmund	S	F19Ba	1661 Jul25	1681 Jul15	1734 Mar 7
Dunham Edmund	S	F43C	1691 Jan15		
Dunham Elizabeth	S	F43B	1689 Nov26		
Dunham Ephraim	S	F43E	1696 May 2		
Dunham Hannah	S	Q13Eam	1625abt		
Dunham Hannah	S	F43H	1704 Apr14		
Dunham Hannah=Q13Eam	S	Q13Gam	1625abt		
Dunham Jonathan	S	F43D	1694 Aug16		
Dunham Mary	S	F43F	1698 Nov26		d. yng
Dunham Mary	S	F43G	1700 Jul 1		
Dunham Mehitabel	S	Q21Gam	1680abt		
Dunham Mercy	S	Q20Bam	1670abt		
Dunham Mercy=Q20Bam	S	Q20Eam	1670abt		
Dunham Persis	S	K31Aam	1660abt		
Dunkhorn Sarah	S	F10Aa	1550abt		
Dunn Hugh	S	F19Eaf	1645ca		
Dunn Mary	S	F19Ea	1671 Jan19	1691	1698living
Dupnak Linda	S	G56Aa	1934ca	1956 Dec26	
Durfee Abigail	S	C61Ea	1755ca		
Durfee Elizabeth	S	W51Ia	1702	1721 Jan 2	1784 Feb18
Durfee Robert	S	W51Iaf	1680abt		
Dutcher Christina	S	C20Aa	1745ca		
Dutton Joseph	S	G11Gaf	1660abt		
Dutton Rebecca	S	G11Ga	1686 Aug13	1705	
Duval Jeane	S	G41Aa	1490 ca		
Duxford Katherine	A	A17/153	1565ca		1631
Dyer Abigail	S	K36Dam	1665abt		
Dyer Abigail	S	R44C	1718 Apr10		

NAME	DIV.	NUMBER	BIRTH	MARRIAGE	DEATH
Dyer Abigail	S	H104D	1738 Jan 9		
Dyer Ambrose	S	H29Da	1709 Dec22	1729 Jan22	1792 May10
Dyer Ambrose	S	H104A	1730 Jan29		
Dyer Charles	S	C95Ga	1710abt		
Dyer Ebenezer	S	R44H	1729 Jun19	unm.	1757
Dyer Edward	S	C80Aa	1670		
Dyer Elijah	S	R44B	1716 Sep10		
Dyer Hannah	S	H104C	1736 Apr 5		
Dyer James	S	R44D	1719 Feb16		
Dyer Jerusha	S	H104G	1747 Jul 9		
Dyer John	S	R117Aa	1692 Apr 9	1713 Oct22	1779 Feb25
Dyer John	S	R44E	1722 May13		
Dyer Joseph	S	R117Aaf	1670abt		
Dyer Joseph	S	R44F	1724 May 9		
Dyer Mary	S	W28Fam	1650abt		
Dyer Mary	S	H104F	1744 Sep 9		
Dyer Naphtali	S	H104E	1741 Dec29		
Dyer Reuben	S	H104H	1753 May25		1780 Apr13
Dyer Sarah	S	R44G	1727 Nov14		
Dyer Sybil	S	R44A	1714 Oct26		
Dyer Thankful	S	H104B	1733 Apr16		
Dyer William	S	H29Daf	1685abt		
Dymoke Frances	A	A10/91	1545abt	1566 Aug20	
Eagleson Barbara F.	D	D33b18	1923Feb 19	1962 Jan25	
Eames Anthony	S	W30Aa	1657ca	1686 Dec 2	1729 Sep17
Eames Elizabeth	S	W18Cam	1635abt		
Eames Mark	S	W30Aaf	1630abt		
Earl Ruhamah	S	R118Ba	1710ca	1734 Aug26	1751bef
Earle Benjamin	S	K48C	1691 May21		
Earle Daniel	S	K48B	1688 Oct28		
Earle ELizabeth	S	K48F	1699 Sep 6		
Earle John	S	K18Aa	1660abt	1686ca	1728bef
Earle John	S	K48A	1687 Aug 7		
Earle Lydia	S	K58F	1704ca		
Earle Martha	S	K20Dam	1650abt		
Earle Mary	S	K20Bam	1650abt		
Earle Mary	S	K48D	1693 Jun 6	unm.	1769
Earle Mary	S	K58C	1697ca		
Earle Oliver	S	K58D	1700ca		
Earle Ralph	S	K18Aaf	1640abt		

NAME	DIV.	NUMBER	BIRTH	MARRIAGE	DEATH
Earle Rebecca	S	K48E	1695 Dec17		1737
Earle Rebecca	S	K58G	1705ca		
Earle Sarah	S	K58E	1702ca	unm.	1734living
Earle Thomas	S	K20Aa	1665ca	1693bef	1727
Earle Thomas	S	K58B	1695ca		
Earle William	S	K20Aaf	1640abt		
Earle William	S	K58A	1693ca		
Eastland Elizabeth	S	X46C	1708 Jan31		
Eastland Hannah	S	X46E	1712 Feb13		d. yng
Eastland Jean	S	X46F	1715 Sep15		d. yng
Eastland John	S	X17Fa	1675ca	1702 Oct29	1726bef
Eastland Joseph	S	X46B	1705 Nov12		
Eastland Joshua	S	X46G	1718 Apr13		d.yng
Eastland Marey	S	X46D	1710 Nov 1		
Eastland Mary	S	X46H	1720 Mar 3		
Eastland Zeruiah	S	X46A	1703 Dec 8		
Easton Waite	S	W45Cam	1660abt		
Eaton Benjamin	S	P22Caf	1640abt		
Eaton Benjamin	S	P22Ca	1664ca	1689 Dec18	1745
Eaton Benjamin	S	P54F	1698ca		
Eaton Benjamin=P22Ca	S	A21Gaf	1664ca	1689 Dec18	1745
Eaton Dorcas	A	A19/19	1754Jul 31	1774 Feb25	1845 Feb 3
Eaton Grace	A	A19/157	1677	1695	
Eaton Hannah	S	P54B	1692 Feb10		
Eaton Jabez	S	P54C	1693 Feb 8		1722 May19
Eaton John	A	A19/76	1696Jan31	1721Dec 28	1759
Eaton John	S	P54E	1697 Oct 6		
Eaton Jonathan	A	A19/152	1655	1691	1743
Eaton Mary	S	P54G	1699ca		
Eaton Mercy	S	H33Fam	1675abt		
Eaton Mercy =H33Fam	S	K31Fam	1670abt		
Eaton Sarah	S	P54D	1695 Oct20		
Eaton Sarah	S	A21Ga	1695 Oct20	1712 Jan 8	1737 Sep13
Eaton Thomas	A	A19/38	1724Feb 17	1747ca	1774 Oct14
Eaton William	S	P54A	1691 Jun 1	unm	1745ca
Ebles I Count of Roucy	D	D30a38	1005abt		
Eddy Abigail	S	C67Aa	1770abt		
Eddy Eleazer	A	A16/26	1681 Oct16	1701 Mar27	1739 Dec 8
Eddy Hannah	A	A16/13	1704ca	1735Mar 7	
Eddy John	A	A16/52	1650abt	1672May 1	1695 Nov27

NAME	DIV.	NUMBER	BIRTH	MARRIAGE	DEATH
Eddy Melatiah	S	Q14Eb	1704ca	1730 Mar22	1798 Oct 8
Eddy Patience	S	C28Gb	1675abt		
Eddy Samuel	S	Q14Ebf	1680abt		
Edgerton Alice	S	R55I	1721 Jul10		1748living
Edgerton Daniel	S	R55J	1725 Jul10		1726 Aug31
Edgerton David	S	R55H	1718 Aug28		
Edgerton Eiljah	S	R55G	1715 Dec 1		
Edgerton John	S	R55E	1710 Apr25	unm.	1730Jul 1
Edgerton Joshua	S	R55C	1707 Feb26		
Edgerton Mary	S	R55F	1713 May17		
Edgerton Peter	S	R55B	1705 Jan14		
Edgerton Richard	S	R19Aaf	1650abt		
Edgerton Samuel	S	R19Aa	1670 May	1703 Apr18	1748 Jun 7
Edgerton Samuel	S	R55A	1704 Mar15		
Edgerton William	S	R55D	1710 Apr25		
Edith of France	D	D30/39	980abt		
Edmunds Benjamin	S	P36G	1724ca		
Edmunds Hannah	S	P36A	1708 Jan13		
Edmunds John	S	P19Aaf	1665abt		
Edmunds John	S	P36B	1711		d. yng
Edmunds Joseph	S	P19Aa	1686 Mar 1	1707 Oct25	1767ca
Edmunds Joseph	S	P36C	1714 Feb 1		
Edmunds Mary	S	P36E	1719 Aug30		
Edmunds Sarah	S	P36F	1721ca		
Edmunds William	S	P36D	1716 Mar14		
Edson Mary	S	Q23Bam	1675abt		
Edwards N	S	N11Bb	1664abt		
Eggleston Hester	A	A12/95	1663 Dec 1	1684 Jun26	
Eggleston James	A	A12/190	1635abt		1679
Eldredge Ann	S	K21Da	1725abt	1747 Jul16	1780aft
Eldridge George	S	N15Na	1800abt		
Elkins Margaret	S	H19Fa	1683 Apr26	1705 Jul12	1772ca
Elkins Thomas	S	H19Faf	1655abt		
Ellis Ann	A	A14/157	1610abt	1632	
Ellis Ann	A	A15/97	1610ca		
Ellis Content	S	T26Fa	1724 Mar15	1745 Mar15	1757 Sep13
Ellis Elijah	S	Q52D	1750abt		
Ellis Elnathan	S	B18Aa	1695abt	1716 Mar 2	
Ellis John	S	Q19Caf	1685abt		
Ellis John	S	C38Aa	1722ca		

NAME	DIV.	NUMBER	BIRTH	MARRIAGE	DEATH
Ellis John	S	Q52C	1748abt		
Ellis Joseph	S	Q19Ca	1709ca	1742 Feb21	1790aft
Ellis Luke	S	Q52B	1746abt		
Ellis Richard	S	T26Faf	1700abt		
Ellis Seth	S	Q52A	1744abt		
Ellison Richard Jr.	A	A3/450	1660		1719
Ellyson Hannah	A	A15/49	1640abt		1727ca
Ellyson Robert	A	A15/98	1625abt		1688bef
Elsey Henry	A	A9/28	1776ca		1844 Apr16
Elsey Mary Ann	A	A9/7	1843 Dec28	1866 Jan25	1900 Oct 6
Elsey Robert	A	A9/14	1817 Jan	1838 Dec25	1850
Ely Amy	A	A4/63	1777ca	1818ca	1876
Ely Daniel	A	A4/252	1693ca	1725 Jan 5	1776 Mar14
Ely Wells	A	A4/126	1729ca	1754ca	1804 Sep 1
Ely William	A	A4/504	1647	1681	1717
Emerson Elizabeth	A	A2/33	1686 Mar6	1708ca	1760 Mar10
Emerson James	A	A2/66	1660ca	1685ca	1756ca
Emerson Jane	S	P21Ham	1780abt		
Emerson Joseph	A	A2/132	1620	1652ca	1680ca
Emerson Mary	A	A16/23	1704 Apr20	1721Sep 23	1777 Jul13
Emerson Nathaniel	A	A16/92	1631ca		1712Dec 29
Emerson Thomas	A	A16/184	1584	1611	1666
Emerson Thomas	A	A16/46	1671ca	1685Nov 20	1738Apr14
Emery Bethia	A	A17/23	1658 Oct15	1681May 4	1726living
Emery John	A	A17/92	1598Sep 29		1683Nov 3
Emery John Jr	A	A17/46	1629ca	1650bef	1693aft
Ensign Hannah	S	X23Eam	1665abt		
Erikson Michael	S	G46Fa	1705abt	1726	
Esten Henry	S	C26Aa	1697		
Esten Henry II	S	C27A	1726		
Esten Jemima	S	C27C	1729		
Esten Jemima E	S	C49Hd	1705ca		
Esten Johanna	S	C24Aa	1645		
Esten John	S	C27B	1727		
Esterbrooks Sally	S	C61Ja	1766ca		
Estes Matthew	S	W45Ga	1689 Jun 7	1712 Jun 5	1774 May11
Estes Richard	S	W45Gaf	1660abt		
Estey Benjamin	S	R28Kaf	1700abt		
Estey Nathan	S	R28Ka	1727 Nov26	1753 Jul22	
Eustace Ann	S	A82G	1737ca		

NAME	DIV.	NUMBER	BIRTH	MARRIAGE	DEATH
Eustace Elizabeth	S	A82B	1723ca		
Eustace Hancock	S	A82F	1735ca		
Eustace Isaac	S	A82E	1732ca		
Eustace John	S	A32Baf	1660abt		
Eustace John	S	A82A	1721ca		
Eustace Sarah	S	A82C	1725ca		
Eustace William	S	A32Ba	1682ca	1720ca	1739
Eustace William	S	A82D	1729ca		
Evans Ann	S	X24Cam	1660abt		
Everetse Cornelia	A	A7/137	1630ca		1707aft
Everson Hannah	S	T21Aa	1732 Jul 6	1751 Aug29	1814 Apr26
Everson Hannah	S	R104A	1753 Apr15		
Everson James	S	R104B	1754 Sep29		
Everson John	S	T21Aaf	1710abt		
Everson Lydia	S	R104D	1759 Jun17	unm.	1813 Apr15
Everson Oliver	S	R104C	1757 Jan 9		
Everson Seth	S	R26Ha	1720ca	1752 Apr28	1768 Sep13
Everson Seth	S	R104E	1761 Jul11		
Everston Katherine	S	G45Ca	1655abt		
Fairbanks Mary	A	A2/217	1647	1665	1682
Fairbanks Mary	D	D21a21	1647	1665	1682
Fairchild Anne	A	A7/51	1710ca	1730ca	1765 Mar 8
Fairchild Richard	A	A7/102	1685abt		1721 Oct
Fairfax Benjamin	S	A11Abf	1590abt		
Fairfax Sarah	S	A11Ab	1615ca		1678ca
Fairfield Abigail	A	A19/179	1698	1718	
Fallowell Ann	S	W12Eam	1615abt		
Farnum Ralph	A	A12/182	1601ca		1648aft
Farnum Sarah	A	A12/91	1638ca	1658 Apr26	
Farr Elizabeth	S	W38Gam	1655abt		
Farrar Joanna	A	A19/151	1661	1680	1733
Farrell Richard	S	G45Aa	1645abt		
Farrow John	S	X22Baf	1660abt		
Farrow Remember	S	X22Ba	1682 Feb 3	1705 Apr 3	1718
Faunce Eleazer	S	W57Ca	1695 Feb 6	1724 Aug 6	1747bef
Faunce Hannah	S	K93D	1718 May30		
Faunce John	S	W11Gaf	1605abt		
Faunce John	S	K26Ba	1683 Dec 3	1709 Feb23	1751 Nov18
Faunce John	S	K93C	1716 Apr13		
Faunce Joseph=K26Baf	S	W57Caf	16670abt		

NAME	DIV.	NUMBER	BIRTH	MARRIAGE	DEATH
Faunce Joseph=W57Caf	S	K26Baf	1660abt		
Faunce Judith	S	K93A	1710 Jan 1		
Faunce Lydia	S	K93B	1714 Jun10		
Faunce Martha	S	W57Eam	1685abt		
Faunce Martha=W57Eam	S	K30Kam	1685abt		
Faunce Mary	S	W37Abm	1640abt		
Faunce Mary	S	K93E	1720 Apr25		
Faunce Mehitable	S	K93F	1722 Apr11		
Faunce Mercy	S	W23Fam	1645abt		
Faunce Priscilla	S	W11Ga	1633ca	1652ca	1707 May15
Faunce Priscilla=W11Ga	S	R12Aam	1633ca	1652ca	1787May 15
Faunce Priscilla=W11Ga	D	D9am23	1633ca	1652ca	1707 May15
Faunce Rebecca	S	K93G	1724 Sep15		
Faunce Sarah	S	W17Kam	1640abt		
Fay Harriet Eleanor	A	A1/9	1829 Oct28	1859 Feb24	1924 Feb27
Fay John	A	A1/288	1700	1721	1732
Fay Jonathan	A	A1/144	1724 Nov21	1746 Jun25	1800 Mar 3
Fay Jonathan Jr	A	A1/72	1752 Jan21	1776 Dec 6	1811 Jun 1
Fay Samuel Howard	A	A1/18	1804 Jul21	1825 Jul 5	1847Aug 16
Fay Samuel Prescott P	A	A1/36	1778 Jan10	1803 Jul31	1856 May18
Fearing Elizabeth	S	W24Ga	1678 Jan25	1702 May8	
Fearing Israel	S	W24Gaf	1650abt		
Fearing Israel	S	W29Haf	1665abt		
Fearing Isreal=W29Ham	S	W24Kaf	1650abt		
Fearing Margaret	S	W29Ha	1689 Jun 8	1708 Aug23	1750 Aug23
Fearing Sarah	S	W24Ka	1689 Dec 1	1716 Sep13	1763 Oct15
Fellows Elizabeth	A	A1/139	1685 Sep14	1708 Mar 2	
Fellows Elizabeth	S	C11Ca	1685Sep 14	1708 Mar 2	=A1/139
Fellows Ephraim	A	A1/278	1641ca	1683ca	1710aft
Fellows Marion	S	C12Ga	1720ca		
Fenton Catherine	S	C63Ba	1786ca		
Ferreri Marie Ann	S	G54Db	1919 Aug16	1989 Oct30	
Ferreri Nicholas	S	G54Dbf	1870		
Ferrers Ann	D	D29a22	1315abt		
Field Elizabeth	S	Q21Aa	1698 Aug 4	1714ca	1768 Apr15
Field John	S	Q21Aaf	1675abt		
Field John	A	A1/118	1770abt	1795 Sep11	
Field Mildred	A	A1/59	1795ca	1815 Mar27	
Field Robert	A	A1/236	1795abt		
Field Ruth	S	C88Ba	1710ca		

NAME	DIV.	NUMBER	BIRTH	MARRIAGE	DEATH
Fillingham Ira W	S	G54Fa	1909 Jan13	1930 Nov 5	1990 Jul
Fillmore John	A	A16/16	1676ca	1701Jun 19	1708
Fillmore John Jr	A	A16/8	1702Mar 18	1735Jun 26	1777Feb 22
Fillmore Millard Pres.	A	A16/1	1800 Jan 7		1881Aug 11
Fillmore Nathaniel Jr	A	A16/2	1771Apr 19	1796ca	1863Mar 28
Fillmore Nathaniel Sr	A	A16/4	1739Mar 20	1767 Oct28	1814Sep 7
Finney Abigail	S	K30Ba	1697 Apr17	1716 Jan10	1765 Mar13
Finney Abigail	S	K30Ib	1715ca	1749 Jan11	1774 Oct17
Finney Elizabeth	S	W56B	1690 Feb 8	1712 Nov18	1775abt
Finney Elizabeth	S	R15Ba	1690 Feb 8	1712 Nov18	1775abt
Finney Hannah	S	W18Fam	1650abt		
Finney Hannah	S	K30Iam	1690abt		
Finney Hannah=W18Fam	S	X17Ham	1650abt		
Finney Jeremiah	S	K30Baf	1675abt		
Finney John	S	W18Eaf	1635abt		
Finney John	S	W56F	1701 Dec13	2/1739 Apr	1791 Mar18
Finney John	S	K30Da	1701 Dec13	1721 Feb22	1791 Mar18
Finney John	S	K111E	1730 Oct18		
Finney Joshua	S	W56H	1708 Jul30	1727 Sep28	1740abt
Finney Josiah	S	W56A	1687 Jan29		1696 Sep19
Finney Josiah	S	W56E	1698 Oct 9	1722 Dec13	1783 Sep 7
Finney Josiah	S	K111C	1726 Feb 5		d.yng
Finney Josiah=K30Daf	S	R15Baf	1660Jan 11	1687Jan19	1726bef
Finney Josiah=R15Baf	S	W18Ea	1660 Jan11	1687 Jan19	1726bef
Finney Josiah=W18Ea	S	K30Daf	1660 Jan11	1687Jan 19	1726bef
Finney Phebe	S	W56G	1705 Feb 1	1726 Sep 8	1753 May23
Finney Phebe	S	K111B	1724 Feb 8		
Finney Priscilla	S	W56D	1694 Mar 9	1717 May23	1731living
Finney Robert	S	W56C	1693 Oct21	1716 Nov15	1764 Jun 1
Finney Ruth	S	K111D	1729 Oct 1		
Finney Sarah	S	K111A	1722 Nov19		
Fish Bartholomew	S	X26Aa	1687 Jun16	1716 Oct 9	1727aft
Fish Cornelius	S	X83D	1743		
Fish Ebenezer	S	X83B	1734		
Fish James #1	S	X83E	1745ca		
Fish James #2	S	X83F	1747ca		
Fish James #3	S	X83G	1747 Oct		
Fish Jedidiah	S	X79B	1738ca		
Fish Lemuel	S	X79A	1727		
Fish Lot	S	X83H	1748		

NAME	DIV.	NUMBER	BIRTH	MARRIAGE	DEATH
Fish Nathan	S	X26Aaf	1665abt		
Fish Nathan	S	X83A	1733		
Fish Nathan=X26Aaf	S	X26Faf	1665abt		
Fish Prince	S	X83I	1751		
Fish Rowland	S	X26Fa	1708 Jul25	1730 Feb16	1751aft
Fish Rufus	S	X83C	1740		
Fisher Elizabeth	S	H10Ab	1595abt	1617Feb 19	1638Feb 4
Fisher Enna Dell	D	D32a22	1861Sep 20	1882Feb 22	1883
Fisher Hannah	S	K18Bam	1640abt		
Fisher Mary	S	K18Cam	1650abt		
Fiske Ann	S	C44Aa	1610		
Fiske Anna	A	A19/141	1656	1689ca	1725bef
Fiske Anne	A	A14/163	1610		1649
Fiske Sarah	S	R117Gam	1680abt		
Fitch Abigail	S	R117A	1687 Feb22	1713 Oct22	1759 May19
Fitch Abigail	S	R50H	1741 Apr19		1749 May 1
Fitch Alice	S	R45A	1713 Jun30		
Fitch Alice	S	R50B	1724 Jan 8		
Fitch Anna	S	R12Ka	1675 Apr 6	1698 Oct 5	1715 Oct 7
Fitch Anna	A	A1/93	1763 Mar 1	1782 Oct 7	1809 Nov15
Fitch Ashael	S	R50G	1738 Aug27		
Fitch Daniel	S	R117C	1692 Feb	1718 Mar 5	1752 Aug 3
Fitch Daniel	S	R46E	1728 Jan 6		1739 Mar 8
Fitch Daniel	S	R49E	1742 Jan30		
Fitch Ebenezer	S	R117B	1689 Jan10	1712 Sep18	1724 Nov20
Fitch Ebenezer	S	R46C	1724 Jul14		
Fitch Ebenezer	S	R45F	1724 Mar10		
Fitch Eleazer	S	R45D	1720 May18		
Fitch Elijah	S	R45C	1717 Feb23		
Fitch Jabez	S	R117G	1702 Jan30	2 Mar	1784 Jan 3
Fitch Jabez	S	R50D	1729 May23		
Fitch James	S	R12Kaf	1655abt		
Fitch James	S	R45B	1715 Jul24		
Fitch James	S	R46B	1722 May27		
Fitch James	S	R49D	1740 Nov 5		
Fitch James Jr	S	R12Db	1649 Aug 2	1687 May 8	1727 Nov10
Fitch James Sr	S	R12Dbf	1625abt		
Fitch Jerusha	S	R117D	1696ca	1717 Mar18	1780 Feb19
Fitch Jerusha	S	R50A	1723 Jan30		
Fitch John	S	R19Haf	1665abt		

NAME	DIV.	NUMBER	BIRTH	MARRIAGE	DEATH
Fitch John	S	R46D	1726 Sep30		
Fitch Lucy	S	R117E	1698ca	1719 Mar19	
Fitch Lucy twin	S	R50F	1736 Jun24		
Fitch Lydia twin	S	R50E	1736 Jun24		
Fitch Mary	S	R12Kbm	1650abt		
Fitch Mary	S	R49F	1744 Apr22		
Fitch Mary Sherwood	S	R12Kb	1674	1715Feb 25	1752 Sep16
Fitch Medina	S	R45E	1722 Nov20		
Fitch Miriam	S	R19Ha	1699 Oct17	1740 Oct16	1744 Dec19
Fitch Perez	S	R50C	1726 Dec 5		
Fitch Phineas	S	R49C	1739 Apr12		d.yng
Fitch Samuel	S	R49A	1735 Jun17		
Fitch Sarah	S	R49G	1748 Mar12		
Fitch Theophilus	S	R117F	1701ca	2 Mar	1751 Jul20
Fitch Theophilus	S	R46F	1731 Jul14		
Fitch Theophulus	S	R49B	1737 May 8		
Fitch William	S	R46A	1720 Jul17		
Fitch William	A	A1/186	1730abt	1752 Apr26	
FitzAlan John	D	D29a20	1365abt		
FitzAlan Margaret	D	D29/19	1390abt		
FitzGoeffrey Hawise	D	D30/31	1210abt		
FitzPiers Goffrey	D	D30a32	1190abt		
Fitzhugh Rosamond	S	A15Ca	1677ca	1698ca	1700
Fitzhugh William	S	A15Caf	1655abt		
Fitzrandolph Edward	S	F19Caf	1630abt		
Fitzrandolph Edward	S	F44G	1698 May25		
Fitzrandolph Elizabeth	S	F44B	1683 Feb18		
Fitzrandolph Francis	S	F44C	1687		1687
Fitzrandolph John	S	F19Ca	1653 Oct 7	1681 Oct 1	
Fitzrandolph John	S	F44F	1693 Nov 2		
Fitzrandolph Mary	S	H24Ebm	1650abt		
Fitzrandolph Sarah	S	F44A	1682 Apr25		
Fitzrandolph Temper.#1	S	F44D	1685 Nov20		1685 Dec27
Fitzrandolph Temper.#2	S	F44E	1687 Jun15		
Flagg Elizabeth	A	A6/67	1656 Mar22	1676 Oct20	1729 Aug 9
Flagg Rebecca	S	R19Gam	1670abt		
Flagg Thomas	A	A6/134	1621ca		1697ca
Fleming Henry	A	A17/210	1575abt		1650living
Fleming Margaret	A	A17/105	1600abt	1627ca	
Fletcher Esther	A	A17/9	1681ca	1707 Jan 5	1767Sep 21

NAME	DIV.	NUMBER	BIRTH	MARRIAGE	DEATH
Fletcher Mary=F17Ba	S	F22Fam	1655ca	1675 Jan	1714bef
Fletcher Mary=F22Bam	S	F17Ba	1655ca	1675 Jan	1714bef
Fletcher Mary=F22Fam	S	F22Bam	1655ca	1675 Jan	1714bef
Fletcher Robert	A	A17/72	1592ca		1677 Apr 3
Fletcher William	A	A17/36	1622ca	1645 Oct 7	1677 Nov 6
Fletcher William Jr	A	A17/18	1656Feb 21	1677Sep 19	1712 May23
Flower William	A	A13/36	1660abt		1693ca
Flowers Enoch	A	A13/18	1693ca		
Flowers Rebecca	A	A13/9	1720 Mar30	1743 Jul 5	1806 Jul20
Floyd Abigail	S	A23Da	1668ca	1698 Jan 7	1732 Oct19
Floyd John	S	A23Daf	1645abt		
Fobes Constant	S	W32Ba	1686 Jun29	1708 Apr 8	1771 Jun29
Fobes William	S	W32Baf	1660abt		
Folger Dorcas	S	P12Fa	1650ca	1674 Feb12	1728living
Folger Joanna	S	P19Iam	1645abt		
Folger Peter	S	P12Faf	1630abt		
Folks Sarah Jane	A	A9/1a	1914Jan 4	1940 Jan24	
Foote Elizabeth	A	A12/175	1615abt	1638	1700
Foote Esther	S	G24Aa	1748	1775	1799
Foote Mary	S	G29A	1753		1785
Foote Nahanial Jr	S	G12Ba	1712	1736	1811
Foote Nathaniel Sr	S	G12Baf	1682	1711	1774
Foote Rebecca	D	D31a24	1630abt		
Forbes Grizel	A	A7/213	1640abt	1666	
Ford Abigail	S	W43F	1679		
Ford Andrew	S	K143E	1721 Sep 2		
Ford Andrew Jr	S	K36Bb	1682ca	1706 Nov27	1750 Nov 8
Ford Andrew Sr	S	K36Bbf	1660abt		
Ford Bathsheba	S	W43E	1675ca		1680 Mar12
Ford Gerald Rudolph	A	A4/1	1913 Jul14	1948 Oct15	
Ford Hannah	S	W43B	1670	1704	1706abt
Ford Hannah	S	R23Ha	1705 Oct18	1726 Nov 9	1800 Apr28
Ford Hannah=W43B	S	W25Ca	1670	1704	1706abt
Ford Hester	S	K143C	1714 Mar 8		
Ford Jacob	S	K143B	1711 Jul20		
Ford James	S	W43D	1675 Apr	1698 Feb28	1735 Jun28
Ford James=W43D	S	R23Haf	1675 Apr	1698Feb28	1735 Jun28
Ford Joanna=A2/173	A	A6/107	1640abt	1662 Sep15	
Ford Joanna=A6/107	A	A2/173	1640ca	1662	
Ford John	S	W52Daf	1665abt		

NAME	DIV.	NUMBER	BIRTH	MARRIAGE	DEATH
Ford Lydia	S	W43A	1668ca	1691ca	1697 Nov 5
Ford Marcy	S	K143A	1708 Nov10		
Ford Mary	S	K143D	1719 Mar11		
Ford Mercy	S	R26Gam	1690abt		
Ford Mercy=R23Bam	S	W44Gam	1660abt		
Ford Mercy=R23Dam	S	R23Bam	1660abt		
Ford Mercy=R26Gam	S	R23Dam	1660abt		
Ford Mercy=W44Gam	S	W42Iam	1660abt		
Ford Michael	S	W25Caf	1645abt		
Ford Michael	S	W16Ca	1650abt	1667 Dec12	1729 Mar27
Ford Patience	S	W43G	1682 Apr 2		
Ford Peleg	S	W52Da	1690 May10	1716 May10	1769 Jan10
Ford Sarah	S	W29Ba	1665ca	1689ca	1728aft
Ford William	S	W16Caf	1625abt		
Ford William	S	W29Baf	1645abt		
Ford William	S	W43C	1672 Dec26	2 Mar	1761 Dec22
Foree Lucretia Green	A	A1/31	1824ca	1843 May 9	
Foree Peter	A	A1/62	1790ca	1816 May18	
Forster Susanna	A	A3/177	1690abt	1714 May 7	
Foster Abraham	S	T25Eaf	1675abt		
Foster Asa	S	T65J	1746 Jul15		
Foster Benjamin	S	W21B	1655ca		1690
Foster Chillingsworth	S	H27Hb	1680 Jul11	1731 Dec 7	1764 Dec22
Foster Daniel	S	T65I	1744 Jul22		
Foster Elizabeth	S	T12Jam	1670abt		
Foster Eunice	S	T65E	1733 Feb29		
Foster Hannah	S	R14Ga	1694 Jul25	1714 Dec 9	1778 Dec17
Foster Hannah	S	T65C	1730 Apr15		
Foster John	A	A8/246	1648ca	1678bef	1711ca
Foster John	S	H27Hbf	1660abt		
Foster John	S	R14Gaf	1670abt		
Foster John=R14Gaf	S	H34Daf	1670abt		
Foster Lois	S	T65D	1732 Jan 7		
Foster Lydia	A	A8/123	1687ca	1706 Oct10	
Foster Mary	S	W21A	1652 Mar8		d.yng
Foster Mary	S	T65A	1725 Oct12		
Foster Mehitable	S	T65F	1737 Feb20		
Foster Mercy	S	H34Da	1697ca	1720 Feb 2	1782 Apr 4
Foster Nathan	S	T25Ea	1700 May17	1724 Nov 3	1753 May26
Foster Nathan	S	T65B	1728 Mar27		

NAME	DIV.	NUMBER	BIRTH	MARRIAGE	DEATH
Foster Phebe	S	T65G	1739 Mar 1		
Foster Renald	A	A16/178	1595abt	1619	1680
Foster Richard	S	W12Ca	1635abt	1651 Sep10	1658ca
Foster Sarah	A	A16/89	1620ca		
Foster Sarah	S	T65H	1742 Jan 4		
Foster Standish	S	T65K	1749 Feb24		
Fout Baltis(Balthazar)	A	A1/154	1700 abt	1721ca	1751 May23
Fout Maria Margareth	A	A1/77	1732 Jan14	1748ca	1795 Oct 6
Fowle Abigail	A	A11/13	1679 Aug7	1699ca	1731aft
Fowle George	A	A11/52	1610 Jan	1634ca	1682 Sep19
Fowle Isaac	A	A11/26	1648ca	1671 Nov30	1718 Oct15
Fox Daniel	S	G28Ca	1722	1761	
Fox Isaac	S	G28Caf	1695abt		
Fox J.	S	N13Ia	1750abt		
Fox Jehiel	S	G30A	1762		1823
France Mary	A	A3/201	1695ca		
Francis Anne A	D	D26/18	1855abt		
Francis Frederick R	D	D26/19	1825abt		
Francis Manning	D	D26a20	1800abt		
Franklin Aaron	A	A19/56	1729	1755	
Franklin Abigail	A	A19/7	1811 Apr18	1838 Dec 5	1892 Oct 3
Franklin Jabez	A	A19/28	1759ca		1829 Feb26
Franklin James Jr	A	A19/224	1682	1706	
Franklin Luther	A	A19/14	1780 Mar 5	1799 Dec 5	1861Apr 18
Franklin Olive	S	C21Ea	1766		
Franklin Philip	A	A19/112	1707 Feb25	1728 Mar31	1797 Feb 5
Franklyn Ellen	A	A17/209	1575abt		1638living
Freeman Alice	S	H27Ea	1675ca	1699ca	1756 Dec24
Freeman Bennet	S	H17Fa	1670 Mar10	1688 Mar14	1716 May30
Freeman Bradford	S	R31C	1713 Aug15		
Freeman Constant	S	H29Aaf	1675abt		
Freeman Elizabeth	S	T13Eam	1650abt		
Freeman Hannah	S	H26Dbm	1660abt		
Freeman Hannah	S	H26Fam	1660abt		
Freeman Hannah	S	H26Gam	1660abt		
Freeman Ichabod	S	R31D	1714 Aug 2		
Freeman John	S	H17Baf	1630abt		
Freeman John	S	H17Faf	1640abt		
Freeman John	S	H23Baf	1655abt		
Freeman Jonathan	S	R14Da	1678 Nov11	1708 Oct12	1714 Apr27

NAME	DIV.	NUMBER	BIRTH	MARRIAGE	DEATH
Freeman Jonathan	S	R31A	1709 Mar26		
Freeman Mercy	S	R22Aam	1660abt		
Freeman Mercy	S	K30Gam	1675abt		
Freeman Mercy	S	H29Aa	1702 Aug31	1719 Oct 8	1786 Dec
Freeman Mercy	S	R31B	1711 Apr24		
Freeman Patience	S	H17Ba	1655ca	1682 Jan31	1745 Feb15
Freeman Patience=H17Ba	S	H28Ham	1655ca	1682 Jan31	1745 Feb15
Freeman Patience=H17Ga	S	H30Gam	1655ca	1682Jan 31	1745Feb 15
Freeman Samuel	S	H27Eaf	1650abt		
Freeman Sarah	S	H23Ba	1676 Sep		1739 Aug23
Freeman Thomas	S	R14Daf	1655abt		
Fritz John Agustus	S	C59Ea	1932		
Frizzell James	A	A2/154	1626ca	1656ca	1716
Frizzell Mary	A	A2/77	1656 May16	1677 Apr10	1745 Mar18
Frost Mehitable	S	P21Mam	1690abt		
Frye Elizabeth	A	A2/193	1620abt	1641ca	
Fuller Aaron	S	F55D	1711 Jun 3		
Fuller Abagail	S	F15F	1674ca		
Fuller Abagail	S	F26E	1704 Jul 5		d. yng
Fuller Abigail	S	F23G	1695 Jan 9		
Fuller Abigail	S	F58C	1718 Apr 3		
Fuller Abigail	S	F26J	1718 Oct19		
Fuller Abner	S	F55I	1724 Dec10		d. yng
Fuller Abraham	S	F61I	1735ca		
Fuller Andrew	S	F60F	1734 Aug11		1758bef
Fuller Ann	S	F26F	1707 Aug29		
Fuller Ann	S	F58B	1716 May28		
Fuller Anne	S	F14Ba	1640aft	1657ca	1691Dec 30
Fuller Anne	S	F15C	1669	1689 Apr29	1722 Jul 2
Fuller Anne	S	F49A	1693 Nov		
Fuller Anne=F14Ba	S	F13D	1640aft	1657ca	1691Dec 30
Fuller Archippus	S	K122A	1721 May17		
Fuller Barnabas	S	F20A	1659ca	1680 Feb25	1738 Apr25
Fuller Benjamin	S	F20D	1665ca		
Fuller Benjamin	S	F23D	1690 Aug 6	m.F48D	
Fuller Benjamin	S	F22I	1701 Oct20		d. yng
Fuller Benjamin	S	F22J	1704ca	unmar.	
Fuller Bethia	S	F18B	1687 Dec	1706 Feb20	1714 Oct26
Fuller Bethia (twin)	S	F40D	1715 Sep 1		
Fuller Consider	S	H117H	1738 Jul 7		

NAME	DIV.	NUMBER	BIRTH	MARRIAGE	DEATH
Fuller Content	S	F49C	1698 Feb19		
Fuller Cornelius	S	F49G	1710		
Fuller Daniel	S	F54H	1731 Apr 4		
Fuller David	S	F49E	1706 Feb		d. yng
Fuller David	S	F58H	1727 Jan26		
Fuller Deborah	S	T38A	1727 Nov23		
Fuller Deborah	S	H117D	1729 Dec14		
Fuller Desire	S	F20E	1670 Dec30	1703 Jun11	
Fuller Desire	S	F55H	1725 Feb		
Fuller Ebenezer	S	F47D	1699 Apr.		
Fuller Ebenezer	S	F24F	1707 Feb20		
Fuller Ebenezer	S	F54A	1715 Oct27		
Fuller Edward	S	F22E	1691ca	1713ca	1730 Jan 7
Fuller Edward	S	F58I	1730 May11		
Fuller Edward MF	D	D6/25	1575 Sep 4		1620Jan11
Fuller Edward MF=D6/25	S	F11A	1575 Sep 4		1620Jan 11
Fuller Eleazer	S	H117A	1723 Nov 3		1736 Aug20
Fuller Eleazer	S	H117I	1740 Apr27		
Fuller Elizabeth	S	F13C	1630aft	1652 Apr22	1715abt
Fuller Elizabeth	S	F14C	1639ca		1683ca
Fuller Elizabeth	S	F14Ham	1640abt		
Fuller Elizabeth	S	T13Ham	1660abt		
Fuller Elizabeth	S	F23E	1692 Sept3		
Fuller Elizabeth	S	F22F	1693ca	1713 Mar 4	1766Janaft
Fuller Elizabeth	A	A2/127	1701 Jul 1	1719 Jan	1786
Fuller Elizabeth	S	F58A	1713ca		
Fuller Elizabeth	S	F54G	1727 Apr30		
Fuller Elkanah	S	F27D	1709 Apr24		
Fuller Ephraim	S	F56B	1711 Sep 8		
Fuller Esther	S	F60B	1724 Jul 6		
Fuller Eunice	S	F58G	1726 May12		
Fuller Ezra	S	H117G	1736 Apr23		
Fuller Grace	S	F61D	1726ca		
Fuller Hannah	S	F14A	1636ca	1658 Jan 1	1686abt
Fuller Hannah	S	F23A	1681 Nov17		
Fuller Hannah	S	F47C	1688 Sept		1735living
Fuller Hannah	S	F50B	1704 May20		
Fuller Hannah	S	F40A	1711 Apr 1	m.F25E	
Fuller Hannah	S	F49H	1713 Jul10		
Fuller Hannah	S	F56E	1718 Apr29		

NAME	DIV.	NUMBER	BIRTH	MARRIAGE	DEATH
Fuller Hannah	S	F26K	1720 Jul 3		
Fuller Hannah	S	F54D	1720 Mar21		
Fuller Hannah	S	H117J	1743 Apr30		
Fuller Isaac	S	F47B	1684 Aug		
Fuller Isaac	S	F61K	1741ca		
Fuller Issacher	S	H117B	1725 Jul 8		
Fuller Jabez	S	F15B	1663ca	1686ca	1711
Fuller Jabez	S	T15Ga	1698ca	1726 Jan12	1728 Oct14
Fuller Jabez	S	F54E	1722 Feb19		
Fuller Jacob	S	F61J	1739ca		
Fuller James	S	F50D	1711 May 1		
Fuller Jean	S	F49D	1704ca		1708
Fuller Jeremiah	S	F61E	1728ca		
Fuller Jerusha	S	T27Ba	1710ca	1737 Nov 2	
Fuller John	S	F13E	1640aft	(2)1687Mar	1691 Jul16
Fuller John	S	F14H	1655ca	1678ca	1726 Mar23
Fuller John	S	T15Gaf	1675abt		
Fuller John	S	F18C	1689 Oct	1710 Jun16	1732 Jul
Fuller John	S	F23H	1696 Apr19		d.yng
Fuller John	S	F22G	1697 Nov10	1721 May10	1758 Jan 5
Fuller John	S	H33Fa	1698 Dec19	1722 Feb 7	1778 Sep25
Fuller John	S	F55A	1704 Nov 3		
Fuller John	S	F50C	1706 Dec25		
Fuller John	S	F40B	1712 Aug 3		
Fuller John	S	F60C	1727 Jan29		
Fuller John	S	H117C	1727 Sep16		1742 Jul30
Fuller John =F14H	D	D6/23	1655ca		1726Mar 23
Fuller Jonathan	S	F24B	1692 Mar10		
Fuller Jonathan	S	F49B	1696 Oct		
Fuller Jonathan	S	F56G	1724 Sep10		d. yng
Fuller Jonathan	S	F54F	1725 Jan12	unmar.	1758bef
Fuller Joseph	A	A2/254	1652	1678ca	1739ca
Fuller Joseph	S	F20B	1661ca	1700ca	1750ca
Fuller Joseph	S	F23B	1683 Jul12		
Fuller Joseph	S	F61A	1723ca		
Fuller Joseph=D6/23	S	F22H	1700Mar1	2/1766Jan	1775Jul 19
Fuller Josiah	S	F47E	1705abt		
Fuller Judah	S	F27G	1715 Aug25		
Fuller Leah	S	F56I	1731 Jun 6		1748bef
Fuller Lois	S	F24E	1704 Sep23		

NAME	DIV.	NUMBER	BIRTH	MARRIAGE	DEATH
Fuller Lydia	S	F18A	1675ca	1699 May17	1755 Nov 6
Fuller Lydia	S	F56A	1709 Sep 1		
Fuller Lydia	S	G27Ab	1710abt		
Fuller Lydia	S	F61F	1729ca		
Fuller Mary	S	F13B	1630aft	1650 Apr17	1691 May11
Fuller Mary	S	P23Aam	1640abt		
Fuller Mary	S	F14E	1644 Jun	1674 Nov18	1720 Nov11
Fuller Mary	S	W49Ab	1685 Aug 6	1731 Sep 1	17560ct23
Fuller Mary	S	F26B	1697 Dec 9	unmar.	1717bef
Fuller Mary	S	F24D	1699ca		
Fuller Mary	S	F27F	1713 Apr 5		
Fuller Mary	S	F26I	1717 Apr		d. yng
Fuller Mary	S	F60A	1721 Feb19		
Fuller Mary	S	F55G	1721 Feb28		
Fuller Mary	S	F26O	1731 Mar18		
Fuller Mary (twin)	S	F40C	1715 Sep 1		
Fuller Mary=W49Ab	S	F23C	1685 Aug 6	1731 Sep 1	1756 Oct23
Fuller Matthew	S	F12A	1610bef		1678 Aug
Fuller Matthew	S	F20C	1663ca	1692 Feb25	1743 Feb 3
Fuller Matthew	S	T27Baf	1715abt		
Fuller Matthew =F12A	S	F14Baf	1610bef		1678 Aug
Fuller Matthias	S	F15E	1672ca	unmar	1697 May 6
Fuller Matthias	S	F26C	1700 Mar24		
Fuller Mehitable	S	F22K	1706 Apr16	1725 Dec 8	1738 May17
Fuller Mehitable	S	F55E	1716 Aug 6		
Fuller Mehitable	S	F60E	1731 Jan 3		
Fuller Mercy	S	F24C	1696 Apr 1		
Fuller Mercy	S	F48D	1710ca	m.F23D	
Fuller Mercy	S	F55F	1718 Jun27		
Fuller Mindwell	S	F61G	1730ca		
Fuller Moses	S	F55C	1708 Jan30		
Fuller Nathan	S	F54C	1719 Apr20		
Fuller Nathaniel	S	F40E	1716 Dec10		
Fuller Nathaniel(twin)	S	F55K	1727 Jun		
Fuller Noadiah	S	F26M	1724 Jul19		1747 Oct27
Fuller Noah	S	H117F	1734 May31		1756 Aug 6
Fuller Nora (twin)	S	F55J	1727 Jun		
Fuller Phoebe	S	F58F	1723 Apr18		
Fuller Rachel	S	F61B	1724ca		
Fuller Rachel	S	F56H	1727 Feb24		

NAME	DIV.	NUMBER	BIRTH	MARRIAGE	DEATH
Fuller Rebecca	S	F27A	1701 Jul22		
Fuller Reliance	S	F18D	1691 Sep 8	1713 Nov16	
Fuller Remember	S	F48A	1701 May26		
Fuller Robert	S	F10A	1550abt		
Fuller Rudolphus	S	F27B	1703 Aug22		
Fuller Ruth	S	F27C	1706 Apr12		
Fuller Ruth	S	F61H	1733ca		
Fuller Samuel	S	F13A	1630ca		1676 Mar26
Fuller Samuel	S	F14B	1637 Feb	1657ca	1691 Dec28
Fuller Samuel	S	G11Daf	1645abt		
Fuller Samuel	S	H33Faf	1675abt		
Fuller Samuel	S	F15G	1676 Aug15	1700 Oct 3	1716 Sep29
Fuller Samuel	S	F47A	1681 Nov		
Fuller Samuel	S	F22B	1682ca	1703 Jun11	1757 Feb12
Fuller Samuel	S	F24A	1687 Feb23		1714bef
Fuller Samuel	S	F23F	1694 Apr12		
Fuller Samuel	S	F55B	1706 Aug31		
Fuller Samuel	S	F26G	1711 Sep 1		
Fuller Samuel MF	S	F12B	1608ca	1635 Apr 8	1683 Oct31
Fuller Samuel Dr MF	S	F11B	1575abt		
Fuller Samuel MF=F12B	D	D6/24	1608ca	1635 Apr 8	1683 Oct31
Fuller Samuel=H33Faf	S	K31Faf	1675abt		
Fuller Sarah	S	F14D	1641abt		d.yng
Fuller Sarah	S	F14G	1654 Dec14		
Fuller Sarah	S	F20F	1670aft		1691living
Fuller Sarah	S	F26D	1702 Aug 7		
Fuller Sarah	S	F58D	1719 Jul 8		
Fuller Sarah	S	F60G	1737 Jun14		
Fuller Seth	S	K31Fa	1692 Aug30	1720 May12	1755ca
Fuller Seth	S	F48B	1705 Sep		1732 Jan 7
Fuller Shubael	S	F22C	1684ca	1708 Dec 7	1748 May29
Fuller Shubael	S	F56F	1720 Jan 6		
Fuller Shubael=F22C	D	D6/22	1684ca	1708 Dec 7	1748 May29
Fuller Silence	S	F58E	1721 May22		
Fuller Susanna	S	H117E	1731 Nov18		
Fuller Temperance	S	F50A	1702 Mar 7		
Fuller Thankful	S	F22D	1688ca	1707 July9	1740Mayaft
Fuller Thankful	S	F48C	1708 Aug 4		1728 Jul 3
Fuller Thankful	S	F56C	1713 Jul10		
Fuller Thankful	S	F40F	1718 Sep19		

NAME	DIV.	NUMBER	BIRTH	MARRIAGE	DEATH
Fuller Thomas	S	F14F	1650 May18		1683bef
Fuller Thomas	S	F15A	1661ca	1680 Dec29	1718 Nov2
Fuller Thomas	S	F22A	1679ca	1714ca	1772 Apr 9
Fuller Thomas	S	F54B	1717 Apr 5		
Fuller Thomas	S	F26N	1726 Jun24		
Fuller Thomas=F15A	S	W49Abf	1661ca	1680Dec 29	1718 Nov 2
Fuller Timothy	S	F15D	1670ca	1694ca	1748 Nov30
Fuller Timothy #1	S	F26A	1695 Aug29		d.yng
Fuller Timothy #2	S	F26H	1715 Oct 9		d. yng
Fuller Timothy #3	S	F26L	1722 May30		
Fuller Timothy=F15D	S	G11Da	1670abt	1694ca	1748 Nov30
Fuller Waitstill	S	F27E	1711 Apr 8		
Fuller William	S	F60D	1729 Jun16		
Fuller Young	S	F49F	1708		
Fuller Zachariah	S	F61C	1725ca		
Fuller Zurviah	S	F56D	1716 Mar29		
Gager Lydia	A	A8/189	1663	1683	1737
Gale Abraham	S	R117Caf	1680abt		
Gale Lydia	S	R117Ga	1699 Jul 9	1722 May29	1753 Aug22
Galliard Sarah	S	A11Abm	1590abt		
Gallop Esther=H34Cam	S	T15Abm	1660abt		
Gallop Esther=T15Abm	S	H34Cam	1660abt		
Gallup Elizabeth	A	A1/277	1650abt		1736aft
Gallup Elizabeth	S	C10Aa	1650abt		=A1/277
Gamlett Anne	S	W12Dam	1615abt		
Gardner Alexander	A	A4/24	1782 Feb28	1805 Feb2?	
Gardner Alexander Jr.	A	A4/12	1810abt	1834	1875 Jun 6
Gardner Dorothy Ayer	A	A4/3	1892 Jul	1912 Sept7	1967 Sep17
Gardner Esther	A	A8/243	1659	1686bef	1706
Gardner John	A	A4/48	1760abt	1781 Jan20	
Gardner Levi Addison	A	A4/6	1861 Apr24	1884 Oct 3	1916 May 8
Gardner Mary	A	A11/21	1648 Apr	1665 Dec13	1722 Jul 8
Gardner Thomas	A	A11/84	1600abt		1638 Nov
Gardner Thomas Jr.	A	A11/42	1620abt	1641 Jul 4	1689 Jul15
Garfield Abram	A	A6/2	1799 Dec28	1820 Feb 3	1833 May 3
Garfield Benjamin	A	A6/64	1643ca	1677 Jan17	1717 Nov28
Garfield Edward	A	A6/128	1575ca	1634ca	1672ca
Garfield James Abram	A	A6/1	1831 Nov19	1853 Nov11	1881 Sep19
Garfield John	S	P18Ba	1664 Jul 7	1687 Nov 3	1708bef
Garfield Samuel	S	P18Baf	1640abt		

NAME	DIV.	NUMBER	BIRTH	MARRIAGE	DEATH
Garfield Solomon	A	A6/8	1743 Jul18	1769 Aug22	1807
Garfield Thomas	A	A6/32	1680 Dec12	1706 Jan 2	1752 Feb 4
Garfield Thomas	A	A6/4	1773 Mar19	1794ca	1801
Garfield Thomas Jr.	A	A6/16	1713 Feb28	1742 Oct21	1774 Jan 3
Garnsey Hannah	A	A19/227	1676	1700	
Garrison Ruth Virginia	D	D33a18	1920 Feb24	1942 Feb19	
Gaskill Hope	A	A3/127	1743 Aug 3	1763 Jul27	
Gaskill Jonathan	A	A3/254	1705ca	1732 May 4	1754
Gaskill Josiah	A	A3/508	1678	1704	1761
Gasque Marie	S	G42Aa	1540ca		
Gastes Merken	A	A7/93	1655ca		
Gates Aaron Jr.	S	G19A	1780	1806	1850
Gates Aaron Sr	S	G18A	1753	1776	1821
Gates Abigail	S	G27D	1714 Nov 8		
Gates Alice	S	G32E	1770		
Gates Ancy B	S	G33E	1800abt		
Gates Beman	S	G20A	1818	1841	1894
Gates Betsey S	S	G21C	1853 Feb26	1875 Oct12	1920 Apr22
Gates Bezaleel	S	G17A	1726	1749	1802
Gates Caleb	S	G24A	1749	1775	1822
Gates Charles B	S	G21B	1844 Oct 3		1864 May31
Gates Cynthia	S	G35A	1844	1864	1903
Gates Daniel Jr	S	G27A	1706 Feb 5	1723 Jun13	
Gates Daniel Sr	S	G11G	1680 May 4	1705	1761 Nov24
Gates David	S	G27B	1709 Jun29	1731 Sep17	1795 Jan16
Gates David	S	G32A	1761 Apr22		
Gates Deborah	S	T13Ea	1683 Feb22	1709 Jun 1	1745 Jan15
Gates Elizabeth	S	G12C	1713	1730	1793
Gates Elizabeth	S	G31A	1727		1791
Gates Elizabeth	S	G28C	1733 Jan15	1761	1779
Gates Ephraim	S	G27H	1724 Aug18		d yng
Gates Eveline	S	G52Ja	1821 Aug21	1845 Oct18	1896 Mar17
Gates Eveline	S	G36A	1821 Aug31	1845 Oct18	1896 Mar17
Gates Geffrey I	S	G3A	1400abt		
Gates Geffrey II	S	G5A	1455abt		
Gates Geffrey III	S	G6A	1485abt		
Gates Geffrey IV	S	G7A	1518ca		
Gates George Capt.	S	F15Daf	1645ca		1725
Gates George Jr	S	G11F	1677 Aug16		d. young
Gates George Sr	S	G10A	1634	1661	1724 Nov12

NAME	DIV.	NUMBER	BIRTH	MARRIAGE	DEATH
Gates H.	S	N14Ea	1770abt		
Gates Harvey	S	G34A	1797	1814	1883
Gates Jesse	S	G31B	1734	1758	1811
Gates Jireh	S	G32B	1763 Oct10		
Gates John	S	G11C	1668 Apr 5		1741after
Gates Joseph	S	G27A	1716 Sep 7		d yng
Gates Joseph Jr	S	G12A	1696Dec 28		1770
Gates Joseph Jr	S	G26A	1735		1779
Gates Joseph Sr	S	G11A	1662 Nov 7	1693ca	1711 Mar18
Gates Judah	S	G27I	1727 Aug 2		
Gates Levi	S	G28A	1735 Feb23	1760 May29	=D1a20
Gates Levi II	S	G33A	1789 Apr15		
Gates Levi Jr	S	G32D	1768		
Gates Levi=G28Aa	D	D1a20	1735 Feb23	1760 May	1802ca
Gates Lydia	S	G33F	1802ca		
Gates Mary	S	G11E	1674 Mar16	1693 Feb14	1742 Mar12
Gates Mary	S	G27F	1719 Mar29		
Gates Mary	S	G28B	1738 Oct22		
Gates Mary B	S	G21A	1842 Aug27	1864 Jan18	1921 Oct28
Gates Miranda	S	G33B	1790abt		
Gates Patience	S	G12B	1712	1736	1799
Gates Peter	S	G8A	1545abt		
Gates Rebecca	S	G27C	1711 Jun 2		
Gates Russel	S	G25A	1786	1820	1834
Gates Russell	S	G32C	1766	1792	
Gates Ruth	S	G27G	1721 Aug16		
Gates Salmon	S	G33C	1790 Jun 6		
Gates Samantha	S	G52Ba	1810abt		
Gates Samuel	S	G11H	1683ca	1710	1737 Jul31
Gates Sarah	S	F15Da	1670 Mar16	1694ca	1712ca
Gates Sarah=F15Da	S	G11D	1670 Mar16	1694ca	1712ca
Gates Susannah	S	G33G	1804ca		
Gates Thomas	S	G1A	1350abt		
Gates Thomas	S	G9A	1575abt		
Gates Thomas	S	T13Eaf	1650abt		
Gates Thomas	S	G11B	1664 Jan21	1692 Oct 3	1734 Apr20
Gates William	S	G2A	1375abt		
Gates William	S	G4A	1425abt		
Gates William	S	G33D	1797		1830ca
Gault Elizabeth	A	A1/57	1792ca	1812 Oct27	

NAME	DIV.	NUMBER	BIRTH	MARRIAGE	DEATH
Gault Jonathan	A	A1/114	1760abt		
Gaunt Lydia	S	B11Ab	1630abt		
Gaunt Peter	S	B11Abf	1600abt		
Gay Abigail	S	R75B	1722 Sept8		1728 Feb 8
Gay Abigail	S	R75E	1729 Aug20 unm.		1804 Apr 7
Gay Calvin	S	R75C	1724 Sep14		
Gay Celia	S	R75F	1731 Aug13		1749 Feb18
Gay David	S	R28Laf	1710abt		
Gay Ebenezer	S	R21Ea	1696 Aug15	1719 Nov13	1787 Mar 8
Gay Ebenezer	S	R75I	1736 Mar 3		1738 Jul 3
Gay Jerusha	S	R75H	1734 Mar17		
Gay Joanna	S	R75K	1741 Nov23 unm.		1772 Jul23
Gay Jotham	S	R75G	1733 Apr11 unm.		1802 Oct16
Gay Martin	S	R75D	1726 Dec29		
Gay Mary	S	R28La	1736 Sep17	1761 Jun18	1815
Gay Nathaniel	S	R21Eaf	1670abt		
Gay Persis	S	R75J	1739 Nov 2		1752 Mar25
Gay Samuel	S	R75A	1721 Jan15		1746 Mar26
George Elizabeth	S	T27Dam	1685abt		
George Mary	S	K23Ca	1670ca	1703 Jul 5	1740bef
George Samuel	S	K23Caf	1645abt		
George Sarah	A	A1/263	1695ca	1715	1732
George Susanna	S	A21Bam	1645abt		
Gibbon Hannah	S	R23Jb	1715ca	1748 May23	1791 Oct23
Gibbons Mary	A	A3/281	1660abt	1692	1730
Gibbs Abigail=A8/221	S	W50B	1677ca	1697 Nov24	1742bef
Gibbs Abigail=D15/24	A	A8/221	1677ca	1697 Nov24	1742bef
Gibbs Abigail=W50B	D	D15/24	1677ca	1697 Nov24	1742bef
Gibbs Bethiah	S	W50A	1675 Dec10		
Gibbs Cornelius	S	W50H	1691ca	1716 Nov 9	1748 Dec31
Gibbs Ebnezer	S	W50F	1687ca		1725ca
Gibbs Elizabeth	S	Q15Bam	1660abt		
Gibbs Jabez	S	W50G	1689ca		1725ca
Gibbs Sarah	S	W50D	1683ca	1700 Jan28	1726 Oct28
Gibbs Sarah =W50D	S	A24Aa	1683ca	1700 Jan28	1726 Oct28
Gibbs Thomas	S	W17Fa	1646 Mar23	1674 Dec23	1732 Jan 7
Gibbs Thomas	S	A24Aaf	1660abt		
Gibbs Thomas	S	W50C	1678 Jan28	1713 Oct22	1725abt
Gibbs Thomas=W17Fa	D	D15a25	1646 Mar23	1674 Dec23	1732 Jan7
Gibbs Warren	S	W50E	1685ca	1714 Apr25	1745abt

NAME	DIV.	NUMBER	BIRTH	MARRIAGE	DEATH
Giddings Joseph	A	A2/196	1645abt	1671	1691
Giddings Joseph Jr.	A	A2/98	1672 Jun 9	1701 Dec25	
Giddings Susanna	A	A2/49	1704 Oct2	1724 Dec29	1794 Jan15
Gifford Adam	S	K119L	1725 Jan 3		
Gifford Benjamin twin	S	K119H	1717 May		
Gifford Catherine	A	A4/237	1718 Jun15	1735 Nov 6	1801 May13
Gifford Christopher	S	B15Fa	1680abt		
Gifford David	S	K119M	1728 Apr 5		
Gifford Elizabeth twin	S	K119E	1712 Oct13		
Gifford Gideon	S	K119B	1705 Mar19		
Gifford Isaac twin	S	K119I	1717 May		
Gifford Jabez	A	A4/474	1686	1716	1761
Gifford Jeremiah	S	K31Ca	1681ca	1703ca	1770ca
Gifford John	S	K119C	1707 Mar 7		
Gifford Jonathan	S	K119A	1704 Mar25		
Gifford Joseph twin	S	K119F	1712 Oct13		
Gifford Margaret	S	A16Aam	1650abt		
Gifford Margaret	S	K119K	1722 Apr15		
Gifford Mary	S	A23Ham	1655abt		
Gifford Mary	S	A22Aa	1688 Jul12	1708 May18	1769 Jan25
Gifford Peleg	S	K119J	1719 Dec 1		
Gifford Philip	S	A22Aaf	1665abt		
Gifford Robert	S	K31Caf	1660abt		
Gifford Sarah	S	K119D	1710 Oct 3		
Gifford William	S	K119G	1714 Jan19		
Gilbert Abigail	S	R71H	1727ca		1747 Sep17
Gilbert Hannah	S	R71B	1712 Feb 9		
Gilbert Joan	D	D30a26	1350abt		
Gilbert Mary	S	R71D	1717ca		
Gilbert Nathaniel	S	R21Aa	1683 Jul19	1709 Jun16	1765 Aug17
Gilbert Nathaniel	S	R71A	1710ca		
Gilbert Rachael	S	C22Aa	1781		
Gilbert Rachel	S	R18Ham	1680abt		
Gilbert Samuel	S	R71E	1723ca		
Gilbert Thomas	S	R21Aaf	1660abt		
Gilbert Thomas	S	R71C	1714ca		
Gilbert Welthia	S	R71F	1725ca		
Giles Eleazer	A	A2/228	1640	1678	
Giles Elizabeth	A	A3/171	1700abt		1764ca
Giles John	A	A2/114	1681 Aug31	1706 Nov 7	1738aft

NAME	DIV.	NUMBER	BIRTH	MARRIAGE	DEATH
Giles Mehitable	A	A2/57	1716ca	1738 Aug10	1799 Apr29
Gilman Bridget	A	A13/129	1580abt	1600	
Gilman Bridget=A18/129	D	D13/24	1575abt	1600ca	
Gilman Edward	D	D13/25	1557		
Gilman Mary	D	D14/24	1600abt		1681
Girton Alfred Franklin	D	D32/22	1863Mar 21	1882Feb 22	1942Feb 18
Girton Jessie S	S	G54Bam	1883 Feb17	1903 Sep 3	1966 May 2
Girton Jessie S	D	D32/21	1883Feb 17	1903Sep 3	1966May 2
Girton John K	D	D32/24	1805Mar 10		1875May 2?
Girton William	D	D32/25	1780abt		
Girton William G	D	D32/23	1830 Apr 2	1855Jun 14	1897May 14
Gladden Mary	S	K35Jam	1670abt		
Gladdine Marie	S	G43Ba	1570abt		
Gladdine Paul	S	G43Baf	1545abt		
Gladdine Suzanne	S	G43Aa	1570abt	1593	
Glascock Elizabeth	S	A31Abm	1670abt		
Glass Hannah	S	W46Bam	1660abt		
Gleason Abigail	A	A12/47	1692 Mar14	1716 Nov21	1721 Apr19
Gleason Isaac	A	A12/94	1654ca	1684 Jun26	1698 May14
Gleason Thomas	A	A12/188	1607ca		1686ca
Glover Hannah	A	A8/231	1646	1663	1722
Goddard Josiah	A	A19/130	1675abt	1695	1720
Goddard Rachel	A	A19/65	1699 Apr18	1717Jul 24	
Godfrey Alice	A	A2/101	1660abt	1680abt	1705 Apr29
Godfrey Benjamin	S	H106Aa	1715ca	1738Aug 23	
Godfrey Benjamin	S	H98J	1720ca		
Godfrey David	S	H98D	1706ca		
Godfrey Deborah	S	H98H	1715ca		
Godfrey Desire	S	H98F	1710ca		
Godfrey Elizabeth	S	T13Aam	1625abt		
Godfrey Elizabeth	S	T13Cam	1625abt		=T13Aam
Godfrey Elizabeth	S	H98I	1718 Mar15		
Godfrey George	S	H28Faf	1640abt		
Godfrey George	S	H98E	1708ca		
Godfrey Jonathan	S	H98A	1700ca		
Godfrey Joshua	S	H98K	1723 Apr30		
Godfrey Mary	S	H98G	1711 Sept4		
Godfrey Moses	S	H28Fa	1667 Jan27	1700ca	1743 Apr16
Godfrey Moses	S	H106Aaf	1690abt		
Godfrey Moses	S	H98C	1704ca		

NAME	DIV.	NUMBER	BIRTH	MARRIAGE	DEATH
Godfrey Penelope	S	C86Aa	1685		
Godfrey Richard	A	A2/202	1630abt	1651aft	1691
Godfrey Richard	S	H98L	1725ca		
Godfrey Samuel	S	H98B	1702ca		
Goffe Martha	A	A1/149	1730abt	1750 Apr26	1808Apr25
Goldstone Anna	A	A11/55	1615 May	1634ca	
Goldstone Henry	A	A11/110	1591 Jul17	1614ca	1638 Jul25
Goldthwaite Elizabeth	A	A2/227	1642	1660	
Gooch Anne	S	A31Bbm	1670abt		
Goodale Samuel	A	A2/116	1669 Dec 3	1697 Dec25	
Goodale Samuel Jr.	A	A2/58	1708 Jun13	1743 Oct20	1769 Apr13
Goodale Sarah	A	A2/29	1745 Mar8	1764 Jun11	1828 Aug28
Goodale Zachariah	A	A2/232	1640	1666	
Goodard Beriah	S	K21Ha	1695abt	1734 Dec 5	1781bef
Goodhue Elizabeth	S	A57F	1710 Dec 1		
Goodhue Grace Anna	A	A19/1a	1879 Jan 3	1905 Oct 4	1957 Jul 8
Goodhue John	S	A57D	1707 Jan 5		
Goodhue Mercy	S	A57E	1709 Feb17		1721 Oct12
Goodhue Nathaniel	S	A23Ga	1670 Aug24	1696 Nov28	1721 Aug16
Goodhue Nathaniel	S	A57C	1702 Nov22		1721Sep 16
Goodhue Sarah	S	A57B	1701 Feb 8		
Goodhue William	S	A23Gaf	1645abt		
Goodhue William	S	A57A	1699 Oct15		
Goodman J	S	N11Ba	1664abt		
Goodman M	S	N11Ab	1665abt		
Goodspeed Benjamin	S	W48Ca	1678 Oct31	1707	1750
Goodspeed Ebenezer	S	W48Caf	1650abt		
Goodspeed Eunice	A	A4/245	1731 Apr 6	1751 Dec12	1809 Dec 3
Goodspeed John	S	F16Aaf	1645abt		
Goodspeed Mercy	S	F16Aa	1669 Feb18	1694 Jan14	
Goodspeed Samuel	A	A4/490	1701		1725bef
Goodwin Elizabeth	A	A19/159	1673	1691	1731
Goolidge Grace	A	A2/253	1663	1688ca	1699
Gorham Elizabeth	S	F15Bam	1645abt		
Gorham James	S	W41Ebf	1685abt		
Gorham John	S	F18Caf	1665ca		
Gorham Thankful	S	F18Ca	1690 Feb15	1710 Jun16	1732 aft
Gorham Thankful	S	W41Eb	1711 May25	1749 Jul27	1755aft
Gosvenor Mary	S	C51Ja	1712ca		
Gould Priscilla	S	H30Fam	1670abt		

NAME	DIV.	NUMBER	BIRTH	MARRIAGE	DEATH
Gould Sarah	S	H30Ham	1660abt		
Gould Sarah	S	X19Dbm	1660abt		
Goulding Arabella	A	A19/81	1692aft	1715ca	1774ca
Goulding Peter	A	A19/i62	1630ca	1672	1703ca
Gove Abigail	A	A4/115	1761 Sep23	1783 Oct 1	1844 Nov29
Gove Edward	A	A4/460	1696	1718	1765
Gove Nathaniel	A	A4/230	1721 Jun24	1743 Sep14	1793 Apr15
Grady Mary E	S	G55Ba	1950abt	1970Sep 12	
Grafton Elizabeth	S	A18A	1667 Dec18	1690ca	1734 Mar26
Grafton Joseph	S	A13Daf	1620abt		
Grafton Nathaniel	S	A13Da	1642ca	1665 Apr 6	1671 Feb11
Grafton Priscilla	S	A18C	1671 Mar12	1690 Oct15	1711living
Grafton Remember	S	A18B	1669 Sep29	1695 Apr10	1696bef
Granger Mary	S	C61Fa	1757ca		
Grant Hannah	A	A16/83	1631ca	1650 Mar	1715 Feb
Grant Jesse Root	A	A5/2	1794 Jan23	1821 Jun24	1873 Jun29
Grant Mary	A	A1/273	1630abt	1668	1681aft
Grant Matthew	A	A5/128	1601	1625	1681
Grant Noah	A	A5/16	1693 Dec11	1717 Jun20	1727 Oct10
Grant Noah III	A	A5/4	1748 Jun20	1792 Mar 4	1819 Feb14
Grant Noah Jr.	A	A5/8	1719 Jul12	1746 Nov 5	1756after
Grant Samuel	A	A5/64	1631 Nov12	1656 May27	1718 Sep10
Grant Samuel Jr.	A	A5/32	1659 Apr20	1688 Apr11	1710 May 8
Grant Thomas	A	A16/166	1600	1624	1643bef
Grant Ulysses Simpson	A	A5/1	1822 Apr27	1848 Aug22	1885 Jul23
Graves Mary	S	R16Aam	1670abt		
Graves Priscilla	A	A12/187	1625ca		1658bef
Graves Rebecca	A	A19/1503	1650abt		
Graves Thomas Jr	A	A19/3006	1620abt		
Gray Andrew	S	T20Db	1707 Sep29	1745 Dec19	1757 Dec19
Gray Ann	S	Q17Ca	1691 Aug 5	1714 Dec30	1730 Sep 6
Gray Edward	S	W13Iaf	1635abt		
Gray Edward	S	W35Iaf	1635abt		
Gray Edward	S	R14Eaf	1675abt		
Gray Edward	S	R22Bbf	1675abt		
Gray Edward =W35Iaf	S	W32Aaf	1650abt		
Gray Elizabeth	S	W44Eam	1660abt		
Gray John	S	Q17Caf	1670abt		
Gray John	S	T20Dbf	1685abt		
Gray Katherine	A	A19/3007	1620abt		

NAME	DIV.	NUMBER	BIRTH	MARRIAGE	DEATH
Gray Samuel	S	W35Ia	1682ca	1699 Jul13	1712 Mar23
Gray Sarah	S	W13Ia	1659 Aug12	1682 May18	1736 Feb14
Gray Sarah	S	R14Ba	1697 Apr25	1714 Oct21	1770 Oct16
Gray Sarah	S	R22Bb	1697 Apr25	1749 Sept7	1770 Oct16
Gray Thomas	S	W32Aa	1670ca	1694 Jul 3	1721 Nov5
Gray Thomas Sr	A	A19/6014	1600abt		
Greeke Margaret	A	A10/67	1549abt		
Green William	S	W17Ea	1650ca	1683ca	1685 Oct7
Green Anne	A	A2/243	1650abt	1673ca	
Green Esther	A	A17/25	1645abt		
Green Hannah	S	F21Cam	1660abt		
Green John	A	A17/50	1620abt		
Green William	S	W49A	1684 Apr24	1709 Mar	1756 Jan28
Greene Anna	S	C82A	1686		
Greene Audry	S	C83A	1694		
Greene Job	S	C76Da	1656		
Greene Mary	S	C80A	1677		
Greene Philip	S	C82B	1705		
Greene Richard	S	C76Ea	.1660		
Greene William	S	C76Aa	1652		
Gregory Rebecca	A	A1/205	1715abt	1734 Jan 9	
Grey Rebecca	S	K29Eam	1670abt		
Grey Susanna	S	K31Dam	1675abt		
Gridge Elizabeth	A	A6/65	1659 Aug17	1677 Jan17	
Gridge Matthew	A	A6/130	1615ca	1643	1700ca
Gridley Elizabeth Ely	A	A4/31	1819ca	1843	1912living
Gridley Jonathan	A	A4/248	1690 Oct	1714 Nov17	1778 Nov16
Gridley Jonathan Jr.	A	A4/124	1726 Dec12	1750 Oct18	
Gridley Theodore	A	A4/62	1757ca	1818ca	1826ca
Gridley Thomas Jr.	A	A4/496	1650ca	1679	1742ca
Griffith Abraham	A	A3/236	1680	1708	1760 Oct 3
Griffith Amos	A	A3/26	1798ca	1820 Dec 7	1871 Sep10
Griffith Ann	A	A3/59	1754 Feb 1		1792 July6
Griffith Eliz. Price	A	A3/13	1827 Apr28	1847 Dec23	1923 May 3
Griffith Elizabeth	A	A3/435	1680abt		1752
Griffith Howell	A	A3/472	1665abt		1710
Griffith Isaac	A	A3/118	1720 Jan 5	1744 Sept	
Griffith Jacob	A	A3/52	1757 Feb27	1778 Apr16	1841 Apr 2
Griffith William	A	A3/208	1690abt		
Griffith William Jr.	A	A3/104	1714		1778 Sep20

NAME	DIV.	NUMBER	BIRTH	MARRIAGE	DEATH
Griffiths Robert B	S	C59Aa	1921		
Griswold Elizabeth	S	P12Ga	1650ca	1679 Aug 5	1727 Jul
Griswold Francis	S	W23Baf	1645abt		
Griswold Hannah	S	W32Bam	1650abt		
Griswold Lydia	S	W23Ba	1671 Oct	1692 Jun 6	1752 Jan6
Griswold Mabel	S	G25Aa	1790	1820	1863
Griswold Matthew	S	P12Gaf	1630abt		
Groce Elizabeth	S	R27Da	1730ca	1748 Oct27	1773 Apr30
Groce Isaac	S	R27Daf	1710abt		
Grover Deborah	S	P23Dam	1660abt		=K39Gam
Grover Deborah =P23Dam	S	K39Cam	1650abt		
Grover Deborah=K39Cam	S	K39Gam	1650abt		
Grover Eleazer	A	A19/62	1728Jan 31	1756	
Grover Priscilla	A	A19/31	1757 Apr 2	1775ca	1820
Grover Stephen	A	A19/248	1655abt	1680	1694
Grover Stephen Jr	A	A19/124	1682ca	1705 Jul 2	1730ca
Grummond Sarah	S	N15Ba	1780ca		
Guild Anne	A	A2/153	1615abt	1637ca	1672
Guild Israel	A	A1/262	1690	1715	1766
Guile Deborah	A	A1/131	1715 Jun26	1739 Sep 6	1783 Aug15
Guile Ephraim	A	A19/238	1661	1686	
Guile Sarah	A	A19/119	1694Jan 20	1730	
Gutch Sarah	S	H19Fam	1655abt		
Guy Mary	S	A11Bam	1590abt		
Gwatney Donald J	S	G59Ba	1951 Nov28	1972 Aug 5	
Haborne Jane	A	A16/167	1602	1634	1696
Haddocks Henry	S	W38Baf	1640abt		
Haddocks John	S	W38Ba	1663 May16	1689Jun 23	1702 Feb 1
Haffield Mary	S	X13Acm	1625abt		
Hager Hannah	A	A19/137	1649	1677ca	1702
Hale Abigail	A	A12/23	1718 Jul 3	1740 Feb28	1796 Jun18
Hale John	A	A12/46	1680 Nov 2	1716 Nov21	1753 May24
Hale Mary	S	A17Bam	1630abt		
Hale Thomas	A	A12/184	1610	1639	1679
Hale Thomas Jr	A	A12/92	1650 Jan	1675 Nov18	1725 Apr 7
Hall Elisha	S	K26Aaf	1660abt		
Hall Elisha =K26Aaf	S	K26Daf	1660abt		
Hall Mary	S	C11Aa	1677		
Hall Mott	S	N15Ib	1790abt		
Hall Phebe	S	K26Da	1689 Mar 3	1716 Apr 3	1728 Jul15

NAME	DIV.	NUMBER	BIRTH	MARRIAGE	DEATH
Hall Tabitha	S	K26Aa	1683abt	1706 Mar18	1740living
Hall Tabitha	S	K31Jam	1685abt		
Hallet Joseph	S	F15Baf	1640abt		
Hallett Mary	S	F15Ba	1665ca	1686ca	1721aft
Hallett Ruhamah	S	W21Cam	1640abt		
Hallock Abigail	A	A14/185	1645ca	1665	1697
Hallock Abigail	A	A14/191	1645ca	1665	1697
Halstead Jennet	A	A10/43	1570abt	1597bef	1623 Aug12
Halstead John	A	A10/86	1550abt		1601 Jul
Hamblen Ebenezer	A	A1/434	1683	1710	1736
Hamblen Thankful	A	A1/435	1689	1710	1768
Hamblen Thankful	A	A1/217	1715 Aug 6	1735 Sep18	
Hamblin John	S	X16Baf	1645abt		
Hamblin Priscilla	S	X16Ba	1670 Apr 3	1696 Apr23	1720ca
Hamilton Daniel	S	H25Ba	1669ca	1693ca	1738 Dec 8
Hamilton Daniel	S	H81F	1708ca		
Hamilton Daniel=H25Ba	S	X16Dbf	1669ca	1693ca	1738 Dec 8
Hamilton Grace	S	H81A	1694 Aug 3		1694 Aug20
Hamilton Lydia	S	H81C	.1697ca		
Hamilton Mary	S	H81D	1700ca		
Hamilton Samuel	S	H81E	1705ca		
Hamilton Sarah	S	X16Db	1680abt	1739 Apr13	
Hamilton Thomas	S	H25Baf	1645abt		
Hamilton Thomas	S	H81B	1695 Sep 1		
Hamlet Abigail	A	A19/73	1689Mar 25	1716	1759 Mar17
Hamlet Jacob	A	A19/146	1641ca	1679	
Hamlin Elizabeth	S	H30Cam	1670abt		
Hamlin John	S	H24Bbf	1645abt		
Hamlin Sarah	S	H24Bb	1671 Jul 1	1732 Nov15	1734living
Hammond Esther	S	R117Fbm	1680abt		
Hammond Barnabas	S	K45H	1694 Jan20		
Hammond Benjamin	S	K17Eaf	1635abt		
Hammond Benjamin	S	K45A	1681 Dec18		
Hammond Jedidah	S	K45K	1703 Sep30		
Hammond Jedidiah	S	K45F	1690 Sep19		
Hammond John	S	K45J	1701 Oct 4		
Hammond Josiah	S	K45G	1692 Sep15		
Hammond Maria	S	K45I	1697 Jan27		
Hammond Rosamond	S	A26Gam	1680abt		
Hammond Rosamond	S	K45C	1684 May 8		

NAME	DIV.	NUMBER	BIRTH	MARRIAGE	DEATH
Hammond Samuel	S	K17Ea	1656ca	1681ca	1728
Hammond Samuel	S	K45D	1685 Mar 8		
Hammond Seth	S	K45B	1682 Feb13		
Hammond Thomas	S	K45E	1687 Sep16		
Hance Content	S	G50Ba	1745abt		
Hance Thomas	S	G50Ca	1745abt		
Hancock Edward	A	A18/82	1590abt		1620ca
Hancock Jane	A	A18/41	1638Feb 24		
Hanks James	A	A13/6	1759ca		1810
Hanks Nancy	A	A13/3	1784 Feb 5	1806 Jun12	1818 Oct 5
Hanson Alice	S	R9Aa	1565abt		
Harberger Eliza	S	N15Ea	1780ca		
Harden Sarah	S	Q22Dbm	1680abt		
Hardenbroeck Andries	A	A8/132	1634ca	1663	
Hardenbroeck Catharina	A	A8/33	1694 Feb20	1713 Jan31	1739aft
Hardenbroeck Johannes	A	A8/66	1665 Sep	1686 Jun16	1714abt
Harding Abigail	S	X84I	1762		
Harding Anna	S	X84E	1745		d.yng
Harding Archelas	S	X80D	1740		
Harding Benjamin	S	X84H	1756		
Harding Cornelius	S	H68I	1716 Mar31		
Harding Cornelius	S	X26I	1716 Mar31	1740 Nov21	
Harding Cornelius	S	X85F	1754		
Harding Ebenezer	S	X84A	1739		
Harding Eleazer twin	S	X84C	1742		
Harding Elizabeth	S	H68F	1708 Apr	1730 Feb16	=X26F
Harding Elizabeth	S	X26F	1708 Apr	1730 Feb16	1751aft
Harding Ephraim	S	X84G	1752		
Harding Hannah	S	X26A	1694 Feb15	1716 Oct 9	1727aft
Harding Hannah	S	X80C	1736		
Harding Hannah	S	X80H	1752		
Harding Hannah=X26A	S	H68B	1694 Feb15	1716 Oct 9	1727aft
Harding James	S	H68D	1702 Nov 2	1724 Oct 8	1732 Apr30
Harding James	S	X26D	1702 Nov 2	1724 OCt 8	1732 Apr30
Harding James	S	X81B	1731		
Harding John	S	H68A	1692ca		
Harding John	S	X26B	1700abt	1731 Sep23	1761
Harding John	S	X80B	1734		
Harding Joseph	S	H22Caf	1645abt		
Harding Joseph	S	X85B	1744		

NAME	DIV.	NUMBER	BIRTH	MARRIAGE	DEATH
Harding Joseph =H22Caf	S	X14Caf	1645abt		
Harding Joshua	S	X80E	1743		
Harding Lucia	S	X85D	1750		
Harding Lydia	S	X84B	1741		
Harding Mary	S	X26E	1706 Apr 2	1728 Nov 7	1737bef
Harding Mary	S	X80A	1732		
Harding Mary =X26E	S	H68E	1706 Apr 2	1728 Nov 7	1737bef
Harding Maziah	S	H22Ca	1671 Nov 1		1734 Jun 5
Harding Maziah	S	X14Ca	1671 Nov 1	1694bef	1734 Jun 5
Harding Mercy	S	C77Aa	1679		
Harding Nathan	S	X26H	1711 Oct29	2 mar.	1801 Mar27
Harding Nathan	S	X84F	1746		
Harding Nathan	S	X85E	1752		
Harding Nathan =X26H	S	H68H	1711 Oct29		1801 Mar27
Harding Nathaniel	S	X80F	1746		
Harding Phebe	S	H68G	1710 Apr	1732 Oct13	
Harding Phebe	S	X85A	1742		
Harding Phebe =H68G	S	X26G	1710 Apr	1732 Oct13	
Harding Priscilla	S	X85C	1747		
Harding Seth	S	X85G	1756		
Harding Tabitha twin	S	X84D	1742		
Harding Thomas	S	H68C	1699 Nov13		1720abt
Harding Thomas	S	X81A	1725		
Harker Sarah	S	C11Ba	1681		
Harlow Abigail	S	K29Ba	1692 Jan27	1716 Nov29	1727 Oct25
Harlow Elizabeth	S	A27A	1683 Feb		
Harlow Hannah	S	Q20Fb	1721 Nov20	1756 Nov30	1766living
Harlow Isaac	S	A27F	1695ca	unm	1724bef
Harlow Joanna	S	W25Aa	1669 Mar24	1697ca	1725 Sep4
Harlow Judith	S	W37Ea	1676 Aug 2	1705 Nov 1	1728living
Harlow Lydia	S	A27E	1693ca		
Harlow Mary	S	A27D	1691ca	unm	1715 Jan 8
Harlow Nathanial	S	W37Ab	1664 Sep30	1691 Mar17	1721 Apr19
Harlow Nathaniel	S	K29Baf	1670abt		=W55Dam
Harlow Nathaniel Jr	S	W55Da	1695 Feb27	1717 Dec19	1756 Nov28
Harlow Nathaniel Sr	S	W55Daf	1670abt		
Harlow Rebecca	S	A14Da	1655 Jun12	1675ca	1727 Sep 3
Harlow Rebecca	S	K19Aa	1678 Feb27	1700 Jul 4	1724living
Harlow Rebecca	S	K21Iam	1680abt		
Harlow Rebecca	S	A27H	1700ca		

NAME	DIV.	NUMBER	BIRTH	MARRIAGE	DEATH
Harlow Rebecca =A14Da	S	W20C	1655 Jun12	1675ca	1727 Sep 3
Harlow Repentance	S	T15Bam	1665abt		
Harlow Repentance	S	K31Bam	1665abt		=T15Bam
Harlow Robert	S	A27G	1698ca		
Harlow Samuel	S	W20B	1652 Jan27	(1)1677ca	1724 Feb17
Harlow Samuel	S	K19Aaf	1755abt		
Harlow Thomas	S	A27B	1686 Mar17		
Harlow William	S	W12Ba	1624	1649 Dec20	1691 Aug25
Harlow William	S	W37Abf	1640abt		
Harlow William	S	W25Aaf	1645abt		
Harlow William	S	W20A	1650 Oct5		d. yng
Harlow William	S	W20D	1657 Jun 2	1683ca	1711 Jan28
Harlow William	S	A27C	1689ca		
Harlow William	S	Q20Fbf	1700abt		
Harlow William =W12Ba	S	A14Daf	1624	1649 Dec20	1691 Aug25
Harlow William =W20D	S	A14Ha	1657 Jun 2	1682ca	1711 Jan28
Harlow William =W25Aaf	S	W37Eaf	1645abt		
Harlow William Sr	S	A14Haf	1635abt		
Harris Abner	S	K87B	1710 Jul29		
Harris Anne	S	K87C	1712 Sep25		
Harris Arthur	S	Q23Ha	1708 Jun25	1730 Nov12	1750bef
Harris Arthur	S	Q76C	1737ca		1750bef
Harris Arthur=Q23Ha	S	K87A	1708 Jun25	1730 Nov12	1750bef
Harris Benjamin	S	Q76A	1731 Sep30		
Harris Elizabeth	S	K87D	1714 Dec 1		1740bef
Harris Isaac	S	K25Da	1685ca	1707 Mar27	1738bef
Harris Isaac =K25Da	S	Q23Haf	1685ca	1707 Mar27	1738bef
Harris Isaac Sr	S	K25Daf	1660abt		
Harris Jane	S	K87E	1716 Jan10		
Harris John	A	A17/56	1607ca	1644ca	1694Feb 15
Harris Lucy	S	Q76D	1739 Jul27		
Harris Sarah	A	A17/7	1729 Jan22	1750 Mar 1	1818May 27
Harris Silas	S	Q76B	1734 Nov 8		
Harris Stephen	A	A17/14	1700 Jun10	1729bef	1775
Harris Susanna	S	T20Bam	1680abt		
Harris Timothy	A	A17/28	1657Dec 1	1682Aug 24	1722Mar 24
Harris William	A	A17/224	1550abt	1579	1599
Harrison Benjamin	A	A14/128	1594 Dec		1645abt
Harrison Benjamin	A	A14/1	1833 Aug20	1853 Oct20	1901 Mar13
Harrison Benjamin Vth	A	A14/8	1726ca	1748ca	1791 Apr24

NAME	DIV.	NUMBER	BIRTH	MARRIAGE	DEATH
Harrison Benjamin III	A	A14/32	1673ca		
Harrison Benjamin IV	A	A14/16	1695ca	1722ca	1745 Jul12
Harrison Benjamin Jr.	A	A14/64	1645 Sep20		1712 Jan30
Harrison John Scott	A	A14/2	1804 Oct 4	1831 Aug12	1878 May25
Harrison William Henry	A	A14/4	1773 Feb 9	1795 Nov22	1841 Apr 4
Harry Hugh	A	A3/428	1660abt	1686	1708
Harry John	A	A3/214	1705abt	1732	1763ca
Harry Miriam	A	A3/107		1756 Sept6	1809 Mar19
Hart Archippus	S	K133A	1703 Aug24		
Hart Hannah	S	K133E	1713 Jun 9		1733living
Hart James	S	C85C	1666		
Hart John	S	C85A	1660abt		
Hart Luke	S	K133C	1708 Sep25		
Hart Mary	S	C85B	1663		
Hart Mary	S	K133F	1715 Nov 7		
Hart Richard	S	K35Baf	1645abt		
Hart Thomas	S	C75Ba	1635ca		
Hart Thomas	S	C85D	1668ca		
Hart Thomas	S	K133B	1706 Aug18	unm	1729 Nov 8
Hart William	S	K35Ba	1670ca	1702 Dec 1	1736bef
Hart William	S	K133D	1710 Dec 1		
Hartley Deborah	A	A3/87	1725abt	1747 Jul27	
Hartley Margaret	A	A10/85	1540abt	1563 Jun 3	
Hartman Daniel H	S	G54Eaf	1884 Jun 4	1903 Sep 3	1962 Dec24
Hartman Daniel H	D	D32a21	1884 Jun 4	1903 Sep 3	=G54eaf
Hartman Ebenezer	S	X80G	1749		
Hartman Helen	S	G54Ea	1908 Aug20	1929 Jan31	
Hartman Helen=G54Ea	D	D32/20	1908Aug 20	1929Jan 31	
Hartridge Alexander	A	A4/98	1760abt		
Hartridge Janet	A	A4/49	1760abt	1781 Jan20	
Harvey Elizabeth	S	G51Fa	1795abt		
Harvey Experience	S	Q20Fam	1690abt		
Harvey Margaret	S	G49Aa	1720ca	1742 May 4	
Harwar Elizabeth	S	A79A	1708ca		d.yng
Harwar Frances	S	A79B	1710ca		d.yng
Harwar Harwar	S	A79C	1713ca		
Harwar Thomas	S	A31Aa	1679ca	1707ca	1713
Harwar Thomas Sr	S	A31Aaf	1655abt		
Harwood James	A	A19/216	1655	1678	1719
Harwood John	A	A19/108	1703May 27	1729	

NAME	DIV.	NUMBER	BIRTH	MARRIAGE	DEATH
Harwood John Jr	A	A19/54	1736Jun 25	1760	1800 Mar12
Harwood Lydia	A	A19/27	1761ca	1780 Aug14	1838Mar 19
Hassell Elizabeth	S	P12Hbm	1650abt		
Hassen Thomas	A	A16/164	1580		1628
Hastings Martha	A	A1/221	1722 Apr27	1750 Sep13	1806 Jun23
Hastings Samuel	S	W38Ca	1665 Mar12	1686 Jan 4	1723 Jul24
Hastings Samuel	A	A1/442	1700abt		
Hastings Thomas	S	W38Caf	1640abt		
Hatch Amy	A	A5/19	1684 Jul15	1704 Jun20	1762 June1
Hatch Amy =A5/19	S	W51Aa	1687 Jul15	1704 Jun20	1762 Jun 1
Hatch Ann	S	W17Aam	1635abt		
Hatch David	S	T23Baf	1710abt		
Hatch David	S	T23Ba	1735 May 2	1755 Jan16	1800
Hatch Gamaliel	S	T59C	1762 Jun		
Hatch Hannah	S	Q15Ab	1681 Feb15	1719 Jul 9	1771 Apr13
Hatch Ichabod	S	T59E	1766ca		
Hatch Jabez	S	T59D	1764ca		
Hatch Jonathan	A	A5/76	1625ca	1646 Apr11	1710 Dec
Hatch Jonathan	S	F17Haf	1640ca		
Hatch Jonathan	S	H111Baf	1685abt		
Hatch Joseph =A5/38	S	W51Aaf	1654	1683 Dec 7	1727 Feb16
Hatch Joseph =W51Aaf	A	A5/38	1654	1683 Dec 7	1727 Feb16
Hatch Joseph Jr	S	W51Da	1689 Aug 3	1712ca	1750 Apr27
Hatch Joseph Sr=A5/38	S	W51Daf	1654	1683 Dec 7	1727 Feb16
Hatch Lydia	S	T59A	1755		
Hatch Mercy	S	F17Ha	1667 Apr27	1690ca	1710 Jan 4
Hatch Nathan	S	H111Ca	1710 Aug22	1732 Dec22	1784 Jun 8
Hatch Peter	S	C17Da	1745ca		
Hatch Phebe	S	T59B	1758 Feb 5		1758 Mar 5
Hatch Samuel	S	Q15Abf	1660abt		
Hatch Sarah	S	A26Ca	1695ca	1722 Dec24	
Hatch Sarah =A26Ca	A	A8/51	1695ca	1722 Dec24	
Hatch Thomas	A	A5/152	1603		1661
Hathaway Abial	S	K42K	1705 Oct21		
Hathaway Abigail	S	K47B	1704 Dec14		
Hathaway Antipas	S	K46A	1698 Oct 5		
Hathaway Apphiah	S	K46B	1701 May13		
Hathaway Arthur	S	B23Aaf	1635	1652	=W14Aa
Hathaway Arthur	S	K42D	1690 Apr 3		
Hathaway Arthur=B23Aaf	S	W14Aa	1635	1652	1711 Dec11

NAME	DIV.	NUMBER	BIRTH	MARRIAGE	DEATH
Hathaway Arthur=B23Aaf	S	K12Aa	1635	1652	1711 Dec11
Hathaway Benjamin	S	K42N	1712 Jan10		
Hathaway Deborah	A	A8/111	1713 Jul10	1730 Oct 9	1794 Jan 7
Hathaway Deborah	S	K47F	1713 Jul10	1730 Oct 9	=A8/111
Hathaway ELizabeth	S	K46D	1706 Oct18		
Hathaway Ebenezer	S	K42P	1717 May12		
Hathaway Elizabeth	A	A19/191	1690	1716	1752aft
Hathaway Elizabeth	S	K47A	1703 Mar11		d.yng
Hathaway Elizabeth	S	K42L	1708 May 6	unm.	1763 Apr29
Hathaway Elnathan	S	K47I	1719 Jan16		
Hathaway Gamaliel	S	K47C	1707 Oct10		
Hathaway Hannah	S	K17C	1662ca		1748
Hathaway Hannah	S	K42E	1692 Feb16		
Hathaway Hannah	S	K47D	1709 Nov 8	unm.	1796 May 1
Hathaway Hepzibah	S	K46H	1718 Mar18		
Hathaway Hunnewell	S	K42J	1703 Apr21		
Hathaway James	S	K42O	1713 Jan24		
Hathaway Jethro	S	K46I	1720 Jul31		
Hathaway Joanna	S	W47Ga	1685 Jan28	1711ca	1749 Mar16
Hathaway Joanna=W47Ga	S	K42B	1685 Jan28	1711ca	1749 Mar16
Hathaway John	S	K17A	1653 Sep17	2 Mar	1732
Hathaway John	S	W47Gaf	1660abt		
Hathaway John	S	K42C	1687 Mar18		
Hathaway Jonathan	S	B23Aa	1665abt		
Hathaway Jonathan	A	A8/222	1671ca	1701	1727ca
Hathaway Jonathan	S	K17G	1672ca	1701 Dec31	=A8/222
Hathaway Jonathan	S	K42G	1697 Jun23		
Hathaway Jonathan	S	K47G	1715 Oct17		
Hathaway Lydia	S	K17D	1663ca	1680ca	1714 Jun23
Hathaway Lydia	S	K21Gam	1685abt		
Hathaway Mary	S	K17E	1665ca	1681ca	1728living
Hathaway Mary	S	K42F	1694 Jun 4		
Hathaway Mary	S	K46E	1709 Oct 3		
Hathaway Nathaniel	S	K46G	1715 Jun23		
Hathaway Parnal	S	K46C	1703 Jun 3		1715 Nov 6
Hathaway Patience	S	K42M	1710 Apr27		
Hathaway Paul	S	K47J	1722 Oct 6		d.yng
Hathaway Richard	S	K42H	1699 May21		
Hathaway Sarah	S	K17B	1655Feb 28		1710bef
Hathaway Sarah	S	K42A	1683 Feb24		

NAME	DIV.	NUMBER	BIRTH	MARRIAGE	DEATH
Hathaway Seth	S	K47E	1711 Aug17		
Hathaway Silas	S	K47H	1717 Dec10 unm.		1754
Hathaway Thomas	S	K17F	1669ca	1696ca	1745ca
Hathaway Thomas	S	K42I	1700 Feb 5		1732bef
Hathaway Thomas	S	K46F	1711 Dec25		
Hathorne John	A	A16/102	1621abt	1643ca	1676Dec12
Hathorne Priscilla	A	A16/51	1649ca		
Hathorne William	A	A16/204	1576	1605	1650
Hathornthwaite Agnes	A	A7/179	1640abt	1664ca	1684ca
Haughton Mercy	A	A8/185	1670ca		
Haven Elizabeth	A	A3/121	1736 Sept2	1754 Nov28	
Haven James	A	A3/242	1709 Mar 4		
Haven Nathaniel	A	A3/484	1664	1689	1746
Haven Richard	S	A23Faf	1660abt		
Haven Sarah	S	A23Fa	1683ca	1702 Feb16	1748aft
Havens Mary	S	W36Bam	1670abt		
Hawes Joseph	S	P21Bcf	1675abt		
Hawes Mary	S	W49Aam	1660abt		
Hawke John	A	A11/188	1580ca		
Hawkes Abigail	S	A55B	1701 Jun 7		
Hawkes Adam	A	A11/94	1605 Jan		1671 Mar13
Hawkes Adam	S	A13Aaf	1610abt		
Hawkes Adam	S	A14Caf	1610abt		
Hawkes Adam	S	A23B	1664 May12	1689ca	1691bef
Hawkes Adam	S	A33C	1702 Dec15 unm		1729 Jul22
Hawkes Anna	S	A23C	1666 May 3		1675 Nov30
Hawkes Ebenezer	S	A23H	1677 Sep 7	3 mar.	1766 Dec 9
Hawkes Ebenezer	S	A58A	1702 Jul14		
Hawkes Elizabeth	S	A58B	1704 Apr24		
Hawkes Elkanah	S	A56C	1715 Feb17		
Hawkes John	S	A13Aa	1633 Aug13	1658 Jun 3	1694 Aug 5
Hawkes John	S	A14Ca	1633 Aug13	1661 Nov11	1694 Aug 5
Hawkes John	S	A23D	1668 Apr25	2 mar.	1750ca
Hawkes John	S	A54A	1690 Apr10		
Hawkes John	S	A33D	1705 Jan27		
Hawkes John	S	A55C	1706 Nov18		
Hawkes Jonathan	S	A56B	1710ca		
Hawkes Margaret	S	A33B	1700 Nov 5		
Hawkes Mercy	S	A23G	1675 Nov14	1696 Nov28	
Hawkes Moses	S	A16A	1659 Nov 9	1698 May10	1708 Jan 1

NAME	DIV.	NUMBER	BIRTH	MARRIAGE	DEATH
Hawkes Moses	S	A33A	1698 Mar 4		
Hawkes Rebecca	S	A23E	1670 Oct18		1675 Nov
Hawkes Rebecca	S	A33E	1708 Aug12		
Hawkes Samuel	S	A58C	1706 May12		
Hawkes Sarah	S	A55A	1699 Dec14		
Hawkes Sarah	S	A56D	1717ca		
Hawkes Susanna	A	A11/47	1633 Aug13	1649ca	1696bef
Hawkes Susannah	S	A23A	1662 Nov29		1675 Nov
Hawkes Thomas	S	A23F	1673 May18	1702 Feb16	1722bef
Hawkes Thomas	S	A56A	1708ca	unm	1736 Sep 4
Hawkins Elijah	S	C27Ca	1725ca		
Hawkins Mary	S	C61Ma	1773ca		
Haws Deborah	S	P21Bc	1696	1719 Jun15	1758 Jan12
Hay Helen	S	G44Ca	1600abt	1637	
Hayes Daniel	A	A12/16	1686 Apr26	1721 May 4	1756 Sep23
Hayes Ezekiel	A	A12/8	1724 Nov	1749 Dec26	1817 Oct17
Hayes George	A	A12/32	1655ca		1685
Hayes Rutherford B.	A	A12/1	1822 Oct 4	1852 Dec30	1893 Jan17
Hayes Rutherford Jr.	A	A12/2	‚1787 Jan 4	1813 Sep13	1822 Jul20
Hayes Rutherford Sr.	A	A12/4	1756 Jul29	1779	1836 Sep25
Hayman Nathaniel	S	W36Aaf	1650abt		
Hayman Sarah	S	W36Aa	1679 Aug27	1698 Feb21	1710abt
Hayward Benjamin	A	A2/40	1689 Feb14		1711ca
Hayward Benjamin Jr.	A	A2/20	1715ca	1734 Feb13	1783 Oct29
Hayward Bethiah	S	Q55A	1722 Apr 7		
Hayward Elisabeth	S	K77A	1685 Jan16		
Hayward Elisha	S	Q20Aa	1670ca	1720 Feb 1	1748
Hayward Elisha	S	Q20Faf	1690abt		
Hayward Elizabeth	A	A2/37	1683 Apr16	1717 May22	1759 Jun15
Hayward Ezra	S	Q55C	1729 Nov16		
Hayward Hannah	S	Q20Fa	1711 Jul 2	1731 Jul11	1756 Aug 1
Hayward James	S	K77C	1689 Jan26		
Hayward Joanna	S	Q21Ga	1704 Aug15	1730 Mar11	1794 Nov23
Hayward John	A	A2/74	1635abt	1662ca	1710
Hayward Joseph	S	Q21Gaf	1680abt		
Hayward Joseph	S	K34Laf	1695abt		
Hayward Marcy	S	C25Ca	1675ca		
Hayward Margery	A	A2/223	1680ca	1699ca	
Hayward Martha	S	K22Ham	1635abt		
Hayward Mary	A	A2/87	1672ca	1689ca	

NAME	DIV.	NUMBER	BIRTH	MARRIAGE	DEATH
Hayward Mary	S	K34La	1718 Jul24	1735 Sep 4	1769 Mar18
Hayward Mary (Howard)	S	Q18Ka	1710ca	1735 Sep 4	1769 Mar18
Hayward Mercy	S	K77B	1687 Feb27		1704 Jan26
Hayward Naomi	S	Q55B	1726 Mar25		
Hayward Nathaniel	S	Q20Aaf	1645abt		
Hayward Patience	S	Q20Cam	1665abt		
Hayward Samuel	A	A2/80	1640abt	1666 Nov28	1713 Jul29
Hayward Samuel	A	A2/174	1645abt	1666 Nov28	1713 Jul29
Hayward Thomas	A	A2/148	1600abt	1627ca	1681
Hayward William	A	A2/160	1610abt	1637ca	1659
Hayward/Howard John	S	K22Ha	1660ca	1685ca	1690
Hazard Martha	S	K18Gbm	1640abt		
Hazen Edward	A	A16/82	1614ca	1650 Mar	1683Jul 22
Hazen Isabel	A	A16/41	1662Jul 21	1680Jan 16	1726aft
Head Elizabeth	A	A4/479	1682	1710	1734
Head Henry	A	A8/210	1647ca	1677ca	1716ca
Head Henry =A8/210	S	K18Haf	1647ca	1677ca	1716ca
Head Innocent	A	A8/105	1695ca	1717 Mar14	
Head Jonathan	S	K18Ha	1678ca	1704 Dec 7	1749bef
Head Joseph	S	K55A	1705 Sep 1		
Hearnden Lydia	S	C79Aa	1670ca		
Hedge Elisha	S	H23Daf	1650abt		
Hedge Elisha	S	H73D	1705 Feb 4		
Hedge Elizabeth	S	W23Eam	1640abt		
Hedge Elizabeth	S	H73E	1708 Apr14		
Hedge Elizabeth=A25Aam	S	R15Cam	1640abt		
Hedge Elizabeth=R15Aam	S	W23Gam	1640abt		
Hedge Elizabeth=R15Cam	S	R15Aam	1640abt		
Hedge Elizabeth=W23Eam	S	A25Aam	1640abt		
Hedge Jabez	S	H73G	1712 Apr13		
Hedge Lamuel	S	H73C	1703 Jan10		1709 Dec13
Hedge Lamuel	S	H73I	1716ca		
Hedge Mary	S	H73B	1701 Nov20		1714 May17
Hedge Samuel	S	H23Da	1675 Jun18	1698 Dec 8	1714 May19
Hedge Samuel	S	H73F	1709 Mar 4		
Hedge Thankful	S	H73A	1699 Aug29		1713 Apr14
Hedge Thankful	S	H73H	1714 Apr17		
Hegeman Grace	S	N15Ma	1800ca		
Heister Elizabeth	S	Q17Aa	1692ca	1709 Dec15	1763bef
Hemingway Elizabeth	A	A2/213	1640abt	1663	

NAME	DIV.	NUMBER	BIRTH	MARRIAGE	DEATH
Hemingway Isaac	A	A3/120	1730 Jul17	1754 Nov28	1778 Jan31
Hemingway James	A	A3/60	1760 Apr12		1822 Jul15
Hemingway James Jr.	A	A3/30	1801 Jul23	1823	1893 Jan28
Hemingway Jane M.	A	A3/15	1824 Aug30	1846 Apr29	1890 Apr 5
Hemingway Joshua III	A	A3/240	1697 Apr 2	1718 July1	1754 Jan30
Hemingway Joshua Jr.	A	A3/480	1668	1694ca	1754aft
Heritage Agnes	D	D11a23	1450abt		
Herrick Daniel	A	A1/356	1708	1731	
Herrick Samuel	A	A1/178	1732 Apr 2	1754 Feb26	1797ca
Herrick Sarah	S	C19Ca	1752ca		
Herrick Sarah	A	A1/89	1764 abt		
Herrington Patience	A	A19/223	1697	1716	1724
Herron Helen	A	A2/1a	1861Jun 2	1886Jun 19	1943May 22
Hersey Hannah	S	R21Fam	1675abt		
Hersey Joshua	S	R14Bb	1678 Mar29	1718 Nov20	1740 Sep30
Hersey Sarah	S	K36Ga	1690ca	1712ca	1714ca
Hersey Sarah	S	K36Ha	1692 Sep26	1717ca	1731aft
Hersey William	S	R14Bbf	1655abt		
Hersey William	S	K36Haf	1670abt		
Hershey Sarah	S	R119A	1719 Jul 4		
Hewes Elizabeth	S	A40A	1685 Apr26		
Hewes Nathaniel	S	A40D	1699 Aug 3		d.yng
Hewes Remember	S	A40B	1687 Mar 7		
Hewes William	S	A18Aa	1665ca	1690ca	1705ca
Hewes William	S	A40C	1691 Jun27	unm	
Hewett Gershom	S	C18Aa	1745ca		
Hewett John	S	W44Aaf	1645abt		
Hewett Solomon	S	W44Aa	1670 Nov25	1695abt	1715 Dec 5
Hicks Hannah	S	W52Eam	1670abt		
Higgins Alice	S	X33D	1707 Nov22		
Higgins Apphia	S	X33E	1709 Nov22		
Higgins Barnabas	S	X33J	1722		
Higgins Benjamin	S	H31Caf	1650abt		
Higgins Beriah	S	X15A	1661 Sep29	1697bef	1699bef
Higgins Beriah	S	X31B	1692ca		
Higgins Beriah	S	X33C	1705 Jan15		
Higgins Dorcas	S	X57D	1731bef		
Higgins Ebenezer	S	X92B	1721		
Higgins Eliakim	S	X92G	1732		
Higgins Elisha	S	X15F	1677ca	3 mar.	1750ca

NAME	DIV.	NUMBER	BIRTH	MARRIAGE	DEATH
Higgins Elisha	S	X33A	1701 Jan 3		
Higgins Elizabeth	S	X19A	1680 Feb11	1701 Apr 3	1721 Nov 4
Higgins Elizabeth	S	X33G	1713		
Higgins Experience	S	X30E	1699ca		
Higgins Hannah	S	X30C	1697bef		1764aft
Higgins Hannah	S	X92A	1719		
Higgins Hannah	S	X57C	1720ca		
Higgins Hannah=H17Ga	S	X15E	1672ca	1699ca	1731 Jan24
Higgins Hannah=H53Cam	S	H17Ga	1672ca	1699ca	1731 Jan24
Higgins Hannah=X15E	S	H53Cam	1672ca	1699ca	1731 Jan24
Higgins James	S	X19D	1688 Jul22	2 mar.	1777 Jul11
Higgins James	S	X57B	1718ca		
Higgins Jemima	S	X15D	1666 Feb14	1699 Nov 1	1723 May 8
Higgins John	S	H112B	1720 Dec16		
Higgins Jonathan	S	X15B	1664 Aug	1687aft	1754ca
Higgins Jonathan	S	X30D	1697ca		
Higgins Jonathan	S	X33F	1711 Oct 8		
Higgins Jonathan	S	X92E	1728		
Higgins Jonathan=X12Da	S	H17Gaf	1637 Jul	1660	1711
Higgins Jonathan=X12Da	S	X12Ha	1637 Jul	1660 Jan 9	1711
Higgins Jonathan=X12Ha	S	X12Da	1637 Jul	1660	1711
Higgins Joseph	S	X15C	1666 Feb14	1689ca	1729bef
Higgins Joseph	S	X31A	1690 Oct 1		
Higgins Joseph	S	X29A	1697bef		1726living
Higgins Joseph	S	X33H	1717		1749bef
Higgins Martha	S	X33B	1703 Jan 5		
Higgins Martha	S	X92C	1723		
Higgins Mary	S	X19B	1682 Jan22	1706 Feb12	1750aft
Higgins Philip	S	X33K	1724 Mar 4		
Higgins Prince	S	X92I	1741		
Higgins Rebecca	S	X19C	1686 Nov30	1715 Aug11	1776 Dec25
Higgins Rebecca	S	X57A	1716ca		
Higgins Richard	S	X12Daf	1610abt		
Higgins Richard	S	X12Haf	1610abt		
Higgins Ruth	S	X31C	1700 Sep11		
Higgins Ruth	S	X33I	1719	unm	1749living
Higgins Samuel	S	H31Ca	1676 Mar 7	1717 Mar20	1761 Dec10
Higgins Samuel	S	X30B	1694 Oct 5	1718 Oct 9	1776 Jul25
Higgins Samuel	S	X92F	1730		
Higgins Sarah	S	X19E	1690 Oct18	1717 Apr10	1741aft

NAME	DIV.	NUMBER	BIRTH	MARRIAGE	DEATH
Higgins Sarah	A	A9/11	1835ca		1870bef
Higgins Silvanus	S	X92H	1736		
Higgins Simeon	S	H112C	1722 Jan16		
Higgins Susanna	S	X92D	1725		
Higgins Thankful	S	X30A	1692ca		1712 Jul13
Higgins William	S	H112A	1719 Aug16		
Higginson Lucy	A	A14/133	1626ca	1646ca	1675 Nov26
Higginson Lucy	A	A14/149	1626ca	1646ca	1675 Nov26
Higginson Robert	A	A14/266	1600abt	1625	1649 Aug
Higginson Robert	A	A14/298	1600abt	1625	1649 Aug
Higley Catherine	S	N11Hb	1680ca		
Higley John	S	N11Hbf	1655abt		
Hildouin IV Montdidier	D	D30a37	1035abt		
Hill Asenath	A	A6/5	1778ca	1794ca	1851 Feb 5
Hill Charity	S	X21Bbm	1650abt		
Hill Eleazer	A	A2/238	1665ca		
Hill John Jr.	A	A2/156	1630ca	1653ca	1717ca
Hill Margery	A	A16/127	1610abt	1640Aug 6	
Hill Mary	A	A1/443	1695abt		
Hill Mary	A	A2/39	1696 Jul15	1719 Jul10	1785ca
Hill Ruth	A	A2/119	1700abt	1718 Mar13	1747 May12
Hill Samuel	A	A2/78	1656ca	1679 Nov 4	1723
Hilliard Abigail	S	W50Ea	1690 Jul12	1714 Apr25	
Hilliard Esther	S	W24Fam	1640abt		
Hilliard Mary	S	X22Bam	1660abt		
Hilliard William	S	W50Eaf	1665abt		
Hills Francis	A	A16/115	1605abt	1626Nov 19	1680aft
Hinckley Mary	A	A1/433	1678	1703	1741
Hinckley Mercy	S	H24Eb	1679 Apr 9	1715 Oct 6	1748bef
Hinckley Samuel	S	H24Ebf	1650abt		
Hinckley Susannah	S	F15Cam	1650abt		
Hincksman Joanna	A	A11/115	1590abt		1661 Dec21
Hinds Abigail	S	A34B	1684ca		
Hinds John	S	A34A	1682 Feb14		
Hinds Rebecca	S	A34C	1686ca		
Hinds William	S	A17Aa	1660ca	1681ca	1636
Hinds William	S	A34D	1688ca		d.yng
Hines Jane	A	A5/25	1715abt		
Hinksman Elizabeth	S	K22Eam	1635abt		
Hinsdale Mary	A	A8/117	1665 Jul22	1685ca	1738 Sep

NAME	DIV.	NUMBER	BIRTH	MARRIAGE	DEATH
Hinsdale Samuel	A	A8/234	1641ca	1660	1675ca
Hoar Charles	A	A11/114	1590abt		1638
Hoar Joanna	A	A11/57	1624 Jun	1648 Jul26	1680 May16
Hobart Caleb	S	W15Aa	1623ca	1657 Jan8	1711 Sep4
Hobart David	S	P21Gaf	1675abt		
Hobart Elizabeth	S	R12Fam	1635abt		
Hobart Hannah	S	X13Ab	1638 May15	1679 Oct21	1691 Sep11
Hobart Jael	S	R11Da	1643ca	1664 May25	1730 Apr14
Hobart Jonathon	S	W34A	1658 Feb 1		1659 Apr20
Hobart Nehemiah	S	P21Ga	1697 Apr27	1739 Apr 5	1740 May31
Hobart Peter	S	R11Daf	1620abt		
Hobart Peter=R11Daf	S	X13Abf	1620abt		
Hobart Sarah	S	R13Bbm	1680abt		
Hobart Thomas	S	W15Aaf	1600abt		
Hobson Alice	A	A14/293	1585ca		
Hodges Abigail	S	K25Ha	1713 May 4	1731 Feb	1764living
Hodges Andrew	S	H124D	1729ca		
Hodges Elizabeth	S	T15Ab	1702ca	1734 Jun12	1782 Oct10
Hodges Elizabeth	S	H124A	1724 Nov24		
Hodges Experience	S	K25Ia	1710ca	1732 Jun17	
Hodges Henry	S	H34Caf	1660abt		
Hodges Henry=H34Caf	S	T15Abf	1660abt		
Hodges John	S	H34Ca	1684ca		1759
Hodges John	S	H124B	1726ca		
Hodges Peter	S	H124C	1727 Sep13		d yng
Hodges Samuel	S	K25Iaf	1690abt		
Hodges William	S	K25Haf	1690abt		
Hodgson Hennetta M	D	D28/19	1815abt		
Hodgson Robert Jr	D	D28/20	1785abt		
Hodgson Robert Sr	D	D28a21	1755abt		
Hoffman Cornelia	A	A8/17	1734 Aug13	1752 Sep22	1789 Nov13
Hoffman Martin	A	A8/34	1706 Feb 6	1733 Oct19	1772 Aug29
Hoffman Mortin Herman.	A	A8/136	1625ca	1664	1688living
Hoffman Nicholas	A	A8/68	1680ca	1704 Dec30	1750 Dec31
Holbrook Daniel	A	A2/106	1676 Mar15	1698 May29	
Holbrook Deborah	A	A2/25	1731 Feb24	1752 Sep 6	1775 Sep13
Holbrook Eunice	A	A6/115	1658 May12	1678ca	
Holbrook Hopestill	A	A2/205	1645abt	1665	1705
Holbrook John	A	A6/230	1618		1699
Holbrook John	A	A2/212	1639ca	1663	1678ca

NAME	DIV.	NUMBER	BIRTH	MARRIAGE	DEATH
Holbrook John	A	A2/236	1667ca	1692ca	1740ca
Holbrook John Jr.	A	A2/118	1694 Mar22	1718 Mar13	1756 May 6
Holbrook Mary	A	A2/109	1686 Nov 2	1709 Jul28	1759 Mar11
Holbrook Peter	A	A2/100	1655 May 7	1680abt	1712 May 3
Holbrook Rebecca	A	A2/53	1699 Feb 9	1726abt	1777 Sep23
Holbrook Samuel	A	A2/218	1643ca	1675	1712ca
Holbrook Silence	A	A2/59	1723 Mar23	1743 Oct20	
Holbrook Thomas Jr.	A	A2/200	1625abt	1651ca	1697
Holbrook William	A	A2/50	1693 Mar28	1722 Apr9	1776 Mar28
Holland Hannah	S	P22Bam	1630abt		
Holliday Adam	A	A1/480	1680ca		
Holliday John James	A	A1/30	1819 Jul23	1843 May 9	1881 Sep18
Holliday Joseph	A	A1/60	1789 Sep15	1816 Mar18	1870 Dec17
Holliday Nannie E	A	A1/15	1848ca	1866 Dec 4	1942 Feb25
Holliday Samuel	A	A1/240	1710ca		
Holliday William	A	A1/120	1755ca		1811ca
Holloway Experiance	S	F16Aam	1645abt		
Holloway Margaret	S	X22Cb	1690ca	1723bef	1768living
Holloway Nathaniel	S	X22Cbf	1665abt		
Holman Abigail	S	P34B	1693 Jan		
Holman Abraham	S	P18E	1672ca	1696ca	1726aft
Holman Abraham	S	P35A	1697ca		
Holman Deborah	S	P18B	1664ca	1687 Nov 3	1709living
Holman Isaac	S	P18A	1663 Apr12		
Holman Jeremiah	S	P12Ea	1629ca	1662ca	1709 Nov30
Holman Jeremiah	S	P18D	1670 Aug29	1700abt	1739 May16
Holman Jeremiah	S	P34C	1695 May11		
Holman Jonathon	A	A2/30	1732 Aug13	1783 Jul10	1814 Feb25
Holman Mary	S	P34A	1690ca		
Holman Mehitabel	S	P18C	1667 Nov12		1709living
Holman Nathaniel	S	P35B	1701ca		
Holman Nathaniel	S	P34D	1704 Jun		d yng
Holman Sarah	S	P18F	1673ca		1679 Dec21
Holman Solomon	A	A2/120	1670abt	1694ca	1753 May 7
Holman Solomon Jr.	A	A2/60	1697 Nov25	1729 Aug28	1785 Apr17
Holman Susan Trask	A	A2/15	1784 Feb22	1802 May19	1849 Nov28
Holman Susanna	S	P35C	1702May 20		
Holman William	S	P12Eaf	1605abt		
Holmes Abigail	S	R103A	1741 Jun 4		1742 Jun20
Holmes Abigail	S	R103C	1746 Jul 6		

NAME	DIV.	NUMBER	BIRTH	MARRIAGE	DEATH
Holmes Abraham	S	H27Dbf	1650abt		
Holmes Bathsheba	S	K27Fam	1670abt		
Holmes Deborah	S	R103B	1743 Apr 3		1748 Jan26
Holmes Desire	S	X28Bam	1680abt		
Holmes Elisha	S	W23Fa	1670 Apr19	1695 Sep2	1753abt
Holmes Elizabeth	S	R103E	1751 Feb18		
Holmes Elkanah	S	A68D	1725 Aug 7		
Holmes Jabez	S	A68C	1723 Sep13		
Holmes Jedidiah	S	A68B	1720 May19		
Holmes John	S	A25Gaf	1670abt		
Holmes John	S	W37Ga	1685abt	1709 Oct 7	
Holmes John	S	R26Gaf	1690abt		
Holmes John	S	A68E	1727 Apr30		
Holmes John=A25Gaf	S	A24Eaf	1670abt		
Holmes Lydia	A	A13/71	1635abt		1693aft
Holmes Lydia	S	R103F	1753 Jun29		
Holmes Marcy	S	Q17Ham	1670abt		
Holmes Mary	S	W24Aam	1645abt		
Holmes Mary	S	R103H	1758 Feb20		
Holmes Mercy	S	Q17Dam	1675abt		
Holmes Mercy	S	K30Cam	1680abt		
Holmes Mercy	S	Q17Ea	1701 Dec26	1724 Oct20	1765ca
Holmes Nathaniel	S	W23Faf	1645abt		
Holmes Nathaniel	S	Q17Eaf	1675abt		
Holmes Nathaniel	S	A25Ga	1692 Aug30	1717 Jun 6	1771aft
Holmes Nathaniel	S	A68A	1718 Jun21		
Holmes Nathaniel	S	R103G	1753 Oct21		
Holmes Obadiah	A	A13/142	1609	1630	1682
Holmes Patience	S	A24Ea	1690 Nov 3	1712 Nov27	1755 Sep 8
Holmes Peleg	S	R26Ga	1715 Sep28	1740 Oct 4	
Holmes Peleg	S	R103D	1749 Jan 6		
Holmes Rachel	S	H26Ham	1675abt		
Holmes Rachel	S	H27Db	1677ca	1740 Jul31	1757 Nov30
Holmes Sarah	S	R27Dbm	1700abt		
Holmes Sarah	S	R103I	1760 Apr23		
Holton Mary	A	A8/119	1678 Jul22	1695 Oct25	1705 Dec 8
Holton William Jr.	A	A8/238	1644ca	1676	1711ca
Hood Sarah	S	A23Hbm	1655abt		
Hooker Sarah	A	A2/147	1620	1647ca	1725
Hooper John	S	Q22Dbf	1680abt		

NAME	DIV.	NUMBER	BIRTH	MARRIAGE	DEATH
Hooper Ruth	S	K41Bam	1690abt		
Hooper Ruth=K41Bam	S	K41Dam	1690abt		
Hooper Sarah	S	Q22Db	1705 Oct 9	1737 Dec14	
Hopkins John	A	A16/112	1610abt		1654bef
Hopkins Abiel	S	H101J	1741 Aug21		
Hopkins Abigail	S	H23Gam	1644 Oct	1667 May23	
Hopkins Abigail	S	H30B	1685 Mar 9	1713 Sept3	
Hopkins Abigail=H23Gam	S	H13D	1644 Oct	1667 May23	
Hopkins Apphia	S	H103F	1734 May 9		
Hopkins Barzillai	S	H106F	1730ca		
Hopkins Benjamin	S	H26H	1690 Feb	1717 Feb13	1745bef
Hopkins Benjamin	S	H87A	1718 Feb17		
Hopkins Bethia	S	H85E	1715 Aug19		
Hopkins Caleb	S	H11E	1622ca		1644living
Hopkins Caleb	S	H13F	1650 Jan		1700abt
Hopkins Caleb	S	H29A	1684ca	1719 Oct 8	1741
Hopkins Caleb	S	H101D	1726 Jul28		
Hopkins Caleb #1	S	H103I	1741 Oct22		d yng
Hopkins Caleb #2	S	H103J	1743 Jul 6		
Hopkins Constance MF	S	X12Cam	1607ca	1628bef	=H11A
Hopkins ConstanceMF	S	H11A	1607ca	1628bef	1677 Oct
Hopkins Constant	S	H101A	1720 Jul28		
Hopkins Damaris =H11G	S	A14Ebm	1627ca	1645aft	1670bef
Hopkins Damaris MF	S	H11C	1618		d yng
Hopkins Damaris(2)H11G	D	D5/24	1627ca	1645aft	1670bef
Hopkins Damaris=A14Ebm	S	K11Ca	1627ca	1645aft	1670bef
Hopkins Damaris=K11Ca	S	H11G	1627ca	1645aft	1670bef
Hopkins David	S	H85A	1707 Jul13		
Hopkins Deborah	S	H11F	1624ca	1646 Apr23	1674ca
Hopkins Deborah	S	H13E	1648 Jun	1668 Jul27	1700abt
Hopkins Deborah	S	H103E	1733ca		d yng
Hopkins Deborah	S	H103G	1736 Apr29		
Hopkins Desire	S	H83G	1714 Nov17		
Hopkins Dorcas	S	R18Aam	1665abt		
Hopkins Ebenezer	A	A16/28	1668 Jul	1691Jan 21	1711
Hopkins Ebenezer	A	A16/14	1699Jun 24	1727Jun 7	1784ca
Hopkins Ebenezer	S	H82G	1706 Jan		
Hopkins EbenezerA16/28	8	R18Gaf	1668Jul	1691Jan 21	1711
Hopkins Edward	S	H87G	1735 Feb24		
Hopkins Elisha	S	H30C	1688 Dec17	1712 Oct 9	1741 Feb 1

NAME	DIV.	NUMBER	BIRTH	MARRIAGE	DEATH
Hopkins Elisha	S	H106C	1721ca		
Hopkins Elisha	S	H102G	1738 May 6	1761 Jan29	
Hopkins Elizabeth	S	H11I	1644 Nov30	unm.	
Hopkins Elizabeth	S	H13J	1664 Nov		d. yng .
Hopkins Elizabeth	S	H26A	1668 Jun		
Hopkins Elizabeth	S	H85C	1711 Apr21		
Hopkins Elizabeth	S	H106A	1717ca	1738 Aug23	
Hopkins Elizabeth	S	H86J	1738 Jun 6		
Hopkins Elizabeth	S	H102I	1741ca		
Hopkins Elkanah	S	H82E	1702 Aug12		1720 Dec25
Hopkins Experience	S	H106E	1728ca		
Hopkins Giles	S	H11B	1610ca	1639 Oct 9	1688 Mar 5
Hopkins Giles	S	H87B	1720 Jan29		
Hopkins Hannah	S	H30G	1700 Mar25	(2)1742May	1793 Oct24
Hopkins Hannah	S	H82J	1714 Nov 4		
Hopkins Hannah	S	H83I	1719 Jun17		1760 Oct22
Hopkins Hannah	S	H86E	1722 Oct22	1741 Oct 8	1772bef
Hopkins Hannah	S	H108C	1729 Jul30		
Hopkins Hannah	S	H103B	1730 May 9	1756 Jan15	1768bef
Hopkins Huldah	S	H84K	1731 Apr18		
Hopkins Isaac	S	H86A	1712 Mar10		
Hopkins Isaac	S	H102C	1725ca		
Hopkins James	S	H85J	1726 Mar20		
Hopkins James	S	H101H	1736 Aug16		
Hopkins Jeremiah	S	H85B	1708 Mar14		
Hopkins Jeremiah	S	H103M	1750 Mar29		
Hopkins John	S	H13C	1643		1643
Hopkins John	S	R18Fbf	1665abt		
Hopkins John	S	H30A	1683 Apr16		1700 Jun24
Hopkins John	S	H83B	1704 Sep23		
Hopkins John	S	H106B	1719 Apr29		
Hopkins John	S	H102F	1732ca		
Hopkins Jonathan	S	H82A	1693 Aug20		1716 Jan24
Hopkins Jonathan	S	H86D	1719 Feb12		
Hopkins Jonathan	S	H101E	1728 Jul27		
Hopkins Joseph	S	H26G	1688	1712 Apr17	1771 Apr24
Hopkins Joseph	S	H86B	1715 May10		
Hopkins Joshua	S	H13H	1657 Jun	1681 May26	1735abt
Hopkins Joshua	S	H30F	1697 Feb20	1724 Oct 1	1780
Hopkins Joshua	S	H108A	1725 Jul18		

NAME	DIV.	NUMBER	BIRTH	MARRIAGE	DEATH
Hopkins Joshua	S	H101I	1738 Jan10		
Hopkins Judah	S	H26D	1677 Jan	2 Mar	1748 Jan 7
Hopkins Judah	S	H83E	1710ca		
Hopkins Lydia	S	H30D	1692 Apr 1	1741 Apr17	
Hopkins Lydia	S	H84D	1713 Jun 1		
Hopkins Lydia	S	H102D	1727ca		
Hopkins Marsy	S	H83A	1703 Apr17		
Hopkins Martha	S	H83C	1705 Mar25		
Hopkins Mary	S	H13A	1640 Nov	1665 Jan 3	1700 Jul 2
Hopkins Mary	S	H20Dam	1650abt		
Hopkins Mary	S	H26I	1692 Apr15	1714 Nov 5	
Hopkins Mary	S	H30E	1694 Jan20	1715 Jun24	1739bef
Hopkins Mary	S	R18Ga	1703ca	1725 Jun20	1796 Aug 9
Hopkins Mary	S	H82H	1708		
Hopkins Mary	S	H86C	1716 Dec15		
Hopkins Mary	S	H102A	1721ca		
Hopkins Mary	S	H101B	1722 Jul18		
Hopkins Mary	S	H106D	1726 Mar12		
Hopkins Mary	S	H103K	1745 Oct 3		
Hopkins Mercy	S	H85G	1719 Feb21		
Hopkins Mercy	S	H101G	1734 Apr26		
Hopkins Michael	S	H103H	1739 Jul 7		1760bef
Hopkins Moses	S	H84C	1711 Dec30		
Hopkins Moses	S	H84H	1721 Mar		
Hopkins Nathan	S	H86F	1726 Aug22		
Hopkins Nathan	S	H84J	1729 Jun16		
Hopkins Nathan	S	H86I	1733 Oct 6		
Hopkins Nathaniel	S	H26F	1684 Mar	1707 May26	1766 Sep13
Hopkins Nathaniel	S	H29B	1684ca		1752
Hopkins Nathaniel	S	H85D	1713 Sep 1		1718bef
Hopkins Nathaniel	S	H85F	1717 Sep15		
Hopkins Oceanus MF	S	H11D	1620ca		d yng
Hopkins Phebe	S	H30H	1702 Mar11	1724 Mar18	1776aft
Hopkins Phebe	S	H82I	1711 Jul11		
Hopkins Phebe	S	H102E	1729ca		
Hopkins Prence #1	S	H86G	1729 Jul 8		
Hopkins Prence #2	S	H86H	1731 Jul 7		
Hopkins Priscilla	S	H108B	1728 Jun 7	unm.	1818
Hopkins Priscilla	S	H102H	1740ca		
Hopkins Rachel	S	H87D	1726 Oct23		

NAME	DIV.	NUMBER	BIRTH	MARRIAGE	DEATH
Hopkins Rebecca	S	H82C	1697ca		
Hopkins Rebecca	S	H83D	1707 Oct10		
Hopkins Rebecca	S	H103D	1732 Oct 3	1754 Dec19	
Hopkins Reliance	S	H84B	1709 Nov17		
Hopkins Reliance	S	H84E	1715 Jul24		
Hopkins Reuben	S	H85H	1722 Apr 4		
Hopkins Richard	S	H84A	1707 Nov26		
Hopkins Ruth	S	H11H	1629ca	unm.	1644living
Hopkins Ruth	S	H13G	1653 Jun		
Hopkins Ruth	S	X19Dam	1660abt		
Hopkins Ruth	S	H26C	1674 Nov		
Hopkins Samuel	S	H26E	1682 Mar		1749
Hopkins Samuel	S	H83J	1720 Mar14		
Hopkins Samuel	S	H85I	1724 Aug30		
Hopkins Samuel	S	H103A	1727 Jul 5		
Hopkins Samuel	S	H87E	1728 Oct22		
Hopkins Sarah	S	H82B	1694ca		
Hopkins Sarah	S	H84F	1717 Jul25	1741 Nov12	
Hopkins Sarah	S	H102B	1723ca		
Hopkins Sarah	S	H103L	1747 Feb 3		
Hopkins Seth	S	H87C	1722 Feb11		
Hopkins Simeon	S	H101F	1731 Feb 7		
Hopkins Solomon	S	H87F	1733 May18		
Hopkins Stephen	A	A16/56	1635ca	1657bef	1689
Hopkins Stephen	S	H13B	1642 Sep	2 Mar	1718 Oct10
Hopkins Stephen	S	H26B	1670 Jul	1692 May19	1733 Apr 9
Hopkins Stephen	S	R18Fb	1689 Nov19	1756 May25	1769 Jan11
Hopkins Stephen	S	H83F	1711 Jan26		
Hopkins Stephen MF	S	H10A	1580ca	1617 Feb19	=K11Caf
Hopkins Stephen MF	S	K11Caf	1588cat	1617 Feb19	1644=D5/25
Hopkins StephenMF H10A	D	D5/25	1580ca	1617 Feb19	1644
Hopkins Susanna	S	H84G	1719 Jul 7		
Hopkins Sylvanus	S	H83H	1716 Feb14		
Hopkins Tabitha	A	A16/7	1745Oct 16	1761Sep 30	
Hopkins Thankful	S	H82D	1700 Apr		
Hopkins Thankful	S	H29D	1709 May27	1729 Jan22	1783 Aug 1
Hopkins Thankful	S	H101C	1724 May30		
Hopkins Theodosius	S	H84I	1726 Nov 9		
Hopkins Theophilus	S	H85K	1728 Mar13		
Hopkins Thomas	S	H29C	1686ca	1724 Feb10	1754

NAME	DIV.	NUMBER	BIRTH	MARRIAGE	DEATH
Hopkins Thomas	S	H82F	1705 Jun		
Hopkins Thomas	S	H103C	1730 Jan28		
Hopkins William	S	H13I	1660 Jan 9 unm.		
Horn Agnes	A	A7/107	1685abt		
Horn James	A	A7/214	1656abt	1674	
Hornby Daniel	S	A31Ca	1690	1741 Nov28	1749 Feb14
Hornell George	S	C21Fa	1760abt		
Horrel Abigail	S	T15Ea	1708 May11	1728 Nov15	1777 Mar29
Horrel Humphrey	S	T15Eaf	1680abt		
Horton Barnabas	A	A14/92	1666 Sep23	1686ca	1696 Dec
Horton Bethia	A	A14/89	1674abt	1690ca	1744 Mar16
Horton Caleb	A	A14/184	1640ca	1665	1702ca
Horton Caleb	A	A14/190	1640ca	1665	1702ca
Horton Caleb	A	A14/46	1687 Dec22	1714 Dec10	1772 Aug 6
Horton Comfort	A	A1/190	1743 Mar29	1768 Dec 8	1805 Jun14
Horton Comfort=A1/190	D	D2a19	1743 Mar29	1768 Dec 8	1805 Jun14
Horton Hezekiah	S	C31Ga	1712ca		
Horton Hope	S	H20Fa	1677ca	1698 Dec22	1734bef
Horton Jonathan	A	A14/178	1648ca	1672	1707ca
Horton Jonathan	A	A1/380	1695	1725	1774
Horton Mary	A	A14/95	1660abt	1682 Nov31	
Horton Phoebe	A	A14/23	1722ca	1738 Mar16	1793 Nov 3
Horton Rachel	A	A19/113	1706 Jun 8	1728 Mar31	1791 Feb24
Horton Rebecca	S	C29Aa	1730abt		
Horton Sarah=A1/95	D	D2/18	1777 Dec28	1797 Feb12	1856 May13
Horton Sarah=D2/18	A	A1/95	1777 Dec28	1797 Feb12	1856 May13
Horton Submit	A	A1/189	1730abt	1753 Jan 4	1778 Apr18
Horton Thomas	A	A19/226	1677	1700	1746
Horton Thomas	A	A1/378	1695ca	1721	1733
Horton Thomas =A01/378	D	D20a25	1695ca	1721	1733
Hoskins Sarah	S	P22Cam	1640abt		
Houghtaling Effie B	S	C57Ba	1881		
House Deborah	A	A1/65	1742 Apr 6	1759 Apr12	1819ca
House Hannah	A	A5/141	1585abt	1610	1633
House John	A	A1/130	1715 Dec 8	1739 Sep 6	1805 Jul 4
House Nathaniel	A	A1/260	1685ca	1710	1763
Hovey Abigail	A	A12/29	1682 Jan 8	1701 Jan27	1764 Jan 9
Hovey Amos	S	P21Ka	1710 Jan26	1737 Jul22	1758bef
Hovey Daniel	A	A12/116	1618 Aug		1692 Apr24
Hovey Ebenezer	S	Q21Cbf	1680abt		

NAME	DIV.	NUMBER	BIRTH	MARRIAGE	DEATH
Hovey Hannah	S	Q21Cb	1703 Feb 4	1741 Aug 6	1760living
Hovey Joseph	S	P21Kaf	1685abt		
Hovey Richard	A	A12/232	1590abt		1676
Hovey Thomas	A	A12/58	1648ca	1677 Nov	1739 Mar 4
Howard Amos	A	A1/296	1696ca	1721	
Howard Benjamin	S	T25Daf	1680abt		
Howard Benjamin	S	T64B	1727 Sept1		
Howard Ebenezer	A	A1/148	1730 Oct12	1750 Apr26	1783ca
Howard Eleazer	S	T64H	1739 May14		
Howard Eunice	S	T64E	1733 Mar 3		
Howard Harriet	A	A1/37	1782 Mar27	1803 Jul31	1847 Jul27
Howard Johadden	S	T64J	1743 Apr24		
Howard John	S	K22Haf	1635abt		
Howard Joseph	S	T64D	1731 Apr11		
Howard Levi	A	A2/10	1752 Sep15	1776 May28	1833 May14
Howard Martha	S	T64F	1735 Mar22		
Howard Mary	S	T64G	1737 Mar 2		
Howard Nathan	S	T64I	1741 Apr23		
Howard Samuel	A	A1/74	1752ca	1777 Apr 3	1797 Jan
Howard Sarah	S	K39Bam	1660abt		
Howard Sarah	S	T64A	1725 Dec 6		
Howard Sarah=K39Bam	S	K39Eam	1660abt		
Howard Susanna	S	L17Bam	1695abt		
Howard Sylvia	A	A2/5	1792 Feb17	1810 Dec5	1866
Howard Thomas	S	T25Da	1702 Jul	1724 Nov 3	1775 Apr28
Howard Thomas	S	T64C	1728 Jan28		
Howard William	S	T64K	1744 Aug30		
Howe Phebe	S	C17Aa	1740ca		
Howes Hannah	S	F12Bam	1595abt		
Howes Joseph Jr	S	Q13Eb	1660ca	1713 Mar 9	1743 Dec24
Howes Joseph Sr	S	Q13Ebf	1635abt		
Howes Peninah	S	H13Bbm	1615abt		
Howes Sarah	S	H26Ba	1673 Oct29	1692 May19	1751aft
Howes Thomas	S	H26Baf	1650abt		
Howland Abigail	A	A4/477	1686	1710	1769
Howland Abigail	D	D18/23	1686	1710	1769
Howland Abigail	S	K25Ga	1702 Oct29	1722 May 6	
Howland Arthur	S	W45Baf	1660abt		
Howland Benjamin	D	D18/24	1655abt		
Howland Caleb	S	P59B	1717 Dec31		

NAME	DIV.	NUMBER	BIRTH	MARRIAGE	DEATH
Howland Elizabeth	A	A3/459	1650abt		1711living
Howland Elizabeth	D	D17/24	1650ca		=A3/459
Howland George	S	P59D	1723 Dec26		
Howland Hannah	S	F22Cam	1661 May15		
Howland Hannah	S	Q14Ba	1694 Oct 6	1716 Dec11	1792 Mar25
Howland Hannah	S	K27Ga	1699 Oct16	1720 Jun29	
Howland Hannah	S	L15Fa	1712 Dec19	1741 Apl10	1795 May23
Howland Hannah=F22Cam	D	D1/22	1661 May15		
Howland Henry Jr	D	D17/25	1595abt		
Howland Henry Sr	D	D1/25	1570abt		
Howland Hope	D	D2/24	1625abt	1647ca	
Howland Hope	S	W41Cam	1645abt		
Howland Isaac	S	P23Eaf	1650abt		
Howland Isaac=P23Eaf	S	Q14Baf	1650abt		
Howland James	S	K27Gaf	1675abt		
Howland James	S	K25Gaf	1680abt		
Howland Joanna	S	L18Bam	1720abt		
Howland John Jr	D	D1/23	1625ca	1651 Dec16	
Howland John Sr MF	D	D29af9	1593abt		1651Oct 26
Howland John Sr MF	S	A14Aaf	1593ca	=D1/24	1651Oct 26
Howland John Sr=A14Aaf	D	D1/24	1593ca	Mayflower	1651 Oct26
Howland John Sr=D1/24	D	D16/25	1593abt		1651 Oct26
Howland Joseph	A	A8/176	1640abt	1664	1703
Howland Joseph	A	A8/22	1749 Sep30	1772 May26	1836 Mar11
Howland Joseph =A8/176	D	D16/24	1640abt	1664	1703
Howland Joseph II	D	D4/21	1749 Sep30	1772 May26	1836 Mar11
Howland Joseph=A8/176	D	D4/24	1640abt	1664	1703
Howland Joseph=A8/176	D	D29a9	1640abt	1664	1703
Howland Lydia	S	K34Bam	1670abt		
Howland Lydia=K34Bam	S	Q18Aam	1670abt		
Howland Nathan	S	P23Ea	1687 Jan17	1712ca	1760bef
Howland Nathaniel	A	A8/88	1671ca	1696 Mar 3	1746 Dec29
Howland Nathaniel Jr	D	D4/22	1705 Jun 9	1739 Nov22	
Howland Nathaniel Jr.	A	A8/44	1705 Jun 9	1739 Nov22	
Howland Nathaniel Sr	D	D4/23	1671ca	1696	1746 Dec29
Howland Prince	S	W45Da	1687ca	1706 Feb13	1714ca
Howland Priscilla	S	P59C	1719 Feb15		
Howland Ruth	S	A14Aa	1640ca	1664 Nov17	1679bef
Howland Ruth	S	P59E	1727 Apr 4		
Howland Seth	S	P59A	1714 Jan 1		

NAME	DIV.	NUMBER	BIRTH	MARRIAGE	DEATH
Howland Susan	A	A8/11	1779 May20	1803 Nov27	1852 Dec
Howland Susan=A08/11	D	D4/20	1779 May20	1803 Nov27	1852 Dec
Howland Susanna	S	K30Jam	1695abt		
Howland Thomas	S	L15Faf	1690abt		
Howland Zoeth	D	D18/25	1625abt		
Hoxie Bathshua	S	W45Bam	1660abt		
Hoyt Jesse	S	N15Fa	1780ca		
Hubbard Amelia	S	R69H	1742		
Hubbard Daniel	S	R69C	1729 Dec24		
Hubbard Elizabeth	S	R69D	1731 Jul 3		
Hubbard John	S	R69B	1727 Jan24		
Hubbard John Jr	S	R118Aa	1703 Nov30	1724 Aug30	1773 Oct30
Hubbard John Sr	S	R118Aaf	1680abt		
Hubbard Jonathan	A	A19/210	1659	1681	1728
Hubbard Leverrett	S	R69A	1725 Jul21		
Hubbard Mary	A	A19/105	1682 Jun 3	1699Apr 27	
Hubbard Nathaniel	S	R69G	1738		1762 Sep30
Hubbard William	S	R69E	1732 Mar20		1736 Nov14
Hubbard William Abdiel	S	R69F	1736 Dec15		
Huckins Elizabeth	S	H76I	1732 Jul 9 unm.		
Huckins Hope	D	D2/22	1665abt		
Huckins Jabez twin	S	H76D	1722 Mar12 unm.		
Huckins James	S	H76H	1730 Apr22		
Huckins John	D	D2a23	1645abt		
Huckins John	S	H76C	1721 May12 unm.		
Huckins Joseph	S	H76F	1726 Jun24 unm.		
Huckins Mary	A	A12/109	1645ca	1666 Dec 6	1683 Sep24
Huckins Samuel	S	H76A	1718 Sep29 unm.		
Huckins Snow twin	S	H76E	1722 Mar12 unm.		
Huckins Thomas	A	A12/218	1620abt	1642ca	1679ca
Huckins Thomas	S	H76B	1719 Nov30 unm.		
Huckins Thomas Jr	S	H23Ha	1687 Jan15	1717 Aug29	1774 Mar 3
Huckins Thomas Sr	S	H23Haf	1660abt		
Hucklin John	S	D2a23	1620abt	1647ca	
Huckstep Lydia	S	W13Cam	1605abt		
Huet Elizabeth	S	W24Ba	1692 Mar5	1716 Feb16	
Huet Timothy	S	W24Baf	1665abt		
Huggins Esther	A	A12/57	1642ca	1664 Oct19	1697 Mar 7
Huggins John	A	A12/114	1609ca		1670 Jun7
Hugh I Count Clermont	D	D30a36	1065abt		

NAME	DIV.	NUMBER	BIRTH	MARRIAGE	DEATH
Huit Susanna	S	R28Eam	1700abt		
Hull Hannah	S	F16Gam	1675ca		
Humphrey Elizabeth	S	C42Aa	1753ca		
Humphrey Elizabeth	S	C53Aa	1800abt		
Hungerford Elizabeth	S	G11Aa	1665abt	1693ca	
Hungerford Esther	S	G11Ha	1685abt	1710	
Hungerford Hannah	S	G27Ba	1710abt	1731 Sep17	
Hungerford Thomas	S	G11Haf	1660abt		
Hunnewell Patience	S	K17Ab	1674ca	1696 Sep29	1732aft
Hunnewell Richard	S	K17Abf	1650abt		
Hunt Abia	S	R79A	1719 Jul 5		
Hunt Elizabeth	S	C50C	1682		
Hunt Elizabeth	A	A8/107	1697ca	1718 Feb 4	1782 Jul 2
Hunt Enoch	S	C46Da	1658ca		
Hunt Enos	S	C50D	1685		
Hunt Ephraim	S	R12Iaf	1635abt		
Hunt Ephraim Jr.	A	A8/214	1650ca	1678ca	1713ca
Hunt Hannah	S	R79D	1726		
Hunt Jane	S	R79C	1723		
Hunt Judeth	S	Q17Db	1700ca	1725 Nov18	1800bef
Hunt Margaret	A	A3/19	1804ca	1824 Sep21	1876
Hunt Martha	S	R26Cam	1690abt		
Hunt Mary	S	W38Bcm	1640abt		
Hunt Mary	S	C50A	1679		
Hunt Mary	S	B15Ca	1680abt	1704 Apr17	
Hunt Mary	S	R22A	1687 Feb18	1706Feb	1716 Jun10
Hunt Mary	S	R79B	1721	unm.	1789 Mar 8
Hunt Peter	S	C46Ba	1655ca		
Hunt Peter	S	C50B	1681		
Hunt Peter	S	C51Ba	1681		
Hunt Samuel	S	R79F	1727		
Hunt Sarah	S	R79E	1726		
Hunt William	S	R12Ia	1655	1687ca	1727 Jan 2
Hunt William	S	R22B	1693 May17	2 Mar	1769 Jul19
Hunt William	A	A3/38	1803		1817
Huntington Christopher	A	A5/68	1626ca	1652 Oct 7	1691
Huntington Elizabeth	S	T72A	1735 Dec 5		1738 Dec 3
Huntington Elizabeth	S	T72D	1743 Jun12		
Huntington John	A	A5/34	1666 Mar15	1683 Dec 9	1700abt
Huntington Joshua	A	A8/94	1698 Dec30	1718 Oct16	1745 Aug26

NAME	DIV.	NUMBER	BIRTH	MARRIAGE	DEATH
Huntington Lydia	A	A8/47	1727 Mar15	1746 Apr 3	1798 Sep23
Huntington Martha	A	A5/17	1696 Dec 6	1717 Jun20	1779 Aug26
Huntington Mary	S	R117Fa	1707 Aug 4	1731 Dec15	1732 Mar12
Huntington Ruth	S	T72B	1738 Apr19		
Huntington Simon	A	A5/136	1600abt		1633
Huntington Simon	S	T27Ca	1710 Jul 6	1734 Dec13	1764 Sep
Huntington Simon	S	T72C	1740 Dec 2		
Huntington Simon III	A	A8/188	1659	1683	1736
Huntington Thomas	S	T27Caf	1680abt		
Huntinton Joseph	S	R117Faf	1680abt		
Hurd Elizabeth	S	X56C	1722ca		
Hurd Jacob	S	R23Iaf	1685abt		
Hurd Jacob	S	X19Ca	1695 Jan12	1715 Aug11	1775ca
Hurd Jacob	S	X56B	1720 Dec17		
Hurd John	S	X19Caf	1670abt		
Hurd Rebecca	S	X56A	1718ca		
Hurd Sarah	S	R23Ia	1712 Nov20	1739 Jan31	
Hussey Elizabeth	A	A3/55	1759 Nov 3	1783 Dec17	1847 Mar26
Hussey John	A	A3/440	1636	1659	1707
Hussey John III	A	A3/212	1715abt	1750ca	1770ca
Hussey John III=A3/212	A	A3/110	1715abt	1750ca	1770
Hussey John Jr.	A	A3/424	1676 Jan18	1703	1733
Hussey John Jr.=A3/424	A	A3/220	1676 Jan18	1703	1733
Hussey Lydia	A	A3/53	1757 Mar27	1778 Apr16	1843 Sep21
Hussey Rebecca	S	A15Eam	1635abt		
Hussey Recond	A	A3/106	1730abt	1756 Sept6	1784 Apr 5
Hutchins Daniel	S	A14Cb	1632ca	1695 Nov 7	
Hutchins Mary	S	W38Ga	1680ca	1702 May14	1750abt
Hutchins Nicholas	S	W38Gaf	1655abt		
Hutchinson Adam	S	A52A	1712 Nov25		
Hutchinson Anna	S	A51D	1719ca		
Hutchinson Benjamin	S	A52D	1715ca		
Hutchinson Edward	A	A8/122	1678 Jun18	1706 Oct10	1752
Hutchinson Elisha	A	A8/244	1641	1677	1717
Hutchinson Elizabeth	S	A51B	1713ca	unm	1770 Mar27
Hutchinson Elizabeth	A	A8/61	1731 Dec31	1757 Jul21	1793 May 2
Hutchinson Francis	S	A14Ba	1630ca	1676ca	1702 Nov12
Hutchinson Francis	S	A22A	1678ca	1708 May18	1755bef
Hutchinson Francis	S	A51F	1722ca		
Hutchinson Hannah	S	A51G	1725ca		

NAME	DIV.	NUMBER	BIRTH	MARRIAGE	DEATH
Hutchinson John	S	A22C	1683ca	1706ca	1762 Aug 2
Hutchinson John	S	A53D	1717 Nov25		1729 Jul30
Hutchinson Lediah	S	A52E	1721 May 7		
Hutchinson Mary	S	A53A	1708 Nov 7		
Hutchinson Mary	S	A51A	1710ca		
Hutchinson Mehitabel	S	A53B	1711 Jan	unm	1780 Feb13
Hutchinson Phebe	S	A53E	1724 May 5		
Hutchinson Sarah	S	A53C	1715 Jun29		
Hutchinson Sarah	S	A51C	1715ca		1756bef
Hutchinson Thomas	S	A22B	1681ca		1755living
Hutchinson Thomas	S	A51E	1722ca		
Hutchinson Thomas #1	S	A52B	1712 Nov25		d. yng
Hutchinson Thomas #2	S	A52C	1715ca		
Hyde Abigail	S	R89I	1744 Nov 4	unm.	1830Feb 20
Hyde Anna	S	R93D	1753ca		
Hyde Anne	S	G44Aa	1620abt	1647 Sep 8	
Hyde Anne	S	R89B	1727 Oct22		
Hyde Avis	S	R93C	1750ca		
Hyde Dan	S	R89E	1733 May 7		
Hyde David	S	R24Ia	1719 Mar22	1740 Feb24	
Hyde David	S	R93A	1741		
Hyde Eleanor	S	R93G	1760ca		
Hyde Elizabeth	S	R93F	1758Apr 8		
Hyde Hannah	S	R89G	1738 Jul19		
Hyde Hester (Esther)	A	A16/87	1630ca	1652 Mar	1703 Nov13
Hyde Joel	S	R93H	1762ca		
Hyde Katherine	A	A13/143	1610ca	1630	
Hyde Priscilla #1	S	R89D	1731 Apr16		d. yng.
Hyde Priscilla #2	S	R89F	1735 Jun 4	unm.	1759 Jul 4
Hyde Richard	S	G44Aaf	1595abt		
Hyde Samuel	S	R89A	1725 Oct24		
Hyde Samuel =R24Caf	S	R24Iaf	1670abt		
Hyde Samuel Jr	S	R24Ca	1691 Sep10	1724 Jan14	1776 Feb14
Hyde Samuel Sr	S	R24Caf	1670ca		
Hyde Simeon	S	R93B	1749 Sept4		
Hyde Sybil	S	R89C	1731 Apr16		1732 Oct 5
Hyde William	A	A16/174	1600abt		1681
Hyde Zebulon	S	R93E	1755ca		
Hyde Zerviah	S	R89H	1740 Dec15		
Ice Peggy Joyce	S	G59Aam	1935abt		

NAME	DIV.	NUMBER	BIRTH	MARRIAGE	DEATH
Ilbrook Elizabeth	S	R11Dam	1620abt		
Ingalls Ebenezer	A	A6/28	1711 Jul14	1735 Jun 5	1771aft
Ingalls Edmund	A	A6/224	1590ca	1618ca	1648ca
Ingalls Edmund	A	A6/56	1680abt	1705 Nov29	
Ingalls Henry	A	A6/14	1738 Oct12	1761 Dec31	1811ca
Ingalls John	A	A6/112	1626ca	1667 May26	1721 Dec31
Ingalls Mehitable	A	A6/7	1764 Jul21	1786 Nov 5	1821 Dec 4
Ingersole John	S	W38Bcf	1640abt		
Ingersole Thomas	S	W38Bc	1668 Mar28	1720 May17	1732 Nov14
Ingham Alexander	S	N13Da	1735ca		
Inglee John	S	H126B	1723ca		
Inglee Jonathan	S	H34Ea	1700abt	1723 Feb27	1748ca
Inglee Jonathan	S	H126A	1721ca		
Ingraham Almy T	S	C64Ab	1815ca		
Inskeep Ann	A	A3/425	1680abt	1703	
Inskeep Ann=A3/425	A	A3/221	1680abt	1703	
Inskeep John	A	A3/442	1650ca		
Irvine Anne	A	A7/13	1770 Jan14	1786 Apr13	1810aft
Irvine Charles	A	A7/52	1696ca	1733 Jun 7	1779 Mar28
Irvine John	A	A7/208	1615abt		1672aft
Irvine John	A	A7/26	1742 Sep15	1765 Sep	1808 Oct15
Irvine Robert	A	A7/104	1639ca		1728ca
Irwin Archbald Jr.	A	A14/12	1734ca	1757ca	1798 Jan23
Irwin Archibald	A	A14/24	1710abt		
Irwin Archibald III	A	A14/6	1772 Feb13	1798 Oct11	1840 Mar 3
Irwin Elizabeth Ramsey	A	A14/3	1810 Jul18	1831 Aug12	1850 Aug15
Jackson Eleazer	S	A26Daf	1680abt		
Jackson Elizabeth	S	A41D	1695 Mar10		
Jackson Frances	A	A11/45	1615abt	1640 Apr10	1696 Feb26
Jackson Joanna	S	Q20Fbm	1700abt		
Jackson Lydia	A	A2/255	1655ca	1678ca	1725ca
Jackson Mary	S	A41E	1698 May24		
Jackson Mary	S	A26Da	1701 Apr15	1731 Aug22	
Jackson Nathaniel	S	A41C	1693 May15		
Jackson Priscilla	S	A41F	1702 Aug27		
Jackson Thomas	S	A18Ca	1670ca	1690 Oct15	1710bef
Jackson Thomas #1	S	A41A	1691 Jul18		d.yng
Jackson Thomas #2	S	A41B	1692 Jul18		
Jacob Craig Edward	D	D33/17a2	1951 Apr21	1985 Jun 8	
Jacob Deborah	D	D14/23	1635abt		

NAME	DIV.	NUMBER	BIRTH	MARRIAGE	DEATH
Jacob Joseph Jr.	A	A12/26	1705 Aug 3		1790 Dec15
Jacob Joseph Sr	A	A12/52	1673ca	1693 Dec18	1764 Dec26
Jacob Mary	S	W32Cam	1650abt		
Jacob Nicholas	D	D14a24	1600abt		
Jacob Penelope	S	L22B	1761 Sep13		
Jacob Samuel	S	L17Baf	1695abt		
Jacob Samuel	S	L22A	1752 Apr11		
Jacob Seth	S	L17Ba	1720 Mar 6	1751 Oct23	1791living
Jacobs Ann	A	A2/231	1660abt	1685ca	1711aft
Jacobs Deborah	S	X21Cbm	1640abt		
James Hannah	S	B17Fa	1715abt	1740 Apr 3	
James Madgalen	A	A3/183	1675abt		
James Morgan	A	A3/366	1670abt	1694	1737
Janes Abigail	S	R94J	1759 Jan24		1759 Feb12
Janes Ann	S	R94K	1761 Dec12		1779 Oct27
Janes Daniel	S	R94G	1751 Mar17		
Janes David	S	R94A	1736 Dec23		
Janes Eliphalet	S	R94D	1742 Feb23		
Janes Irene	S	R94C	1741 Apr 5		1743 Jun28
Janes Irene	S	R94E	1745 Jul30		
Janes Jonathan	S	R24Ja	1713 Mar12	1735 Mar18	
Janes Jonathan	S	R94B	1738 Jan28		1752 Mar16
Janes Jonathan	S	R94I	1756 Jan 8		
Janes Mary	S	R94H	1753 Apr28		
Janes Solomon	S	R94F	1748 Jun20		
Janes William	S	R24Jaf	1685abt		
Jans Catharina	A	A8/135	1640ca	1660	
Jarrett Elizabeth	A	A15/9	1685abt		
Jarrett John	A	A15/18	1660abt		1700abt
Jasper Elizabeth	D	D21a23	1580abt		
Jauncey Sarah	S	A32Bam	1660abt		
Jeanninge Joseph	S	G41Daf	1475abt		
Jeanninge Phillipa	S	G41Da	1500abt	1538May 3	
Jeffreys Alice	A	A18/83	1590abt		
Jelson Mary	S	T26Fam	1700abt		
Jencks Jonathan	S	C87Ha	1707		
Jenney John	S	W12Aaf	1600abt		
Jenney Lettice	S	W47Ca	1662ca	1696ca	1733ca
Jenney Samuel	S	W47Caf	1635abt		
Jenney Samuel	S	K21Faf	1675abt		

NAME	DIV.	NUMBER	BIRTH	MARRIAGE	DEATH
Jenney Susannah	S	W12Aa	1628abt	1654 Apr 4	1655 Aug18
Jenney Susannah	S	K21Fa	1697 Apr 3	1718 Jan15	1763aft
Jenny Caleb	S	T18Ba	1709 Jun20	1738 Apr 6	1761 Aug25
Jenny Desire	S	T46B	1741 Dec 4		1761bef
Jenny Lettice	S	T18Baf	1685abt		
Jenny Ruben	S	T46A	1739		d.yng
Jenny Sarah	S	K17Aam	1645abt		
Jewell Oliver	S	C17Fa	1745ca		
Jewett David	A	A4/246	1736 Oct27	1757 Nov 3	1780ca
Jewett Elizabeth	S	W10Aa	1580abt		
Jewett Elizabeth	A	A4/123	1771 Feb28	1790 Jan13	1860 Mar 8
Jewett Nathan	A	A4/492	1710	1729	1762
Johns Hannah	A	A3/117	1728ca		1791 Nov15
Johnson Ann	S	X21Aam	1640abt		
Johnson Ann	S	K86D	1726ca		
Johnson Ann	S	K88G	1728abt		
Johnson Barbara	S	A30Aa	1690ca	1708ca	1711aft
Johnson Caleb	S	K88D	1722 Apr 2		
Johnson Caleb	S	K86C	1724ca		
Johnson Content	S	K88F	1726abt		
Johnson Daniel	S	K88I	1732abt		
Johnson Elizabeth	A	A17/53	1637Dec 24	1658 Dec20	1683Aug 13
Johnson Elizabeth	S	K88H	1730abt		
Johnson Elizabeth	S	K86E	1730ca		
Johnson Elizabeth	S	G18Aa	1755abt	1776	1816
Johnson Hannah	A	A3/197	1700abt	1719 April1	
Johnson Isaac	A	A17/106	1610abt	1636Jan 20	1675Dec 19
Johnson Jacob	S	K88J	1734abt		
Johnson James	S	K25Ca	1685ca	1716 Feb 6	1743 Mar18
Johnson James	S	K86B	1718ca		
Johnson James	S	A30Aaf	1765abt		
Johnson Jane	S	K88A	1716 Aug15		
Johnson John	A	A17/212	1575abt		1659
Johnson John	S	K86A	1717ca		
Johnson Joseph	S	K88B	1718 Jan 1		
Johnson Joseph	S	K86F	1733ca		1743 Mar18
Johnson Joshua	A	A3/394	1670abt		1747
Johnson Louise C	A	A11/1a	1775 Feb12	1797 Jul6	1852 May15
Johnson Mary	A	A6/229	1614ca	1636ca	
Johnson Mary	S	R25Fa	1715ca	1743 Nov25	1761 Jul13

NAME	DIV.	NUMBER	BIRTH	MARRIAGE	DEATH
Johnson Mehitable	A	A8/235	1644	1660	1689
Johnson Mercy	S	K88E	1724ca		
Johnson Rebecca	A	A6/17	1719 Nov 2	1742 Oct21	1763 Feb 3
Johnson Robert	S	K25Ea	1690ca	1715 Oct27	1758aft
Johnson Ruth	A	A8/121	1703ca	1723 May 2	1737 Jun27
Johnson Samuel	A	A6/34	1660abt		
Johnson Sarah	S	K88C	1720 Feb 9		
Johnson William Jr.	A	A8/242	1656	1686bef	1729
Johnston Susannah	S	C91Aa	1715ca		
Jones Abagail	S	F30A	1689 Jan18		
Jones Abigail	A	A19/37	1729 Jun29	1747Nov 24	1757Sep 15
Jones Abraham	A	A13/66	1630ca	1656ca	1718 Jan25
Jones Anna	S	W29E	1667 Jan26	1693 Dec 5	1723abt
Jones Anna=W29E	S	H33Lam	1667 Jan26	1693 Dec 5	1723abt
Jones Benjamin	S	W29C	1662 Jan8	1686 Dec14	1716abt
Jones Benjamin	S	F28A	1690 Jan 5		
Jones Benjamin	S	F32B	1721 Julca		
Jones Bethia	S	F31D	1706 Apr 9 unm.		1736 Feb28
Jones Bethia	S	P55D	1706 Apr 9 unm.		1735 Feb28
Jones Cornelius	S	F31E	1709 Jul30		
Jones Cornelius	S	P55E	1709 Jul30		
Jones Deborah	S	P55A	1696 Mar		
Jones Deborah	S	F31A	1696 Mar31		
Jones Ebenezer	A	A19/74	1699Jun 18	1719Nov 18	1758Jul 20
Jones Ebenezer	S	F28E	1706 Jun 6		
Jones Elizabeth	S	F31B	1698 Nov25	1692 May	=F29Da
Jones Elizabeth	S	P55B	1698 Nov25		
Jones Elizabeth	S	C21Da	1766		
Jones Ephraim	S	F16H	1670ca		
Jones Ephraim	S	W29H	1673 Aug18	1708 Nov18	1746 Mar23
Jones Experience	S	F28C	1697 Mar 1 unm.		1749living
Jones Hannah	S	F29E	1694 Sep		1731living
Jones Isaac	S	F29C	1690 Apr		
Jones Jedediah	S	F16C	1656Jan 4	1681Mar 18	1725abt
Jones John	S	F16D	1659 Aug14		1728 Feb27
Jones John	S	W29A	1660 Sep16	1697 Feb17	1739ca
Jones John	S	F30C	1703 Feb12		
Jones John	S	A83A	1734ca		
Jones Joseph	S	W13Da	1635abt	1657 Nov11	1714 Jul18
Jones Joseph	S	W29B	1660 Sep16	1689ca	1727 Apr21

NAME	DIV.	NUMBER	BIRTH	MARRIAGE	DEATH
Jones Joseph	S	F32A	1719 Jun 9		
Jones Josiah	S	F28D	1702 Jun14		1749bef
Jones Mary	S	F16I	1672ca		1691living
Jones Mary	S	W29I	1676 Sep 9		
Jones Mary	A	A19/33	1720ca		
Jones Mary	S	F32D	1727 Apr13		
Jones Matthew	S	F16A	1650ca	1694 Jan14	1749
Jones Maurice	S	A32Caf	1680abt		
Jones Mehitable	S	F16J	1675ca		1696living
Jones Mercy	S	F16E	1666 Nov14		1691aft
Jones Mercy	S	F30B	1700 Jul		1729ca
Jones Patience	S	W29D	1665 Feb20		1688 Feb25
Jones Ralph	S	P23Aaf	1640abt		
Jones Ralph	S	F16F	1669 Oct 1	1696bef	1710aft
Jones Ralph	S	F28B	1692 Jan 5		
Jones Ralph=F16F	S	P23Aa	1669 Oct 1	1696bef	1710aft
Jones Rebecca	S	F28F	1710ca		
Jones Reuben	S	F31G	1712ca		
Jones Robert	S	W13Daf	1600abt		
Jones Ruth	S	W29F	1669 Nov26		
Jones Samuel	A	A19/148	1672	1695ca	1753
Jones Samuel	S	F16G	1675ca	1718 Jun26	
Jones Samuel	S	F32C	1723 Apr 4		
Jones Sarah	A	A13/33	1660ca	1685ca	1700abt
Jones Sarah	S	W29G	1671 Sep12	1/1694 Nov	1752living
Jones Sarah	S	R23Eam	1675abt		
Jones Shubael	S	F16B	1654 Aug27		1692aft
Jones Shubael	S	F29A	1683 Jul17		
Jones Silvanus	S	P55F	1710ca		1735 Jan14
Jones Simon	S	F29B	1685 Apr 5		
Jones Swan	S	A32Ca	1705ca	1730ca	1734ca
Jones Sylvanus	S	F31F	1710ca		1735 Jan14
Jones Thankful	S	F31C	1701 Apr12	m.F29D	
Jones Thankful	S	P55C	1701 Apr12		
Jones Thomas	A	A13/132	1602ca		1680ca
Jones Thomas	S	W29J	1679 Aug15	1703 Feb15	1723 Mar19
Jones Timothy	S	F29D	1692 May	m.F31C	
Joseph Thomas D. Carr	D	D33/17a3	1951Jun 26	1979 Jun 8	
Josslyn Mary	S	G8Aa	1545abt		
Joy John	S	W12Ha	1641 Aug10	1668 Dec25	1677bef

NAME	DIV.	NUMBER	BIRTH	MARRIAGE	DEATH
Joy John	S	W26A	1672 Sep30		
Joyce Mary	S	W41Ebm	1685abt		
Judkins Sarah	S	P12Ham	1640abt		
Judson Ruth	A	A4/507	1664		1744
Keeler Elijah	A	A1/218	1727 Mar17		
Keeler Joseph	A	A1/436	1683ca	1705	1757
Keeler Nathan	S	N15Ia	1788ca		
Keeler Rebecca	A	A1/109	1751 Apr29	1774ca	1812 Feb24
Keen Josiah	S	W45Dbf	1655abt		
Keen Benjamin	S	W45Db	1682 Jul26	1719 Mar15	1733bef
Keen Elizabeth	S	Q23Gam	1685abt		
Keen Hannah	S	Q23Eam	1680abt		
Keene Abigail	S	L17Cam	1690abt		
Keene Hannah	S	A15Cc	1676 Feb 4	1720ca	1738aft
Keene John	S	W13Aaf	1605abt		
Keene Josiah	S	W13Aa	1635abt		
Keene Josiah	S	W27A	1650ca	1681ca	1730abt
Keene William	S	A15Ccf	1655abt		
Kelly Mary	A	A4/459	1678	1700	1747
Kelly Rachel	A	A5/5	1750abt	1792 Mar 4	1805 Apr10
Kelsey Stephen	S	N12Ca	1700abt		
Kempton Joanna	S	W25Bam	1650abt		
Kempton Joanna=W25Bam	S	K35Cam	1650abt		
Kendrick Anna	A	A17/3	1768 Oct30	1790Feb 1	1838 Dec
Kendrick Benjamin	A	A17/6	1723 Jan30	1750 Mar 1	1812Nov 13
Kendrick Caleb	A	A17/12	1694Mar 8	1721 Sep15	1771 Mar31
Kendrick John	A	A17/48	1604ca		1686 Aug29
Kendrick John Jr	A	A17/24	1641Oct 3	1673Oct 23	1721Sep 30
Kendrick Solomon	S	H74A	1706ca		
Kendrick Thomas	S	H74B	1708ca		
Kennon Martha	A	A1/313	1685abt		
Kenny Abigail	S	K132E	1707ca		
Kenny Hannah	S	K132F	1709 May27		
Kenny John Jr	S	K35Aa	1670 Jan15	1695ca	1729bef
Kenny John Sr	S	K35Aaf	1645abt		
Kenny Jonathan	S	K132C	1703 Mar12		
Kenny Mary	S	K132D	1705 Nov22		
Kenny Nathaniel	S	K132G	1715ca		1738aft
Kenny Ruth	S	K132A	1696 Aug 3		
Kenny Thomas	S	K132B	1698 Sep19		

NAME	DIV.	NUMBER	BIRTH	MARRIAGE	DEATH
Kenric Hannah	S	R17Dam	1660abt		
Kent Hannah	S	A46A	1702 Oct 3		
Kent Joseph	S	A21Baf	1645abt		
Kent Josiah	S	A46B	1705 Sep 9		
Kent Samuel	S	A21Ba	1668		1737 May15
Kent Susannah	S	C34Da	1722ca		
Kerrington Bridget	A	A12/239	1602	1630	1676
Kilbourn Mary	A	A12/165	1619ca	1641	1697ca
Kimball Margaret	S	A26Bam	1665abt		
Kindreck Edward	S	H23Fa	1690abt	1704 Dec21	1742ca
King Alice	S	K147K	1734 Feb18		
King Barshaba	S	K147G	1726 Sep 5		
King Charles Henry	A	A4/4	1853 Mar12		1930 Feb27
King Deliverance	A	A14/177	1641	1657	1688
King Ebenezer	S	H58D	1700 Jun15		
King Edward I (Eng)	D	D29/25	1239	REIGN	1272-1307
King Elizabeth	A	A2/113	1671 Feb	1699 Dec12	
King Elizabeth	S	X23Cb	1680bef	1706aft	1757 Jun16
King Esther	S	K147D	1721 May23		
King George VI	D	D28a16	1896	REIGN	(1936-1952
King Hezekiah	S	K36Ia	1690ca	1712 May14	1740 Oct18
King Hezekiah		K147A	1715 Apr 4		
King Joanna	S	H58H	1705ca		
King John	A	A2/226	1638	1660	
King John	S	H20Aa	1660abt		1752ca
King John	S	H58E	1701ca		
King John	S	K147I	1730 Sep11		
King Joseph	S	Q20Baf	1670abt		
King Joseph=Q20Baf	S	Q20Eaf	1670abt		
King Leslie Lynch	A	A4/2	1881 Jul25	1912 Sept7	1941
King Lydia	S	X24Ba	1688 Mar 3	1709 Jan 9	1748 Mar31
King Lynch	A	A4/8	1830abt		
King Marcy	S	K147F	1725 Apr29		d.yng
King Marcy #2	S	K147J	1732 Sep12		
King Margaret	D	D21a24	1550abt		
King Mary	A	A2/177	1639ca	1658	1676ca
King Mary	S	K147E	1723 Apr 5		
King Mary=A2/177	A	A2/207	1639ca	1658	1676ca
King Mehitable	S	Q20Ba	1695ca	1719 Nov 4	1747bef
King Mercy	S	Q20Ea	1707 Feb16	1728 Jul11	1789 Mar29

NAME	DIV.	NUMBER	BIRTH	MARRIAGE	DEATH
King Nathaniel #1	S	H58F	1702		
King Nathaniel #2	S	H58G	1704		
King Philip	S	X23Cbf	1650abt		
King Philip=X23Cbf	S	X24Baf	1650abt		
King Roger	S	H58B	1695ca		
King Samuel	S	K36Iaf	1670abt		
King Samuel	S	H58C	1698 Jun 9		
King Samuel	S	K147C	1719 May24		
King Sarah	S	Q12Ga	1670ca	1692 Nov17	1734aft
King Sarah	S	K147B	1717 May 5		
King Stephen	S	H58A	1693ca		
King William	S	K147H	1727 Nov28		
Kingman Joan	A	A2/201	1624	1651ca	1697aft
Kingsley Samuel	A	A1/358	1683abt	1714ca	1730ca
Kingsley Samuel Jr	S	K22Ga	1662 Jun 6	1690ca	1713 Dec17
Kingsley Samuel Sr	S	K22Gaf	1640abt		
Kingsley Sarah	S	C31La	1728		
Kingsley Silence	A	A1/179	1727 Aug30	1754 Feb26	
Kinney Jane	S	G46Ea	1708ca		
Kinney Louise	S	C47Aa	1710ca		
Kinney Martha	D	D32a25	1780abt		
Kinnicut Joanna	S	R12Nam	1670abt		
Kinnicutt Nancy D	S	C64Ba	1815ca		
Kinsley Abigail	S	K76G	1704ca		
Kinsley Benjamin	S	K76E	1701 May16		
Kinsley Bethiah	S	K76H	1706ca		
Kinsley Hannah	S	K76C	1695ca		
Kinsley Mary	S	K76D	1696ca		
Kinsley Samuel	S	K76A	1690ca		
Kinsley Sarah	S	K76B	1691ca		
Kinsley Susanna	S	K76F	1702ca		
Kline Elizabeth	D	D32a23	1831Dec 22	1855Jun 14	1921Nov 19
Kneeland Abigail	S	F62F	1736ca		
Kneeland Benjamin	S	F62C	1731 May 1		1741 Nov27
Kneeland Benjamin Jr.	S	F22Ka	1705 Nov20	1725 Dec 8	1746 Jun20
Kneeland Benjamin Sr.	S	F22Kaf	1670abt		
Kneeland Jabez	S	F62G	1738 Apr14		1747bef
Kneeland Mehitable #1	S	F62D	1732 Dec10		d. yng
Kneeland Mehitable #2	S	F62E	1734 Jun15		1740 Mar27
Kneeland Phebe	S	F62B	1729 Jan15		

NAME	DIV.	NUMBER	BIRTH	MARRIAGE	DEATH
Kneeland Sarah	S	F62A	1728 Aug26		1747bef
Knight Magdalena	A	A4/469	1688ca	1710ca	
Knight Magdalena	A	A1/367	1688cat	1710ca	=A4/469
Knight Priscilla	S	W24Ia	1686 Sep	1706 Mar5	1775 Aug3
Knight Richard	S	A18Ba	1665ca	1695 Apr10	1698
Knowles Barbara	S	H27Gam	1660abt		
Knowles Barbara=H27Gam	S	X19Aam	1660abt		
Knowles Malithiah	S	R78C	1715 Jan 4		1721living
Knowles Mary	S	H28Gam	1665abt		
Knowles Mary	S	R78B	1713 Sep		
Knowles Mehitable	S	H19Eam	1650abt		
Knowles Nathaniel	S	R22Aa	1686 May15	1706Feb	1732
Knowles Rebecca	S	R78A	1710 Jan30		
Knowles Ruth	S	X15Fam	1660abt		
Knowles Samuel	S	R22Aaf	1660abt		
Knowlton Mary	S	F21Ca	1681 Mar29	1706 Jan26	1749 Mar 9
Knowlton Thomas	S	F21Caf	1655abt		
Kunst Heyltje Jans	A	A7/65	1660abt	1682 Dec26	1730ca
Kunst Heyltje Jans	A	A8/65	1660abt	1682 Dec26	1730living
Kunst Jan Barentsen	A	A7/130	1620abt	=A8/130	1670living
Kunst Jan Barentsen	A	A8/130	1620abt	=A7131	1670living
Laeckens Elizabeth	A	A7/149	1645abt		1682aft
Lambe Frances	A	A13/39	1655abt	1678	
Lambe Richard	A	A13/78	1630abt		
Lamoreaux Daniel	D	D33af22	1760abt		
Lamoreaux Mary	D	D33a22	1797 May 6	1813 Dec 2	1847Oct 28
Landon Elizabeth	A	A14/35	1684ca	1701ca	1719 Jul 3
Landon Sylvanus	A	A14/140	1620abt		1681
Landon Thomas	A	A14/70	1655abt		1701ca
Lane Ebenezer	S	R21Faf	1675abt		
Lane Elizabeth	S	W32Gam	1660abt		
Lane George	S	R76D	1731		
Lane Hannah	S	R76A	1724 May27		
Lane Irene	S	R76B	1725 Jan 6		
Lane Jane	S	A29Aam	1685abt		
Lane John	A	A19/212	1660	1683	1714
Lane John Jr	A	A19/106	1691Oct 20	1714Dec 31	1763Sep 23
Lane Lucy	S	R76C	1728 Jun 6		d yng
Lane Lucy	S	R76E	1734 Mar16		
Lane Martha	S	K22Iam	1640abt		

NAME	DIV.	NUMBER	BIRTH	MARRIAGE	DEATH
Lane Peter	S	R21Fa	1697 May25	1723ca	1764 Mar17
Lane Sarah	S	H23Dbm	1650abt		
Lane Sarah	S	P21Oam	1690abt		
Lane Sarah	S	R76H	1745 Oct 6		
Lane Susanna	A	A19/53	1720Apr 8	1741Apr 16	
Lane Sybil	S	R76G	1741 Jul26		
Langdon Mercy	A	A3/461	1655ca		
Langler Sarah	S	K36Ham	1670abt		
Langstaff Henry	S	F19Iaf	1625abt		
Langstaff John	S	F19Ia	1664ca	1694 Nov13	1742aft
Langton Helen	D	D29a15	1490abt		
Langton Joseph	A	A16/78	1630abt	1652bef	
Langton Rachel	A	A16/39	1645ca	1667 Jun10	1673Mar 7
Langton Roger	A	A16/156	1600abt		1671bef
Lapham Rebecca	S	K22Aa	1645ca	1679 Apr16	1717ca
Lapham Thomas	S	K22Aaf	1620abt		
Latham Elizabeth	S	K14Fa	1665ca	1687 Aug 2	1730 Nov16
Latham Hannah	S	K22Da	1655ca	1677ca	1725aft
Latham Mercy	S	K25Dam	1660abt		
Latham Robert	S	K22Daf	1630abt		
Latham Robert=K22Daf	S	K14Faf	1630abt		
Lathrop Abigail	A	A5/35	1665 May	1683 Dec 9	
Lathrop Barnabus	S	W41Eaf	1660abt		
Lathrop Elizabeth	S	F15Aa	1659 Dec18	1680 Dec29	1718aft
Lathrop Elizabeth	S	W49Abm	1660abt		
Lathrop Hannah	A	A8/191	1677	1698	1721
Lathrop Israel Jr	S	R24Fb	1687 Feb 1	1747 Jun 9	1758living
Lathrop Israel Sr	S	R24Fbf	1680abt		
Lathrop John	A	A5/140	1584	1610	1653
Lathrop Joseph	S	F15Aaf	1625abt		
Lathrop Prudence	S	R121A	1748 Mar16		
Lathrop Samuel	A	A5/70	1622ca	1644 Nov28	1700 Feb29
Lathrop Sarah	S	W41Ea	1685ca		
Laughton Margaret	S	Q23Gbm	1685abt		
Lawrence Hannah	A	A19/35	1721 Feb25		
Lawrence Jonathan	A	A19/70	1696Jun 14	1720ca	1773
Lawrence Mary	A	A8/145	1645abt	1671	
Lawrence Nathaniel Jr	A	A19/140	1661	1689ca	1736
Lawson Dorothy	A	A8/255	1665ca	1691	
Lawton Elizabeth	S	K18Gam	1635abt		

NAME	DIV.	NUMBER	BIRTH	MARRIAGE	DEATH
Lazell Abner	S	K96H	1734 Aug22 unm		1757living
Lazell Jacob	S	K96E	1729 Mar25		
Lazell Joshua	S	K26Eaf	1665abt		
Lazell Joshua #1	S	K96A	1717 May 5		d.yng
Lazell Joshua #2	S	K96B	1719 Sep30		
Lazell Lydia	S	K96C	1722 Jan 5		
Lazell Mary	S	K96D	1725ca		
Lazell Sarah twin	S	K96G	1732 Apr30		
Lazell Simon	S	K26Ea	1688 Sep12	1716 Apr 5	1745
Lazell William twin	S	K96F	1732 Apr30		
Le Despencer Hugh	D	D29a23	1290abt		
Le Mahieu Marie	A	A5/145	1570abt	1596 Jan13	
LeBaron Elizabeth	S	R122B	1745 Dec21		
LeBaron Francis	S	R27Cbf	1675abt		
LeBaron Francis	S	R122D	1749 Sep 3 unm.		1773 Sep
LeBaron Isaac	S	R122A	1743 Jan25		
LeBaron Lazarus	S	R27Cb	1698 Dec26	1743 May 2	1733 Sep 2
LeBaron Lemuel	S	R122C	1747 Sep 1		
LeBaron Margaret	S	R122G	1755 Jul 5		1756 Nov20
LeBaron Priscilla	S	R122F	1753 Aug 3		
LeBaron William	S	R122E	1751 Aug 8		
Leach David Jr	S	K29Fa	1706 May20	1734 Jan22	1756bef
Leach David Sr	S	K29Faf	1685abt		
Leach Elizabeth	S	K108B	1735 Mar 2		d.yng
Leach James	S	K108A	1734 May 6		
Leach Mercy	S	K108C	1737 Feb16		
Leach Sarah	S	C51Ga	1700ca		
Leach Sarah	S	K108D	1739 Mar17		
Leach Susannah	S	K108E	1743 Jul 7		
Lecraft Hannah	S	H14Aam	1630abt		
Lee Abigail	S	A26Fa	1713 Apr 9	1730ca	1803 Apr
Lee Alice Hathaway	D	D8a16	1835abt		
Lee Alice Hathaway	A	A07/1a	1861 Jul29	1880 Oct27	1884 Feb14
Lee Ann	S	A32B	1700ca	1720ca	1739living
Lee Ann	S	A85A	1734 Jan30		
Lee David	S	A26Faf	1690abt		
Lee Dorothy	D	D12a19	1586abt		
Lee Elizabeth	S	A32C	1703ca	2 mar.	1750ca
Lee Elizabeth	A	A18/5	1710ca	1738bef	
Lee George Henry	S	A85C	1737 Jul 2		

NAME	DIV.	NUMBER	BIRTH	MARRIAGE	DEATH
Lee Hancock	S	A32E	1709ca	1733 Jan23	1762 Oct
Lee Hancock	S	A85D	1740 Apr 7		
Lee Hancock =A15Fa	A	A18/10	1653ca	1700	1709May 25
Lee Hancock =A18/10	S	A15Fa	1653ca	1700	1709 May25
Lee Henry	S	A85H	1750 Oct28		
Lee Isaac	S	A32A	1701ca	unm	1727ca
Lee John	A	A18/40	1629Feb 23		
Lee John	A	A12/34	1657 Jan 2	1686ca	1711 Nov13
Lee John	S	A32D	1707	unm	1789 Aug11
Lee John	S	A85E	1743 Sep20		
Lee Mary	D	D1a23	1630abt	1651 Dec16	
Lee Mary	S	A85B	1735 Jun 4		
Lee Richard	A	A18/20	1617ca	1641ca	1664ca
Lee Richard	S	A15Faf	1630abt		
Lee Richard	S	A85I	1753 Jul31		1787living
Lee Robert	D	D1af23	1600abt		
Lee Ruth	A	A16/161	1600abt	1619ca	1642
Lee Sarah	A	A12/17	1692 Apr24	1721 May 4	1738 Jul13
Lee Sarah Alexander	S	A85G	1749 Jul 2		
Lee Walter	A	A12/68	1630ca		1717 Feb 9
Lee Willis	S	A85F	1745 Aug16		1776
Leonard Abiel	S	X64I	1717ca		1739
Leonard Abigail	S	X64E	1703 Oct20		
Leonard Anna	S	X64D	1701 Dec16		1724 Jan31
Leonard Ephraim	S	X64F	1705 Jan16		
Leonard Experience	S	K25Iam	1690abt		
Leonard George	S	X21Ca	1671 Apr18	1695 Jul 4	1716 Sep 5
Leonard George	S	X64B	1698 Mar 4		
Leonard Hannah	S	X22Aam	1655abt		
Leonard Marcy	S	X64G	1708 Apr29		d.yng
Leonard Mary	S	X64H	1713 Jan17		
Leonard Nathaniel	S	X64C	1699 Mar 9		
Leonard Phebe	S	X64A	1696 Mar11		
Leonard Thomas	S	X21Caf	1650abt		
Leslie Isabel	A	A7/215	1655abt	1674	
Lester Hannah	A	A3/237	1686	1708	1769aft
Lester Peter	A	A3/474	1660abt	1685	1742ca
Lettice Dorothy	S	W32Aam	1645abt		
Lettice Dorothy=W32Iam	S	W35Iam	1650abt		
Lettice Elizabeth	S	K11Cb	1637ca	1669 Nov18	1693 Oct31

NAME	DIV.	NUMBER	BIRTH	MARRIAGE	DEATH
Lettice Thomas	S	K11Cbf	1610abt		
Lewin John	S	X89A	1727		
Lewin Joseph	S	X28Ca	1700ca	1723 Nov 4	
Lewin Meriah	S	X89B	1730		
Lewis Abigail	A	A8/57	1701 Nov15	1727ca	1776ca
Lewis Esther	S	K30Bam	1675abt		
Lewis George	S	H23Db	1673	1716 Jul21	1769 Nov
Lewis James	S	H23Dbf	1650abt		
Lewis Nathan	S	K30Cbf	1690abt		
Lewis Nathaniel	A	A8/114	1676 Oct 1	1699 Nov25	1752 Feb24
Lewis Rachel	S	G50Aa	1745abt		
Lewis Richard	A	A1/182	1735ca	1758ca	
Lewis Sarah	S	H19Gam	1650abt		
Lewis Sarah	S	H24Eam	1655abt		
Lewis Sarah	S	K30Cb	1713 Jun24	1734 Oct 1	1767 Dec23
Lewis Sarah	S	C37Fa	1763ca		
Lewis Susannah	A	A1/91	1761 Mar25	1779 Feb28	1822 Jul27
Lewis Thomas	S	C31Ba	1705abt		
Lewis William Jr.	A	A8/228	1622ca	1671	1690ca
Light Elizabeth (Lyte)	A	A10/65	1545ca	1565ca	1599ca
Lightfoot Catharine	A	A3/195	1670abt	1700 Dec13	1729
Lightfoot Thomas	A	A3/390	1640ca		1725ca
Lillie Anna	A	A1/75	1760ca	1777 Apr 3	1804 Dec
Lillie John	A	A1/150	1728 Aug 8	1754 Aug16	1765ca
Lillie Theophilus	A	A1/300	1690	1725	1760
Lincoln Abraham	A	A13/4	1744 May13	1770 Jul 9	1786 May
Lincoln Abraham	A	A13/1	1809 Feb12	1842 Nov 4	1865 Apr15
Lincoln Edward	D	D13a24	1575ca	1600ca	1639
Lincoln Edward=D13a24	A	A13/128	1575	1600ca	1639
Lincoln Elizabeth	S	L17Dam	1715abt		
Lincoln Isabella	D	D11a25	1400abt		
Lincoln James	S	H19Ga	1680abt	1714 Feb10	
Lincoln James	S	H56A	1716 May25	1738 Sept2	
Lincoln John	A	A13/8	1716 May 3	1743 Jul 5	1788 Nov
Lincoln Lydia	S	H56B	1718 Jul4		
Lincoln Mary	S	X21Dam	1645abt		
Lincoln Mary	S	W31Jam	1660abt		
Lincoln Mercy	S	W29Jam	1655abt		
Lincoln Mordecai	A	A13/32	1657 Jun14	1685ca	1727 Nov28
Lincoln Mordecai Jr	A	A13/16	1686 Apr24	1714 Sep14	1736 May12

NAME	DIV.	NUMBER	BIRTH	MARRIAGE	DEATH
Lincoln Rachel	S	X15Fc	1680ca	1746 Apr24	
Lincoln Rachel	S	H26Ha	1696 Nov 8	1717 Feb13	1758bef
Lincoln Samuel	A	A13/64	1620ca		1690 May26
Lincoln Sarah	S	P21Ma	1717ca	1731 Jul28	1777 Oct 1
Lincoln Thomas	S	H19Gaf	1650abt		
Lincoln Thomas	S	H26Haf	1675abt		
Lincoln Thomas	S	P21Maf	1690abt		
Lincoln Thomas	A	A13/2	1778 Jan 6	1806 Jun12	1851 Jan17
Lindsey Christopher	A	A12/212	1615abt		1669
Lindsey John	A	A12/106	1640ca	1667 Jun 6	1705ca
Lindsey Sarah	A	A12/53	1674 Mar 2	1693 Dec18	
Linnell Bethia	S	H13Bb	1640ca	1701 Apr 7	1726 Mar25
Linnell David	S	X17Daf	1650abt		
Linnell Hannah	S	F16Cam	1630ca		
Linnell Robert	S	H13Bbf	1615abt		
Linnell Susanna=X30Bam	S	X17Da	1673ca	1695 Nov14	1754 Nov23
Linnell Susannah	S	X30Bam	1675abt		
Lippincott Rebecca	A	A3/509	1684	1704	1748ca
Lippington Daniel	S	F19Aa	1655ca	1677 Sep19	1694
Lippington Daniel	S	F42E	1687 Jul17		1694 Feb17
Lippington Dorothy #1	S	F42B	1679 Sep25		1682 Jan 5
Lippington Dorothy #2	S	F42D	1683 Mar 3		
Lippington Hannah	S	F42C	1681 Feb 1		1682 Jan 2
Lippington Richard	S	F42A	1678 Apr24		
Liscomb Elizabeth	S	K34Dam	1665abt		
Liscomb Elizabeth	S	Q18Cam	1665abt		
Lisk Amy	S	R92G	1752 Jan15		
Lisk Andrew	S	R24Ha	1714ca	1736 Jun15	1797 Feb20
Lisk Andrew	S	R92D	1744 Nov 4		
Lisk Ann	S	R92B	1740 Mar24		
Lisk Betty	S	R92E	1746 Nov22		
Lisk Huldah	S	R92H	1754 Aug18		
Lisk Martha	S	R92C	1742 May30		
Lisk Sarah	S	R92F	1748 Mar 7		
Lisk William	S	R92A	1738 Dec17		1789living
Lister Rosamond	D	D29a12	1565abt		
Little Abigail	S	W13A	1635ca	1656ca	1660bef
Little Abigail	S	W31F	1687ca		
Little Anna	S	W32A	1673 Aug23	1694 Jul 3	1706 Oct16
Little Barnabas	S	W32H	1691 Feb 8		1691 Feb23

NAME	DIV.	NUMBER	BIRTH	MARRIAGE	DEATH
Little Bethia=W31J	S	L15Bbm	1693ca	1712 May22	1751Oct 9
Little Bethiah	S	W31D	1681abt		1689ca
Little Bethiah	S	W31G	1689ca		d. yng
Little Bethiah	S	W31J	1693ca	1712 May22	1751 Oct9
Little Charles	S	W31E	1685 Oct15	1712 Oct 9	1724 Apr25
Little Charles	S	W52Ca	1685 Oct15	1712 Oct 9	1724 Apr25
Little Daniel	A	A4/450	1692	1712	1777
Little David	S	W32D	1680 Mar17	1703 Dec 2	1779 Feb 7
Little Dorothy	S	W31B	1676 Aug11		d.yng
Little Edward	S	W33D	1698 Jul17	1717 Nov 7	1776ca
Little Ephraim	S	W13G	1650 May17	1672 Nov22	1717 Nov24
Little Ephraim	S	W32B	1676 Sep27	1698 Nov29	1723 Nov24
Little Hannah	S	W13C	1637ca	1661 Jan25	1710 May13
Little Isaac	S	W13F	1646ca	1673ca	1699 Nov24
Little Isaac	S	W31C	1677 Feb21	1703ca	1758 Feb 2
Little Isaac=W13F	S	W52Caf	1646ca	1673ca	1699 Nov24
Little Isaac=W31C	S	L15Baf	1677 Feb21	1703ca	1758 Feb 2
Little John	S	W32E	1682 Mar18	1708 Apr 8	1767 Feb26
Little Lemul	S	W31K	1690abt	1717 Oct 1	1723 Mar21
Little Mary	S	W32F	1685 Jul 7		d.yng
Little Mary	S	L15Ba	1704 Sept9	1725 Feb16	1772abt
Little Mercy	S	W13E	1642ca	1666 Nov	1693 Feb 8
Little Mercy	S	W32C	1678 Feb26	1699 Oct 1	1751aft
Little Nathaniel	S	W31H	1690 Apr12		1716bef
Little Patience	S	W13D	1639ca	1657 Nov11	1723 Oct25
Little Ruth	S	W13B	1636ca	unm.	
Little Ruth	S	W32G	1686 Nov23	1710 Nov28	1732 Oct 1
Little Samuel	S	W13I	1656ca	1682 May18	1707 Jan16
Little Samuel	S	W33C	1691 Nov7	2 Mar	1739 Jan8
Little Sarah	S	W33B	1685 Jul23		1741 Mar19
Little Sarah	A	A4/225	1717 Nov11	1741 Jul28	1807 Dec11
Little Thomas	S	W11Ba	1605ca	1633 Apr19	1671ca
Little Thomas	S	W13H	1653abt	unm.	1676ca
Little Thomas	S	W31A	1674 Dec15	1698 Dec 5	1712 Dec22
Little Thomas	S	W33A	1683 Jun28		1699 Apr 2
Little William	S	W31I	1692 Feb27	1712 Jun19	1734
Littlefield Deliver.	A	A16/35	1640abt		1730ca
Littlefield Edmund	A	A16/140	1592	1614	1661
Littlefield Edmund Jr	A	A19/374	1690abt		
Littlefield Esther	A	A19/187	1714	1731	

NAME	DIV.	NUMBER	BIRTH	MARRIAGE	DEATH
Littlefield Francis	A	A16/70	1619ca	1650bef	1712 Jan
Livingston Gilbert	A	A1/360	1690	1711	1746
Livingston Gilbert J	A	A1/90	1758 Oct14	1779 Feb28	1833 Apr 7
Livingston James	A	A1/180	1728 Mar29	1751 Nov11	1790 Jun 2
Livingston Judith	A	A1/45	1785 Sep 4	1806 Jun26	1858 Feb28
Lloyd Henry	A	A8/86	1685 Nov28	1708 Nov27	1763 Mar18
Lloyd James	A	A8/172	1653ca	1676	1693ca
Lloyd Margaret	A	A8/43	1713 Jun 1	1732 Dec19	1756 Sep25
Lobdell Ebenezer	S	T20Fa	1694 Nov 1	1745 Dec18	1748 Mar18
Lobdell Isaac	S	T20Faf	1670abt		
Logan George Lyons	S	G57Aa	1925ca	1946 Dec23	
Logan Katherine H	S	G58A	1948 Oct18	2 Mar	
Logan Lawrence Lyons	S	G58B	1951 Jan29	1970Sep 12	
Logan Thomas	S	G58C	1953 Sep16	1987 April1	
Lombard Benjamin	S	W17Da	1642 Aug26	1672 Sep19	1704aft
Lombard Benjamin Jr	S	W48B	1675 Sep22	(2)1725May	1753 Jan13
Lombard Hope	S	W48C	1682 Mar26	1707	
Lombard Mercy	S	W48A	1673 Nov 2	1701 Mar20	1753 Dec 6
Lombard Mercy	S	B15Ba	1673 Nov 2		1753Dec 6
Lombard Patience	S	X16Ca	1684 Sep	1704 Apr 6	1725ca
Lombard Thomas	S	W17Daf	1615abt		
Longfollow Anne	A	A4/453	1683	1703	1758
Loomis Abigail	S	R24Jam	1685abt		
Loomis Abigail	S	N12Ea	1710ca	1731May 7	
Loomis Joseph	A	A16/238	1590abt	1614	1658
Loomis Philip	S	N12Eaf	1685abt		
Loomis S. (male)	S	N11Fb	1670abt		
Loomis Samuel	S	N11Ja	1680abt		
Loomis Sarah	S	G10Aam	1617ca	1640 Sep28	1667
Loomis Sarah	A	A16/119	1617ca	1640 Sep28	=G10Aam
Lord Deborah	A	A4/493	1698ca	1729	1777ca
Lord Elizabeth	S	G31Ba	1739	1758	1819
Lord Jane	A	A12/185	1615ca	1639	1655abt
Lord Mary	S	F22Eam	1670abt		
Lord Theopolus	S	G31Baf	1715abt		
Loring Hannah	S	K27Bam	1665abt		
Loring Ignatius	S	K40Caf	1700abt		
Loring Mary	S	K40Ca	1725 Feb 1	1745 Oct25	1802 May17
Loring Welthean	S	R11Bam	1600abt		
Lothrop Barnabas	S	H25Aaf	1645abt		

NAME	DIV.	NUMBER	BIRTH	MARRIAGE	DEATH
Lothrop Barnabas	S	F18Ba	1686 Oct22	1706 Feb20	1756 Apr 8
Lothrop Bershuah	S	H25Aa	1671 Jun25	1690 May26	1742aft
Lothrop Bershuah=H25Aa	S	H30Bam	1671 Jun25	1690	1742aft
Lothrop Hannah	S	F39B	1712 Jul 6		
Lothrop Jane	S	F12Ba	1614 Sep	1635 Apr 8	1683bef
Lothrop John	S	F12Baf	1590abt		
Lothrop John	S	F18Baf	1665ca		
Lothrop John	S	F39A	1709 Aug25		1756living
Lothrop Mary	S	K27Gam	1675abt		
Lothrop Mary=K27Gam	S	K25Gam	1675abt		
Lothrop Susanna	S	A25Fam	1670abt		
Lovel Phebe	S	W46Fam	1660abt		
Lowe Joanne	A	A15/19	1660abt		
Lowe Michael	A	A15/38	1635abt		
Lucas Benoni	S	K31Baf	1660abt		
Lucas Benoni	S	T15Baf	1665abt		
Lucas Joanna	S	T15Ba	1691 Feb 9	1721 Sep28	1768 Jan 1
Lucas Joanna	S	R28Iam	1705abt		
Lucas John	S	W55A	1687 Jan24		1696 Jan31
Lucas Joseph	S	W55B	1689 Oct26	2 Mar	1742 Sep 4
Lucas Mary	S	K31Ba	1684 May 4	1708 May20	1759 Sep24
Lucas Patience	S	W55D	1696 Jan 2	1717 Dec17	1760abt
Lucas Samuel	S	W18Da	1661 Sep15	1686 Dec16	1715 Jan17
Lucas Thomas	S	W18Daf	1635abt		
Lucas William	S	W55C	1692 Oct19	1722 May 4	1769
Lucken Johann	A	A7/92	1655abt		1742ca
Lucken Wilhelm	A	A7/184	1620ca		1694aft
Ludden Benjamin	A	A6/114	1650ca	1678ca	1690 Jan28
Ludden Eunice	A	A6/57	1680abt	1705 Nov29	1726af
Ludden James=A6/57	A	A6/228	1611ca	1636ca	1692ca
Ludlow Gabriel	A	A14/138	1587 Feb		1640abt
Ludlow Sarah	A	A14/69	1635ca	1662	1668ca
Ludlow Thomas	A	A14/276	1555ca	1582	1607 Nov
Lukens Elizabeth	A	A7/23	1730abt	1753 Jan16	
Lukens William	A	A7/46	1688 Feb22	1710 Nov27	1739 Jun15
Lukin Alice	A	A15/71	1625ca		1698 Jun22
Lumbart Sarah	S	X17Aa	1666 Dec	1689 May30	1753 May 5
Lumbart Thomas	S	X17Aaf	1640abt		
Lumbert Bathsheba	S	H33Ham	1695abt		
Lumbert Elizabeth	S	R24Aam	1675abt		

NAME	DIV.	NUMBER	BIRTH	MARRIAGE	DEATH
Lumbert Thomas(Lombard	S	X16Caf	1660abt		
Lunt Sarah	S	K36Hbm	1685abt		
Lusher Lydia	S	R21Eam	1670abt		
Luther John	S	C25Ia	1685ca		
Luther Lydia	S	G33Aa	1790abt		
Lyde Edward Jr	S	L13Ba	1662ca	1694 Nov29	1723ca
Lyde Edward Sr	S	L13Caf	1640abt		
Lydia Paine	S	P21Lam	1675abt		
Lyford John	A	A13/130	1595abt		1634abt
Lyford Martha	A	A13/65	1624ca		1693 Apr10
Lyman Benjamin	A	A8/112	1674 Aug10	1698 Oct27	1723 Oct14
Lyman Catherine Robbin	A	A8/7	1825 Jan12	1843 Nov 1	1896 Feb10
Lyman John	A	A8/224	1623	1655	1690
Lyman Joseph	A	A8/56	1699 Aug22	1727ca	1763 Mar30
Lyman Joseph III	A	A8/14	1767 Oct22	1811 Oct27	1847 Dec11
Lyman Joseph Jr.	A	A8/28	1731 May 4	1756 Aug 5	1804 Oct21
Lyon Joshua	S	C72Fa	1710ca		
Lyon Rachel McCoy	S	G50Gb	1755abt		
Lytle Elizabeth	A	A3/21	1794 Aug27		1831 Apr18
Lytle George	A	A3/168	1710abt		1757
Lytle George	A	A3/42	1759ca		
Lytle Guy	A	A3/84	1730abt	1751 Mar25	1764 Mar20
MacVarlo Rachel	S	P210a	1717	1735 Nov27	1736 Mar28
MacVarlo James	S	P210af	1690abt		
Machet Jeanne	A	A4/465	1670abt		1705ca
Mack Deborah	S	G31Bam	1715abt		
Mackay Elizabeth	A	A7/55	1725abt	1766	1766ca
Macomber Abiah	S	X78H	1724 Jun 8		1742living
Macomber Abial	S	K64D	1717 Oct 4	unm.	1740
Macomber Anna	S	X78I	1726 Jan 2		
Macomber Elijah	S	X78F	1718 Oct25		
Macomber Elizabeth	S	Q32D	1715 Feb22		
Macomber Elizabeth	S	X78D	1715 Mar15		
Macomber James	S	X78E	1717 Sep12		
Macomber Joanna	S	Q32F	1722 Apr20		1791 Mar 2
Macomber Job	S	K64G	1723 Feb13		
Macomber John	S	K20Ha	1687 Jul11	1711 Sep11	1723
Macomber John	S	X78C	1713 Feb10		
Macomber John	S	K64E	1719 Jan 8		
Macomber John Jr	S	X24Ca	1681 Mar18	1707 Mar17	1747 Dec14

NAME	DIV.	NUMBER	BIRTH	MARRIAGE	DEATH
Macomber John Sr	S	X24Caf	1660abt		
Macomber Joseph	S	X78J	1732 Mar28		
Macomber Josiah	S	X78B	1711 Feb19		
Macomber Marcy	S	K64B	1714 Mar28		
Macomber Mary	S	K64C	1715 May 4	unm.	1799bef
Macomber Mary	S	X78G	1721 Jul30		1742bef
Macomber Nathaniel	S	X78A	1709 Feb 9		
Macomber Onesimus	S	Q32E	1720 Jun18		
Macomber Philip	S	K64A	1712 Sep11		
Macomber Sarah	S	Q32C	1713 Oct27		
Macomber Thomas	S	Q32A	1710 Apr28		
Macomber Thomas Jr	S	Q15Da	1684 Jul 2	1709 Jun14	1771 Oct 5
Macomber Thomas Sr	S	Q15Daf	1660abt		
Macomber Ursula	S	Q32B	1711 Dec10		1748Nov 10
Macomber William	S	K20Haf	1665abt		
Macomber William	S	K64F	1721 Mar15		
Macomson Jane	A	A1/481	1688ca		
Magny Jean	A	A4/464	1670abt		1703ca
Magoun David	S	T22Caf	1705abt		
Magoun Hannah	S	T22Ca	1729 Jul13	1745 Jan24	1803 Aug23
Mahieu Hester =K10Aa	S	W11Cam	1585abt	1603 Jul 4	1665aft
Mahieu Hester =W11Cam	S	K10Aa	1585abt	1603 Jul 4	1665aft
Mahieu Jennie	S	K10Aaf	1560abt		
Mahurin Bathsheba	S	Q22Ca	1700ca	1724 Apr 8	1748 Jan 5
Mahurin Hugh	S	Q22Caf	1675abt		
Makepeace Abigail	S	X62A	1686 Nov25		
Makepeace Anna	S	X62B	1689 May 4		1745ca
Makepeace Deborah	S	X62F	1699 Jan13		1750living
Makepeace Lydia	S	X62E	1696 Nov 4		
Makepeace Mary	S	X62C	1691 Mar22		
Makepeace Priscilla	S	X62J	1710ca		
Makepeace Remember	S	X62I	1707ca		
Makepeace Seth	S	X62G	1702 Jun23		
Makepeace Susanna	S	X62D	1694 Sep23		1748bef
Makepeace Thomas	S	X62K	1712ca		
Makepeace William	S	X62H	1704ca		
Makepeace William Jr	S	X21Aa	1662	1685 Dec 2	1736 Dec
Makepeace William Sr	S	X21Aaf	1640abt		
Maker Bursel	S	H88G	1727 Dec 6		
Maker David	S	H88H	1731 Jul26		

NAME	DIV.	NUMBER	BIRTH	MARRIAGE	DEATH
Maker Elizabeth	S	H88E	1722 Jun22		
Maker Hannah	S	H88I	1734 Dec11		
Maker James	S	H26Iaf	1670abt		
Maker John	S	H26Ia	1692ca	1714 Nov 5	
Maker Jonathan	S	H88D	1720 Jun13		
Maker Joshua	S	H88F	1725 Sep16		
Maker Mary	S	H88C	1718 Jul13		
Maker Peleg	S	H88A	1720 Aug21		
Maker Thankful	S	H88B	1716 May25		
Malmsbury Benjamin	A	A3/62	1779 Nov 6	1801	1854 June3
Malmsbury Hope	A	A3/31	1804 Sept7	1823	1865 May10
Malmsbury John	A	A3/248	1710ca	1736 Sep18	1770abt
Malmsbury John Jr.	A	A3/124	1744 Jun 7	1771ca	1800abt
Manahan Elizabeth	S	G51Ca	1785ca		
Manahan Hugh	S	G50Da	1745abt		
Manchester Sarah	S	K18Ea	1675ca	1699ca	
Manchester Susanna	S	K20Ga	1686ca	1706ca	1775ca
Manchester William	S	K18Eaf	1650abt		
Manchester William	S	K20Gaf	1665abt		
Manley Hannah	S	R28Kcm	1720abt		
Mann Rebecca	S	W28Ib	1686 Mar22	1716 Jun14	1767 Nov7
Mann Richard	S	W28Ibf	1660abt		
Manney Elida Vanderb.	A	A4/29	1802 Jan 1		1877ca
Manney John	A	A4/232	1698 Aug31	1729 Jan23	
Manney John	A	A4/58	1763 Dec27	1796 Sept1	1839 Jun25
Manney Wines	A	A4/116	1730 Mar22	1758 Sep16	1811 Nov26
Manning Abigail	S	R64C	1722 Nov25		
Manning David	S	R64F	1726 Jan14		
Manning Hezekiah	S	R64B	1721 Aug 8		
Manning Josiah	S	R64A	1720 Mar18		
Manning Samuel	S	R19Ja	1690 Jan14	1719 Apr20	1727 Jun 3
Manning Samuel	S	R64E	1725 Oct22		
Manning Sarah	S	R64D	1724 Feb22		1727living
Mansfield Hannah	S	W23ca	1670ca	1712 Apr24	
Margaret of Montdidier	D	D30/36	1065abt		
Mariner Mary	S	T25Cam	1670abt		
Maris Elizabeth	A	A3/413	1665	1685	1708aft
Markham Priscilla	A	A12/93	1654ca	1675 Nov18	1682 Apr18
Markham William	A	A12/186	1621ca		1689
Marot Anne	A	A15/15	1700abt		

NAME	DIV.	NUMBER	BIRTH	MARRIAGE	DEATH
Marot Jean	A	A15/30	1680abt		
Marquet Anne	S	G43Bam	1545abt		
Marsh John	A	A12/246	1586ca		1627ca
Marsh Lydia	A	A12/123	1625ca	1645 Nov17	1658aft
Marshall Elizabeth	D	D30a17	1602	1627	=A12/153
Marshall Elizabeth	A	A12/153	1602		1641
Marshall Mary	S	N11Ea	1675abt		
Marshall Rebecca	S	W56Cam	1670abt		
Marshall Samuel Jr	S	W56Da	1694abt	1717 May23	1731living
Marshall Samuel Sr	S	W56Daf	1670abt		
Marshfield Josiah	S	R18Haf	1675abt		
Marshfield Katherine	S	R18Ha	1702 Feb 2	1722 Oct 4	1788 Jun 7
Marshfield Sarah	A	A8/239	1656	1676	
Marston Benjamin	S	L20A	1730 Sep22	1755 Nov13	1792 Aug10
Marston Benjamin Jr	S	L15Da	1696 Feb24	1729 Nov20	1754 May22
Marston Benjamin Sr	S	L15Daf	1670abt		
Marston Elizabeth	S	L20B	1731 Mar 4	1756 Sep22	1798 Sep 2
Marston John	S	L20F	1740 May29	unm	1761 Apr25
Marston Lucy	S	L20H	1744 Sep		d. yng.
Marston Lucy	S	L20I	1748 Feb 4	1769 Apr15	1793 Oct25
Marston Patience	S	L20C	1733 Jan2	1754 Nov7	1767 Apr20
Marston Penelope	S	L20E	1739 Jul29		d. yng.
Marston Penelope	S	L20G	1742 Aug		1754 bef
Marston Sarah	S	L20D	1735 Mar19	unm	1772 Apr 2
Martiau Elizabeth	A	A10/23	1615abt	1641ca	1686 Feb10
Martiau Nicholas	A	A10/46	1591ca		1657ca
Martin Abi Cumberland	S	C41G	1764		
Martin Abigail	S	Q19Eam	1700abt		
Martin Abigail	S	C34E	1725ca		
Martin Abigail	S	C36J	1763		
Martin Albert H	S	C56C	1858		
Martin Amanda	S	C60G	1805		
Martin Amasa	S	C63C	1791		
Martin Anderson	S	C42C	1776		
Martin Andruss	S	C52D	1795		
Martin Ann	S	C25E	1678		
Martin Ann	S	C28B	1699		
Martin Ann	S	C31J	1725		
Martin Anne	S	C36C	1745		
Martin Anthony	S	C42B	1760		

NAME	DIV.	NUMBER	BIRTH	MARRIAGE	DEATH
Martin Asa	S	C41F	1760		
Martin Augusta R	S	C56A	1854		
Martin Barbery	S	C31F	1713		
Martin Benjamin	S	C32J	1720abt		
Martin Benjamin	S	C31L	1734		
Martin Benjamin	S	C41C	1751		
Martin Benjamin	S	C37F	1762		
Martin Benjamin	S	C60E	1797		
Martin Bosworth	S	C63B	1785		
Martin Bruth	S	C58D	1907		
Martin Calvin	S	C61K	1768		
Martin Caroline	S	C55A	1826		
Martin Charles August	S	C56B	1856		
Martin Chloe	S	C40G	1756		
Martin Constant	S	C41A	1745		
Martin Cyrus	S	C61I	1763		
Martin Daniel	S	C28C	1702		
Martin Daniel Jr	S	C29A	1730abt		
Martin David	S	C35E	1748		
Martin Desire	A	A6/61	1684 Mar20	1707 Jul10	1727 Sep12
Martin Ebenezer	S	C25H	1684		
Martin Ebenezer	S	C34C	1720ca		
Martin Ebenezer	S	C52C	1791		
Martin Edna	S	C57C	1882		
Martin Edna Rosamond	S	C58A	1900		
Martin Edward	S	C32A	1700		
Martin Edward	S	C39B	1744		
Martin Edward	S	C61A	1746		
Martin Elhanan	S	C61M	1771		
Martin Elizabeth	S	C31I	1722		
Martin Elizabeth	S	C60A	1787		
Martin Ephraim	A	A1/370	1676	1699	1734
Martin Ephraim=A1/370	S	C25D	1676	1699	1734
Martin Ephriam	S	C36H	1758		
Martin Ephriam	S	C53B	1800abt		
Martin Ephriam II	S	C39A	1736		
Martin Ephriam Jr	S	C32C	1704		
Martin Erford A	S	C57B	1879		
Martin Ernest J	S	C57A	1878		
Martin Freelove	S	C41B	1748		

NAME	DIV.	NUMBER	BIRTH	MARRIAGE	DEATH
Martin George B	S	C56E	1861		
Martin Gideon	S	C36D	1747		
Martin Gideon	S	C37B	1753		
Martin Grace	A	A12/61	1656ca	1676 Aug11	172? Aug 2
Martin Hannah	S	C31B	1705abt		
Martin Hannah	S	C36A	1741		
Martin Hannah	S	C40H	1763		
Martin Hannah	S	C60H	1807		
Martin Helen	S	C56D	1860		
Martin Hezekiah	S	C28A	1697		
Martin Hezekiah	S	C31H	1719		
Martin Hezekiah	S	C36B	1743		
Martin Hezekiah	S	C52A	1787		
Martin Hezekiah Sr	S	C36E	1748		
Martin Holden	S	C37H	1765		
Martin Hopestill	S	C32E	1710		
Martin Hopestill	S	C38B	1725		
Martin Hopestill	S	C61C	1750		
Martin Horace Anderson	S	C64B	1812ca		
Martin Hosea	S	C60B	1790		
Martin Ira K	S	C60I	1812		
Martin James	S	C37D	1757		
Martin James	S	C40I	1766		
Martin James W	S	C55B	1829		
Martin James W	S	C69Ia	1829		
Martin Jemima	S	C25A	1672		
Martin Jemima	S	C34A	1717		
Martin Jemima	S	C31K	1727ca		
Martin Jesse	S	C54A	1782		
Martin Joanna	S	C31C	1705abt		
Martin Johanna	S	C25G	1682		
Martin John	S	C24A	1634		
Martin John	A	A6/122	1652 Jan	1681 Jun27	1720 Aug28
Martin John	S	C25C	1674		
Martin John	S	C31D	1709		
Martin John	S	C34B	1718ca		
Martin John	S	C30B	1732		
Martin John	S	C35A	1735		
Martin John	S	C52B	1789		
Martin John	S	C53A	1800abt		

NAME	DIV.	NUMBER	BIRTH	MARRIAGE	DEATH
Martin Joseph	S	C35C	1739		
Martin Joseph	S	C61G	1758		
Martin Joseph S	S	C60C	1791		
Martin Joseph Winthrop	S	C52E	1801		
Martin Josiah	S	C62C	1798		
Martin Judeth	S	C32F	1714		
Martin Judeth	S	C40C	1747		
Martin Judith	S	C25I	1686		
Martin Kent	S	C63A	1783		
Martin Kingsley	S	C37H	1767		
Martin Levi	S	C40D	1749		
Martin Lippit	S	C54B	1785		
Martin Lois	S	C38E	1733		
Martin Lucy	S	C41D	1755		
Martin Lucy	S	C36G	1756		
Martin Luther	S	C42A	1752		
Martin Luther	S	C64A	1811		
Martin Lydia	S	C32H	1715ca		
Martin Lydia	A	A1/185	1718 Jul17	1737 Oct 6	1798 Dec21
Martin Lydia	S	C40J	1770		
Martin Lydia	S	G33Da	1800abt		
Martin Manassah	S	C32I	1720ca		
Martin Manasseh	S	C25F	1681		
Martin Manley Eugene	S	C58C	1904		
Martin Marcy	S	C31E	1710abt		
Martin Marcy	S	C37A	1750		
Martin Martha	S	C61H	1761		
Martin Mary	S	C31G	1715		
Martin Mary	S	C38A	1723		
Martin Mary	S	C35B	1737		
Martin Mary	S	C36F	1753		
Martin Meletiah	S	C25B	1673		
Martin Meletiah	S	C28E	1706		
Martin Meletiah	S	C30C	1736		
Martin Molly	S	C40F	1754		
Martin Nathan	S	C28D	1704		
Martin Nathan	S	C35D	1743		
Martin Nathaniel	S	C34D	1721ca		
Martin Otis	S	C53C	1800abt		
Martin Patience	S	C40A	1743		

NAME	DIV.	NUMBER	BIRTH	MARRIAGE	DEATH
Martin Peleg	S	C30A	1731		
Martin Perservance	S	C32D	1706		
Martin Phebe	S	C40E	1751		
Martin Phebe	S	C54D	1791		
Martin Philip	S	C61F	1756		
Martin Porter	S	C58B	1902		
Martin Rebecca	S	C28F	1708		
Martin Rebeckah	S	C38D	1729		
Martin Richard	A	A6/244	1609	1631	1694ca
Martin S.	S	N13Ib	1750abt		
Martin Samuel Perry	S	C41E	1758		
Martin Sarah	S	C31A	1705abt		
Martin Sarah	S	C36I	1761		
Martin Sarah	S	C54C	1788		
Martin Sarah	S	C60D	1794		
Martin Serepta	S	C61L	1769		
Martin Seth	S	C32G	1715		
Martin Seth	S	C40B	1745		
Martin Simeon	S	C61E	1754		
Martin Simeon	S	C37C	1755		
Martin Sterry	S	C62B	1794		
Martin Sullivan	S	C62A	1789		
Martin Sylvanus Jr	S	C61B	1748		
Martin Sylvanus Sr	S	C38C	1727		
Martin Thankful	S	C32B	1702		
Martin Thomas	S	C37E	1759		
Martin Thomas P	S	C60F	1802		
Martin Timothy	S	C28G	1711		
Martin Valentine	S	C61D	1753		
Martin Wheeler	S	C61J	1765		
Martin Whipple	S	C54E	1796		
Martin William	A	A12/122	1620ca	1645 Nov17	
Martin Zattie	S	C56F	1866		
Mason Abigail	A	A1/355	1700abt	1731	1749
Mason Agnes	A	A17/225	1550abt		
Mason Arthur	A	A11/62	1630ca	1655 Jul 5	1707 Mar4
Mason Esther	S	C37Ca	1756ca		
Mason Hezekiah	S	C28Fa	1705ca		
Mason John	S	C31Ja	1725ca		
Mason Mary	A	A11/31	1655abt	1678 Nov29	1740 June

NAME	DIV.	NUMBER	BIRTH	MARRIAGE	DEATH
Mason Priscilla	S	R12Kam	1655abt		
Mason Prudence	S	C37Ha	1768ca		
Mason Samuel	S	C61Ca	1749ca		
Masters Lydia	S	K12Cam	1620abt		
Masters Lydia =K12Dam	S	K16Dam	1620abt		
Masters Lydia =K16Dam	S	K12Dam	1620abt		
Masterson Mary	S	R11Bcm	1620abt		
Matchett Susannah	A	A16/37	1623ca	1650ca	1717Dec 10
Mathewson Deborah	S	C87Ea	1714		
Matthews Miriam	A	A3/29	1786 Aug11	1807 Dec 9	1860after
Matthews Oliver	A	A3/464	1670abt		
Matthews Oliver	A	A3/116	1721 Nov28		1824 Jan17
Matthews Thomas	A	A3/232	1693 Mar29	1718 Jul28	1766 Dec19
Matthews William	A	A3/58	1755 Mar		1844 Feb20
Maverick Abigail	S	A13C	1644ca	1662ca	1685bef
Maverick Elizabeth	S	A13D	1649ca	2 mar.	1690ca
Maverick Elizabeth	S	A13F	1649ca		
Maverick John	S	A11Baf	1590abt		
Maverick Mary	S	A13B	1640ca		1655 Feb24
Maverick Moses	S	A11Ba	1611ca	1635bef	1685 Jan28
Maverick Rebecca	S	A13A	1639ca	1658 Jun 3	1659 Nov 4
Maverick Remember	S	A13G	1652ca	1670ca	1690ca
Maverick Samuel	S	A13E	1647ca		1668living
Maxson Rebecca	S	K20Cam	1650abt		
May Dorothy	D	D27a25	1597ca	1613 Dec10	1620 Dec 7
May Elizabeth	A	A1/67	1730 Dec 3	1754ca	1789aft
May Henry	S	R10Aaf	1575abt		
May Hezekiah	A	A1/134	1696 Dec14	1721 Apr27	1783 Sep 5
May Joanna	S	Q23Cam	1675abt		
May John	S	W46Da	1688ca	1712 Apr 8	1754 Jun 3
May John Jr	A	A1/268	1663ca	1684	1729
May Susanna	S	C61Ka	1770ca		
Mayhew Abiah	S	R22Bam	1675abt		
Mayhew Mary	S	W31Aa	1680 May25	1698 Dec 5	1753aft
Mayhew Matthew	S	W31Aaf	1655abt		
Mayhieu Hester	S	H11Gam	1590abt		
Maynard A.K.	S	N17Eaf	1830abt		
Maynard Lulie E	S	G54Aam	1862 Nov27	1883 Nov18	1940 Apr
Maynard Lulie E=G54Aam	S	N17Ea	1862 Nov 7	1883 Nov18	1940 Apr
Mayo Abigail	S	X38C	1728 Jun18		d.yng

NAME	DIV.	NUMBER	BIRTH	MARRIAGE	DEATH
Mayo Alice	S	H17Fb	1686 Apr29	1719 Mar 3	1748 Oct12
Mayo Bathsheba	S	X54C	1705 Apr27		
Mayo Deborah	S	H31D	1708		1717bef
Mayo Eliakim	S	X54D	1707 Apr 1		1736bef
Mayo Elizabeth	S	Q13Ebm	1635abt		
Mayo Elizabeth	S	X14Dam	1650abt		
Mayo Elizabeth	S	H22Eam	1655abt		
Mayo Elizabeth	S	H23Aam	1655abt		
Mayo Elizabeth	S	X54A	1702 May 1		
Mayo Hannah	S	H31B	1678ca	1707ca	1760abt
Mayo Hannah	S	H26Da	1680ca	1702 Apr14	1719 Jul 5
Mayo Hannah	S	H26Db	1681 Jan 8	1720 May12	1746aft
Mayo John	S	H14Aaf	1630abt		
Mayo John	S	H26Dbf	1660abt		
Mayo John	S	H26Faf	1660abt		
Mayo John	S	H26Gaf	1660abt		
Mayo John	S	H31A	1676ca		1717bef
Mayo John #1	S	X38A	1724 Mar15		d.yng
Mayo John #2	S	X38B	1725 Oct 4		1760living
Mayo Joshua	S	X54E	1712 May28		
Mayo Lydia	S	H27Ga	1694 Jun12	1714 Jun 4	1745 Mar18
Mayo Mary	S	H26Ga	1694 Oct26	1712 Apr17	1771 Jan15
Mayo Mehitable	S	X38D	1732 May 9		
Mayo Mercy	S	H27Ham	1655abt		
Mayo Mercy	S	H26Fa	1688 Apr23	1707 May26	1764aft
Mayo Mercy	S	X54F	1718 Feb27		
Mayo Nathaniel Jr	S	X16Ga	1681 Jul 7	1721 Mar15	1761ca
Mayo Nathaniel Sr	S	H17Fbf	1660abt		=X16Gaf
Mayo Nathaniel Sr	S	X16Gaf	1660abt		
Mayo Ruth	S	X38E	1734 Jul31		1760living
Mayo Samuel	S	H26Daf	1655abt		
Mayo Samuel	S	X19Daf	1660abt		
Mayo Sarah	S	X19Da	1690ca		1726bef
Mayo Thankful	S	H31C	1680ca	1717 Mar20	1730abt
Mayo Thankful	S	X54B	1703 Jan10		
Mayo Thomas Jr	S	X19Aa	1678 Apr 3	1701 Apr 3	1769 Jul
Mayo Thomas Sr	S	X19Aaf	1655abt		
Mayo Thomas Sr=X19Aaf	S	H27Gaf	1655abt		
Mayo William	S	H14Aa	1654 Oct 7	1676aft	1690abt
McCleary Samuel	S	C17Ja	1750ca		

NAME	DIV.	NUMBER	BIRTH	MARRIAGE	DEATH
McComas Alexander	A	A3/172	1695ca	1713 Nov19	1761 Jan
McComas Alexander Jr.	A	A3/86	1720abt	1747 Jul27	
McComas Daniel	A	A3/344	1670abt		1697
McComas Elizabeth	A	A3/43	1760ca		
McCulley Elizabeth	A	A3/123	1730abt	1753ca	
McCulley John	A	A3/246	1705abt		1773
McCune Nancy R	A	A1/61	1799 Jun16	1816 Mar18	1834
McDowell Jane	A	A14/13	1736 Apr19	1757ca	1814 Aug 6
McDowell William	A	A14/26	1680ca	1715ca	1759ca
McElwain Jane	A	A3/37	1755ca	1780ca	1834abt
McElwain Moses	A	A3/74	1726abt		1760ca
McElwain Robert	A	A3/148	1700abt		1760
McFarlain Catharine	A	A9/27	1801 Jan 1	1815 Jan15	1883 Feb21
McFarlin Abigail	S	R112F	1756ca		
McFarlin David	S	R112H	1759ca		
McFarlin Elijah	S	R28Ea	1722ca	1745 Nov14	1777 Nov29
McFarlin Elijah	S	R112B	1751ca		
McFarlin Hannah	S	R112C	1752ca		
McFarlin Joseph	S	R112D	1754ca		
McFarlin Laurana	S	R112E	1755 Aug18		
McFarlin Mary	S	R112A	1746 Jul18		
McFarlin Saba	S	R112G	1758ca		
McFarlin Solomon	S	R28Eaf	1700abt		
McHenry Daniel	S	C21Ca	1759		
McLelland Catharine	A	A1/49	1765ca	1785 Feb22	
McNeal Mary J	S	G52Fa	1815ca		
McQueen Nancy	S	G32Da	1770ca		
McVeagh Edmond	A	A7/90	1675abt		1739
McVeagh Elizabeth	A	A7/45	1699ca	1726 May25	1791 Jan
Meddowes Mary	A	A19/209	1644	1665	
Meeker Mary	S	R16Bbm	1670abt		
Meeks John	S	C14Ca	1715ca		
Mendall John	S	Q12Caf	1635abt		
Mendall Mercy	S	Q12Ca	1666 Aug 3	1690ca	1711aft
Mendenhall Aaron	A	A3/206	1690 Sep20	1715 Mar16	1765 Apr30
Mendenhall Benjamin	A	A3/408	1662	1689	1740
Mendenhall Benjamin Jr	A	A3/204	1691 Mar 5	1717 Mar 9	1743 May13
Mendenhall Jemima	A	A3/51	1757 Dec 9	1779 Jun30	1851 Dec 5
Mendenhall John	A	A3/412	1659	1685	1759
Mendenhall Joshua	A	A3/102	1727 Nov11	1755	1816 Feb 5

NAME	DIV.	NUMBER	BIRTH	MARRIAGE	DEATH
Mendenhall Lydia	A	A3/103	1730abt	1755	
Mercer Harriet	A	A1/25	1802ca	1821 May22	1869 Oct24
Mercer John	A	A1/50	1775ca	1793 Oct11	
Mercer Robert	A	A1/200	1696 Dec19	1727 Aug 1	
Mercer Robert	A	A1/100	1737 Dec22		
Mercer Thomas	A	A1/400	1671abt		
Merll Mary	S	H30Bam	1660abt		
Merrett Mary	S	P21Kam	1685abt		
Merrick Abigail	S	H90A	1700abt		
Merrick Abigail	A	A12/31	1702 Apr 5	1725 Jan18	1791 Aug16
Merrick Abigail	S	H92D	1724 Jul10	1742 Sep 9	
Merrick Alice	S	H91H	1713ca		
Merrick Barnabas	S	H92F	1728ca		
Merrick Benjamin	S	H27D	1674	2 Mar	1745abt
Merrick Benjamin	S	H91I	1717 Mar20		
Merrick Benjamin	S	H90F	1719 May 2		
Merrick Bezaleel	S	H92I	1736 Nov12		
Merrick Constant	S	H91B	1701ca		
Merrick Deborah	S	H75C	1712 Jun20		
Merrick Elizabeth	S	X26Bam	1690abt		
Merrick Gideon	S	H91E	1702ca		
Merrick Hannah	S	H91A	1700ca	1721 Oct12	1764 Feb
Merrick Hannah	S	H92G	1731 Oct 9		
Merrick Isaac	S	H90D	1713ca		
Merrick Jabez	S	H75H	1722 Feb		
Merrick Jethro	S	H75I	1725 Aug		
Merrick John	A	A12/62	1658 Nov 9	1687 Feb 4	1748 Apr10
Merrick John	S	H27F	1680ca	1703Jun	1753 Apr18
Merrick John	S	H90B	1709ca		1743living
Merrick Joseph	S	H92C	1722 Jun 6		
Merrick Joshua	S	H27G	1680ca	1714 Jun 4	1738ca
Merrick Joshua	S	H75A	1708 Apr17		
Merrick Lydia	S	H92E	1726 Sep20		
Merrick Mary	S	H13Ba	1650 Nov 4	1667 May22	1700abt
Merrick Mary	S	H92H	1734 May17		
Merrick Mercy	S	H91D	1705ca	1726 Oct13	
Merrick Nathaniel	S	H27E	1675	1699ca	1743 Nov13
Merrick Nathaniel	S	H90E	1714 Feb23		
Merrick Oliver	S	H75E	1716 Dec14		
Merrick Priscilla	S	H91F	1705ca		

NAME	DIV.	NUMBER	BIRTH	MARRIAGE	DEATH
Merrick Rebecca	S	H27A	1668 Nov28	1690ca	1724bef
Merrick Rebecca	S	H90C	1711ca	1728 Sep30	1743living
Merrick Ruth	S	H27H	1684	1710 Nov 2	1766 Feb13
Merrick Ruth	S	H91G	1709ca		
Merrick Samuel	S	H27I	1686ca		1715bef
Merrick Samuel	S	H75D	1714 Jan 5		
Merrick Sarah	S	H23Bam	1655abt		
Merrick Sarah	S	K26Gam	1690abt		
Merrick Sarah	S	H91J	1720 Jul 5		
Merrick Sarah=K26Gam	S	K39Jam	1690abt		
Merrick Seth	S	H92B	1720 May13		
Merrick Simeon	S	H75G	1721 Apr		
Merrick Snow	S	H75B	1709 Jan15		
Merrick Stephen	S	H23Ga	1673 Mar26	1706 Nov21	1731 Mar11
Merrick Stephen	S	H27C	1673 Mar26	1706 Nov21	1731 Mar11
Merrick Thomas	A	A12/124	1620ca	1653 Aug21	1704 Sep 7
Merrick Thomas	S	H92A	1717 Feb10		
Merrick Thomas	S	H75F	1718 Dec12		
Merrick William	S	H13Baf	1625abt		
Merrick William	S	H23Gaf	1650abt		
Merrick William	S	H27B	1670 Aug 1		1670 Mar20
Merrick William	S	H91C	1703ca		
Merrick William Jr	S	H13Da	1643 Sep15	1667 May23	1732 Oct30
Merrick William Sr	S	H13Daf	1625abt		
Merrill Abel	A	A17/10	1690ca	1714 Nov15	1753 Mar29
Merrill Daniel	S	R20Caf	1675abt		
Merrill Elizabeth	A	A17/5	1727 Feb22	1746 Aug 2	
Merrill John	A	A17/20	1662 Feb16		1705May15
Merrill Nathaniel	A	A17/160	1570	1592	1626
Merrill Nathaniel	A	A17/80	1601ca	1630ca	1654Mar 16
Merrill Nathaniel Jr	A	A17/40	1634ca	1661Oct 15	1682 Jan 1
Merrill Susannah	S	R20Ca	1700 Aug18	1717ca	1746living
Messenger Andrew	A	A16/120	1620abt		1681bef
Messenger Daniel	A	A16/30	1683ca	1703Jan 28	1751ca
Messenger Samuel	A	A16/60	1650bef		1685
Messenger Susannah	A	A16/15	1704Nov 30	1727Jun 7	
Metcalf Abiel	S	R43C	1709 Nov15	twin	
Metcalf Abigail	S	R43A	1708 Jun13		
Metcalf Abijah	S	R43B	1709 Nov15	twin	
Metcalf Alice	S	R43D	1712 May 2	twin	

NAME	DIV.	NUMBER	BIRTH	MARRIAGE	DEATH
Metcalf Azuba	S	R43K	1723		
Metcalf Delight	S	R43H	1719 May 1		
Metcalf Elizabeth	S	R43G	1716 Mar 6		
Metcalf Hannah	S	R43E	1712 May 2 twin		
Metcalf Jonathan	S	R17Daf	1660abt		
Metcalf Joseph	S	R17Da	1683 Apr 2	1707 Sep 3	1723 May24
Metcalf Mary	S	R43F	1715 Dec17		
Metcalf Sarah	S	R43I	1720 Feb10		
Metcalf Sybil	S	R43J	1722 Nov10		1722Dec 26
Mickle Robert	A	A3/386	1650abt		1696living
Mickle Sarah	A	A3/193	1675 Oct13	1696 Jan25	
Miles Katherine	D	D23a25	1595abt		
Milhous Franklin	A	A3/6	1848 Nov 4	1879 Apr16	1919 Feb 2
Milhous Hannah	A	A3/3	1885 Mar 7	1908 Jun25	1967 Sep30
Milhous John	A	A3/192	1669 June	1696 Jan25	1710 May10
Milhous Joshua Vickers	A	A3/12	1820 Dec31	1847 Dec23	1893 Apr15
Milhous Thomas	A	A3/384	1650abt		1669living
Milhous Thomas	A	A3/96	1699 Mar14	1721 Apr 1	1770
Milhous William	A	A3/48	1738 Jun12	1767 Oct22	1826 Jan24
Milhous William Jr.	A	A3/24	1783 June4	1807 Jun10	1874 Mar15
Millard Abiathar	A	A16/6	1744Jun 22	1761Sep 30	1811
Millard Ann	A	A1/381	1708	1725	1751
Millard John	A	A16/96	1610abt		1685ca
Millard Nehemiah	A	A16/24	1668 Jun 6	1696 Mar 3	1751 Jul23
Millard Phebe	A	A16/3	1781Aug 12	1796ca	
Millard Robert	A	A16/48	1632ca	1662Dec24	1699Mar 16
Millard Robert	A	A16/12	1702Apr 20	1725Mar 7	1784ca
Miller Agnes	A	A3/75	1730abt		1762living
Miller David	S	P57C	1708 Apr17		
Miller Elias	S	P57D	1711 Aug17		
Miller Elizabeth	S	W51Ea	1688 Feb18	1709 Jul 7	1729living
Miller Elizabeth	A	A3/179	1713 May 7	1732 Aug25	1771after
Miller Faith	S	W44Dam	1645abt		
Miller Faith	S	W29Aam	1650abt		
Miller Faith =W29Aam	S	W42Cam	1650abt		
Miller Francis	S	P57A	1702 Jan11		
Miller Gayen	A	A3/358	1675abt		1742
Miller Hannah	S	P16Ba	1670ca	1696ca	1745bef
Miller Hannah	S	P57E	1723 Apr12		d. yng.
Miller James	A	A3/194	1669 Apr24	1700 Dec13	1749

NAME	DIV.	NUMBER	BIRTH	MARRIAGE	DEATH
Miller James	A	A3/150	1700abt		
Miller John	S	K14Caf	1640abt		
Miller John	S	W51Eaf	1660abt		
Miller John	S	P57B	1704 Oct28		
Miller John Jr	S	P23Ca	1669	1701 Feb12	1727 Aug 8
Miller John Sr	S	P16Baf	1645abt		
Miller John Sr =P16Baf	S	P23Caf	1645abt		
Miller Lucy	S	C19Ea	1760ca		
Miller Lydia	S	K14Ca	1661 May18	1681 Dec29	1727 Mar 1
Miller Robert	A	A3/388	1645abt		
Miller Sally	A	A4/13	1819 Apr18	1834	1873 Jan30
Miller Sarah	A	A3/97	1701 Oct10	1721 Apr 1	1775 Aug26
Miller Susan	S	C64Aa	1812ca		
Mills William W	S	G21Ca	1855abt	1875 Oct12	
Miner Grace	A	A5/33	1670 Sep20	1688 Apr11	1753 Apr16
Miner John	A	A5/66	1635 Aug30	1658 Oct21	1719 Sep17
Miner Thomas	A	A5/132	1608	1634	1690
Mitchell Alice	S	R30B	1714 Dec23		
Mitchell Benjamin	S	K82E	1710 Jan23		
Mitchell Betty	S	X58F	1741 Mar22		
Mitchell Edward	S	R14Ba	1647ca	1708 Aug26	1716 Mar15
Mitchell Edward	S	R30C	1715 Feb 7		
Mitchell Elizabeth	S	K13A	1628	1645 Dec 6	1685bef
Mitchell Elizabeth	S	A60I	1722 Apr27		
Mitchell Experience	S	K11Ba	1609ca	1627aft	1687ca
Mitchell Experience	A	A2/150	1620abt		1689
Mitchell Experience	S	R14Baf	1625abt		
Mitchell George	S	K82B	1685ca		
Mitchell Isaac	S	A60G	1714 Jan20	unm	1738 Aug24
Mitchell Jacob	S	A24Ba	1671ca	1701 Nov18	1744 Dec21
Mitchell Jacob Sr	S	A24Baf	1650abt		
Mitchell James	S	X58A	1718 Nov 4		
Mitchell Jeremiah	S	K84C	1710ca		1747living
Mitchell John	S	K23B	1664ca	1690ca	1699aft
Mitchell John	S	K83A	1695abt		
Mitchell John	S	K84B	1707 Aug19		1757bef
Mitchell Jonathan	S	K84A	1704 May25		
Mitchell Joseph	S	K23C	1669ca	1703 Jul 5	1764bef
Mitchell Joseph	S	K82C	1690ca		
Mitchell Joseph	S	H33Haf	1695abt		

NAME	DIV.	NUMBER	BIRTH	MARRIAGE	DEATH
Mitchell Lydia	S	A60E	1710 Jun20		
Mitchell Margaret	S	K82D	1695ca		
Mitchell Mary	S	A60D	1707 Mar 7		
Mitchell Mary	S	R30A	1709 Jul19		
Mitchell Mary	S	K84E	1714 Feb 5		
Mitchell Mercy	S	X58C	1722 May 4		
Mitchell Noah	S	A60F	1712 Sep16		
Mitchell Rebeckah	S	A60B	1704 Oct19		
Mitchell Sara	S	H33Ha	1719 Oct14	1747 Jan21	
Mitchell Sarah	A	A2/75	1641	1662ca	1731aft
Mitchell Sarah	S	A60H	1717 Apr29		
Mitchell Seth	S	A60C	1705 Mar16		
Mitchell Seth	S	X58E	1738 Dec11		
Mitchell Susannah	S	A60A	1702 Jan15		
Mitchell Tabitha	S	X58B	1720 Jul19		
Mitchell Thomas	S	K13B	1631ca	1659ca	1688bef
Mitchell Thomas	S	K23A	1660ca	1682bef	1738aft
Mitchell Thomas	S	K82A	1682ca		
Mitchell Thomas	S	K84D	1712 May30		
Mitchell William	S	X58D	1725 Jun31		
Mitchell William Jr	S	X19Ea	1691ca	1717 Apr10	1767aft
Mitchell William Sr	S	X19Eaf	1670abt		
Moigne Anne	S	G44Aam	1595abt		
Montanje Phebe	S	C17Ia	1755ca		
Montfort Clarissa	A	A1/39	1760 abt	1794 Jun19	1845
Montgomery Elizabeth	S	P14Aam	1625abt		
Moor Hiram D	A	A19/6	1812 Dec26	1838 Dec 5	1888 Jan 9
Moor John	A	A19/12	1785ca	1811 Sep 9	
Moor JosephineVictoria	A	A19/3	1846 Mar14	1868May 6	1885Mar 14
Moore Ann	A	A3/109	1744 Feb16	1760 Oct25	1784 Sep16
Moore James	A	A3/176	1690abt	1714 Jul 7	1759
Moore James	A	A3/88	1735abt	1759 Apr 5	1777ca
Moore Joseph	A	A3/44	1759 Dec15	1782 Jan10	1832 Feb18
Moore Joseph Dickinson	A	A3/22	1794 Oct21	1825 Jun23	1860
Moore Margaret	S	K13Aam	1600abt		
Moore Mary	S	A13Dam	1620abt		
Moore Mary Louise	A	A3/11	1832 Dec24	1850 May30	1918 Nov18
Morey Ann	S	C49Hc	1705ca		
Morey Hannah	S	W21E	1674abt	1694ca	1730bef
Morey John	S	W21D	1666ca		1699aft

NAME	DIV.	NUMBER	BIRTH	MARRIAGE	DEATH
Morey Jonathan	S	W12Cb	1633ca	1659 Jul 8	1700ca
Morey Jonathan	S	W21C	1661ca	1690 Jan24	1732ca
Morey Uriah	S	C49Ka	1705ca		
Morgan Daniel	S	G12Ca	1712	1730	1773
Morgan Desire	S	G13A	1736	1752	1801
Morgan Hannah	A	A16/63	1642Jul 18	1660Nov 20	1706 Dec16
Morgan James	A	A16/126	1607ca	1640Aug 6	1685
Morgan James	S	G12Caf	1680	1704ca	1721
Moris Elizabeth	A	A13/37	1660abt		
Morrill Hannah	A	A17/55	1636 Sep	1652 Nov 5	1717 Oct 6
Morrill Isaac	A	A17/110	1588ca		1661Dec 20
Morrill Mary	S	P12Fam	1630abt		
Morris Lewis	A	A3/452	1655ca		1694
Morris Mary	A	A15/11	1685abt		
Morris Mary	S	C51Ca	1691ca		
Morris Richard	A	A3/226	1690ca		1763
Morris Sarah	A	A3/113	1715abt	1739ca	
Morse Abigail	A	A3/241	1696 Jan 1	1718 July1	1739 May25
Morse Elizabeth	D	D21/22	1610abt		
Morse John	D	D22/22	1635abt		
Morse Joseph	A	A3/482	1671	1691	1709
Morse Joseph II=A3/482	D	D22/21	1671	1691	1709
Morse Joseph Jr	D	D22/23	1610abt		
Morse Joseph Sr	D	D22/24	1576abt		
Morse Richard	D	D22/25	1550abt		
Morse Samuel	D	D21/23	1576		1645
Morse Thomas Jr	D	D21/24	1550abt		
Morse Thomas Sr	D	D21/25	1520abt		1566
Morton Ann	S	W56Ca	1694 May19	1716 Nov15	
Morton David	S	X48E	1716 Mar19		1746living
Morton Deborah	S	P13Ba	1652ca	1672ca	1678ca
Morton Deborah	S	H34E	1698 Sep15	1723 Feb27	1725ca
Morton Deborah	S	H125F	1730 Jul15		
Morton Deborah =P13Ba	S	F16Fam	1652ca	1672ca	1679ca
Morton Ebenezer	S	H34D	1696 Oct19	1720 Feb 2	1750 May12
Morton Ebenezer	S	H125D	1726 Aug27		
Morton Eleazer	S	W56Caf	1670abt		
Morton Elizabeth	S	K134A	1704 Jul10		
Morton Ephraim	S	W18Faf	1650abt		
Morton Ephraim	S	W57Daf	1690abt		

NAME	DIV.	NUMBER	BIRTH	MARRIAGE	DEATH
Morton Ephraim =W18Faf	S	X17Haf	1650abt		
Morton George	S	K35Caf	1645abt		
Morton George	S	W25Baf	1650abt		
Morton Hannah	S	W37Cam	1650abt		
Morton Hannah	S	F13Eb	1659abt	1687 Mar24	1738 Oct
Morton Hannah	S	W18Fa	1677 Nov 7	1687 Apr22	1715 Nov 3
Morton Hannah	S	H34C	1694 Sep 1		
Morton Hannah	S	H125E	1728 Oct 8		
Morton James	S	X48D	1714 May13		
Morton Joanna	S	Q17Cam	1670abt		
Morton Joanna	S	K134F	1723ca		
Morton John	S	F13Ebf	1635abt		
Morton John	S	K16Jaf	1665abt		
Morton John	S	X17Ha	1680 Jul20	1705 Dec27	1738 Feb 4
Morton John	S	H34B	1693 Jun		
Morton John	S	X48A	1706 Nov15		1765 Apr 6
Morton John	S	H125C	1724 Oct18		
Morton John =F13Ebf	S	P13Baf	1625abt		
Morton John Jr.	S	H14Da	1650 Dec21	1687 Mar 4	1717 Mar20
Morton John Sr.=F13Ebf	S	H14Daf	1625abt		
Morton Jonathan	S	X48B	1707 Feb10		d.yng
Morton Josiah	S	X48C	1709 Feb28		
Morton Lucia	S	H125J	1737 Jan 7		
Morton Manasseh	S	K35Ca	1668 Feb 3	1703ca	1746ca
Morton Mary	S	H34A	1689 Dec15	1715 Dec13	1781 Mar20
Morton Mary	S	K16Ja	1689 Dec15	1715 Dec13	1781 Mar20
Morton Mary	S	H125B	1723 Apr29		
Morton Mary	S	K134G	1725ca		
Morton Mary =K16Ja	S	K39Iam	1689 Dec15	1715 Dec13	1781 Mar20
Morton Mercy	S	H125A	1721 Jan20		
Morton Nathaniel	S	H125I	1735 Nov10		
Morton Patience	S	W11Gam	1605abt		
Morton Ruth	S	W25Ba	1676 Dec20	1696 Dec10	1709 Dec21
Morton Ruth	S	K134D	1713 Feb 8		
Morton Sarah	S	K30Fa	1706 Jul 6	1727 Apr 4	1785 Dec23
Morton Sarah	S	W57Da	1718 May 6	1734 May23	1792 Dec27
Morton Sarah	S	H125H	1733 Jan30	unm.	1751 Sep 4
Morton Seth	S	K134E	1721 Jan20		
Morton Seth	S	H125G	1731 Mar11		
Morton Susanna	S	W57Dam	1695abt		

NAME	DIV.	NUMBER	BIRTH	MARRIAGE	DEATH
Morton Taber	S	K134C	1709 Mar 3		
Morton Thomas	S	K30Faf	1685abt		
Morton Zeffaniah	S	K134B	1707 Jan 6		
Mosher Hugh	S	K20Caf	1650abt		
Mosher Joseph	S	K20Ca	1670ca	1693aft	1755bef
Mosher/Mosier Benjamin	S	K60G	1709 Feb22		
Mosher/Mosier James	S	K60E	1704 Dec14		
Mosher/Mosier Jonathan	S	K60C	1699 Mar13		
Mosher/Mosier Joseph	S	K60D	1701 Jun23		1730abt
Mosher/Mosier Lydia	S	K60I	1717 Jun11		
Mosher/Mosier Philip	S	K60B	1697 Dec20		
Mosher/Mosier Rebecca	S	K60A	1695 Dec28		
Mosher/Mosier Ruth	S	K60F	1707 Sep17		
Mosher/Mosier William	S	K60H	1713 Jul29		1743bef
Mosier Maxom	S	B21Fa	1730abt	1751	
Mosier Philip	S	B21Ea	1725abt	1750	
Mounce Ann	A	A1/201	1702 Jan 9	1727 Aug 1	
Mounce Christopher	A	A1/402	1675abt		
Mudge Martha	S	W28Ia	1695abt	1714 Dec30	1715 Oct 3
Mudge Mehitable	S	P14Da	1670ca		1718living
Mudge Micah	S	W28Iaf	1670abt		
Muhullen M.A.	S	G52La	1825ca		
Mulcahey Catherine	A	A9/9	1829 Aug	1852 Oct31	1906aft
Mulcahey Patrick	A	A9/18	1805abt		1852aft
Mulford John	S	X15Da	1670 Jul	1699 Nov 1	1730 Apr20
Mulford Thomas	S	X15Daf	1645abt		
Mullins Priscilla MF	A	A11/39	1605abt	1624bef	1680after
Mullins William MF	A	A11/78	1595abt		1621
Munford James	A	A1/156	1709abt	1727	1754
Munford Robert	A	A1/312	1680abt		1735ca
Munford Robert	A	A1/78	1730abt	1755 Feb11	1774 abt
Murdock Phebe	S	W17Ia	1666ca	1692abt	1746
Murray Elizabeth	A	A8/31	1756 May14	1785 Nov	1837 Dec17
Murray James	A	A8/62	1713 Aug 9	1744 May14	1781 Nov 8
Murray John	A	A8/248	1650abt		1712
Murray John	A	A8/124	1677 Feb	1712 Apr20	1728 Feb27
Myatt Sarah	S	R18Fam	1660abt		
Nash Alice	S	K36Da	1685ca	1703ca	1751 Dec 5
Nash Alice =K36Da	S	K39Ham	1685abt	1703ca	1751 Dec 5
Nash Elizabeth	S	A19Dbm	1655abt		

NAME	DIV.	NUMBER	BIRTH	MARRIAGE	DEATH
Nash Jacob	S	K36Daf	1665abt		
Nash Mary	S	K39Fam	1680abt		
Nathaniel Giles	A	A3/342	1680abt		
Neal Alice	S	P49C	1750 Jul 1		
Neal Benjamin	S	P21Laf	1675abt		
Neal Jerusha	S	P49B	1747 Nov23		
Neal Jonathan	S	P21La	1700 Oct13	1741 Dec 8	1770bef
Neal Joseph	S	P49D	1752 Dec12		
Neal Sarah	S	P49A	1743 Jan12		
Negus Hannah	S	L20Aam	1710abt		
Nelson Hannah	D	D2/21	1690abt		
Nelson John	S	W12Gb	1644ca		1697 Apr29
Nelson John	A	A8/174	1654		1734
Nelson John =A8/174	D	D12/17	1654		1734
Nelson Mehitable	S	W55Cam	1670abt		
Nelson Mercy	S	T15Gam	1675abt		
Nelson Rebecca	A	A8/87	1688 Nov15	1708 Nov27	1728 Jul27
Nelson Robert	D	D12a18	1620abt		
Nelson Samuel	S	W25C	1683 Jul4	1704 Dec13	1756abt
Nelson Samuel=W25C	S	W43Ba	1683 Jul 4	1704 Dec13	1756abt
Nelson Sarah	S	R27Aam	1700abt		
Nelson Thomas	D	D2a22	1665abt		
Newberry Rebecca	A	A12/73	1630abt	1651ca	1687 Jan 5
Newberry Thomas	A	A12/146	1594	1630	1635
Newcomb Andrew	S	H28Daf	1635abt		
Newcomb Anne	S	R40C	1720 Apr 4		
Newcomb Daniel	A	A1/66	1729 Nov29	1754ca	1789aft
Newcomb Deborah	S	H96D	1702ca		
Newcomb Ebenezer	S	H96H	1712ca		
Newcomb Edward	S	H96A	1695 Aug 3		
Newcomb Elizabeth	S	H96G	1709ca		
Newcomb Elizabeth	S	R40G	1727 Dec19		
Newcomb Hezekiah	S	R16Ca	1693ca	1716 Nov14	1772 Aug15
Newcomb Hezekiah	S	R40D	1722 Dec27		
Newcomb James	S	R40J	1732 Feb 7		
Newcomb Jemima	S	R40I	1730 Dec14		
Newcomb Jerusha	S	R40F	1726 Mar24		
Newcomb Joseph	S	H96I	1715ca		
Newcomb Josiah	S	H96F	1706ca		
Newcomb Judith	A	A1/181	1733 May31	1751 Nov11	1808 Aug31

NAME	DIV.	NUMBER	BIRTH	MARRIAGE	DEATH
Newcomb Lydia	A	A1/33	1763 Apr28	1791 Jul26	1835 Sep14
Newcomb Mary	S	H96E	1704ca		
Newcomb Obadiah	A	A1/132	1695ca		1761 May 4
Newcomb Peter	S	R40B	1718 Nov28		
Newcomb Samuel	S	R40H	1729 Sept2		1748 Sept9
Newcomb Silas	S	R40A	1717 Sept2		
Newcomb Simeon	S	R16Caf	1670abt		
Newcomb Simon	A	A1/264	1665ca	1687	1744
Newcomb Simon	S	H96C	1699 Nov30		
Newcomb Thomas	S	H28Da	1668ca	1693 Oct	
Newcomb Thomas	A	A1/362	1691ca	1720	1761ca
Newcomb Thomas	S	H96B	1698ca		
Newcomb Thomas	S	R40E	1724 Sep 3		
Newell William	S	C18Ba	1750ca		
Newland Jabez	S	T20Ea	1707ca	1728 Sep23	1787 Apr 7
Newland Jeremiah	S	T20Eaf	1680abt		
Newton Allerton	S	A30B	1691ca		d.yng
Newton Benjamin	S	A78F	1719ca		
Newton Elizabeth	S	W43Dam	1650abt		
Newton Elizabeth	S	A78E	1717ca		
Newton Frances	S	A78B	1711ca		
Newton John	S	A15Da	1657ca	1685ca	1699bef
Newton John	S	A78A	1709ca	unm	1744bef
Newton John Sr	S	A15Daf	1635abt		
Newton Sarah	S	A78D	1715ca		
Newton William	S	A30A	1686ca	2 mar.	1722bef
Newton William	S	A78C	1713ca		
Nickerson Ebenezer	S	H36C	1697 Jun13		
Nickerson Jane	S	H36D	1699 Apr 6		
Nickerson Mary	S	X16Iam	1670abt		
Nickerson Mary	S	H36E	1701 Aug13		
Nickerson Mary	S	X26Da	1701 Aug13	1724 Oct 8	
Nickerson Mercy	S	X19Eam	1670abt		
Nickerson Mercy	S	H36A	1691 Mar17		
Nickerson Nicholas	S	H16Baf	1635abt		
Nickerson Nicholas	S	B13Aaf	1650abt		
Nickerson Nicholas	S	H36B	1693 Mar19		
Nickerson Sarah	S	B13Aa	1674ca		1723Feb 4
Nickerson Thankful	S	H36F	1705 Jul26		
Nickerson William	S	H16Ba	1658 Jan12	1690 Jan22	1720abt

NAME	DIV.	NUMBER	BIRTH	MARRIAGE	DEATH
Nickerson William	S	X26Daf	1680abt		
Niles Nathaniel	S	R17Abf	1650abt		
Niles Samuel	S	R17Ab	1674 May 1	1737 Dec22	1762 May 1
Ninian Joanna	A	A17/41	1627ca	1661Oct 15	1717Feb 8
Nixon Francis Anthony	A	A3/2	1878 Dec 3	1908 Jun25	1956 Sept4
Nixon George	A	A3/32	1752ca	1775 Aug17	1842 Aug 5
Nixon George III	A	A3/8	1821ca	1843 Jan10	1863 Jul14
Nixon George Jr.	A	A3/16	1784ca	1806ca	1860aft
Nixon James	A	A3/64	1725 abt		1775 Jun26
Nixon Richard Milhous	A	A3/1	1913 Jan 9	1940 Jun21	
Nixon Samuel Brady	A	A3/4	1847 Oct 9	1873 Apr10	1814 Apr28
Noble Aaron	S	N13H	1748 Nov25		
Noble Abigail	S	N13G	1745 Feb16		
Noble Arthur Jackson	S	N16B	1816 Sep30		
Noble Asa	D	D26/23	1715abt		
Noble Asiel	S	N15E	1782 Aug 7		
Noble Bethia	D	D26a23	1715abt		
Noble Carlton Monroe	S	N16D	1821 Jan27		
Noble Catherine Sophia	S	N16G	1827 Aug25	unm	
Noble Charles Albert	S	N17A	1851 Nov17		
Noble Charles Harris	S	N16J	1834 Jun30	unm	
Noble Clarissa	S	N15N	1798 Feb28		1802Jul 15
Noble Daniel	S	N12B	1700 Nov25		
Noble Daniel	S	N14F	1768ct 1		
Noble David	S	N12E	1709Mar	1731May 7	1761Feb 18
Noble David	S	N13A	1732 Jan25	1753 Feb21	1776 Aug 5
Noble David	S	N15B	1778 Jun26		
Noble David Jr	S	N14B	1755 Mar19	1774 Nov23	
Noble David William	S	N16A	1814 Oct29		
Noble Electa	S	N15I	1789 Apr 5		
Noble Elizabeth	S	N11F	1673 Feb 9		
Noble Enoch	S	N13F	1742Dec 25		d yng
Noble Enoch	S	N14D	1763 Jun14		
Noble Enoch George	S	N16H	1829 Sep25		
Noble Ernest Wheeler	S	N17D	1856 Dec20		
Noble Esther	S	N15F	1784 Feb 6		
Noble Ezekial	S	N14E	1767abt		
Noble Hannah	S	N11B	1664 Feb24		
Noble Hannah	S	N13J	1752 May15		
Noble Helen	S	G54Aa	1890abt	1907 Dec24	1964

NAME	DIV.	NUMBER	BIRTH	MARRIAGE	DEATH
Noble Helen Grace	S	N17C	1854 Nov 5		d. yng
Noble Helen L	S	N18B	1888 Jul18		1964 Feb14
Noble Henry Orville	S	G54Aaf	1860 May31	1883 Nov18	=N17E
Noble Henry Orville	S	N17E	1860 May31	1883Nov18	1934 Jan 2
Noble James	S	N13C	1736 Jul 9		
Noble James	S	N15G	1785 May16		1794
Noble James	S	N15M	1796 Apr 3		
Noble James Jr	S	N12A	1699Mar 29		d. yng
Noble James Jr	S	N12D	1707 Jan12		1739
Noble James Sr	S	N11H	1677 Oct 1	1698abt	1712 Apr22
Noble James Taylor	S	N16I	1832 May15	unm	
Noble John	S	N11A	1662 Mar 6		
Noble John	S	N13K	1755Mar 15		d yng
Noble Katherine	S	N13D	1738 Jul 5		
Noble Lucy	S	N14I	1774 Oct		
Noble Luke	S	N11G	1675 Jul15		
Noble Luke	D	D26a24	1685abt		
Noble Lydia	S	N12C	1704 Dec 7		
Noble Lydia	S	N13I	1750		
Noble Mary	S	N11I	1680 Jun29		
Noble Mary	S	N15D	1781 May 7		
Noble Matthew	S	N11D	1670ca		
Noble Miranda	S	N15K	1793 Feb 4		
Noble Norman Wheeler	S	N18D	1902 Jun29	1926 Jan26	
Noble Olive Blanch	S	N18C	1891 Feb 3	unm	1965Dec 5
Noble Oliver	S	N13B	1734 Mar 1		
Noble Orville M	S	N18A	1885 Mar 4		d yng
Noble Polly	S	N14H	1772 Jun15		
Noble Rebecca	S	N11J	1683 Jan 4		
Noble Rebecca	S	N14C	1760ca		
Noble Roswell	S	N15H	1787 Oct 3		1825abt
Noble Ruth	S	N13Aa	1732ca	1753 Feb21	
Noble Ruth	D	D26/22	1740abt		
Noble Ruth	S	N14A	1753 Aug12		
Noble Sallie	S	N15A	1776 Jan26		
Noble Sarah	S	N16C	1818 Nov13		1820
Noble Sarah Maria	S	N16F	1825 Aug22		
Noble Sophia	S	N15L	1794 Dec 3		
Noble Thirza	S	N13E	1740 Jul27		
Noble Thirza	S	N14G	1770ca		d yng

NAME	DIV.	NUMBER	BIRTH	MARRIAGE	DEATH
Noble Thirza	S	N15C	1779 Nov 3		
Noble Thomas Jr	S	N11C	1666 Jan14		
Noble Thomas Sr	S	N10A	1632abt	1660 Nov 1	1704 Jan20
Noble Truman Wilgus	S	N17B	1853 Jul11		1857
Noble Washington A.	S	N16E	1823 Mar 3		
Noble William Taylor	S	N15J	1791 Jun16	1814 Jan11	1861 Jan7
Norris Mary	S	A10Aa	1590ca	1611 Nov 4	1620 Feb25
Norton Elizabeth	A	A11/15	1695 Mar15	1715 Oct6	
Norton John	A	A11/30	1651ca	1678 Nov29	1716 Oct3
Norton Lyman	S	G35Aa	1843	1864	1906
Norton Margaret	D	D30a23	1430abt		
Norton William	A	A11/120	1575abt		
Norton William	A	A11/60	1625abt	1649ca	1694 Apr30
Noyes Elizabeth	A	A4/227	1708 Jan16	1728 Apr22	1787
Noyes Hannah	S	K36Hb	1709 Jul23	1732 Dec21	1777ca
Noyes James	S	R21Dbf	1660abt		
Noyes John	S	R21Db	1685 Jun13	1739 Mar13	1751 Sep17
Noyes John Jr.	A	A4/454	1667	1703	1719
Noyes Nicholas	S	K36Hbf	1685abt		
Nye Benjamin	S	B11Daf	1600abt		
Nye Bethiah	S	H111Bam	1685abt		
Nye Caleb	S	W51Gaf	1670abt		
Nye Ebenezer	S	W51Ga	1690abt		1759 Jul 2
Nye Mary	S	B11Da	1630abt	1670 Jun 1	
Nye Mary =B11Da	S	W48Aam	1630abt	1670 Jun 1	
Ochard Joan	D	D30a22	1460abt		
Oldham Alice	S	Q23Ea	1703 Jun22	1723 Feb13	1771aft
Oldham Isaac	S	Q23Eaf	1680abt		
Olfertsen Sioert	A	A7/132	1640abt		1702
Oliver Magdalene	S	L9Aa	1570abt		
Oliver Sybil	D	D30a29	1260abt		
Olmstead Elizabeth	A	A16/59	1640ca		1681 Oct12
Olmstead James	A	A16/236	1580	1605	1640
Olmstead Nicholas	S	G10Aaf	1612ca	1640bef	1684Aug 31
Olmstead Nicholas	A	A16/118	1612ca	1640bef	=G10Aaf
Olmstead Sarah	S	G10Aa	1641	1661	1709Nov 7
Olmstead Sarah	S	F15Dam	1645ca		
Olney Amey	S	C90F	1725abt		
Olney Anthony	S	C90D	1725abt		
Olney Charles	S	C87Fa	1714ca		

NAME	DIV.	NUMBER	BIRTH	MARRIAGE	DEATH
Olney Charles	S	C90B	1720abt		
Olney Elizabeth	S	C76Ba	1666		
Olney Epenetus	S	C78Aa	1675		
Olney Freeborn	S	C90H	1730abt		
Olney James	S	C87Da	1688		
Olney James	S	C90A	1715abt		
Olney Joseph	S	C90C	1725abt		
Olney Lydia	S	C75Fa	1645		
Olney Lydia	S	C87Ia	1726		
Olney Martha	S	C90G	1730abt		
Olney Mary	S	C90E	1725abt		
Onion Jonathon	S	C71Ca	1695ca		
Orcutt Elizabeth	S	K79B	1700abt		
Orcutt Huldah	S	P48A	1734 Oct25		
Orcutt Ignatius	S	P48C	1738 Apr 1 unm		1828
Orcutt Jane	S	P21Ha	1704 Dec18	1732 Oct 5	1751bef
Orcutt Joanna	S	K79A	1698abt		
Orcutt John	S	P21Jaf	1670abt		
Orcutt Samuel	S	P21Ja	1697 Oct 9	1724 Sep12	1743 Mar 5
Orcutt Sybil	S	P48B	1736 Oct16		
Orcutt Thomas	S	P21Haf	1780abt		
Orcutt William	S	K22Ia	1665ca	1690aft	1739 Apr10
Orcutt William Sr	S	K22Iaf	1640abt		
Ormsby Martha	A	A19/225	1680	1706	
Orr Janet	A	A4/101	1700abt	1720	
Orr William	A	A4/202	1690ca		
Osborn Agnes E	S	G53E	1854 Jan21		(twin)
Osborn Alice Cora	S	G53A	1846 Aug20		
Osborn Charles T	S	G53F	1860 May31		
Osborn Clarinda	S	G52I	1818ca		
Osborn Cora Eveline	S	G53G	1864 Sep 5	1886 Oct11	1918 Apr
Osborn Elizabeth	S	G52H	1817ca		
Osborn Emily	S	G52G	1816		
Osborn Frances Amelia	S	G53C	1851 Oct 9		
Osborn Hannah	A	A2/125	1679Dec 2	1701 Nov26	
Osborn Harrison	S	G52F	1813 Jan13		(twin)
Osborn Jane	S	G52A	1804 Mar 1		
Osborn John	S	G52D	1810abt		
Osborn John A	S	G52N	1830 ca		
Osborn Lewis	S	G52B	1806 Aug 6		

NAME	DIV.	NUMBER	BIRTH	MARRIAGE	DEATH
Osborn Narcissa	S	G52L	1827		
Osborn Phebe	S	G52E	1813 Jan13		(twin)
Osborn Philander	S	G52M	1828		
Osborn Thomas	S	G36Aa	1819 Dec12	1845 Oct18	1910 Feb28
Osborn Thomas	S	G52J	1819 Dec12	1845 Oct18	1910 Feb28
Osborn Urville	S	G52K	1820ca		
Osborn William	A	A2/250	1650ca	1672ca	
Osborn William	S	G36Aaf	1773 Aug 3	1802abt	1869 Mar25
Osborn William	S	G51Aa	1773 Aug 3	1802abt	1869 Mar25
Osborn William D	S	G53D	1854 Jan21		(twin)
Osborn William Jr	S	G52C	1809 Sep 4		
Osborn Winfield Scott	S	G52B	1849 Aug10		
Oswald Joseph	A	A7/30	1745abt		1786ca
Oswald Susannah	A	A7/15	1770 Nov 2	1768 Jan18	1807 Dec20
Otis Hannah	S	X23Ea	1686 May16	1709 Nov28	1739bef
Otis Job	S	W32Ca	1677 Mar20	1699 Oct 1	1758
Otis John	S	W32Caf	1650abt		
Otis John	S	W31Caf	1660abt		
Otis Mary	S	F18Cam	1665ca		
Otis Mary	S	W31Ca	1685 Dec10	1703ca	1733bef
Otis Mary =W31Ca	S	L15Bam	1685 Dec10	1703ca	1733bef
Otis Mercy	S	L19Aa	1728 Sep14	1754 Nov14	1814 Oct19
Otis Ruth	S	L18Cam	1715abt		
Otis Stephen	S	X23Eaf	1665abt		
Owen Abigail	S	C49Ga	1697ca		
Owen Deliverance	A	A16/53	1654Feb 15	1672May 1	1726May 3
Owen William	A	A16/106	1625abt	1650Sep29	1702 Jan17
Pabodie Elizabeth	S	R12Ham	1647 Apr24	1666 Nov	=X13Aa
Pabodie Elizabeth	S	X13Aa	1647 Apr24	1666 Nov	1678ca
Pabodie Hannah	S	W19Ca	1662 Oct15	1683 Aug2	1723 Apr29
Pabodie Martha	S	W30Dam	1655abt		
Pabodie Martha	S	W32Eam	1660abt		
Pabodie Mary	S	T16Aam	1655abt		
Pabodie Mercy	S	T16Bam	1655abt		
Pabodie Mercy =T16Bam	S	W35Jam	1650abt		
Pabodie Priscilla	S	R21Bbm	1670abt		
Pabodie Rebecca	S	W32Dam	1660abt		
Pabodie Ruth	S	W19Aa	1658 Jun27	1677ca	1725ca
Pabodie Ruth =R12Lam	S	R14Aam	1658 Jun27	1677ca	1725ca
Pabodie Ruth =W19Aa	S	R12Lam	1658 Jun27	1677ca	1725ca

NAME	DIV.	NUMBER	BIRTH	MARRIAGE	DEATH
Pabodie Ruth =W19Aa	S	R21Gam	1658 Jun27	1677ca	1725ca
Pabodie William Jr	S	W28Ea	1664 Nov24	1693 Jun27	1744 Sep17
Pabodie William Sr	S	W28Eaf	1630abt		
Pabodie William=W19Aaf	S	W19Caf	1630abt		
Pabodie William=W19Aaf	S	X13Aaf	1630abt		
Pabodie William=X13Aaf	S 1	W19Aaf	1630abt		
Packard Abel	S	K153B	1729 Sep 8		
Packard Abiah	S	K153C	1731 Aug 5		
Packard Abigail	S	K153D	1733 Oct 8		
Packard Abigail	S	K150E	1735 May14		
Packard Barnabas	S	K153F	1737 Mar 3		
Packard Benjamin	S	R28Kc	1743ca	1765 Apr30	1825 Feb18
Packard Deborah	S	K22Ca	1655ca	1677ca	1725aft
Packard Deliverance	S	K22Ba	1652ca	1684bef	1711bef
Packard Jacob	S	K150C	1728 Apr12		
Packard Jedediah	S	R123C	1771 Feb18		
Packard John	S	K39Ea	1695 Oct 8	1725 Feb 2	1738 Jun 3
Packard John	S	K153E	1735 Nov 6		
Packard John	S	R123A	1765 Dec19		
Packard Jonathan	S	K39Ba	1684 Dec 7	1723 Nov27	1746 Jun 7
Packard Jonathan #1	S	K150A	1724 Aug28		d. yng
Packard Jonathan #2	S	K150D	1730 Nov12		
Packard Joseph	S	R28Kcf	1720abt		
Packard Lois	S	R123B	1767 Aug31		
Packard Lydia	S	K153A	1726 Dec27		
Packard Mary	S	Q22Bam	1680abt		
Packard Melatiah	S	R123G	1773 Jul31		
Packard Samuel	S	K22Baf	1630abt		
Packard Samuel	S	K22Caf	1630abt		
Packard Susanna	S	K150B	1726 Feb21		
Packard Zaccheus	S	K39Baf	1660abt		
Packard Zaccheus	S	K39Eaf	1660abt		=K39Baf
Paddy Elizabeth	S	L12Cam	1650abt		
Paddy Margaret	A	A11/35	1610abt	1630abt	1661 Feb13
Page John	A	A15/70	1626ca		1691Jan23
Page Mary	A	A15/35	1635abt		
Page Susanna	A	A12/189	1610abt		1691
Paine Abigail	S	H43A	1686 Jan 5		
Paine Abigail	S	C72C	1699		
Paine Abigail	S	H45E	1707 Aug 3		

NAME	DIV.	NUMBER	BIRTH	MARRIAGE	DEATH
Paine Abigail	S	H109D	1729 Jul29		1750aft
Paine Abigail (Payne)	S	C69B	1823		
Paine Abigail #1	S	H42F	1687 Mar 4		1688 Jan21
Paine Abigail #2	S	H42G	1689 Nov10		
Paine Abigial	S	X32E	1707 Aug 3		
Paine Abijah	S	C49M	1713		
Paine Abraham	S	H43C	1691ca		
Paine Albert B (Payne)	S	C69L	1842		
Paine Alice	S	H44Q	1728 Dec 4	1775 Dec12	1777 Apr18
Paine Alma (Payne)	S	C69A	1822		
Paine Ann E (Payne)	S	C69J	1838		
Paine Anna	S	C50Ba	1686		
Paine Anna	S	C51B	1686		
Paine Arnold (Payne)	S	C68A	1800		
Paine Arnold Jr	S	C69E	1830		
Paine Barnabas	S	H42N	1705 Nov13		
Paine Benjamin	S	H44D	1696 Feb22		1713Dec 15
Paine Benjamin	S	C49H	1699		
Paine Benjamin	S	H44M	1714 May18		1716 Jan14
Paine Bethiah #1	S	H46C	1695 Feb22		1697 Jul29
Paine Bethiah #2	S	H46D	1698 May23	1735 Dec11	1755aft
Paine Constance	S	H43H	1704 Feb17		
Paine Daniel	S	C51H	1702		
Paine David H (Payne)	S	C69K	1839		
Paine Day C (Payne)	S	C68F	1831		
Paine Dorcas	S	H17J	1668ca	1689ca	1707 Oct30
Paine Dorcas	S	H43G	1699 Feb24		
Paine Dorcas	S	H47E	1701 May27		
Paine Dorothy	S	C72A	1695		
Paine Dwight Z (Payne)	S	C69G	1831		
Paine Ebenezer	S	H47A	1692 Apr 8		
Paine Ebenezer	S	H41D	1692 Jun17	1722 Dec13	1734
Paine Ebenezer	S	C51J	1711		
Paine Ebenezer	S	H109A	1722 Nov26		
Paine Ebenezer =H41D	S	H30Ga	1692 Jun17	1722 Dec13	1734
Paine Eleazer	S	H17D	1658 Mar10		
Paine Elisha	S	H17E	1658ca	1685 Jan20	1735 Feb 7
Paine Elisha	S	H43D	1693 Dec29		
Paine Elizabeth	S	C46F	1664		
Paine Elizabeth	S	C49A	1682		

NAME	DIV.	NUMBER	BIRTH	MARRIAGE	DEATH
Paine Elizabeth	S	H41E	1694 Jun11		
Paine Elizabeth	S	H44G	1702 Jun 2		
Paine Elizabeth	S	C72F	1712		
Paine Elizabeth	S	H109B	1724 Jul 7		
Paine Elkanah	S	H42I	1692 Feb 1		
Paine Experience	S	H46F	1702 Mar17		
Paine Experience	S	H47K	1713 May27		
Paine Ezekial	S	C49N	1715		
Paine Fidelia	S	C67C	1775abt		
Paine Gideon	S	C49J	1703		
Paine Hannah	S	H42A	1679 Apr 6		1681 Nov17
Paine Hannah	S	H42D	1684 May12		
Paine Hannah	S	W36Ea	1685 Apr20	1703 May20	1755 Oct16
Paine Hannah	S	H47B	1694 Jul 5		
Paine Hannah	S	H45F	1709 Sep24		
Paine Hannah	S	X32F	1709 Sep24		
Paine Hannah	S	H44N	1720 Jan11		1723 Jan28
Paine Hannah	S	H44R	1728 Dec 4 unm.		1807ca
Paine Hannah	S	H43I	1729 Jan		
Paine Hannah	S	H109E	1732ca		
Paine Hugh	S	H42B	1680 Jul 5		1681 Nov29
Paine Isaac	S	H41G	1698 Jan 3 unm.		1760abt
Paine Isaiah	S	C49P	1718ca		
Paine James	S	H17H	1665	1691 Apr 9	1728 Nov12
Paine James	S	H46A	1691 Mar24		1711 Jul13
Paine James	S	H44O	1723 Dec17		1724 Feb23
Paine James L (Payne)	S	C69C	1825		
Paine John	S	C46C	1658		
Paine John	S	H17F	1660 Mar14	2 Mar	1731 Oct
Paine John	S	C49B	1684		
Paine John Jr	S	H44A	1690 Sep18		
Paine John Sr	S	H43J	1707 Jul		
Paine Jonathan	S	H42E	1685 Feb 1		
Paine Jonathan	S	C72D	1701		
Paine Jonathan	S	H47J	1710 Dec10		
Paine Joseph	S	H17I	1667ca	1691 May27	1712 Oct 1
Paine Joseph	S	C49E	1693		
Paine Joseph	S	H47C	1697 Mar29		
Paine Joshua	S	H41F	1696 May20		
Paine Joshua	S	H42K	1697 Aug28		

NAME	DIV.	NUMBER	BIRTH	MARRIAGE	DEATH
Paine Josiah	S	C49D	1687		
Paine Josiah	S	H44I	1705 Mar 8		1728 May 7
Paine Judith	S	C51E	1695		
Paine Lois	S	X32D	1705 Sep29		
Paine Lois =X32D	S	H45D	1705 Sep29		
Paine Lucy (Payne)	S	C69H	1833		
Paine Lydia	S	H42M	1700 Dec 4		
Paine Lydia	S	H53Ca	1705ca	1729Mar 5	1794bef
Paine Lydia	S	H45G	1710ca		
Paine Lydia	S	X32G	1710ca		
Paine Mary	S	H17A	1650abt	2 Mar	1723bef
Paine Mary	S	H24Bam	1650abt		
Paine Mary	S	C46D	1659		
Paine Mary	S	H44B	1692 Jan28		
Paine Mary	S	H43E	1695 Feb 1		
Paine Mary	S	H46E	1700 Aug13		
Paine Mary	S	H41H	1703 Feb24		
Paine Mary	S	H47I	1708 Dec 1		
Paine Mary =H17A	S	X12Ga	1650ca	1670 Jan11	1723bef
Paine Mary A	S	C55Ba	1836		
Paine Mary A (Payne)	S	C69I	1836		
Paine Mathewson W	S	C67B	1775abt		
Paine Mercy	S	H28Ha	1686 Aug 5	1710 Nov23	1718aft
Paine Mercy	S	H44L	1712 Apr 3		
Paine Mercy =H28Ha	S	H41B	1686 Aug 5	1710 Nov23	1718bef
Paine Moses	S	H42J	1695 Sep28		
Paine Nathan	S	C49I	1701		
Paine Nathan	S	C66A	1741		
Paine Nathaniel	S	W36Eaf	1660abt		
Paine Nathaniel	S	C46H	1667		
Paine Nathaniel	S	H41C	1689 Jul 9		1706 Mar14
Paine Nathaniel	S	C72B	1697		
Paine Nathaniel	S	H44J	1707 Nov18		1728 Nov 4
Paine Nathaniel	S	H109C	1727 Aug15		
Paine Nicholas	S	H17G	1663ca	1699ca	1732
Paine Nicholas	S	H53Caf	1670ca	1699ca	1733bef
Paine Nicholas	S	X15Ea	1670ca	1699ca	1733bef
Paine Noah	S	C51F	1696		
Paine Phebe	S	H42H	1690 Mar14		1695 Jan21
Paine Phebe	S	H42L	1698		

NAME	DIV.	NUMBER	BIRTH	MARRIAGE	DEATH
Paine Phebe	S	H47F	1703 Jul30		
Paine Philip =H45C	S	X32C	1704 Nov18		1725 Apr10
Paine Phillip	S	H45C	1704 Nov18		1725 Apr10
Paine Priscilla	S	X32B	1701 Oct16		
Paine Priscilla=X32B	S	H45B	1701 Oct16		
Paine Rachel	S	C72E	1705		
Paine Rebecca	S	C46B	1656		
Paine Rebecca	S	H43B	1690ca		
Paine Rebecca	S	C49F	1694		
Paine Rebecca	S	H46G	1705 Apr 8 unm.		1726Jun 30
Paine Rebecca	S	H44K	1709 Oct30		
Paine Rebecca	S	C51I	1710		
Paine Reliance	S	H47G	1705 Jan27		
Paine Richard	S	H47D	1699 Mar25		
Paine Samuel	S	H17B	1652ca	1682 Jan31	1712 Oct13
Paine Samuel	S	H28Haf	1660abt		
Paine Samuel	S	C46E	1662		
Paine Samuel	S	H30Gaf	1670abt		
Paine Samuel	S	H41A	1683 Oct30		1706 Oct 5
Paine Samuel	S	C51A	1686		
Paine Samuel	S	C49O	1717		
Paine Sarah	S	C46G	1666		
Paine Sarah	S	C51D	1692		
Paine Sarah	S	H44E	1699 Apr14		
Paine Seth	S	C51C	1690		
Paine Seth	S	H41I	1706 Oct 5 unm.		1722 Mar23
Paine Solomon	S	C49G	1696		
Paine Solomon	S	H43F	1698 May16		
Paine Stephen	S	C45Aa	1629		
Paine Stephen	S	C46A	1654		
Paine Stephen	S	C49C	1686		
Paine Stephen	S	C51G	1699		
Paine Stephen	S	C65A	1716		
Paine Stephen Jr	S	C47A	1708		
Paine Thankful	S	X32A	1699 Mar14		
Paine Thankful=X32A	S	H45A	1699 Mar14		
Paine Theophilus	S	H44H	1703 Feb 7		
Paine Thomas	S	H17C	1656ca	2 mar	1721 Jun23
Paine Thomas	S	H42C	1681 Feb28		
Paine Thomas	S	H46B	1694 Apr 9		

NAME	DIV.	NUMBER	BIRTH	MARRIAGE	DEATH
Paine Thomas	S	H47H	1708 Dec 1		
Paine Thomas	S	H44P	1725 Apr 6		
Paine Thomas =H12Da	S	X15Eaf	1628ca	1652bef	1706 Aug16
Paine Thomas =X15Eaf	S	X12Gaf	1628ca	1652bef	1706 Aug16
Paine Thomas Jr=X12Gaf	S	H12Ba	1628ca	1652bef	1706 Aug16
Paine Thomas R (Payne)	S	C69M	1845		
Paine Thomas Sr	S	H12Baf	1600abt		
Paine Urania	S	C49K	1706		
Paine William	S	H44C	1695 Jun 6		
Paine William	S	C49L	1711		
Paine William (Payne)	S	C69D	1828		
Paine Zatto	S	C67A	1770abt		
Palfrey Peter	A	A8/162	1615ca		1663ca
Palfrey Remembrance	A	A8/81	1638 Sep	1661 Feb12	1700
Palmer Abel	S	C16Da	1730ca		
Palmer Esther	S	C23Fa	1795ca		
Palmer Grace	A	A5/133	1610abt	1634	1690
Panton Elinor	A	A16/173	1600abt		1670
Pares Judith	A	A11/113	1600abt	1623 Jul14	1654 Mar29
Park Elizabeth	A	A7/99	1685abt		1747living
Park James	A	A7/198	1635abt	1673ca	
Parker Elizabeth	A	A19/79	1705 Jan	1723Apr 30	
Parker Jacob	A	A17/34	1630abt		1669bef
Parker Joanna	A	A11/63	1635 Jun 1	1655 Jul 5	1704 Jan2
Parker John Jr	A	A19/158	1668	1691	1740
Parker Loanna	S	C68Aa	1802		
Parker Nicholas	A	A11/126	1600abt	1629ca	1655aft
Parker Tabitha	A	A17/17	1658 Feb28	1676Nov 18	1741 Jan31
Parkman Esther	A	A19/89	1724Jul 17	1743Aug 4	
Parkman John	A	A19/178	1693	1718	1727
Parlour Susanna =Q18Ca	S	K34Da	1688ca	1713 Dec10	1734 Jun 9
Parlour Thomas	S	K34Daf	1665abt		
Parlow Joanna	S	Q15Ba	1685ca	1709ca	1730ca
Parlow Susanna	S	Q18Ca	1688ca	1713 Dec10	1734 Jun 9
Parlow Thomas	S	Q15Baf	1660abt		
Parlow Thomas(Parlour)	S	Q18Caf	1665abt		=K34Daf
Parmelee John	A	A12/142	1600abt		1659abt
Parmelee Mary	A	A12/71	1635abt	1660 Sep16	1667 Mar
Parris Elizabeth	S	W33Dam	1670abt		
Parsons Deborah	S	A28Da	1690ca	1713 Apr 9	

NAME	DIV.	NUMBER	BIRTH	MARRIAGE	DEATH
Parsons Mary	A	A3/433	1660abt		1718
Parsons Rachel/Varney	A	A16/79	1630abt	1652bef	1707Feb15
Partirdge Sarah	S	Q13Fbm	1640abt		
Partridge Elizabeth	A	A5/79	1640abt		1722 Aug 7
Partridge George	A	A5/158	1610abt	1638	
Partridge Lydia	S	A21Dam	1655abt		
Partridge Mary	A	A12/81	1638ca	1673 Nov12	1683 May20
Partridge Mary	A	A12/85	1638ca	1673 Nov12	1683 May20
Partridge Ruth	S	F15Gam	1655ca		
Partridge S	S	N11Bc	1665abt		
Partridge William	A	A12/162	1620ca	1644	1668
Partridge William	A	A12/170	1620ca	1644	1668ca
Passmore Rebecca	A	A3/81	1720abt	1741 Jan	
Patton J.E.R.	S	N16Fa	1825ca		
Paul Elizabeth	A	A19/47	1754ca	1777Dec 27	
Paul James	A	A19/94	1725ca	1749Nov 16	1814ca
Paul William	A	A19/188	1691	1716	1732
Peabody Mary	S	W35Cam	1640abt		
Pearce Mary	A	A3/505	1690abt	1714	1727ca
Pearce Thomas	A	A17/64	1583ca		1666 Oct 7
Pearson John	A	A17/58	1635abt		1693Dec 22
Pearson Phebe	A	A17/29	1660Apr 13	1682Aug 24	1732Oct 16
Peck Ann	S	C46Ea	1663ca		
Peck Belinda	S	C62Aa	1790ca		
Peck Daniel	S	C51Da	1690ca		
Peck Hannah	S	R20Aam	1660abt		
Peck Ichabod	S	C51Ea	1694ca		
Peck Joel	S	C48B	1680		
Peck Judith	S	C48D	1683ca		
Peck Mehitable	S	C35Ea	1750ca		
Peck Noah	S	C48A	1678		
Peck Rebecca	S	C48C	1681		
Peck Rebecca	S	C72Da	1702ca		
Peck Rebekah	S	C32Aa	1700		
Peck Samuel	S	C46Bb	1655ca		
Peckham Almy	S	K67B	1732 Feb26		
Peckham Elizabeth	S	K35Eam	1660abt		
Peckham Hannah	S	W51Bb	1691 Jan28	1716ca	1770abt
Peckham Jean =A8/49	S	W51La	1702 Jan23	1727 Nov 4	
Peckham Jean =W51La	A	A8/49	1702 Jan23	1727 Nov 4	

NAME	DIV.	NUMBER	BIRTH	MARRIAGE	DEATH
Peckham John	A	A8/196	1600ca	1648	1681ca
Peckham Philip	S	W47Ea	1680 Oct27	1705ca	1722 Dec20
Peckham Rebecca	S	W47Dam	1655abt		
Peckham Rebecca	S	K35Dam	1655abt		=W47Dam
Peckham Sarah	S	K67A	1730 Jan14		
Peckham Stephen	S	K21Eaf	1655abt		
Peckham Stephen	S	W51Bbf	1665abt		
Peckham Stephen	S	W51Laf	1675abt		
Peckham Stephen	A	A8/98	1680abt		
Peckham Thomas	S	W47Eaf	1655abt		
Peckham William	S	K21Ea	1688 Oct27	1726 Nov 6	1771bef
Peeck Hannah	A	A7/35	1696 Jun12	1716 Mar10	1769 Oct 8
Peeck Jan	A	A7/140	1625abt	1650	1664abt
Peeck Johannes	A	A7/70	1653 Oct	1683 Jul18	
Peirce Elizabeth	S	H113D	1736 Jan28		
Peirce Esther	S	H113C	1734 Jul17		
Peirce Hannah	S	H113A	1723 Mar10		
Peirce Joseph	S	H32Da	1695ca	1719 Nov20	
Peirce Joseph	S	H113B	1725 April		
Peirce William	S	H32Daf	1670abt		
Peirson Rose	A	A3/207	1693	1715 Mar16	1771
Pelham Penelope	S	L11Ca	1633	1651ca	1703 Dec 7
Pemberton Alice	S	C73Aa	1564		
Penn Christian	A	A6/247	1606ca	1634ca	1684ca
Pennell Ann	A	A3/409	1667May	1689	1709 May
Penniman Sarah	S	X24Aam	1645abt		
Pepper Ann	S	C70C	1705		
Pepper Benjamin	S	C70E	1713		
Pepper Jacob	S	C46Fa	1660ca		
Pepper Mary	S	C70D	1707		
Pepper Rebecca	S	C70B	1687		
Pepper Robert	S	C70A	1687		
Percival Elizabeth	S	G24Ab	1750abt	1800	
Perdue Elizabeth	A	A1/445	1715abt		
Perkins Edward	S	A44A	1695 May 1		d.yng
Perkins Elizabeth	S	A44F	1701 Oct13		
Perkins Ezra	S	T66D	1748 Mar18		
Perkins Hannah	A	A8/95	1701 Jul 7	1718 Oct16	1745
Perkins Hannah	S	T66A	1742 Apr23		1766 Jan30
Perkins Jabez	A	A8/190	1677	1698	1741

NAME	DIV.	NUMBER	BIRTH	MARRIAGE	DEATH
Perkins Jacob	A	A16/94	1646ca	1667 Dec25	1719 Nov26
Perkins John	A	A16/188	1609	1635ca	1686
Perkins Joseph	S	T66B	1743 Jan21		
Perkins Mary #1	S	A44D	1698 Dec13		d.yng
Perkins Mary #2	S	A44E	1700 Mar27		
Perkins Philippa	A	A16/47	1670Nov 28	1685Nov 20	1738Apr26
Perkins Rebecca	A	A3/441	1635abt	1659	
Perkins Thomas	S	A20Aa	1673	1694 Jul26	1701bef
Perkins Thomas #1	S	A44B	1696 Apr24		d.yng
Perkins Thomas #2	S	A44C	1697 Oct19		d.yng
Perkins Thomas Jr	S	T25Fa	1695 Sep22	1740 Mar10	1770
Perkins Thomas Sr	S	T25Faf	1670abt		
Perkins Tryphena	S	T66C	1746 Feb 6		1770living
Perley Elizabeth	A	A19/117	1705 Oct10	1725ca	1742 Mar 4
Perley Isaac	A	A19/234	1680	1704	1711
Perne Rachel	A	A2/145	1620ca		1677
Perrin Ruth	S	C51Aa	1687ca		
Perry Meribah	S	W50Ha	1695 Jun11	1716 Nov 9	1774 Nov16
Perry Benjamin	S	B14E	,1670 Jan15		
Perry Benjamin	S	W50Haf	1670abt		
Perry Deborah	S	K57B	1693 Jun16		
Perry Deborah	A	A8/27	1754 Oct14	1777 Apr19	1808ca
Perry Deborah=A8/213	S	B14B	1654	1675ca	1710
Perry Deborah=B14B	S	W37Fam	1654	1675ca	1710
Perry Deborah=B14B	A	A8/213	1654	1675ca	1710
Perry Deborah=B14B	S	K17Gam	1654	1675ca	1710
Perry Ebenezer	S	P29A	1707 Jan10		
Perry Ebenezer=A8/108	S	K57H	1705 Mar 5	1728ca	1775aft
Perry Ebenezer=K57H	A	A8/108	1705 Mar 5	1728ca	1775aft
Perry Elizabeth	S	K57A	1690 Jul15		
Perry Ezra	S	B11Ca	1625abt	1652 Feb12	
Perry Ezra	S	K19Baf	1645abt		
Perry Ezra	S	B14A	1653 Feb11		
Perry James	S	P29C	1711 Dec27		
Perry Joanna	S	Q17Iam	1685abt		
Perry John	S	B14C	1657 Jan 1		
Perry John	S	P15Ga	1699 Mar 3	1706 Dec19	1725 Aug 6
Perry John Sr	S	P15Gaf	1675abt		
Perry Mary	S	K57G	1702 Dec10		
Perry Mary	S	C61Da	1755ca		

NAME	DIV.	NUMBER	BIRTH	MARRIAGE	DEATH
Perry Mercy	S	P29B	1709 Aug 8		
Perry Mercy	S	K57J	1710 Dec 8		
Perry Nathan	S	K57F	1700 Jan12		
Perry Rebecca	S	K57E	1698ca		
Perry Remembrance	S	B14F	1676 Jan 1		
Perry Ruth	S	Q21Fbm	1690abt		
Perry Samuel	A	A8/54	1731 Jun27	1754 Apr14	1805 Apr15
Perry Samuel=A8/216	S	B14D	1667	1689	1751
Perry Samuel=B14D	S	K19Ba	1667	1689	1751
Perry Samuel=K19Ba	A	A8/216	1667	1689	1751
Perry Sarah	S	K57D	1696 Jun 8		d.yng
Perry Seth	S	K57I	1707 Feb24		1729Oct18
Perry Thomas	S	K57C	1693 Feb24		d.yng
Peterson Joseph	S	W29Gb	1669 Apr 1	1704 Aug23	1750abt
Phelps Abigail	A	A12/15	1731 Nov11	1749 Dec21	1816 Jan
Phelps D.	S	N15Kb	1790abt		
Phelps Nathaniel	A	A12/120	1627ca	1650 Sep17	1702 May27
Phelps Nathaniel Jr	A	A12/60	1653 Jun 2	1676 Aug11	1719 Jun20
Phelps Timothy	A	A12/30	1697ca	1725 Jan18	1788 Dec 5
Phelps William	A	A12/240	1605abt		1672
Phillips Andrew Jr	A	A19/142	1662	1683	1717
Phillips Benjamin	S	R81B	1719 Aug 3		
Phillips Benjamin Jr	S	R23Ca	1687 May20	1716 Jan17	1750 May
Phillips Benjamin Sr	S	R23Caf	1665abt		
Phillips Ebenezer	A	A1/290	1695		1745
Phillips Experience	S	K36Iam	1670abt		
Phillips Jeremiah	S	R81A	1717 Nov17		
Phillips Joanna	A	A19/71	1697Sep 8	1720ca	
Phillips Joanna	A	A1/145	1729 May17	1746 Jun25	1788 Jun10
Phillips Marcy	S	C81Aa	1730		
Phillips Rebecca	S	R26Kam	1700abt		
Phillips Rebecca	S	R26Lam	1700abt		
Phillips Ruth	S	A23Hc	1686ca	1732 Nov 9	1760 Jan15
Phillips Thomas	S	B20Ba	1705abt	1729 Dec 4	
Phillips Walter	S	A23Hcf	1665abt		
Phinney Abigail	S	X43C	1704 Jun 8		
Phinney Alice	S	X42A	1694 Apr 1		
Phinney Barnabas	S	X49C	1715 Mar28		
Phinney Benjamin	S	X17I	1682 Jun18	2 mar.	1758bef
Phinney Bethiah	S	X45A	1715 Jul 9		

NAME	DIV.	NUMBER	BIRTH	MARRIAGE	DEATH
Phinney David	S	X44G	1710 Jun10		
Phinney Ebenezer	S	X17D	1673 Feb18	1695 Nov14	1754 Apr10
Phinney Ebenezer	S	X30Baf	1673Feb 18	1695 Nov14	=X17D
Phinney Ebenezer	S	X44F	1708 May26		
Phinney Elizabeth	S	X41A	1690 Apr11		
Phinney Elizabeth	S	R12Na	1695ca	1713 Feb23	1746living
Phinney Elizabeth	S	X50G	1722ca		
Phinney Experience	S	X42H	1716 Apr 8		d.yng
Phinney Gershom	S	X43A	1699 Mar21		
Phinney Hannah	S	X17K	1687 Mar28		d.yng
Phinney Hannah	S	X41D	1700 Apr 8		
Phinney Hannah	S	X42I	1720 Apr 8		d. yng
Phinney Jabez	S	X41H	1708 Jul16		
Phinney James	S	X43D	1706 Apr15		
Phinney John	S	X17A	1665 May 5	1689 May30	1746 Nov27
Phinney John	S	X41B	1696 Apr 8		
Phinney John	S	X42B	1696 Dec17		
Phinney John Jr	S	X12Fa	1638 Dec24	1664 Aug10	1718
Phinney John Sr	S	X12Faf	1610abt		
Phinney Jonathan	S	R12Naf	1665abt		
Phinney Jonathan	S	X17J	1684 Jul30	2 mar.	1738
Phinney Jonathan	S	X50C	1718 Sep22		1739bef
Phinney Joseph	S	X17B	1667 Jan28	2 mar.	1726 Jun29
Phinney Joseph	S	X42E	1709 Apr10		
Phinney Joseph	S	X50B	1716 Jan24		
Phinney Joshua	S	X50F	1721 Jan10		
Phinney Lusanna	S	X49F	1725ca		1758living
Phinney Marcy	S	X42D	1707 Sep19		
Phinney Martha	S	X44C	1700 Apr22		
Phinney Martha	S	X41G	1706 Jul12		
Phinney Mary	S	X17F	1678 Sep 3	2 mar.	1745ca
Phinney Mary	S	X44B	1698 Mar23		
Phinney Mary	S	X42C	1700 May 5		
Phinney Mary	S	X45D	1723ca		
Phinney Mehitable	S	X30Ba	1696 Aug14	1718 Oct 9	1778 May28
Phinney Mehitable	S	X44A	1696 Aug14	1718 Oct 9	=X30Ba
Phinney Mehitable	S	X50D	1720ca		
Phinney Melatiah	S	X49B	1712 Jul26		
Phinney Mercy	S	X17G	1679 Jul10	1715 Jan26	1730ca
Phinney Mercy	S	X43E	1708 Aug24		

NAME	DIV.	NUMBER	BIRTH	MARRIAGE	DEATH
Phinney Patience	S	X41F	1704 Sep12		
Phinney Patience	S	X42G	1713 Aug19		
Phinney Pelatiah	S	X42F	1710 Mar21		
Phinney Rebecca	S	X44E	1703ca		
Phinney Reliance	S	X17H	1681 Aug27	1705 Dec27	1735 Dec 4
Phinney Rhoda	S	X45C	1718 Feb 1		
Phinney Samuel	S	X17E	1676 Nov 4	1713 Apr30	1723living
Phinney Samuel	S	X44D	1702 Apr 1		
Phinney Sarah	S	X41E	1702 Oct 8		
Phinney Seth	S	X49E	1723 Jun27		
Phinney Temperance	S	X49A	1710 Mar28		
Phinney Thankful	S	X50A	1713 Dec24		
Phinney Thankful	S	X45B	1716ca		
Phinney Thomas	S	X17C	1671 Jan	1698 Aug25	1755 Nov30
Phinney Thomas	S	X41C	1697 May25		
Phinney Thomas	S	X43B	1702 Feb17		
Phinney Timothy	S	X50E	1720ca		1739living
Phinney Zaccheus	S	X49D	1720 Aug 4		
Phippeny Rebecca	S	H17Jam	1645abt		
Pierce Barbara	A	A1/1a	1925 Jun 8	1945 Jan 6	
Pierce Barbara	D	D2a12	1925 Jun 8	1945 Jan 6	
Pierce Benjamin	A	A17/4	1726 Nov25	1746 Aug 2	1764 Jun16
Pierce Benjamin Jr	A	A17/2	1757 Dec25	1790Feb 1	1839 Apr 1
Pierce Ebenezer	S	W28Hb	1680abt		
Pierce Elizabeth Slade	A	A1/23	1822 Mar22	1840 Dec16	1901 Mar 1
Pierce Elizabeth=A1/23	D	D2/16	1822 Mar22	1840 Dec16	1901 Mar 1
Pierce Franklin Pres	A	A17/1	1804 Nov23		1869 Oct 8
Pierce Hester	D	D22a23	1610abt		
Pierce Isaac	A	A1/92	1763 Sep22	1782 Oct 7	1849 Nov26
Pierce Levi	A	A1/46	1797 Jun 8	1818 Mar 9	1838
Pierce Levi	D	D2a17	1797 Jun 8	1818 Mar 9	1838
Pierce Mary	A	A2/219	1650abt	1675	1735
Pierce Mary	S	C36Ba	1745ca		
Pierce Mial	A	A1/368	1692	1711	1786ca
Pierce Nathan	A	A1/184	1716 Feb21	1737 Oct 6	1793 Apr14
Pierce Stephen	A	A17/16	1651 Jul16	1676Nov 18	1733 Jun10
Pierce Stephen Jr	A	A17/8	1679ca	1707 Jan 5	1749 Sep 9
Pierce Thomas	A	A17/32	1608ca	1635 May 6	1683Nov 6
Pierson Thomas	A	A3/414	1665abt	1690	1722
Pieters Heyltje	A	A7/135	1635abt		1700ca

NAME	DIV.	NUMBER	BIRTH	MARRIAGE	DEATH
Pike Hannah	A	A6/97	1630abt		1718
Pike Robert	A	A6/194	1600abt		1674ca
Pinney Isaac	A	A4/498	1663	1685	1709
Pinney Jonathan	A	A19/30	1754ca	1775ca	1812
Pinney Mary	A	A4/249	1690 Mar 4	1714 Nov17	
Pinney Priscilla	A	A19/15	1778ca	1799 Dec 5	1811Oct 18
Pinson Hannah	S	F20Cam	1640abt		
Pitcher Abigail(Mary)	S	W28La	1688 Apr26	1710 Jan11	1758 Jun25
Pitcher Nathaniel	S	W28Laf	1660abt		
Pitney Martha	S	W36Cam	1640abt		
Pitney Sarah	S	W28Dam	1640abt		
Place Smith W	S	C67Ca	1775abt		
Plantagenet Joan	D	D29/24	1265abt		
Platt Mary	S	W38Bam	1630abt		
Platts Ann	S	W31Kam	1675abt		
Plum Dorcas	A	A8/225	1623ca	1655	
Plummer Ann	S	T12Dam	1640abt		
Pomeroy Medad	A	A8/226	1638	1661	1716
Pomeroy Thankful	A	A8/113	1679 May31	1698 Oct27	1773 Sep18
Pontus Mary	S	T12Cam	1635abt		
Pope Anne	A	A10/9	1635abt	1658 Dec 1	1668ca
Pope Elizabeth	S	W51Ka	1706 Jan 3	1727 Oct 9	
Pope Hannah	S	W12Ea	1639	1662ca	1709 Mar12
Pope Hannah	S	K14Ham	1639	1662ca	1709Mar 12
Pope Hannah=	S	W19Eam	1639	1662ca	1709Mar 12
Pope Joanna=K17Aa	S	W47Gam	1667ca	1682 Mar15	1695 Dec25
Pope Joanna=W47Gam	S	K17Aa	1667ca	1682 Mar15	1695 Dec25
Pope John	S	W51Kaf	1680abt		
Pope Lemuel	A	A8/106	1696 Feb21	1718 Feb 4	1771 May23
Pope Mary	S	W37Fa	1686 Sep11	1705ca	1728living
Pope Mercy	A	A8/53	1729 Jan26	1751 Sep21	1780bef
Pope Nathaniel	A	A10/18	1637ca		1659ca
Pope Seth =B14Ba	A	A8/212	1648	1675ca	1727ca
Pope Seth=A8/212	S	B14Ba	1648	1675ca	1727ca
Pope Seth=B14Ba	S	W37Faf	1648	1675ca	1727ca
Pope Seth=B14Ba	S	K17Gaf	1648	1675ca	1727ca
Pope Susanna	S	A24Bam	1650abt		
Pope Susannah=A8/223	S	B23A	1681	1701 Dec31	1760 Feb 5
Pope Susannah=B23A	S	K17Ga	1681 Jul31	1701 Dec31	1760 Feb 5
Pope Susannah=K17Ga	A	A8/223	1681	1701 Dec31	1760 Feb 5

NAME	DIV.	NUMBER	BIRTH	MARRIAGE	DEATH
Pope Thomas	S	W12Eaf	1615abt		
Pope Thomas	S	K17Aaf	1645abt		
Poppell Calvin	S	G55Bb	1910abt	1945 Aug	1964
Poppell Edgar Broward	S	G55Aa	1910	1933 Aug20	1959
Porter Abner	S	K141J	1718 Nov27		
Porter Bathsheba	S	K141A	1697ca		d.yng
Porter Bathsheba	S	K141E	1707 Sep17		
Porter Daniel	S	K141F	1708 Jun15		
Porter Elizabeth	A	A17/107	1610abt	1636Jan 20	1683Aug 13
Porter Elizabeth	A	A14/15	1754 Nov 6	1776 Feb15	
Porter Esther	S	K141I	1716 Jun20		
Porter Hannah	S	K39Fa	1712 Dec16	1740 Mar13	1787 May 2
Porter Job	S	K141H	1713 Jun 6		
Porter John	A	A5/130	1600abt	1620	1648
Porter John	S	K36Aaf	1650abt		
Porter John	S	H21Db	1666 Dec12	1728 Dec26	1747ca
Porter Martha Alice	A	A4/5	1853 Nov17		1930 Jul14
Porter Mary	A	A5/65	1638ca	1656 May27	
Porter Nicholas	S	K36Aa	1672 Apr11	1688ca	1770 Dec31
Porter Nicholas #1	S	K141B	1699 Oct27		d.yng
Porter Nicholas #2	S	K141C	1700 Oct26		
Porter Samuel	S	H21Dbf	1640abt		
Porter Samuel	S	K39Faf	1680abt		
Porter Sarah	S	K141K	1722 Apr 3	unm	1798 Jun25
Porter Susanna	S	K141G	1711 Mar20		
Porter William	S	K141D	1702 Aug19		
Porteus Mildred	D	D28/21	1755abt		
Porteus Robert Jr	D	D28/22	1730abt		
Porteus Robert Sr	D	D28a23	1700abt		
Post John	A	A16/86	1626ca	1652 Mar	1710Feb 10
Post Mary	A	A16/43	1662Nov	1685Apr 16	1705 Nov
Post Stephen	A	A16/172	1600abt	1625	1659
Potter Abel	S	C49Fa	1693ca		
Potter Fisher	S	C87Ba	1706		
Potter Hopestill	S	R25Daf	1690abt		
Potter Ichabod	S	K18Gbf	1640abt		
Potter Martha	S	K54A	1721ca		
Potter Susannah	S	R25Da	1715 Oct15	1733 Nov 4	
Potter Thomas	S	K18Gb	1663ca	1720 Dec 8	1727ca
Potts David	A	A7/88	1670ca	1693	1730 Nov16

NAME	DIV.	NUMBER	BIRTH	MARRIAGE	DEATH
Potts Elizabeth	A	A7/11	1750 Jan27	1778 Sep22	1807 Aug20
Potts John	A	A7/44	1696 Aug 8	1726 May25	1767abt
Potts Jonas	A	A3/478	1686		1754
Potts Rachel	A	A3/239	1690abt		
Potts Thomas	A	A7/22	1729ca	1753 Jan16	1776 Jul29
Powell Isaac	A	A1/444	1705abt		
Powell John	A	A1/222	1735abt		
Powell Mary	S	W28Ba	1660 May 7	1689ca	1726abt
Powell Mary	A	A1/111	1763 Jul	1779 Jan14	1841
Powell Roland	S	W28Baf	1635abt		
Power Rebecca	S	C75Ea	1643ca		
Powers Abigail	A	A16/1a	1798 Mar13	1826 Feb 5	1853 Mar30
Pratt Aaron	S	P12H	1649ca	2 mar.	1735 Feb23
Pratt Aaron	S	P21C	1690 Mar10	1724 Jun 8	1767 Mar28
Pratt Aaron	S	P45B	1732ca		
Pratt Aaron Jr	S	P43D	1734 Apr 8		
Pratt Abigail	S	K26Dbm	1665abt		
Pratt Abigail	S	P21L	1708 Aug 4	1741 Dec 8	1796 Oct18
Pratt Ann	S	P25B	1690abt		
Pratt Anna	S	P42E	1728 Sep18		
Pratt Anna	S	Q70B	1730ca		
Pratt Anne	S	P26B	1710ca		
Pratt Benajah	S	K31Aaf	1660abt		
Pratt Benjamin	S	P19D	1681 Jan19		d. yng
Pratt Benjamin	S	P21N	1710 Mar13	1749 Dec30	1763 Jan 6
Pratt Benjamin	S	P51B	1758ca	No issue	1783bef
Pratt Bernard	S	P50A	1731 Oct21		
Pratt Bethia	S	P19C	1679 Feb11	1701ca	1741
Pratt Charity	S	P42C	1725 Jul26		
Pratt Constantine	S	P50B	1734 Jun 5		
Pratt Daniel	S	P12D	1640ca		1685abt
Pratt Daniel	S	K31Aa	1680ca	1700 Jan23	1739 May 7
Pratt Daniel	S	P21B	1687 Feb 2	1719 Jun15	1749 Feb17
Pratt Daniel	S	P40G	1722		d. yng
Pratt Daniel	S	P42D	1726 Dec 2		1754living
Pratt Deborah	S	P42A	1721 Sep27		
Pratt Delivered	S	P14A	1664 Nov13	1688ca	1726living
Pratt Dorcas	S	P19E	1683 Apr 2		d. yng
Pratt ELizabeth	S	P21G	1697 Dec 5	2 mar.	
Pratt Ebenezer	S	P14D	1669 Aug31		1718bef

NAME	DIV.	NUMBER	BIRTH	MARRIAGE	DEATH
Pratt Ebenezer	S	P41I	1724 Feb23		
Pratt Elizabeth	S	P40A	1711 Jul24		1730 Sep19
Pratt Elizabeth	S	P42B	1723 Apr 5		
Pratt Elizabeth	S	P44F	1744		1754 Dec 3
Pratt Frederick	S	P51D	1762ca		1782living
Pratt George	S	P51C	1759ca	No issue	1782living
Pratt Hannah	S	Q22Aam	1675abt		
Pratt Hannah	S	T18Dam	1680abt		
Pratt Hannah	S	P25E	1700abt		
Pratt Hannah	S	P21K	1706 Apr	1737 Jul22	1739bef
Pratt Hannah	S	P32E	1708 May17		
Pratt Hannah	S	P41C	1714 Mar16		
Pratt Hannah	S	P44A	1732ca		
Pratt Henry	S	P21A	1685 Jun 5	1709 Dec	1750 Nov 1
Pratt Henry	S	P41E	1717 Nov29		
Pratt Isabella	S	P51A	1753ca		
Pratt Jane	S	Q17Gb	1710abt	1736 Nov 9	1788 Feb22
Pratt Jane	S	P47B	1735ca		
Pratt Jared/Gerard	S	P50D	1939 Sep22		
Pratt Jeremiah	S	P14G	1674 Oct13	1700abt	1718living
Pratt Jeremiah	S	P41J	1726 Jul25		d yng
Pratt Joanna	S	A26Ba	1690 Oct26	1715 Jan19	1747living
Pratt John	S	P12A	1631ca	1663ca	1697aft
Pratt John	S	A26Baf	1665abt		
Pratt John	S	P14C	1667 Oct	1690abt	
Pratt John	S	P21E	1693 Mar 4	1725 Jan 8	1780
Pratt John	S	P32B	1700 Aug22		
Pratt John	S	P43A	1728 Dec17		
Pratt John	S	P45A	1730ca		
Pratt Jonathan	S	P25A	1690abt		
Pratt Jonathan	S	P21D	1692 Nov 6	1729 Mar14	1786
Pratt Jonathan	S	P44B	1734 Apr15		1754 Nov25
Pratt Joseph	S	P12Haf	1640abt		
Pratt Joseph	S	P12F	1645ca	1674 Feb12	1712 Dec24
Pratt Joseph	S	Q22Faf	1675abt		
Pratt Joseph	S	P19B	1677 Oct19		1712bef
Pratt Joseph	S	P43F	1742 Nov19		
Pratt Joseph=Q22Faf	S	Q22Daf	1675abt		
Pratt Joshua	S	P14F	1672 Jan10		
Pratt Joshua	S	P19G	1686 Jun28	1722 May22	1737living

NAME	DIV.	NUMBER	BIRTH	MARRIAGE	DEATH
Pratt Joshua	S	K117A	1701 Dec27		1730abt
Pratt Joshua	S	P38A	1733bef		
Pratt Leah	S	P44C	1736 Aug 5		1754 Dec 5
Pratt Lemuel	S	P41F	1719 May19		
Pratt Lucy	S	P44G	1754ca		
Pratt Lydia	S	P19H	1688 Nov28		1694 Aug31
Pratt Lydia	S	P42H	1738 Sep 5		1753living
Pratt Malatiah	S	Q14Ebm	1680abt		
Pratt Martha twin	S	P42G	1732 Sep25		1761living
Pratt Mary	S	P12B	1633ca	1655 Mar 2	1702 Feb11
Pratt Mary	S	P14B	1666 Apr		
Pratt Mary	S	P19A	1675 Sep16	1707 Oct25	1746bef
Pratt Mary	S	P21I	1701 Dec10		d.yng
Pratt Mary	S	P32G	1716 Jul11		
Pratt Mary	S	P40E	1717 Jan 6		d. yng
Pratt Mary	S	P43B	1730		
Pratt Mary	S	P45D	1736ca		
Pratt Mary twin	S	P42F	1732 Sep25 unm		1804 Mar 1
Pratt Mehitabel	S	W55Bam	1670abt		
Pratt Mehitabel	S	P40B	1712 Oct12		1730 Sep19
Pratt Mercy	S	P12E	1642ca	1662ca	1692ca
Pratt Mercy	S	P14H	1676 Dec23		
Pratt Mercy	S	P25C	1695abt		
Pratt Mercy	S	P21J	1703 Dec 6	1724 Sep12	1757living
Pratt Mercy	S	P41M	1733 Mar16		
Pratt Moses	S	P21H	1699 Dec31	1732 Oct 5	1751bef
Pratt Moses	S	P41L	1729 Jun27		
Pratt Moses Jr	S	P47A	1733ca		
Pratt Nathan	S	P32C	1703 Jun20		1746living
Pratt Nathaniel	S	Q22Fa	1700 Mar23	1728ca	1749 Dec24
Pratt Nathaniel	S	P21O	1712ca	1735 Nov27	1736 Mar29
Pratt Noah	S	P41D	1715 Sep10		
Pratt Olive	S	P50E	1741 Oct12		
Pratt Oliver	S	P26A	1700ca		
Pratt Oliver twin	S	P41A	1712 Nov25		
Pratt Patience	S	Q15Aa	1682ca	1703 Oct28	1718 Mar29
Pratt Peter	S	P12G	1647ca	1679 Aug 5	1688 Mar24
Pratt Peter	S	P20A	1680ca	1709 Sep 7	1730 Nov22
Pratt Peter	S	P40D	1716 Jul19		
Pratt Phineas	S	P11Aa	1593ca	1630ca	1680 Apr19

NAME		DIV.	NUMBER	BIRTH	MARRIAGE	DEATH
Pratt Phineas		S	P14E	1671 Apr		
Pratt Phineas		S	P19F	1683 Mar18		
Pratt Phineas		S	P21M	1709 Dec31	1731 Jul28	1779 Sep 5
Pratt Phineas		S	P32F	1713 Jun11		
Pratt Phineas		S	P40F	1720 Oct20		
Pratt Phineas		S	P50F	1743 Mar27		
Pratt Priscilla		S	P45C	1734 Feb12		
Pratt Rachel		S	P17A	1675ca		1715bef
Pratt Rachel		S	P44D	1739 Aug 4		1754 Nov19
Pratt Rhoda		S	P50C	1735 Feb22		
Pratt Rhoda		S	P44E	1742 May14		1754 Nov25
Pratt Samuel		S	P12C	1636ca	1667ca	1676 Mar26
Pratt Samuel		S	P16B	1670ca	1696ca	1745
Pratt Samuel		S	P32A	1697 May15		
Pratt Sarah		S	P12Ha	1664 May31	1684ca	1706 Jul22
Pratt Sarah		S	P20Aam	1665abt		
Pratt Sarah		S	P16A	1668ca	1691 Jul30	1702 May14
Pratt Sarah		A	A4/511	1680	1697	
Pratt Sarah		S	P19I	1690	1714 Jan11	1762 Jun 4
Pratt Sarah		S	P21F	1695 Oct23	1720 Jul 4	1721 Oct14
Pratt Sarah		S	P25D	1695abt		
Pratt Sarah		S	K117B	1703 Oct 1		
Pratt Sarah		S	P32D	1705 Aug18		
Pratt Sarah		S	Q22Da	1705ca	1728ca	1737 Jun23
Pratt Sarah		S	P40C	1714 Sep 1		d. yng
Pratt Sarah		S	P41G	1721 Jun10		
Pratt Sarah		S	P43C	1731 Dec27		
Pratt Seth		S	Q70A	1729 Jun21		
Pratt Silas		S	P41K	1727 Mar23		
Pratt Susanna		S	R20Cam	1675abt		
Pratt Sybil		S	P41H	1723 Jun19		
Pratt Temperance		S	P40H	1723 Dec20		
Pratt Thomas		S	P43E	1736 Nov14		
Pratt Zebediah	twin	S	P41B	1712 Nov25		
Prence Elizabeth		S	W45Dam	1660abt		
Prence Hannah		S	H17Iam	1650abt		
Prence Jane		S	H12Ab	1637 Nov 1	1660 Jan 9	1712 Jun
Prence Mary		S	H17Fam	1640abt		
Prence Mary		S	X18Aam	1650abt		
Prence Mercy		S	H17Bam	1630abt		

NAME	DIV.	NUMBER	BIRTH	MARRIAGE	DEATH
Prence Thomas	S	H12Abf	1610abt		
Prentice Grace	S	R117Fb	1704 Jan26	1734 Oct 2	
Prentice Samuel	S	R117Fbf	1680abt		
Presbury Abigail	A	A8/109	1703ca	1728ca	1749 Jun25
Presbury Stephen	S	W41Ba	1672ca	1693ca	1730
Presbury Stephen=W41Ba	A	A8/218	1672ca	1693ca	1730ca
Prescott Abel	A	A1/146	1718 Apr 7	1742ca	1805 Oct22
Prescott Jonathan Jr	A	A1/292	1677	1701	1729
Prescott Lucy	A	A1/73	1757 Apr24	1776 Dec 6	1792 Oct10
Price Daniel	A	A3/54	1761 Oct22	1783 Dec17	1846 Aug 2
Price Edith	A	A3/27	1801 May 9	1820 Dec 7	1873 Feb11
Price Hugh	S	K15Fa	1660abt	1685bef	1691bef
Price John	S	K33B	1688 Dec 7	unm.	1711bef
Price Mary	S	K33A	1685 Jul25	1706 Jan20	1748 May29
Price Mordecai	A	A3/432	1660ca		1715ca
Price Mordecai Jr.	A	A3/216	1698ca	1724Apr 28	
Price Samuel	A	A3/108	1739 Feb28	1760 Oct25	1825 Apr16
Price Walter	A	A3/218	1710abt		1782Nov 11
Priest Degory	S	P10A	ˏ1579ca	1611 Nov 4	1620 Jan 1
Priest Hannah	A	A19/17	1751ca	1779 Sep 8	1829May 2
Priest James	A	A19/34	1720ca		1750Sep 8
Priest Joseph	A	A19/136	1650ca	1677ca	
Priest Joseph Jr	A	A19/68	1678Mar 18	1701 Dec25	1756Apr 28
Priest Mary	S	P11A	1613ca	1630ca	1689bef
Priest Sarah	S	P11B	1615ca	1631ca	1648living
Prince Charles	D	D28/14	1948	1981	
Prince Hannah	S	F41E	1738 Dec13		
Prince John	S	F18Da	1693 Mar	1713 Nov16	
Prince John	S	F41A	1716 Sep18		
Prince Joseph	S	F41B	1718 May10		
Prince Philip	D	D28a15	1921		
Prince Rebecca	S	F41C	1719 Sep 9		
Prince Ruth	S	H33Dam	1675abt		
Prince Ruth	S	K29Dam	1680abt		
Prince Samuel	S	F41D	1724 Apr26		
Princess Diana Spencer	D	D28a14	1961	1981	
Prothero Elizabeth	A	A3/367	1670abt	1694	
Proudfoot Margaret	S	G52Ma	1830ca		
Provoest Ralph Martin	S	C59Ca	1931		
Prowne John	D	D30a24	1400abt		

NAME	DIV.	NUMBER	BIRTH	MARRIAGE	DEATH
Prowse Agnes	D	D30/18	1570abt		
Prowse John II	D	D30/22	1460abt		
Prowse John III	D	D30/20	1510abt		
Prowse John IV	D	D30/19	1540abt		
Prowse Richard	D	D30/23	1430abt		
Prowse Robert	D	D30/21	1490abt		
Pulsipher David	A	A19/220	1685	1707	
Pulsipher David Jr	A	A19/110	1708 May 7	1740Oct 2	
Pulsipher Mary	A	A19/55	1744 Jan19	1760	1827 Jan19
Purchase Abigail	A	A16/101	1624abt		
Purchase Aquila	A	A16/202	1590abt	1613	1633
Purchase Ruth	S	A23Hcm	1665abt		
Putnam Priscilla	A	A19/45	1751 Aug22	1774Dec3	1837 Oct 6
Putnam Tarrant	A	A19/180	1688	1715	1732
Putnam Tarrant Jr	A	A19/90	1716 Apr 3	1742Dec 9	1794Aug 27
Pyle Jane (Pile)	A	A14/277	1560ca	1582	1607aft
Queen Elizabeth I	D	D28/16	1900		
Queen Elizabeth II	D	D28/15	1926	REIGN	(1952-
Quincy Daniel	A	A11/28	1650 Feb7	1682 Nov9	1690 Aug10
Quincy Edmund	A	A11/112	1602 May	1623 Jul14	1637
Quincy Edmund Jr.	A	A11/56	1627 Mar	1648 Jul26	1697 Jan7
Quincy Elizabeth	A	A11/7	1721 Dec	1740 Oct16	1775 Oct1
Quincy John	A	A11/14	1689 Jul21	1715 Oct6	1767 Jul13
Rainiar IV of Hainault	D	D30a39	980abt		
Rainsford Dorothy	S	W36Eam	1660abt		
Ramsey James	A	A14/28	1725ca		
Ramsey James Jr.	A	A14/14	1751 Jun 8	1776 Feb15	1810 Mar17
Ramsey Mary	A	A14/7	1781 Mar30	1798 Oct11	1813 Feb10
Randall Elizabeth	A	A16/27	1673 Jul 3	1701 Mar27	
Ransom Hannah	S	A26Dam	1680abt		
Ransom Sybil	S	C20Ha	1760ca		
Rathbone John	S	K23Aaf	1635abt		
Rathbone John=K23Aaf	S	K23Baf	1635abt		
Rathbone Margaret	S	K23Aa	1660ca	1682bef	1736aft
Rathbone Martha	S	C16Aa	1731		
Rathbone Mary	S	C14Da	1720ca		
Rathbone Sarah	S	K23Cam	1645abt		
Rathbone Sarah	S	K23Ba	1665ca	1690ca	1699aft
Rathborn Sarah	S	G51Db	1790abt		
Rawlins Edith	S	W46Cam	1660abt		

NAME	DIV.	NUMBER	BIRTH	MARRIAGE	DEATH
Rawson Abner	A	A2/18	1721 Apr27	1745 May17	1794 Nov14
Rawson Edmund	A	A2/36	1689 Jul 8	1717 May22	1765 May20
Rawson Edward	A	A2/144	1615		1693
Rawson Grindall	A	A2/72	1659 Jan23	1682 Aug30	1714 Feb 6
Rawson Rhoda	A	A2/9	1749 Oct4	1769 Jun 1	1827 Jun 9
Ray Bridget	A	A17/231	1576ca		
Ray James	S	G58Ab	1950abt	1990 Nov10	
Raymond Ann	S	R12Ca	1664 May12	1681ca	1705bef
Raymond Anna	S	R19Gbm	1665abt		
Raymond James	S	Q16Aa	1689 Jun 1	1716 Dec27	1753aft
Raymond John	S	Q16Aaf	1665abt		
Raymond Joshua	S	R12Caf	1640abt		
Raymond Mercy	S	Q34B	1720 Apr 3		
Raymond Paul	S	C19Ba	1747ca		
Raymond Peter	S	Q34A	1718 Mar27		
Raynor Edward	D	D4amf24	1580 abt		
Raynor Elizabeth	D	D4am24	1615abt		
Read Elizabeth	A	A19/215	1665	1686	
Read Hopestill	A	A2/51	1693 Apr 1	1722 Apr 9	1762 Mar15
Read Samuel	A	A2/204	1645ca	1665	1717
Read Samuel Jr.	A	A2/102	1669 Nov 3	1693ca	1724 Feb14
Reade Andrew	A	A10/88	1545abt		1623 Jul 8
Reade George	A	A10/22	1608 Oct25	1641ca	1674aft
Reade Mildred=A10/11	D	D28a25	1645abt	1671ca	1694ca
Reade Mildred=D28a25	A	A10/11	1645abt	1671ca	1694ca
Reade Robert	A	A10/44	1570abt	1600 Jul31	1627ca
Reagan John Edward	A	A9/2	1883 Jul13	1904 Nov 8	1941 May18
Reagan John Michael	A	A9/4	1854ca	1878 Feb27	1889 Jan10
Reagan Michael	A	A9/8	1829 Sep 3	1852 Oct31	1884 Mar2
Reagan Ronald Wilson	A	A9/1	1911 Feb 6	1/1940Jan	=D26a16
Reagan Ronald Wilson	D	D26a16	1911 Feb 6	1952 Mar 4	U.S. Pres.
Reagan Thomas	A	A9/16	1825abt		1852 Oct31
Reames Mary	A	A3/157	1730abt	1751 July1	
Record Margaret	A	A3/213	1715abt	1733	
Reder Sarah	S	A11Cam	1685abt		
Reed Abigail	S	K156H	1745 Apr10		
Reed Alice	S	K144A	1703 Oct19		d.yng
Reed Alice	S	K144E	1711 Apr 4		1724 Sep29
Reed Alice	S	K144J	1725 Apr19		
Reed Anne	S	W46Eb	1701ca	1737 Jul27	1770 Jan 8

NAME	DIV.	NUMBER	BIRTH	MARRIAGE	DEATH
Reed Barnabas	S	K156I	1748 Apr30		
Reed Bathsheba	S	K36A	1676ca	1688ca	1725ca
Reed Benjamin	S	K145I	1730 Apr 8		d.yng
Reed Betty #1	S	K146F	1731 Mar 1		d.yng
Reed Betty #2	S	K146G	1734 Oct 1		
Reed Daniel	s	K144F	1713 Dec 6		
Reed David twin	S	K156D	1740 Jul 9		
Reed Ebenezer	S	K144D	1709 Jul13	1723Feb 21	1790 Apr16
Reed Ebenezer	S	K156A	1733 Dec11		d.yng
Reed Ebenezer	S	K156J	1751 Dec13		1764Jul 12
Reed Ebenezer=K144D	S	K39Ha	1709 Jul13	1723 Feb21	1790 Apr16
Reed Elijah	S	K146E	1727 Feb14		
Reed Ezekiel	S	K145E	1722 ca		
Reed Hannah	S	K36Bam	1650abt		
Reed Hannah	S	K146C	1722 Feb26		
Reed Hester	S	K36F	1685ca		1705living
Reed Ichabod	S	K156C	1738 Apr26		
Reed Jacob	S	K36H	1691 Nov 6	2 mar.	1766
Reed Jacob	S	K146B	1720 Jul 7		
Reed James	S	W46Ebf	1675abt		
Reed James	S	K144G	1716 Mar 3		
Reed James	S	K145B	1716 Oct12		
Reed John	S	K36C	1680 Oct21		d.yng
Reed John	S	K36G	1687 Jul10	2 mar.	1739bef
Reed John	S	K145A	1713 Aug10		
Reed Jonathan twin	S	K156E	1740 Jul 9		
Reed Joseph	S	K145C	1717 Feb13		
Reed Martha	A	A2/123	1670ca	1697 Mar 3	
Reed Mary	S	K36E	1684ca		1705living
Reed Mary	S	K145D	1719 Dec21		
Reed Mercy	S	K36B	1676ca	2 mar.	1737 Feb 4
Reed Moses	S	K144I	1722 Jan15		
Reed Obadiah	S	K144C	1706 Mar14		
Reed Paul twin	S	K156F	1743 Mar 3		d.yng
Reed Peter	S	K145F	1723 ca		
Reed Samuel	S	K145J	1732 Jul13		
Reed Sarah	S	K36I	1694 Mar21	1712 May14	1750 May17
Reed Sarah	S	K146A	1718 May 2		
Reed Silas twin	S	K156G	1743 Mar 3		d.yng
Reed Silence	S	K145H	1728 Aug10		d.yng

NAME	DIV.	NUMBER	BIRTH	MARRIAGE	DEATH
Reed Solomon	S	K144H	1719 Oct22		
Reed Squire	S	K145G	1725 May25		
Reed William	S	K36D	1682 May24	1703ca	1753 Jun 3
Reed William	S	K39Haf	1685abt		
Reed William	S	K144B	1705 Dec15		1724 Nov21
Reed William	S	K146D	1725 Sep20		
Reed William	S	K156B	1735 Oct23		
Reed William Jr	S	K16Ea	1639 Dec15	1675ca	1706ca
Reed William Sr	S	K16Eaf	1615abt		
Reynolds Elizabeth	S	L20Iam	1725abt		
Reynor Elizabeth	D	D29a10	1615abt		
Rice David	A	A19/166	1659	1687	
Rice Elizabeth	A	A19/161	1648	1668ca	1739
Rice Hannah	A	A19/211	1659	1681	1747
Rice Hannah	A	A19/83	1691 Jan 5	1711Nov 15	
Rice Martha	A	A19/165	1657	1688ca	
Rice Sally	A	A19/21	1761ca	1782 Feb18	1835 Jan 3
Rich Lydia	S	H26Ea	1686ca		1748aft
Rich Richard	S	H26Eaf	1660abt		
Richard Alice	S	W19Bam	1614	1650	1683
Richard Alice	D	D27a24	1614	1650	1683
Richard Sarah	S	T25Fam	1670abt		
Richards Alice=W18Aam	S	X20Aam	1627ca	1650aft	1671 Dec12
Richards Alice=X20Aam	S	W18Aam	1627ca	1650aft	1671 Dec12
Richards Alice=X20Aam	S	R11Ba	1627ca	1650	1671 Dec12
Richards Elizabeth	S	T13Fa	1684ca	1703 Feb 8	1729 Jan26
Richards Sarah	S	C12Ha	1720ca		
Richards Thomas	S	R11Baf	1600abt		
Richards William	S	T13Faf	1655abt		
Richardson Aaron	S	P27F	1702 Dec16		
Richardson Abigail	S	P27E	1696 Jan15		
Richardson Elizabeth	S	P27B	1689 Oct20	unm.	1735 Aug11
Richardson Ezekiel	A	A17/76	1604ca		1647 Oct21
Richardson Ezekiel	S	P15Ca	1655 Oct28	1687 Jul27	1733 Mar13
Richardson Ezekiel	S	P27D	1694 Apr22		
Richardson Josiah	A	A17/38	1635ca	1659 Jun 6	1695 Jun22
Richardson Sarah	A	A17/19	1659Mar 25	1677Sep 19	1748Jan 30
Richardson Theophilus	S	P15Caf	1630abt		
Richardson Theophilus1	S	P27A	1688		d yng
Richardson Theophilus2	S	P27C	1691 Jan 7		

NAME	DIV.	NUMBER	BIRTH	MARRIAGE	DEATH
Richardson Thomas	A	A17/152	1560abt		1633
Richmond Abigail	S	X23G	1678 Feb26	1708 Jul29	1763 Feb28
Richmond Abigail	S	X69E	1697ca		
Richmond Anna	S	X74C	1704 Oct14		
Richmond Christopher	S	X69B	1689ca		
Richmond Ebenezer	S	X23F	1676 May12	1701bef	1729
Richmond Ebenezer	S	X74A	1701 Mar31		
Richmond Edward	S	X20Caf	1650abt		
Richmond Edward	S	X23B	1665 Feb 8	1685abt	1741bef
Richmond Edward	S	X70B	1696ca		
Richmond Elizabeth	S	X60B	1696 May10		
Richmond Elizabeth	S	X74E	1708 Sep 1		
Richmond Elizabeth	S	X70F	1708ca		
Richmond Hannah	S	X71D	1702 Aug29		
Richmond Hannah	S	X60H	1709 Jul 9		1728 Jan20
Richmond Henry	S	X69C	1692ca		
Richmond Ichabod	S	X60F	1704 Feb27		
Richmond John	S	X13Ca	1627ca	1660abt	1715 Oct 7
Richmond John	S	X23E	1673 Dec 5	1709 Nov28	1760bef
Richmond John	S	X69D	1695ca		
Richmond John	S	X73A	1710ca		
Richmond John Sr	S	X13Caf	1600abt		
Richmond Joseph	S	X23A	1663 Dec 8	1685 Jun26	1730ca
Richmond Joseph	S	X69A	1686ca		
Richmond Josiah	S	X70C	1697ca		
Richmond Josiah	S	X69H	1700ca		
Richmond Lydia	S	X71E	1704 May14		
Richmond Margaret	S	X69I	1702ca		1737living
Richmond Mary	S	X69F	1699ca		
Richmond Mary	S	X73B	1712ca		1739living
Richmond Mary	S	X60J	1713 Nov29		
Richmond Mary	S	X70I	1716ca		1738aft
Richmond Mehitable	S	X71G	1712ca		
Richmond Mercy	S	X70A	1694ca		1760 Jan27
Richmond Nathaniel	S	X70D	1700ca		1740ca
Richmond Oliver	S	X71B	1697 Aug25		
Richmond Peleg	S	X60D	1700 Oct25		
Richmond Perez	S	X60E	1702 Oct 5		
Richmond Phebe	S	X70G	1713ca		
Richmond Priscilla	S	X70J	1718ca		

NAME	DIV.	NUMBER	BIRTH	MARRIAGE	DEATH
Richmond Rachel	S	X74D	1707 May 6		1730living
Richmond Robert	S	X74B	1702 Sep18		
Richmond Rogers	S	X60K	1716 May25		
Richmond Ruth	S	X60G	1705 Mar 7		
Richmond Samuel	S	X23C	1668 Sep23	2 mar.	1736
Richmond Samuel	S	X71A	1695 Oct16		
Richmond Sarah	S	X23D	1670 Feb26	1699 Oct 6	1727 Nov27
Richmond Sarah	S	X60I	1711 Oct31		
Richmond Sarah	S	X70H	1714ca		
Richmond Seth	S	X70E	1705ca		
Richmond Silas	S	X71F	1710ca		
Richmond Silvester	S	X20Ca	1673ca	1693	1754 Nov20
Richmond Silvester	S	X60C	1698 Jun30		
Richmond Stephen	S	X73C	1719ca		
Richmond Susanna	S	W46Ebm	1675abt		
Richmond Sylvester	S	X74F	1711 Nov25		
Richmond Thomas	S	X71C	1700 Sep10		1737living
Richmond William	S	X60A	1694 Oct10		
Richmond William	S	X69G	1699ca		
Rickard Abner	S	Q77C	1744 Sep28		
Rickard Amasa	S	Q75D	1738 Jul10		
Rickard Benjamin	S	K102C	1726 Jun 7		
Rickard Bethiah	S	Q23D	1698 Oct15	1724 May 6	1764aft
Rickard Deborah	S	Q77H	1758 May26		1784 Aug26
Rickard Eleazer	S	Q23I	1709 Mar 8	1739 Aug 2	1784 Jan 7
Rickard Eleazer	S	Q77B	1742 Jul22		
Rickard Elijah	S	Q77G	1756 Jan24		
Rickard Elizabeth	S	K27F	1694ca	1720 Jun 9	1731 Dec 7
Rickard Elizabeth	S	Q72E	1732 Mar 2		
Rickard Elkanah	S	Q23G	1704 Jun 7	2 mar.	1777 Jul21
Rickard Elkanah	S	Q75B	1732 Aug19		1788 Aug16
Rickard Esther	S	K27E	1691 Apr 1		1713 Jun26
Rickard Giles Jr	S	Q13Ea	1659	1683 Nov 7	1709 Jan29
Rickard Giles Sr	S	Q13Eaf	1625abt		=Q13Gaf
Rickard Giles=Q13Eaf	S	Q13Gaf	1625abt		
Rickard Hannah	S	Q23B	1693 Sep25	1720 Apr12	1771 Oct17
Rickard Hannah	S	K102F	1736 Mar10		
Rickard Henry	S	Q23E	1700 Feb 4	1723 Feb13	1771aft
Rickard Isaac	S	Q74C	1728 Feb 6		
Rickard James	S	K27G	1696 Sep25	1720 Jun29	

NAME	DIV.	NUMBER	BIRTH	MARRIAGE	DEATH
Rickard James	S	K100A	1706 Nov15		
Rickard James	S	K102A	1721 Jun11		
Rickard John	S	K14Da	1657 Nov24	1678ca	1712 Apr25
Rickard John	S	K27A	1679 Feb26		d.yng
Rickard John	S	K27C	1684 Feb 3	1706ca	1742
Rickard John	S	K102B	1723 Jul22		
Rickard John Sr	S	K14Daf	1635abt		
Rickard Judah	S	Q74B	1725 Mar 1		
Rickard Judith	S	K26Bam	1660abt		
Rickard Judith	S	W57Cam	1670abt		
Rickard Keturah	S	Q75F	1744 Jun13		
Rickard Keziah	S	Q77F	1753 Aug26		
Rickard Lazarus	S	Q72D	1730 May29		
Rickard Lemuel	S	Q72A	1722 Nov 6		
Rickard Lothrop	S	K102D	1730 Mar10		
Rickard Marcy	S	Q77A	1740 Jul		
Rickard Margaret	S	K100B	1708 Apr 5		
Rickard Mariah	S	K100D	1711 Sep29		
Rickard Mary	S	K27D	1688ca		1711living
Rickard Mary	S	Q23F	1702 Apr 8		
Rickard Mary	S	K100C	1709 Oct 4		
Rickard Mary	S	Q77D	1747 Aug29		
Rickard Mehitable	S	Q23H	1707 Apr 1	1730 Nov12	1741bef
Rickard Mercy	S	K27B	1682 Feb 3	1710 Apr 4	1717?
Rickard Nathaniel	S	Q75A	1730 Jul13		
Rickard Rachel	S	Q72F	1736 May17		
Rickard Rebecca	S	Q72G	1740 Apr17		1757 Feb24
Rickard Rebeckah	S	Q23A	1690 Feb 9		
Rickard Rececca	S	R14Dbm	1655abt		
Rickard Samuel	S	Q13Ga	1662 Jan14	1689 Dec31	1727 Sep 7
Rickard Samuel	S	Q23C	1696 May21	1721 Oct19	1768 Aug21
Rickard Samuel	S	Q74A	1724 Sep26		
Rickard Samuel	S	Q72C	1727 Oct12		
Rickard Sarah	S	Q77E	1749 Oct 9		
Rickard Seth	S	Q75C	1735 Dec14		
Rickard Theophilus	S	Q72B	1725 Jan26		
Rickard Uriah	S	Q75E	1740 Jun27		
Rickard William	S	K102E	1733 Nov21		
Ricketson Jonathan	A	A4/476	1688	1710	=D18a/23
Ricketson Jonathan Jr	A	A4/238	1725 Mar	1747 Oct12	1772 Feb21

NAME	DIV.	NUMBER	BIRTH	MARRIAGE	DEATH
Ricketson Jonathan Jr	D	D18/22	1725 Mar	1747 Oct12	=A04/238
Ricketson Jonathan Sr	D	D18a23	1688	1710	1768
Ricketson Rhoda	A	A4/119	1748 Aug 8	1765 Dec19	1828ca
Rider John	S	W22B	1663ca	1692ca	1736bef
Rider Joseph	S	W57Ba	1691 Jul	1722 Nov 1	1737 Jul18
Rider Samuel	S	W22A	1657ca		d. yng
Rider Samuel	S	W57Baf	1665abt		
Rider Samuel Jr	S	W12Da	1632 Nov	1656 Dec23	1715 Jul18
Rider Samuel Sr	S	W12Daf	1610abt		
Rider Sarah	S	W57Iam	1690abt		
Ridley Elizabeth	S	H21Ea	1680ca	1700 Feb25	
Ridley Mark	S	H21Eaf	1655abt		
Riggs Mary	A	A2/159	1635abt	1660ca	
Rightmire James	S	G50Ebf	1720abt		
Rightmire Phebe	S	G50Eb	1750abt		
Rindge Susanna	A	A2/197	1645abt	1671	
Ring Andrew	S	H11Fa	1618ca	1646 Apr23	1692 Feb22
Ring Andrew	S	H33B	1689 Nov14		1695abt
Ring Andrew	S	T20Da	1696 Mar28	1724 May20	1744 Nov17
Ring Andrew	S	H33E	1696 Mar28	1724 May20	1744 Nov17
Ring Andrew	S	T51B	1727 Sep14		1729 Sep13
Ring Andrew	S	H116B	1727 Sep14		d yng
Ring Andrew	S	H119A	1748 Dec28		d yng
Ring Deborah	S	H14E	1660ca	unm.	
Ring Deborah	S	H32A	1694 Jan24		1696 May29
Ring Deborah	S	H33F	1698 Jul10	1722 Feb 7	1763 Nov 8
Ring Deborah	S	H32F	1708 Feb 5	1737 May12	1738 Aug29
Ring Deborah	S	T51H	1742 Jul21		
Ring Deborah	S	H116H	1742 Jul21		
Ring Eleazer	S	H14C	1655ca	1687 Jan11	1749 Nov21
Ring Eleazer	S	H33A	1688 Nov 7		1688 Dec 3
Ring Eleazer	S	H32E	1704 Jan16		1734 Feb 3
Ring Eleazer	S	T51G	1740 May 7		
Ring Eleazer	S	H115K	1744 Jul29		d yng
Ring Eleazer	S	H119B	1749 Dec31		
Ring Eleazer=T12Kaf	S	T20Daf	1665abt		
Ring Eleazer=T15Faf	S	T12Kaf	1665abt		
Ring Eleazer=T20Daf	S	T15Faf	1665abt		
Ring Eleazer=T51G	S	H116G	1740 May 7		
Ring Eliphaz	S	H115J	1742 Jan 7		

NAME	DIV.	NUMBER	BIRTH	MARRIAGE	DEATH
Ring Elizabeth	S	H12Eam	1605abt		
Ring Elizabeth	S	H12Aam	1615abt		
Ring Elizabeth	S	H14A	1652 Apr19	1676aft	1690abt
Ring Elizabeth	S	H32D	1701 Feb15	1719 Nov20	1775 Oct17
Ring Elizabeth	S	H33K	1708 May 9	1736 Jun26	1768 Nov11
Ring Elizabeth	S	H115G	1736 Aug 5		
Ring Elizabeth=H12Aam	S	H13Eam	1600abt		
Ring Elkanah	S	H33J	1706 Oct19		1759living
Ring Elkanah	S	H119G	1762 Oct 6		d yng
Ring Francis	S	H115H	1737 Jan28		
Ring George	S	H115A	1726 May19		
Ring Grace #1	S	H115B	1727 Nov14		d. yng
Ring Grace #2	S	H115C	1730 Apr 6		
Ring Hannah	S	H32B	1697 May26		1715 June1
Ring Hannah	S	T51D	1733 Jan10		
Ring Hannah	S	H116D	1733 Jan10		
Ring Jonathan	S	H33H	1702 Dec23	1747 Jan21	1774ca
Ring Jonathan	S	H119E	1757 Mar 1		
Ring Joseph	S	H119C	1751 Nov 3		
Ring Louisa	S	H115I	1740 Jul16		d yng
Ring Lydia	S	H33L	1710 Nov20		1788 Mar 3
Ring Lydia twin	S	H115D	1730 Apr 6		
Ring Mary	S	H14D	1658ca	1687 Mar 4	1731 Oct31
Ring Mary	S	K16Jam	1665abt		
Ring Mary	S	H116A	1714 Feb28		
Ring Mary	S	H115E	1731 Mar17		
Ring Mary =T15Fa	S	H33G	1700 Dec 9	1722 Nov 7	1739living
Ring Mary=H116A	S	T51A	1724 Feb28		
Ring Mary=H33G	S	T15Fa	1700 Dec 9	1722 Nov 7	1739living
Ring Mary=T15Fa	S	R25Fbm	1700 Dec 9	1722 Nov 7	1739living
Ring Molly	S	H119F	1760 Jul29		
Ring Phebe	S	T12Ka	1691 Jan26	1719 Nov26	1756 May15
Ring Phebe	S	H33C	1691 Jan26	1719 Nov26	1756 May15
Ring Samuel	S	H33D	1693 Mar12	1724 Jan28	1768 May 8
Ring Samuel	S	H115F	1733 Feb14		1747Sep 1
Ring Sarah	S	H116F	1737 Sep 2		
Ring Sarah	S	H119D	1754 Jun12	unm.	1827 Oct23
Ring Susanna	S	H14F	1662ca	unm.	
Ring Susanna	S	H33I	1705 Apr 9	1725 Jan27	1728 Sep10
Ring Susanna	S	H116C	1730 Jun 3		

NAME	DIV.	NUMBER	BIRTH	MARRIAGE	DEATH
Ring Susannah	S	T51C	1730 June3		
Ring William	S	H11Faf	1590abt		
Ring William	S	H14B	1653ca	1693 Jun13	1730ca
Ring William	S	H32C	1699 Jul24		1728 Dec25
Ring William	S	H116E	1735		
Ring William	S	T51E	1735 Aug 7		
Ripley Alethea	S	R63H	1738 Apr24		
Ripley Alice	S	R19A	1683 Sep18	1703 Apr18	1730 Dec18
Ripley Ann	S	R63C	1726 Aug24		
Ripley Anna	S	R19L	1704 Nov 1	1730ca	1747bef
Ripley Bradford	S	R63K	1744 Dec26	unm.	1775
Ripley David	S	R19I	1697 May20	1720 Mar21	1781 Feb16
Ripley David	S	R63E	1730 Feb 7		
Ripley Ebenezer	S	R58G	1729 Jun27		
Ripley Elizabeth	S	R58E	1724 Nov 4		
Ripley Faith	S	R19C	1686 Sep20	1708 Jan 5	1720 Feb11
Ripley Faith	S	R63A	1722 May 1		
Ripley Gamaliel	S	R63G	1736 Apr19		1737 May30
Ripley Gamaliel	S	R63I	1740 Oct20		
Ripley Hannah	S	R19B	1685 Mar 2	1711 Oct 8	1751 Mar19
Ripley Hannah	S	R58C	1718 Jan12	unm.	1750 Nov 8
Ripley Hannah	S	R63L	1750 Feb27		
Ripley Hezekiah	S	R19H	1695 Jun10	2 Mar	1779 Feb 4
Ripley Hezekiah	S	R63J	1743 Feb 3		
Ripley Hezekiah	S	R62A	1748 Sep25		
Ripley Irena	S	R19J	1700 Aug28	1719 Apr20	1726 Jan20
Ripley Irene	S	R63D	1728 Feb11		
Ripley Jerusha	S	R19K	1704 Nov 1	1744 Sep 9	1792 Nov 8
Ripley John	S	R12Faf	1635abt		
Ripley John	S	T21Baf	1710abt		
Ripley John	S	R58I	1738 Mar31		
Ripley Joshua	S	R12Fa	1658 Nov 9	1682 Nov28	1739 May18
Ripley Joshua	S	R16Bcf	1670abt		
Ripley Joshua	S	R19D	1688 May13	1712 Dec 3	1773 Nov18
Ripley Joshua	S	R58F	1726 Oct30		
Ripley Leah	S	R19G	1693 Apr17	2 Mar	1775 Apr28
Ripley Leah=R19G	S	R16Bc	1693 Apr19	1752 Nov 9	1775 Apr28
Ripley Lydia	S	R63B	1723 Feb20		
Ripley Margaret	S	R19E	1690 Nov 4		1774 May 3
Ripley Mary	S	R58A	1714 Nov18		

NAME	DIV.	NUMBER	BIRTH	MARRIAGE	DEATH
Ripley Mary	S	T21Ba	1730 Mar14	1748 Jun30	
Ripley Nathaniel	S	R58D	1721 Jun30		
Ripley Phineas	S	R58B	1716 Nov25	unm.	1746 Aug 4
Ripley Rachel	S	R19F	1693 Apr17	1714 Jun21	1782 Apr 4
Ripley Sarah	S	K40Abm	1710abt		
Ripley William	S	R58H	1733 Feb12		
Ripley William	S	R63F	1734 Jul12		
Roath Benjamin	S	F52C	1701 Oct31		
Roath John	S	F21Aa	1669 Nov	1695 Aug 6	1743 Mar 9
Roath John	S	F52A	1697 Nov		
Roath Joseph	S	F52B	1699 Nov11		
Roath Robert	S	F21Aaf	1645abt		
Robbins Ann Francis	D	D26/16	1921 Jul 6	1952 Mar 4	=A9/1b
Robbins Anne Frances	A	A9/1b	1921Jul 6	1952 Mar 4	=D26/16
Robbins Anne Jean	A	A8/15	1789 Jul 3	1811 Oct27	1867 May25
Robbins Edward Hutch.	A	A8/30	1758 Feb19	1785 Nov	1829 Dec29
Robbins Honor	D	D26a21	1770abt		
Robbins Jeduthan	S	T18Daf	1680abt		
Robbins John Newell	D	D26a18	1855abt		
Robbins Kenneth S	D	D26/17	1885abt		
Robbins Mehitable	S	T18Da	1713 Jul 9	1738 Dec17	1766 Nov3
Robbins Nathaniel	A	A8/60	1726 Apr12	1757 Jul21	1795 May19
Robbins Nathaniel Jr.	A	A8/240	1677	1695	1741
Robbins Thomas	A	A8/120	1703 Aug11	1723 May 2	1791 Jan30
Roberts Abigail	A	A19/77	1701ca	1721Dec 28	1758aft
Roberts Abraham	A	A19/154	1655ca	1700	1731ca
Roberts Hannah	A	A5/13	1740abt	1762 Nov25	1821ca
Roberts Lewis	A	A5/26	1715abt		
Roberts Lydia	A	A3/205	1694ca	1717 Mar 9	
Roberts Owen	A	A3/410	1670abt		1716living
Roberts Sarah	S	H26Eam	1660abt		
Robinson Elizabeth	S	X27Dam	1680abt		
Robinson Hannah	S	X24Aa	1670 Mar 8		1757 Dec 2
Robinson Increase	S	X24Aaf	1645abt		
Robinson Mercy	S	F17Iam	1645abt		
Rockwell Ruth	A	A5/69	1633 Aug	1652 Oct 7	
Rockwell William	A	A5/138	1590	1624	1640
Rockwood Joanna	A	A6/53	1669 Aug25	1684 Nov 4	1710ca
Rockwood John=A2/172	A	A6/106	1641	1662	1724
Rockwood John=A6/106	A	A2/172	1641 Dec 1	1662	1724

NAME	DIV.	NUMBER	BIRTH	MARRIAGE	DEATH
Rockwood Joseph	A	A2/86	1671 May27	1689ca	1713ca
Rockwood Mary	A	A2/43	1690 Jul31		
Rockwood Richard	A	A6/212	1610abt	1636ca	1660aft
Roelofs Itie	A	A7/133	1640abt		
Rogers Abigail	S	X13C	1640ca	1660abt	1727 Aug 1
Rogers Abigail	S	X51E	1708 Aug 3	1748Feb 23	1785
Rogers Abigail=H40C	S	X18C	1677 Mar 2	1698 Jan11	1746ca
Rogers Abigail=X18C	S	H40C	1677 Mar 2	1698 Jan11	1746ca
Rogers Abijah	S	X28G	1714 Aug 4	1738 Sep14	1755aft
Rogers Ann	A	A3/253	1715abt	1738 May18	
Rogers Ann	S	X87A	1747		
Rogers Benjamin	S	X26Ga	1704Nov 19	1732 Oct13	
Rogers Benjamin=X26Ga	S	X34E	1704Nov 19	1732 Oct13	
Rogers Bridget	A	A17/115	1605abt		1678living
Rogers Crisp =X36B	S	X53Aa	1704Feb17		
Rogers Crisp =X53Aa	S	X36A	1704Feb17		
Rogers Daniel	S	X37H	1732 Mar16		1759bef
Rogers Desire	S	X88B	1725		
Rogers Ebenezer	S	X34A	1697 Feb17		
Rogers Eleazer	S	H22F	1673 Nov 3	1697ca	1739living
Rogers Eleazer	S	X14E	1673 Nov 3	1698bef	1739living
Rogers Eleazer	S	X16F	1685 May19	1712 Aug22	1760ca
Rogers Eleazer	S	H70E	1710 Oct 2		
Rogers Eleazer	S	X28E	1710 Oct 2		
Rogers Eleazer	S	X37F	1723 Nov15		
Rogers Eleazer	S	X88F	1735		
Rogers Elizabeth	S	H17Gam	1639 Sep29	1660 Jan 9	1678ca
Rogers Elizabeth	S	X13D	1652bef	1688 Nov17	1703aft
Rogers Elizabeth	S	A15Ccm	1655abt		
Rogers Elizabeth	S	H22A	1666 Oct 8		1704bef
Rogers Elizabeth	S	X14A	1666 Oct 8		1704bef
Rogers Elizabeth	S	X20C	1673 Apr16	1693	1724 Oct23
Rogers Elizabeth	S	X16E	1682 Oct23		1713living
Rogers Elizabeth	S	H67B	1693 Sep22		1698living
Rogers Elizabeth	S	X25B	1693 Sep22		
Rogers Elizabeth	S	H70A	1698 Oct15		
Rogers Elizabeth	S	X28A	1698 Oct15		
Rogers Elizabeth	S	H69C	1706 Mar27		
Rogers Elizabeth	S	X27C	1706 Mar27		
Rogers Elizabeth	S	X37B	1715 Nov14		

NAME	DIV.	NUMBER	BIRTH	MARRIAGE	DEATH
Rogers Elizabeth	S	X40B	1718 Jan10	1740	
Rogers ElizabethH17Gam	S	X12D	1639 Sep29	1660 Jan 9	1678ca
Rogers Elkanah	S	X53Ba	1700ca		
Rogers Elkanah	S	X36B	1706 Feb13		
Rogers Ensign	S	X37G	1729 Jul 9		
Rogers Experience	S	H70D	1707 Apr28	1727Apt 17	=X28D
Rogers Experience	S	X28D	1707 Apr28	1727 Apr17	1750aft
Rogers Hanna	S	X13B	1645ca	3 mar.	1704aft
Rogers Hannah	S	X12H	1652 Aug 8	1679aft	1690aft
Rogers Hannah	S	R12Ha	1668 Nov16	1689 Jul31	1750ca
Rogers Hannah	S	X20A	1668 Nov16	1689 Jul31	1750ca
Rogers Hannah	S	H22C	1669 Mar20		1733 Jul19
Rogers Hannah	S	X14C	1669 Mar20	1694bef	1733bef
Rogers Hannah	S	X16H	1689 Aug 5	1712 Feb19	1754aft
Rogers Hannah	S	H70C	1703 Feb26		
Rogers Hannah	S.	X28C	1703 Feb26	1723 Nov 4	1736bef
Rogers Hannah	S	H69E	1710 Apr 6	1755 Dec25	
Rogers Hannah	S	X27E	1710 Apr 6	1755 Dec25	
Rogers Hannah	S	X35D	1717ca		1745aft
Rogers Hannah	S	X88E	1734		
Rogers Henry	S	X37A	1713 Aug19		
Rogers Huldah	S	H69H	1717 Aug13		
Rogers Huldah=H69H	S	X27G	1717 Aug13		
Rogers Isaac	S	X51B	1701 Dec 8		1767bef
Rogers Jabez	S	X40E	1727 Jun30		
Rogers James	S	H17Aa	1648 Oct18	1670 Jan11	1678 Apr13
Rogers James	S	X12G	1648 Oct18	1670 Jan11	1678 Apr13
Rogers James	S	H40A	1673 Oct30		
Rogers James	S	X18A	1673 Oct30	1697 Feb17	1751 Sep 8
Rogers James	S	X51D	1706 May 2		
Rogers James=H17Aa	S	H24Baf	1648 Oct18	1670Jan 11	1678 Apr13
Rogers John	A	A17/230	1570abt	1595ca	1636
Rogers John	S	X11B	1614ca	1639 Apr16	1692ca
Rogers John	S	X12E	1642 Apr 3	1669 Aug19	1714ca
Rogers John	S	X20B	1670 Sep22	unm	1696 Nov 2
Rogers John	S	X16B	1672 Nov 4	2 mar.	1738 Jan10
Rogers John	S	X34C	1701 Aug 1		
Rogers John	S	X88G	1740		
Rogers John	S	X40J	1741 Apr 9		
Rogers John=R12Haf	S	X13A	1640ca	3 mar.	1732 Jun28

NAME	DIV.	NUMBER	BIRTH	MARRIAGE	DEATH
Rogers John=X13A	S	R12Haf	1640ca	3 Mar	1732 Jun28
Rogers Jonathan	S	X34D	1703 Mar20		
Rogers Joseph	S	H17Aaf	1620abt		
Rogers Joseph	S	X12B	1635 Jul19		1660 Dec27
Rogers Joseph	S	H22B	1667 Feb 1		1696 Apr24
Rogers Joseph	S	X14B	1667ca	1690abt	1696 Apr24
Rogers Joseph	S	X16D	1679 Feb22	2 mar.	1757bef
Rogers Joseph	S	H67C	1694ca		1698living
Rogers Joseph	S	X25C	1695ca		
Rogers Joseph	S	X34G	1708 Sep20		
Rogers Joseph	S	H69G	1715 Mar24		1728 Aug 8
Rogers Joseph MF =X11A	S	H12Gaf	1610ca		1677 Jan
Rogers JosephMF=H12Gaf	S	X11A	1610ca		1677 Jan
Rogers Judah	S	X16C	1677 Nov23	1704 Apr 6	1739ca
Rogers Judah	S	X51Ca	1700ca		
Rogers Judah	S	X35A	1704 Dec29		
Rogers Lucy	S	X27D	1708 Jun 6	2 mar.	1758 Jun 1
Rogers Lucy	S	H69D	1708 Jun 8		
Rogers Martha	S	X36C	.1708 Feb26		
Rogers Martha	S	X37E	1723 Jan 9		
Rogers Mary	S	X12F	1644 Sep22	1664 Aug10	1718aft
Rogers Mary	S	W44Fam	1660abt		
Rogers Mary	S	X18B	1675 Nov 9	1694bef	1731 Feb17
Rogers Mary	S	X51A	1698 Nov12		
Rogers Mary	S	X35B	1706 Oct 1		
Rogers Mary=H24Ba	S	H40B	1675 Nov 9	1693ca	1731 Feb17
Rogers Mary=H40B	S	H24Ba	1675 Nov 9	1693ca	1731 Feb17
Rogers Mehitable	S	X16G	1686 Mar13	1721 Mar15	1760aft
Rogers Mehitable	S	X40G	1731 Dec 9		
Rogers Mercy	S	X37C	1718 Sep 1		
Rogers Meriah=X28G	S	H70G	1714 Aug 4	1738 Sep14	1755aft
Rogers Meriah=X28H	S	H70H	1716 Oct21		d. yng
Rogers Moriah	S	X28H	1716 Oct21		d. yng
Rogers Moses	S	X37D	1720 Mar13		
Rogers Nathaniel	S	H22G	1675 Jan18		1705bef
Rogers Nathaniel	S	X16I	1693 Oct 3	2 mar.	1743living
Rogers Nathaniel	S	X40I	1738 Apr29		
Rogers Nathaniel=H22G	S	X14F	1675 Jan18		1705bef
Rogers Nehemiah	S	X40C	1723 Oct31		
Rogers Patience	S	L15Dam	1675		

NAME	DIV.	NUMBER	BIRTH	MARRIAGE	DEATH
Rogers Patience	S	X35C	1710 Nov 9		
Rogers Phebe	S	X27B	1703 Nov 1		
Rogers Phebe=X27B	S	H69B	1703 Nov 1		
Rogers Priscilla	S	X34H	1710ca		
Rogers Ruth	S	X20D	1675 Apr18		1725 Apr28
Rogers Ruth	S	H70I	1718		1720 Apr18
Rogers Ruth	S	X28I	1718		d yng
Rogers Ruth	S	X88A	1722		
Rogers Ruth	S	X40D	1725 Jul31		
Rogers Samuel	S	X16A	1671 Nov 1		d.yng
Rogers Samuel	S	X88C	1728		
Rogers Sarah	S	X12A	1633 Aug 6		d.yng
Rogers Sarah	S	X20E	1677 May 4	1694	1770ca
Rogers Sarah	S	X25A	1691 Nov20		1696living
Rogers Sarah	S	H69A	1701 Oct27		
Rogers Sarah	S	X27A	1701 Oct27		
Rogers Sarah	S	X34F	1706 Jul21		
Rogers Sarah	S	X40A	1717 Apr 4		
Rogers Sarah	S	X40H	1735 Oct17		
Rogers Sarah=X27A	S	H67A	1691 Nov20		1696living
Rogers Susannah	S	X51C	1703 Jan19		
Rogers Temperance	S	X40F	1729 Dec 3	1763Jul 11	
Rogers Thankful	S	X34B	1699 Oct24		1739bef
Rogers Thomas	S	X14D	1672 May 6	2 mar.	1749 Sep23
Rogers Thomas	S	X28B	1701 Oct 8	1721 Oct31	1740aft
Rogers Thomas	S	X51F	1710 Oct21		
Rogers Thomas	S	H69F	1712 Dec11		
Rogers Thomas	S	X27F	1712 Dec11	1744 Jun21	1749 Oct10
Rogers Thomas	S	X88D	1730		
Rogers Thomas #1	S	H22D	1670 Mar 6		d yng
Rogers Thomas #2	S	H22E	1672 May 6	2 Mar	1749 Sep23
Rogers Thomas =X12C	S	H12Ga	1638 Mar29	1665 Dec13	1678
Rogers Thomas =X28B	S	H70B	1701 Oct 8	1721 Oct31	1740aft
Rogers Thomas MF	S	X10A	1590bef		1621
Rogers Thomas=H12Ga MF	S	X12C	1638 Mar29	1665 Dec13	1678
Rogers Willis	S	H70F	1712		1713 May27
Rogers Willis	S	X28F	1712ca		d yng
Rogerson Lydia	S	C62Ab	1790ca		
Rood Abigail	S	T68B	1746 Oct28		
Rood Asa	S	T63A	1717 Mar20		

NAME	DIV.	NUMBER	BIRTH	MARRIAGE	DEATH
Rood Asa	S	T68A	1744 Oct13		1762 Aug28
Rood Elijah	S	C20Da	1750abt		
Rood Elijah Jr	S	C20Fa	1755ca		
Rood Eunice	S	T63H	1734 Jun23		
Rood Jabez	S	T25Ca	1693 Feb 7	1716ca	1760 May17
Rood Jabez	S	T63D	1724ca		
Rood Jabez =T25Ca	S	T26Daf	1693 Feb 7	1716ca	1760 May17
Rood Jeremiah	S	T63F	1729 Jan		
Rood Josiah Standish	S	T63E	1726 Jul		
Rood Lydia	S	T63G	1731 Sep12		
Rood Mehitable	S	T63C	1721 Oct23		
Rood Rufus	S	T26Da	1719 Jul 5	1743 Dec29	1779 Apr12
Rood Rufus =T26Da	S	T63B	1719 Jul 5	1743 Dec29	1779 Apr12
Rood Samuel	S	T25Caf	1670abt		
Roos Cornelia	A	A8/71	1688 May 6	1708 Mar14	1760ca
Roos Johannes	A	A8/142	1660abt		1695
Roosevelt Anna Eleanor	D	D4a17	1884 Oct12	1905 Mar17	1962 Nov 7
Roosevelt Anna Eleanor	A	A8/1a	1884Oct 12	1905 Mar17	1962Nov 7
Roosevelt Cornelius	A	A7/4	1794 Jan30	1822ca	=D8/18
Roosevelt Cornelius V.	D	D8/18	1794 Jan30	1822ca	1871 Jun17
Roosevelt Franklin D	D	D4/17	1882 Jan30	1905 Mar17	1945 Apr 5
Roosevelt Franklin D.	A	A8/1	1882 Jan30	1905 Mar17	1945 Apr 5
Roosevelt Isaac	A	A8/16	1726 Dec 8	1752 Sep22	1794 Oct13
Roosevelt Isaac	A	A8/4	1790 Apr21	1827 Apr26	1863 Oct23
Roosevelt Isaac	D	D4a19	1790 Apr21	1827 Apr26	1863 Oct23
Roosevelt Jacobus	A	A7/16	1724 Aug	1746 Dec 4	1777 Mar12
Roosevelt Jacobus Jr	D	D8/19	1759 Oct25	1793 Mar 8	1840Aug 13
Roosevelt Jacobus Sr	D	D8a20	1724 Aug 9	1746 Dec 4	1777 Mar12
Roosevelt James	A	A8/32	1692 Feb28	1713 Jan31	1776 May
Roosevelt James	A	A8/8	1760 Jan10	1786 Nov15	1847 Feb 6
Roosevelt James	D	D4/18	1828 Jul16	1880 Oct 7	1900 Dec 8
Roosevelt James J.	A	A7/8	1759 Oct	1793 Mar 8	1840 Aug13
Roosevelt James=D4/18	A	A8/2	1828 Jul16	1880 Oct 7	1900 Dec 8
Roosevelt Johannes	A	A7/32	1689 Mar	1708 Sep25	1750 Apr 4
Roosevelt Nicholas	A	A7/64	1658 Oct	1682 Dec26	1742 Jul30
Roosevelt Nicholas	A	A8/64	1658 Oct	1682 Dec26	1742 Jul30
Roosevelt Theodore Jr.	A	A7/1	1858 Oct27	1880 Oct27	1919 Jan 6
Roosevelt Theodore Sr	A	A7/2	1831 Sep22	1853 Dec22	1878 Feb 9
Roosevelt Theodore Sr	D	D8/17	1831Sep 22	1853 Dec22	1878 Feb 9
Roosevelt Theordore Jr	D	D8/16	1858 Oct27	1880 Oct27	=A7/1

NAME	DIV.	NUMBER	BIRTH	MARRIAGE	DEATH
Root Elizabeth R	D	D26/20	1800abt		
Root Exekial	D	D26a22	1740abt		
Root George Bridges	D	D26/21	1770abt		
Root John	A	A12/164	1608	1641	1684
Root John Jr	A	A12/82	1642ca	1664 Oct18	1687 Sep24
Root Mary	A	A12/41	1667 Sep22	1687ca	
Rose Dorcas	S	T26Fbm	1695abt		
Rose Elizabeth	A	A19/129	1665abt	1686	1732bef
Rothbottom Joseph	S	W36Fa	1680abt	1700ca	1718bef
Roude Laura	S	C23Ea	1790ca		
Round Anne	S	C33A	1704		
Round Elizabeth	S	C33G	1719		
Round Hannah	S	C33C	1710		
Round Joanna	S	C33D	1713		
Round John	S	C33E	1715		
Round Judith	A	A1/369	1687	1711	1744
Round Nathaniel	S	C33F	1717		
Round Richard	S	C25Ea	1675ca		
Round Richard	S	C33B	1706		
Rouse John	S	T14Fb	1690ca	1739 Nov18	1756 May 4
Rouse Simon	S	T14Fbf	1670abt		
Rowe Hugh	A	A16/38	1645ca	1667 Jun10	1696 Dec11
Rowe John	A	A16/76	1620ca		1661 Mar 9
Rowe Ruth	A	A16/19	1671 Jun26	1689Feb 13	1736 May10
Rowely Abigail	S	F59B	1716 Feb13		
Rowely Abijah	S	F59F	1725 Jul13		
Rowely Elizabeth	S	F59G	1728 Jun27		
Rowely Nathan	S	F59A	1714 Jan22		
Rowely Prudence	S	F59H	1732 Jul29		
Rowely Samuel	S	F59C	1718 Aug17		
Rowely Thankful	S	F59E	1723 Jul15		
Rowely Thomas	S	F59D	1721 Mar24		
Rowley Aaron	S	F17I	1666 May 1	1696 Mar 7	1743 Jun 9
Rowley Aaron	S	F37C	1693abt		
Rowley Ebenezer	S	F34G	1695ca		
Rowley Elizabeth	S	F37D	1694 Nov25		1730bef
Rowley Elizabeth	S	F35E	1694ca		
Rowley Elizabeth	S	F36C	1695 May		
Rowley Elnathan	S	F37F	1699 Apr23		
Rowley Elnathan	S	F35F	1700ca		

NAME	DIV.	NUMBER	BIRTH	MARRIAGE	DEATH
Rowley Hannah	S	F34D	1687ca	unm.	1735living
Rowley Hatch	S	F36H	1706 March		
Rowley Henry	A	A5/154	1600abt		
Rowley Isaac	S	F35A	1684ca		
Rowley Jabez	S	F35H	1702ca		
Rowley John	S	F17J	1667 Oct22		1705bef
Rowley John	S	F34F	1630ca		
Rowley John	S	F36G	1706 May25		
Rowley Jonathan	S	F34I	1703ca		
Rowley Mary	S	F17A	1653 Mar20	1675 Jan 7	
Rowley Mary	S	F34A	1677ca		
Rowley Mary	S	F37E	1695ca	m.F33F	
Rowley Mary	S	F36D	1699 Sep		
Rowley Mary	S	F35G	1701ca		
Rowley Matthew	S	F17K	1669ca		
Rowley Matthew	S	F35D	1692ca		1715living
Rowley Mehitable	S	F14Ha	1660 Jan11	1678ca	1732ca
Rowley Mehitable	S	F17F	1660Jan11		
Rowley Mehitable	S	F14Ha	1660ca	1678	1732
Rowley Mehitable	S	F34H	1698ca		
Rowley Mehitable	S	F36I	1709 May		
Rowley Mercy	S	F37A	1690 Jan22		1730bef
Rowley Mercy	S	F36A	1691 Aug		
Rowley Moses	S	F17B	1654 Nov10	1675 Jan	1735 Jul16
Rowley Moses	S	F22Baf	1660abt		
Rowley Moses	S	F22Faf	1665abt		
Rowley Moses	S	F34B	1679ca		
Rowley Moses	S	F36F	1704 Feb		
Rowley Moses Sr	S	F14Haf	1635abt		
Rowley Naomi	S	F34C	1685ca	1703 Jun11	1764ca
Rowley Naomi =F34C	S	F22Ba	1685ca	1703 Jun11	1764ca
Rowley Nathan	S	F17H	1664ca	1690ca	1742 May
Rowley Nathan	S	F36E	1700 Apr		
Rowley Patience	S	G29Aam	1720abt	1736	
Rowley Samuel	S	F34E	1688ca	m.(F22Fa)	
Rowley Samuel=F34E	S	F22Fa	1688ca	1713 Mar 4	1767 Jan 7
Rowley Sarah	A	A5/77	1630ca	1646 Apr11	
Rowley Sarah	S	F17Ham	1640ca		
Rowley Sarah	S	F17G	1662Sep 10		living1700
Rowley Sarah	S	F36B	1693 Oct	m.F37C	

NAME	DIV.	NUMBER	BIRTH	MARRIAGE	DEATH
Rowley Shubael	S	F17E	1660 Jan11		1714 Mar28
Rowley Shubael	S	F35B	1686ca		
Rowley Thomas	S	F35C	1690ca		
Rowley Timothy	S	F37B	1692 Nov19		1759aft
Rowlson Esther	S	C19Da	1755ca		
Royce Lydia	A	A16/31	1680May 28	1703Jan 28	1750ca
Royce Nehemiah	A	A16/62	1636ca	1660Nov 20	1706 Nov
Royce Robert	A	A16/124	1610abt		1676
Royce Sarah	S	T13Gam	1635abt		
Ruck Abigail	D	D14a22	1670abt		
Ruck Hannah	A	A1/301	1702ca	1725	1767ca
Rudd Jonathan	A	A16/84	1625abt	1647	1658
Rudd Mary	S	R19Cam	1665abt		
Rudd Mary	A	A16/21	1695 Feb 3	1718Mar 12	1757aft
Rudd Nathaniel	A	A16/42	1652ca	1685Apr 16	1727 Apr
Rudolph Lucretia	A	A06/1a	1832 Apr19	1853Nov 11	1918Mar 13
Ruggles Rachel	A	A6/235	1640abt	1664ca	
Rumzel Dorothy	S	C58Cb	1905ca		
Russel Mable	S	R118Aam	1680abt		
Russel Rebecca	A	A12/9	1723 Feb 6	1749 Dec26	1773 May27
Russell John	A	A12/144	1597ca		1680 Aug
Russell John	A	A12/18	1687 Jan24	1707 Dec17	1757 Jul 4
Russell John Jr	A	A12/72	1627ca	1651ca	1692Dec20
Russell Samuel	A	A12/36	1660 Nov 4		1731 Jun24
Rust Elizabeth	A	A1/357	1713	1731	1741
Rutherford Barbara	A	A8/251	1660abt	1682	=A8/253
Rutherford Barbara	A	A8/253	1660abt	1682	1705aft
Rutherford Henry	A	A12/154	1510abt		1668
Rutherford Sarah	A	A12/77	1641 Jul31	1657 Jun24	1687 Jan 5
Ryan Thelma C. (Pat)	A	A3/1a	1912Mar 16	1940 Jun21	
Sabin Elizabeth	A	A16/49	1642ca	1662Dec 24	1717 Feb 7
Sabin William	A	A16/98	1620abt	1639abt	1686Feb
Sachet A	S	N11Aa	1665abt		
Safford Esther	S	C12Da	1710ca		
Sale Benjamin	S	K78A	1693 Mar 5		
Sale Edward	S	K22Hb	1665ca	1692ca	1699ca
Sale John	S	K78B	1697 Apr10		
Salisbury Ebenezer	S	C26C	1700abt		
Salisbury Jemima	S	C26A	1695ca		
Salisbury Joanna	S	C26B	1700abt		

NAME	DIV.	NUMBER	BIRTH	MARRIAGE	DEATH
Salisbury Joseph	S	C26D	1700abt		
Salisbury Martin	S	C26E	1700abt		
Salisbury Rebecca	S	C36Ha	1760ca		
Salisbury Samuel	S	C25Aa	1670ca		
Salter Deborah	S	X20Eam	1640abt		
Salter Elizabeth	A	A6/245	1610abt	1631	
Salter Hannah	A	A13/17	1690ca	1714 Sep14	1727
Salter Richard	A	A13/34	1665abt		1728after
Sampson Abraham Jr	S	T12Aa	1658ca	1680ca	1727
Sampson Abraham Sr	S	T12Aaf	1620abt		
Sampson Benjamin	S	K94E	1728 Feb11		
Sampson Cornelius	S	K94C	1724 May		
Sampson Deborah	S	K94B	1720		
Sampson Deborah	S	R113E	1760Dec 17		
Sampson Elisha	S	R113B	1754ca		
Sampson Ephraim	S	H118G	1740ca		
Sampson Ephraim	S	R113D	1757ca		
Sampson Hannah	S	R113C	1755ca		
Sampson Isaac	S	H33Gaf	1675abt		
Sampson John	S	W36Fb	1680abt	1717 Sep11	1734 Jan12
Sampson Jonathan	S	H118D	1733 Oct25		
Sampson Jonathan	S	R113A	1753ca		
Sampson Jonathan Jr	S	R28Ia	1729 Apr 3	1751 Oct27	1811ca
Sampson Jonathan Sr	S	R28Iaf	1705abt		
Sampson Josiah	S	K94F	1731 Oct		d.yng
Sampson Judith	D	D18a24	1655abt		
Sampson Mary	S	H118A	1724 Jan 6		
Sampson Mercy	S	H118C	1731 May15		
Sampson Micah	S	K94A	1717 Jan26		
Sampson Nehemiah	S	R113F	1764Jul 17		
Sampson Peleg	S	H118B	1726 Nov19		
Sampson Priscilla	S	H118F	1738ca		
Sampson Rebecca	S	K94D	1726 Apr27	unm	1748 Aug24
Sampson Simeon	S	H118E	1736 Aug		
Sampson Sylvia	S	R113G	1766Apr 1		
Samson Abigail	S	T35D	1727 Apr12		
Samson Abigail	S	T36A	1729 Oct25		
Samson Abigail	S	T32E	1738 Jan 4		
Samson Abner	S	T29H	1726 July		
Samson Abraham	S	T14B	1686ca	1712ca	1775 Nov16

NAME	DIV.	NUMBER	BIRTH	MARRIAGE	DEATH
Samson Abraham	S	T30E	1721 Jul31		
Samson Alice	S	T31B	1716 Feb21		
Samson Andrew	S	T31A	1714 Sep28		
Samson Anna	S	T29G	1722 Mar 1		
Samson Anna	S	T34F	1736 Apr25		
Samson Anna (Hannah)	S	T32H	1747 Apr30	unm	1831 May13
Samson Barnabas	S	T15H	1704 Feb12	1728 Nov 6	1749ca
Samson Barnabas	S	T39A	1730 Feb26		
Samson Benjamin	S	K26Ca	1687ca	1716 Mar19	1758 Apr19
Samson Benjamin	S	T33C	1726 Dec11	unm	1747bef
Samson Beriah	S	T31F	1728 Nov 1		
Samson Bethiah	S	T35F	1731 Apr22		
Samson Caleb	S	T12Da	1665ca	1684ca	1745abt
Samson Caleb	S	T17E	1698ca		
Samson David	S	T17A	1686ca		
Samson Deborah	S	T31E	1726 Jun12		
Samson Ebenezer	S	T14E	1696ca	1728 Apr23	1778 Nov25
Samson Ebenezer	S	T32C	1734 Mar27	unm	1771bef
Samson Elizabeth	S	X23Fam	1650abt		
Samson Elizabeth	S	A25Db	1692 Dec22	1726 Sep15	1744 Apr17
Samson Elizabeth	S	T36B	1732 Mar29		
Samson Elizabeth	S	T39C	1734 Dec18		
Samson Elizabeth	S	T34J	1744ca		
Samson Ephraim	S	T15E	1698 May 8	1728 Nov15	1787 Apr11
Samson Eunice	S	T36D	1737 May15		
Samson Eunice	S	T32F	1740 Mar18	unm	1812 Oct 4
Samson Experience	S	T39B	1733 Jan 1		
Samson Fear	S	T29C	1708 Nov16		
Samson George	S	A25Dbf	1670abt		
Samson Grace	S	T14G	1701	unm.	1786 Jan 2
Samson Hannah	S	T30B	1715 Nov 4		
Samson Hannah #1	S	T34A	1716 Apr21		
Samson Hannah #2	S	T34I	1743ca		
Samson Henry	S	T12Daf	1640abt		
Samson Henry	S	T30G	1724 Aug 4		
Samson Isaac	S	T12Ba	1661ca	1686	1726 Sept3
Samson Isaac	S	T15A	1688 Apr18	1715Oct	1748ca
Samson Isaac	S	T34H	1741ca		
Samson Jacob	S	T34G	1739 Feb		
Samson James	S	T14Baf	1660abt		

NAME	DIV.	NUMBER	BIRTH	MARRIAGE	DEATH
Samson James	S	T30D	1720 Feb19 unm		1741 June2
Samson James =T14Baf	S	T14Faf	1660abt		
Samson Jerusha	S	T17H	1705ca		
Samson Joanna	S	T35B	1723 Jul31 unm.		1784 Jan22
Samson Joanna	S	T32B	1732 Oct23		
Samson John	S	T33A	1724 Jan10 unm		1747 Jun23
Samson John	S	T34D	1724ca		
Samson Jonathan	S	T15B	1689 Feb 9	1721 Sep28	1758 Feb 3
Samson Jonathan	S	T35E	1729 Apr 3		
Samson Jonathan	S	T37D	1733 Oct25		
Samson Joseph	S	T14Fa	1696ca	1719 May 6	1738 Feb26
Samson Joseph	S	T31C	1719 Nov16		
Samson Joseph	S	T33B	1726 Dec11		
Samson Joshua	S	T17F	1700ca		
Samson Josiah	S	T15C	1692 Jun 5 unm.		1730 Mar29
Samson Josiah	S	T35G	1734 Jan23		1750 Jun21
Samson Judah	S	T31H	1735 Aug10		
Samson Keturah	S	T29F	1718 Jan14		
Samson Lois	S	T33D	1728 Nov29		
Samson Lora	S	T17B	1688ca		
Samson Lusanna	S	T36C	1734 Nov 7		
Samson Lydia	S	T15D	1694 Apr22 unm.		1734 Apr30
Samson Lydia	S	T34K	1745ca		
Samson Marcy	S	T37C	1731 May15		
Samson Margaret	S	T34E	1728 Apr15		
Samson Mary	S	T35A	1722 Jul 6		
Samson Mary	S	T37A	1724 Jan 6		
Samson Mary	S	T36F	1745 Apr10		
Samson Miles	S	T14C	1690ca	1713 Apr28	1784 Nov26
Samson Miles	S	T31G	1731 May13		
Samson Nathan	S	T32G	1744 Apr 1 unmr		1806 Oct11
Samson Nathaniel	S	T14A	1682ca	1703 Jan19	1750ca
Samson Nathaniel	S	T29E	1715 Feb22		1788
Samson Noah	S	T29A	1704 Jan24		
Samson Peleg	S	T15F	1700 Nov12	1722 Nov 7	1741 Apr27
Samson Peleg	S	H33Ga	1700 Nov12	1722 Nov 7	1741 Apr27
Samson Peleg	S	T37B	1726 Nov19		
Samson Peleg =T15F	S	R25Fbf	1700 Nov12	1722 Nov 7	1741 Apr27
Samson Penelope	S	T14Ba	1686ca	1712ca	1727living
Samson Penelope	S	T30H	1726 Jun 2 unm		1819 Aug31

NAME	DIV.	NUMBER	BIRTH	MARRIAGE	DEATH
Samson Perez	S	T29B	1706 Oct21		1733bef
Samson Phebe	S	T34L	1747ca		
Samson Priscilla	S	T17D	1697ca	unm.	1758 Jul 7
Samson Priscilla	S	T15G	1700 Nov12	1726 Jan12	1733living
Samson Priscilla	S	T35C	1726 Apr14		
Samson Priscilla	S	T37F	1739 Mar18		
Samson Priscilla	S	T36G	1745 Apr10		
Samson Rachel	S	T17C	1700abt		
Samson Rachel	S	T32A	1728 Dec25	unm	1789 Apr20
Samson Rebecca	S	T14D	1694ca		1725living
Samson Rebecca	S	T30C	1718 Oct26		
Samson Robert	S	T29D	1712 Apr 2		
Samson Ruhamah	S	T33F	1735ca		
Samson Ruth	S	T17G	1702ca		
Samson Ruth	S	T30A	1713 Jul 2		
Samson Sarah	S	T14F	1698ca	1719 May 6	1747living
Samson Sarah	S	T17I	1706ca	unm.	1721living
Samson Sarah	S	T34C	1719 Jan 4		
Samson Sarah	S	T31D	1723 Mar25		
Samson Sarah	S	T33E	1733 May 5		
Samson Sarah	S	T36E	1742 Jan31		
Samson Simeon	S	T37E	1736 Aug		
Samson Stephen	S	K26Caf	1665abt		
Samson Stephen	S	T30F	1722 Oct23		
Samson Uriah	S	T34B	1717 Jul30		
Samson Zerviah	S	T32D	1735 Jun10		1737 Jun19
Sand Sarah	S	R17Abm	1650abt		
Sandys Hester	D	D12a20	1555abt		
Sanford Joseph	S	C37Aa	1748ca		
Sanford Mary	S	W51Iam	1680abt		
Santvoort Jacob Abrah.	A	A8/146	1650abt	1677	1685aft
Santvoort Mary	A	A8/73	1678 Nov	1698 Sept7	1768 Sept3
Sarson Jane	S	W31Ka	1700 May25	1717 Oct 1	
Sarson Samuel	S	W31Kaf	1675abt		
Saturlee Frances	S	C20Ka	1770ca		
Savage Alice	A	A18/51	1655ca	1674Apr 13	1701bef
Savage Anthony	A	A18/102	1630abt		1695ca
Savell Ann	A	A11/37	1601 Apr	1625 Apr25	1693 Sep 5
Savell Anna =A11/37	A	A19/1467	1601 Apr	1625 Apr25	1693 Sep 5
Savil William	A	A11/74	1580abt		

NAME	DIV.	NUMBER	BIRTH	MARRIAGE	DEATH
Sawin Rebecca	S	C61Jb	1770Ca		
Sawtelle Elizabeth	A	A3/483	1671	1691	
Sawtelle Elizabeth	D	D22a21	1671	1691	
Sawyer Abigail	S	T73F	1742 Dec29		
Sawyer Anne	S	W30F	1682 Dec15		
Sawyer Cornelius	S	T73J	1751 Jul 6		1759living
Sawyer Dinah	S	T73G	1744 Apr20		
Sawyer Elizabeth	S	T73B	1733 Jan18		
Sawyer Ephraim	S	T27Daf	1685abt		
Sawyer Ephraim	S	T73E	1740 Feb10		
Sawyer Eunice	S	T73C	1736 May22		
Sawyer Jacob	S	T27Da	1706 Dec14	1730 Sep 3	1758 Aug22
Sawyer Jacob Standish	S	T73K	1754 Apr10		
Sawyer Jemima	S	T73A	1731 Mar 6		1747 Jun23
Sawyer Jemima	S	T73I	1749 Mar 7		
Sawyer Jeremiah	S	T73H	1746 Jul26		
Sawyer John	S	W13Ea	1640ca	1666 Nov	1706abt
Sawyer Josiah	S	W30D	1675ca	1705 Dec20	1733ca
Sawyer Mary	S	W30E	1677 Oct12		
Sawyer Mercy	S	W30A	1668 Feb 1	1686 Dec 2	1729 Sep22
Sawyer Prudence	S	T73D	1738 Apr30		
Sawyer Susanna	S	W30B	1671 May27		
Sawyer Thomas	S	W30C	1672 Feb11		
Sayles Catherine	S	C76F	1671		
Sayles Deborah	S	C76G	1673ca		
Sayles Eleanor	S	C76E	1671		
Sayles Isabel	S	C76C	1655ca		
Sayles John Jr	S	C76B	1654		
Sayles John Sr	S	C75Aa	1633		
Sayles Mary	S	C76A	1652		
Sayles Phebe	S	C76D	1658		
Sayles Richard	S	C81A	1695		
Sayles Thomas	S	C81B	1699		
Scarlet Elizabeth	S	A23Db	1667 Nov18	1735 Sep 4	1750 May23
Scarlet John	S	A23Dbf	1645abt		
Schuyler David P.	A	A7/150	1636	1657	1690
Schuyler Maria	A	A7/75	1666 Sep29	1689 Feb 3	1742 June7
Scolley James	S	R23Fa	1695ca	1720 Dec29	1721 Oct30
Scothorn Elenor	A	A3/35	1764ca	1790 Feb 4	1819 Nov22
Scothorn Nathan	A	A3/140	1705 Nov10	1730ca	1731 Jan10

NAME	DIV.	NUMBER	BIRTH	MARRIAGE	DEATH
Scothorn Nathan Jr.	A	A3/70	1730ca	1759 Oct29	1764ca
Scothorn Robert	A	A3/280	1659	1692	1708
Scott Caroline L	A	A14/1a	1832Oct 1	1853Oct 20	1892Oct 25
Scott Elizabeth	A	A3/357	1675abt	1698	
Scott Esther	S	C81Ba	1700		
Scott Jean	A	A7/199	1635abt	1673ca	
Scott Margaret	A	A8/249	1650abt		
Scott Margaret	A	A4/99	1760abt		
Scudder Elizabeth	A	A5/71	1625abt	1644 Nov28	1690aft
Scudder Experience	S	H30Ca	1692 Apr28	1712 Oct 9	1756aft
Scudder John	S	H30Caf	1670abt		
Seabury Abigail	S	R59A	1715		1802Jun12
Seabury Benjamin	S	R19Ea	1689 Sep24		1797 Apr 9
Seabury Elisha	S	R59B	1721		
Seabury Elizabeth	S	Q15Gam	1670abt		
Seabury Hopestill	S	K30Jc	1722 May31	1772 Oct15	1790 May21
Seabury Martha	S	W30Da	1679 Sep23	1705 Dec20	1733aft
Seabury Samuel	S	W30Daf	1655abt		
Seabury Samuel	S	R19Eaf	1665abt		
Seabury Samuel	S	K30Ccf	1695abt		
Seabury Samuel =K30Ccf	S	K30Jcf	1695abt		
Seabury Sarah	S	K30Cc	1718 Jul21	1770 Mar19	1802 Nov 4
Seabury Sarah	S	R59C	1723 Jan29		
Seamans William	S	C31Ia	1720ca		
Searle Deborah	S	X61A	1695 Nov17		
Searle John	S	X61B	1698 Mar12		1714 Mar20
Searle Nathaneil	S	X20Ea	1662 Jun 9	1694	1749 Feb 5
Searle Nathaniel	S	X61D	1703 Apr26		
Searle Robert	S	X20Eaf	1640abt		
Searle Sarah	S	X61C	1700 Apr 2		
Sears Abigail	S	H93A	1711 Nov23		
Sears Betty	S	K113A	1735ca		
Sears Chloe	S	K113C	1740ca		
Sears Desire	S	H93D	1716 Mar 9		
Sears Elizabeth	S	K25Aa	1675	1705Nov 22	1725bef
Sears Hannah	S	H19Kam	1670abt		
Sears Hannah	S	H16Ea	1672 Dec	1692 Feb 8	1702 Mar21
Sears Hannah	S	H93F	1720 Jun 3		
Sears Isaac	S	H93H	1723 Oct 5		1724 Jan13
Sears Lydia	S	H16Eb	1666 Oct24	1706 Sep30	1748

NAME	DIV.	NUMBER	BIRTH	MARRIAGE	DEATH
Sears Mary	S	H93E	1718 Aug 9	1738 Nov30	1762bef
Sears Mercy	S	H93B	1713 Oct21		
Sears Paul	S	H16Ebf	1640abt		
Sears Paul	S	K30Gaf	1675abt		
Sears Rebecca	S	K113B	1737ca		
Sears Ruth	S	H93C	1715 Jul 4		
Sears S.	S	N14Eb	1770abt		
Sears Samuel	S	H93G	1721 Dec 5		
Sears Samuel Jr.	S	H27Ha	1687 Sep15	1710 Nov 2	1727ca
Sears Samuel Sr.	S	H27Haf	1655abt		
Sears Sarah	S	K113D	1742ca		
Sears Seth	S	H93I	1725 Apr 9	1765 May16	1770
Sears Silas	S	H16Eaf	1645abt		
Sears Silas	S	K25Aaf	1650abt		
Sears Thomas	S	K30Ga	1699 Jun 6	1734 May16	1755 Jul
Sears Thomas	S	K113E	1746ca		
Sears Willard	S	K113F	1748ca		
Seaver Elizabeth	A	A2/215	1643	1661	1731
Seeds Sarah	A	A3/33	1755ca	1775 Aug17	
Seeley Ruth	S	C49Na	1716ca		
Segar Anna	S	C12Fa	1715ca		
Selden Rebecca	A	A4/127	1730ca	1754ca	
Selden Samuel	A	A4/494	1695 May17	1721ca	1745 Feb28
Selden Samuel =A4/254	A	A4/494	1695 May17	1721ca	1745 Feb28
Selden Sarah	A	A4/247	1735 Nov15	1757 Nov 3	1811 May16
Seldon Joseph	A	A4/508	1651	1676	1724
Sever Ann Warren	S	L28D	1763 Sep25	unm	1788 Jan19
Sever James	S	L28C	1761 Nov 3		
Sever John	S	L28E	1766 May 7		
Sever Nicholas	S	L19Caf	1720abt		
Sever Sarah	S	L28A	1757 Oct 3		
Sever William	S	L19Ca	1730ca	1755 Aug16	1809 Jun15
Sever William	S	L28B	1759 Jun23		
Severence Martha	S	Q19Cam	1685abt		
Sewell Philippa	A	A16/191	1628	1647ca	1669
Sexton Sarah	S	F21Aam	1645abt		
Shatswell Mary	A	A17/85	1610ca		1694Apr 28
Shaw Anthony	S	W35Aaf	1640abt		
Shaw Grace	S	W35Aa	1667ca	1688ca	1737 Mar 1
Shaw Grace =W35Aa	A	A8/209	1667ca	1688ca	1737 Mar 1

NAME	DIV.	NUMBER	BIRTH	MARRIAGE	DEATH
Shaw Hannah	S	H17Ca	1661ca	1678 Aug 5	1713 Jul24
Shaw Hannah	S	Q21Ea	1704 Jul31	1722 Nov19	1762 Mar30
Shaw Jonathan	S	H14Caf	1635abt		
Shaw Jonathan	S	W55Baf	1665abt		
Shaw Jonathan =H16Caf	S	H16Caf	1635abt		
Shaw Jonathan =H16Caf	S	H17Caf	1635abt		
Shaw Joseph	S	T24Eaf	1675abt		
Shaw Joseph =C21Caf	S	Q21Eaf	1675abt		
Shaw Joseph =T24Eaf	S	Q21Caf	1675abt		
Shaw Lydia	S	H16Ca	1665ca	1689 Apr 4	1711aft
Shaw Mary	S	H14Ca	1665ca	1687 Jan11	1730 Nov28
Shaw Mary	S	Q23Iam	1695abt		
Shaw Mary =H14Ca	S	T12Kam	1665ca	1687 Jan11	1730 Nov28
Shaw Mary =T12Kam	S	T15Fam	1665ca	1687 Jan11	1730 Nov28
Shaw Mary =T15Fam	S	T20Dam	1665abt	1687 Jan11	1730 Nov28
Shaw Persis	S	W55Ba	1692 Mar10	1714 Mar10	1726 Jun 6
Shaw Ruth	S	Q21Ca	1698 Jan25	1719bef	1738ca
Shaw Sarah	S	T24Ea	1702 Mar18	1721 Feb 8	1730 Jun12
Sheffield Mary	A	A1/375	1701	1729	
Shelby Hannah	S	X17Dam	1650abt		
Sheldon Benjamin	A	A8/58	1697ca	1723 Jun12	1773 Aug28
Sheldon Dinah	A	A4/475	1697	1716	1761aft
Sheldon Flora	A	A1/5	1872 Mar17	1894 Jun20	1920 Sep 4
Sheldon Flora =A1/5	D	D2/14	1872 Mar17	1894 Jun20	1920 Sep 4
Sheldon Isaac =A8/232	D	D26/26	1629ca	1653ca	1708
Sheldon Isaac =D26/26	A	A8/232	1629ca	1653ca	1708
Sheldon Mary	A	A8/29	1731ca	1756 Aug 5	1805 Oct18
Sheldon Michael	A	A1/40	1790ca		
Sheldon Robert E=A1/10	D	D2a15	1845 Jan 1	1869 Feb24	1917 Jan21
Sheldon Robert Emmet	A	A1/10	1845 Jun 1	1869 Feb24	1917 Jan21
Sheldon Rosalana	S	C52Aa	1789ca		
Sheldon Ruth	D	D26/25	1660abt		
Sheldon Thomas	A	A8/116	1661 Aug 6	1685ca	1725 Jun 7
Sheldon Thomas H	A	A1/20	1818 May12	1844 Jan21	1854 Nov22
Shelley Mary	S	W25Aam	1645abt		
Shelley Mary =W25Aam	S	W37Eam	1645abt		
Shellman John	A	A1/76	1723ca	1748ca	1816 Sep25
Shellman John Jr	A	A1/38	1756 May 5	1794 Jun19	1838 Apr17
Shellman Susan	A	A1/19	1808 Feb20	1825 Jul 5	1887 Jan12
Shepard Anna	A	A11/29	1663 Sep 8	1682 Nov9	1708 Jul24

NAME	DIV.	NUMBER	BIRTH	MARRIAGE	DEATH
Shepard Anna	A	A8/85	1684 Jan30	1704 Jan 9	1735 May 7
Shepard Bethia	S	R67C	1720 Oct23		
Shepard James	S	R67B	1714 Apr27		
Shepard John	S	R67A	1710 Apr28		
Shepard THomas	A	A11/116	1605 Nov5	1632ca	1649 Aug25
Shepard Thomas III	A	A8/170	1658	1682	1685
Shepard Thomas III	D	D24/25	1658	1682	=A08/170
Shepard Thomas Jr	D	D23a23	1635 Apr 5	1656 Nov 3	=A11/58
Shepard Thomas Jr	A	A8/340	1635 Apr 5	1656 Nov 3	=A11/58
Shepard Thomas Jr.	A	A11/58	1635 Apr5	1656 Nov3	1677 Dec22
Sheperd John	S	R20Aaf	1660abt		
Sheperd Rebecca	A	A4/9	1830abt		
Sheperd Samuel	S	R20Aa	1682 Feb 2	1709 May17	1750 Jun 5
Sherman Abigail	S	R80E	1723ca		
Sherman Alice	S	R80C	1719 Jul29		
Sherman Benjamin	S	K53E	1712		
Sherman Bethiah	S	R80F	1724 Jan26		
Sherman Daniel	S	K53B	1706 Nov26		
Sherman Elizabeth	S	T22Eam	1720abt		
Sherman Experience	S	T12Ea	1678 Sep23	1702 Jul 5	1744 Mar31
Sherman George	S	K53D	1710		
Sherman Hannah	S	H14Ba	1668 Feb21	1693 Jun13	1745 Jul 8
Sherman Jane	S	R80B	1716 Oct 2		
Sherman John	S	R23Aa	1682 Oct17	1712 Mar26	1765 Jul26
Sherman John	S	R80D	1721 Jul27		
Sherman Josiah	S	K53A	1702 Mar 2		
Sherman Keziah	S	R80H	1728 Oct28		
Sherman Peleg	S	K18Gaf	1635abt		
Sherman Ruth	S	K53C	1708		
Sherman Samuel	S	R80I	1730 Jan 2		
Sherman Sarah	S	R80A	1714 Aug15		
Sherman Susannah	S	K53F	1715		
Sherman Thomas	S	K18Ga	1658 Aug 8	1702 May26	1720bef
Sherman William	S	H14Baf	1645abt		
Sherman William	S	T12Eaf	1655abt		
Sherman William	S	R80G	1726 Jan11		
Sherwood Esther	S	R24Ka	1717 Nov20	1736 Dec15	1799 Dec10
Sherwood Matthew	S	R12Kbf	1650abt		
Sherwood Samuel	S	R24Kaf	1690abt		
Shields Anne	A	A15/7	1742Jul 31	1760ca	

NAME	DIV.	NUMBER	BIRTH	MARRIAGE	DEATH
Shields James	A	A15/28	1675abt		1727Jun 2
Shields James Jr	A	A15/14	1700abt		1750abt
Shinn Jane	A	A3/255	1710abt	1732 May 4	
Shinn John Jr.	A	A3/510	1685abt	1707	1736
Shipley Lucy	A	A13/7	1765ca		1785abt
Shipley Robert Jr	A	A13/14	1713 Oct	1737bef	1771
Shipman Betsey	S	G20Aa	1820abt	1841	
Shoemaker Margaret	D	D32a24	1804Jan 29		1890Mar 14
Shore Jonathan	A	A16/50	1649ca		1668Jan 15
Shore Phoebe	A	A16/25	1674 Apr20	1696 Mar 3	1717 Mar11
Shore Sampson	A	A16/100	1625abt	1639abt	
Short Hannah	S	C37Ea	1760ca		
Short Joanna	A	A1/383	1715	1748	
Short Joanna	D	D2a20	1715	1748	
Short Philip	S	C25Ga	1680ca		
Shriner Catharine	A	A1/53	1785ca		
Shurtleff Abiel	S	K29Caf	1680abt		
Shurtleff Hannah	S	K29Ca	1705ca	1724 Mar 4	1789 Nov14
Shurtleff Sarah	S	K40Cam	1700abt		
Shurtleff Susannah	S	A25Fa	1691ca	1709 Dec29	1763 Jan16
Shurtleff William	S	A25Faf	1670abt		
Sijbrantsz Aeffe Jans	A	A8/133	1637	1663	
Silvester Israel	S	H33Daf	1675abt		
Silvester Israel	S	K29Daf	1675abt		=H33Dam
Silvester Lois	S	A26Eam	1690abt		
Silvester Ruth	S	H33Da	1701 Jun26	1724 Jan28	1775abt
Silvester Ruth	S	K29Da	1702 Jun26	1719 Feb 4	1779bef
Simmons Aaron	S	T16Iaf	1655abt		
Simmons Aaron	S	T41C	1724 Mar25		
Simmons Abiah	S	T41E	1730 Oct23		1751living
Simmons Benjamin	S	T16Ba	1678ca	1715ca	1748bef
Simmons Betty	S	T41B	1720 Feb25		
Simmons Hannah	S	T41A	1718 Jun16		
Simmons John	S	W35Jaf	1645abt		
Simmons John =W35Jaf	S	T16Baf	1645abt		
Simmons Joshua	S	T16Ia	1688ca	1728 Apr 4	1774 Jan15
Simmons Mary	S	Q13Dam	1640abt		
Simmons Priscilla	S	T41D	1727 Dec30		
Simmons Rebecca=Q14Aam	S	T12Fam	1640abt		
Simmons Rebecca=T12Fam	S	K15Aam	1640abt		

NAME	DIV.	NUMBER	BIRTH	MARRIAGE	DEATH
Simmons Rebecca=T12Fam	S	K16Ham	1640abt		
Simmons Rebecca=T12Fam	S	Q14Aam	1640abt		
Simmons William	S	W35Ja	1672 Feb24	1696ca	1760 Abt
Simpson Hannah	A	A5/3	1798 Nov23	1821 Jun24	1883 May11
Simpson John	A	A5/12	1738ca	1762 Nov25	1804 Aug
Simpson John Jr.	A	A5/6	1767ca	1793 Oct17	1837 Jan20
Simpson Thomas	A	A5/48	1683ca		1761 June
Simpson William	A	A5/24	1710ca		1794 May15
Sinclair Shirley Ann	S	C59Ba	1930		
Sioerts Heyltje	A	A7/33	1688 Sept2	1708 Sep25	1752ca
Sioerts Olfert	A	A7/66	1661ca	1682 Sep 9	1710ca
Sisson Content	S	K44G	1700ca		
Sisson Hannah	S	K44H	1702ca		1734living
Sisson James	S	K17Da	1660ca	1680ca	1734
Sisson James	S	K21Gaf	1685abt		
Sisson James	S	K44C	1686ca		
Sisson Jonathan	S	K44D	1690ca		
Sisson Mary	S	K44B	1684 Feb26		1734living
Sisson Philip	S	K44E	1694ca		1730ca
Sisson Rebecca	S	K21Ga	1710ca	1729ca	1789aft
Sisson Rebecca	S	K44J	1710ca		
Sisson Richard	S	K17Daf	1635abt		
Sisson Richard	S	K44A	1682 Feb19		
Sisson Sarah	S	K44I	1705ca		
Sisson Thomas	S	K44F	1698ca		1734living
Skeffe Abigail	S	W41A	1666 May 2	1684 Dec 3	1718 Jun 7
Skeffe Deborah	S	W41B	1668 Jul14	1693ca	1743 Mar11
Skeffe James	S	W16Aaf	1615abt		
Skeffe Lydia	S	W41D	1675ca	1701 May 7	1733aft
Skeffe Lydia =W41D	S	W47Aa	1675ca	1701 May 7	1735aft
Skeffe Marcy	S	W41C	1671 Nov13	1691ca	1711 Mar12
Skeffe Stephen	S	W16Aa	1641 Apr14	1665ca	1710abt
Skeffe Stephen	S	W47Aaf	1650abt		
Skeffe Stephen	S	W41E	1685 Feb 4	2 Mar	1756
Skidmore Joseph	S	N15Ca	1775ca		
Skiffe Deborah	A	A8/219	1668	1693ca	1743
Skiffe Mary	S	W31Aam	1655abt		
Skinner Abigail	S	A19D	1685ca	2 mar.	1730ca
Skinner Agnes	S	A19C	1682ca		1698living
Skinner John	S	A19B	1679 Apr 2		

NAME	DIV.	NUMBER	BIRTH	MARRIAGE	DEATH
Skinner Mary	S	R19Hb	1703ca	1746 Nov25	1787 Nov17
Skinner Rebecca	S	A19A	1677 Jan22		
Skinner Richard	S	G29Aaf	1716	1736	1790
Skinner Sarah	S	A19E	1687 Sep18		d.yng
Skinner Stephen	S	G29A	1753		1842
Skinner Thomas	S	A13Db	1644ca	1676ca	1690 Dec28
Slade Hannah	A	A3/499	1679		1710ca
Slater Abraham	S	F45G	1699 Sep 8		
Slater Aleeshia	S	F45H	1702 Oct29		
Slater Caleb (Edward)	S	F45E	1695 Aug10		1740living
Slater Edward	S	F19Da	1644ca	1684 Jan 9	
Slater Elizabeth	S	F45B	1686 Mar14		d. yng
Slater Elizabeth	S	F45F	1697 Aug 8		
Slater Phebe	S	F45D	1693 Jul28		
Slater Philoreta #1	S	F45A	1685 Nov 6		1687 Sep 2
Slater Philoreta #2	S	F45C	1690 Feb23		
Small Edward	S	H30Gaf	1675abt		
Small Mary	A	A2/235	1645abt	1668	1675ca
Small Zachariah	S	H30Gb	1698	1742 May22	1778 Apr24
Smalley Benjamin	S	H21Da	1667ca	1694ca	1722bef
Smalley Benjamin #1	S	H63C	1700 Jan23		d. yng.
Smalley Benjamin #2	S	H63D	1702 Oct15		
Smalley Elisha	S	X27Db	1711ca	1749 Oct 6	1774bef
Smalley Elizabeth	S	H63J	1716ca		
Smalley Francis	S	H21Daf	1640abt		
Smalley Francis	S	H63I	1714ca		
Smalley Hannah	S	H63A	1695 Nov25		
Smalley James	S	H63F	1707 Oct28		
Smalley John	S	H12Faf	1625abt		
Smalley Joseph	S	H63H	1712ca		
Smalley Mary	S	H12Fa	1647 Dec11	1667 Sep19	1699 Dec 7
Smalley Mary	S	H63E	1705 Mar15		
Smalley Phebe	S	H63G	1709 Dec13		
Smalley Rebecca	S	H63B	1697 Apr27		
Smith A.	S	N13Cb	1740abt		
Smith Abigail	A	A14/75	1656 Mar11		1692 Nov12
Smith Abigail	S	C72Ba	1700abt		
Smith Abigail	A	A11/3	1744 Nov23	1764 Oct25	1818 Oct28
Smith Abigail =A14/75	A	A14/67	1656 Mar11		1692 Nov12
Smith Abraham Jr.	A	A3/456	1647ca		

NAME	DIV.	NUMBER	BIRTH	MARRIAGE	DEATH
Smith Anna	A	A17/49	1605ca		1656
Smith Anne	S	F25D	1695 Nov 8		
Smith Anthony	A	A14/150	1625abt	1651ca	1665abt
Smith Anthony	A	A3/114	1723 Jul26	1746 May16	1810
Smith Anthony =A14/158	A	A14/134	1625abt	1651ca	1665abt
Smith Bathshua #1	S	H107A	1716 Apr17		d yng
Smith Bathshua #2	S	H107C	1724 Aug 8		
Smith Benjamin	A	A12/42	1673 Jan10	1699 Mar14	1754ca
Smith Benjamin	S	F25M	1711 Dec 5		1746bef
Smith Benjamin	S	C88Ea	1715ca		
Smith Benjamin	S	X39F	1724 Oct 3		
Smith Bethiah	S	H61H	1708ca		
Smith Bethya	S	X17Ba	1680ca	1713 Apr30	
Smith Chloe	A	A12/5	1762 Nov10	1779	1847 Feb17
Smith Cynthia	S	C54Ba	1798ca		
Smith Daniel	S	X16Haf	1660abt		
Smith Daniel	S	F25G	1700 Apr11		
Smith Daniel Jr	A	A1/272	1642	1668	1681
Smith David	S	F25H	1702 May24		
Smith David	S	H61I	1711ca		1734living
Smith Dean	S	H61C	1698ca		
Smith Ebenezer	S	F25F	1698 Mar21		1699 May27
Smith Ebenezer	S	F25N	1714 Sep26		1746bef
Smith Elizabeth	D	D31a25	1602	1624	1686
Smith Elizabeth	A	A12/161	1602	1624	=A12/169
Smith Elizabeth	S	R12Cam	1640abt		
Smith Elizabeth	A	A4/505	1662	1681	1750
Smith Elizabeth	S	T15Eam	1680abt		
Smith Elizabeth	A	A12/21	1703 May 5	1727	1778 Jan12
Smith Elizabeth	S	F25I	1704 Apr19		
Smith Elizabeth	S	G27Bb	1710abt		
Smith Elizabeth=A4/505	A	A12/169	1602	1624	1686
Smith Ephraim	A	A1/68	1704 Oct 5	1743 Jan 3	1774 Mar24
Smith Frances D	D	D28/18	1840abt		
Smith Gertrude	S	C58Ba	1902		
Smith Grace	S	H25E	1676 Sept5		1691 Dec 1
Smith Grace	S	X39E	1722 Dec17		
Smith Hannah	S	Q17Bam	1660abt		
Smith Harriett	A	A1/17	1800 May12	1821 Nov 8	1867 Jun21
Smith Henry	A	A8/84	1678 Jan19	1704 Jan 9	1766 Oct31

NAME	DIV.	NUMBER	BIRTH	MARRIAGE	DEATH
Smith Henry	D	D33a21	1827 May25	1848 Jul15	1910Apr 30
Smith Hulda	S	H107E	1732 Jul28		
Smith Israel	A	A12/10	1739 Apr 2	1761ca	1811 Jun 7
Smith James	S	X16Ha	1685 Apr	1712 Feb19	1755ca
Smith James	S	F25C	1693 Dec18		
Smith James	S	H61A	1694 Feb13		1696 May27
Smith James	S	X39C	1718 Apr 8		1754living
Smith Jemima	S	F25L	1709 Nov 9		
Smith John	S	W41Aaf	1630abt		
Smith John	A	A12/80	1637ca	1673 Nov12	1676 May30
Smith John	S	H19Aaf	1645abt		
Smith John	S	F15Caf	1645abt		
Smith John	A	A1/136	1672 Jul13	1695 aft	1739 May 8
Smith John	S	H25D	1673 May26	1694 May14	1717bef
Smith John	S	Q21Abf	1675abt		
Smith John	S	H61F	1703ca		
Smith John =A12/80	A	A12/84	1637ca	1673 Nov12	1676 May30
Smith John =H25D	S	H20Da	1673 May26	1694 May14	1717bef
Smith John III	A	A12/20	1697 Feb 1	1727	1784
Smith John Jr	D	D28a24	1670abt		
Smith John Jr.	A	A12/40	1665 May15	1687ca	1724 Jan20
Smith Joseph	S	F15Ca	1667 Dec 6	1689 Apr29	1746 Mar14
Smith Joseph	S	H25C	1671 Apr10		1692 Sep22
Smith Joseph	S	F25B	1691 Oct28		
Smith Joseph	S	H30Ea	1692 Oct 9	1715 Jun24	1778ca
Smith Joseph =H30Ea	S	H80B	1692 Oct 9	1715 Jun24	1778ca
Smith Joshua	S	X39D	1720 Jul19		
Smith Judith	A	A3/57	1751 May 9	1768	1836 Mar 5
Smith Leah	S	C51Ha	1703ca		
Smith Levi	S	X39A	1713 Mar15		
Smith Lola Josephine	D	D33/20	1857 Sep 4	1877Jan 23	1958Sep 1
Smith Lucy	A	A11/43	1620abt	1641 Jul 4	1687 Nov4
Smith Marcy	S	Q21Ab	1696ca	1768aft	1782 Nov10
Smith Margaret	D	D11a24	1420abt		
Smith Margaret M.	A	A18/1a	1788Jun 21	1810 Jun21	
Smith Mary	A	A12/171	1625ca	1644	1680
Smith Mary	S	H25B	1669 Jan 3	1693ca	1708bef
Smith Mary	S	R14Eam	1675abt		
Smith Mary	S	R22Bbm	1675abt		
Smith Mary	A	A1/291	1697		1745

NAME	DIV.	NUMBER	BIRTH	MARRIAGE	DEATH
Smith Mary	S	H61E	1702ca		
Smith Mary	S	F25K	1707 Dec22	unmar	1728 Sep16
Smith Mary	S	G15Aa	1713	1734	1802
Smith Mary	S	H107B	1718 Oct 4	1737 Sep24	
Smith Mary A12/171	A	A12/163	1625ca	1644	1680
Smith Matthias	S	F25E	1697 Jul10		
Smith Mercy	S	H61D	1700ca		
Smith Mildred	D	D28/23	1700abt		
Smith Oswald	D	D28a19	1815abt		
Smith Philip	D	D31/24	1630abt		
Smith Ralph	S	H13Aaf	1620abt		
Smith Rebecca	A	A1/271	1668ca	1686ca	1750
Smith Rebecca	S	H25F	1678 Dec10		
Smith Rebecca	A	A8/21	1734ca	1766 Jun 5	1809 Nov25
Smith Rebecca=A1/271	D	D31/23	1668ca	1686ca	1750
Smith Rebecca=A8/21	D	D4am20	1734ca	1766 Jun 5	1809 Nov25
Smith Samuel	A	A12/160	1601ca	1624	1680
Smith Samuel	S	H13Aa	1641 Jul11	1665 Jan 3	1696 Mar22
Smith Samuel	S	H25A	1668 May26	1690 May26	1692 Sep22
Smith Samuel	S	H80A	1690 Feb13		
Smith Samuel	S	H61B	1696 May25		
Smith Samuel	S	H107D	1729 Dec21		
Smith Samuel =A12/160	D	D31/25	1601ca	1624	1680
Smith Samuel =A12/160	A	A12/168	1601ca	1624	1680
Smith Samuel =H13Aa	S	H20Daf	1641 Jul11	1665 Jan 3	1696 Mar22
Smith Samuel =H25A	S	H30Eaf	1668 May26	1690 May26	1692 Sep22
Smith Sanford	A	A1/34	1760 Feb27		1815 Jun25
Smith Sarah	S	X16Dbm	1650abt		
Smith Sarah	A	A19/143	1661	1683	
Smith Sarah	S	H19Aa	1671 Mar27	1690 Dec15	1715bef
Smith Seth	S	H61J	1713ca		
Smith Shubal	S	W41Aa	1653 Mar13	1684 Dec 3	1734 Apr 5
Smith Solomon	S	X39B	1715 Mar 8		
Smith Stephen	S	H61G	1706ca		
Smith Susannah	S	F25A	1690 Jan12	unm.	1746living
Smith Thomas	A	A11/24	1640abt	1663ca	1690 Feb14
Smith Thomas	A	A3/228	1672ca	1717ca	1732
Smith Thomas	S	F25J	1705 Feb 6		
Smith William	A	A8/168	1654	1675	1704
Smith William	A	A11/12	1666 Mar24	1699ca	1730 Jun 3

NAME	DIV.	NUMBER	BIRTH	MARRIAGE	DEATH
Smith William	S	C56Aa	1855ca		
Smith William Henry	A	A8/42	1708 Oct29	1732 Dec19	1776 Oct 2
Smith William Jr.	A	A11/6	1706 Jan29	1740 Oct16	1783 Sep1?
Smitherman G. Scott	S	G57Ab	1930abt	1966 Dec30	
Smiton Sarah	S	K20Fam	1650abt		
Snao Isaac	S	H65D	1717abt		
Snell Amos	S	Q22Baf	1680abt		
Snell Jemima	S	Q22Ba	1704 May 3	1721 Mar 7	1784 Feb 6
Snider Arlene	S	C59A	1923		
Snider Audrey	S	C59C	1926		
Snider Dale R	S	C59B	1924		
Snider Margaret	S	C59E	1929		
Snider Rex A	S	C58Aa	1894		
Snider Virginia	S	C59D	1928		
Snow Aaron	S	H62F	1707 Mar23		
Snow Aaron	S	H38H	1710 Feb15		
Snow Abiah	S	W42I	1691ca	1716 Jan 2	1717 Feb 1
Snow Abigail	S	W16C	1650ca	1667 Dec12	1682 Jun25
Snow Abigail	S	W42A	1670 Dec 6	unm.	
Snow Abigail	S	H21C	1673 Oct14		
Snow Abigail	A	A19/149	1677	1695ca	1753aft
Snow Abigail	S	Q61E	1727 May27		
Snow Abigail =W16C	S	W25Cam	1650ca	1667 Dec12	1682 Jun25
Snow Abijah	S	Q61B	1721 Feb12		
Snow Alice	S	W16F	1657 Jan18	1680abt	1697 Sep5
Snow Amasa	S	H64K	1720 Jan 9		
Snow Ambrose	S	H64J	1718 Jan 6		
Snow Ann	S	H64B	1703 Jul1?		
Snow Anna	S	H16A	1656 Jul 7	1683 Feb14	1714 Jul 7
Snow Anthony	S	W11Ea	1620abt	1639 Nov 8	1692 Aug
Snow Anthony	S	H64F	1709 Jul28		
Snow Bathsheba	S	Q67B	1732ca		
Snow Bathshuah	S	H20A	1664 Jul25		1706ca
Snow Bathshuah	S	H62L	1723 Oct 4		
Snow Benjamin	S	Q13F	1669ca	2 mar.	1743 May28
Snow Benjamin	S	H19B	1673 Jun 9	1700 Jun 6	1750ca
Snow Benjamin	S	Q22B	1696 Jun23	1721 Mar 7	1760 Oct29
Snow Benjamin	S	H52A	1700 Feb 5		
Snow Benjamin	S	H65C	1716abt		
Snow Benjamin	S	Q66B	1724 Aug25		

NAME	DIV.	NUMBER	BIRTH	MARRIAGE	DEATH
Snow Bethia	S	Q20A	1688 Sep28	1720 Feb 1	1747bef
Snow Bethiah	S	H25Da	1672 Jul 1	1694 May14	1747ca
Snow Bethiah	S	W42F	1681 Dec	1706ca	1761 Oct 1
Snow Bethiah =H25Da	S	H20D	1672 Jul 1	1694 May14	1747ca
Snow Betty	S	Q58A	1729 Mar 9		
Snow Caleb	S	Q68D	1736 Jun 8		
Snow Daniel	S	Q66C	1726 Jul26		
Snow Daniel	S	Q60F	1727ca		
Snow Daniel	S	Q58E	1742 Apr30		
Snow David	S	Q21G	1703 Sep27	1730 Mar11	
Snow David	S	H60F	1711 Oct30		
Snow David	S	H64L	1722 Mar15		d yng
Snow David	S	H64M	1723ca		
Snow David	S	Q65A	1732 Dec12		1753 May25
Snow David twin	S	H39G	1709 Dec22		
Snow Deborah	S	W42D	1677 Dec21		1681
Snow Deborah	S	H23G	1685abt	1706 Nov21	1731aft
Snow Deborah	S	H51D	1698ca		
Snow Ebenezer	S	H20F	1675ca	1698 Dec22	1725 Apr 9
Snow Ebenezer	S	H38D	1700 Feb14	1741 Feb24	1758Dec 21
Snow Ebenezer	S	Q22D	1701 Mar29	2 mar.	1790living
Snow Ebenezer	S	H62C	1703 Feb16		
Snow Ebenezer	S	Q68A	1729 Nov16		
Snow Edward	S	H23B	1672 Mar26		1755ca
Snow Edward	S	H71G	1711 May18		
Snow Eleazer	S	Q20E	1701 Jul14	1728 Jul11	1796 Feb18
Snow Eleazer	S	Q58C	1734 Oct30		
Snow Elijah	S	Q66D	1728 Nov 6		
Snow Elisha	S	H21H	1686 Jan10		1750abt
Snow Elisha	S	H64G	1711 Oct20		
Snow Elisha	S	H62I	1716 Oct 9		
Snow Elisha	S	H66B	1720ca		
Snow Elizabeth	S	H16D	1666 May 9		1675 Jan18
Snow Elizabeth	S	H16H	1676 Jun22		1677 Mar22
Snow Elizabeth	S	H23F	1690bef	1704 Dec21	1710abt
Snow Elizabeth	S	H38A	1693 Oct	1719 Oct20	
Snow Elizabeth	S	H52B	1702 Oct10		
Snow Elizabeth	S	H71C	1702ca		
Snow Elizabeth	S	H64C	1705 Mar27		
Snow Elizabeth	S	Q22E	1705 May 5	1725 May 4	1755 Jul 6

NAME	DIV.	NUMBER	BIRTH	MARRIAGE	DEATH
Snow Elizabeth	S	Q60C	1719 May 4		
Snow Elizabeth	S	H57A	1721 Jul18		
Snow Elizabeth	S	Q66E	1730 Apr 2		
Snow Elizabeth =H12G	S	X12Ca	1640ca	1665 Dec13	1678 Jun16
Snow Elizabeth =H38A	S	H19Ka	1693 Oct	1719 Oct20	
Snow Elizabeth=X12Ca	S	H12G	1640ca	1665 Dec13	1678 Jun16
Snow Elkins	S	H55E	1713 Mar24		
Snow Francis	S	Q68E	1740 Mar26		
Snow Grace	S	H23D	1674 Feb	2 Mar	1715aft
Snow Hannah	S	Q13E	1664ca	2 mar.	1723 Mar29
Snow Hannah	S	H20B	1666 Jan 2	1686 Dec 2	1737 Jun23
Snow Hannah	S	H21A	1670 Aug26		
Snow Hannah	S	H16I	1679 Sep16		
Snow Hannah	S	H39B	1701 Nov29		
Snow Hannah	S	H38E	1702 Mar21		
Snow Hannah	S	H62K	1720 Dec15		
Snow Hannah	S	Q63A	1723 Nov14		
Snow Henry	S	H62E	1707 Jan6		
Snow Hope	S	H62J	1718 Nov18		
Snow Isaac	S	H21F	1683 Aug10		1748bef
Snow Isaac	S	Q21E	1700 Jul22	1722 Nov19	1737 Jul10
Snow Isaac	S	H64H	1713 Feb11		
Snow Isaac	S	Q63B	1726 Feb16		
Snow Jabez	S	H12H	1642ca	1671bef	1690 Dec27
Snow Jabez	S	H23A	1670 Sep 6	1695ca	1750 Oct14
Snow Jabez	S	H71A	1696 Jul22		
Snow Jabez	S	H39A	1699 Nov11		
Snow Jabez	S	H72B	1703ca		
Snow James	S	Q13H	1673ca		1691ca
Snow James	S	H19I	1689 Mar31		
Snow James	S	Q20B	1691 Oct14	1719 Nov 4	1749 Aug28
Snow James	S	Q21C	1693 Aug16	2 mar.	1760
Snow James	S	H52I	1716ca		
Snow James	S	H66C	1722ca		
Snow James	S	Q57C	1729 Apr 4		
Snow James	S	Q60G	1730 Dec30		
Snow Jane	S	H19J	1692 Mar27		
Snow Jane	S	H52H	1714 Mar 4		
Snow Jane	S	H55F	1716 Apr22		
Snow Jedediah	S	Q61G	1731 Mar15		

NAME	DIV.	NUMBER	BIRTH	MARRIAGE	DEATH
Snow Jemima	S	Q66A	1723 Jan 5		
Snow Jesse	S	H60E	1709 Oct27		
Snow Jesse	S	H66D	1724ca		
Snow Jesse	S	Q64B	1730 Feb 8		
Snow Joanna	S	Q65C	1735 Nov27		
Snow John	S	H12F	1638ca	1667 Sep19	1692 Apr 4
Snow John	S	H21E	1678 May 3	1700 Feb25	1738 Oct14
Snow John	S	H60A	1700 May26		
Snow John	S	Q20F	1704 Aug14	2 mar.	1786bef
Snow John	S	H64D	1706 Dec27		
Snow John	S	H65A	1710abt		
Snow John	S	Q60B	1717 Apr19		1738 Dec 3
Snow John	S	H55H	1720 Mar30	1746 Dec10	1764 Jan20
Snow John	S	H66F	1730abt		
Snow John	S	Q61I	1736 Mar31		
Snow John	S	Q59B	1762 Jan 4		
Snow Jonathan	S	H37A	1691 Jan30		
Snow Jonathan	S	H60C	1703 Jan16		
Snow Jonathan	S	Q21F	1703 Sep27	2 mar.	1783 Jan17
Snow Jonathan	S	H39F	1709 Dec22	twin	
Snow Jonathan	S	Q64E	1735 Mar10		
Snow Joseph	S	H12D	1634ca		1722 Jan 3
Snow Joseph	S	Q13D	1664ca	1689ca	1753 Dec18
Snow Joseph	S	H19A	1671 Nov24	1690 Dec15	1705 Jan21
Snow Joseph	S	Q21A	1690 Sep 7	2 mar.	1773 Jul24
Snow Joseph	S	H51B	1694ca		
Snow Joseph	S	Q60A	1715 Mar26		
Snow Joseph	S	H72G	1718 Sep14		
Snow Joseph	S	Q65B	1734 Jun27		
Snow Joseph	S	Q63E	1734 May23		
Snow Joseph	S	H66H	1735abt		
Snow Joshua	S	H37D	1700 Aug18		
Snow Joshua	S	H71B	1700 Mar12		
Snow Joshua	S	H64A	1701 Sep22		
Snow Joshua	S	H66E	1725abt		
Snow Josiah	S	W16B	1645abt	1669ca	1692 Aug
Snow Josiah	S	H19K	1694 Nov27	1719 Oct20	
Snow Josiah	S	H38C	1699 Jan27		
Snow Josiah	S	H57B	1723 Sep18		
Snow Josiah =W16B	S	W44Baf	1645abt	1669ca	1692 Aug

NAME	DIV.	NUMBER	BIRTH	MARRIAGE	DEATH
Snow Judith	S	Q63F	1736 Dec 7		
Snow Lemuel	S	Q67A	1729		
Snow Lucretia	S	C21Hb	1764ca		
Snow Lucy	S	Q66F	1735 May27		
Snow Lusannah	S	W42G	1682 Mar 7	1709 Jun16	1732 Mar 7
Snow Lusannah =W42G	S	W44Ba	1682 Mar 7	1709 Jun16	1732 Mar 7
Snow Lydia	S	W16A	1640ca	1665ca	1712ca
Snow Lydia	S	Q13B	1661ca		1698living
Snow Lydia	S	W42B	1672 Jul 5	1692	1716 Apr 8
Snow Lydia	S	H19G	1684 Jul20	1714 Feb10	1738 Mar18
Snow Lydia	S	H21G	1685 Sep29		
Snow Lydia	S	H38F	1707 Jul24		
Snow Lydia	S	H55C	1710 Mar26		
Snow Lydia	S	Q65E	1740 Feb16		
Snow Lydia =W16A	S	W47Aam	1640ca	1665ca	1712ca
Snow Margaret	S	H55A	1706 May14		
Snow Mark	S	H12A	1628 May 9	2 Mar	1694
Snow Mark	S	H37B	1695 Apr30		
Snow Martha	S	H72D	1707 Oct		
Snow Martha	S	Q63C	1728 Nov15		
Snow Mary	S	X12Gam	1620abt		
Snow Mary	S	H12B	1630ca	1652bef	1704 Apr28
Snow Mary	S	Q13A	1660ca		1698living
Snow Mary	S	H16B	1661 Nov30	1690 Jan22	1720abt
Snow Mary	S	H21B	1671 Mar10		
Snow Mary	S	H19C	1674 Oct17		
Snow Mary	S	X26Dam	1680abt		
Snow Mary	S	Q21B	1691 Nov. 1		
Snow Mary	S	H52C	1705 Feb18		
Snow Mary	S	H39H	1712 Sep10		
Snow Mary	S	H64I	1716 Aug16		
Snow Mary	S	Q61C	1724 Feb28		
Snow Mary	S	H57C	1725 Nov21		
Snow Mary	S	Q57D	1731 Aug12		
Snow Mary	S	Q60H	1733 Apr20		1751Feb 12
Snow Mary =X12Gam	S	X15Eam	1620abt		
Snow Mehitabel	S	Q65D	1737 Sep18		1766 Mar23
Snow Mehitable	S	H20E	1674ca	unm.	1706living
Snow Mercy	S	W42C	1675 Aug29	1698 Feb 7	1755abt
Snow Mercy	S	H39D	1705 Nov18		

NAME	DIV.	NUMBER	BIRTH	MARRIAGE	DEATH
Snow Mercy	S	H60G	1713 Sep26		
Snow Mercy	S	H55I	1721 Feb24		
Snow Mercy	S	Q58D	1737 Mar22		
Snow Micajah	S	H20C	1669 Dec22	1697 Nov25	1753ca
Snow Micajah	S	H60H	1716 Dec15		
Snow Moses	S	Q64F	1737 Sep27		
Snow Nathan	S	H72F	1716ca		
Snow Nathan	S	Q61D	1725 Jul 9		
Snow Nathaniel	S	H51C	1696ca		
Snow Nathaniel	S	H37C	1697 Oct16		
Snow Nathaniel	S	H62D	1705 Feb 7		
Snow Nathaniel	S	H72E	1709ca		
Snow Nathaniel	S	Q68B	1731 Jun 6		
Snow Nicholas	S	H11Aa	1605ca	1628	1676 Nov15
Snow Nicholas	S	X12Caf	1615abt		
Snow Nicholas	S	H16C	1663 Dec 6	1689 Apr 4	1752ca
Snow Peter	S	Q63D	1731 Jul25		
Snow Phebe	S	H21I	1689 Jun27		
Snow Phebe	S	H37G	1705 Nov17		
Snow Phebe	S	H60D	1707 Jul17	1729 Mar19	
Snow Phebe	S	H71H	1713ca		
Snow Phebe	S	H66G	1732abt		
Snow Phineas	S	H64E	1706 Dec27	twin	1706Jan 16
Snow Prence	S	H16G	1674 May22		
Snow Prence	S	H37H	1707 Dec26		
Snow Prence	S	H39E	1707 Oct26		
Snow Rachel	S	H23H	1685abt	1717 Aug29	1765 Mar22
Snow Rebecca	S	Q13G	1671ca	1689 Dec31	1740 Apr 4
Snow Rebecca	S	H21D	1676 Jul23	2 mar	1753 Aug31
Snow Rebecca	S	W42H	1685 Jun16	unm.	
Snow Rebecca	S	H19H	1686 Dec 4		
Snow Rebecca	S	Q22A	1694 Nov 7	1738bef	1763 Sep 4
Snow Rebecca	S	H72C	1705ca		1723 Apr 2
Snow Rebecca	S	H52F	1710 Sep26		
Snow Rebecca	S	Q64D	1734 Oct16		
Snow Rebecca	S	Q68G	1742 Mar 5		
Snow Rebeckah	S	Q21D	1696 Jun25	1722 Dec20	1740ca
Snow Reuben	S	Q58B	1731 Apr16		
Snow Rhoda	S	Q65F	1742 Oct 7		
Snow Robert	S	H55G	1717 Feb22		

NAME	DIV.	NUMBER	BIRTH	MARRIAGE	DEATH
Snow Ruth	S	H12I	1644ca	1666 Dec12	1716 Jan27
Snow Ruth	S	H19E	1679 Oct14	1704 Apr13	1720ca
Snow Ruth	S	H38I	1712 Feb23		1717 Jul15
Snow Ruth	S	H60I	1717 Mar14		
Snow Ruth	S	Q61A	1720 May12		
Snow Ruth	S	H55J	1725 Dec11		
Snow Ruth	S	Q64G	1747ca		
Snow Ruth =H12I	S	X18Bam	1644ca	1666 Dec12	1716 Jan27
Snow Samuel	S	H39C	1703 Dec16		
Snow Samuel	S	H71F	1708 Jan22		
Snow Samuel	S	H62G	1709 Feb14		1728 Jun10
Snow Samuel	S	Q64A	1729 Sep20		
Snow Sarah	S	H12C	1632ca	1654 Feb25	1697living
Snow Sarah	S	X16Fam	1670abt		
Snow Sarah	S	H16F	1671 May10		
Snow Sarah	S	H23C	1673 Feb		
Snow Sarah	S	H19D	1677 Apr30	1699 Feb15	1742ca
Snow Sarah	S	W42E	1680 Nov 6	1699	1720abt
Snow Sarah	S	H37F	1703 Mar20		
Snow Sarah	S	Q22F	1706 Aug20	1728ca	1732 Apr28
Snow Sarah	S	H55D	1712 Feb13		
Snow Sarah	S	Q60E	1725 Feb 3		1745 Jan 8
Snow Sarah	S	Q61H	1732 Apr 6		
Snow Sarah	S	Q64C	1732 Dec 3		
Snow Sarah	S	Q68C	1733 Jul27		
Snow Sarah	S	Q59A	1758 Mar23		
Snow Sarah =W16D	S	W19Fam	1651	1673ca	1730abt
Snow Sarah =W16D	S	W42Gam	1651	1673ca	1730abt
Snow Sarah =W19Fam	S	W16D	1651	1673ca	1730abt
Snow Seth	S	H52J	1718ca		
Snow Seth	S	Q57B	1725 Aug 7		
Snow Silas	S	H66A	1718		
Snow Solomon	S	Q22C	1698 Apr 6	1724 Apr 8	1741bef
Snow Solomon	S	Q68F	1741 Dec13		
Snow Stephen	S	H12E	1636ca	2 Mar	1705 Dec17
Snow Stephen	S	H19F	1681 Feb24	1705 Jul12	1769bef
Snow Stephen	S	H60B	1702 May19		
Snow Stephen	S	H55B	1708 Mar21	1730 Oct 8	1773living
Snow Susanna	S	Q20C	1694 Sep27	1717 Dec25	1730ca
Snow Susanna	S	H62A	1699 Feb 6		

NAME	DIV.	NUMBER	BIRTH	MARRIAGE	DEATH
Snow Susanna	S	H52E	1708 Nov12		
Snow Susanna	S	Q60D	1722 Dec12		
Snow Susanna	S	Q61F	1729 Feb15		
Snow Susanna	S	Q57E	1735 Mar 2		
Snow Sylvanus	S	H71D	1704 Feb16		
Snow Tabitha	S	H71E	1707 Mar21		
Snow Thankful	S	H51A	1692 Dec15		
Snow Thankful	S	H37E	1701 Feb 7		
Snow Thankful	S	H52G	1712 Jan18		
Snow Thankful	S	H62H	1714 Jul23		
Snow Thomas	S	H16E	1668 Aug 6	2 Mar	
Snow Thomas	S	H23E	1677ca	unm	1697 Apr 2
Snow Thomas	S	H62B	1701 Feb 1		
Snow Thomas	S	H72A	1701ca		1730ca
Snow Thomas	S	H52D	1706 Feb 6		
Snow Thomas	S	H38G	1709 Jun15		
Snow Thomas =H16E	S	H19Kaf	1668 Aug 6	1792 Feb 8	1702 Mar21
Snow William	S	Q11Ca	1617ca	1654ca	1708 Jan31
Snow William	S	Q13C	1662ca	1686 Dec	1726bef
Snow William	S	Q20D	1697 Aug14	1722 Nov 8	1774aft
Snow William	S	H65B	1715abt		
Snow William	S	Q57A	1723 Aug10		
Snow Zebedee	S	Q68H	1743 Feb26		
Soanes Patience	S	T22Dam	1700abt		
Somes Lucy	S	X86A	1735		
Somes Nehemiah	S	X27Da	1704 Aug22	1734 Oct15	
Somes Nehemiah	S	X86B	1737		
Somes Timothy	S	X27Daf	1680abt		
Soper Esther	A	A19/93	1738May 10	1754Oct 31	1812 Jul 9
Soper Samuel Jr	A	A19/186	1709	1731	1751bef
Soule Benjamin	S	T12Fa	1666ca	1694ca	1729 Dec 1
Soule Benjamin	S	T19E	1704 Jun 4		
Soule Deborah	S	T19D	1702 Apr23		
Soule Ebenezer	S	T19F	1710 Feb16		
Soule Esther	S	Q24D	1707 Apr16		1793 May15
Soule Hannah	S	T19B	1696 Mar18		
Soule Isaac	S	K38C	1698 Jun16	unm.	1736bef
Soule Jacob	S	K38E	1702 Aug30		
Soule James	S	K16Ha	1659ca	1693 Dec14	1744 Aug27
Soule James	S	Q24F	1711 Apr15		

NAME	DIV.	NUMBER	BIRTH	MARRIAGE	DEATH
Soule John	S	K16Haf	1635abt		
Soule John	S	K34Eaf	1680abt		
Soule John	S	Q24C	1705 Apr13		
Soule John =K16Haf	S	K15Aaf	1635abt		
Soule John =K34Eaf	S	Q18Daf	1680abt		
Soule John =Q14Aaf	S	T12Faf	1635abt		
Soule John =Q18Daf	S	Q21Faf	1680abt		
Soule John Jr	S	Q14Aa	1675ca	1701 Dec 8	1743 May19
Soule John Sr =T12Faf	S	Q14Aaf	1635abt		
Soule Joshua	S	T14Eaf	1680abt		
Soule Martha	S	K38B	1696 Apr11		
Soule Martha	S	K34Ea	1702 Apr11	1732 Apr25	1772 Mar18
Soule Martha=K34Ea	S	Q18Da	1702 Apr11	1732 Apr25	1772 Mar18
Soule Martha=Q18Da	S	Q24A	1702 Apr11	1732Apr 25	1772 Mar18
Soule Mary	S	K38A	1694 Oct 2		d. yng
Soule Mary	S	Q24E	1709 Mar14		
Soule Nathan	S	Q24H	1717 Oct 1		1731 Feb 8
Soule Rachel	S	Q14Eam	1670abt		
Soule Rachel	S	T22Cam	1705abt		
Soule Rachel	S	Q24I	1719 Nov16		
Soule Rachel =Q14Cam	S	T20Bam	1670abt		
Soule Rachel =T20Bam	S	Q14Cam	1670abt		
Soule Rebecca	S	T20Fbm	1675abt		
Soule Rebecca	S	K38D	1700 Apr21	unm.	1747 Jun21
Soule Rebecca	S	Q24G	1713 Oct 1		1759 Jan24
Soule Sarah	S	K15Aa	1660ca	1680bef	1699ca
Soule Sarah	S	T19C	1699 May 9	unm.	1716 Nov19
Soule Sarah	S	Q21Fa	1703 Oct 8	1728 Dec18	1743 Apr12
Soule Sarah =Q21Fa	S	Q24B	1703 Oct 8	1728 Dec18	1743 Apr12
Soule Zachariah	S	T19A	1694 Mar21		
Soule Zerviah	S	T14Ea	1705 Nov 2	1728 Apr23	1782 Dec21
Southworth Alice	S	W15Ca	1646ca	1667 Dec26	1718 Mar5
Southworth Benjamin	S	T16Aa	1681ca	1715 Aug 4	1756 May12
Southworth Christopher	D	D29a16	1465abt		
Southworth Constant	S	W15Caf	1620abt		
Southworth Constant	S	T40G	1731 Jul 9		1751living
Southworth Deborah	S	T40H	1734 Mar11		
Southworth Edward	D	D29/11	1590abt		
Southworth Edward	S	T16Aaf	1655abt		
Southworth Edward	S	T40B	1717 Dec10		1739 Jan17

NAME	DIV.	NUMBER	BIRTH	MARRIAGE	DEATH
Southworth Elizabeth	A	A8/177	1640abt	1664	1717
Southworth Elizabeth	D	D4a/24	1640abt	1664	=D4a/24
Southworth Elizabeth	D	D29/9	1640abt	1664	=A8/177
Southworth Elizabeth	S	W32Da	1686 Sep24	1703 Dec12	1743 Apr10
Southworth Elizabeth	S	T40C	1719 Dec15	unm.	1761living
Southworth Hannah	S	T40A	1715 Oct29		
Southworth John Sir	D	D29/15	1490abt		
Southworth JohnII Sir	D	D29/13	1540abt		
Southworth Josher	S	T40J	1738 Nov 1		
Southworth Mercy	S	H27Eam	1655abt		
Southworth Obed	S	T40I	1736 Nov11		
Southworth Rebekah	S	T40F	1727 Dec 6		1739 Jan 8
Southworth Sarah	S	T40E	1725 Sep18		1739 Jan 6
Southworth Thomas	D	D4af24	1615abt		
Southworth Thomas	S	T40D	1722 Apr 1		
Southworth Thomas II	D	D29/12	1565abt		
Southworth Thomas III	D	D29/10	1615abt		=D4af24
Southworth Thomas Sir	D	D29/14	1515abt		
Southworth William	S	W32Daf	1660abt		
Sparrow Abigail	S	H89E	1700ca		
Sparrow Hannah	S	H89D	1699ca		
Sparrow John	S	H22Ebf	1660abt		
Sparrow John	S	H89C	1698ca		
Sparrow John=H22Ebf	S	X14Dbf	1660abt		
Sparrow Jonathan	S	H17Iaf	1650abt		
Sparrow Jonathan	S	H89A	1695ca	1721 Oct12	1790
Sparrow Jonathan Jr.	S	H27Aa	1665 Jul 5	1690ca	1739 Mar 9
Sparrow Jonathan Sr	S	X15Baf	1635abt		=H27Aaf
Sparrow Jonathan Sr.	S	H27Aaf	1635abt		=X15Baf
Sparrow Joseph	S	H89B	1697ca		
Sparrow Lydia	S	X15Ba	1660aft	1687aft	1708aft
Sparrow Patience	S	H17Ia	1670abt	1691 May27	1745 Oct25
Sparrow Rebbeca	S	R14Dam	1655abt		
Sparrow Rebecca	S	H22Eb	1684 Dec23	1730 Feb11	1765abt
Sparrow Rebecca	S	H89F	1700abt	1720 Oct20	1736 Sep15
Sparrow Rebecca=H22Eb	S	X14Db	1684 Dec23	1730 Feb11	1765abt
Spaulding Dinah	S	R117Bam	1670abt		
Speed Mary	S	W43Aam	1645abt		
Spencer Dorothy	D	D12a22	1490abt		
Spencer Grace	S	F22Ham	1675abt		

NAME	DIV.	NUMBER	BIRTH	MARRIAGE	DEATH
Spencer Henry	D	D11/25	1400abt		1448
Spencer Julian	D	D11/22	1490abt		
Spencer Susan	D	D12/21	1520abt		
Spencer Thomas	D	D11/24	1420abt		
Spencer Thomas	D	D12/22	1490abt		
Spencer William	D	D11/23	1450abt		
Spooner Benjamin	S	A26Ga	1705abt	1731 Nov23	
Spooner Benjamin	S	A74C	1745ca		
Spooner Eleanor	S	A74A	1742ca		
Spooner Eleazer	S	A74B	1745ca		
Spooner Elizabeth	S	K35Da	1683 Jun19	1701 Jan28	1738bef
Spooner Elizabeth	S	Q19Bam	1685abt		
Spooner Jane	S	K30Jb	1729 Aug21	1770 Feb22	1772 Jun22
Spooner John	S	A26Gaf	1680abt		
Spooner John=K35Daf	S	W47Daf	1655abt		
Spooner John=K35Eaf	S	K35Daf	1655abt		
Spooner John=W47Daf	S	K35Eaf	1655abt		
Spooner Mary	S	A74F	1746		
Spooner Phebe	S	K35Ea	1687 May11	1710ca	
Spooner Phebe	S	A74E	1745ca		
Spooner Samuel	S	A74D	1745ca		
Spooner Sarah	S	R27Aa	1726 Jan31	1746 Nov24	1782 Jul 1
Spooner Thomas	S	K30Jbf	1705abt		
Spooner Thomas=K30Jbf	S	R27Aaf	1705abt		
Spooner William	S	W47Da	1680 May11	1699ca	1729
Sprague Anthony	S	W12Fa	1636	1661 Dec26	1729 Sept3
Sprague Anthony	S	W24A	1663 Aug18	1689 Aug1	1730bef
Sprague Benjamin	S	W24B	1665 Aug16		1690 Sep27
Sprague Dorcas	S	K18Aam	1640abt		
Sprague Elizabeth	S	W24D	1669 Sep5		1690 Oct11
Sprague Elizabeth	S	A25Dbm	1670abt		
Sprague James	S	W24G	1677 Jan23	1702 May8	1742aft
Sprague Jeremiah	S	W24I	1682 Jul24	1706 Mar5	1759 Mar5
Sprague Jerusha	S	C37Ba	1755ca		
Sprague Joanna	S	W15Ga	1645 Dec	1667 Dec16	1678 Jul11
Sprague John	S	W24C	1667 Sep30		1690 Oct23
Sprague John	S	W42Fa	1682ca	1706ca	1739 Dec14
Sprague John Jr	S	T13Gb	1662ca	1726 Mar21	1728 Mar 6
Sprague John Sr	S	T13Gbf	1635abt		
Sprague Josiah	S	W24H	1680 Apr23	1705 May17	1760 Mar23

NAME	DIV.	NUMBER	BIRTH	MARRIAGE	DEATH
Sprague Matthew	S	W24K	1688 Mar27	1716 Sep13	1783 Jun16
Sprague Richard	S	W24J	1685 Apr10		1754bef
Sprague Samuel	S	W42Faf	1655abt		
Sprague Samuel	S	W24E	1671 Mar8	1716 Feb16	1723abt
Sprague Sarah	S	W24F	1674 May23	1716 Jun10	1751 Oct9
Sprague William	S	W15Gaf	1620abt		
Spring Phineas	S	G34Aaf	1768		1846
Spring Polly	S	G34Aa	1798	1814	1879
Sproat Anna	S	X23Fa	1671 Mar	1701bef	1739aft
Sproat Robert	S	X23Faf	1650abt		
Spur Joanna	S	X22Ca	1685ca	1710aft	
Squire Ann	A	A16/203	1591	1613	1662
Squire Edith	A	A11/33	1587 May29	1609 Oct19	1672 Jan21
Squire Grizell	A	A6/117	1668 May 4	1690ca	1738aft
Squire Henry	A	A11/66	1563ca	1586ca	
Squire Philip	A	A6/234	1640abt	1664ca	1692ca
Stacey Joseph	S	W52Ea	1694ca	1721 Apr11	1741 Aug25
Stacey Thomas	S	W52Eaf	1670abt		
Stackhouse Amos	A	A1/110	.1757ca	1770 Jan14	1825 Apr
Stackhouse Esther	A	A1/55	1787 Oct17	1807 Oct29	1819 Sep2?
Stackhouse James	A	A1/220	1725 Nov11	1750 Sep13	1759 Aug16
Stackhouse Robert	A	A1/440	1692		1788
Stafford Thomas	S	C82Aa	1682		
Standish Abigail	S	T26D	1717 Feb 9	1743 Dec29	1747 Aug31
Standish Abigail	S	T49A	1724 Oct 6		d.yng
Standish Abigail	S	T48D	1731 Dec16		
Standish Abigail	S	T67C	1760abt		
Standish Abigail	S	T58F	1779 Apr 2		
Standish Alexander	S	T11B	1626ca	(1)unkn	1702 Jul 6
Standish Alexander	S	H33Caf	1670abt		
Standish Amasa	S	T69F	1756 Jan 8		
Standish Amos	S	T22A	1718 Nov18		
Standish Amos	S	T56A	1748 Jan16		
Standish Amy	S	T27C	1709 Mar14	1734 Dec13	1798 Feb24
Standish Asa	S	T67D	1760abt		
Standish Asa	S	T70C	1763 Sep28		
Standish Betty	S	T22G	1739 Sep 6		
Standish Betty Bisbe	S	T56B	1750 Nov 2		1792 Jun12
Standish Charles	S	T11A	1624ca		1630abt
Standish Charles	S	T11G	1634aft	unm	1655aft

NAME	DIV.	NUMBER	BIRTH	MARRIAGE	DEATH
Standish David	S	T12H	1670ca		1689bef
Standish David	S	T22C	1723 Sept4	1745 Jan24	1795 Jun 4
Standish David	S	T55F	1758 Sep19		
Standish Deborah	S	T26A	1711 Dec27	unm.	1805
Standish Desire	S	T12I	1689 May 5	1715 Feb21	1766 Jun20
Standish Desire	S	T22B	1720 Dec18		
Standish Desire	S	T23B	1725 Mar30	1755 Jan16	1782 Dec 3
Standish Desire	S	H114B	1725 Mar30		
Standish Dorcas	S	T69J	1768 Nov19		
Standish Ebenezer	S	T12G	1672ca	1697ca	1755 Mar19
Standish Ebenezer	S	T48A	1721 Oct16		
Standish Ebenezer=T12G	S	H33Eaf	1672ca	1697ca	1755 Mar19
Standish Eleazer	S	T25A	1690ca		1755 Jun11
Standish Elisha	S	T69C	1750 May24		
Standish Elizabeth	S	T12C	1664ca	1683ca	1731living
Standish Elizabeth	S	T27A	1706 Feb 7		
Standish Elizabeth	S	T71C	1740ca		
Standish Experience	S	T47D	1744 Sep24		
Standish Hadley	S	T56E	1759 Feb 4		
Standish Hannah	S	T20C	1703 Mar 6	1721 Jan 4	1774 Apr 5
Standish Hannah	S	T25E	1705 Mar	1724 Nov 3	1763 Dec 6
Standish Hannah	S	T48B	1723 Dec15		
Standish Hannah	S	T47E	1746 Apr27		
Standish Hannah	S	T69A	1746 Nov 3		
Standish Hannah	S	T55C	1750 Dec 1	unm	1825 Jul23
Standish Ichabod	S	T12K	1693 Jun10	1719 Nov26	1772 Feb29
Standish Ichabod	S	H33Ca	1693 Jun10	1719 Nov26	1772 Feb29
Standish Ichabod	S	H114D	1729 Nov27		d. yng
Standish Ichabod=H114D	S	T23D	1729 Nov27		d yng
Standish Israel	S	T13F	1682ca	1703 Feb 8	1729bef
Standish Israel	S	T26F	1721 Mar 1	2 Mar	1802 Mar 4
Standish Israel	S	T71A	1738 Apr22		
Standish Israel	S	T69B	1748 Oct22		
Standish James	S	T55G	1760 Jan13		d.yng
Standish James	S	T55H	1763 Oct24		
Standish Jehoden	S	T25B	1690ca	unm.	1768 Jun23
Standish Job	S	T58E	1776 Nov21		
Standish John	S	T11C	1627ca	unm.	1651bef
Standish John	S	T49G	1739 Nov24		
Standish Jonas	S	T69D	1751 Nov 3		

NAME	DIV.	NUMBER	BIRTH	MARRIAGE	DEATH
Standish Josiah	S	T11F	1633ca		1690 Mar19
Standish Josiah	S	T11F	1633ca		1690 Mar19
Standish Josiah	S	T13D	1669ca		1753 Mar26
Standish Josiah	S	T25G	1700abt	unm.	1725 Nov 8
Standish Josiah	S	T71B	1739 Nov11		
Standish Judith	S	T58A	1767 Jul 4		
Standish Lemeul	S	T70D	1765ca		
Standish Lemuel	S	T55A	1746 Jun24		
Standish Levi	S	T69H	1764 May24		
Standish Lois	S	T13G	1684ca	2 Mar	1731aft
Standish Lois	S	T26C	1716 Jan 9	unm.	1753 Aug11
Standish Lois	S	T67B	1757Aug 23		
Standish Lora	S	T11E	1627aft		1655bef
Standish Lora	S	T12A	1660abt	1680ca	1725bef
Standish Lucy	S	T70A	1758 Sept4		
Standish Lucy #1	S	T55D	1754 Mar 6		d. yng
Standish Lucy #2	S	T55I	1766 Mar 1	unm.	1794bef
Standish Lydia	S	T12B	1662ca	1686	1734living
Standish Lydia	S	H33Gam	.1675abt		
Standish Lydia	S	T47C	1743 May 1		
Standish Lydia	S	T70B	1761 Apr21		
Standish Martha	S	T13B	1662ca	unm.	1730
Standish Mary	S	T13A	1660ca	1681 Jan 4	1731living
Standish Mary	S	T25F	1705 Mar18	1740 Mar10	1770 Apr 7
Standish Mary	S	T23A	1722 Jan14	unm	1789 Nov10
Standish Mary	S	H114A	1722 Jan14	unm.	1789 Nov10
Standish Mary	S	T22E	1733 Jan21	1769 Dec25	1780living
Standish Mary	S	T55J	1771 May16	unm.	1828bef
Standish Mehitable	S	T25C	1694ca	1716ca	1755bef
Standish Mehitable	S	T26Dam	1694ca	1716ca	=T25C
Standish Mercy	S	T12D	1665ca	1684ca	1725abt
Standish Mercy	S	T13H	1686ca	1726 Sep30	1748 Nov 4
Standish Mercy	S	T20F	1716 Oct17	1745 Dec18	1794 Feb22
Standish Miles	S	T27B	1709 Nov18	1737 Nov 2	1790aft
Standish Miles	S	T18D	1713 Mar11	1738 Dec17	1797 Nov3
Standish Miles	S	T47A	1740ca		
Standish Molly	S	T58C	1772ca		
Standish Moses	S	T20B	1701 Aug30	1723 Nov23	1769 Apr24
Standish Moses	S	K40Gaf	1705abt		
Standish Moses	S	T49E	1733 Apr20		

NAME	DIV.	NUMBER	BIRTH	MARRIAGE	DEATH
Standish Moses	S	T70E	1767ca		
Standish Myles	S	T10A	1584ca		1656 Oct 3
Standish Myles	S	T11D	1629ca	1660 Jul19	1661 Mar20
Standish Myles	S	T12E	1665ca	1702 Jul 5	1759 Sep15
Standish Myles	S	T13C	1665ca	2 Mar.	1728 Apr 9
Standish Myles	S	T58D	1774ca		
Standish Nathan	S	T69E	1753 Sep27		
Standish Olive	S	T55B	1748 May29		
Standish Patience	S	T18B	1707 Aug16	1738 Apr 6	1746bef
Standish Peleg	S	T48E	1734 Jan21		1758 Aug17
Standish Penelope	S	T18E	1717 Apr13	unm.	1739 Nov11
Standish Penelope	S	T47B	1741 Jun27		
Standish Phebe	S	H114C	1727 Apr19	unm.	1817 Dec31
Standish Phebe=T23C	S	T23C	1727 Apr19	unm.	1817 Dec31
Standish Priscilla	S	T18C	1710 Apr 1		
Standish Priscilla	S	T47G	1755 Apr24	unm	1805 Nov
Standish Priscilla	S	T55E	1756 Apr24		
Standish Prudence	S	T27D	1711 May 9	2 Mar	1769 Dec25
Standish Rachel	S	T49B	1726 Apr24		
Standish Rebecca	S	T49D	1731 Jan24		
Standish Samuel	S	T13E	1680ca	1709 Jun 1	1753 Aug 4
Standish Samuel	S	T26B	1713 Dec 1	1752 Mar31	1764living
Standish Samuel	S	T67A	1753 May 8		
Standish Sarah	S	T12F	1666ca	1694ca	1740 Mar 4
Standish Sarah	S	T25D	1696ca	1724 Nov 3	1744aft
Standish Sarah	S	T18A	1704 Apr15	1729 Mar 2	1779 Feb
Standish Sarah	S	T20E	1709 Nov	1728 Sep23	1792 Aug25
Standish Sarah	S	T26E	1719 Jan20	unm.	1753 Aug11
Standish Sarah	S	T48C	1729 Aug 5		
Standish Sarah	S	T49F	1736 Apr26		
Standish Sarah	S	T47F	1748 May		
Standish Sarah	S	T56C	1754 Apr22	unm.	1773 Aug28
Standish Sarah	S	T69I	1766 Nov15	unm	1846living
Standish Silas	S	T69G	1762 Sep11		
Standish Thomas	S	T12J	1690 Jan29	1717 Jan20	1774living
Standish Thomas	S	T26G	1724 May12	1757 Dec22	1798 Mar 1
Standish Thomas	S	T22D	1725 Jan23	2 Mar	1759 Jun18
Standish Thomas	S	T56D	1757 May 8	unm	1776 Mar
Standish William	S	T22F	1737 Jun24	1763 Dec 8	1828 Nov 1
Standish William	S	T58B	1770 Oct		

NAME	DIV.	NUMBER	BIRTH	MARRIAGE	DEATH
Standish Zachariah	S	T20A	1698 Oct12	1720 Oct13	1770 Mar30
Standish Zachariah	S	T48F	1739 May30		
Standish Zerviah	S	H33Ea	1706 Jan 8	1724 May20	1798 Apr26
Standish Zerviah	S	K40Ga	1728 Aug26	1745 Sep30	1769 Jul25
Standish Zerviah=H33Ea	S	T20D	1706 Jan 8	2 mar	1798 Apr26
Standish Zerviah=K40Ga	S	T49C	1728 Aug26	1745 Sep30	1769 Jul25
Stanhope Rebecca	A	A3/481	1670	1694ca	
Stanley Hannah	S	H21Dbm	1640abt		
Stanton Dorothy	S	R21Dbm	1660abt		
Staples Anne	S	T50D	1731ca	unm	1763Dec 3
Staples Benjamin	S	Q16Caf	1675abt		
Staples Hannah	S	T50A	1724ca		
Staples John	S	T20Caf	1675abt		
Staples John	S	T50G	1743ca		
Staples Mary	S	Q16Ca	1700ca	1719 Dec 1	1749ca
Staples Mary	S	T50E	1735ca		
Staples Ruth	S	T50H	1744 Apr 3		
Staples Sarah	S	T50B	1725ca		
Staples Seth	S	T20Ca	1700ca	1721 Jan 4	1778 Mar20
Staples Silence	S	T21Aam	1710abt		
Staples Susanna	S	T50C	1727ca		
Staples Zerviah	S	T50F	1740ca		
Starbuck Hepsibah	S	K17Fa	1680 Apr 2	1696ca	1740 Apr 7
Starbuck Nathaniel	S	K17Faf	1655abt		
Starr Benjamin	S	A15Aa	1647 Feb 6	1675 Dec23	1678
Starr Comfort	A	A19/232	1661	1683	1729
Starr Comfort III	A	A19/58	1731Aug 10	1754 Dec22	1812Nov 30
Starr Comfort Jr	A	A19/116	1696 Aug 9	1725ca	1775 Feb13
Starr Lydia	S	A15Abm	1630abt		
Starr Sarah	A	A19/29	1760Nov 28		1805 Aug20
Starr Thomas	S	A15Aaf	1625abt		
Stearns Abigail	D	D22a22	1635abt		
Stebbing Editha	A	A12/253	1610ca	1637	1688
Stebbins Hannah	S	N11Ga	1677ca		
Stebbins R	S	N12Ba	1700abt		
Steele Abiel	S	R18F	1693 Oct8	2 mar	1769living
Steele Bethia	S	R20A	1690ca	1709 May17	
Steele Bradford	S	R68G	1734 Sep22		
Steele Daniel	S	R18G	1697 Apr 3	1725 Jun20	1788 Mar13
Steele Daniel	S	R68D	1725ca		

NAME	DIV.	NUMBER	BIRTH	MARRIAGE	DEATH
Steele Daniel	S	R53A	1726 Jun19		
Steele Ebenezer	S	R20C	1695 Aug13	1717ca	1746ca
Steele Elijah	S	R54G	1735		
Steele Eliphalet	S	R18H	1700 Jun23	1722 Oct 4	1773 Jul
Steele Eliphalet #1	S	R54A	1723		
Steele Eliphalet #2	S	R54J	1742		
Steele Eliphaz	S	R54F	1732		
Steele Elisha	S	R68H	1737ca		
Steele Elizabeth	S	R18B	1682ca		1711bef
Steele Huldah	S	R68E	1729 Mar8		
Steele James	S	R12Gaf	1640abt		
Steele James	S	R51F	1719 Dec22		
Steele Jerusha	S	R51A	1710 Jul 1		
Steele Jerusha	S	R54K	1746		
Steele Jerusha (twin)	S	R18D	1684 Feb15		1711bef
Steele John	S	R12Eaf	1630abt		
Steele John	S	R12Ga	1660ca	1689ca	1697ca
Steele John	S	R20B	1692ca		1710abt
Steele John	S	R68A	1718 Feb22		
Steele John	S	R51H	1723ca		
Steele Josiah	S	R54B	1723		
Steele Katherine	S	R54C	1726		
Steele Katherine	S	R54I	1738		
Steele Lemuel	S	R53G	1742ca		
Steele Mary	S	R68C	1721ca		
Steele Mary	S	R53B	1728 Feb 2		
Steele Meletiah	S	R68F	1731	unm.	1760 Apr22
Steele Mercy	S	R54D	1727		
Steele Nathaniel	S	R51G	1721		
Steele Rachel	S	R54H	1737		
Steele Roswell	S	R53E	1738 Feb 4		
Steele Samuel	S	R12Ea	1652 Mar15	1680 Sep16	1709 Jan 2
Steele Samuel	S	R51B	1712 Mar11		
Steele Samuel (twin)	S	R18C	1684 Feb15		1709bef
Steele Submit	S	R53H	1746abt		
Steele Susanna	S	R51D	1715 Dec15		
Steele Susanna	S	R68B	1720 Jun30		
Steele Theophilus	S	R54E	1730		
Steele Thomas	S	R18A	1681 Sep 9	1709 May10	1739 Jun
Steele Thomas	S	R51E	1717ca		

NAME	DIV.	NUMBER	BIRTH	MARRIAGE	DEATH
Steele Thomas	S	R53F	1740		
Steele Timothy	S	R53D	1736 Jun19		
Steele Welthia	S	R53C	1730 Feb14		
Steele William	S	R18E	1687 Feb20		1712bef
Steele William	S	R51C	1713 Dec10		
Stehens Henry Jr	S	C11C	1681		
Stephens Abigail	S	C18C	1756		
Stephens Abigail	S	C22F	1800ca		
Stephens Amy	S	C17F	1747		
Stephens Andrew	S	C12D	1709		
Stephens Andrew	S	C17G	1749		
Stephens Anna	S	C20E	1753		
Stephens Benjamin	S	C12E	1713		
Stephens Benjamin	S	C21A	1750abt		
Stephens Benjamin	S	C19D	1754		
Stephens Christina	S	C23H	1795		
Stephens Clarissa	S	C23A	1768		
Stephens Cynthia	S	C20K	1768		
Stephens Cynthia	S	C23Da	1787		
Stephens Cynthia	S	C22G	1800ca		
Stephens Desire	S	C17K	1755Ca		
Stephens Dorothy	S	C17E	1746		
Stephens Drusilla	S	C18D	1759		
Stephens Elias	S	C21H	1764		
Stephens Elijah	S	C21I	1765ca		
Stephens Elijah	S	C22Fa	1800ca		
Stephens Elizabeth	S	C15C	1730ca		
Stephens Elizabeth	S	C18A	1746		
Stephens Esther	S	C17D	1745		
Stephens Eunice	S	C20F	1755		
Stephens Ezra	S	C23D	1786		
Stephens Hannah	S	C13B	1706ca		
Stephens Hannah	S	X65F	1710 Oct 6		
Stephens Hannah	S	C13F	1714		
Stephens Henry II	S	C14A	1709		
Stephens Henry Sr	S	C10A	Stephens=	Stevens	=A1/276
Stephens Hepzibah	S	C13E	1712		
Stephens Hilda	S	C22D	1796		
Stephens Ira	S	C20H	1759		
Stephens Ira	S	C23G	1793ca		

NAME	DIV.	NUMBER	BIRTH	MARRIAGE	DEATH
Stephens Isaac	S	X65D	1706 Oct11	1727aft	1768aft
Stephens Jedediah	S	C14D	1716		
Stephens Jedediah	S	C20G	1757		
Stephens Jedediah	S	C23F	1793ca		
Stephens Jesse	S	C12H	1721		
Stephens Jesse	S	C15B	1730ca		
Stephens Joanna	S	C19A	1746		
Stephens John	S	C13A	1705		
Stephens John	S	C17A	1737		
Stephens John	S	C21E	1766		
Stephens Jonathan	S	C19F	1767		
Stephens Joseph	S	X65C	1704 Apr23		
Stephens Joshua	S	C20A	1745		
Stephens Joshua	S	C22C	1793		
Stephens Josiah	S	X65E	1707 Nov23		
Stephens Katharine	S	X21Bam	1650abt		
Stephens Leander	S	C23B	1771		
Stephens Lucy	A	A1/69	1717ca	1743 Jan 3	1806 May 4
Stephens Martha	S	C20D	1750		
Stephens Martha	S	C21F	1760abt		
Stephens Martin	S	C13D	1710		
Stephens Mary	S	C14C	1715ca		
Stephens Mary	S	C17B	1740		
Stephens Mary	S	C20B	1746		
Stephens Mary	S	C18B	1750		
Stephens Mary	S	C21C	1758		
Stephens Nathan	S	C20J	1766		
Stephens Nathan	S	C22A	1783		
Stephens Nathaniel	S	C17I	1753		
Stephens Nicholas	S	X21Da	1669ca	1696bef	1747bef
Stephens Nicholas	S	X65B	1702 Feb24		
Stephens Noah	S	C15A	1730ca		
Stephens Olive	S	C17J	1755		
Stephens Olive	S	C22B	1790		
Stephens Oliver	S	C17L	1760ca		
Stephens Pamelia	S	C22H	1800ca		
Stephens Patience	S	C13G	1716		
Stephens Phineas	S	C12B	1705		
Stephens Phineas	S	C21G	1760ca		
Stephens Phineas	S	C22Da	1794		

NAME	DIV.	NUMBER	BIRTH	MARRIAGE	DEATH
Stephens Rachel	S	C19B	1749		
Stephens Rhoda	S	C22Ca	1795		
Stephens Richard	S	X21Daf	1645abt		
Stephens Richard	S	X65A	1698 Apr21		
Stephens Richard Sr	S	C11B	1679		
Stephens Rufus	S	C20I	1762		
Stephens Rufus	S	C23C	1773		
Stephens Safford	S	C17C	1742		
Stephens Samuel	S	C12F	1714		
Stephens Sarah	S	C12Ca	1708		
Stephens Sarah	S	C13C	1708		
Stephens Sarah	S	C21B	1750abt		
Stephens Sarah	S	C18E	1763		
Stephens Silas	S	C22I	1800abt		
Stephens Simeon	S	C14B	1710ca		
Stephens Stephen	S	C17H	1751		
Stephens Sylvania	S	C20Ia	1764		
Stephens Sylvania	S	C22E	1800ca		
Stephens Thankful	S	C20C	1748		
Stephens Thomas	S	C19E	1760		
Stephens Thomas Jr	S	C12A	1703		
Stephens Thomas Sr	S	C11A	1678		
Stephens Uriah	S	C12C	1708		
Stephens Uriah	S	C21D	1761		
Stephens William	S	C21J	1777		
Stephens William R	S	C23E	1788ca		
Stephens Zebulon	S	C12G	1717		
Stephens Zebulon	S	C19C	1751		
Stetson Abigail	S	T22Fa	1740 Aug10	1763 Dec 8	1825 Jun26
Stetson Ebenezer	S	W45Ha	1693 Jul22	1728 Apr 2	1778 Dec22
Stetson Elisha	S	R25Caf	1700abt		
Stetson Hannah	S	R14Gam	1670abt		
Stetson Hannah	S	H34Dam	1670abt		
Stetson John	S	T22Faf	1715abt		
Stetson Thomas	S	W45Haf	1670abt		
Stetson Zeresh	S	R25Ca	1712 Nov29	1731 Dec18	1763 Apr 6
Stevens Christopher	S	R70C	1738 Sep13		
Stevens Elizabeth	S	R118A	1703ca	1724 Aug30	1744 Aug25
Stevens Henry Jr	A	A1/138	1681 Nov20	1708 Mar 2	
Stevens Henry=C10A	A	A1/276	1650abt		1726ca

NAME	DIV.	NUMBER	BIRTH	MARRIAGE	DEATH
Stevens Jessie Ann	D	D26a19	1825abt		
Stevens John	S	R70D	1740 Aug 4		
Stevens Joseph	S	C17Kb	1760ca		
Stevens Leverett	S	R70E	1742 Sep19		
Stevens Lucy	S	C16D	1730ca		
Stevens Mary	S	C16B	1725ca		
Stevens Moses	S	R70F	1747 Aug30		1762bef
Stevens Noah	S	C16Ca	1730ca		
Stevens Phineas	S	C16E	1730ca		
Stevens Ruhamah	S	R70A	1735 Apr20		1754living
Stevens Samuel	S	R12Gb	1656 Mar 1	1702 Jun23	1712 Jul12
Stevens Sarah	S	C15Aa	1730ca		
Stevens Sarah	S	C16C	1730ca		
Stevens Uriah	S	C13Ca	1708		
Stevens Uriah Jr	S	C16A	1724		
Stevens William	S	R118B	1705 Feb 2	1734 Aug26	1751 Sep
Stevens William	S	R70B	1736 Sep 1		
Steward Mary	S	K34Cam	1685abt		
Steward Mary	S	Q18Bam	1685abt		
Stewart Daniel	A	A7/14	1761ca	1786 Jan18	1829 May17
Stewart John	A	A7/56	1700abt		
Stewart John Jr	A	A7/28	1725 Feb13		1776 Sept4
Stewart Martha	A	A7/7	1799 Aug	1831 May 8	1862ca
Stickney Moses	A	A4/462	1677	1707	1756
Stickney Susanna	A	A4/231	1724 Apr10	1743 Sep14	1769aft
Stille Neeltje C	A	A7/139	1648ca	1669	
Stillman Anna	A	A1/135	1699 Apr 6	1721 Apr27	1767 Nov 7
Stillman George	A	A1/270	1654ca	1686ca	1728
Stillman George=A1/270	D	D31a23	1654ca	1686ca	1728
Stobo Archibald	A	A7/98	1685abt		1736 Feb25
Stobo Jean	A	A7/49	1705abt	1729ca	
Stockbridge Benjamin	S	W28Ga	1677 Oct 9	1701 Jul23	1725 Jun11
Stockbridge Benjamin	S	L18Caf	1715abt		1784abt
Stockbridge Charles	S	K37Aaf	1665abt		
Stockbridge Charles Jr	S	W28Ca	1663 Feb 4	1689ca	1731 Apr 7
Stockbridge Charles Sr	S	W28Caf	1640abt		
Stockbridge Elizabeth	S	L18Ca	1737 Mar 6	1768 Oct25	1801 Nov
Stockbridge Rachel	S	K37Aa	1690 Apr 9	1711 Jun28	1785bef
Stoddard Eunice	S	A26Ea	1715 Apr16	1740 Mar 3	1758living
Stoddard Hezekiah	S	A26Eaf	1690abt		

NAME	DIV.	NUMBER	BIRTH	MARRIAGE	DEATH
Stodder Mary	S	P21Cam	1680abt		
Stodder Mary	S	P21Dam	1680abt		
Stonard Alice	S	W35Aam	1640abt		
Stone Margaret	A	A1/441	1695ca		
Stone Mary	A	A19/233	1664	1683	1735
Storrs Mary	A	A12/27	1710 May		
Storrs Mehitable	S	C51Fa	1697ca		
Storrs Samuel	A	A12/108	1640 Dec	1666 Dec 6	
Storrs Samuel Jr=B13Fa	A	A12/54	1677 May17	1700 Oct31	1727 Aug 9
Storrs Samuel=Jr	S	B13Fa	1677 May17	1700 Oct31	=A12/54
Storrs Sarah	S	B13Ba	1675abt	1696 Feb26	
Storrs Thomas	A	A12/216	1605		
Story Philippa	A	A16/11	1726May 21	1745Dec 10	1796aft
Story Samuel	A	A16/44	1659ca		1726
Story Stephen	A	A16/22	1697Oct 7	1721Sep 23	1766 Dec13
Story William	A	A16/88	1614ca		1702bef
Stover Elizabeth	S	K17Abm	1650abt		
Stover Hannah	S	W37Ba	1665ca	1697 Feb 2	1735 Oct14
Stowell David Jr	A	A19/222	.1693	1716	1763bef
Stowell Elizabeth	A	A19/111	1719 Aug21	1740Oct 2	
Stream Elizabeth	A	A6/231	1624ca		1688ca
Strode Elizabeth	A	A3/91	1720abt	1747 Sep30	
Strode George	A	A3/364	1690abt		1682ca
Strode John	A	A3/182	1670abt		1744ca
Strong Ebenezer	A	A8/236	1643ca	1668	1729ca
Strong Ebenezer Jr.	A	A8/118	1671 Aug 2	1695 Oct25	1729 Nov12
Strong Hannah	S	R18Fbm	1665abt		
Strong Hannah	S	G32Ba	1770ca		
Strong Jedidiah	S	A21Caf	1650abt		
Strong King	S	N13Ja	1750abt		
Strong Lydia	S	A26Fam	1690abt		
Strong Mary	A	A8/59	1701 Jan16	1723 Jun12	1770abt
Strong Ozias	S	G32Baf	1734 Sep 3		1808
Strong Sarah	S	A21Ca	1674		1726 Dec25
Strong Sarah	S	K26Fam	1685abt		
Strother Francis	A	A18/12	1700ca		1752ca
Strother Sarah D	A	A18/3	1760Dec14	1779Aug 20	1822Dec13
Strother William	A	A18/48	1640abt		1700ca
Strother William	A	A18/6	1725ca	1752bef	1808ca
Strother William Jr	A	A18/24	1665ca		1726Jul 26

NAME	DIV.	NUMBER	BIRTH	MARRIAGE	DEATH
Strout Hannah	S	H29Dam	1685abt		
Studley Joanna	S	T14Eam	1680abt		
Studley Sarah	S	T14Ca	1689ca	1713 Apr28	1782 Nov 2
Sturtevant Ann	S	A25Eam	1660abt		
Sturtevant Ann=A25Eam	S	A26Aam	1660abt		
Sturtevant Ann=A26Aam	S	A24Cam	1660abt		
Sturtevant Caleb	S	K103B	1715 Mar16		
Sturtevant David	S	R27Dbf	1700abt		
Sturtevant David	S	H122E	1742 Jan16		
Sturtevant Desire	S	K126A	1708 Mar 8		
Sturtevant Elizabeth	S	A64E	1719 Apr 7		
Sturtevant Elizabeth	S	K103H	1735ca		1747Jul 28
Sturtevant Ephraim	S	H33La	1704 Feb 5		1787 Jan12
Sturtevant Ephraim	S	H122A	1732		1757
Sturtevant Fear	S	A64D	1719 Apr 7		
Sturtevant Francis	S	K103A	1711 Jan15		
Sturtevant Hannah	S	T12Ga	1680ca	1697ca	1759 Jan23
Sturtevant Hannah	S	H33Eam	1680ca	1697ca	=T12Ga
Sturtevant Hannah	S	A64B	1711 Aug20		
Sturtevant Hannah	S	H122G	1747ca		d yng
Sturtevant Isaac	S	A64A	1708 Aug10		
Sturtevant Isaac	S	H122F	1745 Jan20		d yng
Sturtevant James	S	K29Aa	1687ca	1710 Feb15	1756 May 8
Sturtevant James	S	R25Gaf	1700abt		
Sturtevant James	S	K103C	1718 Sep15		
Sturtevant James	S	H122H	1750ca		d yng
Sturtevant Jane	S	H122I	1753 Mar18		d yng
Sturtevant John	S	H122D	1739ca	unm.	
Sturtevant Joseph	S	W29Ea	1666 Jul16	1693 Dec 5	1723abt
Sturtevant Joseph	S	H33Laf	1680abt		
Sturtevant Joseph	S	H122C	1737ca		d yng
Sturtevant Lemuel	S	K126B	1710 Mar 5		
Sturtevant Lydia	S	K103E	1723 Mar 2		
Sturtevant Lydia	S	H122B	1735ca		
Sturtevant Mary	S	W13Ga	1651 Dec7	1672 Nov22	1717 Feb10
Sturtevant Mary=K103F	S	R25Ga	1728 Feb16	1761 Jan17	1813 May
Sturtevant Mary=R25Ga	S	K103F	1728 Feb16	1761 Jan17	1813 Nat
Sturtevant Mercy	S	K41Aam	1680abt		
Sturtevant Mercy	S	H33Iam	1770abt		
Sturtevant Rebecca	S	A64C	1715 Jul		d.yng

NAME	DIV.	NUMBER	BIRTH	MARRIAGE	DEATH
Sturtevant Samuel	S	W13Gaf	1625abt		
Sturtevant Samuel	S	W29Baf	1640abt		
Sturtevant Samuel	S	K29Aaf	1655abt		=K33Aaf
Sturtevant Samuel	S	K33Aaf	1655abt		=K29Aaf
Sturtevant Samuel	S	A24Faf	1660abt		
Sturtevant Samuel	S	K33Aa	1677ca	1706 Jan20	1743 Jun18
Sturtevant Samuel	S	K126C	1716 Jun 5		1744
Sturtevant Sarah	S	R27Db	1732 Oct28	1776 Mar19	1796 Oct11
Sturtevant Sarah	S	K103G	1732ca	unm	1770
Sturtevant Susanna	S	K103D	1720 Feb 4		
Sturtevant William	S	A24Fa	1683ca	1707 Feb12	1753 Aug28
Sutphen Noami	S	G50Ga	1755abt		
Sutton Elizabeth	S	W28Ibm	1660abt		
Sutton Isabel	D	D29/16	1465abt		
Sutton Margaret	A	A6/241	1635ca	1655	1700ca
Sutton Thomas Sir	D	D29a17	1440abt		
Swan Ebenezer	S	P15H	1672 Nov14	1698 Mar 2	1740 May27
Swan Ebenezer	S	P30C	1703 Mar23		
Swan Elizabeth	S	P15C	1661 Jul14	1687 Jul27	1735bef
Swan Elizabeth	S	P30A	1699 Mar29		
Swan Hannah	S	P15F	1667 Feb27		
Swan Hannah	S	P28D	1701 Mar12		
Swan John	S	P12Ba	1620ca	1655 Mar 2	1708 Jun 5
Swan John	S	P15E	1665 May 1	1692 Apr11	1738bef
Swan John #1	S	P28A	1693		d yng
Swan John #2	S	P28C	1698 Jul 5		
Swan Judith	S	A32Cam	1680abt		
Swan Lydia	S	P15D	1663 Jul28		
Swan Mary	S	P15B	1659 May 2		
Swan Mary	S	P30D	1706 Mar 4	unm.	1750bef
Swan Mercy	S	P15G	1670ca	1706 Dec19	1748 Jun23
Swan Samuel	S	P15A	1657	unm	1678 Jun
Swan Samuel	S	P28E	1708 Feb20		
Swan Samuel	S	P30E	1711 Apr 5		
Swan Sarah	S	P28B	1695 Jan31		
Swan Sarah	S	P30B	1700 Feb26		
Swan William	S	P30F	1713 Jan31		
Swett Joseph	S	L20Aaf	1710abt		
Swett Sarah	S	L20Aa	1734 Feb	1755 Nov13	1780abt
Swift Abigail	S	K148E	1730ca		

NAME	DIV.	NUMBER	BIRTH	MARRIAGE	DEATH
Swift Alice =D1a21	S	G28Aam	1698 Jul23	1721 Nov21	1783Jan15
Swift Alice =G28Aam	D	D1a21	1698 Jul23	1721 Nov21	1783 Jan 1
Swift Alice=G28Aam	D	D3/21	1698 Jul23	1721 Nov21	1783 Jan15
Swift Alice=G28Aam	D	D15/23	1698 Jul23	1721 Nov21	1783 Jan15
Swift Dinah	S	W50Ham	1670abt		
Swift Elizabeth	S	K148D	1720ca		
Swift Henrietta	S	R24Ba	1701	1730 Mar	1758 Oct
Swift Jireh Jr.	A	A8/110	1709 Nov23	1730 Oct 9	1782 Mar16
Swift Jireh=A8/220	S	W50Ba	1675abt	1697 Nov24	1746abt
Swift Jireh=D15a24	A	A8/220	1675abt	1697 Nov24	1746aby
Swift Jireh=W50Ba	D	D15a24	1675abt	1697 Nov24	1746abt
Swift Joanna	S	W50Ca	1692 Mar 9	1713 Oct22	1720abt
Swift John	S	K148C	1718ca		
Swift Rachel	S	K148F	1732ca		
Swift Ruth	S	K148B	1715ca		
Swift Susannah	A	A8/55	1734ca	1754 Apr14	1806 Jun8
Swift Thomas	S	K16Fa	1659 Jul30	1687aft	1697bef
Swift Thomas	S	K37A	1687 Nov15	1711 Jun28	1753aft
Swift Thomas	S	K148A	1712 Mar29		
Swift Thomas Sr	S	K16Faf	1635abt		
Swift William	S	W50Baf	1640abt		
Swift William=W50Baf	S	W50Caf	1640abt		
Sylvester Grizzell	A	A8/173	1655abt	1676	1688ca
Sylvester Joseph Jr	S	W23Da	1664 Nov11	1690 Apr	1754abt
Sylvester Joseph Sr	S	W23Daf	1640abt		
Sylvester Mary	S	R19Aam	1650abt		
Sylvester Ruth	S	C52Da	1796ca		
Symmes Anna Tuthill	A	A14/5	1775 Jul25	1795 Nov22	1864 Feb25
Symmes John Cleves	A	A14/10	1742 Jul21	1760 Oct30	1814 Feb26
Symmes Timothy	A	A14/40	1683ca	1710 Jul31	1765ca
Symmes Timothy Jr.	A	A14/20	1714 May27	1740ca	1756 Apr 6
Symmes William	A	A14/80	1626 Jan	1675ca	1691 Sep22
Symmes Zachariah	A	A14/160	1599	1622	1670
Symonds Mary	S	L21Da	1750ca	1776bef	1813ca
Taber Abigail	S	K20E	1678 Oct27	unm.	1714 Jan25
Taber Abigail	S	K35J	1693 May 2	1715 Dec 1	1765living
Taber Abigail	S	K135M	1725 Apr16		
Taber Amaziah	S	K56C	1704 Jul 9		
Taber Amaziah	S	K136G	1724 Nov23		
Taber Amos	S	K135A	1703 Apr29		

NAME	DIV.	NUMBER	BIRTH	MARRIAGE	DEATH
Taber Amy	S	K139K	1740ca		
Taber Bartholomew	S	K137D	1717 Sep11		
Taber Benjamin	S	K135C	1706 Dec 2		
Taber Bethia	S	W47Fa	1687 Sep 3	1708ca	1758 Aug 6
Taber Bethia	S	K20H	1689 Apr18	1711 Sep11	1782bef
Taber Bethiah	S	K35H	1687 Sep 3	1709ca	1758 Aug 6
Taber Comfort	S	K61D	1707 Aug 3		
Taber Cordelia	D	D33/21	1831 May 2	1848 Jul15	1896Sep 10
Taber Daniel	S	K139J	1739ca		
Taber Deborah	S	K136B	1714 Apr29		d.yng
Taber Deborah	S	K136I	1731 May25		
Taber Ebenezer	S	K35Ja	1693ca	1715 Dec 1	1772bef
Taber Eleanor	S	K135G	1713 Mar28		
Taber Elezebeth	S	K135J	1718 Nov 2		
Taber Elizabeth	S	Q51B	1743 Feb 5		
Taber Elnathan	S	K136E	1720 Sep15		
Taber Esther	S	K19B	1671 Apr17	1689 Oct23	1749 Jan14
Taber Esther	S	K20F	1680 Feb23	1698 Nov15	1714living
Taber Esther	S	K56D	1709 Mar 6		
Taber Esther=K19B	A	A8/217	1671 Apr17	1689 Oct23	1749 Jan15
Taber Eunice	S	K137A	1711 Jul10		
Taber Hannah	S	K140E	1723 Sep13		
Taber Hannah	S	Q51D	1750 Aug30		
Taber Huldah	S	K139G	1724 Mar 3		
Taber Jabez	S	K136H	1727 Jun22		
Taber Jacob	S	K35F	1683 Jul26	1710ca	1773 Apr 4
Taber Jacob	S	K137G	1723 May21		
Taber Jacob	S	K140I	1735 Oct 2		
Taber Jemima	S	Q51E	1753 Dec17		
Taber Jerusha	S	K137C	1715 Aug27		
Taber Jesse	S	K139E	1719 Nov21		
Taber John	S	K35E	1681 Feb22	1710ca	
Taber John	S	K20G	1684 Jul18	1706ca	1727bef
Taber John	S	K135H	1715 Aug 8		
Taber John	S	K63F	1718aft		
Taber John	S	K61I	1723 Feb 7		
Taber John	S	K137H	1726 Nov28	unm	1761 Aug27
Taber Jonathan	S	K35G	1685 Sep22		
Taber Jonathan	S	K56B	1702 Feb24	1730ca	1770
Taber Jonathan	S	K61F	1712 Oct 5		

NAME	DIV.	NUMBER	BIRTH	MARRIAGE	DEATH
Taber Jonathan	S	K70F	1741 Jan 8		
Taber Jonathan=K56B	S	K21Ia	1702 Feb24	1730ca	1770
Taber Joseph	S	K35Jaf	1670abt		
Taber Joseph	S	K35D	1679 Mar 7	2 mar.	1750ca
Taber Joseph	S	K135E	1709 Feb15		
Taber Joseph	S	K63G	1718aft		
Taber Joseph	S	K140D	1721 Sep21		
Taber Joseph Jr	S	Q19Ba	1710 Feb15	1739 Sep15	1772
Taber Joseph Sr=K35Da	S	Q19Baf	1683 Jun19	1701 Jan28	1738bef
Taber Josiah	S	K61G	1715 Jun 4		
Taber Lois	S	K137E	1719 Aug23		
Taber Lois	S	K70D	1737ca		d. yng.
Taber Lydia	S	K35A	1673 Aug 8	1695ca	1723aft
Taber Lydia	S	K20C	1673 Sep28	1693aft	1754aft
Taber Lydia	S	K63H	1718aft		
Taber Lydia	S	K140G	1728 Oct24		
Taber Margaret	S	K61J	1727 Apr 8		
Taber Martha	S	K61A	1700 Oct 6		
Taber Mary	S	K20A	1668 Jan28	1693bef	1728ca
Taber Mary	S	K35C	1677 Mar17	1703ca	1745aft
Taber Mary	S	K63A	1707 Mar21		
Taber Mary	S	K135D	1708 Jun 6		
Taber Mary	S	K61E	1710 Feb25		
Taber Mary	S	K56E	1711 Nov12		
Taber Mary	S	K136D	1717 Aug25		
Taber Mary	S	K140C	1719 Aug24		
Taber Mary	S	K70A	1731 Sep11		
Taber Mary	D	D33a24	1742Apr 26	1761 Jul31	
Taber Mercy	S	K70B	1733 Jul31		
Taber Noah	S	K139H	1727 Jul 7		
Taber Pardon	D	D33/24	1742	1761 Jul31	
Taber Paul	S	K140A	1716 Mar30		
Taber Peace	S	K139F	1722 Feb22		
Taber Peleg	D	D33/22	1791 May13	1813 Dec 2	1871May 26
Taber Peter	S	K135K	1721 Apr 6		
Taber Phebe	S	K136F	1723 Mar 6		
Taber Philip	S	K12Da	1640ca	1667ca	1693bef
Taber Philip	S	K20D	1675 Feb29	1700bef	1750ca
Taber Philip	S	K35I	1689 Feb 7	1710ca	1766aft
Taber Philip	S	K61B	1702 Oct 4		1763

NAME	DIV.	NUMBER	BIRTH	MARRIAGE	DEATH
Taber Philip	S	K63B	1708 Dec14		
Taber Philip	S	K139I	1730 Oct31		
Taber Philip	D	D33/23	1766Jul 11		1821
Taber Philip=K12Caf	S	K16Daf	1625abt		
Taber Philip=K12Daf	S	K12Caf	1625abt		
Taber Philip=K61B	D	D33/25	1702 Oct 4		1763 Mar 8
Taber Priscilla	S	K56A	1701 Jun28		
Taber Rebecca	S	K136C	1715 Jan24		
Taber Rebecca	S	K61H	1719 Apr18		
Taber Rebecca	S	K70C	1735 Dec18		d.yng.
Taber Rebeckah	S	K135F	1711 Oct11		
Taber Richard	S	K139A	1711 Nov25		
Taber Rube	S	Q51C	1745 Mar22		
Taber Samuel	S	K56F	1714 Dec 4		d yng
Taber Sarah	S	K20B	1671 Mar26	1693aft	1733bef
Taber Sarah	S	K35B	1674 Jan28	1702 Dec 1	1735aft
Taber Sarah	S	K135B	1704 Mar 2		
Taber Sarah	S	K63D	1713 Sep13		
Taber Sarah	S	K137F	1721 Jul23	unm	1745 Apr16
Taber Seth	S	K56G	1719 Jul 5		1739living
Taber Stephen	S	K137B	1712 Feb22		
Taber Stephen	S	K70G	1744 Mar13		
Taber Thomas	S	W47Faf	1650abt		
Taber Thomas	S	W14Ca	1650abt		
Taber Thomas	S	K19A	1668 Oct22	1700 Jul 4	1722
Taber Thomas	S	K21Iaf	1680abt		
Taber Thomas	S	K136A	1712 Jul18		
Taber Thomas	S	K139B	1713 Nov18		
Taber Thomas	S	K63E	1716 Apr30		
Taber Thomas	S	K140B	1717 Oct28		
Taber Thomas	S	K135I	1717 Sep20		
Taber Thomas	S	K70E	1739 Feb 1		
Taber Thomas=K12Ca	S	K16Da	1646 Feb	1670ca	1730 Nov11
Taber Thomas=K16Da	S	K12Ca	1646 Feb	1670ca	1730 Nov11
Taber Tucker	S	K139D	1717 Oct10		
Taber Water #1	S	K140F	1725 Sep 4		d. yng
Taber Water #2	S	K140H	1731 Oct 1		
Taber William	S	K61C	1704 Feb18		
Taber William	S	K63C	1711 Apr28		
Taber William	S	K135L	1722 Mar15		

NAME	DIV.	NUMBER	BIRTH	MARRIAGE	DEATH
Taber William	S	Q51A	1741 Feb24		
Taber Zephaniah	S	K139C	1715 Oct 1		
Tabor Hannah	S	R28Lam	1710abt		
Taft Aaron	A	A2/8	1743 May28	1769 Jun 1	1808 Mar26
Taft Alphonso	A	A2/2	1810 Nov5	1853 Dec26	1891 May21
Taft Huldah	A	A2/55	1718 Jun28	1737 Jan25	
Taft Israel	A	A2/110	1698 Apr26	1717 Dec19	1753ca
Taft Joseph	A	A2/32	1680ca	1708ca	1747 Jul18
Taft Peter	A	A2/16	1715ca	1736 Apr20	1783 Dec12
Taft Peter Rawson	A	A2/4	1785 Apr14	1810 Dec5	1867 Jan 1
Taft Robert	A	A2/64	1640ca	1670abt	1725 Feb 8
Taft Robert Jr.	A	A2/220	1674ca	1694ca	1748ca
Taft William Howard	A	A2/1	1857 Sep15	1886Jun 19	1930 Mar 8
Tailer Elizabeth	A	A8/175	1667		1734
Tarpley Elizabeth	S	A80C	1720 May28		d.yng
Tarpley John	S	A31Baf	1660abt		
Tarpley John	S	A31Ab	1695 Jul16	1715ca	1736bef
Tarpley John	S	A80B	1720 May28		d.yng
Tarpley John Sr	S	A31Abf	1670abt		
Tarpley Travers	S	A80A	1717ca		
Tart Elizabeth	S	X16Bbm	1675abt		
Taverner John	S	A15Cbf	1655abt		
Taverner John	S	A31Ba	1682 Mar 7	1711ca	1711
Taverner Sarah	S	A15Cb	1679 Jan 7	1702ca	1720bef
Taylor Abigail #1	S	H105D	1721 Jun14		d yng
Taylor Abigail #2	S	H105F	1726 Oct 6	unm.	1747living
Taylor Anne	A	A14/147	1625abt		
Taylor Anne	S	H105C	1719 Mar25	unm.	
Taylor Asabel	S	N14Baf	1730abt		
Taylor Benjamin	S	F51A	1705ca		
Taylor Edward	S	H30Baf	1660abt		
Taylor Edward	S	H105E	1723 Apr24		
Taylor Elizabeth	D	D12a17	1667		1734
Taylor Elizabeth	S	A84B	1739ca		
Taylor Hancock	S	A84C	1742ca	unm	1774
Taylor Hannah	S	W48Bbm	1665abt		
Taylor Hannah	S	B17Ha	1715abt	1738 Jan	
Taylor James	A	A18/16	1650abt		1698Apr 30
Taylor James	A	A18/8	1674Mar14	1699Feb 23	1729Jun23
Taylor James	S	A32Cbf	1685abt		

NAME	DIV.	NUMBER	BIRTH	MARRIAGE	DEATH
Taylor John	S	F20Ea	1665ca	1703 Jun11	1737living
Taylor John	S	H30Ba	1685ca	1713 Sept3	1750abt
Taylor John	S	F51C	1707ca		
Taylor John	S	H105B	1717 Apr17		
Taylor Joseph	S	F14Ca	1660abt		1727 Sep13
Taylor Joseph	S	T16Eaf	1660abt		
Taylor Mary	S	T16Ea	1691 Aug18	1731 Apr 1	
Taylor Mary	S	H105A	1714 Nov 1		
Taylor Richard=A18/2	S	A84D	1744 Apr 3	1779Aug 20	1829
Taylor Richard=A84D	A	A18/2	1744Apr 3	1779Aug 20	1829
Taylor Sarah	S	F51B	1706ca		
Taylor Sarah	S	N14Ba	1755abt	1774 Nov23	
Taylor Thomas	A	A14/294	1626		1643
Taylor Zachary	S	A84A	1735 Feb26		
Taylor Zachary Pres	A	A18/1	1784Nov 24	1810Jun 21	1852Aug 14
Taylor Zachary Sr	A	A18/4	1707Apr 17	1735ca	1768bef
Taylor Zachary=A18/4	S	A32Cb	1707 Apr17	1735ca	1768bef
Temple John	D	D12a21	1520abt		
Temple John II, Sir	D	D12/19	.1585abt		
Temple Mary	D	D12/18	1620abt		
Temple Thomas Sir	D	D12/20	1555abt		
Terbosch Aeltje	A	A4/471	1692	1709bef	
Terry Abiel	S	X66C	1714 Dec 3		
Terry Benjamin	S	X22C	1683aft	2 mar.	1770ca
Terry Benjamin	S	X68C	1719ca		
Terry Dinah	S	X68N	1741 Sep 7	1768Dec22	1792aft
Terry George	S	X68E	1723 Nov30		
Terry Joanna	S	X68F	1725 Jul 6		
Terry John	S	X22B	1684bef	1705 Apr 3	1711bef
Terry John	S	X67B	1708 May26		
Terry John	S	X68D	1721ca		
Terry Lydia	S	X66A	1701bef		
Terry Lydia	S	X68G	1726 Oct10		
Terry Margaret	S	X68J	1732 Oct22		
Terry Mary	S	X68A	1715ca		
Terry Miriam	S	X68L	1737 May18		
Terry Nathaniel	A	A14/94	1656 Jan	1682 Nov30	
Terry Phebe	A	A14/47	1698ca	1714 Dec10	1776 Dec24
Terry Phebe	S	X68H	1729 Sep15		
Terry Richard	A	A14/188	1618		1676

NAME	DIV.	NUMBER	BIRTH	MARRIAGE	DEATH
Terry Robert	S	X68B	1717ca		
Terry Sarah	S	X68M	1739 Aug13		
Terry Silas	S	X67A	1707 Apr 8		
Terry Solomon	S	X68K	1734 Jan13		
Terry Thomas	S	X13Bb	1631ca	1680ca	1691 Oct
Terry Thomas	S	X22A	1679bef	1699 Jan 4	1757bef
Terry Thomas	S	X66B	1707ca		1748living
Terry William	S	X68I	1731 Apr17		
Tew Anna	S	B17Ea	1710abt	1730 Jan	
Thacher Bethiah	S	H17Ha	1671 Jul10	1691 Apr 9	1734 Jul 8
Thacher John	S	H17Haf	1650abt		
Thatcher Elizabeth	S	F15Ga	1672 Mar 1	1700 Oct 3	1730bef
Thatcher Elizabeth	S	T13Cb	1675abt	1724 Jul24	1729living
Thatcher Rudolphus	S	F15Gaf	1650ca		
Thaxter Abigail #1	S	W39A	1667 Sep29		1667 Oct22
Thaxter Abigail #2	S	W39C	1670 Nov18		1671 May 8
Thaxter David	S	W39D	1672 Apr 6	1695 Jun24	1760 Jun14
Thaxter John	S	W39F	1675 Jul27		1675 Aug11
Thaxter Mary	S	W39E	1674 May16		1674 Jul 9
Thaxter Samuel	S	W15Ha	1641 May19	1666 Dec19	1725 May27
Thaxter Samuel	S	W39G	1677 Apr23		1678 Oct20
Thaxter Sarah	S	W39B	1668 Nov16	1691 Mar25	1719aft
Thaxter Thomas	S	W15Haf	1615abt		
Thayer Bethia	S	R28Jam	1710abt		
Thayer Bethia	S	R28Kbm	1710abt		
Thomas Abigail	S	R82A	1722 Dec4		
Thomas Anna	S	R82C	1726 Aug7		
Thomas Bethiah	S	W52Cam	1650ca	1673ca	1718 Sep23
Thomas Bethiah=W32Cam	S	W13Fa	1650ca	1673ca	1718 Sep23
Thomas David	S	P16Aaf	1640abt		
Thomas Eleanor	S	R82F	1732 Feb10		
Thomas Elizabeth	S	Q18Aa	1690 Nov19	1723 Oct24	1776 Aug
Thomas Elizabeth	S	P31D	1698 Oct27		d yng
Thomas Elizabeth	S	R82D	1729 May10	unm.	1761 May 3
Thomas Elizabeth=Q18Aa	S	K34Ba	1690 Nov19	1723 Oct24	1776 Aug
Thomas Ephrain	S	W36Ca	1667 Oct	1686 Dec18	1715abt
Thomas Gideon	S	R23Da	1692 Dec23	1720 Feb 9	1766 Dec14
Thomas James	S	W28Da	1663 Nov	1692 Jan3	1718 Apr25
Thomas Jeremiah	S	Q18Aaf	1665abt		
Thomas Jeremiah=Q18Aaf	S	K34Baf	1665abt		

NAME	DIV.	NUMBER	BIRTH	MARRIAGE	DEATH
Thomas Joanna	S	P31A	1693 May10		
Thomas Joanna	S	K40Dam	1695abt		
Thomas Joanna	S	K34Ca	1707 Feb28	1734 Nov 6	1795 Mar 9
Thomas Joanna	S	Q18Ba	1707 Feb28	1734 Nov 6	1795 Mar 9
Thomas John	S	W28Daf	1640abt		
Thomas John	S	W36Caf	1640abt		
Thomas John	S	W44Ga	1683 Nov 8	1714 Dec23	1770 Apr14
Thomas Jonathan	S	K34Caf	1685abt		
Thomas Jonathan	S	Q18Baf	1685abt		
Thomas Margaret	A	A1/303	1708	1727	1765
Thomas Margaret=A1/303	D	D14/21	1708	1727	1765
Thomas Mary	S	P31F	1701 Dec 4		
Thomas Mercy	S	R82B	1725 Jun27		
Thomas Nathan=R23Ba	S	W42Ia	1688 Nov21	1715 ca	1741 Nov 3
Thomas Nathan=W42Ia	S	R23Ba	1688 Nov21	1715ca	1741 Nov 3
Thomas Nathaniel	S	W13Faf	1625abt		
Thomas Nathaniel	D	D14a23	1635abt		
Thomas Nathaniel Jr	S	X21Cb	1664 Oct18	1730 Sep 3	1738 Feb24
Thomas Nathaniel Jr	S	W52Ga	1700 Jun24	1722 Jul23	1745 Sep 3
Thomas Nathaniel Sr	S	X21Cbf	1640abt		
Thomas Nathaniel Sr	S	W52Gaf	1675abt		
Thomas Priscilla	S	L20Bam	1710abt		=L20Cam
Thomas Priscilla	S	L20Cam	1710abt		
Thomas Samuel	S	W42Iaf	1660abt		
Thomas Samuel=R23Daf	S	R23Daf	1660abt		
Thomas Samuel=W21Iaf	S	W44Gaf	1660abt		
Thomas Samuel=W44Gaf	S	R23Baf	1660abt		
Thomas Sarah	S	R23Cam	1665abt		
Thomas Sarah	S	A24Eam	1665abt		
Thomas Sarah	A	A3/233	1690abt	1718 Jul28	
Thomas Sarah	S	P31C	1696 Dec 6		
Thomas Sarah	S	R82E	1732 Feb10		
Thomas Sarah=A24Eam	S	A25Gam	1665abt		
Thomas Susanna	S	P31B	1694 Feb15		
Thomas William	S	P16Aa	1665ca	1691 Jul30	1734 Apr 5
Thomas William	D	D14/22	1670abt		
Thomas William	S	P31E	1699 Mar18		
Thomasson Eleanor	A	A3/143	1700abt	1721 Feb16	1760abt
Thomasson Paul	A	A3/286	1670abt		1707
Thompson Abigail	S	R21Cam	1670abt		

NAME	DIV.	NUMBER	BIRTH	MARRIAGE	DEATH
Thompson Elizabeth	A	A11/93	1592abt	1615 Sep10	1676 Jun 2
Thompson Elizabeth	A	A19/3003	1595a	1615Sep10	=A11/93
Thompson Frances	A	A14/313	1590ca	1608	
Thompson George	A	A6/124	1638ca		1674 Sep 7
Thompson James	A	A19/144	1649	1674	1693
Thompson James Jr	A	A19/72	1680May	1716	1763Jul 3
Thompson John	A	A2/162	1619ca	1641ca	1685
Thompson John	A	A6/62	1660 Mar24		
Thompson Jonathan	S	P15Eaf	1645abt		
Thompson Martha	A	A18/9	1679ca	1699Feb 23	1762Nov 19
Thompson Martha=A18/9	S	A32Cbm	1679ca	1699Feb 23	1762Nov 19
Thompson Mehitable	A	A2/81	1645abt	1666 Nov28	=A2/175
Thompson Mehitable	A	A2/175	1645abt	1666 Nov28	1711
Thompson Mehitable	A	A6/31	1701 May17	1728 May11	1747 Feb10
Thompson Sarah	S	A11Ebm	1610abt		
Thompson Sarah	S	P15Ea	1670 Jun 1	1692 April1	1738 Apr
Thompson Sarah	A	A19/9	1789 Apr 3	1814 Dec 9	1856 Nov19
Thompson Susanna	A	A19/155	1661	1700	1725
Thompson William	A	A11/186	1570abt		1623
Thompson William	A	A19/36	1723Oct 19	1747Nov 24	1808 May
Thompson William	A	A19/18	1754Jun 30	1774 Feb25	1830Oct 23
Thornton Anne=A10/71	D	D11/20	1550abt	1573Jun 16	1614 Dec27
Thornton Anne=D11/20	A	A10/71	1550abt	1573 Jun16	1614 Dec27
Thornton Francis	A	A18/50	1651Nov 5	1674Apr 13	1726ca
Thornton Henry	D	D11a21	1520abt		
Thornton Margaret	A	A18/25	1678Apr2		1727living
Thornton William	A	A18/100	1630abt		1708aft
Thorton Sarah	S	C65Aa	1718ca		
Throope Lydia	S	R19Iam	1685abt		
Thurber James	S	P21Eaf	1675abt		
Thurber Priscilla	S	P21Ea	1697 Feb 3	1725 Jan 8	1746
Thurber Samuel	S	C38Ba	1724ca		
Thurlo Mary	A	A4/455	1682	1703	1747
Thurston Abigail	S	T60B	1716 Jul11		
Thurston Bethiah	A	A2/89	1672 Apr30		
Thurston David	S	T24Ca	1685ca	1713 Apr28	1759 May31
Thurston David	S	T60D	1721 Mar27		
Thurston Hannah	A	A2/69	1650 Apr28	1667 Mar12	1690 Dec29
Thurston James	S	T60C	1718 Sep 3		
Thurston John	A	A2/138	1601	1633ca	1685

NAME	DIV.	NUMBER	BIRTH	MARRIAGE	DEATH
Thurston John	S	T24Caf	1660abt		
Thurston John	S	T60A	1714 May22		
Thurston John Jr.	A	A2/178	1635	1660ca	1711ca
Thurston Joseph	S	B17Ja	1722ca		
Thurston Judith	S	W48Bam	1655abt		
Thurston Mary	S	T60E	1723 Jun30 unm		1776 May 4
Tiffany Esther	S	C62Ac	1795ca		
Tilden Abigail	S	W28C	1666 Jul11	1689ca	1716abt
Tilden David	S	W28L	1685 Nov 6	1710 Jan11	1756 Jul3
Tilden Ebenezer	S	W28K	1682 Jun16	1713 Mar23	1760abt
Tilden Ephraim	S	W28J	1680 Nov20	unmar.	
Tilden Hannah	S	W28A	1662 Oct14		
Tilden Isaac	S	W28I	1678 Aug28	2 Mar	1771 Apr15
Tilden Joseph	S	W28F	1672 May13	1701 Jan23	1712
Tilden Judith	S	W28E	1670 Jun 1	1693 Jun27	1714 Jul20
Tilden Lydia	S	K22Aam	1620abt		
Tilden Lydia	S	W57Bam	1665abt		
Tilden Lydia	S	K29Bb	1700 Apr23	1727aft	1742 Apr 6
Tilden Mary	S	W24Aa	1665ca	1689 Aug1	1731abt
Tilden Mary	S	W28D	1668 Apr7	1692 Jan3	1724 Aug13
Tilden Mercy	S	W28G	1674 May 1	1701 Jul23	1743
Tilden Nathaniel	S	W13Caf	1605abt		
Tilden Nathaniel	S	W28Ha	1678 Mar27	1700 Dec18	1733 Nov21
Tilden Ruth	S	W28H	1676 Jun 1	1700 Dec18	
Tilden Samuel	S	K29Bbf	1680abt		
Tilden Stephen	S	W13Ca	1629ca	1661 Jan25	1711 Aug22
Tilden Stephen	S	W28B	1663 Feb 5	1689ca	1727 Oct 3
Tilden Thomas	S	W24Aaf	1645abt		
Tilley Elizabeth	A	A12/125	1625ca	1653 Aug21	1684 Aug21
Tilley Elizabeth MF	D	D1a24	1606ca		=A14Aam
Tilley Elizabeth MF	S	A14Aam	1606ca	=D1a/24	1687Dec 21
Tilley Elizabeth=D1a24	D	D16a25	1606ca		1687 Dec21
Tilley John	D	D1af24	1580abt		1621ca
Tilson Anna	S	K31Ga	1703 Jun12	1722 Aug 2	1792 Nov16
Tilson Anna	S	T21Dam	1710abt		
Tilson Edmund	S	K39Aaf	1675abt		
Tilson Edmund=K39Aaf	S	K31Gaf	1675abt		
Tilson Elizabeth	S	F19Bam	1640ca		
Tilson Elizabeth	S	K39Aa	1700 May 6	1730 Jan 7	1773 Aug 8
Tilson Mary	A	A8/179	1630ca	1652	

NAME	DIV.	NUMBER	BIRTH	MARRIAGE	DEATH
Tilson Mary=A08/179	D	D4am23	1630ca	1652	
Tilton Abigail	A	A16/17	1679 Apr 1	1701Jun 19	1727Nov 13
Tilton Abraham	A	A16/34	1640ca		1728Mar 28
Tilton Jane	S	R22Ba	1697 Aug 2	1718 Jun 2	1732 Oct19
Tilton William	A	A16/68	1589ca		1683
Tilton William	S	R22Baf	1675abt		
Tinkham Abaisha	S	Q25F	1727 May23		
Tinkham Abigail	S	Q50G	1753ca	unm	1799bef
Tinkham Abijah	S	Q27E	1727 Mar21		
Tinkham Amos	S	Q25G	1729 Jul10		
Tinkham Amy	S	Q50C	1745 Sep15		
Tinkham Ann	S	Q40E	1726 Aug 6		
Tinkham Arthur	S	Q45B	1742 Jun 7		
Tinkham Barbara	S	Q50E	1749 Jul14		
Tinkham Bathsheba	S	Q37A	1726 Jun10		
Tinkham Caleb	S	Q17E	1693 Oct12	1724 Oct20	1748bef
Tinkham Caleb	S	Q42F	1738 Mar20		
Tinkham Charles	S	Q53A	1747 Jun16		
Tinkham Clark	S	Q53B	1748 Feb 7		
Tinkham Cornelius	S	Q25A	1717 Aug31		1739 Apr16
Tinkham Daniel	S	Q54I	1767 Apr30		
Tinkham Deborah	S	Q36E	1728 Sep 7		
Tinkham Deborah	S	Q50F	1751 May22		
Tinkham Ebenezer	S	Q12B	1651 Sep30	1676bef	1718 Apr 8
Tinkham Ebenezer	S	Q15A	1679 Mar23	2 mar.	1726 Aug31
Tinkham Ebenezer	S	Q17G	1698 May 3	2 mar.	1764living
Tinkham Ebenezer	S	Q31C	1714 Dec16		
Tinkham Ebenezer	S	Q33E	1728 Jan 2		
Tinkham Ebenezer	S	Q38I	1732 Jun26		1748living
Tinkham Ebenezer	S	Q43B	1741 Apr14		
Tinkham Edward	S	Q40B	1719 Feb 2		
Tinkham Eleanor(Nelle)	S	Q42G	1740ca		
Tinkham Elizabeth	S	Q15E	1688ca		1715 Mar27
Tinkham Elizabeth	S	Q30A	1704 Oct13		
Tinkham Elizabeth	S	Q38B	1713 Jul 5		
Tinkham Elizabeth	S	Q33A	1719 Oct 1		
Tinkham Elizabeth	S	Q37D	1737 May11		1777 Feb 3
Tinkham Elizabeth	S	Q50A	1741 Jul17	unm.	1794bef
Tinkham Elizabeth	S	Q54A	1748ca		
Tinkham Elizabeth	S	Q53E	1755ca		

NAME	DIV.	NUMBER	BIRTH	MARRIAGE	DEATH
Tinkham Ephraim	S	Q14C	1682 Oct 7	1708 Jun24	1713 Jul11
Tinkham Ephraim	S	Q26B	1711 Feb13		1730 May13
Tinkham Ephraim	S	Q27A	1718 Nov 8		1734 Jan10
Tinkham Ephraim	S	Q40D	1724 Mar25		
Tinkham Ephraim	S	Q28A	1733 Apr30		
Tinkham Ephraim	S	Q53C	1750 jan27		
Tinkham Ephraim Sr	S	K15Caf	1625abt	1646ca	=Q11Aa
Tinkham Ephraim=K15Ca	S	Q12A	1649	1676aft	1714 Oct13
Tinkham Ephraim=K15Caf	S	Q11Aa	1625ca	1646ca	1685ca
Tinkham Ephraim=K16Caf	D	D10af24	1625abt	1646ca	1685ca
Tinkham Ephraim=Q11Aa	S	K16Caf	1625abt	1646ca	1685ca
Tinkham Ephraim=Q12A	S	K15Ca	1649	1675 aft	1714 Oct13
Tinkham Ephraim=Q14C	S	K32C	1682 Oct 7	1798 Jun24	1713Jul11
Tinkham Esther	S	Q25C	1721 Apr26		
Tinkham Fear	S	Q42C	1731 Nov 5		
Tinkham Fear	S	Q28E	1740 Mar14		1773bef
Tinkham Gideon	S	Q36F	1731 Apr24		
Tinkham Grizzell	S	Q54G	1760ca		
Tinkham Hannah	S	Q38A	.1710 Oct31	unm	1748living
Tinkham Hannah	S	Q25D	1723 Apr10		
Tinkham Hannah	S	Q41B	1730ca		
Tinkham Hannah	S	Q50H	1754 Dec 3		
Tinkham Helkiah	S	Q12D	1655 Feb 8	1684ca	1725ca
Tinkham Helkiah	S	Q17A	1685 Aug15	1709 Dec15	1746bef
Tinkham Hezekiah	S	Q19E	1725 Nov10	1745 Dec28	1809
Tinkham Hezekiah	S	Q53F	1759 Oct 8		
Tinkham Hilkiah	S	Q45C	1750ca		1773 Dec25
Tinkham Huldah	S	Q50J	1758ca		
Tinkham Isaac	S	Q12G	1666 Apr11	1692 Nov17	1730ca
Tinkham Isaac	S	K32D	1685 Jun		
Tinkham Isaac	S	Q14D	1685 Jun	1717 Dec12	1750 Apr 7
Tinkham Isaac	S	Q38C	1715 Dec27		
Tinkham Isaac	S	Q27B	1720 Apr21		
Tinkham Jabez	S	Q30D	1711 Dec29		
Tinkham Jacob	S	Q17D	1691 Jun15	2 mar.	1733 Jul18
Tinkham Jacob	S	Q41A	1723 Feb28		
Tinkham Jacob	S	Q45A	1738 May29		
Tinkham James	S	Q43C	1743 Jan19		
Tinkham Jeremiah	S	Q15B	1681 Aug 7	1709ca	1715 Apr 5
Tinkham Jeremiah	S	Q31B	1712 Feb20		

NAME	DIV.	NUMBER	BIRTH	MARRIAGE	DEATH
Tinkham Joanna	S	Q15D	1685ca	1709 Jun14	1766 Apr29
Tinkham Joanna	S	Q16B	1695ca	1716 Apr16	1738 Jun28
Tinkham Joanna	S	Q31A	1711 Dec 8	unm	1763
Tinkham Joanna	S	Q36G	1734 May15		
Tinkham Joanna	S	Q37E	1740 Jan 1	unm	1813 Feb24
Tinkham Joanna	S	Q54B	1750ca		
Tinkham John	S	Q12F	1663 Nov15	1720bef	1740bef
Tinkham John	S	K32B	1680 Aug22		
Tinkham John	S	Q14B	1680 Aug22	1716 Dec11	1766 Apr14
Tinkham John	S	Q17C	1689 Mar27	1714 Dec30	1730 May12
Tinkham John	S	Q25B	1719 May 8		
Tinkham John	S	Q19A	1720bef	1741 May13	1785bef
Tinkham John	S	Q40C	1721		
Tinkham John	S	Q50B	1743 May10		
Tinkham John	S	Q54D	1753ca		
Tinkham Joseph	S	Q33B	1721 Dec16		
Tinkham Joseph	S	Q40F	1728 May14		
Tinkham Kezia	S	Q36H	1738 Aug15		
Tinkham Lois	S	Q28G	1745 Oct 2		
Tinkham Lydia	S	Q41C	1732ca		
Tinkham Lydia	S	Q38J	1734 Mar10		
Tinkham Marcy	S	Q42A	1726 may 8		
Tinkham Marmaduke	S	Q50I	1756ca		
Tinkham Martha	S	Q36A	1720 Aug23		
Tinkham Martha	S	Q19C	1722 May19	1742 Feb21	1790aft
Tinkham Martha	S	Q38G	1726 Dec29		
Tinkham Martha	S	Q28F	1743 Mar27		1773bef
Tinkham Martha=K32A	S	Q14A	1678ca	1701 Dec 8	1758 Feb16
Tinkham Martha=K32A	S	Q21Fam	1678ca	1701 Dec 8	1758Feb 16
Tinkham Martha=K34Eam	S	K32A	1678ca	1701 Dec 8	1758 Feb16
Tinkham Martha=Q14A	S	K34Eam	1678ca	1701 Dec 8	1758 Feb16
Tinkham Martha=Q14A	S	Q18Dam	1678ca	1701 Dec 8	1758 Feb16
Tinkham Mary	D	D10a24	1650abt		
Tinkham Mary	S	K16Ca	1661 Aug 5	1680ca	1731
Tinkham Mary	S	Q12E	1661 Aug 5	1680ca	1731
Tinkham Mary	S	Q17B	1687 Aug13	1709 Jan19	1717 Mar17
Tinkham Mary	S	K32F	1691ca		
Tinkham Mary	S	Q14F	1691ca	1717 Dec24	1751living
Tinkham Mary	S	Q30B	1705 Jan30		
Tinkham Mary	S	Q40A	1718 Jun25		1730 Jul25

NAME	DIV.	NUMBER	BIRTH	MARRIAGE	DEATH
Tinkham Mary	S	Q19B	1721bef	1739 Sep15	1772aft
Tinkham Mary	S	Q38F	1724 Sep14		
Tinkham Mary	S	Q25H	1731 Jan17		
Tinkham Mary	S	Q43A	1739 Apr 9		
Tinkham Mary	S	Q50D	1747 Sep 4		
Tinkham Mercy	S	Q16A	1692ca	1716 Dec27	1723 Apr17
Tinkham Mercy	S	Q36D	1726 Aug24		
Tinkham Mercy	S	Q37B	1732 Jul25		
Tinkham Moses	S	Q26A	1709 Aug16		1730 Apr27
Tinkham Moses	S	Q27F	1730 Feb 3		1750 Apr15
Tinkham Nathan	S	Q27D	1725 Apr18		
Tinkham Nathaniel	S	Q42E	1736 Aug12		
Tinkham Nehemiah	S	Q54H	1766		
Tinkham Noah	S	Q27C	1722 Jul25		
Tinkham Patience	S	Q30E	1714ca		
Tinkham Patience	S	Q42B	1729 Jul16	unm	1799living
Tinkham Patience	S	Q28B	1734 Jan 9	unm	1773
Tinkham Perez	S	Q33F	1736 Aug 4		1760 Nov25
Tinkham Peter	S	Q12C	,1653 Dec25	1690ca	1709 Dec30
Tinkham Peter	S	Q15C	1683 Apr20		1713 Jul10
Tinkham Peter	S	Q17I	1706 Apr 1	1736 Jan 6	1765living
Tinkham Peter	S	Q30C	1709 Sep 5		
Tinkham Peter	S	Q36B	1722 May16		
Tinkham Peter	S	Q19D	1723 Feb 8	1746 Jun12	1768living
Tinkham Peter	S	Q54F	1757		1776 Nov17
Tinkham Phebe	S	Q43D	1746 Jul12		
Tinkham Philip	S	Q54K	1770ca		
Tinkham Priscilla	S	Q15F	1690ca		1715 Apr16
Tinkham Priscilla	S	Q30F	1716ca		
Tinkham Priscilla	S	Q33D	1726 Jun10		
Tinkham Priscilla	S	Q43F	1755 Jul26		
Tinkham Renew	S	Q54C	1751ca		
Tinkham Ruth	S	Q17H	1701 Feb13	1722 Jul28	1726 Oct 7
Tinkham Ruth	S	Q38H	1729 Jul 9	unm	1748living
Tinkham Samuel	S	Q14E	1687 Mar19	2 mar.	1775 Mar16
Tinkham Samuel	S	Q16C	1697ca	1719 Dec 1	1747bef
Tinkham Samuel	S	Q36C	1723 Mar13		
Tinkham Samuel	S	Q28C	1737 Apr16		1773bef
Tinkham Samuel	S	Q54J	1769		
Tinkham Samuel =Q14E	S	K32E	1687 Mar19		1775 Mar16

NAME	DIV.	NUMBER	BIRTH	MARRIAGE	DEATH
Tinkham Sarah	S	Q17F	1696 Jan30		1714 Feb22
Tinkham Sarah	S	Q38D	1718 Aug 5	unm	1748living
Tinkham Sarah	S	Q33C	1723 Feb23		
Tinkham Sarah	S	Q42D	1733 Dec28		
Tinkham Sarah	S	Q28H	1748 Jun18		1773bef
Tinkham Sarah	S	Q53D	1753 Dec14		
Tinkham Sarah	S	Q54E	1755ca		
Tinkham Seth	S	Q16D	1704 May15	1724ca	1750 Feb 9
Tinkham Seth	S	Q25I	1734 Aug27		1758 Jul11
Tinkham Seth	S	Q37C	1734 Nov13		
Tinkham Shuball	S	Q15G	1692ca	1718 Dec17	1739 Mar29
Tinkham Silas	S	Q28D	1739 Apr25		
Tinkham Susanna	S	Q50K	1760ca		1818living
Tinkham Susannah	S	Q25E	1724 Mar19		
Tinkham Susannah	S	Q43E	1748 Sep15		
Tinkham Zedekiah	S	Q38E	1721 Jul11		
Tinkham Zilpah	S	Q25J	1737 Jul25		
Tirrell Mary	S	K26Db	1689 Aug22	1728 Jan21	
Tirrell William	S	K26Dbf	1665abt		
Tisdale Abigail	S	X21A	1667 Jul15	1685 Dec 2	1725ca
Tisdale Abigail	S	X63E	1711ca		
Tisdale Abraham	S	X63B	1707ca	unm	1737
Tisdale Anna	S	X21C	1672 Jan27	2 mar.	1733 Sep
Tisdale Anna	S	X63H	1718ca		
Tisdale Deborah	S	X63D	1709ca		
Tisdale Ephraim	S	X63F	1714bef		
Tisdale Hannah	S	K25Ham	1690abt		
Tisdale Israel	S	X63C	1708ca	1735Aug 7	1769 Oct27
Tisdale Jedediah	S	X63G	1715ca		1735ca
Tisdale John	S	X13Baf	1615abt		
Tisdale John	S	X13Ba	1640ca	1664 Nov23	1677 Dec
Tisdale John	S	X21B	1669 Aug10	2 mar.	1728 Jan26
Tisdale John	S	X63A	1702ca		
Tisdale Remember	S	X21D	1675 Jul 8	1696bef	1710ca
Titus Abigail	S	A14Ab	1652 Feb18	1679 Oct16	1734 May31
Todd Mary Ann	A	A13/1a	1818Dec 13	1842 Nov 4	1882 Jul16
Tokesy Joanna	A	A14/267	1600abt	1625	
Tokesy Joanna	A	A14/299	1600abt	1625	
Tomas Jannetje=A7/129	A	A8/129	1625abt	1650abt	1660ca
Tomas Jennetje=A8/129	A	A7/129	1625abt	1650abt	1660ca

NAME	DIV.	NUMBER	BIRTH	MARRIAGE	DEATH
Tompkins John Jr	D	D10/24	1650abt		
Tompkins Sarah=A2/225	A	A2/245	1642	1663	1707aft
Tompkins Sarah=A2/245	A	A2/225	1642	1663	1707aft
Tomson Abel twin	S	K154K	1752 Apr10		d. yng
Tomson Abigail	S	K39B	1696 Feb14	1723 Nov27	1776aft
Tomson Abigail	S	K149A	1735 Nov26		
Tomson Abigail	S	K154A	1740 Feb12		d.yng
Tomson Abigail	S	K158D	1748 Oct25		d.yng
Tomson Abigail	S	K157I	1755 Aug18		
Tomson Adam	S	K16A	1646bef		d yng.
Tomson Adam	S	K154M	1754 Apr24		
Tomson Amasa	S	H123D	1722 Apr18		
Tomson Amasa=H123D	S	K40D	1722 Apr18	1743 Feb23	1807 May 7
Tomson Andrew	S	H123E	1724 Mar20		d yng
Tomson Andrew	S	K40E	1724 Mar20		d.yng
Tomson Andrew	S	K158B	1741 Jan18		
Tomson Asa	S	K154F	1745 Sep 3		d.yng
Tomson Asa	S	K160B	1747 Mar 4		
Tomson Barnabas	S	K39F	1704 Jan28	1740 Mar13	1798 Dec20
Tomson Barnabas	S	K154B	1741 Feb13		d.yng
Tomson Betty	S	K166A	1734 May16		
Tomson Bezer	S	K160J	1765 Feb27		d.yng
Tomson Caleb	S	K39J	1712 Nov 4	1736 May20	1787 Jan19
Tomson Caleb	S	K157H	1752 Oct18		
Tomson Caleb	S	K160K	1767 Mar23		
Tomson Daniel	S	Q49E	1750 Oct24		
Tomson Daniel=Q49E	S	K131G	1750 Oct24		
Tomson David	S	K154J	1750 Sep 2		d.yng
Tomson Deborah	S	K158A	1740 Jul27		
Tomson Ebenezer	S	Q18I	1699 Jun19	unm	1725ca
Tomson Ebenezer	S	K40F	1725 Mar11	1748 Jul13	1813 Sep10
Tomson Ebenezer	S	K131B	1737 Oct14		
Tomson Ebenezer	S	K162C	1753 Oct18		
Tomson Ebenezer=K131B	S	Q49B	1737 Oct14		
Tomson Ebenezer=K40F	S	H123F	1725 Mar11	1748 Jul13	1813Sep 10
Tomson Ebenezer=Q18I	S	K34J	1699 Jun19	unm	1725ca
Tomson Elisabeth	S	K127B	1726 Aug 7		
Tomson Elisabeth	S	K149C	1741 Jun29		d.yng
Tomson Elizabeth	S	K16F	1654 Jan28	1687aft	1717
Tomson Elizabeth	S	Q46B	1726 Aug 7		

NAME	DIV.	NUMBER	BIRTH	MARRIAGE	DEATH
Tomson Ephraim	S	Q18B	1683 Oct16	1734 Nov 6	1744 Nov13
Tomson Ephraim	S	Q49D	1748 Aug 1		
Tomson Ephraim #1	S	K128B	1742 Apr 8		d. yng
Tomson Ephraim #2	S	K128C	1744 May 8		d. yng
Tomson Ephraim=Q18B	S	K34C	1683 Oct16	1734 Nov 6	1744 Nov13
Tomson Ephraim=Q49D	S	K131F	1748 Aug 1		
Tomson Esther	S	K16E	1652 Jul28	1675ca	1706ca
Tomson Esther	S	K39G	1706 Feb18	1737 Oct25	1776 Jul 5
Tomson Eunice	S	K162E	1765 Sep10		
Tomson Francis	S	Q18J	1700 Jan27		1734bef
Tomson Francis	S	Q48B	1734 Mar15		
Tomson Francis=Q18J	S	K34K	1700 Jan27	unm	1734bef
Tomson Francis=Q48B	S	K130B	1734 Mar15		
Tomson Hannah	S	K39H	1708 Mar10	1732 Feb21	1787 Nov27
Tomson Hannah	S	K165A	1741 Dec12		d.yng
Tomson Hannah	S	K166E	1748 May19		d.yng
Tomson Hannah	S	K154H	1748 May30		
Tomson Hannah #1	S	K157A	1737 Jul24		d.yng
Tomson Hannah #2	S	K157D	1743 Aug 8	unm	1797living
Tomson Ichabod	S	K154N	1756 Apr23		
Tomson Ignatius	S	K160C	1750 Aug24	unm	1770 Jan22
Tomson Isaac	S	K34I	1696 Mar10		1724bef
Tomson Isaac	S	Q18H	1696 Mar10		1724bef
Tomson Isaac	S	K129A	1714 Sep24		1740 Apr30
Tomson Isaac	S	Q47A	1714 Sep24		1740Apr 30
Tomson Isaac	S	K154I	1749 May29		
Tomson Jabez	S	K154E	1744 Mar26		d.yng
Tomson Jacob	S	K16I	1662 Apr24	1693 Dec28	1726 Sep 1
Tomson Jacob	S	K40Aaf	1690abt		
Tomson Jacob	S	K39A	1695 Apr17	1730 Jan 7	1789 Mar10
Tomson Jacob	S	K34L	1703 Jun24	1735 Sep 4	1750 Feb17
Tomson Jacob	S	Q18K	1703 Jun24	1735 Sep 4	1750 Feb17
Tomson Jacob	S	K131A	1736 Jul 9		
Tomson Jacob	S	Q49A	1736 Jul 9		
Tomson Jacob	S	K149B	1738 Mar28		
Tomson Jacob	S	K154D	1743 Mar14	twin	d.yng
Tomson James	S	K41C	1702 Feb 2	unm.	1739 Nov23
Tomson James	S	K130D	1739 Nov11		
Tomson James	S	Q48D	1739 Nov11		
Tomson Joanna	S	K128A	1738 Jul23		d. yng

NAME	DIV.	NUMBER	BIRTH	MARRIAGE	DEATH
Tomson Joanna	S	K152B	1751 Aug 9		
Tomson Joanna	S	K158F	1772 Jan19		
Tomson John	S	K11Ea	1617ca	1645 Dec26	1696 Jun16
Tomson John	S	H34Aaf	1640abt		
Tomson John	S	K16B	1648		d yng
Tomson John	S	Q12Ea	1649 Nov24	1680ca	1725 Nov25
Tomson John	S	K34B	1682 Aug 9	1723 Oct24	1757
Tomson John	S	K39D	1700 Mar19	1735ca	1790 Dec 6
Tomson John	S	K129C	1717 Jun11		
Tomson John	S	K127A	1724 Feb18		
Tomson John	S	K166C	1737 Oct14		
Tomson John #2=Q12Ea	S	K16C	1649 Nov24	1680ca	1725 Nov25
Tomson John =D10a/25	S	Q12Eaf	1625abt		
Tomson John Sr=Q12Eaf	D	D10a25	1625abt		
Tomson John=K127A	S	Q46A	1724 Feb18		
Tomson John=K129C	S	Q47C	1717 Jun11		
Tomson John=K34B	S	Q18A	1682 Aug 9	1723 Oct24	1757
Tomson Joseph	S	K41D	1706 Jun 3	1732 Feb 7	1788bef
Tomson Joseph	S	K166B	1735 Mar 3		
Tomson Joshua	S	K160A	1746 Jul22		d.yng
Tomson Josiah	S	K162B	1751 Jun 9	unm	1828 Jul23
Tomson Lois	S	K160G	1758 Apr12		
Tomson Loring	S	K160F	1756 Apr25		
Tomson Lucia	S	K157C	1741 Jul12		d.yng
Tomson Lucy	S	K158E	1755 Dec 4		
Tomson Lydia	S	K16H	1659 Oct 5	1693 Dec14	1741 Mar14
Tomson Lydia	S	K39E	1703 Apr22	1725 Feb 2	1738living
Tomson Lydia	S	Q46C	1730 Aug13		
Tomson Lydia	S	K161C	1752 May 9		
Tomson Lydia=Q46C	S	K127C	1730 Aug13		
Tomson Martha	S	K34F	1689 Jan 4	unm.	1770ca
Tomson Martha	S	Q18E	1689 Jan 4		1765ca
Tomson Martha	S	K131E	1745 Jan 1		d.yng
Tomson Mary	S	K16D	1651ca	1673ca	1723aft
Tomson Mary	S	K34A	1681 May 2	unm.	1742 May30
Tomson Mary	S	K39I	1711 May19	1739 Nov 8	1769 Jul19
Tomson Mary	S	K40B	1718 May 8	1737 Mar16	1756 Apr 9
Tomson Mary	S	K129D	1719 Sep24		1734 Jun23
Tomson Mary	S	K131D	1743 Sep 7		d.yng
Tomson Mary	S	K157E	1745 Aug12		

NAME	DIV.	NUMBER	BIRTH	MARRIAGE	DEATH
Tomson Mary	S	K160E	1754 Sep16		
Tomson Mary	S	K162D	1757 Apr28		
Tomson Mary=K129D	S	Q47D	1719 Sep24		1734Jun 23
Tomson Mary=K16D	S	W47Fam	1651ca	1673ca	1723aft
Tomson Mary=K39I	S	K40Aa	1711 May19	1739 Nov 8	1769 Jul19
Tomson Mary=K40B	S	H123B	1718 May 8	1737 Mar16	1756 Apr 9
Tomson Mercy	S	K16L	1671ca	unm.	1756 Apr19
Tomson Mercy	S	K39C	1699 Oct13	1721 May 4	1799 Sep 4
Tomson Mercy	S	K158C	1745 Sep21		d.yng
Tomson Mercy	S	K163F	1756 Oct28		
Tomson Molly	S	K161D	1756 Dec13		
Tomson Moses	S	K163H	1762 Jul 1		
Tomson Nathan	S	Q48C	1736 Dec10		
Tomson Nathan=Q48C	S	K130C	1736 Dec10		
Tomson Nathaniel	S	Q49C	1740 Jul23	unm	1761bef
Tomson Nathaniel	S	K157G	1750 Sep13		
Tomson Nathaniel=Q49C	S	K131C	1740 Jul23	unm.	1761bef
Tomson Noah	S	K154G	1746 Mar20		
Tomson Olive twin	S	K154L	1752 Apr10		1776 Feb12
Tomson Peter	S	K16K	1670ca	1699ca	1732bef
Tomson Peter	S	K34H	1694 May11	unm.	1726bef
Tomson Peter	S	Q18G	1694 May11		1725ca
Tomson Peter	S	K41B	1701 Jun30	2 mar.	1791 Nov28
Tomson Peter	S	K130A	1733 Oct 8		
Tomson Peter	S	Q48A	1733 Oct 8		
Tomson Peter	S	K165B	1747 Apr27		d.yng
Tomson Rachel #1	S	K163B	1748 Jan22		d.yng
Tomson Rachel #2	S	K163I	1767 Oct22		
Tomson Rebecca	S	K163A	1746 Mar 5		
Tomson Reuben=K39Ia	S	K40A	1716 Oct11	2 mar.	1793 Sep28
Tomson Reuben=K40A	S	H123A	1716 Oct11	1739 Nov 8	1793 Sep28
Tomson Reuben=K48A	S	K39Ia	1716 Oct11	2 Mar	1793 Sep28
Tomson Ruth	S	K161A	1744 Jan14		
Tomson Samuel	S	K154C	1743 Mar14	twin	d.yng
Tomson Sarah	S	K16G	1657 Apr 4		1697aft
Tomson Sarah	S	K34G	1691 Mar 3	unm.	1770ca
Tomson Sarah	S	Q18F	1691 Mar 3		1765ca
Tomson Sarah	S	K41A	1699 Oct30	1729 Mar26	1776 May 9
Tomson Sarah	S	K157B	1738 Nov15		
Tomson Sarah	S	K166D	1744 Apr17		

NAME	DIV.	NUMBER	BIRTH	MARRIAGE	DEATH
Tomson Sarah	S	K160D	1752 Apr 5 unm		1769 Nov27
Tomson Sarah	S	K160L	1770 Jan12		
Tomson Seth	S	K160H	1760 Jun18		
Tomson Shubael	S	K34D	1686 Apr11	1713 Dec10	1733 Jul 7
Tomson Shubael	S	Q47B	1716 Mar27		1734 Jun18
Tomson Shubael=K34D	S	Q18C	1686 Apr11	1713 Dec10	1733
Tomson Shubael=Q47B	S	K129B	1716 Mar27		1734 Jun18
Tomson Silva	S	K157J	1757ca		
Tomson Susanna	S	K162A	1749 Jun 4		
Tomson Thomas	S	H34Aa	1664 Oct19	1715 Dec13	1742 Oct26
Tomson Thomas	S	K34E	1688 Jul29	1732 Apr25	1760ca
Tomson Thomas	S	K39Iaf	1695abt		
Tomson Thomas	S	K130E	1743 Jun 1		d. yng
Tomson Thomas	S	K163E	1754 Nov17 unm		1837Dec 10
Tomson Thomas	S	K160I	1762 May27		
Tomson Thomas =Q47E	S	K129E	1721 Jul28		
Tomson Thomas=H123C	S	K40C	1720 Apr21	1745 Oct25	1769 Sep14
Tomson Thomas=H34Aa	S	K16J	1664 Oct19	1715 Dec13	1742 Oct26
Tomson Thomas=K129E	S	Q18D	1688 Jul29	1732 Apr25	1760ca
Tomson Thomas=K129E	S	Q47E	1721 Jul28		
Tomson Thomas=K40C	S	H123C	1720 Apr21	1745 Oct25	1769 Sep14
Tomson William	S	K157F	1747 Feb15		
Tomson Zaccheus	S	K152A	1743 Jul22		d. yng
Tomson Zadock	S	K161B	1747 May11 unm		1786 Dec 4
Tomson Zebadiah	S	K40G	1728 Aug18	1745 Dec 5	1775 Sep30
Tomson Zebadiah	S	K163D	1752 Dec17		d.yng
Tomson Zebadiah #2	S	K163G	1758 Dec15		
Tomson Zebadiah=K40G	S	H123G	1728 Aug18	1745 Dec 5	1775 Sep30
Tomson Zerviah	S	K163C	1750 Mar17		
Tone Andrew	S	G50A	1743 Feb17		
Tone Antoine	S	G44E	1600 Feb 7		
Tone Clementine	S	G40D	1460ca		
Tone Clementine	S	G41E	1498 Jan11		
Tone Elizabeth	S	G50D	1749		
Tone Flibton	S	G43A	1568 Apr 7	1593	
Tone Francis	S	G49D	1725 Oct 3		
Tone Francois	S	G44A	1595 Jun11	1647 Sep 8	1661 May 3
Tone Guillane	S	G42D	1542 Oct 3		
Tone Hannah	S	G50C	1747 Aug23		
Tone Henri	S	G43C	1570 Mar 4	1600	

NAME	DIV.	NUMBER	BIRTH	MARRIAGE	DEATH
Tone Henri	S	G44B	1596 May 9		
Tone Hugh	S	G44D	1598 Sep 1		
Tone Hugh	S	G45B	1650 May 5	1676 Jun 8	
Tone Jacques	S	G46D	1704 Jan 9		
Tone Jane	S	G46B	1685ca		1700
Tone Jane	S	G51G	1796 Jan20		
Tone Jaques	S	G44C	1597 Apr17	1637	
Tone Jean	S	G42C	1541 Sep15		
Tone Jean	S	G43B	1569 Feb16		
Tone Jean I	S	G37A	1385	1409	
Tone Jean II	S	G38A	1410abt		1456bef
Tone Jean III	S	G39A	1430abt	1451	1515
Tone Jean IV	S	G40A	1452 Aug17	1485 Jun 3	1527
Tone Jean V	S	G41A	1486 Apr 7		
Tone Jerome	S	G42B	1540 May 7	1565 Jun11	1619
Tone Joan	S	G46C	1690abt		1702
Tone John II	S	G51C	1785 Dec 2		
Tone John Jr =G50E	D	D7a19	1750ca	1778 Apr26	1808
Tone John Jr=D7a19	S	G50E	1750ca	1778 Apr26	1808
Tone John Sr	S	G49A	1719 Oct11	1742 May 4	1791ca
Tone Joseph	S	G40B	1455ca		
Tone Joseph	S	G49B	1721 May17	1752 Jun 7	
Tone Joseph Alfred	S	G41C	1493 Sep 5		
Tone Joseph Jr	S	G42A	1539 Jun14		
Tone Joseph Pierre	S	G41D	1496 Mar12	1538May 3	
Tone Lewis	S	G49E	1725abt		
Tone Lewis	S	G51D	1788 Feb 8		
Tone Margaret	S	G51A	1782	1802abt	
Tone Margaret=G51A	S	G36Aam	1782	1802abt	
Tone Marie	S	G42E	1544 May 9		
Tone Mary	S	G45A	1648 Aug11		
Tone Mary	S	G50H	1757 Oct22		
Tone Mary Louise	S	G41B	1487 Aug17		
Tone Nancy	S	G51E	1790abt		
Tone Peter	S	G47A	1735abt		
Tone Philip	S	G39B	1435abt		
Tone Pierre	S	G40B	1455ca		
Tone Sally	S	G46F	1708May12	1726	
Tone Sarah	S	G50F	1754ca		
Tone Theobold Wolfe	S	G48A	1763Jun 20	1785ca	1798Nov 11

NAME	DIV.	NUMBER	BIRTH	MARRIAGE	DEATH
Tone Thomas	S	G45C	1651 Jul21		
Tone Thomas	S	G46A	1682 Feb12	1718	
Tone Thomas	S	G50B	1745 Feb17		
Tone Thomas	S	G51F	1793 Jan16		
Tone William	S	G46E	1706 Oct14		
Tone William	S	G49C	1723 Dec 9		
Tone William	S	G50G	1755 Aug19		
Tone William	S	G51B	1784ca		
Toorey William	A	A2/192	1620abt	1641ca	1690
Torgerson Thelma	S	C58Ca	1905		
Torrey Angel	A	A2/96	1657 Jun10	1688ca	1725ca
Torrey David	S	W46Ca	1687 Jan 4	1710 Jun12	1770 Jan
Torrey James	S	W17Aaf	1635abt		
Torrey James	S	W46Caf	1660abt		
Torrey Joseph	A	A2/24	1727ca	1752 Sept6	1760 Nov29
Torrey Louisa Maria	A	A2/3	1827Sept11	1853 Dec26	1907 Dec8
Torrey Samuel D.	A	A2/6	1789 Apr14	1824 Jan27	1877 Dec23
Torrey Sarah	S	W17Aa	1660 Feb9	1678ca	1722aft
Torrey William	A	A2/48	1700 Dec17	1724 Dec29	1779 Mar1
Torrey William	A	A2/12	1754 Nov23	1788 Jul20	1817 Sep16
Totman Deborah	S	X90B	1731		
Totman Experience	S	X90E	1743		
Totman Hannah	S	X90C	1734		
Totman Joshua	S	X90D	1737		
Totman Samuel	S	X28Da	1693 Jul20	1727 Apr17	1750bef
Totman Samuel	S	X90A	1729		
Totman Stephen	S	X28Daf	1670abt		
Touchet Anne	D	D29/17	1440abt		
Touchet James	D	D29a18	1415abt		
Touteville Margaret	A	A11/117	1606 Aug	1632ca	1635 Feb
Towneley Lawrence	A	A10/84	1540abt	1563 Jun 3	1597 Jan19
Towneley Lawrence	A	A10/42	1570abt	1597bef	1654 Feb
Towneley Mary	A	A10/21	1614 May13	1638ca	1662 Aug11
Townsend Deborah	S	P24D	1696ca		1747
Townsend James	S	P14Aa	1647ca	1688ca	1698
Townsend John	S	P14Aaf	1625abt		
Townsend Joseph	S	P24A	1690ca	unm.	1710abt
Townsend Joshua	S	P24C	1694ca		
Townsend Patience	S	P24B	1692ca		
Townsend Ruemourn	S	P24E	1698ca		

NAME	DIV.	NUMBER	BIRTH	MARRIAGE	DEATH
Tracy Aphiah	S	X14Dbm	1660abt		
Tracy Aphiah=X14Dbm	S	H22Ebm	1660abt		
Tracy Eliphalet	S	R60D	1720 Nov14		
Tracy John	S	X18Aaf	1650abt		
Tracy John	S	R19Faf	1665abt		
Tracy Joshua	S	R60A	1715 Jun19		1715 Dec13
Tracy Josiah	S	R60C	1718 May10		
Tracy Mary	S	W23Bam	1645abt		
Tracy Nehemiah	S	R60E	1722 Mar18		
Tracy Perez	S	R60B	1716 Nov13		
Tracy Rebecca	S	H13Bam	1625abt		
Tracy Rebecca	S	H13Dam	1625abt		
Tracy Samuel	S	R60F	1724 Dec 5 unm.		1774
Tracy Sarah	A	A5/159	1610abt	1638	
Tracy Solomon	S	R60G	1728 May23		
Tracy Susanna	S	X18Aa	1675ca	1697 Feb17	
Tracy Winslow	S	R19Fa	1688 Feb 9	1714 Jun21	1767 Nov26
Train Hannah	A	A19/139	1657	1678	
Trask John	A	A2/124	1678ca	1701 Nov26	
Trask Samuel	A	A2/62	1721 Dec17	1757 Jan 6	1790 Mar 7
Trask Susanna	A	A2/31	1759 Oct11	1783 Jul10	1843 Feb25
Trask William Jr.	A	A2/248	1640	1677	1691
Travers Elizabeth	A	A3/485	1667	1689	
Travers Elizabeth	S	A31A	1689ca	2 mar.	1720bef
Travers Frances	S	A31D	1697 Aug20		
Travers Rebecca	S	A31B	1692 Oct15	2 mar.	1726 Dec29
Travers Samuel	S	A15Ea	1660ca	1685 Jul 1	1698bef
Travers William	S	A15Eaf	1635abt		
Travers Winifred	S	A31C	1694	1741 Nov28	1749 Aug10
Treat Elizabeth	S	H23Aa	1676 Jul24	1695ca	1755 Mar 3
Treat Jane	S	H29Aam	1675abt		
Treat Samuel=H22Eaf	S	X14Daf	1655abt		
Treat Samuel=H23Aaf	S	H22Eaf	1655abt		
Treat Samuel=X14Daf	S	H23Aaf	1655abt		
Treat Sarah	S	H22Ea	1678 Jun20	1700 Dec10	1728 Sep26
Treat Sarah	S	X14Da	1678 Jun20	1700 Dec10	1728 Sep26
Treddeawy Jonathan	S	W48Baf	1655abt		
Treddeway Hannah	S	W48Ba	1680 Jun14	1711 May23	1714 Sep19
Trimmer Anthony	A	A3/72	1724ca	1749ca	1754 Nov
Trimmer Anthony	A	A3/18	1781ca	1824 Sep21	1841

NAME	DIV.	NUMBER	BIRTH	MARRIAGE	DEATH
Trimmer John	A	A3/144	1700abt	1721ca	1750
Trimmer Margaret Ann	A	A3/9	1826ca	1843 Jan10	1865 Mar18
Trimmer Paul	A	A3/36	1750ca	1780ca	1834abt
Trowbridge John	D	D30a18	1570abt		
Trowbridge Sarah	A	A12/19	1686 Nov26	1707 Dec17	1761 Jan23
Trowbridge Thomas	D	D30/17	1597	1627	=A12/152
Trowbridge Thomas	A	A12/152	1597	1627	1672 Aug
Trowbridge Thomas III	A	A12/38	1663 Feb14	1685 Oct16	1711 Sep15
Trowbridge Thomas Jr	A	A12/76	1631 Dec	1657 Jun24	1702 Aug22
Tucker Elizabeth	S	H111D	1712 Sep		
Tucker Eunice	S	H111H	1722 Jun12		
Tucker Hannah	S	H111E	1714 Sep		
Tucker John	S	W15Baf	1615abt		
Tucker John	S	H31Baf	1655abt		
Tucker John	S	H111B	1709 Sep		d yng
Tucker John	S	H111F	1715 Mar20		
Tucker Keziah	S	H111A	1707 Nov		
Tucker Mary	S	W15Ba	1640 Oct 8	1660 Dec13	1710 Mar21
Tucker Mary	D	D28a20	1785abt		
Tucker Samuel	S	H31Ba	1680ca	1707ca	1765ca
Tucker Samuel	S	H111G	1719 Mar16		
Tucker Sarah	S	A15Cam	1655abt		
Tucker Susannah	S	K35Ia	1690ca	1710ca	
Tucker Thankful	S	H111C	1710 Sep	1732Dec 22	1741bef
Tufts Elizabeth	S	R23Iam	1690abt		
Tunstall Martha	A	A8/169	1652	1675	1709
Tupper Rebecca	S	Q14Fam	1650abt		
Turell Lydia	A	A8/247	1660	1678bef	1688bef
Turner Catherine	S	K65B	1705abt		
Turner Christopher	S	K21Aa	1680ca		1775bef
Turner Mary	S	K65A	1705abt		
Turney Cora Louise	S	G53Ab	1910 Jul 6	1936	1962 Jun10
Tuthill Anna	A	A14/11	1741 Oct	1760 Oct30	1776 Jul25
Tuthill Henry	A	A14/88	1665 May 1	1690bef	1750 Jan 4
Tuthill Henry III	A	A14/22	1715abt	1738 Mar16	1793 Sep17
Tuthill Henry Jr.	A	A14/44	1690ca		1775 Sep 1
Tuthill John	A	A14/176	1635	1657	1717
Tuttle Abigail	S	A38C	1701 Apr25		
Tuttle Daniel	S	R24Fa	1710ca	1731bef	
Tuttle John	S	A17Ea	1666 Apr22	1689 Dec 3	1715 Feb27

NAME	DIV.	NUMBER	BIRTH	MARRIAGE	DEATH
Tuttle John	S	R90A	1736		1756 Feb17
Tuttle Martha	S	A38A	1690 Nov21		
Tuttle Mary	S	A38B	1696 Jul 7		
Tuttle Remember	S	A38D	1703ca		
Tuttle Sarah	S	A17Fa	1672 Sep 3	1699 Nov13	1719living
Tuttle Sarah	S	A38F	1706ca		
Tuttle Susanna	S	A38G	1708ca		
Tuttle Symon	S	A17Eaf	1645abt		
Tuttle Symon	S	A17Faf	1645abt		
Tuttle William	S	A38E	1705ca	unm	1726 Dec10
Twigden Amphyllis	A	A10/17	1601 Feb2	1633 Dec	1654 Jan19
Twigden John	A	A10/34	1580abt		1610ca
Twigden Thomas	A	A10/68	1545abt		1580ca
Twiggs Hannah	A	A3/71	1735ca	1759 Oct29	
Twiggs John	A	A3/142	1700abt	1721 Feb16	1760
Twining Barnabas	S	H77F	1705 Sep29		
Twining Elizabeth	S	X12Ea	1645ca	1669 Aug19	1724 Mar10
Twining Elizabeth	S	H77A	1690 Aug25		
Twining Hannah	S	H77D	1702 Apr 2		
Twining Mercy	S	H77G	1708 Feb20		
Twining Ruth	S	H77C	1699 Aug27		
Twining Thankful	S	H77B	1696 Jan11		
Twining William	S	X12Eaf	1620abt		
Twining William	S	H77E	1704 Sept2		
Twining William Jr	S	H24Aa	1665abt	1688 Mar21	1734 Jan23
Twining William Sr	S	H24Aaf	1640abt		
Twitchell Benjamin	A	A2/158	1635abt	1660ca	1680
Twitchell Hannah	A	A2/79	1661ca	1679 Nov 4	1690
Tying Anna=A11/59	D	D23/23	1639 Jan 6	1656 Nov 3	1709 Aug 5
Tying Anna=A11/59	A	A8/341	1639 Jan 6	1656 Nov 3	1709 Aug5
Tying Anne=A8/341	A	A11/59	1639 Jan6	1656 Nov3	1709 Aug5
Tying Eunice	S	W31Iam	1665abt		
Tying William	D	D23a24	1605	1636ca	1652Jan 18
Tying William	A	A11/118	1605ca	1636ca	1652 Jan18
Tyler Henry	A	A15/32	1604ca	1655ca	1672Apr13
Tyler Henry	A	A15/16	1660abt	1683ca	1729Dec
Tyler John (III)	A	A15/2	1747Feb 28	1776 ca	1813Jan 6
Tyler John Jr	A	A15/4	1710ca		1773
Tyler John Sr.	A	A15/8	1685ca		
Tyler John U.S. Pres.	A	A15/1	1790Mar 29	1813Mar 29	1889Jul 10

NAME	DIV.	NUMBER	BIRTH	MARRIAGE	DEATH
Tyson Elizabeth	A	A7/47	1690 Oct 7	1710 Nov27	1765 Feb18
Tyson Rynear	A	A7/94	1659ca		1745 Sep27
Uncles James	A	A1/42	1794 Aug 5	1816 Sep26	1835 Jan25
Uncles Martha	A	A1/21	1824 Jan 7	1844 Jan21	1912 Jul 9
Underwood Mary	A	A16/229	1585abt	1600	
Underwood Remembrance	A	A17/39	1639Feb25	1659Jun 6	1718Feb 20
Underwood William	A	A17/78	1615ca		1697Aug 12
Valentine Ethel	S	N18Da	1905abt	1926 Jan26	
Vallet Sarah	S	C49Ca	1687ca		
Van Bommel Huybertsie	A	A7/153	1650ca		1730
Van Deursen Tryntje	A	A8/141	1654ca	1673	
Van Dyck Cornelis	A	A7/148	1642ca	1663ca	1663ca
Van Dyck Hendrick	A	A7/74	1665ca	1689 Feb 3	1707 Apr11
Van Dyck Lydia	A	A7/37	1704 Jul16	1728 Oct 6	1785 Jun10
Van Hoesen Anna Janse	A	A7/147	1660abt		
Van Imbroch Elizabeth	A	A7/71	1659ca	1683 Jul18	
Van Imbroch Gysbert	A	A7/142	1630abt		1665
Van Kleeck Johannes	A	A4/470	1680ca	1709bef	1754ca
Van Kleeck Sarah	A	A4/235	1722 Nov	1739ca	
Van Laer Sara	A	A8/67	1665abt	1686 Jun16	1743 Nov17
Van Laer Stoffel G.	A	A8/134	1639ca	1660	1665living
Van Rosenvelt Claes M.	A	A7/128	1625abt	1650aft	1658ca
Van Rosenvelt Claes M.	A	A8/128	1625abt	1650 bef	1658ca
Van Vleck Magdaleentje	A	A8/147	1650abt	1677	1699living
VanDenBergh Cornelis G	A	A7/158	1650ca	1684ca	1717ca
VanDenBergh Tryntje C	A	A7/79	1684ca	1698 Sep 9	1753 Mar3
VanDerPoel Cornelia	A	A7/159	1660ca	1684ca	
VanSchaick Adrian	D	D7/25	1580ca		
VanSchaick Arie C	D	D7/23	1642ca		1699
VanSchaick Belitje	A	A7/69	1672Apr 2	1695Jun 28	1707ca
VanSchaick Belitze	D	D8/22	1672Apr 2	1695Jun 28	=A07/69
VanSchaick Claas G.	A	A7/144	1655abt		1677living
VanSchaick Cornelis A.	D	D7/24	1610ca	1635ca	1669
VanSchaick Cornelius	A	A7/36	1705 Oct17	1728 Oct 6	1776 Oct13
VanSchaick Cornelius	A	A7/18	1734 Sep15	1772 Dec 1	1797 Mar18
VanSchaick Emanuel	A	A7/72	1680ca	1703 Jun11	1706 Nov19
VanSchaick Francis S.	D	D7/21	1689 Jul	1722ca	1754ca
VanSchaick Hendrick C	A	A7/138	1646ca	1669	1709
VanSchaick Henrikje	D	D8/23	1646	1669	1709
VanSchaick Iden	D	D7/22	1665ca	1685 Oct28	1728

NAME	DIV.	NUMBER	BIRTH	MARRIAGE	DEATH
VanSchaick Janet	S	G50Ea	1755 Apr11	1778 Apr26	
VanSchaick Janet G50Ea	D	D7/19	1755 April	1778 Apr26	
VanSchaick John	S	G50Eaf	1730abt		
VanSchaick John H.	D	D7/20	1723ca	1747 Aug11	
VanSchaick Maria	A	A7/9	1773 Dec 8	1793 Mar 8	1845 Feb 3
VanStoutenburg Engelt.	A	A7/157	1653	1671	
Vanderburgh Aeltje	A	A4/117	1741 Dec 7	1758 Sep16	1817 Feb18
Vanderburgh Henry	A	A1/366	1685ca	1710ca	=A4/468
Vanderburgh Henry	A	A4/468	1685ca	1710ca	1750
Vanderburgh Henry Jr.	A	A4/234	1717 Apr 3	1739ca	1792bef
Vanderburgh Susanna	A	A1/183	1725	1758ca	
Vaughan Elizabeth	S	P23Eam	1650abt		
Vaughan George	S	K22Eaf	1635abt		1694ca
Vaughan Mary	S	K22Ea	1660ca	1683ca	
Vaughn Elizabeth	S	Q14Bam	1670abt		
Ver Planck Catalyntie	A	A7/151	1640ca		
Vermayes Benjamin	S	R11Ca	1624ca	1648 Dec21	1665bef
Vickers Abraham	A	A3/200	1691 Sep11		1756
Vickers Martha	A	A3/25	1786 Mar27	1807 Jun10	1873 May29
Vickers Thomas	A	A3/400	1670abt		1695
Vickers Thomas	A	A3/100	1720ca	1746 Sep13	1793 Dec30
Vickers Thomas Jr.	A	A3/50	1757 Mar 8	1779 Jun30	1829 Dec25
Vickery Benjamin	S	H17Ja	1665ca	1689ca	1718 Jan10
Vickery Benjamin	S	H48B	1693 Mar 3		1712 Apr24
Vickery Dorcas	S	H48D	1698 Mar13		
Vickery George	S	H17Jaf	1640abt		
Vickery Ichabod	S	H48G	1707 Oct30		
Vickery Joseph	S	H48A	1690 Jan 4		
Vickery Phebe	S	H48E	1701 Nov20		1718 May20
Vickery Sarah	S	H48F	1705 Apr11		
Vickery Thomas	S	H48C	1695 Nov15		
Vinal Martha	A	A14/167	1628ca	1646	
Vinall Mary	S	W28Ka	1684ca	1713 Mar23	1760bef
Vinall Stephen	S	W28Kaf	1660abt		
Vincent Ella Augustus	S	C56Ba	1858		
Vincent Mary	S	K17Eam	1635abt		
Vining Sarah	S	T24Gam	1675abt		
Vose Elizabeth	S	K16Fam	1635abt		
Wade David	S	Q62D	1732 Mar14		
Wade Deborah	S	X17Jb	1691	1735 Oct16	1738aft

NAME	DIV.	NUMBER	BIRTH	MARRIAGE	DEATH
Wade Hopestill	S	Q62A	1725 Jul13		
Wade Keziah	S	Q62C	1729 Oct18		
Wade Mary	S	Q62B	1727 Nov25		
Wade Rebecca	S	Q62E	1734 Jul29		
Wade Thomas Jr	S	Q21Da	1680ca	1722 Dec20	1789 Jan22
Wade Thomas Sr	S	Q21Daf	1655abt		
Wade Thomas Sr=Q21Daf	S	X17Jbf	1655abt		
Wadsworth Abigail	S	K16Ia	1670 Oct25	1693 Dec28	1744 Jan15
Wadsworth Abigail	S	K40Aam	1670 Oct25	1693 Dec28	=K16Ia
Wadsworth Alice	S	L14Da	1697 Apl15	1722 May10	1791 Jun 9
Wadsworth Elisha	S	L14Daf	1670abt		
Wadsworth John	S	K16Iaf	1645abt		
Wadsworth Mary	S	X23Aam	1640abt		
Wadsworth Mary=X23Aam	S	X23Cam	1640abt		
Wadsworth Robert	A	A3/20	1785 Nov 5		1867 Oct18
Wadsworth Sarah Ann	A	A3/5	1852 Oct15	1873 Apr10	1886 Jan18
Wadsworth Thomas	A	A3/80	1715abt	1741 Jan	
Wadsworth Thomas Jr.	A	A3/40	1747 Mar19	1768 Aug18	1830aft
Wadsworth Thomas W.	A	A3/10	1826 Feb10	1850 May30	1879 Sep11
Wainwright Francis	A	A16/190	1620ca	1647ca	1692
Wainwright Sarah	A	A16/95	1650ca		1688 Feb 3
Waite Thomas	S	C49Aa	1680ca		
Walcott Elizabeth	S	L16A	1688 Mar30	unm	1702 Jul12
Walcott Josiah	S	L13Aa	1649ca	1684 Feb19	1728 Feb 9
Walcott Josiah	S	L16B	1690 Dec21		1691 Jan 4
Walden Ann	S	H12Fam	1625abt		
Waldo Bethia	A	A19/375	1690abt		
Waldo Cornelius	A	A19/1500	1635abt		
Waldo Daniel	A	A19/750	1670abt		
Waldron Pieter	A	A7/78	1675 Jun25	1698 Sep 9	1725 May 3
Waldron Rebecca	A	A7/39	1719 Aug	1737 Nov28	
Waldron Willem	A	A7/156	1647	1671	
Wales Hannah	S	W33Bam	1650abt		
Walker Abigail	S	X75B	1711 Dec 3		
Walker David Davis	A	A1/12	1840 Jan19	1862 Dec25	1918 Oct 4
Walker Deborah	S	X75F	1719 Aug13		1795ca
Walker Dorothy	A	A1/3	1901 Jul 1	1921 Aug 6	1972 Oct 8
Walker Dorothy=A1/3	D	D2a13	1901 Jul 1	1921 Aug 6	1972 Oct 8
Walker Eliakim	S	X72C	1705ca		
Walker Elizabeth	S	H18E	1664 Sep28		

NAME	DIV.	NUMBER	BIRTH	MARRIAGE	DEATH
Walker Elnathan	S	X72D	1707ca		
Walker George E	A	A1/24	1797ca	1821 May22	1864 Oct28
Walker George Herbert	A	A1/6	1875 Jun11	1899 Jan17	1953 Jun24
Walker Hannah	A	A19/145	1648	1674	1686
Walker Hannah	A	A19/167	1669	1687	1704
Walker Jabez	S	H18F	1668 Jul 8		1741ca
Walker Jabez	S	H50F	1706ca		
Walker James	S	X23Gaf	1645abt		
Walker James	S	X72B	1704ca		
Walker James Jr	S	X23Da	1674 Dec24	1699 Oct 6	1749 Sep12
Walker James Sr=X23Gaf	S	X23Daf	1645abt		
Walker Jeremiah	S	H50D	1702 May17		
Walker John	S	H18A	1655		1676 Mar26
Walker John	S	H49B	1694ca		
Walker Lydia	S	X75E	1717 Jul31		
Walker Mary	S	K20Aam	1640abt		
Walker Mary	S	W33Da	1698 Jul28	1717 Nov 7	1739 Jan25
Walker Mary	S	H50C	1699 Sep14	1748 Mar 9	
Walker Mehitable	S	H49D	1698ca		
Walker Mercy	S	H50E	1704 Nov 7	1733 Jan 3	
Walker Nathan	S	X23Ga	1667 Jan28	1708 Jul29	1747 Dec23
Walker Nathan	S	X75A	1709 Oct27		
Walker Patience	S	H50H	1709ca		
Walker Peter	S	X72E	1710ca		1767 Aug 6
Walker Phebe	S	X75C	1713 Sep29		
Walker Rejoice	S	H50B	1697 May13	1732 Nov 9	
Walker Richard	S	H50A	1695 Jun 1		
Walker Sarah	S	X13Bam	1615abt		
Walker Sarah	A	A8/195	1622	1645	1700
Walker Sarah	S	W11Fa	1622ca	1645 Nov19	1700 Nov24
Walker Sarah	S	H18D	1662 Jul30		
Walker Sarah	S	X72A	1702ca		
Walker Sarah	S	H50G	1708ca		
Walker Sarah=A8/195	A	A5/75	1622	1645	1700
Walker Susanna	S	H49C	1696ca		
Walker Thomas	S	W33Daf	1670abt		
Walker Thomas	A	A1/48	1765ca	1785 Feb22	1800ca
Walker William	S	W11Faf	1595abt		
Walker William	S	H12Ca	1620ca	1654 Feb25	1697living
Walker William	S	H49A	1692ca		

NAME	DIV.	NUMBER	BIRTH	MARRIAGE	DEATH
Walker William	A	A5/150	1700abt		
Walker William	S	X75D	1715 Aug17		
Walker William #1	S	H18B	1657 Aug 2		d yng
Walker William Jr #2	S	H18C	1659 Aug 2		1743 Jan
Walling Elizabeth	S	C78Ca	1680ca		
Wallingford Judith	A	A1/297	1699	1721	
Walsingham Elizabeth	S	G6Aa	1485abt		
Walsingham William	S	G6Aaf	1460abt		
Walton Abraham	A	A8/18	1739ca	1766ca	1796 Dec21
Walton Jacob	A	A8/36	1703 Jul 3	1726 May14	1749 Oct17
Walton Maria Eliza	A	A8/9	1769 Mar15	1786 Nov15	1810 Mar22
Walton Thomas	A	A8/144	1650abt	1671	1689
Walton William	A	A8/72	1675ca	1698 Sept?	1747 May23
Wanton Edward	S	W45Abf	1650abt		
Wanton Michael	S	W45Ab	1679 Apr 9	1717 April1	1741 Jun13
Ward Abigail	S	A17A	1650abt	1681ca	1688
Ward Abigail	S	A39D	1706ca		
Ward Elizabeth	S	A17D	1670ca		d.yng
Ward Esther	S	F22Gam	1670abt		
Ward Martha	S	A17E	1672ca	1689 Dec 3	1724bef
Ward Mary	S	A17C	1660abt	2 mar.	1706living
Ward Rebecca	S	A17G	1678ca		d.yng
Ward Remember	S	A17B	1650abt	1679 May 1	1684 Jan 6
Ward Samuel	S	A17F	1673ca	1699 Nov13	1713bef
Ward Samuel	S	A39A	1702 Jun16		d.yng
Ward Samuel Jr	S	A13Ca	1638ca	1662ca	1690
Ward Samuel Sr	S	A13Caf	1610abt		
Ward Sarah #1	S	A39B	1703 May 7		d.yng
Ward Sarah #2	S	A39C	1705 bef		
Wardwell Grace	A	A2/99	1675ca	1701 Dec25	
Wardwell Sarah	A	A4/463	1680abt	1707	
Wardwell Uzal	A	A2/198	1639	1678ca	1742
Ware Lucy	A	A12/1a	1831 Aug28	1852Dec 30	1889Jun25
Warfield Clara J	S	N16Ha	1830ca		
Warner Augustine	A	A10/20	1611 Sep28	1638ca	1674 Dec24
Warner Augustine Jr.	A	A10/10	1642 Jun 3	1671ca	1681 Jun19
Warner AugustineA10/10	D	D28/25	1642 Jun 3	1671ca	1681 Jun19
Warner Mary	S	R12Eam	1630abt		
Warner Mildred	A	A10/5	1671ca	1689ca	1701 Mar26
Warner Mildred=A10/5	D	D28/24	1671ca	1689ca	1701Nar 26

NAME	DIV.	NUMBER	BIRTH	MARRIAGE	DEATH
Warren Abigail	S	W11E	1618ca	1639 Nov 8	1692ca
Warren Abigail	S	W18B	1655 Mar15		1689bef
Warren Abigail	S	W57B	1700 May 9	1722 Nov 1	1766 Dec 5
Warren Alice	S	W52D	1695 Sep 3	1716 May10	1733 May30
Warren Alice=A24Aam	S	W17F	1656 Aug2	1674 Dec23	1692ca
Warren Alice=D15/25	S	A24Aam	1656 Aug 2	1674 Dec23	1692ca
Warren Alice=W17F	D	D15/25	1656 Aug 2	1674 Dec23	1692ca
Warren Ann	S	L19B	1728 Jul 5	unm.	1757 Oct16
Warren Anna	S	W11B	1612ca	1633 Apr19	1675Feb19
Warren Anne	S	W46D	1690ca	1712 Apr 8	1740abt
Warren Benjamin	S	W18F	1670 Jan 8	1697 Apr22	1746 May30
Warren Benjamin	S	W57A	1698 Mar15		d. yg.
Warren Charles	S	L27C	1762 Apr14		1784 Nov30
Warren Daniel	S	W38Haf	1640abt		
Warren Deborah	S	W50Eam	1665abt		
Warren Edward	S	W52B	1690 Sep14		1691 Feb28
Warren Elizabeth	S	W11D	1616ca	1635Mar 14	1669 Mar9
Warren Elizabeth	S	W17E	1654 Sep15	1683ca	1689abt
Warren Elizabeth	S	W18E	1662 Aug15	1687 Jan19	1720ca
Warren Elizabeth	S	W52J	1710 Jan17	unmar	1744 Nov 5
Warren Elizabeth=W18E	S	R15Bam	1662Aug 15	1687 Jan19	1720ca
Warren Elizabeth=W18E	S	K30Dam	1662Aug 15	1687Jan19	1720ca
Warren George	S	L27E	1766 Sep20		
Warren Hannah	S	W57C	1704 Mar 1	1724 Aug 6	1768 Jan25
Warren Henry	S	L27D	1764 Mar21		
Warren Hope	S	W17C	1650bef		1688abt
Warren Hope	S	W46C	1690abt	1710 Jun12	1745 Dec
Warren Hope	S	W52G	1702 Aug 2	1722 Jul23	1728 May 3
Warren Jabez	S	W17L	1667ca		1701 Apr19
Warren James	S	W46A	1679 Jan13		1709 Dec25
Warren James	S	L19A	1726 Sep28	1754 Nov14	1808 Nov28
Warren James	S	L27A	1757 Oct18		
Warren James Jr	S	L15Ca	1700 Apl14	1737 Jan30	1757 Jul 2
Warren James Jr=L15Ca	S	W52F	1700 April14	1723 Jan30	1757 Jul 2
Warren James Sr=L15Caf	S	W31Eaf	1665ca	1687Jun 21	1715May 29
Warren James Sr=W17K	S	L15Caf	1665cat	1687Jun 21	1715May 29
Warren James Sr=W31Eaf	S	W17K	1665ca	1687 Jun21	1715 May29
Warren Jane	S	W17D	1652 Jan10	1672 Sep19	1682 Feb27
Warren Joanna	S	W46F	1690ca	1717 Aug 1	
Warren John	S	W17J	1663 Oct23		1688abt

NAME	DIV.	NUMBER	BIRTH	MARRIAGE	DEATH
Warren John	S	W52A	1688 Nov27		1689 Mar 1
Warren John	S	W46E	1689ca	(2)1737Jul	1768 Mar 3
Warren Joseph	S	W18C	1657 Jan8	1692 Dec20	1696 Dec28
Warren Joseph	S	W54A	1690abt		d yng
Warren Joseph	S	W54B	1693 Jan17	1722 Aug22	1750abt
Warren Joseph	S	W57H	1717 Sep 4		1746before
Warren Joseph= W11G	D	D9af23	1626ca	1652ca	1689 May
Warren Joseph=D9af23	S	R12Aaf	1626ca	1652ca	1689 May
Warren Joseph=R12Aaf	S	W11G	1626ca	1652ca	1689 May
Warren Joshua	S	W38Ha	1668 Jul 4	1695ca	1760 Jan30
Warren Josiah	S	L19E	1735 Mar 2		1736 Apr22
Warren Marcy	S	W52H	1704 Mar21	unmar	1745 Jan17
Warren Mary	S	W11A	1610	1629ca	1683 Mar27
Warren Mary	A	A6/133	1624	1642	1691
Warren Mary	S	W17H	1660 Mar9		1690bef
Warren Mary	S	W52I	1707 Jan14	unmar	1795 Feb 4
Warren Mercy	S	W17G	1657 Feb20	1677 Feb28	1727aft
Warren Mercy	S	W57I	1721 May15	1762 Jan 7	1798 Mar21
Warren Mercy =R12Aa	S	W18A	1653 Sep23	1674 Jan6	1747 Mar
Warren Mercy=A24Abm	D	D9a23	1653Sep23	1674 Jan 6	1747 Mar
Warren Mercy=A5/37	A	A8/97	1658 Feb20	1678 Feb28	1727aft
Warren Mercy=A8/97	A	A5/37	1658 Feb20	1678 Feb28	1727aft
Warren Mercy=D9a23	S	R12Aa	1653 Sep23	1674 Jan 6	1747 Mar
Warren Mercy=R12Aa	S	A24Abm	1653Sep 23	1674Jan 6	1747 Mar
Warren Nathaniel	A	A5/74	1624ca	1645	=A8/194
Warren Nathaniel	S	W15D	1642ca	1665ca	
Warren Nathaniel	S	W57D	1706 Jul20	1734 May23	1767 Feb26
Warren Nathaniel 2nd	S	W17I	1661 Mar10	1692abt	1707 Oct29
Warren Nathaniel=A5/74	S	W11F	1624ca	1645	1667
Warren Nathaniel=W11F	A	A8/194	1624ca	1645	1667
Warren Patience	S	W18D	1660 Mar15	1686 Dec16	1719aft
Warren Patience	S	W52E	1697 Jan13	1721 April11	1729 Jan31
Warren Patience	S	W57G	1715 Oct27		1789 Nov27
Warren Priscilla	S	W54C	1696 Jun10	unm.	1716living
Warren Priscilla	S	W57F	1712Aug12	unm.	
Warren Richard 2d	S	W17A	1646	1678ca	1696 Jan23
Warren Richard MF	S	W10A	1580ca	1610bef	=A5/148
Warren Richard MF=W10A	A	A5/148	1580ca	1610bef	1673 Oct 2
Warren Richard MF=W10A	D	D25/25	1580ca	1610bef	1673 Oct 2
Warren Richard MF=W10A	S	K11Aaf	1580ca	1610bef	1673 Oct 2

NAME	DIV.	NUMBER	BIRTH	MARRIAGE	DEATH
Warren Samuel	S	W46B	1682 Mar 7	1703 Jan26	1750ca
Warren Sarah	S	L19Cam	1720abt		
Warren Sarah	S	L19C	1730 May23	1755 Aug16	1797 Mar15
Warren Sarah=K11Aa	S	W11C	1610	1634 Mar28	1695aft
Warren Sarah=K35Ham	S	W41Dam	1649Aug 29	1673ca	1692aft
Warren Sarah=W11C	S	K11Aa	1610	1634 Mar28	1695aft
Warren Sarah=W17B	S	K35Ham	1649Aug 29	1673ca	1692aft
Warren Sarah=W31Aa	S	W52C	1692 May27	2 Mar	1756 Aug25
Warren Sarah=W41Dam	S	W17B	1649 Aug29	1673ca	1692aft
Warren Sarah=W52C	S	W31Ea	1692 May27	1712 Oct 9	1756 Aug25
Warren Winslow	S	L19D	1733 May23		1747 Mar 9
Warren Winslow	S	L27B	1759 Mar24		
Warriner Hannah	S	N10Aa	1643 Aug17	1660 Nov 1	1721bef
Warriner William	S	N10Aaf	1620abt		
Washburn Abigail	S	K71E	1688 Jun 2		
Washburn Anna	S	K80B	1695 Feb 1	unm	1747 Jan14
Washburn Benjamin	S	K22F	1655ca	unm.	1690
Washburn Benjamin	S	K75C	1687 Jan17		
Washburn Benjamin	S	K73E	1689ca		
Washburn Benjamin	S	K74H	1693ca		
Washburn Cornelius	S	K75I	1702 May 6		
Washburn Deborah	S	T21Bam	1710abt		
Washburn Deliverance	S	K72G	1700abt		
Washburn Ebenezer	S	K75D	1690 Feb23	no issue	1727 Oct10
Washburn Ebenezer	S	K74F	1691ca		
Washburn Edward	S	K74C	1684		
Washburn Edward	S	K80D	1700 Dec 8		
Washburn Elisabeth	S	K75A	1684 Oct12		
Washburn Elisabeth	S	K80I	1710 Apr 5		
Washburn Elizabeth	S	K22H	1662ca	2 Mar	1741 Feb27
Washburn Elizabeth	S	K72A	1675abt		
Washburn Ephraim	S	K74I	1695ca		
Washburn Gideon	S	K80F	1704 Aug16		
Washburn Hannah	S	K73F	1690ca		
Washburn Hannah	S	K74G	1692ca		
Washburn Hepzibah	S	K72C	1685abt		
Washburn Israel	S	K73C	1683 Feb24		
Washburn James	S	Q20Daf	1670abt		
Washburn James	S	K22J	1672 May15	1693 Dec20	1749 Jun11
Washburn James	S	K80C	1698 Oct 6		

NAME	DIV.	NUMBER	BIRTH	MARRIAGE	DEATH
Washburn Jane	S	K22I	1672bef	1690aft	1698bef
Washburn Joanna	S	K75F	1693 Oct12	unm	1728living
Washburn John	S	K22A	1646ca	1679 Apr16	1719
Washburn John	S	K71B	1682 Apr 5		
Washburn John Jr	S	K13Aa	1620ca	1645 Dec 6	1686 Nov12
Washburn John Sr	S	K13Aaf	1600abt		
Washburn Jonathan	S	K22E	1655ca	1683ca	1726bef
Washburn Jonathan	S	K74D	1686ca		
Washburn Joseph	S	K22D	1653ca	1677ca	1733 Apr20
Washburn Joseph	S	K71C	1683 Jul 7		
Washburn Joseph	S	K74E	1690ca		
Washburn Josiah	S	K71A	1679 Feb11		
Washburn Josiah	S	K75B	1686 May12		
Washburn Martha	S	K75E	1692 Feb27		
Washburn Martha	S	K80H	1708 Jan10		
Washburn Mary	S	K22G	1661ca	1690ca	1740 Feb28
Washburn Mary	S	Q20Da	1694 Oct28	1722 Nov 8	1774 Mar31
Washburn Mary=Q20Da	S	K80A	1694 Oct28	1722 Nov 8	1774 Mar31
Washburn Miles	S	K74A	1675abt		
Washburn Moses	S	K80E	1702 Sep 9		
Washburn Nathan	S	K75G	1699 Jan29		1728bef
Washburn Nathaniel	S	K72B	1680abt		living1729
Washburn Nehemiah	S	K73D	1686 May20		
Washburn Noah	S	K73B	1682 Jul11		
Washburn Patience	S	K72E	1690abt		
Washburn Rebecca	S	K71F	1690ca		
Washburn Samuel	S	K22C	1652ca	1677ca	1720 Mar24
Washburn Samuel	S	K73A	1678 Apr 6		
Washburn Sarah	S	K22K	1675ca	1696 Jan12	1746
Washburn Sarah	S	K80G	1706 Oct 2		
Washburn Thomas	S	K22B	1648ca	3 Mar	1730ca
Washburn Thomas	S	K72D	1690abt		
Washburn Timothy	S	K72F	1700abt		
Washburn William	S	K71D	1686 Feb16		
Washington Augustine	A	A10/2	1694ca	1731 Mar 6	1743 Apr12
Washington George	A	A10/1	1732 Feb22	1759 Jan 6	1799 Dec14
Washington John	A	A10/8	1634ca	1658 Dec 1	1677ca
Washington Lawrence	A	A10/32	1568ca	1588 Aug3	1616 Dec13
Washington Lawrence	A	A10/16	1602ca	1633 Dec	1653 Jan21
Washington Lawrence	A	A10/4	1659	1689ca	1697 Feb

NAME	DIV.	NUMBER	BIRTH	MARRIAGE	DEATH
Washington Robert	A	A10/64	1544ca	1565ca	1621ca
Wateman Joseph Jr	S	W42Ga	1676 Jan 2	1709 Jun16	1715 Nov23
Water Samuel	S	R28Jaf	1710abt		
Waterhouse Eleaser	S	C17Ka	1755ca		
Waterman Abigail	S	W44D	1681 Dec31	1703ca	1729 Aug15
Waterman Anna	S	A61H	1720 Mar 6		d.yng
Waterman Anthony	S	W44E	1684 Jun 4	1709ca	1715 Apr 3
Waterman Anthony	S	A69D	1716 Jun23		
Waterman Benjamin	S	K159G	1748 Jul15		d.yng
Waterman Bethiah	S	W44F	1687 Aug20	1710 Feb20	1746 Nov28
Waterman Ebenezer	S	K159A	1738 May12		d.yng
Waterman Eleazer	S	A69F	1721 Aug 3		
Waterman Elizabeth	S	R19Ham	1665abt		
Waterman Elizabeth	S	K31Gam	1670abt		=K39Aam
Waterman Elizabeth	S	K39Aam	1670abt		=K31Gam
Waterman Elizabeth	S	W19Fa	1679 Sep7	1699 Dec28	=W44C
Waterman Elizabeth	S	W44C	1679 Sep 7	1699 Dec28	1708 Oct
Waterman Elizabeth	S	K31Ia	1707ca	1731 Nov17	1778aft
Waterman Isaac	S	A61A	1703 May10		
Waterman John	S	A24Caf	1660abt		
Waterman John	S	A25Eaf	1660abt		
Waterman John	S	A26Aaf	1660abt		
Waterman John	S	A26Aa	1685 Sep23	1709 Dec29	1761 Jun 8
Waterman John	S	A69E	1718 Jul 3		
Waterman Joseph	S	W44B	1676 Jan16	1709 Jun16	1715 Nov23
Waterman Joseph	S	A69B	1710 Feb 2		
Waterman Joseph=W16Da	S	W42Gaf	1650ca	1673ca	1710 Jan 3
Waterman Joseph=W19Faf	S	W16Da	1650ca	1673ca	1710 Jan3
Waterman Joseph=W42Gaf	S	W19Faf	1650ca	1673ca	1710 Jan3
Waterman Josiah	S	A61B	1704 Mar 5		
Waterman Lydia	S	W44G	1689 Feb20	1714 Dec23	1750 Jan17
Waterman Lydia	S	A69G	1724 Apr 7		
Waterman Mary	S	A61F	1715 Feb25		
Waterman Mary	S	K159H	1750 Nov14		d.yng
Waterman Nathaniel #1	S	K159F	1746 Jun 9		d.yng
Waterman Nathaniel #2	S	K159I	1752 Sep23		d.yng
Waterman Perez	S	A69C	1713 Oct 8		
Waterman Rebecca	S	A61D	1710 Oct 9		
Waterman Robert	S	W16Daf	1625abt		
Waterman Robert	S	A24Ca	1681 Feb 9	1702 Mar19	1749 Jan16

NAME	DIV.	NUMBER	BIRTH	MARRIAGE	DEATH
Waterman Robert	S	A25Ea	1681 Feb 9	1723 Dec 5	1749 Jan16
Waterman Robert	S	K40Baf	1695abt		
Waterman Robert	S	A61E	1712 Mar 2		
Waterman Robert	S	K159J	1755 Jan15		d.yng
Waterman Samuel	S	K31Iaf	1685abt		
Waterman Samuel	S	K159D	1743 Jun25		
Waterman Samuel=A61G	S	K40Ba	1718 Aug11	1737 Mar16	1787 Nov16
Waterman Samuel=K40Ba	S	A61G	1718 Aug11	1737 Mar16	1787 Nov16
Waterman Sarah	S	W44A	1674 May 4	1695abt	1758 Apr25
Waterman Sarah	S	A69A	1709 Nov 8		
Waterman Seth	S	K159C	1740 Feb 1		
Waterman Thomas	S	A61C	1707 Oct		
Waterman Thomas	S	K159E	1745 May 9		d.yng
Waterman Zebediah	S	K159B	1739 Jun17		1756 May 5
Waters Asa	A	A2/28	1741 Jan11	1764 Jun11	1813 Nov2
Waters Asa	S	R114B	1760 Feb11		
Waters Asa Jr	A	A2/14	1769 Oct2	1802 May19	1841 Dec24
Waters Bethia	S	R115A	1757 Dec28		
Waters Chloe	S	R114J	1775 Sep19		
Waters Daniel	S	R28Kb	1735ca	1757ca	
Waters Daniel	S	R114E	1765 Jul 5		1781
Waters Hannah	S	A37A	1700ca		
Waters Hannah	S	R114F	1767 Jan12		
Waters Isaac (Watrous)	S	P20Aaf	1665abt		
Waters John	A	A2/224	1640	1663	1707
Waters Jonathan	A	A2/56	1715 Jul31	1738 Aug10	1786 Sep13
Waters Lucee	S	R115B	1759 Oct20		
Waters Matilda	S	R114C	1761 May31		
Waters Mehitable	S	P20Aa	1690ca	1709 Sep 7	1723aft
Waters Mercy	A	A2/61	1697 Jul24	1729 Aug28	1785after
Waters Moley	S	R114I	1773 Apr6		
Waters Nathaniel	A	A2/112	1671 Feb 6	1699 Dec12	1718ca
Waters Nehemiah	S	R114A	1758 Jul 9		1790bef
Waters Rebecca	S	R114D	1762 Oct 8		
Waters Richard	A	A2/122	1669 Nov19	1697 Mar 3	1725ca
Waters Samuel	S	R28Kbf	1710abt		
Waters Samuel	S	R115C	1762 Nov27		
Waters Samuel	S	R114H	1770 Oct 6		1790living
Waters Susan Holman	A	A2/7	1803 Apr	1824 Jan27	1866 Feb3
Waters William	S	A17Cb	1660abt	1699 Jul17	1703ca

NAME	DIV.	NUMBER	BIRTH	MARRIAGE	DEATH
Waters Zebulon	S	R28Ja	1734 Jan 3	1757 Sep21	1730 May29
Waters Zebulon	S	R114R	1768 Aug23		
Watson Benjamin	S	L29C	1761 Feb 8		1781 Jun24
Watson Benjamin M.	S	L31D	1774 Nov		
Watson Brooke	S	L31J	1788 Jun		
Watson Daniel	S	L31F	1779 Dec		
Watson Elizabeth	S	L29B	1759 Feb17		
Watson Elkanah	S	L20Ca	1732 Feb27	1754 Nov7	1804 Sept7
Watson Elkanah	S	L30B	1758 Jan22		
Watson Ellen	S	L29D	1764 Apr12		
Watson George	S	L31B	1771 Apr		
Watson John	S	L20Iaf	1725abt		
Watson John	S	L20Ia	1748 Aug26	1769 Apr15	1826 Feb 1
Watson John	S	L31A	1769		
Watson John=L20Baf	S	L20Caf	1710abt		
Watson John=L20Caf	S	L20Baf	1710abt		
Watson Lucia	S	L30E	1765 Nov11 unm		792 Mar20
Watson Lucia	S	L31E	1776		
Watson Marston	S	L30A	1756 May28		
Watson Mary	S	X21Cam	1650abt		
Watson Patty	S	L30D	1762 Oct16		
Watson Phebe	S	H14Cam	1640abt		
Watson Phebe	S	H16Cam	1640abt		
Watson Phebe	S	H17Cam	1640abt		
Watson Priscilla	S	L30C	1760 Sep30		
Watson Sarah Marston	S	L31C	1772		
Watson William	S	L20Ba	1730 May 6	1756 Sep22	1815 Apr27
Watson William	S	L29A	1757 Aug18 unm		1781 Mar 4
Watson William #1	S	L31G	1781 Oct		d. yng.
Watson William #2	S	L31H	1783 Oct		
Watson Winslow	S	L31I	1786 Apr		
Wear James Hutchenson	A	A1/56	1789 Sep30	1812 Oct27	1832 Apr
Wear James Hutchenson	A	A1/14	1838 Sep30	1866 Dec 4	1893 Jun14
Wear Jonathan	A	A1/112	1755 abt		1832 abt
Wear Lucretia(Loulie)	A	A1/7	1874 Sep17	1899 Jan17	1961 Aug28
Wear William Gault	A	A1/28	1817 Dec11	1837 Nov 2	
Weatherstone Donnie	S	G54Cb	1905abt	1941	
Webb Aaron	S	P46A	1721		d yng
Webb Christopher	S	P21Fa	1689 Dec30	1720 Jul 4	1724
Webb Ebenezer	S	R56A	1712 Apr26		1713 Jun 8

NAME	DIV.	NUMBER	BIRTH	MARRIAGE	DEATH
Webb Ebenezer	S	R56C	1718 Jan12		
Webb Hannah	S	R56B	1715 Jun29		
Webb Joshua	S	R56D	1721 Feb 2		
Webb Peter	S	P21Faf	1660abt		
Webb Samuel Jr	S	R19Ba	1690 May14	1711 Oct 8	1779 Mar 6
Webb Samuel Sr	S	R19Baf	1665abt		
Webster Aaron	S	R52C	1716 Feb24		
Webster Abiel	S	R52D	1718 Jul31		
Webster Abigail	S	R52J	1731 Sep23		
Webster Ann	S	R52G	1724 Apr18		
Webster Elisha	S	R52A	1713 Nov12		
Webster Elizabeth	A	A3/85	1723 Nov 1	1751 Mar25	
Webster Jerusha	S	R52B	1714 Jan 8		
Webster John	A	A17/84	1605ca	1630ca	1645ca
Webster John	A	A17/42	1632	1653 Jun13	1716aft
Webster John	A	A3/340	1662		1753
Webster John	S	R52I	1728 Sep 4		
Webster John Jr	S	R18Fa	1680ca	1712 Dec25	1753ca
Webster John Sr	S	R18Faf	1655abt		
Webster Jonathan	S	R18Aaf	1665abt		
Webster Lucy	A	A17/21	1664Dec 19		1718living
Webster Mary	S	R52E	1720 Jul23		
Webster Michael	A	A3/170	1700abt		1764
Webster Osee	S	R52K	1734 Apr 7		
Webster Robert	S	R52L	1736 Apr 8		
Webster Sarah	S	R52F	1722 Apr17		
Webster Susanna	S	R18Aa	1686 Apr25	1739 May10	1757 Nov27
Webster Susannah	S	R52H	1726 Jul 8		
Weeden Elizabeth	S	G9Aa	1575abt		
Weeks Abagail	S	F33G	1690 Jan28		
Weeks Ebenezer	S	F33F	1688 Mar29		
Weeks Elizabeth	S	F33D	1683 May17		
Weeks John	S	F17Aa	1655ca	1675 Jan 7	1730bef
Weeks John	S	F33B	1678 Aug18		
Weeks Mary	S	F17Ia	1669 Jan16	1696 Mar 7	1743aft
Weeks Mary	S	F33J	1696 Sep 3		
Weeks Mehitable	S	F33H	1693ca		
Weeks Nathaniel	S	F33A	1676		
Weeks Renew	A	A6/121	1660 Aug12	1679ca	1703 Jul29
Weeks Shubael	S	F33E	1685 Mar15		

NAME	DIV.	NUMBER	BIRTH	MARRIAGE	DEATH
Weeks Thomas M	S	N15La	1794ca		
Weeks Uriah	S	F33I	1693 Feb 3		d. yng
Weeks William	A	A6/242	1628ca	1649	1677ca
Weeks William	S	F17Iaf	1645abt		
Weeks William	S	F33C	1680 Feb11		
Weir Rebecca	A	A5/7	1770abt	1793 Oct17	1802ca
Weir Samuel	A	A5/14	1731ca		1811
Welch Betsey	S	G51Da	1790ca		
Weld Lucy	S	N13Ba	1735ca		
Welles Samuel	A	A4/506	1662		1733
Wellington Mary	S	W38Bam	1640abt		
Wells Bethia	A	A14/179	1655	1672	1733
Wells Hannah	S	C17Ca	1745ca		
Wells Mary	A	A12/219	1620abt	1642ca	1648
Wells Ruth	A	A4/253	1697 Jan29	1725 Jan 5	1731 Apr 2
Wells Susan	S	C19Fa	1770ca		
Welson John	S	W43Baf	1660abt		
Wensley John	S	L12Caf	1645abt		
Wensley Sarah	S	L12Ca	1673 Aug11	1700 Jul11	1753 Dec16
Wensley Sarah	S	W52Fam	1680abt		
Wentworth Joane	S	G7Aa	1520 ca		
West Abigail	S	X26Hb	1716 Jul23	1750 Nov15	1785 Sep28
West Almy	S	K68E	1729 Jan11	unm.	1763 Jan 3
West Amy	S	K21E	1693 May22	1726 Nov 6	1757aft
West Ann	S	K21C	1688 Jul 9	unm.	1761abt
West Anne	S	K68D	1727 Oct 8		
West Audria	S	K66A	1748 Jan 2		
West Bartholomew	S	K12Eaf	1630abt		
West Bartholomew	S	K21D	1690 Jul31	1747 Jul16	1770abt
West Bartholomew	S	K68G	1734 Nov 8		
West Bartholomew 1	S	K66C	1753 Nov26		d.yng
West Bartholomew 2	S	K66D	1756 May30	unm.	
West Benjamin	S	X26Hbf	1690abt		
West Edward	S	K66E	1758ca		
West Elizabeth=A1/377	A	A6/59	1694	1716	
West Elizabeth=A6/59	A	A1/377	1694	1716	
West Esther	S	X17Bb	1680 Sep30	1706 Sep19	1726living
West Eunice	S	K21H	1699 Jun21	1734 Dec 5	1745bef
West Grizzell	S	Q19Ea	1729 Oct 9	1745 Dec28	1810ca
West Hannah	S	X26Hbm	1690abt		

NAME	DIV.	NUMBER	BIRTH	MARRIAGE	DEATH
West Hannah	S	K68A	1720 Apr21		
West John	A	A6/118	1670abt		
West John	S	K21G	1697 Apr27	1729ca	1778
West John	S	Q19Eaf	1700abt		
West John	S	K69C	1735ca		1789aft
West Katharine	S	K21A	1684 Sep 9		1775bef
West Katherine	S	K69A	1730 May22		d.yng
West Lois	S	K21I	1701 Apr12	1730ca	1770aft
West Marcy	S	K68B	1722 Jul 7	unm.	1762 Apr23
West Marcy/Mary	S	K69B	1732 Feb19		
West Mercy	S	K66G	1761aft		1780living
West Peter	S	X17Bbf	1655abt		
West Samuel	S	K68C	1725 Apr 3		
West Sarah=K21B	S	K35Fa	1686 Aug 1	1710ca	1775 Dec 5
West Sarah=K35Fa	S	K21B	1686 Aug 1	1710ca	1775 Dec 5
West Stephen	S	K12Ea	1654ca	1683ca	1748 Aug12
West Stephen	S	K35Faf	1665abt		
West Stephen	S	K21F	1695 May19	1718 Jan15	1769 Jul 7
West Stephen	S	K68F	1732 Mar14		
West Susannah	S	K68H	1737 Dec29		
West Susannah	S	G32Bam	1737 Mar28		1827 Jun
West Thomas	S	K66F	1759ca	unm.	1780bef
West William	S	K66B	1750 Feb 1		
Weston Abner	S	T18Aa	1708ca	1729 Mar 2	1786ca
Weston Abraham	S	T52G	1772ca		
Weston Anna	S	T53E	1758 Mar29	unm	1833 Sep19
Weston Benjamin	S	T20Fb	1701 Nov14	1765 Mar13	1773 May 5
Weston Benjamin	S	T52C	1758ca		
Weston Deborah	S	T45D	1743		
Weston Desire	S	T21D	1730 Apr 4	1750 Oct31	1796 Jul23
Weston Desire	S	T52A	1752ca		
Weston Edmund	S	T20Fbf	1675abt		
Weston Hannah	S	T45C	1740	unm.	1823 Jan29
Weston Hannah	S	T52F	1770ca		
Weston Isaac	S	T21B	1724 Jun14	1748 Jun30	1763living
Weston Isaac	S	T53C	1754 Feb27		
Weston Jacob	S	T21C	1727 May14	unm.	1760bef
Weston Jacob	S	T53D	1756 Sep20		
Weston John	S	T18Aaf	1680abt		
Weston Joseph	S	T52E	1765ca	unm.	

NAME	DIV.	NUMBER	BIRTH	MARRIAGE	DEATH
Weston Mary	S	T53B	1752 May 6		
Weston Mary	S	T52H	1775ca	unm.	
Weston Micah	S	T45A	1730ca		
Weston Nathan	S	T12Ia	1688 Feb 8	1715 Feb21	1754 Oct11
Weston Nathan	S	T21A	1723 Jul11	1751 Aug29	
Weston Nathan	S	T52B	1754ca		
Weston Patience	S	T53A	1749 Mar23		
Weston Poly	S	C53Ca	1800abt		
Weston Seth	S	T45B	1732ca		1764 Mar22
Weston Zadoc	S	T52D	1760ca		
Westwood Sarah	A	A12/119	1644ca	1661 May30	1730 Mar24
Westwood William	A	A12/238	1603ca	1630	1669ca
Wetmore Charity	D	D33am22	1760		
Wheat Anna	S	R66D	1736		
Wheat Hannah	S	R66E	1738 Jul16		
Wheat Jemima	S	R66F	1740		
Wheat Mary	S	R66C	1733		
Wheat Samuel	S	R19Laf	1675abt		
Wheat Sarah	S	R66A	1731 Oct 3		
Wheat Solomon	S	R19La	1700ca	1730ca	1797 Oct24
Wheat Solomon	S	R66B	1731 Dec19		
Wheaton Benjamin	A	A2/84	1661 Feb	1693abt	1726abt
Wheaton Mary	A	A2/21	1718 Oct23	1734 Feb13	
Wheaton Robert	A	A2/168	1610abt	1636ca	1696ca
Wheaton Samuel	A	A2/42	1693 Aug20		1717 Feb24
Wheeler Abigail	S	C25Ha	1685Ca		
Wheeler Betsey S	A	A1/47	1800 May30	1818 Mar 9	1881 Feb23
Wheeler Betsey S	D	D2/17	1800 May30	1818 Mar 9	=A1/147
Wheeler Elizabeth	A	A6/29	1717 Jun 9	1735 Jun 5	
Wheeler Helen H	S	N16Ba	1816ca		
Wheeler Heman	S	N16Baf	1780abt		
Wheeler Henry	A	A6/232	1635ca	1659ca	1696bef
Wheeler James	A	A6/116	1667 May27	1690ca	1740abt
Wheeler James Jr	A	A1/376	1697	1716	1740
Wheeler James Jr	A	A6/58	1697 Mar27	1716 Mar 8	1740abt
Wheeler Jarvis	A	A1/94	1774 Sep22	1797 Feb12	1852 Mar 3
Wheeler Jarvis	D	D2a18	1774 Sep22	1797 Feb12	1852 Mar 3
Wheeler Jeremiah	A	A1/188	1731 Mar23	1753 Jan 4	1811 Feb26
Wheeler Martha	A	A3/399	1670abt		
Wheeler Martha	S	C38Ca	1727		

NAME	DIV.	NUMBER	BIRTH	MARRIAGE	DEATH
Wheeler Mary	S	K36Gb	1690ca	1715 Dec 1	1740aft
Wheeler Simeon	S	N14Ha	1770abt		
Wheelock Eleazer	S	T13Haf	1660abt		
Wheelock Mary	S	T28A	1728 Nov26	1746 Dec29	1809 Jan29
Wheelock Ralph	S	T13Ha	1682 Feb12	1726 Sep30	1748 Oct13
Wheelwright Mary	S	L13Cam	1640abt		
Whelden Catherine	S	H11Ba	1615ca	1639 Oct 9	1688living
Whelden Gabriel	S	H11Baf	1590ca		
Whipple Susannah	A	A19/213	1662	1683	1713
Whippo Priscilla	A	A1/35	1763ca		1838 Aug26
Whitcomb Hannah	S	P21Da	1706	1729 Mar14	
Whitcomb Israel	S	P21Caf	1680abt		
Whitcomb Israel	S	P21Daf	1680abt		=P21Caf
Whitcomb Mary	S	P21Ca	1703 Mar 9	1724 Jun 8	1776 Aug 8
White Alice	D	D30a20	1510abt		
White Ann	A	A5/131	1600	1620	1648
White Ann	A	A11/11	1685 Jul 4	1704ca	1772 Mar
White Barbara Elin	D	D33/17/3	1949 Oct29	1979 Jun 8	
White Benjamin	A	A11/22	1626ca	1681 Jan21	1722 Jan9
White Elizabeth	A	A3/217	1708	1724Apr 28	
White Gideon	S	L18Baf	1720abt		
White Guy Jr.	A	A3/434	1680abt		1712
White H Leslie 3rd	D	D33/17/1	1942Nov25		1968Feb25
White H Leslie Jr	D	D33/18	1921Dec 16	2 Mar	
White H Leslie Sr	D	D33/19	1897 Feb3	1919Sep 3	1982Sep 9
White Joanna	S	L18Ba	1744ca	1770 Jun16	1829 May 2
White John	A	A11/44	1615abt	1640 Apr10	1691 Apr15
White John	A	A19/190	1690abt	1716	1752
White Mary	A	A16/239	1590	1614	1652
White Mary	A	A4/449	1690	1711	1777
White Robert Furneau	D	D33a20	1851 Dec 8	1877Jan 23	1938Mar 14
White Sarah	A	A19/95	1719Feb 19	1749Nov 16	1789ca
White Susanna	S	L10Ab	1600ca	1621 May12	1654 Dec18
White Timothy Joshua	D	D33/17/4	1962Dec 27		
White Virginia Louise	D	D33/17/2	1946Nov 28	1985 Jun 8	
Whitfield Abigail	S	R12Dbm	1625abt		
Whiting Abigail	A	A12/37	1665ca		1733 May 7
Whiting Anne	S	R41A	1698 Jan 2		
Whiting Azariah	S	R26Ea	1711 Aug 9	1753 Jul12	
Whiting Bernice	S	R74H	1733		

NAME	DIV.	NUMBER	BIRTH	MARRIAGE	DEATH
Whiting Charles	S	R21Da	1692 Jul 5	1716 Jan10	1738 Mar 7
Whiting Charles	S	R74D	1725	twin	
Whiting Ebenezer	S	R74I	1735 May18		
Whiting Eliphalet	S	R41J	1715 Apr 8		1736 Aug 9
Whiting Elisha	S	R41K	1717 Jan17		1725living
Whiting Elizabeth	S	R41C	1702 Feb11		
Whiting Elizabeth	S	R74E	1725	twin	
Whiting Elizabeth	S	R102D	1759 Oct 6		
Whiting Ephraim	A	A1/354	1699	1731	1788
Whiting Ephraim	S	R102B	1757 Jan21		
Whiting Gamaliel	S	R74F	1727 Sep		
Whiting John	A	A12/74	1635ca	1654ca	1689 Sep 8
Whiting John	S	R26Eaf	1685abt		
Whiting John	S	R41F	1705 Feb20		
Whiting John	S	R74B	1719 Aug 3		
Whiting John	S	R102A	1754 Aug 6		
Whiting John=A12/174	S	R17Aaf	1645abt		
Whiting Joseph	S	R41E	1705 Feb17	unm.	1722 Mar 1
Whiting Joseph	S	R41M	1722ca		1725living
Whiting Katherine	A	A19/107	1691ca	1714Dec 31	1731 Apr 1
Whiting Martha	S	R41H	1710 Mar12		1719 Jun29
Whiting Mary	S	R17Bam	1655abt		
Whiting Mary	S	R41I	1712 Nov24		1736 Aug 9
Whiting Mary	S	R74A	1717		
Whiting Nathan	S	R41N	1724 May 4		
Whiting Patience	S	R102C	1757 Jan21		
Whiting Samuel	S	R17Aa	1670ca	1696 Sep14	1725 Sep27
Whiting Samuel	S	R41B	1700 Feb20		1718
Whiting Samuel	S	R41L	1720 May15		
Whiting Samuel III	A	A19/214	1662	1686	1714
Whiting Susanna	A	A1/177	1734 Sep14	1757 Jan14	
Whiting Sybil	S	R41G	1708 May 6		
Whiting Sybil	S	R74C	1722		
Whiting William	A	A12/148	1600abt		1643abt
Whiting William	S	R21Daf	1670abt		
Whiting William	S	R41D	1704 Jan22		
Whiting William	S	R74G	1731		
Whitman Abigail	S	T20Aa	1702 Sep22	1720 Oct13	1778 Aug30
Whitman Ebenezer	S	T20Aaf	1675abt		
Whitman Elizabeth	S	T62B	1732 Aug 6	unm.	1765 Feb 8

NAME	DIV.	NUMBER	BIRTH	MARRIAGE	DEATH
Whitman Hannah	S	K29Fam	1685abt		
Whitman James	S	T62D	1738 Jan 2		1747 Jun 9
Whitman John	A	A13/134	1603ca		1692ca
Whitman John	S	G31Aaf	1700abt		
Whitman John	S	T24Ga	1703 Feb28	1729 Nov10	1792 Jan 7
Whitman John	S	T62C	1735 Mar17		
Whitman Judith	S	X23Cbm	1650abt		
Whitman Judith=X23Cbm	S	X24Bam	1650abt		
Whitman Naomi	S	Q13Ca	1664ca	1686 Dec	1711aft
Whitman Nicholas	S	T24Gaf	1675abt		
Whitman Samuel	S	T62A	1730 Sep26		
Whitman Sarah	A	A13/67	1632ca	1656ca	1718 Jun11
Whitman Sarah	S	C78Ga	1696		
Whitman Susanna	A	A6/49	1658 Feb28	1683 Jul25	1725ca
Whitman Thomas	S	Q13Caf	1640abt		
Whitman Valentine	A	A6/98	1630abt	1650ca	1701 Jan26
Whitman Zachariah Jr	S	G23A	1747		1806
Whitman Zachariah Sr	S	G31Aa	1722		1793
Whitmarsh Ann	A	A19/185	1702	1726	1750
Whitmarsh Judith	S	T24Eam	1675abt		
Whitmarsh Judith	S	Q21Cam	1675abt		=Q21Eam
Whitmarsh Judith	S	Q21Eam	1675abt		=T24Eam
Whitmarsh Mary	A	A19/189	1698	1716	
Whitmarsh Nicholas	S	K142A	1698 Mar20		
Whitmarsh Nicholas Jr	S	K36Ba	1673 Aug21	1698ca	1706bef
Whitmarsh Nicholas Sr	S	K36Baf	1650abt		
Whitney Amy	S	C17Ib	1755ca		
Whitney Elizabeth	A	A1/437	1684ca	1705	1763
Whiton Azariah	S	R26Maf	1710abt		
Whiton Phebe	S	R26Ma	1736 Mar16	1755 Jan23	1793 Nov16
Whiton Rachel	S	Q23Ca	1700 Jul12	1721 Oct19	1792 Jan30
Whiton Thomas	S	Q23Caf	1675abt		
Wicks Elizabeth	S	C82Ba	1706		
Wightman James	S	C74Da	1621		
Wignol Judith	A	A16/179	1600abt	1619	1664
Wilbour Clark	S	B22L	1742 Nov 1		
Wilbour Daniel	S	B22G	1729 Jun 1		
Wilbour Deborah	S	B22K	1738 Aug29		
Wilbour Esther	S	B22C	1721 May 8		
Wilbour Esther	S	B22I	1733 Nov12		

NAME	DIV.	NUMBER	BIRTH	MARRIAGE	DEATH
Wilbour Lydia	S	B22D	1723 Apr16		
Wilbour Lydia	S	B22J	1735 Nov 2		
Wilbour Mary	S	B22B	1719 Sep 7		
Wilbour Samuel	S	B22E	1725 Dec10		
Wilbour Thomas	S	B22A	1718 May31		
Wilbour William	S	B17Ca	1695abt	1717 Jun20	
Wilbour William	S.	B22F	1727 Jul24		
Wilbur Benjamin	A	A4/478	1670	1710	1729
Wilbur Charles	S	B22H	1732 Aug22		
Wilbur Meribah	A	A4/239	1729 Aug22	1747 Oct12	1825 Nov 6
Wilcox Barjona	S	K51F	1708 Nov23		
Wilcox Daniel	S	K12Ba	1622bef	1661 Nov28	1702 Jul 2
Wilcox Daniel	S	K50B	1699 Dec29		1734bef
Wilcox Daniel	S	K51B	1701 Feb25		
Wilcox Edward	S	K12Baf	1600abt		
Wilcox Edward	S	K18E	1675ca	1699ca	1718 May
Wilcox Elezebeth	S	K50D	1704 Jan18		
Wilcox Elizabeth	S	K51C	1702 Dec13		
Wilcox Ephraim	S	K52B	1704 Aug 9		
Wilcox Freelove	S	K52D	1709 Dec18		
Wilcox Jabez	S	K51E	1707 Mar21		
Wilcox Jacob	S	K51A	1699 Oct14		1726living
Wilcox John	S	K18D	1670ca	1698	1718bef
Wilcox John	S	K51D	1704 Sep22		
Wilcox John	S	K50F	1725		
Wilcox Josiah	S	K52A	1701 Sep22		
Wilcox Lydia	S	K18G	1677ca	2 Mar	1756
Wilcox Mary	S	K18A	1665ca	1686ca	1735
Wilcox Rebecca	S	K51G	1711 Aug14		
Wilcox Sarah	S	K18B	1667ca	1692ca	1751bef
Wilcox Stephen	S	K18C	1668ca	2 Mar	1736 Nov13
Wilcox Stephen	S	K50E	1708 Jan10		
Wilcox Susanna	S	K18H	1680ca	1704 Dec 7	1748aft
Wilcox Susannah	S	K50A	1696 Feb14		
Wilcox Thomas	S	K18F	1676ca	unm.	1712
Wilcox Thomas	S	K50C	1701 Oct12		
Wilcox Thomas	S	K51H	1713ca		1726living
Wilcox William	S	K52C	1706 Dec26		
Wilder Edward	S	W18Caf	1635abt		
Wilder Elizabeth	S	W24Gam	1650abt		=W12Kam

NAME	DIV.	NUMBER	BIRTH	MARRIAGE	DEATH
Wilder Elizabeth	S	W29Ham	1650abt		=W24Gam
Wilder Elizabeth	S	W24Kam	1665abt		
Wilder Elizabeth	S	W24Ha	1679 Apr12	1705 May17	1755 Oct21
Wilder John	S	W24Haf	1650abt		1708abt
Wilder Mary	S	R27Cbm	1675abt		
Wilder Mehitable	S	W18Ca	1661	1692 Dec20	1716aft
Wiles Asamy	S	C37Dc	1760abt		
Wiley Luke	A	A3/164	1706ca		1771
Wiley Mary	A	A3/41	1750ca	1768 Aug18	
Wiliams Peleg Jr	S	C91D	1720ca		
Wiliams Robert	S	C91B	1715ca		
Willard Deborah	S	H16Ebm	1640abt		
Willard Hannah	S	W31Ia	1690 Dec	1712 Jun19	1715 Apr12
Willard Samuel	S	W31Iaf	1665abt		
Willets Hope	A	A3/460	1652		1703
Willets Lydia	A	A3/115	1726 Jan16	1746 May16	
Willets Timothy	A	A3/230	1687 Dec25		1760abt
Willey Lawrence E	S	G55Ca	1920abt	1948 Feb12	
William Jeremish	S	C94B	1700abt		
William Rogers	S	C74B	1599		
Williams Abigail	S	C95E	1710abt		
Williams Anna	S	P12Aam	1620abt		
Williams Anna	S	P12Cam	1620abt		
Williams Anna	S	P13Bbm	1620abt		
Williams Anne	S	C96B	1706		
Williams Barbara	S	C94F	1700abt		
Williams Benjamin	S	F53B	1715 Jul 4		1732 Jul15
Williams Bethia	S	X77D	1716 Nov 1		1745ca
Williams Charles	A	A8/38	1700ca		1773 Jul 2
Williams Daniel	S	C75E	1642		
Williams Daniel	S	C78D	1680abt		
Williams Daniel	S	C91A	1713ca		
Williams Edmund	S	X77A	1710 Dec 4		
Williams Elizabeth	S	C46Aa	1655ca		
Williams Elizabeth	S	X24C	1686 Apr18	1707 Mar17	1732 May 2
Williams Elizabeth	S	C96G	1717		
Williams Elizabeth	S	X77F	1721 Mar21		
Williams Elizabeth	S	C91G	1725abt		
Williams Elizabeth	S	C92A	1732abt		
Williams Experience	S	X76B	1705 Nov30		

NAME	DIV.	NUMBER	BIRTH	MARRIAGE	DEATH
Williams Freeborn	S	C75B	1635		
Williams Freelove	S	C94G	1700abt		
Williams Freelove	S	C91F	1725abt		
Williams Grace	A	A8/19	1745ca	1766ca	
Williams Hannah	S	H19Aam	1645abt		
Williams Hannah	S	F21D	1683 Sep30		
Williams Hannah	S	C96H	1719		
Williams James	S	C73A	1560abt		
Williams James	S	C79D	1680		
Williams James	S	C96A	1704		
Williams Jemima	S	C94H	1700abt		
Williams John	S	F14Eaf	1625abt		
Williams John	S	X24A	1675 Aug27		1724 Aug18
Williams John	S	F21C	1679 Feb17	1706 Jan26	1741 Jan11
Williams John	S	X76D	1708 Oct31		1736bef
Williams John	S	C95D	1710abt		
Williams Jonathan	S	C95F	1710abt		
Williams Joseph	S	C75F	1643		
Williams Joseph	S	F14Ea	1647 Apr18	1674 Nov18	1719aft
Williams Joseph	S	C78G	1695abt		
Williams Joseph	S	C96D	1709		
Williams Joseph	S	T26Gaf	1710abt		
Williams Joseph	S	C95A	1710abt		
Williams Joseph	S	F53C	1717 Jan22		1719 May27
Williams Joseph	S	F53E	1723 Apr23		
Williams Joseph Jr	S	C79A	1670		
Williams Judith	S	X77E	1721ca		1743 Oct 1
Williams Katherine	S	C74D	1621		
Williams Lydia	S	C79E	1683		
Williams Lydia	S	C94D	1700abt		
Williams Lydia	S	X77C	1713ca		1796 Jan19
Williams Lydia	S	C96I	1724		
Williams Martha	S	C94E	1700abt		
Williams Mary	S	C75A	1633		
Williams Mary	S	T13Fam	1655abt		
Williams Mary	S	H13Fa	1655ca		1715abt
Williams Mary	S	C79C	1676		
Williams Mary	S	F21B	1677 Nov29		
Williams Mary	S	C78A	1677abt		
Williams Mary	S	C94C	1700abt		

NAME	DIV.	NUMBER	BIRTH	MARRIAGE	DEATH
Williams Mary	S	C95G	1710abt		
Williams Mary	S	C96E	1711		
Williams Mary	S	F53A	1713 Feb17		
Williams Mercy	S	C75D	1640		
Williams Mercy	S	C94A	1700abt		
Williams Meribah	S	C94I	1700abt		
Williams Nathan	S	C96J	1728		
Williams Nathaniel	S	X13Da	1639 Nov17	1688 Nov17	1692 Aug16
Williams Nathaniel	S	X24B	1679 Apr	1709 Jan 9	1726 Aug24
Williams Nathaniel	S	X76A	1702 Dec30		1746 Dec29
Williams Nathaniel	S	X77B	1711 Jan 4		
Williams Nathaniel	S	C96F	1714		
Williams Patience	S	C78E	1680ca		
Williams Peleg Sr	S	C78B	1679		
Williams Providence	S	C75C	1638		
Williams Providence	S	C78F	1690		
Williams Rebecca	S	F22Hbm	1680abt		
Williams Rebecca	S	C92B	1735		
Williams Richard	S	X13Bcf	1610abt		
Williams Robert	S	C74C	1621		
Williams Roger II	S	C78C	1680		
Williams Samuel	S	X13Bc	1637ca	1695ca	1697 Aug
Williams Sarah	S	F21A	1675 Nov17	1695 Aug 6	1702 Sep10
Williams Sarah	S	X16Bb	1700ca	1728 Apr18	1744aft
Williams Sarah	S	C96C	1707		
Williams Sarah	S	T26Ga	1734 Apr22	1757 Dec22	1820 Apr30
Williams Sarah J	S	N16Ea	1825ca		
Williams Sidrach	S	C74A	1621		
Williams Silas	S	X76C	1707 Jan16		
Williams Silas	S	C91C	1717ca		
Williams Simeon	S	X76F	1717 Feb21		
Williams Stephen	S	C95C	1710abt		
Williams Thomas	S	H13Faf	1630abt		
Williams Thomas	S	C79B	1672		
Williams Thomas	S	X16Bbf	1675abt		
Williams Thomas	S	C95B	1710abt		
Williams Thomas	S	C16Ba	1725ca		
Williams Timothy	S	X76E	1714 Sep28		
Williams Timothy	S	C91E	1720abt		
Williams Zipporah	S	F53D	1720 Jul28		

NAME	DIV.	NUMBER	BIRTH	MARRIAGE	DEATH
Williamson Experience	S	T16Eam	1660abt		
Williamson Harvey G	S	G59Aaf	1935abt		
Williamson Marilyn Kay	S	G55Aa	1955abt	1972 Jul29	
Willis Hannah	S	Q20Aam	1645abt		
Willis Henry	S	A32Eaf	1690abt		
Willis Mary	S	A32Ea	1716 Aug 5	1733 Jan23	1766 Dec 4
Willis Richard	S	H22Faf	1650abt		
Willis Richard	S	X14Eaf	1650abt		
Willis Ruhamah=H22Fa	S	X14Ea	1675ca	1698bef	1739aft
Willis Ruhamah=X14Ea	S	H22Fa	1675ca	1698bef	1739aft
Willis Sarah	S	K22Kam	1650abt		
Williston Susannah	S	B17Ia	1720abt	1739 Sep	
Willoughby Elizabeth	S	A11Eb	1635ca	1663ca	1672aft
Willoughby Elizabeth	A	A18/23	1635ca	1663ca	=A11Eb
Willoughby Thomas	A	A18/46	1598ca		1658bef
Willoughby Thomas	S	A11Ebf	1610abt		
Wilmer Anne	D	D11/21	1520abt		
Wilmer William	D	D11a22	1490abt		
Wilson Edward	S	A17Baf	1630abt		
Wilson Hannah	A	A3/251	1715abt	1739 Dec13	
Wilson Hannah	A	A3/17	1790ca	1806ca	1827ca
Wilson John	S	A35A	1681 Sep29		
Wilson John	A	A9/12	1812 Feb 9	1841 Nov28	1883 Mar 9
Wilson John Jr.	A	A2/146	1621	1647ca	1691
Wilson Nelle Clyde	A	A9/3	1883 Jul24	1904 Nov 8	1962 Jul24
Wilson Samuel	S	A35B	1683 Aug17		d, yng
Wilson Susanna	A	A2/73	1664 Dec 1	1682 Aug30	1748 Jul 8
Wilson Thomas	A	A9/6	1844 Apr28	1866 Jan25	1909 Dec12
Wilson William	S	A17Ba	1650abt	1679 May 1	1732bef
Wilson William	A	A3/34	1764ca	1790 Feb 4	1837 Nov12
Windebank Mildred	A	A10/45	1584ca	1600 Jul31	1630abt
Windebank Thomas	A	A10/90	1545abt	1566 Aug20	1607 Nov25
Wines Ann	A	A4/233	1700abt	1729 Jan23	
Wines Barnabas Jr.	A	A14/186	1636ca		1711ca
Wines Sarah	A	A14/93	1668ca	1686ca	1733 Apr16
Wing Lydia	S	H25Bam	1645abt		
Wing Sarah	S	K31Cam	1660abt		
Winne Catelyntje	A	A7/77	1691ca	1706 Jul12	
Winslow Anna	S	L15E	1709 Jan29	unmarried	1723 Sep16
Winslow Brooke Watson	S	L32M	1797ca		

NAME	DIV.	NUMBER	BIRTH	MARRIAGE	DEATH
Winslow Catherine W.	S	L32L	1796ca		1805ca
Winslow Christiana B.	S	L32I	1791ca	unm	1815ca
Winslow Daniel Murray	S	L32A	1777abt		1814 Mar20
Winslow Edward	S	L10A	1595 Oct	1621 May12	1655 May 8
Winslow Edward	S	L11A	1624	unmar	1626 Aft
Winslow Edward	S	L12B	1667 May14		d. yng
Winslow Edward	S	L15F	1714 June7	1741 Apl10	1784 June8
Winslow Edward	S	L21D	1746 Feb20	1776bef	1815 May13
Winslow Edward	S	L32F	1785ca	unm	1820 May21
Winslow Edward Sr	S	L9A	1570abt		
Winslow Eleanor	S	R12Jam	1635abt		
Winslow Eleanor=R12Jam	S	W27Aam	1635abt		
Winslow Elinor	S	W29Aa	1677 Jul 2	1697 Feb17	1737aft
Winslow Eliza Chipman	S	L32K	1794 Dec		
Winslow Elizabeth	S	L11D	1635abt	1656bef	1697 Sep23
Winslow Elizabeth	S	L12A	1664 Apr 8	1684 Sept4	1735 Jul11
Winslow Elizabeth	S	L15D	1707 Dec13	1729 Nov20	1761 Sep20
Winslow Elizabeth	S	L26A	1769 Nov14		
Winslow Gilbert	S	W42Ca	1673 Jul 1	1698 Feb 7	1731 Jun12
Winslow Hannah	S	L32G	1787ca	unm	1820living
Winslow Isaac	S	L18C	1739 Apr27	1768 Oct25	1819 Oct24
Winslow Isaac	S	L26E	1777 Apr12		1778
Winslow Isaac=L12C	S	W52Faf	1671ca	1700 Jul11	1738 Dec14
Winslow Isaac=W52Faf	S	L12C	1671ca	1700 Jul11	1738 Dec14
Winslow Joanna	S	L25B	1773 Jun30		
Winslow John	S	T11Daf	1615abt		
Winslow John	S	L11B	1626ca	unmar	1626 Aft
Winslow John	S	L15B	1703 May27	1725 Feb16	1774 Apl17
Winslow John	S	L21A	1741 May14		1742 Jul17
Winslow John	S	L26C	1774 Jul14		
Winslow John Francis	S	L32J	1793		
Winslow Josiah	S	L11C	1629ca	1651ca	1680 Dec18
Winslow Josiah	S	L15A	1701 Jul27	unm.	1724 May 1
Winslow Josiah	S	L18A	1730		1730
Winslow Kenelm	S	W44Da	1675 Sep22	1703ca	1757 Jun10
Winslow Margaret	S	K14Cam	1640abt		
Winslow Mary	S	W13Iam	1635abt		
Winslow Mary	S	R19Fam	1665abt		
Winslow Mary	S	L25A	1771 Jul28		
Winslow Mary	S	L32B	1778ca		

NAME	DIV.	NUMBER	BIRTH	MARRIAGE	DEATH
Winslow Nathaniel Jr	S	W42Ba	1667 Jul29	1692	1736 Mar13
Winslow Nathaniel Sr	S	W29Aaf	1645abt		=W44Daf
Winslow Nathaniel Sr	S	W42Baf	1645abt		=W42Ca
Winslow Nathaniel Sr	S	W42Caf	1645abt		
Winslow Nathaniel Sr	S	W44Daf	1650abt		=W42Cam
Winslow Pelham	S	L18B	1737 Jun 8	1770 Jun16	1780abt
Winslow Penelope	S	W52Fa	1704 Dec21	1723 Jan30	1737 May25
Winslow Penelope	S	L15C	1704 Dec21	1723 Jan30	1737 May25
Winslow Penelope	S	L21B	1743 Apr19	unm	1810 Jan23
Winslow Penelope	S	L25D	1758ca		
Winslow Penelope	S	L32E	1783ca		
Winslow Rebecca	S	H17Ham	1650abt		
Winslow Ruth S	S	L26B	1771 Dec17		
Winslow Sarah	S	T11Da	1638ca	1660 Jul19	1726 Apr 9
Winslow Sarah	S	L26D	1775 Aug14		
Winslow Sarah (Sally)	S	L21C	1744 Feb24	unm	1821
Winslow Sarah Ann	S	L32H	1789ca		
Winslow Susanna	S	K14Fam	1630abt		=K22Dam
Winslow Susanna	S	K22Dam	1630abt		=K14Fam
Winslow Thomas Astor C	S	L32C	1779ca	unm	1810
Winslow Ward Chipman	S	L32D	1781ca		1783
Winsor Ann	S	C87Ib	1737		
Winsor Deborah	S	C87F	1715		
Winsor Freelove	S	C87H	1720		
Winsor Hannah	S	C77B	1680ca		
Winsor Hannah	S	C87D	1711		
Winsor Joseph	S	C87E	1713		
Winsor Joshua	S	C77C	1682		
Winsor Joshua Jr	S	C89B	1709		
Winsor Lillis	S	C65Aa	1744		
Winsor Lydia	S	C87C	1709		
Winsor Martha	S	C87A	1703		
Winsor Mary	S	C87B	1707		
Winsor Mary	S	C88Ca	1718		
Winsor Mary	S	C89E	1718		
Winsor Mercy	S	C87G	1718		
Winsor Samuel	S	C75Da	1644		
Winsor Samuel	S	C77A	1677		
Winsor Samuel	S	C89C	1712		
Winsor Samuel	S	C87I	1722		

NAME	DIV.	NUMBER	BIRTH	MARRIAGE	DEATH
Winsor Sarah	S	C89A	1707		
Winsor Susannah	S	C89D	1715		
Winston David	S	C60Aa	1785ca		
Winston John	A	A12/78	1621ca		1696 Feb21
Winston Mary	A	A12/39	1667 Jun24	1685 Oct16	1742 Sep16
Winter Elizabeth	A	A19/237	1678	1697	
Winter Martha	S	W44Aam	1645abt		
Winthrop Lucy	A	A11/123	1600 Jan 9	1622 Apr19	
Wise Anthony John III	S	G56A	1933 Nov 5	1956 Dec26	
Wise Anthony John Jr	S	G55Ba	1911 abt	1932 May10	
Wise Patricia Eliz.	S	G56B	1934 Oct29	1956 Jun30	
Wiswall Elizabeth	S	L14Dam	1675abt		
Wiswall Ichabod	S	R21Bbf	1670abt		
Wiswall Priscilla	S	R21Bb	1690 Jul25	1716Oct23	1780 Sep12
Wiswell Deborah	S	K30Ccm	1695abt		
Wiswell Sarah	S	K30Jcm	1700abt		
Witherell Joseph	S	T22Eaf	1720abt		
Witherell Joseph	S	T57D	1780 Jan15		
Witherell Joshua	S	T22Ea	1741ca	1769 Dec25	1812 Dec28
Witherell Joshua	S	T57A	1771 Apr 2	unm.	1810 Sept2
Witherell Mary	S	T57C	1776 Sep16		
Witherell Thomas	S	T57B	1774 Apr 2		
Withering Matilda	S	G48Aa	1765abt	1785ca	
Wixon Elizabeth	S	X16Gam	1660abt		=H17Fbm
Wixon Elizabeth=X16Gam	S	H17Fbm	1660abt		
Wixon Prince	S	B18Ba	1695abt	1720 Apr 1	
Wolcott Anna	S	P12Gam	1630abt		
Wood Abiel	S	Q14Daf	1665abt		
Wood Abigail	S	G23Aa	1750		1816
Wood Abijah	S	Q14Da	1688 Feb20	1717 Dec12	1777 Dec25
Wood Bethia	S	T28Aam	1700abt		
Wood Coffil	S	N13Ga	1745ca		
Wood Ebenezer	A	A16/20	1698 Sep 8	1718Mar 12	1744
Wood Ebenezer	A	A16/10	1726Nov 15	1745Dec 10	1796
Wood Edward	A	A16/160	1598	1619ca	1642
Wood Ephraim	S	K30Jaf	1695abt		
Wood Henry	S	Q14Fa	1677ca	1717 Dec24	1750ca
Wood Henry	S	Q29D	1726 Feb27		
Wood Hepzibah	A	A16/5	1747Apr 14	1767 Oct28	1783May 11
Wood Jabez Jr	A	A1/382	1719	1748	1793

NAME	DIV.	NUMBER	BIRTH	MARRIAGE	DEATH
Wood Jabez Jr=A1/382	D	D2/20	1719	1748	1793
Wood Jabez Sr	D	D2a21	1690abt		
Wood Jesse Jr	A	A1/238	1750abt		1824ca
Wood Joanna	S	Q29B	1722 Mar30	unm.	1797 Apr 7
Wood Joanna=A1/191	D	D2/19	1750	1768 Dec 8	1813
Wood Joanna=D2/19	A	A1/191	1750	1768 Dec 8	1813
Wood John	S	R11Bcf	1620abt		
Wood John	A	A16/40	1656Nov 2	1680Jan 16	1738aft
Wood John	S	B17Ga	1712ca		
Wood John Jr	S	W35Ca	1664ca	1688ca	1739 Feb22
Wood John Sr	S	W35Caf	1640abt		
Wood Margaret	S	K20Da	1675ca	1700bef	1755ca
Wood Mary	A	A2/179	1642	1660ca	1726
Wood Mary	S	R11Bc	1643ca	1676	1714 Jan 6
Wood Mildred	A	A1/117	1770abt	1793 Oct14	
Wood Moses	S	Q29E	1730 Feb 3		
Wood Rebecca	S	K30Ja	1717 Nov29	1733 Nov21	
Wood Sally	A	A1/119	2770abt	1795 Sep11	
Wood Samuel	S	Q14Faf	1650abt		
Wood Samuel	S	Q29A	1718 Sep27		1751bef
Wood Silence	A	A2/237	1675ca		1756ca
Wood Susanna	S	Q29C	1724 Apr24		
Wood Thomas	A	A16/80	1633ca		1687 Sep
Wood William	S	K20Daf	1650abt		
Wood William	A	A1/234	1740abt		1808ca
Woodbury Samuel	S	W36Fc	1683 Aug30	1739 Jun18	1757 Mar24
Woodford Mary=A08/233	D	D26a26	1635	1653ca	1684
Woodford Mary=D26a26	A	A8/233	1635	1653ca	1684
Woodin Martha	S	Q16Aam	1665abt		
Woodman Cornelius	S	A20G	1684ca		
Woodman Edward	S	A13Ga	1650ca	1670ca	1695ca
Woodman Edward	S	A20B	1675ca		d.yng
Woodman John	S	A20C	1676ca		1693living
Woodman Mary	S	H30Gam	1675abt		
Woodman Maverick	S	A20E	1680ca		
Woodman Moses	S	A20D	1678ca		
Woodman Remember	S	A20A	1673ca	1694 Jul26	1702bef
Woodman Samuel	S	A20F	1682ca		1708bef
Woodmansey Elizabeth	A	A2/133	1625ca	1652ca	1665aft
Woodruff Sadie	S	C57Aa	1877		

NAME	DIV.	NUMBER	BIRTH	MARRIAGE	DEATH
Woodward Elizabeth	A	A2/221	1671ca	1694ca	1748aft
Woodward Experience	A	A8/227	1643	1661	1686
Woodward Freedom	S	A21Cam	1650abt		
Woodward Martha	A	A14/271	1600abt		
Woodward Martha	S	A14/303	1600abt		=A14/271
Woodworth Judith	A	A1/363	1701ca	1720	
Woodworth Mary	S	T16Iam	1655abt		
Worden Abigail	S	G45Ba	1725abt	1752 Jun 7	
Worden Mary=A12/111	S	B11Ba	1635abt	1657 Sep 8	1723
Worden Mary=B11Ba	A	A12/111	1635abt	1657 Sep 8	1723
Worden Peter	S	B11Baf	1600abt		
Worden Peter	A	A12/222	1630abt		1680
Wright Adam	S	K15A	1645ca	2 Mar	1724 Sep20
Wright Adam	S	K118F	1724 Sep27		
Wright Benjamin	S	K118D	1715 Mar20	unm.	1792 Mar10
Wright Easter	S	K118A	1709 Mar 4		
Wright Ebenezer	S	K124B	1736 Feb14		
Wright Edmund	S	T21Da	1730 Oct28	1750 Oct31	1762 Aug 7
Wright Edmund	S	K123E	1730 Oct28		
Wright Edmund	S	T54D	1750abt		
Wright Elizabeth	A	A19/251	1664	1686	
Wright Elizabeth	S	X91A	1740		
Wright Elizabeth	S	T54B	1750abt		
Wright Enoch	S	T54C	1750abt		d.yng
Wright Esther	S	K15C	1649	1675 aft	1717 May28
Wright Esther	S	K31A	1680ca	1700 Jan23	1705ca
Wright Esther=K15C	S	Q12Aa	1649	1675aft	1717 May28
Wright Hannah	S	K124A	1735 Sep22		
Wright Hannah	S	K125D	1743 Jun27		
Wright Hannah	S	X91D	1752ca		
Wright Isaac	S	K15D	1652 Aug 2		1677bef
Wright Isaac	S	K120E	1736 Sep 3		
Wright Isaac=K31D	S	K40Faf	1685 Jan19	1717Dec 19	1766 Jan11
Wright Isaac=K40Faf	S	K31D	1685 Jan19	1717 Dec19	1766 Jan11
Wright Jacob	S	K123F	1733 Apr17		
Wright James	S	K31I	1707ca	1731 Nov17	1778aft
Wright Jemima	S	C28Ga	1675abt		
Wright John	S	K15B	1656bef	unm.	1677ca
Wright John	S	K31B	1681ca	1708 May20	1774 May
Wright John	S	K118B	1711 Oct11		

NAME	DIV.	NUMBER	BIRTH	MARRIAGE	DEATH
Wright Joseph	D	D26a25	1660abt		
Wright Joseph	S	K120B	1721 Jun16		
Wright Josiah	S	P12Hbf	1650abt		
Wright Lydia	S	K123G	1736 Sep22		
Wright Lydia	S	K125F	1749 Jan26		
Wright Lydia	S	T54A	1750abt	unm	1848 Jan 5
Wright Mary	S	K15F	1654ca	1685bef	1711living
Wright Mary	S	K31C	1681ca	1703ca	1760aft
Wright Mary	S	K120C	1726 Jan30	1748 Jul13	1804 Nov29
Wright Mary=K120C	S	K40Fa	1726 Jan30	1748 Jul13	1804 Nov29
Wright Moses	S	K31H	1703ca	1733 Jan12	
Wright Moses	S	K124C	1739 Jun15		
Wright Nathan	S	K31J	1711aft	1736 Dec 7	1762bef
Wright Nathan	S	K125A	1737 Sep10		1748 Oct 7
Wright Priscilla	S	K125E	1746 Jul 3		d. yng
Wright Priscilla	S	X91E	1755ca		
Wright Rachel	S	K31E	1689ca	1719 Nov18	1779 Dec 7
Wright Rachel	S	K120D	1732 Mar23	unm	1760ca
Wright Repentance	S	K118C	1713 Oct18		1800 May 7
Wright Richard	A	A16/198	1598ca		
Wright Richard	S	K11Da	1608ca	1644	1691 Jun 9
Wright Richard	S	Q12Aaf	1625abt		
Wright Ruth	D	D26/24	1685abt		
Wright Ruth #1	S	K123A	1723 Aug12		d. yng
Wright Ruth #2	S	K123B	1724 Mar 1		d. yng
Wright Samuel	S	K15E	1653ca	unm.	1677bef
Wright Samuel	S	K31G	1699ca	1722 Aug 2	1773 Jan 5
Wright Samuel	S	T21Daf	1710abt		
Wright Samuel	S	K123D	1728 Oct 6		
Wright Samuel	S	T54E	1750abt		
Wright Sara	A	A11/163	1559 Feb	1588 Nov30	1607 Nov3
Wright Sarah	S	P12Hb	1670 Feb25	1707 Sep 4	1752 Dec13
Wright Sarah	S	K31F	1693ca	1720 May12	1726 Jun 7
Wright Sarah	S	K118E	1719 Nov17		1809 May10
Wright Sarah	S	K123C	1726 Jun 3		
Wright Sarah	S	X91C	1748ca		
Wright Susannah	S	K120A	1719 Dec 9		1736 Mar15
Wright Tabitha	S	K125C	1740 Mar16		
Wright Thomas	S	X28Ga	1710ca	1738 Sep14	1755aft
Wright William	S	X91B	1743		

NAME	DIV.	NUMBER	BIRTH	MARRIAGE	DEATH
Wright Zadock	S	K125B	1739 Apr 3		1748 Oct 8
Wyngaart Luykas G.	A	A7/146	1660abt		1709ca
Wyngaart Maria	A	A7/73	1685 Feb15	1703 Jun11	
Wynne Elizabeth	S	C12Aa	1705ca		
Yancey David	A	A1/58	1790ca	1815 Mar27	
Yancey Jechonias	A	A1/116	1765abt	1793 Oct14	
Yancey Jeremiah	A	A1/232	1748ca		1788ca
Yancey Sarah Amanda	A	A1/29	1819 Jun11	1837 Nov 2	1879 Dec 4
Yates Angeltje	A	A7/19	1752 Jul 6	1772 Dec 1	
Yates Christoffel	A	A7/76	1684 Apr16	1706 Jul12	1754 Feb
Yates Deborah	S	X53D	1714ca		
Yates Experience	S	X53C	1708ca		
Yates Hannah	S	X53G	1722ca		
Yates Johannes G.	A	A7/38	1716 Oct14	1737 Nov28	1775ca
Yates John	S	X53E	1718ca		
Yates John Jr	S	X18Ca	1675ca	1698 Jan11	1730bef
Yates John Sr	S	X18Caf	1650abt		
Yates Joseph	A	A7/152	1647		1730
Yates Mary	S	X53A	1700ca		
Yates Mercy	S	X53F	1720ca		
Yates Reliance	S	X53B	1704ca		
Young Benjamin	S	H19Da	1675ca	1699 Feb15	1730abt
Young Benjamin	S	H53E	1715ca	1748 Apr14	
Young Daniel	S	H53C	1704 Apr 4		
Young David	S	H24Ecf	1660abt		
Young Elisha	S	X26Baf	1690abt		
Young Elizabeth	S	F20Aa	1660ca	1680 Feb25	1738 aft
Young Elizabeth	S	X17Ib	1690abt	1747 Nov 5	
Young Elizabeth	S	X26Ba	1711 May24	1731 Sep23	1752aft
Young Elizabeth	S	X55H	1723 Sep17		
Young George	S	F20Caf	1640abt		
Young Hannah	S	H29Cam	1680abt		
Young Hannah	S	X55G	1719 Feb12		
Young Henry	S	X17Ibf	1665abt		
Young Henry= X17Ibf	S	X16Raf	1665abt		
Young James	S	X19Ba	1685 Apr 4	1706 Feb12	1750 Jun18
Young James	S	X55I	1725 May30		
Young John	S	H20Caf	1645abt		
Young John	S	H53B	1702 Apr19		
Young John =H20Caf	S	H19Daf	1645abt		

NAME	DIV.	NUMBER	BIRTH	MARRIAGE	DEATH
Young Joseph	S	X19Baf	1660abt		
Young Joseph	S	H53D	1708ca	1735 Aug	
Young Lydia #1	S	X55E	1717 Aug17		d yng
Young Lydia #2	S	X55F	1718 Sep 8		
Young Martha	S	X16Fa	1695 Jul28	1712 Aug22	1765ca
Young Mary	S	X16Ham	1660abt		
Young Mary	S	X55D	1715 Mar25		
Young Mary	S	H53G	1715abt		
Young Mercy	S	H20Ca	1670ca	1697 Nov25	1753ca
Young Patience	S	F20Ca	1673 Mar 3	1692 Feb25	1746 Jun25
Young Phebe	S	X55A	1707 Jun 3		
Young Rebecca	S	H24Ec	1689 Oct14	1747 Nov25	1764 Feb25
Young Samuel	S	X55C	1712 Dec11		
Young Sarah	S	X55B	1709 Feb 2		
Young Sarah	S	H53F	1710ca	1730 Sep23	
Young Thankful	S	H53A	1700 Dec20		
Zuille Margaret	S	A77E	1737ca		
Zuille Matthew	S	A29Ba	1701ca	1734ca	1766bef
Zuille Robert	S	A77C	1740ca		
Zuille Sarah	S	A77A	1735ca	unm	1766aft

```
[A10]  ALLERTON                      A13B  MARY
       unk                           A13C  ABIGAIL
       unk                                 a Samuel Ward Jr  [A17]
       ======                              f Samluel Ward Sr
A10A  ISAAC=A18/44      [A11]              m Mary --
      a Mary Norris                  A13D  ELIZABETH
      b Fear Brewster=A18/45               a Nathaniel Grafton  [A18]
      f William Brewster MF=A18/90         f Joseph Grafton
      ======                              m Mary Moore
[A11]  ALLERTON                            b Thomas Skinner    [A19]
       Isaac Allerton      A10A     A13E  SAMUEL
       Mary Norris         A10Aa    A13F  ELIZABETH
       Fear Brewster       A10Ab    A13G  REMEMBER
       ------                              a Edward Woodman    [A20]
A11A  BARTHOLOMEW     [A12]                ======
      a Margaret --                 [A14]  CUSHMAN
      b Sarah Fairfax                      Thomas Cushman      A11Ca
      f Benjamin Fairfax                   Mary Allerton       A11C
      m Sarah Galliard                     ------
A11B  REMEMBER        [A13]         A14A  THOMAS              [A21]
      a Moses Maverick                    a Ruth Howland
      f John Maverick                     f John Howland  MF =D1/24
      m Mary Guy                          m Elizabeth Tilley =D1a/24
A11C  MARY                                b Abigail Titus
      a Thomas Cushman  [A14]       A14B  MARY
      f Robert Cushman                    a Francis Hutchinson  [A22]
      m Sarah Reder                 A14C  SARAH
A11D  SARAH                               a John Hawkes        [A23]
A11E  ISAAC           [A15]               f Adam Hawdes
      a Elizabeth --                      b Daniel Hutchins
      b ELizabeth Willoughby        A14D  ISAAC               [A24]
      f Thomas Willoughby                 a Rebecca Harlow
      m Sarah Thompson                    f William Harlow =W12Ba
      ======                              m Rebecca Bartlett =W12B
[A12]  ALLERTON                     A14E  ELKANAH             [A25]
       Bartholomew Allerton A11A          a Elizabeth Cole
       Margaret --          A11Aa         f James Cole
       Sarah Fairfax        A11Ab         m Abigail Davenport
       ------                              b Martha Cooke
A12A  ISAAC                               f Jacob Cooke =H11Ga
A12B  MARY                                m Damaris Hopkins =H11G
A12C  DOROTHY                       A14F  FEAR
A12D  JOHN                          A14G  ELEAZER             [A26]
      ======                              a Elizabeth Coombs =P22A
[A13]  MAVERICK                            f John Coombs
       Moses Maverick      A11Ba          m Elizabeth --
       Remember Allerton   A11B  A14H  LYDIA
       ------                              a William Harlow Jr  [A27]
A13A  REBECCA                             f William Harlow Sr
      a John Hawkes      [A16]            m Rebecca Bartlett
      f Adam Hawkes                       ======
      m Ann --
```

[A15] ALLERTON
    Isaac Allerton   A11E
    Elizabeth --   A11Ea
    Elizabeth Willoughby
    ------   A11Eb
A15A ELIZABETH
  a Benjamin Starr
  b Simon Ayers Jr   [A28]
  f Simon Ayers Sr
  m Lydia Starr
A15B ISAAC
A15C WILLOUGHBY   [A29]
  a Rosamond Fitzhugh
  f William Fitzhugh
  m Sarah Tucker
  b Sarah Taverner
  f John Taverner
  m Elizabeth --
  c Hannah Keene
  f William Keene
  m Elizabeth Rogers
A15D MARY
  a John Newton Jr   [A30]
  f John Newton Sr
  m Joan Barr
A15E FRANCES
  a Samuel Travers   [A31]
  f William Travers
  m Rebecca Hussey
A15F SARAH=A18/11
  a Hancock Lee=A18/10 [A32]
  f Richard Lee
  m Ann Constable

    ======
[A16] HAWKES
    John Hawkes   A13Aa
    Rebecca Maverick A13A

A16A MOSES   [A33]
  a Margaret Cogswell
  f John Cogswell
  m Margaret Gifford
    ======
[A17] WARD
    Samuel Ward   A13Ca
    Abigail Maverick A13C

A17A ABIGAIL
  a William Hinds   [A34]
A17B REMEMBER
  a William Wilson   [A35]
  f Edward Wilson
  m Mary Hale

A17C MARY
  a Peter Doliber [A36]
  f Joseph Doliber
  m Margaret --
  b William Waters [A37]
A17D ELIZABETH
A17E MARTHA
  a John Tuttle   [A38]
  f Symon Tuttle
  m Sarah Cogswell
A17F SAMUEL   [A39]
  a Sarah Tuttle
  f Symon Tuttle
  m Sarah Cogswell
A17G REBECCA
    ======
[A18] GRAFTON
    Nathaniel Grafton A13Da
    Elizabeth Maverick A13D

A18A ELIZABETH
  a William Hewes   [A40]
A18B REMEMBER
  a Richard Knight
A18C PRISCILLA
  a Thomas Jackson   [A41]
    ======
[A19] SKINNER
    Thomas Skinner   A13Db
    Elizabeth Maverick A13D

A19A REBECCA
A19B JOHN
A19C AGNES
A19D ABIGAIL
  a Ebenezer Ager   [A42]
  b Nathaniel Coney   [A43]
  f John Coney
  m Elizabeth Nash
A19E SARAH
    ======
[A20] WOODMAN
    Edward Woodman   A13Ga
    Remember Maverick A13G

A20A REMEMBER
  a Thomas Perkins   [A44]
A20B EDWARD
A20C JOHN
A20D MOSES
A20E MAVERICK
A20F SAMUEL
A20G CORNELIUS

[A21] CUSHMAN
    Thomas Cushman A14A
    Ruth Howland   A14Aa
    Abigail Titus A14Ab

A21A ROBERT by Ruth [A45]
  a Persis --
  b Prudence Sherman
  f Samuel Sherman
A21B DESIRE
  a Samuel Kent   [A46]
  f Joseph Kent
  m Susanna George
A21C THOMAS   [A47]
  a Sarah Strong
  f Jedidiah Strong
  m Freedom Woodward
A21D JOB by Abigail [A48]
  a Lydia Brewster
  f William Brewster
  m Lydia Partridge
A21E BARTHOLOMEW
A21F SAMUEL   [A49]
  a Fear Corser
A21G BENJAMIN   [A50]
  a Sarah Eaton
  f Benjamin Eaton
  m Mary Coombs
  b Sarah --
    ======
[A22] HUTCHINSON
    Francis Hutchinson A14Ba
    Mary Cushman   A14B

A22A FRANCIS   [A51]
  a Mary Gifford
  f Philip Gifford
  m Mary Davis
A22B THOMAS   [A52]
  a Mary Colson
  f Adam Colson
  m Mary Dastin
A22C JOHN   [A53]
  a Mary--
    ======
[A23] HAWKES
    John Hawkes A14Ca
    Sarah Cushman A14C

A23A SUSANNAH

A23B ADAM   [A54]
  a Elizabeth--
A23C ANNA
A23D JOHN   [A55]
  a Abigail Floyd
  f John Floyd
  m Sarah Doolittle
  b Elizabeth Scarlet
  f John Scarlet
  m Thomasin --
A23E REBECCA
A23F THOMAS   [A56]
  a Sarah Haven
  f Richard Haven
  m Susannah --
A23G MERCY
  a Nathaniel Goodhue [A57]
  f William Goodhue
  m Hannah Dane
A23H EBENEZER   [A58]
  a Elizabeth Cogswell
  f John Cogswell
  m Mary Gifford
  b Sarah Bassett
  f William Bassett
  m Sarah Hood
  c Ruth Phillips
  f Walter Phillips
  m Ruth Purchase
    ======
[A24] CUSHMAN
    Isaac Cushman A14D
    Rebecca Harlow A14Da

A24A ISAAC   [A59]
  a Sarah Gibbs
  f Thomas Gibbs
  m Alice Warren
  b Mercy Bradford
  f John Bradford
  m Mercy Warren
A24B REBEKAH
  a Jacob Mitchell Jr [A60]
  f Jacob Mitchell Sr
  m Susanna Pope
A24C MARY
  a Robert Waterman [A61]
  f John Waterman
  m Ann Sturtevant

A24D SARAH
  a James Bryant   [A62]
  f John Bryant
  m Sarah Bonham
A24E ICHABOD   [A63]
  a Patience Holmes
  f John Holmes
  m Sarah Thomas
A24F PEAR
  a William Sturtevant [A64]
  f Samuel Sturtevant
  m Mercy --
A24G MERCY
  ======
[A25] CUSHMAN
  Elkanah Cushman A14E
  Elizabeth Cole A14Ea
  Martha Cooke A14Eb

A25A ELKANAH by Cole   [A65]
  a Hester Barnes
  f Jonathan Barnes
  m Elizabeth Hedge
A25B JAMES
A25C JABEZ
A25D ALLERTON by Cooke [A66]
  a Mary Buck
  f James Buck
  m Abigail Church
  b Elizabeth Samson
  f George Samson
  m Elizabeth Sprague
A25E ELIZABETH
  a Robert Waterman
  f John Waterman
  m Ann Sturtevant
A25F JOSIAH   [A67]
  a Susannah Shurtleff
  f William Shurtleff
  m Susanna Lothrop
A25G MARTHA
  a Nathaniel Holmes [A68]
  f John Holmes
  m Sarah Thomas
A25H MEHITABLE
  ======
[A26] CUSHMAN
  Eleazer Cushman A14G
  Elizabeth Coombs A14Ga

A26A LYDIA
  a John Waterman Jr [A69]
  f John Waterman Sr
  m Ann Sturtevant

A26B JOHN   [A70]
  a Joanna Pratt
  f John Pratt
  m Margaret Kimball
A26C JAMES   [A71]
  a Sarah Hatch
A26D MOSES   [A72]
  a Mary Jackson
  f Eleazer Jackson
  m Hannah Ransom
A26E ELEAZER
  a Eunice Stoddard
  f Hezekiah Stoddard
  m Lois Silvester
A26F WILLIAM   [A73]
  a Abigail Lee
  f David Lee
  m Lydia Strong
A26G SARAH
  a Benjamin Spooner [A74]
  f John Spooner
  m Rosamond Hammond
  ======
[A27] HARLOW
  William Harlow A14Ha
  Lydia Cushman A14H

A27A ELIZABETH
A27B THOMAS
A27C WILLIAM
A27D MARY
A27E LYDIA
A27F ISAAC
A27G ROBERT
A27H REBECCA
  ======
[A28] AYERS
  Simon Ayers A15Ab
  Elizabeth Allerton A15A

A28A LYDIA
A28B SIMON
A28C ISAAC
A28D BENJAMIN   [A75]
  a Deborah Parsons
A28E ELIZABETH
  ======
[A29] ALLERTON
  Willoughby Allerton A15C
  Sarah Taverner A15Cb

A29A Isaac   [A76]
  a Ann Corbin
  f Gawin Corbin m Jane Lane

A29B ELIZABETH
   a Matthew Zuille   [A77]
   ======
[A30]   NEWTON
      John Newton A15Da
      Mary Allerton A15D

A30A WILLIAM   [A78]
   a Barbara Johnson
   f James Johnson
   m Elizabeth --
   b Elizabeth Berryman
   f Benjamin Berryman
   m Sarah --
A30B ALLERTON
   ======
[A31]   TRAVERS
      Samuel Travers A15Ea
      Frances Allerton A15E

A31A ELIZABETH
   a Thomas Harwar Jr   [A79]
   f Thomas Harwar Sr
   b John Tarpley Jr   [A80]
   f John Tarpley Sr
   m Elizabeth Glascock
A31B REBECCA
   a John Taverner Jr
   f John Taverner Sr
   b Charles Colston   [A81]
   f William Colston
   m Anne Gooch
A31C WINIFRED
   a Daniel Hornby
A31D FRANCES
   ======
[A32]   LEE
      Hancock Lee A15Fa
      Sarah Allerton A15F

A32A ISAAC
A32B ANN
   a William Eustace   [A82]
   f John Eustace
   m Sarah Jauncey
A32C ELIZABETH
   a Swan Jones   [A83]
   f Maurice Jones
   m Judith Swan
   b Zachary Taylor   [A84]
   f James Taylor
   m Martha Thompson

A32D JOHN
A32E HANCOCK   [A85]
   a Mary Willis
   f Henry Willis
   m Anne Alexander
   ======
[A33]   HAWKES
      Moses Hawkes A16A
      Margaret Cogswell A16Aa

A33A MOSES
A33B MARGARET
A33C ADAM
A33D JOHN
A33E REBECCA
   ======
[A34]   HINDS
      William Hinds A17Aa
      Abigail Ward   A17A

A34A JOHN
A34B ABIGAIL
A34C REBECCA
A34D WILLIAM
   ======
[A35]   WILSON
      William Wilson A17Ba
      Remember Ward   A17B

A35A JOHN
A35B SAMUEL
   ======
[A36]   DOLIBER
      Peter Doliber A17Ca
      Mary Ward A17C

A36A MARGARET
A36B JOSEPH
A36C ABIGAIL
A36D PETER #1
A36E SAMUEL
A36F JOHN
A36G HANNAH
A36H THOMAS
A36I PETER #2
   ======
[A37]   WATERS
      William Waters A17Cb
      Mary Ward   A17C

A37A HANNAH
   ======

[A38]   TUTTLE
    John Tuttle   A17Ea
    Martha Ward   A17E

A38A MARTHA
A38B MARY
A38C ABIGAIL
A38D REMEMBER
A38E WILLIAM
A38F SARAH
A38G SUSANNA
    ======

[A39]   WARD
    Samuel Ward A17F
    Sarah Tuttle A17Fa

A39A SAMUEL
A39B SARAH #1
A39C SARAH #2
A39D ABIGAIL
    ======

[A40]   HEWES
    William Hewes A18Aa
    Elizabeth Grafton A18A

A40A ELIZABETH
A40B REMEMBER
A40C WILLIAM
A40D NATHANIEL
    ======

[A41]   JACKSON
    Thomas Jackson A18Ca
    Priscilla Grafton A18C

A41A THOMAS #1
A41B THOMAS #2
A41C NATHANIEL
A41D ELIZABETH
A41E MARY
A41F PRISCILLA
    ======

[A42]   AGER
    Ebenezer Ager A19Da
    Abigail Skinner A19D

A42A EBENEZER Jr
    ======

[A43]   CONEY
    Nathaniel Coney A19Db
    Abigail Skinner A19D

A43A ABIGAIL

A43B THOMAS
A43C ELIZA
A43D SAMUEL
A43E MARY
A43F PRISCILLA
A43G JOSEPH
A43H WILLIAM
A43I ANNA
    ======

[A44]   PERKINS
    Thomas Perkins A20Aa
    Remember Woodman A20A

A44A EDWARD
A44B THOMAS #1
A44C THOMAS #2
A44D MARY #1
A44E MARY #2
A44F ELIZABETH
    ======

[A45]   CUSHMAN
    Robert Cushman A21A
    Persis --   A21Aa

A45A ROBERT
A45B RUTH
A45C ABIGAIL
A45D HANNAH
A45E THOMAS
A45F JOSHUA
A45G JONATHAN
    ======

[A46]   KENT
    Samuel Kent A21Ba
    Desire Cushman A21B

A46A HANNAH
A46B JOSIAH
    ======

[A47]   CUSHMAN
    Thomas Cushman A21C
    Sarah Strong A21Ca

A47A WILLIAM
A47B THOMAS
A47C ZIBIAH
A47D ELEAZER
A47E RUTH
A47F LYDIA
    ======

[A48]   CUSHMAN
        Job Cushman A21D
        Lydia Brewster A21Da

A48A MARIA
A48B JOB
A48C LYDIA
======

[A49]   CUSHMAN
        Samuel Cushman A21F
        Fear Corser   A21Fa

A49A DESIRE
A49B MERCY
A49C SAMUEL
A49D JOSEPH
A49E JACOB
A49F JEMIMA #1
A49G BARTHOLOMEW
A49H JEMIMA #2
======

[A50]   CUSHMAN
        Benjamin Cushman A21G
        Sarah Eaton   A21Ga

A50A JABEZ
A50B CALEB
A50C SOLOMON
A50D JERUSHA #1
A50E BENJAMIN
A50F SARAH
A50G ABIGAIL
A50H THOMAS
A50I JERUSHA #2
A50J HULDAH
======

[A51]   HUTCHINSON
        Francis Hutchinson A22A
        Mary Gifford   A22Aa

A51A MARY
A51B ELIZABETH
A51C SARAH
A51D ANNA
A51E THOMAS
A51F FRANCIS
A51G HANNAH
======

[A52]   HUTCHINSON
        Thomas Hutchinson A22B
        Mary Colson   A22Ba

A52A ADAM twin
A52B THOMAS twin
A52C THOMAS twin
A52D BENJAMIN twin
A52E LEDIAH
======

[A53]   HUTCHINSON
        John Hutchinson A22C
        Mary --   A22Ca

A53A MARY
A53B MEHITABEL
A53C SARAH
A53D JOHN
A53E PHEBE
======

[A54]   HAWKES
        Adam Hawkes A23B
        Elizabeth -- A23Ba

A54A JOHN
======

[A55]   HAWKES
        John Hawkes A23D
        Abigail Floyd A23Da
        Elizabeth Scarlett A23Db

A55A SARAH
A55B ABIGAIL
A55C JOHN
======

[A56]   HAWKES
        Thomas Hawkes A23F
        Sarah Haven   A23Fa

A56A THOMAS
A56B JONATHAN
A56C ELKANAH
A56D SARAH
======

[A57]   GOODHUE
        Nathaniel Goodhue A23Ga
        Mercy Hawkes   A23G

A57A WILLIAM
A57B SARAH
A57C NATHANIEL

A57D JOHN
A57E MERCY
A57F ELIZABETH
======

[A58] HAWKES
    Ebenezer Hawkes A23H
    Elizabeth Cogswell A23Ha
    Sarah Bassett   A23Hb
    Ruth Phillips   A23Hc

A58A EBENEZER by Eliz.
A58B ELIZABETH
A58C SAMUEL
======

[A59] CUSHMAN
    Isaac Cushman A24A
    Sarah Gibbs   A24Aa
    Mercy Bradford A24Ab

A59A PHEBE by Sarah
A59B ALICE
A59C REBEKAH
A59D SARAH
A59E NATHANIEL
A59F FEAR
A59G PRISCILLA by Mercy
A59H ISAAC
A59I ABIGAIL
======

[A60] MITCHELL
    Jacob Mitchell A24Ba
    Rebekah Cushman A24B

A60A SUSANNAH
A60B REBECKAH
A60C SETH
A60D MARY
A60E LIDIA
A60F NOAH
A60G ISAAC
A60H SARAH
A60I ELIZABETH
======

[A61] WATERMAN
    Robert Waterman A24Ca
    Mary Cushman   A24C

A61A ISAAC
A61B JOSIAH
A61C THOMAS
A61D REBECCA
A61E ROBERT

A61F MARY
A61G SAMUEL
A61H ANNA
======

[A62] BRYANT
    James Bryant A24Da
    Sarah Cushman A24D

A62A REBECKAH #1
A62B BARNABAS #1
A62C HOPESTILL
A62D BARNABUS #2
A62E SETH
A62F REBECKAH #2
======

[A63] CUSHMAN
    Ichabod Cushman A24E
    Patience Holmes A24Ea

A63A JOANNA
A63B WILLIAM
A63C SARAH
A63D EXPERIENCE
A63E PATIENCE
A63F MARY
A63G ICHABOD
A63H REBEKAH
A63I ISAAC
======

[A64] STURTEVANT
    William Sturtevant A24Fa
    Fear Cushman   A24F

A64A ISAAC
A64B HANNAH
A64C REBECCA
A64D FEAR twin
A64E ELIZABETH twin
======

[A65] CUSHMAN
    Elkanah Cushman A25A
    Hester Barnes A25Aa

A65A ELIZABETH
A65B ELKANAH
A65C JAMES
A65D HANNAH
======

[A66] CUSHMAN
    Allerton Cushman A25D
    Mary Buck   A25Da
    Elizabeth Samson A25Db

A66A ALLERTON by Mary
A66B JAMES
A66C MARY
A66D EPHRAIM
A66E ALICE   by Eliz.
A66F JOSEPH
    ======

[A67] CUSHMAN
    Josiah Cushman A25F
    Susannah Shurtleff A25Fa

A67A SUSANNAH #1
A67B MARTHA
A67C SUSANNAH #2
A67D ANNA
A67E JOSIAH
A67F ELCANAH
A67G WILLIAM
A67H ELIZABETH
A67I ISAIAH
    ======

[A68] HOLMES
    Nathaniel Holmes A25Ga
    Martha Cushman   A25G

A68A NATHANIEL
A68B JEJIDIAH
A68C JABEZ
A68D ELKANAH
A68E JOHN
    ======

[A69] WATERMAN
    John Waterman A26Aa
    Lidia Cushman A26A

A69A SARAH
A69B JOSEPH
A69C PEREZ
A69D ANTHONY
A69E JOHN
A69F ELEAZER
A69G LYDIA
    ======

[A70] CUSHMAN
    John Cushman A26B
    Joanna Pratt A26Ba

A70A ELEAZER
A70B CHARLES
A70C JOHN
    ======

[A71] CUSHMAN
    James Cushman A26C
    Sarah Hatch A26Ca

A71A LYDIA
A71B JAMES
A71C EBENEZER
A71D THOMAS
A71E MARY
A71F SARAH
A71G SETH
A71H ELISHA
A71I ELIZABETH
A71J TEMPERANCE
A71K PATIENCE
    ======

[A72] CUSHMAN
    Moses Cushman A26D
    Mary Jackson A26Da

A72A ABNER
A72B ELIJAH
A72C MARY
A72D SARAH
A72E ISAAC
A72F HANNAH
A72G BETTEE
A72H DEBORAH
A72I HULDAH
A72J MOSES
A72K ELEAZER
    ======

[A73] CUSHMAN
    William Cushman A26F
    Abigail Lee   A26Fa

A73A HANNAH twin
A73B SARAH twin
A73C SOLOMON
A73D LYDIA
A73E WILLIAM

A73F	JOB	
A73G	ABIGAIL	
A73H	MARY	
A73I	ALDERTON	
A73J	JOSHUA	
A73K	BENJAMIN	
A73L	JOSEPH	
	======	

[A74] SPOONER
    Benjamin Spooner A26Ga
    Sarah Cushman A26G

A74A	ELEANOR
A74B	ELEAZER
A74C	BENJAMIN
A74D	SAMUEL
A74E	PHEBE
A74F	MARY
	======

[A75] AYERS
    Benjamin Ayers A28D
    Deborah Parsons A28Da

A75A	BENJAMIN
A75B	ELIZABETH
A75C	CLEMENS
	======

[A76] ALLERTON
    Isaac Allerton A29A
    Ann Corbin A29Aa

A76A	GAWIN
A76B	WILLOUGHBY
A76C	ISAAC
	======

[A77] ZUILLE
    Matthew Zuille A29Ba
    Elizabeth Allerton A29B

A77A	SARAH
A77B	MARGARET
A77C	ROBERT
	======

[A78] NEWTON
    William Newton A30A
    Barbara Johnson A30Aa
    Elizabeth Berryman A30Ab

A78A	JOHN by Barbara
A78B	FRANCES

A78C	WILLIAM by Elizabeth
A78D	SARAH
A78E	ELIZABETH
A78F	BENJAMIN
	======

[A79] HARWAR
    Thomas Harwar A31Aa
    Elizabeth Travers A31A

A79A	ELIZABETH
A79B	FRANCES
A79C	HARWAR
	======

[A80] TARPLEY
    John Tarpley A31Ab
    Elizabeth Travers A31A

A80A	TRAVERS
A80B	JOHN twin
A80C	ELIZABETH twin
	======

[A81] COLSTON
    Charles Colston A31Bb
    Rebecca Travers A31B

A81A	TRAVERS
A81B	CHARLES
A81C	SUSANNAH
A81D	ELIZABETH
A81E	WINIFRED
	======

[A82] EUSTACE
    William Eustace A32Ba
    Ann Lee A32B

A82A	JOHN
A82B	ELIZABETH
A82C	SARAH
A82D	WILLIAM
A82E	ISAAC
A82F	HANCOCK
A82G	ANN
	======

[A83] JONES
    Swan Jones A32Ca
    Elizabeth Lee A32C

A83A	JOHN
	======

```
[A84]   TAYLOR
          Zachary Taylor  A32Cb
          Elizabeth Lee   A32C
          ------
A84A  ZACHARY
A84B  ELIZABETH
A84C  HANCOCK
A84D  RICHARD=A18/2
          ======
[A85]   LEE
          Hancock Lee     A32E
          Mary Willis     A32Ea
          ------
A85A  ANN
A85B  MARY
A85C  GEORGE HENRY
A85D  HANCOCK
A85E  JOHN
A85F  WILLIS
A85G  SARAH ALEXANDER
A85H  HENRY
A85I  RICHARD
A85J  MARY WILLIS
          ======
```

```
      ======
[B10]    BURGESS              B13G  PATIENCE
         unk                 B13H  MERCY
         unk                 B13I  MARY
      ------                 B13J  SARAH
B10A  THOMAS Sr    [B11]           ======
   a  Dorothy --            [B14]   PERRY
                                  Ezra Perry        B11Ca
      ======                      Elizabeth Burgess B11C
[B11]    BURGESS                  ------
         Thomas Burgess Sr B10A  B14A  EZRA
         Dorothy --     B10Aa B14B  DEBORAH
      ------                     a  Seth Pope      [B23]
B11A  THOMAS Jr     [B12]   B14C  JOHN
   a  Elizabeth Bassett     B14D  SAMUEL
   f  William Bassett       B14E  BENJAMIN
   b  Lydia Gaunt           B14F  REMEMBRANCE
   f  Peter Gaunt                 ======
B11B  JOHN          [B13]   [B15]   BURGESS
   a  Mary Worden                 Jacob Burgess B11D
   f  Peter Worden                Mary Nye      B11Da
B11C  ELIZABETH                   ------
   a  Ezra Perry     [B14]   B15A  SAMUEL
B11D  JACOB          [B15]   B15B  EBENEZER
   a  Mary Nye                 a  Mercy Lombard
   f  Benjamin Nye           B15C  JACOB          [B20]
B11E  JOSEPH         [B16]     a  Mary Hunt
   a  Patience --            B15D  THOMAS
      ======                    a  Joanna --
[B12]    BURGESS            B15E  BENJAMIN
         Thomas Burgess Jr B11A    a  Priscilla
         Lydia Gaunt    B11Ab B15F  MARY
      ------                     a  Christopher Gifford
B12A  THOMAS II      [B17]         ======
   a  Esther --              [B16]   BURGESS
      ======                       Joseph Burgess B11E
[B13]    BURGESS                   Patience --    B11Ea
         John Burgess B11B         ------
         Mary Worden  B11Ba  B16A  REBECCA
      ------                     a  -- Ross
B13A  JOHN Jr        [B18]   B16B  DOROTHY
   a  Sarah Nickerson          a  -- Clifton
   f  Nicholas Nickerson     B16C  BENJAMIN
B13B  THOMAS         [B19]   B16D  ICHABOD
   a  Sarah Storrs                 ======
B13C  JOSEPH                 [B17]   BURGESS
   a  Thomasine Baggs                Thomas Burgess B12A
   f  Jonathan Baggs                 Esther ---    B12Aa
B13D  SAMUEL                         ------
   a  Elizabeth --          B17A  EDWARD         [B21]
B13E  JACOB                    a  Elizabeth Coe
   a  Sarah --              B17B  DEBORAH
B13F  MARTHA                B17C  ESTHER
   a  Samuel Storrs           a  William Wilbour [B22]
```

320

----

cont'd
B17D LYDIA
  a --Collins
B17E JOSEPH
  a Ann Tew
B17F JOHN
  a Hannah James
B17G MARY
  a John Wood
317H THOMAS
  a Hannah Taylor
B17I JACOB
  a Susannah Williston
B17J MERCY
  a Joseph Thurston
B17K REBECCA
B17L MARTHA
B17M NATHANIEL
  a Ruth Chandler

======
[B18] BURGESS
  John Burgess Sr B13A
  Sarah Nickerson B13Aa

B18A MARY
  a Elnathan Ellis
B18B ELIZABETH
  a Prince Wixon
B18C JOSEPH
B18D BENJAMIN
B18E SAMUEL
B18F EZEKIEL
B18G THANKFUL
  a John Blossom
B18H JOHN Jr
======
[B19] BURGESS
  Thomas Burgess B13B
  Sarah Storrs B13Ba

B19A MARY
  a Ebenezer Babcock
B19B THOMAS
B19C HANNAH
B19D MARTHA
B19E SARAH
B19F THANKFUL
  a Daniel Cole
B19G EBENEZER
B19H MATTHIAS
B19I DAVID

======
[B20] BURGESS
  Jacob Burgess B15C
  Mary Hunt B15Ca

B20A ZACCHEUS
B20B JEDIDAH
  a Thomas Phillips
B20C ABIA
B20D ABIGAIL
  a -- Swift
B20E SAMUEL
B20F JACOB
======

[B21] BURGESS
  Edward Burgess B17A
  Elizabeth Coe B17Aa

B21A BENJAMIN #1
B21B THOMAS
B21C ESTHER
B21D BENJAMIN #2
B21E SARAH
  a Philip Mosier
B21F LYDIA
  a Maxon Mosier
======
[B22] WILBOUR
  William Wilbour B17Ca
  Esther Burgess B17C

B22A THOMAS
B22B MARY
B22C ESTHER
B22D LYDIA
B22E SAMUEL
B22F WILLIAM
B22G DANIEL
B22H CHARLES
B22I ESTHER
B22J LYDIA
B22K DEBORAH
B22L CLARK
======
[B23] POPE
  Seth Pope B14Ba
  Deborah Perry B14B

B23A SUSANNAH
  a Jonathan Hathaway
  f Arthur Hathaway W14Aa)
  m Sarah Cooke (W14A)

```
          ======     Note:Stephens/Stevens Same family
[C10]    STEPHENS                    ======
          unk              [C14]    STEPHENS
          unk                       Henry Stephens Jr C11C
          ------                    Elizabeth Fellows C11Ca
C10A HENRY Sr.=A1/276  [C11]        ------
     a Elizabeth Gallup        C14A HENRY II
          ======                    a Sarah Babcock
[C11]    STEPHENS              C14B SIMEON
          Henry Stephens Sr C10A     a Mercy Coates
          Elizabeth Gallup C10Aa C14C MARY
          ------                    a John Meeks
C11A THOMAS Sr         [C12]   C14D JEDEDIAH        [C20]
     a Mary Hall                    a Mary Rathbone
C11B RICHARD Sr        [C13]        ======
     a Sarah Harker            [C15]    STEPHENS
C11C HENRY Jr=A1/138   [C14]        Thomas Stephens C12A
     a Elizabeth Fellows            Elizabeth Wynne C12Aa
          ======                C15A NOAH
[C12]    STEPHENS                   a Sarah Stevens
          Thomas Stephens C11A  C15B JESSE
          Mary Hall       C11Aa C15C ELIZABETH
C12A THOMAS Jr         [C15]        ======
     a Elizabeth Wynne         [C16]    STEVENS
C12B PHINEAS                        Uriah Stevens Jr C12C
C12C URIAH             [C16]        Sarah Stevens   C12Ca
     a Sarah Stephens            ------
C12D ANDREW            [C17]   C16A URIAH Jr        [C21]
     a Esther Safford               a Martha Rathbone
C12E BENJAMIN          [C18]   C16B MARY
     a Elizabeth --                 a Thomas Williams
C12F SAMUEL                    C16C SARAH
     a Anna Segar                   a Noah Stevens
C12G ZEBULON           [C19]   C16D LUCY
     a Marion Fellows                a Abel Palmer
C12H JESSE                     C16E PHINEAS
     a Sarah Richards               ======
          ======               [C17]    STEPHENS
[C13]    STEPHENS                   Andrew Stephens C12D
          Richard Stephen C11B      Esther Safford  C12Da
          Sarah Harker    C11Ba     ------
          ------               C17A JOHN
C13A JOHN                           a Phebe Howe
C13B HANNAH                    C17B MARY
C13C SARAH                          a Thomas Dickenson
     a Uriah Stevens           C17C SAFFORD
C13D MARTIN                         a Hannah Wells
C13E HEPZIBAH                  C17D ESTHER
C13F HANNAH                         a Peter Hatch
C13G PATIENCE                  C17E DOROTHY
```

C17F AMY
  a Oliver Jewell
C17G ANDREW
  a Cynthia Brownell
C17H STEPHEN
C17I NATHANIEL
  a Phebe Montanje
  b Amy Whitney
C17J OLIVE
  a Samuel McCleary
C17K DESIRE
  a Eleaser Waterhouse
  b Joseph Stevens
C17L OLIVER
  a Nancy Chittenden
  ======
[C18]   STEPHENS
    Benjamin Stephens C12E
    Elizabeth --   C12Ea

C18A ELIZABETH
  a Gershom Hewett
C18B MARY
  a William Newell
C18C ABIGAIL
C18D DRUSILLA
  a Obadiah Brown
C18E SARAH
  ======
[C19]   STEPHENS
    Zebulon Stephens C12G
    Marion Fellows   C12Ga

C19A JOANNA
  a John Bacon
C19B RACHEL
  a Paul Raymond
C19C ZEBULON
  a Sarah Herrick
C19D BENJAMIN
  a Esther Rowlson
C19E THOMAS
  a Lucy Miller
C19F JONATHAN
  a Susan Wells

  ======

[C20]   STEPHENS
    Jedediah Stephens C14D
    Mary Rathbone   C14Da

C20A JOSHUA   [C23]
  a Christina Dutcher

C20B MARY
C20C THANKFUL
C20D MARTHA
  a Elijah Rood
C20E ANNA
  a Jeremiah Baker
C20F EUNICE
  a Elijah Rood
C20G JEDEDIAH   [C22]
  a Abigail Corey
C20H IRA
  a Sybil Ransom
C20I RUFUS
  a Sylvania Stephens
C20J NATHAN
C20K CYNTHIA
  a Frances Saturlee
  ======
[C21]   STEPHENS
    Uriah Stephens C16A
    Martha Rathbone C16Aa

C21A BENJAMIN
C21B SARAH
C21C MARY
  a Daniel McHenry
C21D URIAH
  a Elizabeth Jones
C21E JOHN
  a Olive Franklin
C21F MARTHA
  a George Hornell
C21G PHINEAS
  a Mary Clark
C21H ELIAS
  a Lucille Chapman
  b Lucretia Snow
  c Polly Crosby
C21I ELIJAH
  a Jane --
C21J WILLIAM
  a Anne Ayres
  ======
[C22]   STEPHENS
    Jedediah Stephens C20G
    Abigail Corey   C20Ga

C22A NATHAN
  a Rachael Gilbert
C22B OLIVE
C22C JOSHUA
  a Rhoda Stephens
C22D HILDA
  a Phineas Stephens
  b Jeremiah Baker

```
C22E  SYLVINA                      C25I  JUDITH
C22F  ABIGAIL                        a  John Luther
  a  Elijah Stephens                ======
C22G  CYNTHIA                    [G26]   SALISBURY
C22H  PAMELIA                         Samuel Salisbury C25Aa
C22I  SILAS                           Jemima Martin    C25A
      ======                         ------
[C23]   STEPHENS                 C26A  JEMIMA
      Joshua Stephens   C20A       a  Henry Esten    [C27]
      Christine Dutcher C20Aa    C26B  JOANNA
      ------                     C26C  EBENEZER
C23A  CLARISSA                   C26D  JOSEPH
  a  William Baker               C26E  MARTIN
C22B  LEANDER                          ======
C22C  RUFUS                      [C27]   ESTEN
  a  Thankful Baker                  Henry Esten      C26Aa
C22D  EZRA                            Jemima Salisbury C26A
  a  Cynthia Stephens               ------
C22E  WILLIAM R                  C27A  HENRY II
  a  Laura Roude                 C27B  JOHN
C22F  JEDEDIAH                   C27C  JEMIMA
  a  Esther Palmer                 a  Elijah Hawkins
C22G  IRA                            ======
C22H  CHRISTINA                  [C28]   MARTIN
      ======                         Meletiah Martin C25B
[C24]   MARTIN                       Rebecca Brooks  C25Ba
      unk                            ------
      unk                       C28A  HEZEKIAH
      ------                    C28B  ANN
C24A  JOHN          [C25]          a  Joseph Bowen
  a  Johanna Esten            C28C  DANIEL        [C29]
      ======                       a  Tabatha Carpenter
[C25]   MARTIN                 C28D  NATHAN
      John Martin   C24A       C28E  MELETIAH       [C30]
      Johanna Esten C24Aa          a  Abigail --
      ------                   C28F  REBECCA
C25A  JEMIMA                       a  Hezekiah Mason
  a  Samuel Salisbury[C26]    C28G  TIMOTHY
C25B  MELETIAH        [C28]
  a  Rebecca Brooks
  b  Jemima Wright                 ======
  c  Patience Eddy            [C29]   MARTIN
C25C  JOHN          [C31]          Daniel Martin  C28C
  a  Marcy Hayward                 Tabitha CarpenterC28Ca
C25D  EPHRAIM        [C32]         ------
  a  Thankful Bullock        C29A  DANIEL Jr
C25E  ANN                          a  Rebecca Horton
  a  Richard Round  [C33]          ======
C25F  MANASSEH                 [C30]   MARTIN
  a  Hannah Carpenter              Meletiah Martin C28E
C25G  JOHANNA                       Abigail --     C28Ea
  a  Philip Short                  ------
C25H  EBENEZER       [C34]     C30A  PELEG
  a  Abigail Wheeler          C30B  JOHN
                              C30C  MELETIAH
```

```
======                    ------
[C31]  MARTIN              C33A  ANNE
       John Martin  C25C   C33B  RICHARD
       Marcy Hayward C25Ca C33C  HANNAH
       ------             C33D  JOANNA
C31A  SARAH                C33E  JOHN
   a  Caleb Boomer         C33F  NATHANIEL
C31B  HANNAH               C33G  ELIZABETH
   a  Thomas Lewis         ======
C31C  JOANNA
   a  Joseph Barney        [C34]  MARTIN
C31D  JOHN        [C35]           Ebenezer Martin  C25H
   a  Mary Andrus                 Abigail Wheeler  C25Ha
C31E  MARCY                       ------
   a  Squire Bullock       C34A  JEMIMA
C31F  BARBERY              C34B  JOHN
   a  Obadiah Bowen        C34C  EBENEZER
C31G  MARY                 C34D  NATHANIEL      [C42]
   a  Hezekiah Horton         a  Susannah Kent
C31H  HEZEKIAH    [C36]    C34E  ABIGAIL
   a  Hannah Andrus               ======
C31I  ELIZABETH            [C35]  MARTIN
   a  William Seamans              John Martin   C31D
C31J  ANN                          Mary Andrus   C31Da
   a  John Mason                   ------
C31K  JEMIMA               C35A  JOHN
   a  Valentine Bowen      C35B  MARY
C31L  BENJAMIN    [C37]    C35C  JOSEPH
   a  Sarah Kingsley       C35D  NATHAN
       ======             C35E  DAVID
[C32]  MARTIN                      ======
       Ephraim Martin  C25D [C36]  MARTIN
       Thankful Bullock C25Da      Hezekiah Martin  C31H
       ------                      Hannah Andrus    C31Ha
C32A  EDWARD      [C38]            ------
   a  Rebekah Peck         C36A  HANNAH
C32B  THANKFUL             C36B  HEZEKIAH
C32C  EPHRIAM Jr  [C39]       a  Mary Pierce
   a  Elizabeth --         C36C  ANNE
C32D  PERSERVANCE          C36D  GIDEON
C32E  HOPESTILL            C36E  HEZEKIAH(2) Sr  [C52]
C32F  JUDETH                  a  Mehitable Peck
C32G  SETH        [C40]    C36F  MARY
   a  Hannah --            C36G  LUCY
C32H  LYDIA                C36H  EPHRAIM         [C53]
C32I  MANASSAH                a  Rebecca Salisbury
C32J  BENJAMIN    [C41]    C36I  SARAH
   a  Lucy --              C36J  ABIGAIL
       ======                    ======
[C33]  ROUND               [C37]  MARTIN
       Richard Round C25Ea         Benjamin Martin C31L
       Ann Martin    C25E          Sarah Kingsley  C31La
       ------                      ------
```

C37A MARCY
   a Joseph Sanford
C37B GIDEON
   a Jerusha Sprague
C37C SIMEON
   a Esther Mason
C37D JAMES   [C54]
   a Hannah Chase
   b Freelove--
   c Asany Wiles
C37E THOMAS   [C60]
   a Hannah Short
C37F BENJAMIN
   a Sarah Lewis
C37G HOLDEN
   a Sarah Cole
C37H KINGSLEY
   a Prudence Mason
     ======

[C38] MARTIN
    Edward Martin C32A
    Rebecca Peck C32Aa

C38A MARY
   a John Ellis
C38B HOPESTILL
   a Samuel Thurber
C38C SYLVANUS Sr [C61]
   a Martha Wheeler
C38D REBECKAH
   a John Barney
C38E LOIS
   a Joseph Barney
     ======

[C39] MARTIN
    Ephraim Martin C32C
    Elizabeth -- C32Ca

C39A EPHRAIM II
   a Ann --
C39B EDWARD
   a Ruth --
     ======

[C40] MARTIN
    Seth Martin C32G
    Hannah -- C32Ga

C40A PATIENCE
C40B SETH
C40C JUDETH
C40D LEVI
C40E PHEBE

C40F MOLLY
C40G CHLOE
C40H HANNAH
C40I JAMES
C40J LYDIA

     ======

[C41] MARTIN
    Benjamin Martin C32J
    Lucy --   C32Ja

C41A CONSTANT
C41B FREELOVE
C41C BENJAMIN
   a Sarah --
C41D LUCY
C41E SAMUEL
C41F ASA
C41G ABI C
     ======

[C42] MARTIN
    Nathaniel Martin C34D
    Susannah Kent C34Da

C42A LUTHER   [C62]
   a Elizabeth Humphrey
C42B ANTHONY   [C63]
   a Susanna Allen
C42C ANDERSON   [C64]
   a Nancy Alger
     ======

[C43] CHICKERING
    unk
    unk

C43A HENRY   [C44]
   a Mary --
     ======

[C44] CHICKERING
    Henry Chickering C43A
    Mary --   C43Aa

C44A FRANCIS   [C45]
   a Ann Fiske
     ======

[C45] CHICKERING
    Francis Chickering C44A
    Ann Fiske   C44A

C45A ANN
   a Stephen Paine [C46]

[C46]   PAINE
    Stephen Paine C45Aa
    Ann Chitering C45A

C46A STEPHEN   [C47]
  a Elizabeth Williams
  b Mary Brinstall
C46B REBECCA
  a Peter Hunt
  b Samuel Peck   [C48]
C46C JOHN   [C49]
  a Elizabeth Belcher
C46D MARY
  a Enoch Hunt   [C50]
C46E SAMUEL   [C51]
  a Ann Peck
C46F ELIZABETH
  a Jacob Pepper   [C70]
C46G SARAH
  a Daniel Aldis   [C71]
C46H NATHANIEL   [C72]
  a Mary Chaffee
  ======

[C47]   PAINE
    Stephen Paine   C46C
    Elizabeth Wilson C46Ca

C47A STEPHEN Jr
  a Louise Kinney
  b -- Spaulding
  ======

[C48]   PECK
    Samuel Peck   C46Bb
    Rebecca Paine C46B

C48A NOAH
C48B JOEL
C48C REBECCA
C48D JUDITH
  ======

[C49]   PAINE
    John Paine   C46C
    Elizabeth Belcher C46Ca

C49A ELIZABETH
  a Thomas Waite
C49B JOHN
  a Mary Davis
  b Hannah --
C49C STEPHEN   [C65]
  a Sarah Vallet
C49D JOSIAH

C49E JOSEPH
C49F REBECCA
  a Abel Potter
C49G SOLOMON
  a Abigail Owen
C49H BENJAMIN
  a Elizabeth --
  b Ann Arnold
  c Ann Morey
  d Jemima E Esten
C49I NATHAN
  a Hannah --
C49J GIDEON
  a Rebecca Corses
C49K URANIA
  a Uriah Morey
C49L WILLIAM
C49M ABIJAH
C49N EZEKIAL
  a Ruth Seeley
C49O SAMUEL
C49P ISAIAH
  a Martha --
  ======

[C50]   HUNT
    Enoch Hunt C46Da
    Mary Paine C46D

C50A MARY
C50B PETER
  a Anna Paine
C50C ELIZABETH
C50D ENOS
  ======

[C51]   PAINE
    Samuel Paine C46E
    Ann Peck   C46Ea

C51A SAMUEL
  a Ruth Perrin
C51B ANNA
  a Peter Hunt
C51C SETH
  a Mary Morris
C51D SARAH
  a Daniel Peck
C51E JUDITH
  a Ichabod Peck
C51F NOAH
  a Mehitable Storrs
C51G STEPHEN
  a Sarah Leach

C51H DANIEL
  a Leah Smith
  b Abigail Frissell
C51I REBECCA
  a D. Cleveland
C51J EBENEZER
  a Mary Grosvenor
  ======

[C52] MARTIN
  Hezekiah Martin C36E
  Mehitable Peck C36Ea

C52A HEZEKIAH
  a Rosalana Sheldon
C52B JOHN
  a Nancy Bemas
C52C EBENEZER
  a Hannah Bingham
C52D ANDRUSS
  a Ruth Sylvester
C52E JOSEPH W
  a Almira D Baxter
  ======

[C53] MARTIN
  Ephraim Martin   C36H
  Rebecca SalisburyC36Ha

C53A JOHN
  a Elizabeth Humphrey
C53B EPHRIAM
  a Phidelia Chase
C53C OTIS
  a Poly Weston
  ======

[C54] MARTIN
  James Martin C37D
  Freelove -- C37Da

C54A JESSE
C54B LIPPIT
  a Rhoda --
C54C SARAH
C54D PHEBE
C54E WHIPPLE   [C55]
  a Cynthia Smith
  ======

[C55] MARTIN
  Whipple Martin C54E
  Cynthia Smith C54Ea

C55A CAROLINE
C55B JAMES W   [C56]
  a Mary A Paine

[C56] MARTIN
  James W Martin C55B
  Mary A Paine   C55Ba

C56A AUGUSTA R
  a William Smith
C54B CHARLES AUGUST   [C57]
  a Ella Augustus Vincent
C54C ALBERT H
C54D HELEN
C54E GEORGE B
C54F ZATTIE
  ======

[C57] MARTIN
  Charles A Martin C56B
  Ella A Vincent   C56Ba

C57A ERNEST   [C58]
  a Sadie Woodruff
C54B ERFORD A
  a Effie B Houghtaling
C54C EDNA
  ======

[C58] MARTIN
  Ernest J Martin C57A
  Sadie Woodruff   C57Aa

C58A EDNA ROSAMOND
  a Rex A Snider   [C59]
C58B PORTER
  a Gertrude Smith
C58C Manley Eugene
  a Thelma Torgerson
  b Dorothy Rumzek
C58D BRUTH
  a Myrl Ann Bloss
C58E MARIAN CHARLES
  a Winnifred M McMichael
  ======

[C59] SNIDER
  Rex A Snider C58Aa
  Edna R Martin C58A

C59A ARLENE
  a Robert B Griffiths
C59B DALE R
  a Shirley Ann Sinclair
C59C AUDREY
  a Ralph Martin Provoast
C59D VIRGINIA
  a Harold Frank Chase
C59E MARGARET
  a John H Fritz

[C60]   MARTIN
    Thomas Martin C37E
    Hannah Short C37Ea

C60A ELIZABETH
  a David Winston
C60B HOSEA
C60C JOSEPH S
C60D SARAH
C50E BENJAMIN
  a Sally Coats
C60F THOMAS P
C60G AMANDA
C60H HANNAH
C60I IRA K

    ======
[C61]   MARTIN
    Sylvanus Martin SrC38C
    Martha Wheeler C38Ca

C61A EDWARD
  a Deborah Brown
C61B SYLVANUS Jr
C61C HOPESTILL
  a Samuel Mason
C61D VALENTINE
  a Mary Perry
C61E SIMEON
  a Abigail Durfee
C61F PHILIP
  a Mary Granger
C61G JOSEPH
C61H MARTHA
  a Christopher Blanding
C61I CYRUS
  a Charlotte Bridgham
C61J WHEELER
  a Sally Esterbrooks
  b Rebecca Sawin
C61K CALVIN
  a Susanna May
C61L SEREPTA
C61M ELHANAN
  a Mary Hawkins
    ======
[C62]   MARTIN
    Luther Martin   C42A
    Elizabeth Humphrey C42Aa

C62A SULLIVAN
  a Belinda Peck
  b Lydia Rogerson
  c Esther Tiffany

C62B STERRY
  a Mary Davis
C62C JOSIAH
  a Charlotte Davis
    ======
[C63]   MARTIN
    Anthony Martin C42B
    Suanna Allen   C42Ba

C63A KENT
  a Catherine Bump
C63B BOSWORTH
  a Catherine Fenton
C63C AMASA
  a Desire Ballou
    ======
[C64]   MARTIN
    Anderson Martin C42C
    Nancy Alger   C42Ca

C64A LUTHER
  a Susan Miller
  b Almy T Ingraham
C64B HORACE ANDERSON
  a Nancy D Kinnicutt
    ======
[C65]   PAINE
    Stephen Paine C49C
    Sarah Vallet C49Ca

C65A STEPHEN   [C66]
  a Sarah Thorton
    ======
[C66]   PAINE
    Stephen Paine C65A
    Sarah Thorton C65Aa

C66A NATHAN   [C67]
  a Lillis Winsor
    ======
[C67]   PAINE
    Nathan Paine C66A
    Lillis Winsor C66Aa

C67A ZATTO   [C68]
  a Abigail Eddy
C67B MATHEWSON W
  a Fidelia Darling
C67C FIDELIA
  a Smith W Place
    ======

```
======                              ------
[C68]  PAINE                        C72A  DOROTHY
       Zatto Paine  C67A            C72B  NATHANIEL
       Abigail Eddy C67Aa                 a  Abigail Smith
       ------                       C72C  ABIGAIL
C68A  ARNOLD Sr          [C69]      C72D  JONATHAN
      a  Loanna Parker                    a  Rebecca Peck
       ======                       C72E  RACHEL
[C69]  PAINE                              a  Timothy Borden
       Arnold Paine Sr C68A         C72F  ELIZABETH
       Loanna Parker   C68Aa              a  Joshua Lyon
       ------                             ======
C69A  ALMA
C69B  ABIGAIL
C69C  JAMES L
C69D  WILLIAM
C69E  ARNOLD Jr
C69F  DAY C
C69G  DWIGHT
C69H  LUCY
C69I  MARY A
      a  James W Martin
C69J  ANN E
C69K  DAVID H
C69L  ALBERT B
C69M  THOMAS R
       ======
[C70]  PEPPER
       Jacob Pepper   C46Fa
       Elizabeth Paine C46F
       ------
C70A  ROBERT
C70B  REBECCA
C70C  ANN
C70D  MARY
C70E  BENJAMIN
       ======
[C71]  ALDIS
       Daniel Aldis C46Ga
       Sarah Paine  C46G
       ------
C71A  SARAH
C71B  DANIEL
C71C  ANN
      a  Jonathan Onion
C71D  SARAH
       ======
[C72]  PAINE
       Nathaniel Paine C46H
       Mary Chaffee   C46Ha
       ------
```

```
    ======
[C73]   WILLIAMS
        unk
        unk
    ------
C73A  JAMES            [C74]
   a  Alice Pemberton
    ======
[C74]   WILLIAMS
        James Williams  C73A
        Alice Pemberton C73Aa
    ------
C74A  SIDRACH
C74B  ROGER            [C75]
   a  Mary Barnard
C74C  ROBERT
C74D  KATHERINE
   a  James Wightman
   b  John Davis
    ======
[C75]   WILLIAMS
        Roger Williams  C74B
        Mary Barnard    C74Ba
    ------
C75A  MARY
   a  John Sayles Sr [C76]
C75B  FREEBORN
   a  Thomas Hart      [C85]
C75C  PROVIDENCE
C75D  MERCY
   a  Samuel Winsor    [C77]
C75E  DANIEL           [C78]
   a  Rebecca Power
C75F  JOSEPH           [C79]
   a  Lydia Olney
    ======
[C76]   SAYLES
        John Sayles Sr C75Aa
        Mary Williams  C75A
    ------
C76A  MARY
   a  William Greene  [C80]
C76B  JOHN Jr          [C81]
   a  Elizabeth Olney
C76C  ISABEL
C76D  PHEBE
   a  Job Greene       [C82]
C76E  ELEANOR
   a  Richard Greene  [C83]
C76F  CATHERINE
C76G  DEBORAH
   a  Caleb Carr       [C84]
```

```
    ======
[C77]   WINSOR
        Samuel Winsor  C75Da
        Mercy Williams C75D
    ------
C77A  SAMUEL           [C87]
   a  Mercy Harding
C77B  HANNAH
   a  Daniel Angell Sr [C88]
C77C  JOSHUA Sr        [C89]
   a  Mary Barker
    ======
[C78]   WILLIAMS
        Daniel Williams C75E
        Rebecca Power   C75Ea
    ------
C78A  MARY
   a  Epenetus Olney  [C90]
C78B  PELEG Sr         [C91]
   a  Elizabeth Carpenter
C78C  ROGER I!         [C92]
   a  Elizabeth Walling
C78D  DANIEL
C78E  PATIENCE
   a  William Ashton  [C93]
C78F  PROVIDENCE
   a  Elizabeth --
C78G  JOSEPH
   a  Sarah Whitman
    ======
[C79]   WILLIAMS
        Joseph Williams C75F
        Lydia Olney     C75Fa
    ------
C79A  JOSEPH           [C94]
   a  Lydia Hearnden
C79B  THOMAS           [C95]
   a  Mary Blackmar
C79C  MARY
C79D  JAMES            [C96]
   a  Elizabeth Blackmar
C79E  LYDIA
    ======
[C80]   GREENE
        William Greene C76Aa
        Mary Sayles    C76A
    ------
C80A  MARY
   a  Edward Dyer
    ======
[C81]   SAYLES
        John Sayles Jr  C76B
        Elizabeth Olney C76Ba
    ------
```

C81A RICHARD
    a Marcy Phillips
C81B THOMAS
    a Esther Scott
    ======
[C82] GREENE
    Job Greene   C76D
    Phebe Sayles C76Da

C82A ANNE
    a Thomas Stafford
C82B PHILIP
    a Elizabeth Wicks
    ======
[C83] GREENE
    Richard Greene C76Ea
    Eleanor Sayles C76E
C83A AUDRY
    a Thomas Stafford
    ======
[C84] CARR
    Caleb Carr   C76Ga
    Deborah Sayles C76G

C84A MERCY
    a Esek Brown
    ======
[C85] HART
    Thomas Hart   C75Ba
    Freeborn Williams C75B

C85A JOHN
C85B MARY
    a Samuel Cranston   [C86]
C85C JAMES
C85D THOMAS
    ======
[C86] CRANSTON
    Samuel Cranston C85Ba
    Mary Hart   C85B

C86A JOHN
    a Penelope Godfrey
    ======
[C87] WINSOR
    Samuel Winsor C77A
    Mercy Harding C77Aa

C87A MARTHA
    a Robert Colwell
C87B MARY
    a Fisher Potter
C87C LYDIA
    a John Angell

C87D HANNAH
    a James Olney
C87E JOSEPH
    a Deborah Mathewson
C87F DEBORAH
    a Clarles Olney
C87G MERCY
    a Nedebiah Angell
C87H FREELOVE
    a Jonathan Jencks
C87I SAMUEL
    a Lydia Olney
    b Ann Winsor
    ======
[C88] ANGELL
    Daniel Angell Sr C77Ba
    Hannah Winsor   C77B

C88A SAMUEL
C88B JOHN
    a Ruth Field
C88C Nedebiah
    a Mary Winsor
C88D JOSHUA
C88E MERCY
    a Benjamin Smith
C88F JOB
C88G DANIEL
C88H EZEKIAL
C88I WAIT
    ======
[C89] WINSOR
    Joshua Winsor Sr C77C
    Mary Barker   C77Ca

C89A SARAH
C89B JOSHUA Jr
C89C SAMUEL
C89D SUSANNAH
C89E MARY
C89F ABRAHAM
C89G JOHN
    a Mercy Smith
    ======
[C90] OLNEY
    Epenetus Olnay C78A
    Mary Williams C78Aa

C90A JAMES
C90B CHARLES
C90C JOSEPH
C90D ANTHONY

C90E MARY
C90F AMEY
C90G MARTHA
  a Stephen Angell
C90H FREEBORN
   ======
[C91] WILLIAMS
    Peleg Williams Sr C78B
    Elizabeth Carpenter C78Ba

C91A DANIEL
  a Susannah Johnston
C91B ROBERT
  a Anne Chase
C91C SILAS
C91D PELEG Jr
C91E TIMOTHY
C91F FREELOVE
C91G ELIZABETH
   ======
[C92] WILLIAMS
    Roger Williams Jr C78C
    Elizabeth Walling C78Ca

C92A ELIZABETH
C92B REBECCA
   ======
[C93] ASHTON
    William Ashton C78Ea
    Patience Williams C78E
C93A JOSHUA
C93B WILLIAM
C93C THOMAS
C93D REBECCA
   ======
[C94] WILLIAMS
    Joseph Williams C79A
    Lydia Hearnden C79Aa

C94A MERCY
C94B JEREMIAH
C94C MARY
C94D LYDIA
C94E MARTHA
C94F BARBARA
C94G FREELOVE
C94H JEMIMA
C94I MERIBAH

   ======
[C95] WILLIAMS
    Thomas Williams C79B
    Mary Blackmar C79Ba

C95A JOSEPH
C95B THOMAS
C95C STEPHEN
C95D JOHN
C95E ABIGAIL
C95F JONATHAN
C95G MARY
  a Charles Dyer
   ======
[C96] WILLIAMS
    James Wilians   C79D
    Elizabeth Blackmar C79Da

C96A JAMES
C96B ANNE
C96C SARAH
C96D JOSEPH
C96E MARY
C96F NATHANIEL
C96G ELIZABETH
C96H HANNAH
C96I LYDIA
C96J NATHAN

DIVISION S
F10-F16

[F10]   FULLER
   unkn
   unkn

F10A   Robert Fuller
  a   Sara Dunkhorn
   ======

[F11]   Fuller
   Robert Fuller F10A
   Sara Dunkhorn F10Aa

F11A   EDWARD FULLER MF   [F12]
  a   unkn
F11B   SAMUEL FULLER Dr. MF
   ======

[F12]   FULLER
   EDWARD FULLER F11A
   unkn

F12A   MATTHEW   [F13]
  a   Frances --
F12B   SAMUEL MF   [F14]
  a   Jane Lothrop
  f   John Lothrop
  m   Hannah Howes
   ======

[F13]   FULLER
   Matthew Fuller F12A
   Frances --   F12Aa

F13A   SAMUEL   [F15]
  a   unkn
F13B   MARY
  a   Ralph Jones   [F16]
F13C   ELIZABETH
  a   Moses Rowley   [F17]
F13D   ANNE
F13E   JOHN   [F18]
  a   Bethia --
  b   Hannah Morton
  f   John Morton
  m   Lettice Handford
   ======

[F14]   FULLER
   Samuel Fuller   F12B
   Jane Lothrop   F12Ba

F14A   HANNAH
  a   Nicholas Bonham   [F19]
F14B   SAMUEL   [F20]
  a   Anne Fuller
  f   Matthew Fuller
  m   unkn

F14C   ELIZABETH
  a   Joseph Taylor
F14D   SARAH
F14E   MARY
  a   Joseph Williams   [F21]
  f   John Williams
  m   Jane --
F14F   THOMAS
F14G   SARAH
F14H   JOHN   [F22]
  a   Mehitable Rowley
  f   Moses Rowley Sr
  m   Elizabeth Fuller
   ======

[F15]   Fuller
   Samuel Fuller   F12B
   Jane Lothrop   F12Ba

F15A   THOMAS   [F23]
  a   Elizabeth Lathrop
  f   Joseph Lathrop
  m   Mary Ansel
F15B   JABEZ   [F24]
  a   Mary Hallett
  f   Joseph Hallett
  m   Elizabeth Gorham
F15C   ANNE
  a   Joseph Smith   [F25]
  f   Rev. John Smith
  m   Susannah Hinkley
F15D   TIMOTHY   [F26]
  a   Sarah Gates
  f   George Gates
  m   Sarah Olmstead
  b   Mary Champion
  f   Thomas Champion
  m   Hannah Brockway
F15E   MATTHIAS
F15F   ABAGAIL
F15G   SAMUEL [F27]
  a   Elizabeth Thatcher
  f   Rodolphus Thatcher
  m   Ruth Partridge
   ======

[F16]   JONES
   Ralph Jones   F13Ba
   Mary Fuller F13B

F16A   MATTHEW
  a   Mercy Goodspeed
  f   John Goodspeed
  m   Experience Holloway

F16B SHUBAEL
F16C JEDEDIAH [F29]
 a Hannah Davis
 f John Davis
 m Hannah Linnell
F16D JOHN [F30]
 a Abagail --
F16E MERCY
F16F RALPH [F31]
 a Deborah Coombs
 f Frances Coombs
 m Deborah Morton
F16G SAMUEL [F32]
 a Mary Blish
 f Joseph Blish
 m Hannah Hull
F16H EPHRAIM
F16I MARY
F16J MEHITABLE
  ======
[F17] ROWLEY
  Moses Rowley F13Ca
  Elizabeth Fuller F13C

F17A MARY
 a John Weeks [F33]
F17B MOSES [F34]
 a Mary Fletcher
 b Mary Crippen
F17C CHILD
F17D CHILD
F17E SHUBAEL [F35]
 a Catherine Crippen
 f Thomas Crippen
 m Frances --
F17F MEHITABLE =F14Ha
F17G SARAH
F17H NATHAN [F36]
 a Mercy Hatch
 f Jonathan Hatch
 m Sarah Rowley
F17I AARON [F37]
 a Mary Weeks
F17J JOHN
F17K MATTHEW
  ======
[F18] FULLER
  John Fuller F13E
  Bethia -- F13Ea

F18A LYDIA
 a Joseph Dimmock [F38]
 f Shubael Dimmock
 m Joanna Bursley
F18B BETHIA
 a Barnabas Lothrop [F39]
 f John Lothrop
 m Mary Cole
F18C JOHN [F40]
 a Thankful Gorham
 f John Gorham
 m Mary Otis
F18D RELIANCE
 a John Prince [F41]
  ======
[F19] BONHAM
  Nicholas Bonham F14Aa
  Hannah Fuller F14A

F19A HANNAH
 a Daniel Lippington [F42]
F19B MARY
 a Edmund Dunham [F43]
 f Benajah Dunham
 m Elizabeth Tilson
F19C SARAH
 a John Fitzrandolph [F44]
 f Edward Fitzrandolph
 m Elizabeth Blossom
F19D ELIZABETH
 a Edward Slater [F45]
 b John Drake Sr.
F19E HEZEKIAH [F46]
 a Mary Dunn
 f Hugh Dunn
 m Elizabeth Drake
F19F ELIJAH
F19G SAMUEL
F19H JANE
F19I PRICILLA
 a John Langstaff
 f Henry Langstaff
  ======
[F20] FULLER
  Samuel Fuller F14B
  Anne Fuller F14Ba

F20A BARNABAS [F47]
 a Elizabeth Young
F20B JOSEPH [F48]
 a Thankful Blossom
 f Peter Blossom
 m Sarah Bodfish

F20C MATTHEW   [F49]
   a Patience Young
   f George Young
   m Hannah Pinson
F20D BENJAMIN   [F50]
   a unknown
F20E DESIRE
   a John Taylor [F51]
F20F SARAH
   ======
[F21] WILLIAMS
     Joseph Williams F14Ea
     Mary Fuller   F14E

F21A SARAH
   a John Roath [F52]
   f Robert Roath
   m Sarah Sexton
F21B MARY
F21C JOHN   [F53]
   a Mary Knowlton
   f Thomas Knowlton
   m Hannah Green
F21D HANNAH
   ======
[F22]   FULLER
     John Fuller   F14H
     Mehitable Rowley F14Ha

F22A THOMAS   [F54]
   a Elizabeth --
F22B SAMUEL   [F55]
   a Naomi Rowley=F34C
   f Moses Rowley
   m Mary Fletcher
F22C SHUBAEL   [F56]
   a Hannah Crocker=D1/22
   f Jonathan Crocker
   m Hannah Howland
F22D THANKFUL
   a Jabez Crippen   [F57]
   f Thomas Crippen
   m Frances --
F22E EDWARD   [F58]
   a -- Bate
   f James Bate
   m Mary Lord
F22F ELIZABETH
   a Samuel Rowley =F34E[F59]
   f Moses Rowley
   m Mary Fletcher

F22G JOHN   [F60]
   a Mary Cornwall
   f William Cornwall
   m Esther Ward
F22H JOSEPH   [F61]
   a Lydia Day
   f John Day
   m Grace Spencer
   b Zerviah Dewey
   f Jedediah Dewey
   m Rebecca Williams
F22I BENJAMIN #1
F22J BENJAMIN #2
F22K MEHITABLE
   a Benjamin Kneeland Jr
   f Benjamin Kneeland Sr
   m Abagail --
   ======
[F23]   FULLER
     Thomas Fuller   F15A
     Elizabeth Lathrop F15Aa

F23A HANNAH
F23B JOSEPH
F23C MARY
F23D BENJAMIN m. F48D
F23E ELIZABETH
F23F SAMUEL
F23G ABIGAIL
F23H JOHN
   ======
[F24]   FULLER
     Jabez Fuller F15B
     Mary Halet   F15Ba

F24A SAMUEL
F24B JONATHAN
F24C MERCY
F24D MARY
F24E LOIS
F24F EBENEZER
   ======
[F25] SMITH
     Joseph Smith F15Ca
     Anne Fuller   F15C

F25A SUSANNA
F25B JOSEPH
F25C JAMES
F25D ANNE
F25E MATTHIAS m.F40A
F25F EBENEZER
F25G DANIEL
F25H DAVID

F25I	ELIZABETH	[F29]	JONES
F25J	THOMAS		Jedediah Jones F16C
F25K	MARY		Hannah Davis F16Ca
F25L	JEMIMA		------
F25M	BENJAMIN	F29A	SHUBAEL
F25N	EBENEZER	F29B	SIMON
	======	F29C	ISAAC
[F26]	FULLER	F29D	TIMOTHY (m.F31C)
	Timothy Fuller F15D	F29E	HANNAH
	Sarah Gates F15Da		======
	Mary Champion F15Db	[F30]	JONES
	------		John Jones F16D
F26A	TIMOTHY #1 by Sarah		Abagail -- F16Da
F26B	MARY		------
F26C	MATTHIAS	F30A	ABAGAIL
F26D	SARAH	F30B	MERCY
F26E	ABAGAIL	F30C	JOHN
F26F	ANN		======
F26G	SAMUEL	[F31]	JONES
F26H	TIMOTHY #2 by Mary		Ralph Jones F16F
F26I	MARY		Deborah Coombs F16Fa
F26J	ABIGAIL		------
F26K	HANNAH	F31A	DEBORAH
F26L	TIMOTHY #3	F31B	ELIZABETH
F26M	NOADIAH	F31C	THANKFUL (m. F29D)
F26N	THOMAS	F31D	BETHIA
F26O	MARY	F31E	CORNELIUS
	======	F31F	SYLVANUS
[F27]	FULLER	F31G	REUBEN
	Samuel Fuller F15G		======
	Elizabeth Thatcher F15Ga	[F32]	JONES
	------		Samuel Jones F16G
F27A	REBBECCA		Mary Blish F16Ga
F27B	RUDOLPHUS		------
F27C	RUTH	F32A	JOSEPH
F27D	ELKANAH	F32B	BENJAMIN
F27E	WAITSTILL	F32C	SAMUEL
F27F	MARY	F32D	MARY
F27G	JUDAH		======
	======	[F33]	WEEKS
[F28]	JONES		John Weeks F17Aa
	Matthew Jones F16A		Mary Rowley F17A
	Mercy Goodspeed F16Aa		------
	------	F33A	NATHANIEL
F28A	BENJAMIN	F33B	JOHN
F28B	RALPH	F33C	WILLIAM
F28C	EXPERIENCE	F33D	ELIZABETH
F28D	JOSIAH	F33E	SHUBAEL
F28E	EBENEZER	F33F	EBENEZER mar.F36D
F28F	REBECCA	F33G	ABIGAIL
	======	F33H	MEHITABLE

F33I	URIAH	{F38]	DIMMOCK
F33J	MARY		Joseph Dimmock F18Aa
	======		Lydia Fuller F18A
[F34]	ROWLEY		------
	Moses Rowley F17B	F38A	THOMAS
	Mary Fletcher F17Ba	F38B	BETHIAH
	------	F38C	MEHITABLE
F34A	MARY	F38D	ENSIGN
F34B	MOSES	F38E	ICHABOD
F34C	NAOMI=F22Ba	F38F	ABIGAIL
F34D	HANNAH	F38G	PHAROH
F34E	SAMUEL=F22Fa	F38H	DAVID
F34F	JOHN		======
F34G	EBENEZER	[F39]	LOTHROP
F34H	MEHITABLE		Barnabas Lothrop F18Ba
F34I	JONATHAN		Bethia Fuller F18B
	======		------
[F35]	ROWLEY	F39A	JOHN
	Shubael Rowley F17E	F39B	HANNAH
	Catherine Crippen F17Ea		======
	------	[F40]	FULLER
F35A	ISAAC		John Fuller F18C
F35B	SHUBAEL		Thankful Gorham F18Ca
F35C	THOMAS		------
F35D	MATTHEW	F40A	HANNAH m. F25E
F35E	ELIZABETH	F40B	JOHN
F35F	ELNATHAN	F40C	MARY
F35G	MARY	F40D	BETHIA
F35H	JABEZ	F40E	NATHANIEL
	======	F40F	THANKFUL
[F36]	ROWLEY		======
	Nathan Rowley F17H	[F41]	PRINCE
	Mercy Hatch F17Ha		John Prince F18Da
	------		Reliance Fuller F18D
F36A	MERCY		------
F36B	SARAH	F41A	JOHN
F36C	ELIZABETH	F41B	JOSEPH
F36D	MARY mar..F33F	F41C	REBECCA
F36E	NATHAN	F41D	SAMUEL
F36F	MOSES	F41E	HANNAH
F36G	JOHN		======
F36H	HATCH	[F42]	LIPPINGTON
F36I	MEHITABLE		Daniel Lippington F19Aa
	======		Hannah Bonham F19A
[F37]	ROWLEY		------
	Aaron Rowley F17I	F42A	RICHARD
	Mary Weeks F17Ia	F42B	DOROTHY #1
	------	F42C	HANNAH
F37A	MERCY	F42D	DOROTHY #2
F37B	TIMOTHY	F42E	DANIEL
F37C	AARON		======
F37D	ELIZABETH		
F37E	MARY		
F37F	ELNATHAN		

[F43]	DUNHAM		F47C	HANNAH
	Edmund Dunham	F19Ba	F47D	EBENEZER
	Mary Bonham	F19B	F47E	JOSIAH
	------			======
F43A	BENAJAH		[F48]	FULLER
F43B	ELIZABETH			Joseph Fuller F20B
F43C	EDMUND			Thankful Blossom F20Ba
F43D	JONATHAN		F48A	REMEMBER
F43E	EPHRAIM		F48B	SETH
F43F	MARY		F48C	THANKFUL
F43G	MARY		F48D	MERCY m. F23D
F43H	HANNAH			======
	======		[F49]	FULLER
[F44]	FITZRANDOLPH			Matthew Fuller F20C
	John Fitzrandolph F19Ca			Patience Young F20Ca
	Sarah Bonham	F19C		------
	------		F49A	ANNE
F44A	SARAH		F49B	JONATHAN
F44B	ELIZABETH		F49C	CONTENT
F44C	FRANCES		F49D	JEAN
F44D	TEMPERANCE		F49E	DAVID
F44E	TEMPERANCE		F49F	YOUNG
F44F	JOHN		F49G	CORNELIUS
F44G	EDWARD		F49H	HANNAH
	======			======
[F45]	SLATER		[F50]	FULLER
	Edward Slater	F19Da		Benjamin Fuller F20D
	Elizabeth Bonham F19D			unk
	------			------
F45A	PHILORETA		F50A	TEMPERANCE
F45B	ELIZABETH		F50B	HANNAH
F45C	PHILORETA		F50C	JOHN
F45D	PHEBE		F50D	JAMES
F45E	CALEB			======
F45F	ELIZABETH		[F51]	TAYLOR
F45G	ABRAHAM			John Taylor F20Ea
F45H	ALEESHIA			Desire Fuller F20E
	======			------
[F46]	BONHAM		F51A	BENJAMIN
	Hezekiah Bonham	F19E	F51B	SARAH
	Mary Dunn	F19Ea	F51C	JOHN
	------			======
F46A	MARY		[F52]	ROATH
F46B	SAMUEL			John Roath F21Aa
F46C	HANNAH			Sarah Williams F21A
F46D	SARAH			------
	======		F52A	JOHN
[F47]	FULLER		F52B	JOSEPH
	Barnabas Fuller F20A		F52C	BENJAMIN
	Elizabeth Young F20Aa			======

F47A	SAMUEL			
F47B	ISAAC			

[F53]	WILLIAMS		[F57]	CRIPPEN	
	John Williams F21C			Jabez Crippen F22Da	
	Mary Knowlton F21Ca			Thankful Fuller F22D	
	------			------	

F53A	MARY		F57A	SUSANNA	
F53B	BENJAMIN		F57B	FRANCES	
F53C	JOSEPH		F57C	LYDIA	
F53D	ZIPPORAH		F57D	THOMAS	
F53E	JOSEPH		F57E	JABEZ	
	======		F57F	JOHN	
[F54]	FULLER		F57G	MEHITABLE	
	Thomas Fuller F22A		F57H	SAMUEL	
	Elizabeth -- F22Aa		F57I	JOSEPH	
	------		F57J	THANKFUL	
				======	
F54A	EBENEZER		[F58]	FULLER	
F54B	THOMAS			Edward Fuller F22E	
F54C	NATHAN			-- Bate F22Ea	
F54D	HANNAH			------	
F54E	JABEZ				
F54F	JONATHAN		F58A	ELIZABETH	
F54G	ELIZABETH		F58B	ANN	
F54H	DANIEL		F58C	ABIGAIL	
	======		F58D	SARAH	
[F55]	FULLER		F58E	SILENCE	
	Samuel Fuller F22B		F58F	PHOEBE	
	Naomi Rowley F22Ba		F58G	EUNICE	
	------		F58H	DAVID	
F55A	JOHN		F58I	EDWARD	
F55B	SAMUEL			======	
F55C	MOSES		[F59]	ROWLEY	
F55D	AARON			Samuel Rowley F22Fa	
F55E	MEHITABLE			Elizabeth Fuller F22F	
F55F	MERCY			------	
F55G	MARY		F59A	NATHAN	
F55H	DESIRE		F59B	ABIGAIL	
F55I	ABNER		F59C	SAMUEL	
F55J	NORA (twin)		F59D	THOMAS	
F55K	NATHANIEL (twin)		F59E	THANKFUL	
	======		F59F	ABIJAH	
[F56]	FULLER		F59G	ELIZABETH	
	Shubael Fuller F22C		F59H	PRUDENCE	
	Hannah Crocker F22Ca			======	
	------		[F60]	FULLER	
F56A	LYDIA			John Fuller F22G	
F56B	EPHRAIM			Mary Cornwall F22Ga	
F56C	THANKFUL			------	
F56D	ZURVIAH		F60A	MARY	
F56E	HANNAH		F60B	ESTHER	
F56F	SHUBAEL		F60C	JOHN	
F56G	JONATHAN		F60D	WILLIAM	
F56H	RACHEL		F60E	MEHITABLE	
F56I	LEAH		F60F	ANDREW	
	======		F60G	SARAH	

340

DIVISION S
F61/F62

```
[F61]    FULLER                      [F62]    KNEELAND
         Joseph Fuller   F22H                 Benjamin Kneeland F22Ka
         Lydia Day       F22Ha                Mehitable Fuller   F22K
         ------                               ------

F61A    JOSEPH                       F62A    SARAH
F61B    RACHEL                       F62B    PHEBE
F61C    ZACHARIAH                    F62C    BENJAMIN
F61D    GRACE                        F62D    MEHITABLE
F61E    JEREMIAH                     F62E    MEHITABLE
F61F    LYDIA                        F62F    ABIGAIL
F61G    MINDWELL                     F62G    JABEZ
F61H    RUTH                                 ======
F61I    ABRAHAM
F61J    JACOB
F61K    ISAAC
        ======
```

341

```
[G1]    GATES                    G8A  PETER     [G9]
        unk                           a  Mary Josseyin
        unk                           ======
        ------
                                 [G9]    GATES
G1A  THOMAS      [G2]                    Peter Gates    G8A
     ======                             Mary Josselyn G8Aa
[G2]    GATES                           ------
        Thomas Gates G1A
        unk                       G9A  THOMAS     [G10]
        ------                         a  Elizabeth Weeden
                                       ======
G2A  WILLIAM      [G3]           [G10]   GATES
     unk                                 Thomas Gates      G9A
     ======                              Elizabeth Weeden G9Aa
[G3]    GATES                            ------
        William Gates G2A
        unk                       G10A  GEORGE Sr.    [G11]
        ------                          a  Sarah Olmstead
                                        f  Nicholas Olmstead
G3A  SIR GEFFREY  [G4]                  m  Sarah Loomis
     a  Agnes Baldington                ======
     ======
[G4]    GATES                    [G11]   GATES
        Sir Geffrey Gates G3A            George Gates Sr. G10A
        Agnes Baldington  G3Aa           Sarah Olmstead   G10Aa
        ------                           ------

G4A  WILLIAM   [G5]              G11A  JOSEPH Sr.   [G12]
     a  Mabell Caplow    .             a  Elizabeth Hungerford
     ======                      G11B  THOMAS              [G14]
[G5]    GATES                          a  Hannah Brainard
        William Gates G4A         G11C  JOHN
        Mabell Caplow G4Aa        G11D  SARAH
                                       a  Timothy Fuller
G5A  SIR GEFFREY II [G6]               f  Samuel Fuller
     a  Elizabeth Clopton        G11E  MARY
     f  Sir William Clopton            a  Daniel Cone Jr   [G15]
                                       f  Daniel Cone Sr
                                 G11F  GEORGE Jr
[G6]    GATES                    G11G  DANIEL SR        [G27]
        Sir Geffrey II    G5A          a  Rebecca Dutton
        Elizabeth Clopton G5Aa         f  Joseph Dutton
        ------                   G11H  SAMUEL
G6A  GEFFREY III    [G7]               a  Esther Hungerford
     a  Elizabeth Walsingham           f  Thomas Hungerford
     f  William Walsingham             ======
     ======                     [G12]   GATES
[G7]    GATES                            Joseph Gates Sr     G11A
        Geffrey Gates III G6A            Elizabeth Hungerford G11Aa
        Elizabeth Walsingham G6Aa        ------
        ------
                                 G12A  Joseph Jr          [G17]
G7A  GEFFREY IV     [G8]               a  Hannah Brainard
     a  Joane Wentworth                f  Daniel Brainard
     ======                      G12B  PATIENCE
[G8]    GATES                          a  Nathaniel Foote Jr [G29]
        Geffrey Gates IV G7A           f  Nathaniel Foote Sr
        Joane Wentworth  G7Aa
        ------
```

G12C ELIZABETH
  a Daniel Morgan [G13]
  f James Morgan
  m Bridget --
  ======
[G13] MORGAN
  Daniel Morgan   G12Ca
  Elizabeth Gates G12C

G13A DESIRE MORGAN
  a William Belcher
  ======
[G14] GATES
  Thomas Gates   G11B
  Hannah Brainard G11Ba

[G14A JOSHUA
  a Lydia Brainard
  ======
[G15] CONE
  Daniel Cone G11Ea
  Mary Gates G11E

G15A JOSEPH Sr [G26]
  a Mary Smith
  ======
[G16] GATES
  Joseph Gates Sr   G11A
  Elizabeth Hungerford G11Aa

G16A JOSEPH Jr   [G17]
  a Hannah Brainard
  ======
[G17] GATES
  Joseph Gates Sr G16A
  Hannah Brainard G16Aa

G17A BEZALLEL   [G18]
  a Mary Brainard
  ======
[G18] GATES
  Bazaleel Gates G17A
  Mary Brainard G17Aa

G18A AARON Sr   [G19]
  a Elizabeth Johnson
  ======
[G19] GATES
  Aaron Gates Sr   G18A
  Elizabeth Johnson G18Aa

G19A Aaron Gates Sr
  a Ruth Beman

[G20] GATES
  Aaron Gates Jr G19A
  Ruth Beman   G19Aa

G20A BEMAN   [G21]
  a Betsey Shipman
  ======
[G21] GATES
  Beman Gates   G20A
  Betsey Shipman G20Aa

G21A MARY
  a Rufus R Dawes [G22]
G21B CHARLES B
G21C BETSEY S
  a William M Mills
  ======
[G22] DAWES
  Rufus R Dawes G21A
  Mary Gates   G21Aa

G22A CHARLES GATES DAWES
  30th U.S. Vice Pres.
  Calvin Coolidge Pres.

[G23]   WHITMAN
   Zachariah Whitman Sr G31Aa
   Elizabeth Gates   G31A

G23A ZACHARIAH Jr
  a Abigail Wood
======
[G24]   GATES
   Joshua Gates G14A
   Lydia Brainard G14Aa

G24A CALEB [G25]
  a Esther Foote
  b Elizabeth Percival
======
[G25]   GATES
   Caleb Gates G24A
   Esther Foote G24Aa

G25A RUSSEL
  a Mabel Griswold
======
[G26]   CONE
   Joseph Cone Sr G15A
   Mary Smith   G15Aa

G26A JOSEPH Jr
  a Martha Brainard
======
[G27]   GATES
   Daniel Gates Sr G11G
   Rebecca Dutton G11Ga

G27A DANIEL Jr [G31]
  a Sarah Cone
  b Lydia Fuller
C27B DAVID   [G28]
  a Hannah Hungerford
  b Elizabeth Smith
C27C REBECCA
C27D ABIGAIL
C27E JOSEPH
C27F MARY
C27G RUTH
C27H EPHRAIM
C27I JUDAH
======
[G28]   GATES
   David Gates   G27B
   Hannah Hungerford G27Ba

G28A LEVI   [G32]
  a Lydia Crocker
  f James Crocker
  m Alice Swift

G28B MARY
G28C ELIZABETH
  a Daniel Fox [G30]
  f Isaac Fox
======
[G29]   FOOTE
   Nathaniel Foote G12Ba
   Patience Gates G12B

G29A MARY FOOTE
  a Stephen Skinner
  f Richard Skinner
  m Patience Rowley
======
[G30]   FOX
   Daniel Fox   G28Ca
   Elizabeth Gates G28C

G30A JEHIEL
  a Jerusha Baldwin
======
[G31]   GATES
   Daniel Gates G27A
   (1) Sarah Cone G27Aa
   (2) Lydia Fuller G27Ab
------
by Cone
G31A ELIZABETH
  a Zachariah WhitmanSr[G23]
  f John Whitman
  m Margaret Clark
by Fuller
G31B JESSE
  a Elizabeth Lord
  f Theopolus Lord
  m Deborah Mack
======
[G32]   GATES
   Levi Gates   G28A
   Lydia Crocker G28Aa

G32A DAVID
G32B JIREH   [G33]
  a Hannah Strong
  f Ozias Strong
  m Susannah West
G32C RUSSELL
  a Esther Briggs
G32D LEVI Jr   [G34]
  a Nancy McQueen
G32E ALICE

344

[G33]   GATES
    Jireh Gates   G32A
    Hannah Strong G32Aa
    ======
G33A LEVI II
  a Lydia Luther
G33B MIRANDA
  a Alanson Cunning
  b -- Wood
G33C SALMON
G33D WILLIAM   [G36]
  a Lydia Martin
  b Diadama Clarke
G33E ANCY B
  a -- Bower
  b -- Bradley
G33F LYDIA
G33G SUSANNAH
    ======

[G34]   GATES
    Levi Gates Jr G32D
    Nancy McQueen G32Da

G34A HARVEY   [G35]
  a Polly Spring
  f Phineas Spring
    ======
[G35]   GATES
    Harvey Gates G34A
    Polly Spring G34Aa

G35A CYNTHIA
  a Lyman Norton
    ======
[G36]   GATES
    William Gates G33D
    Lydia Martin G33Da

G36A EVELINE
  a Thomas Osborn [G53]
  f William Osborn
  m Margaret Tone

[G37]   TONE
    unkn
    unkn

G37A JEAN   [G38]
  a Phillipa Daniel
    ======
[G38]   TONE
    Jean Tone   G37A
    Phillipe Daniel G37Aa

G38A JEAN II   [G39]
  a Phillipe Daniel II
  f Jean Daniel
    ======
[G39]   TONE
    Jean Tone II   G38A
    Phillipe Daniel G38Aa

G39A JEAN III   [G40]
  a Jeanne DuFour
  f Galhard DuFour
  m Jean DeLomagne
G39B PHILIP
    ======
[G40]   TONE
    Jean Tone III G39A
    Jeanne DuFour G39Aa
    ======

G40A JEAN IV   [G41]
  a Marie Bascom
  f Guillaume Bascom
  m Adelaide Chabane
G40B PIERRE
G40C JOSEPH
G40D CLEMENTINE
G40E MARIE CELINE
  a Henry Broquin
    ======
[G41]   TONE
    Jean Tone IV G40A
    Marie Bascom G40Aa

G41A JEAN V
  a Jeane Duval
G41B MARIE LOUISE
  a Jean Breman
G41C JOSEPH ALFRED
G41D JOSEPH PIERRE [G42]
  a Philippa Jeanninge
  f Joseph Jeanninge
  m Philippa Daniel
G41E CLEMENTINE

[G42] TONE
  Joseph Pierre Tone Sr G41D
  Philippa Jeanninge G41Da

G42A JOSEPH Jr
 a Marie Gasque
G42B JEROME [G43]
 a Henrietta Augar
 f Pierre Auger
 n Desiree DuVergier
G42C JEAN
G42D GUILLAME
G42E MARIE
 a Maurice Bodine
======
[G43] TONE
  Jerome Tone G42B
  Henrietta Auger G43Ba

G43A FLIBTON
 a Suzanne Gladdine
G43B JEAN [G44]
 a Marie Gladdine
 f Paul Gladdine
 n Anne Marquet
G43C HENRI
 a Cecile Baringer
======
[G44] TONE
  Jean Tone G43B
  Marie Gladdine G43Ba

G44A FRANCOIS [G45]
 a Anne Hyde
 f Richard Hyde
 n Anne Moigne
G44B HENRI
G44C JAQUES
 a Helen Hay
G44D HUGH
G44E ANTOINE
======
[G45] TONE
  Francois Tone G44A
  Anne Hyde G44Aa

G45A MARY
 a Richard Farrell
G45B HUGH [G46]
 a Sarah Bodine
 f Daniel Bodine
 n Marie Crois
G45C THOMAS
 a Katherine Everston

[G46] TONE
  Hugh Tone G45B
  Sarah Bodine G45Ba

G46A THOMAS [G49]
 a Susanna Budd
 f Thomas Budd
 n Susana Caldwell
G46B JANE
G46C JOAN
G46D JACQUES
 a Sarah Carroll
G46E WILLIAM [G47]
 a Jane Kinney
G46F SALLY
 a Michael Eriksson
======
[G47] TONE
  William Gates G46E
  Jane Kinney G46Ea

G47A PETER [G48]
======
[G48] TONE
  Peter Tone G47A
  unk

G48A THEOBOLD WOLFE TONE
 a Matilda Withering
======
[G49] TONE
  Thomas Tone G46A
  Susanna Budd G46Aa

G49A JOHN Sr. [G50]
 a Margaret Harvey
G49B JOSEPH
 a Abigail Worden
G49C WILLIAM
G49D FRANCIS
G49E LEWIS
======
[G50] TONE
  John Tone Sr G49A
  Margaret Harvey G49Aa

G50A ANDREW
 a Rachel Lewis
G50B THOMAS
 a Content Hance
G50C HANNAH
 a Thomas Hance
G50D ELIZABETH
 a Hugh Mananan

G50E JOHN Jr   [G51]
  a Janet VanSchaick
  f John Van Schaick
  m Ann Clendinnan
  b Phebe Rightmire
  f James Rightmire
G50F SARAH
  a James Combs
G50G WILLIAM
  a Noami Sutphen
  b Rachel M Lyon
G50H MARY
  ======

[G51]   TONE
    John Tone Jr   G50E
    Janet VanSchaick G50Ea

G51A MARGARET
  a William Osborn [G52]
G51B WILLIAM
G51C JOHN 2d
  a Elizabeth Manahan
G51D LEWIS
  a Betsey Welch
  b Sarah Rathborn
G51E NANCY
  a Richard Carman
G51F THOMAS
  a Elizabeth Harvey
G51G JANE
  a Ezra Bourne
  ======

[G52]   OSBORN
    William Osborn G51Aa
    Margaret Tone G51A

G52A JANE
  a David Chamber
G52B LEWIS
  a Samantha Gates
G52C WILLIAM Jr
  a Abigail Davis
G52D JOHN
G52E PHEBE
  a James Davis
G52F HARRISON
  a Mary J McNeal
G52G EMILY
  a Galesha Bridge
G52H ELIZABETH
  a G. David
G52I CLARINDA

G52J THOMAS   [G53]
  a Eveline Gates
G52K URVILLE
G52L NARCISSA
  a M.A.Mulhullen
G52M PHILANDER
  a Margaret Proudfoot
G52N JOHN A
  ======

[G53]   OSBORN
    Thomas Osborn G52J, G36Aa
    Eveline Gates G52Ja.G36A

G53A ALICE CORA
G53B WINFIELD SCOTT
G53C FRANCES AMELIA
G53D WILLIAM D
G53E AGNES E
G53F CHARLES T
G53G CORA EVELINE
  a George W. Burgess [G54]
  ======

[G54]   BURGESS
    George W Burgess   G53Ga
    Cora Eveline Osborn G53G

G54A CLARENCE PERRY   [G55]
  a Helen Noble
  f Henry Orville Noble
  m Lulie E Maynard
  b Cora Louise Turney
G54B ALBERT CARL Sr
  a Helen Briswalter
  f John Briswalter
  m Myrtle --
  b Lera Brown
G54C CLYDE CECIL
  a Ines DeWitt
  b Donnie Weatherstone
G54D RAY ELMER   [G57]
  a Elizabeth Alexander
  f Eben Alexander
  m Hattie Blanton
  b Marie Ann Ferreri
  f Nicholas Ferreri
  m Carmela DiBingo
G54E ROY ARTHUR
  a Helen Hartman
  f Daniel Hartman
  m Jessie Girton
G54F ETHEL MAY
  a Ira W. Fillingham

```
    =======
[G55]   BURGESS
        Clarence Perry G54A
        Helen Nobie   G54Aa
    ------
G55A ESTHER
     a Edgar Broward Poppell
G55B MARGARET ELIZABETH
     a Anthony Wise Jr   [G56]
     b Calvin Poppell
G55C CORA LOUISE
     a Lawrence E Willey
    ======
[G56]   WISE
        Anthony Wise Jr   G55Ba
        Margaret E Burgess G55B
    ------
G56A ANTHONY JOHN III
     a Linda Dupnak
G56B PATRICIA ELIZABETH
     a Willian D Bazemore
    ======
[G57]   BURGESS
        Ray Burgess      G54D
        Elizabeth Alexander G54Da
    ------
G57A MARGARET LOUISE
     a George Lyons Logan  [G58]
     b G. Scott Smitherman
G57B GEORGE MILTON        [G59]
     a Elayne Carruthers
    ======
 [G58]  LOGAN
        George Logan        G57Aa
        Margaret Louise Burgess G57A
    ------
G58A KATHERINE
     a Michael Abbiatti
     b James Ray
G58B LAWRENCE L
     a Mary E Grady
G58C THOMAS
     a Wendy Barto
    ======
[G59]   BURGESS
        George M Burgess G57B
        Elayne Carruthers G57Ba
    ------
G59A ROGER GLENN
     a Marilyn Kay Williamson
     f Harvey G Williamson
     m Peggy Joyce Ice
G59E BARBARA ELLEN
     a Donald J Gwatney
```

```
[H10]   HOPKINS                      b  Mary Cottle
        unknown parents              f  Edward Cottle
        ------                       m  Judith --
H10A    STEPHEN MF [H11]     H12F    JOHN              [H21]
   a    Unknown                 a    Mary Smalley
   b    Elizabeth Fisher        f    John Smalley
        ======                  m    Ann Walden
[H11]   HOPKINS              H12G    ELIZABETH
        Steven Hopkins  H10A    a    Thomas Rogers     [H22]
        unknown         H10Aa   f    Joseph Rogers
        Elizabeth Fisher H10Ab  m    Hannah --
        ------               H12H    JABEZ             [H23]
H11A    CONSTANCE by wife #1    a    Elizabeth --
   a    Nicholas Snow Jr [H12] H12I  RUTH
   f    Nicholas Snow Sr        a    John Cole         [H24]
H11B    GILES by wife #1 [H13]  f    Daniel Cole
   a    Catherine Whelden       m    Ruth --
   f    Gabriel Whelden      H12J    Child
H11C    DAMARIS #1 by Elizabeth      H12K   Child
H11D    OCEANUS          "    H12L    Child
H11E    CALEB            "            ======
H11F    DEBORAH          "    [H13]   HOPKINS
   a    Andrew Ring     [H14]        Giles Hopkins H11B
   f    William Ring                 Catherine Wheldon H11Ba
   m    Mary Durrant                 ------
H11G    DAMARIS #2 by Elizabeth H13A MARY
   a    Jacob Cooke     [H15]   a    Samuel Smith      [H25]
   f    Francis Cooke MF        f    Ralph Smith
   m    Hester Hayhieu      H13B    STEPHEN           [H26]
H11H    RUTH    by Elizabeth    a    Mary Merrick
H11I    ELIZABETH       "       f    William Merrick
        ======                  m    Rebecca Tracy
[H12]   SNOW                    b    Bethia Linnell
        Nicholas Snow H11Aa     f    Robert Linnell
        Constance Hopkins H11A  m    Penina Howes
        ------               H13C    JOHN
H12A    MARK            [H16]  H13D    ABIGAIL
   a    Ann Cooke               a    William Merrick Jr.[H27]
   f    Josiah Cooke            f    William Merrick Sr.
   m    Elizabeth Ring Deane    m    Rebecca Tracy
   b    Jane Prence          H13E    DEBORAH
   f    Thomas Prence          a    Josiah Cooke Jr.   [H28]
   m    Mary Collier           f    Josiah Cooke Sr.
H12B    MARY                    m    Elizabeth Ring
   a    Thomas Paine Jr [H17] H13F  CALEB              [H29]
   f    Thomas Paine Sr        a    Mary Williams
H12C    SARAH                   f    Thomas Williams
   a    William Walker [H18]    m    Elizabeth --
H12D    JOSEPH          [H19] H13G  RUTH
   a    Mary --              H13H    JOSHUA            [H30]
H12E    STEPHEN         [H20]   a    Mary Cole
   a    Susannah Deane         f    Daniel Cole
   f    Stephen Deane       H13I    WILLIAM
   m    Elizabeth Ring      H13J    ELIZABETH
```

[H14] RING
     Andrew Ring H11Fa
     Deborah Hopkins H11F

H14A ELIZABETH
  a William Mayo   [H31]
  f John Mayo
  m Hannah Lecraft
H14B WILLIAM   [H32]
  a Hannah Sherman
  f William Sherman
  m Desire Doty
H14C ELEAZER   [H33]
  a Mary Shaw
  f Jonathan Shaw
  m Phebe Watson
H14D MARY
  a John Morton Jr   [H34]
  f John Morton Sr
  m Lettice --
H14E DEBORAH
H14F SUSANNA
    ======
[H15] COOKE
     Jacob Cooke H11Ga
     Damaris Hopkins H11G

H15A ELIZABETH
H15B CALEB
H15C JACOB
H15D MARY
H15E MARTHA
H15F FRANCIS
H15G RUTH
    ======
[H16] SNOW
     Mark Snow H12A
     Ann Cooke H12Aa
     Jane Prence H12Ab

H16A ANNA
  a Eldad Atwood   [H35]
  f Stephen Atwood
  m Abigail Dunham
H16B MARY
  a William Nickerson [H36]
  f Nicholas Nickerson
  m Mary Derby
H16C NICHOLAS   [H37]
  a Lydia Shaw
  f Jonathan Shaw
  m Phebe Watson
H16D ELIZABETH

H16E THOMAS   [H38]
  a Hannah Sears
  f Silas Sears
  m Anna --
  b Lydia Sears
  f Paul Sears
  m Deborah Willard
H16F SARAH
H16G PRENCE   [H39]
  a Hannah Storrs
  f Samuel Storrs
  m Mary Huckins
H16H ELIZABETH
H16I HANNAH
    ======
[H17] PAINE
     Thomas Paine H12Ba
     Mary Snow H12B

H17A MARY
  a James Rogers [H40]
  f Joseph Rogers
  m Hannah --
  b Israel Cole [H127]
  f Daniel Cole
  m Ruth --
H17B SAMUEL   [H41]
  a Patience Freeman
  f John Freeman
  m Mercy Prence
H17C THOMAS   [H42]
  a Hannah Shaw
  f Jonathan Shaw
  m Phebe Watson
  b Elizabeth --
H17D ELEAZER
H17E ELISHA   [H43]
  a Rebecca Doane
  f John Doane
  m Hannah Bangs
H17F JOHN   [H44]
  a Bennet Freeman
  f John Freeman
  m Mary Prence
  b Alice Mayo
  f Nathaniel Mayo
  m Elizabeth Wixam
H17G NICHOLAS   [H45]
  a Hannah Higgins
  f Jonathan Higgins
  m Elizabeth Rogers
H17H JAMES   [H46]
  a Bethia Thatche

```
        f John Thatcher              H19H   REBECCA
        m Rebecca Winslow            H19I   JAMES
H17I    JOSEPH           [H47]       H19J   JANE
     a  Patience Sparrow             H19K   JOSIAH           [H57]
        f Jonathan Sparrow              a  Elizabeth Snow
        m Hannah Prence                 f  Thomas Snow
H17J    DORCAS                          m  Hannah Sears
     a  Benjamin Vickery [H48]              ======
        f George Vickery             [H20]   Snow
        m Rebecca Phippeny                    Stephen Snow    H12E
            ======                            Susanna Deane   H12Ea
[H18]    WALKER                                Mary Cottle    H12Eb
         William Walker H12Ca                 ------
         Sarah Snow      H12C        H20A   BATHSHUAH
            ------                       a  John King        [H58]
H18A    JOHN                         H20B   HANNAH
H18B    WILLIAM #1                       a  William Cole     [H59]
H18C    WILLIAM #2       [H49]           f  Daniel Cole
     a  Susanna --                       m  Ruth --
H18D    SARAH                        H20C   MICAJAH          [H60]
H18E    ELIZABETH                        a  Mercy Young
H18F    JABEZ            [H50]           f  John Young
     a  Elizabeth --                     m  Ruth Cole
            ======                   H20D   BETHIA
[H19]    SNOW                            a  John Smith       [H61]
         Joseph Snow H12D               f  Samuel Smith
         Mary -- H12Da                   m  Mary Hopkins
            ------                   H20E   MEHITABLE
H19A    JOSEPH           [H51]       H20F   EBENEZER         [H62]
     a  Sarah Smith                      a  Hope Horton
        f John Smith                         ======
        m Hannah Williams            [H21]   SNOW
H19B    BENJAMIN         [H52]               John Snow       H12F
     a  Thankful Bordman                     Mary Smalley H12Fa
        f Thomas Bordman                     ------
        m Elizabeth Ryder            H21A   HANNAH
H19C    MARY                         H21B   MARY
H19D    SARAH                        H21C   ABIGAIL
     a  Benjamin Young   [H53]       H21D   REBECCA
        f John Young                     a  Benjamin Smalley  [H63]
        m Ruth Cole                      f  Francis Smalley
H19E    RUTH                             m  Elizabeth --
     a  James Brown      [H54]           b  John Porter
        f George Brown                   f  Samuel Porter
        m Mehitable Knowles              m  Hannah Stanley
H19F    STEPHEN          [H55]       H21E   JOHN             [H64]
     a  Margaret Elkins                  a  Elizabeth Ridley
        f Thomas Elkins                  f  Mark Ridley
        m Sarah Gutch                    m  Hannah --
H19G    LYDIA                        H21F   ISAAC            [H65]
     a  James Lincoln    [H56]           a  Alice --
        f Thomas Lincoln             H21G   LYDIA
        m Sarah Lewis                H21H   ELISHA           [H66]
                                         a  Elizabeth Bedwell
                                     H21I   PHEBE
```

```
[H22]   ROGERS                      H23Haf  Thomas Huckins Sr
        Thomas Rogers H12Ga                n Hannah Chipman
        Elizabeth Snow H12G                ======
        ------                     [H24]   COLE
H22A  ELIZABETH                            John Cole H12Ia
H22B  JOSEPH            [H67]              Ruth Snow H12I
   a  Prudence --                          ------
H22C  HANNAH                       H24A  RUTH
   a  Maziah Harding  [H68]           a  William Twining Jr [H77]
   f  Joseph Harding                  f  William Twining Sr
   n  Bethiah Cooke                   n  Elizabeth Dean
H22D  THOMAS #1                    H24B  JOHN              [E78]
H22E  THOMAS #2         [H69]         a  Mary Rogers
   a  Sarah Treat                     f  James Rogers
   f  Samuel Treat                    n  Mary Paine
   n  Elizabeth Mayo                  b  Sarah Hamlin
   b  Rebecca Sparrow                 f  John Hamlin
   f  John Sparrow                    n  Sarah Bearse
   n  Apphia Tracy               H24C  HEPZIBAH
H22F  ELEAZER          [H70]     H24D  HANNAH
   a  Ruhamah Willis             H24E  JOSEPH            [H79]
   f  Richard Willis                a  Elizabeth Cobb
   n  Patience Bonum                 f  James Cobb
H22G  NATHANIEL                      n  Sarah Lewis
      ======                         b  Mercy Hinkley
[H23]   SNOW                         f  Samuel Hinckley
        Jabez Snow H12H              n  Mary Fitzrandolph
        Elizabeth -- H12Ha          c  Rebecca Young
        ------                       f  David Young
H23A  JABEZ            [H71]         n  Ann Doane
   a  Elizabeth Treat            H24F  MARY
   f  Samuel Treat              H24G  SARAH
   n  Elizabeth Mayo                  ======
H23B  EDWARD           [H72]    [H25]   SMITH
   a  Sarah Freeman                   Samuel Smith H13Aa
   f  John Freeman                    Mary Hopkins H13A
   n  Sarah Merrick                   ------
H23C  SARAH                     H25A  SAMUEL            [H80]
H23D  GRACE                        a  Bershuah Lothrop
   a  Samuel Hedge     [H73]        f  Barnabas Lothrop
   f  Elisha Hedge                  n  Susannah Clark
   n  Mary --                    H25B  MARY
   b  George Lewis                  a  Daniel Hamilton [H81]
   f  James Lewis                   f  Thomas Hamilton
   n  Sarah Lane                    n  Lydia Wing
H23E  THOMAS                    H25C  JOSEPH
H23F  ELIZABETH                 H25D  JOHN
   a  Edward Kindreck  [H74]    H25E  GRACE
H23G  DEBORAH                   H25F  REBECCA
   a  Stephen Merrick  [H75]          ======
   f  William Merrick
   n  Abigail Hopkins
H23H  RACHEL
   a  Thomas Huckins Jr  [H76]
```

[H26] HOPKINS
   Stephen Hopkins H13B
   Mary Merrick   H13B
   Bethia Linnell H13Bb

H26A ELIZABETH
H26B STEPHEN   [H82]
  a Sarah Howes
  f Thomas Howes
  m Sarah Bangs
H26C RUTH
H26D JUDAH   [H83]
  a Hannah Mayo
  f Samuel Mayo
  m Ruth --
  b Hannah Mayo
  f John Mayo
  m Hannah Freeman
H26E SAMUEL   [H84]
  a Lydia Rich
  f Richard Rich
  m Sarah Roberts
H26F NATHANIEL   [H85]
  a Mercy Mayo
  f John Mayo
  m Hannah Freeman
H26G JOSEPH   [H86]
  a Mary Mayo
  f John Mayo
  m Hannah Freeman
H26H BENJAMIN   [H87]
  a Rachel Lincoln
  f Thomas Lincoln
  m Rachel Holmes
H26I MARY
  a John Maker   [H88]
  f James Maker
  m Rachel --
  ======
[H27] MERRICK
   William Merrick H13Da
   Abigail Hopkins H13D

H27A REBECCA
  a Jonathan Sparrow Jr [H89]
  f Jonathan Sparrow Sr
  m Rebecca Bangs
H27B WILLIAM
H27C STEPHEN
H27D BENJAMIN   [H90]
  a Rebecca Doane
  f Daniel Doane
  b Rachel Holmes
  f Abraham Holmes
  m Elizabeth Arnold

H27E NATHANIEL   [H91]
  a Alice Freeman
  f Samuel Freeman
  m Mercy Southworth
H27F JOHN
H27G JOSHUA   [H92]
  a Lydia Mayo
  f Thomas Mayo
  m Barbara Knowles
H27H RUTH
  a Samuel Sears Jr [H93]
  f Samuel Sears Sr
  m Marcy Mayo
  b Chillingsworth Foster
  f John Foster
  m Mary Chillingsworth
H27I SAMUEL
  ======
[H28] COOKE
   Josiah Cooke H13Ea
   Deborah Hopkins H13E

H28A ELIZABETH #1
H28B JOSIAH   [H94]
  a Mary --
H28C RICHARD   [H95]
  a Hannah --
H28D ELIZABETH #2
  a Thomas Newcomb [H96]
  f Andrew Newcomb
  m Sarah --
H28E CALEB   [H97]
  a Deliverance Crowell
  f John Crowell
  m Hannah --
H28F DEBORAH
  a Moses Godfrey [H98]
  f George Godfrey
H28G JOSHUA   [H99]
  a Patience Doane
  f Ephraim Doane
  m Mary Knowles
H28H BENJAMIN   [H100]
  a Mercy Paine
  f Samuel Paine
  m Patience Freeman
  ======
[H29] HOPKINS
   Caleb Hopkins H13F
   Mary Williams H13Fa

H29A CALEB   [H101]
  a Mercy Freeman
  f Constant Freeman
  m Jane Treat

H29B NATHANIEL   [H102]
  a Lydia --
  b Sarah --
H29C THOMAS   [H103]
  a Deborah Bickford
  f Jeremiah Bickford
  m Hannah Young
H29D THANKFUL
  a Ambrose Dyer   [H104]
  f William Dyer
  m Hannah Strout
    ======
[H30] HOPKINS
    Joshua Hopkins H13H
    Mary Cole H13Ha

H30A JOHN
H30B ABIGAIL
  a John Taylor   [H105]
  f Edward Taylor
  m Mary Merll
H30C ELISHA   [H106]
  a Experience Scudder
  f John Scudder
  m Elizabeth Hamlin
H30D LYDIA
H30E MARY
  a Joseph Smith   [H107]
  f Samuel Smith
  m Bershuah Lothrop
H30F JOSHUA   [H108]
  a Priscilla Curtis
  f John Curtis
  m Priscilla Gould
H30G HANNAH
  a Ebenezer Paine [H109]
  f Samuel Paine
  m Patience Freeman
  b Zachariah Small
  f Edward Small
  m Mary Woodman
H30H PHEBE
  a Moses Bixbee   [H110]
  f Joseph Bixbee
  m Sarah Gould
    ======
[H31] MAYO
    William Mayo H14Aa
    Elizabeth Ring H14A

H31A JOHN

H31B HANNAH
  a Samuel Tucker [H111]
  f John Tucker
  m Susanna --
H31C THANKFUL
  a Samuel Higgins [H112]
  f Benjamin Higgins
  m Lydia Bangs
H31D DEBORAH
    ======
[H32] RING
    William Ring H14B
    Hannah Sherman H14Ba

H32A DEBORAH
H32B HANNAH
H32C WILLIAM
H32D ELIZABETH
  a Joseph Peirce [H113]
  f William Peirce
H32E ELEAZER
H32F DEBORAH
    ======
[H33] RING
    Eleazer Ring H14C
    Mary Shaw H14Ca

H33A ELEAZER
H33B ANDREW #1
H33C PHEBE
  a Ichabod Standish [H114]
  f Alexander Standish
  m Desire Doty
H33D SAMUEL   [H115]
  a Ruth Sylvester
  f Israel Sylvester
  m Ruth Prince
H33E ANDREW #2   [H116]
  a Zerviah Standish
  f Ebenezer Standish
  m Hannah Sturtivant
H33F DEBORAH
  a John Fuller   [H117]
  f Samuel Fuller=H31Faf
  m Mercy Eaton=H31Fam
H33G MARY
  a Peleg Sampson [H118]
  f Isaac Sampson
  m Lydia Standish

H33H JONATHAN   [H119]   [H36]   NICKERSON
    a Sara Mitchell   William Nickerson H16Ba
    f Joseph Mitchell   Mary Snow H16B
    m Bathsheba Lumbert   ------
H33I SUSANNA   H36A   MERCY
    a Nehemiah Bosworth [H120] H36B   NICHOLAS
    f David Bosworth   H36C   EBENEZER
    m Mercy Sturtevant   H36D   JANE
H33J ELKANAH   H36E   MARY
H33K ELIZABETH   H36F   THANKFUL
    a James Claghorn Jr [H121]   ======
    f James Claghorn Sr   [H37]   SNOW
H33L LYDIA   Nicholas Snow H16C
    a Ephraim Sturdevant [H122]   Lydia Shaw H16Ca
    f Joseph Sturdevant   ------
    m Anna Jones   H37A   JONATHAN
    ======   H37B   MARK
[H34]   MORTON   H37C   NATHANIEL
    John Morton H14Da   H37D   JOSHUA
    Mary Ring H14D   H37E   THANKFUL
    ------   H37F   SARAH
H34A MARY   H37G   PHEBE
    a Thomas Tomson [H123]   H37H   PRENCE
    f John Tomson   ======
    m Mary Cooke   [H38]   SNOW
H34B JOHN   Thomas Snow H16E
H34C HANNAH   [H124]   Hannah Sears H16Ea
    a John Hodges   ------
    f Henry Hodges   H38A   ELIZABETH
    m Esther Gallop   H38B   MARY
H34D EBENEZER   [H125]   H38C   JOSIAH
    a Mercy Foster   H38D   EBENEZER
    f John Foster   H38E   HANNAH
    m Hannah Stetson   H38F   LYDIA
H34E DEBORAH   H38G   THOMAS
    a Jonathan Inglee [H126]   H38H   AARON
    ======   H38I   RUTH
[H35]   ATWOOD   ======
    Eldad Atwood H16Aa   [H39]   SNOW
    Anna Snow H16A   Prence Snow H16G
    ------   Hannah Storrs H16Ga
H35A MARY   ------
H35B JOHN   H39A   JABEZ
H35C ANNA   H39B   HANNAH
H35D DEBORAH   H39C   SAMUEL
H35E SARAH   H39D   MERCY
H35F ELDAD   H39E   PRENCE
H35G EBENEZER   H39F   JONATHAN
H35H BENJAMIN   H39G   DAVID
    ======   H39H   MARY
                                      ======

```
[H40]   ROGERS                        H43C  ABRAHAM
        James Rogers H17Aa            H43D  ELISHA
        Mary Paine H17A               H43E  MARY
        ------                        H43F  SOLOMON
H40A  JAMES                           H43G  DORCAS
H40B  MARY                            H43H  HANNAH
H40C  ABIGAIL                         H43I  JOHN
        ======                                ======
[H41]   PAINE                         [H44]   PAINE
        Samuel Paine    H17B                  John Paine H17F
        Patience Freeman H17Ba                Bennet Freeman H17Fa
        ------                                Alice Mayo H17Fb
H41A  SAMUEL                                  ------
H41B  MERCY                           H44A  JOHN    by Bennet
H41C  NATHANIEL                       H44B  MARY
H41D  EBENEAZER                       H44C  WILLIAM
H41E  ELIZABETH                       H44D  BENJAMIN #1
H41F  JOSHUA                          H44E  SARAH
H41G  ISAAC                           H44F  CHILD
H41H  MARY                            H44G  ELIZABETH
H41I  SETH                            H44H  THEOPHILUS
        ======                        H44I  JOSIAH
[H42]   PAINE                         H44J  NATHANIEL
        Thomas Paine H17C             H44K  REBECCA
        Hannah Shaw  H17Ca            H44L  MERCY
        ------                        H44M  BENJAMIN #2
H42A  HANNAH #1                       H44N  HANNAH #1 by Alice
H42B  HUGH                            H44O  JAMES
H42C  THOMAS                          H44P  THOMAS
H42D  HANNAH #2                       H44Q  ALICE
H42E  JONATHAN                          a James Knowles
H42F  ABIGAIL  #1                       f Richard Knowles
H42G  ABIGAIL  #2                       n Martha Cobb
H42H  PHEBE #1                        H44R  HANNAH #2
H42I  ELKANAH                                 ======
H42J  MOSES
H42K  JOSHUA                          [H45]   PAINE
H42L  PHEBE #2                                Nicholas Paine H17G
H42M  LYDIA                                   Hannah Higgins H17Ga
H42N  BARNABAS                                ------
        ======                        H45A  THANKFUL
[H43]   PAINE                         H45B  PRISCILLA
        Elisha Paine  H17E            H45C  PHILLIP
        Rebecca Doane H17Ea           H45D  LOIS
        ------                        H45E  ABIGAIL
H43A  ABIGAIL                         H45F  HANNAH
H43B  REBECCA                         H45G  LYDIA
        ======                                ======
```

356

DIVISION S
H46-H53

[H46] PAINE
    James Paine H17H
    Bethiah Thacher H17Ha

H46A JAMES
H46B THOMAS
H46C BETHIAH #1
H46D BETHIAH #2
    a Samuel Russell
    f Jonathan Russell
    m Martha Moody
H46E MARY
H46F EXPERIENCE
H46G REBECCA
    ======

[H47] PAINE
    Joseph Paine H17I
    Patience Sparrow H17Ia

H47A EBENEZER
H47B HANNAH
H47C JOSEPH
H47D RICHARD
H47E DORCAS
H47F PHEBE
H47G RELIANCE
H47H THOMAS
H47I MARY
H47J JONATHAN
H47K EXPERIENCE
    ======

[H48] VICKERY
    Benjamin Vickery H17Ja
    Dorcas Paine H17J

H48A JOSEPH
H48B BENJAMIN
H48C THOMAS
H48D DORCAS
H48E PHEBE
H48F SARAH
H48G ICHABOD
    ======

[H49] WALKER
    William Walker H18C
    Susanna -- H18Ca

H49A WILLIAM
H49B JOHN
H49C SUSANNA
H49D MEHITABLE
    ======

[H50] WALKER
    Jabez Walker H18F
    Elizabeth -- H18Fa

H50A RICHARD
H50B REJOICE
    a Joseph Lewen
H50C MARY
    a John Berry
    f Samuel Berry
    m Elizabeth Bell
H50D JEREMIAH
H50E MERCY
    a Nathaniel Smith Jr
    f Nathaniel Smith Sr
H50F JABEZ
H50G SARAH
H50H PATIENCE
    ======

[H51] SNOW
    Joseph Snow H19A
    Sarah Smith H19Aa

H51A THANKFUL
H51B JOSEPH
H51C NATHANIEL
H51D DEBORAH
    ======

[H52] SNOW
    Benjamin Snow H19B
    Thankful Bowerman H19Ba

H52A BENJAMIN
H52B ELIZABETH
H52C MARY
H52D THOMAS
H52E SUSANNA
H52F REBECCA
H52G THANKFUL
H52H JANE
H52I JAMES
H52J SETH
    ======

[H53] YOUNG
    Benjamin Young H19Da
    Sarah Snow H19D

H53A THANKFUL
H53B JOHN
H53C DANIEL
    a Lydia Paine
    f Nicholas Paine
    m Hannah Higgins

H53D JOSEPH
   a Rebecca Newcomb
   f Simon Newcomb
   m Hannah Carter
H53E BENJAMIN
   a Thankful Atwood
   f Eleazer Atwood
   m Joanna Strout
H53F SARAH
   a Thomas Snow
   f Benjamin Snow
   m Thankful Bowerman
H53G MARY
   ======

[H54] BROWN
   James Brown H19Ea
   Ruth Snow H19E

H54A JOSEPH
H54B JESSE
H54C ZILPHA
H54D RUTH
H54E JANE
H54F JAMES
H54G GEORGE
H54H REBECCA
H54I BENJAMIN
   ======

[H55] SNOW
   Stephen Snow H19F
   Margaret Elkins H19Fa

H55A MARGARET
   a Eldad Atwood Jr
   f Eldad Atwood Sr
   m Anne Snow
   b Isaac Thayer
   c Joseph Lovering
H55B STEPHEN
   a Rebecca Snow
   f Benjamin Snow
   m Thankful Bowerman
H55C LYDIA
H55D SARAH
H55E ELKINS
H55F JANE
H55G ROBERT
H55H JOHN
   a Phebe Hatch
   f Thomas Hatch
   m Mary Cathcart
H55I MERCY
H55J RUTH
   ======

[H56] LINCOLN
   James Lincoln H19Ga
   Lydia Snow   H19G

H56A JAMES
   a Rebecca Brown
   f James Brown
   m Ruth Snow
H56B LYDIA
   ======

[H57] SNOW
   Josiah Snow H19K
   Elizabeth Snow H19Ka

H57A ELIZABETH
H57B JOSIAH
H57C MARY
   ======

[H58] KING
   John King H20Aa
   Bathshuah Snow H20A

H58A STEPHEN
H58B ROGER
H58C SAMUEL
H58D EBENEZER
H58E JOHN
H58F NATHANIEL #1
H58G NATHANIEL #2
H58H JOANNA
   ======

[H59] COLE
   William Cole H20Ba
   Hannah Snow H20B

H59A ELISHA
H59B DAVID
H59C HANNAH
H59D JANE
   ======

[H60] SNOWA
   Micajah Snow H20C
   Mercy Young H20Ca

H60A JOHN
H60B STEPHEN
H60C JONATHAN
H60D PHEBE
   a Joshua Paine
   f Samuel Paine
   m Patience Freeman
H60E JESSE
H60F DAVID

```
H60G  MERCY                      [H64]   SNOW
H60H  MICAJAH                       John Snow H21E
H60I  RUTH                          Elizabeth Ridley H21Ea
      ======                        ------
[H61]   SMITH                    H64A  JOSHUA
   John Smith H20Da              H64B  ANN
   Bethiah Snow H20D             H64C  ELIZABETH
      ------                     H64D  JOHN
H61A  JAMES                      H64E  PHINEAS
H61B  SAMUEL                     H64F  ANTHONY
H61C  DEAN                       H64G  ELISHA
H61D  MERCY                      H64H  ISAAC
H61E  MARY                       H64I  MARY
H61F  JOHN                       H64J  AMBROSE
H61G  STEPHEN                    H64K  AMASA
H61H  DAVID                      H64L  DAVID #1
H61I  SETH                       H64M  DAVID #2
      ======                           ======
[H62]   SNOW                     [H65]   SNOW
   Ebenezer Snow H20F               Isaac Snow  H21F
   Hope Horton   H20Fa              Alice --   H21Fa
      ------                        ------
H62A  SUSANNA                    H65A  JOHN
H62B  THOMAS                     H65B  WILLIAM
H62C  EBENEZER                   H65C  BENJAMIN
H62D  NATHANIEL                  H65D  ISAAC
H62E  HENRY                            ======
H62F  AARON                      [H66]   SNOW
H62G  SAMUEL                        Elisha Snow H21H
H62H  THANKFUL                      Elizabeth Bedwell H21Ha
H62I  ELISHA                        ------
H62J  HOPE                       H66A  SILAS
H62K  HANNAH                     H66B  ELISHA
H62L  BATHSHUAH                  H66C  JAMES
      ======                     H66D  JESSE
[H63]   SMALLEY                  H66E  JOSHUA
   Benjamin Smalley H21Da        H66F  JOHN
   Rebecca Snow H21D             H66G  PHEBE
      ------                     H66H  JOSEPH
H63A  HANNAH                          ======
H63B  REBECCA                    [H67]   ROGERS
H63C  BENJAMIN #1                   Joseph Rogers H22B
H63D  BENJAMIN #2                   Prudence --   H22Ba
H63E  MARY                          ------
H63F  JAMES                      H67A  SARAH
H63G  PHEBE                      H67B  ELIZABETH
H63H  JOSEPH                     H67C  JOSEPH
H63I  FRANCIS                         ======
H63J  ELIZABETH
      ======
```

[H68] HARDING
     Maziah Harding H22Ca
     Hannah Rogers H22C

H68A JOHN
H68B HANNAH
H68C THOMAS
H68D JAMES
    a Mary Nickerson
    f William Nickerson
    m Mary Snow
H68E MARY
H68F ELIZABETH
H68G PHEBE
H68H NATHAN
H68I CORNELIUS
    ======
[H69] ROGERS
     Thomas Rogers H22E
     Sarah Treat   H22Ea
     Rebecca Collins H22Eb

H69A SARAH by Treat
H69B PHEBE
H69C ELIZABETH
H69D LUCY
H69E HANNAH
H69F THOMAS
H69G JOSEPH
H69H HULDAH
    ======
[H70] ROGERS
     Eleazer Rogers H22F
     Ruhamah Willis H22Fa

H70A ELIZABETH
H70B THOMAS
H70C HANNAH
H70D EXPERIENCE
H70E ELEAZER
H70F WILLIS
H70G ABIJAH
H70H MERIAH
H70I RUTH
    ======
[H71] SNOW
     Jabez Snow H23A
     Elizabeth Treat H23Aa

H71A JABEZ
H71B JOSHUA
H71C ELIZABETH

H71D SYLVANUS
H71E TABITHA
H71F SAMUEL
H71G EDWARD
H71H PHEBE
    ======
[H72] SNOW
     Edward Snow H23B
     Sarah Freeman H23Ba

H72A THOMAS
H72B JABEZ
H72C REBECCA
H72D MARTHA
H72E NATHANIEL
H72F NATHAN
H72G JOSEPH
    ======
[H73] HEDGE
     Samuel Hedge H23Da
     George Lewis H23Db
     Grace Snow   H23D

H73A THANKFUL #1 by Hedge
H73B MARY
H73C LAMUEL
H73D ELISHA
H73E ELIZABETH
H73F SAMUEL
H73G JABEZ
H73H THANKFUL #2
H73I LAMUEL
    ======
[H74] KINDRECK
     Edward Kindreck H23Fa
     Elizabeth Snow H23F

H74A SOLOMON
H74B THOMAS
    ======
[H75] MERRICK
     Stephen Merrick H23Ga
     Deborah Snow   H23G

H75A JOSHUA
H75B SNOW
H75C DEBORAH
H75D SAMUEL
H75E OLIVER
H75F THOMAS
H75G SIMEON
H75H JABEZ
H75I JETHRO
    ======

[H76] HUCKINS
    Thomas Huckins H23Ha
    Rachel Snow   H23E

H76A SAMUEL
H76B THOMAS
H76C JOHN
H76D JABEZ
H76E SNOW
H76F JOSEPH
H76G son
H76H JAMES
H76I ELIZABETH
    ======

[H77] TWINING
    William Twining H24Aa
    Ruth Cole H24A

H77A ELIZABETH
H77B THANKFUL
H77C RUTH
H77D HANNAH
H77E WILLIAM
H77F BARNABAS
H77G MERCY
    ======

[H78] COLE
    John Cole H24B
    Mary Rogers H24Ba
    Sarah Hamlin H24Bb

H78A JONATHAN by Mary
H78B JOHN
H78C MARY
H78D JAMES
H78E NATHAN
H78F JOSHUA
H78G MOSES
H78H PHEBE
H78I THANKFUL #1
H78J JOSEPH
H78K THANKFUL #2
    ======

[H79] COLE
    Joseph Cole H24E
    Elizabeth Cobb H24Ea
    Mercy Hinkley H24Eb
    Rebecca Young H24Ec

H79A GERSHOM by Elizabeth
H79B RUTH

H79C PATIENCE
    a Judah Rogers Jr
    f Judah Rogers Sr
    m Patience Lombard
H79D ELIZABETH
H79E SARAH
    a Joshua Cole
    f John Cole
    m Mary Rogers
H79F RELIANCE
H79G MERCY by Mercy
H79H JOSEPH
H79I MARY
    ======

[H80] SMITH
    Samuel Smith H25A
    Bershuah Lothrop H25Aa

H80A SAMUEL
H80B JOSEPH
    ======

[H81] HAMILTON
    Daniel Hamilton H25Ba
    Mary Smith   H25B

H81A GRACE
H81B THOMAS
H81C LYDIA
H81D MARY
H81E SAMUEL
H81F DANIEL
    ======

[H82] HOPKINS
    Stephen Hopkins H26B
    Sarah Howes   H26Ba

H82A JONATHAN
H82B SARAH
H82C REBECCA
H82D THANKFUL
H82E ELKANAH
H82F THOMAS
H82G EBENEZER
H82H MARY
H82I PHEBE
H82J HANNAH
    ======

[H83] HOPKINS
    Judah Hopkins H26D
    Hannah Mayo   H26Da
    Hannah Mayo   H26Db (sic)

H83A MARSY by Hannah (a)
H83B JOHN
H83C MARTHA
H83D REBECCA
H83E JUDAH
H83F STEPHEN
H83G DESIRE
H83H SYLVANUS
H83I HANNAH
H83J SAMUEL by Hannah (b)
======
[H84] HOPKINS
       Samuel Hopkins H26E
       Lydia Rich   H26Ea

H84A RICHARD
H84B RELIANCE #1
H84C MOSES
H84D LYDIA
H84E RELIANCE #2
H84F SARAH
    a Abner Bangs
    f Jonathan Bangs
    m Experience Berry
H84G SUSANNA
H84H MOSES
H84I THEODOSIUS
H84J NATHAN
H84K HULDAH
======
[H85] HOPKINS
       Nathaniel Hopkins H26F
       Mercy Mayo   H26Fa

H85A DAVID
H85B JEREMIAH
H85C ELIZABETH
H85D NATHANIEL #1
H85E BETHIA
H85F NATHANIEL #2
H85G MERCY
H85H REUBEN
H85I SAMUEL
H85J JAMES
H85K THEOHPILUS
======
[H86] HOPKINS
       Joseph Hopkins H26G
       Mary Mayo   H26Ga

H86A ISAAC
H86B JOSEPH

H86C MARY
H86D JONATHAN
H86E HANNAH
    a Thomas Merrick
    f Stephen Merrick
    m Deborah Snow
H86F NATHAN #1
H86G PRENCE #1
H86H PRENCE #2
H86I NATHAN #2
H86J ELIZABETH
======
[H87] HOPKINS
       Benjamin Hopkins H26H
       Rachel Lincoln   H26Ha

H87A BENJAMIN
H87E GILES
H87C SETH
H87D RACHEL
H87E SAMUEL
H87F SOLOMON
H87G EDWARD
======
[H88] MAKER
       John Maker H26Ia
       Mary Hopkins H26I

H88A PELEG
H88B THANKFUL
H88C MARY
H88D JONATHAN
H88E ELIZABETH
H88F JOSHUA
H88G BURSEL
H88H DAVID
H88I HANNAH
======
[H89] SPARROW
       Jonathan Sparrow H27Aa
       Rebecca Merrick H27A

H89A JONATHAN
    a Dorcas Vickery
    f Benjamin Vickery
    m Dorcas Paine
H89B JOSEPH
H89C JOHN
H89D HANNAH
H89E ABIGAIL
H89F REBECCA
    a Joshua Paine
    f Thomas Paine
    m Hannah Shaw

[H90] MERRICK
    Benjamin Merrick H27D
    Rebecca Doane   H27Da
    Rachel Lincoln   H27Db

H90A ABIGAIL by Rebecca
H90B JOHN
H90C REBECCA
    a John Baker
H90D ISAAC
H90E NATHANIEL
H90F BENJAMIN
    ======

[H91] MERRICK
    Nathaniel Merrick H27E
    Alice Freeman   H27Ea

H91A HANNAH
    a John Snow
    f Micajah Snow
    m Mercy Young
H91B CONSTANT
H91C WILLIAM
H91D MERCY
    a Eleazer King
    f John King
    m Bathshua Snow
H91E GIDEON
H91F PRISCILLA
H91G RUTH
H91H ALICE
H91I BENJAMIN
H91J SARAH
    ======

[H92] MERRICK
    Joshua Merrick H27G
    Lydia Mayo   H27Ga

H92A THOMAS
H92B SETH
H92C JOSEPH
H92D ABIGAIL
    a Nathaniel Hopkins Jr
    f Nathaniel Hopkins Sr
    m Mercy Mayo
H92E LYDIA
H92F BARNABAS
H92G HANNAH
H92H MARY
H92I BEZALEEL
    ======

[H93] SEARS
    Samuel Sears H27Ha
    Ruth Merrick H27H

H93A ABIGAIL
H93B MERCY
H93C RUTH
H93D DESIRE
H93E MARY
    a Joseph Snow
    f Edward Snow
    m Sarah Freeman
H93F HANNAH
H93G SAMUEL
H93H ISAAC
H93I SETH
    a Kezia Wing
    f John Wing
    m Mary Knowles
    ======

[H94] COOKE
    Josiah Cooke H28B
    Mary --   H28Ba

H94A DESIRE
H94B DEBORAH
    a Joseph Hatch
    f Thomas Hatch
    m Sarah Elmes
H94C JOHN
H94D MARY
H94E JOSHUA
    a Zerviah Hatch
    f Josiah Hatch
    m Desire Hawes
    b Hannah Rogers
    f Thomas Rogers
    m Sarah Treat
H94F ELIZABETH
    a Thomas Doty Jr
    f Thomas Doty Sr
    m Elizabeth Harlow
H94G HANNAH
    a Isaiah Atkins
H94H JACOB
H94I SOLOMON
    ======

[H95] COOKE
    Richard Cooke H28C
    Hannah --   H28Ca

H95A THOMAS
H95B HANNAH

```
H95C  CALEB                          H98I  ELIZABETH
H95D  ELIZABETH                      H98J  BENJAMIN
H95E  SARAH                          H98K  JOSHUA
H95F  DEBORAH                        H98L  RICHARD
     a Sylvanus Snow                       ======
     f Jabez Snow
     m Elizabeth Treat         [H99]  COOKE
H95G  ANNE                              Joshua Cooke H28G
H95H  ABIGAIL                           Patience Doane H28Ga
H95I  THANKFUL                          ------
     a Jesse Nickerson
     f John Nickerson          H99A  MARTHA
     m Sarah Bassett           H99B  JOSIAH
     ======                    H99C  JOSHUA
[H96]  NEWCOMB                          a Zilpha Brown
     Thomas Newcomb  H28Da              f James Brown
     Elizabeth Cooke H28D               m Ruth Snow
     ------                    H99D  MERCY
                               H99E  EBENEZER
H96A  EDWARD                            a Mercy Paine
H96B  THOMAS                            f John Paine
H96C  SIMON                             m Bennet Freeman
H96D  DEBORAH                   H99F  EPHRAIM
H96E  MARY                      H99G  RUHAMA #1
H96F  JOSIAH                    H99H  SIMEON
H96G  ELIZABETH                 H99I  MOSES
H96H  EBENEZER                  H99J  ZACCHEUS
H96I  JOSEPH                    H99K  RUHAMA #2
     ======                     H99L  JONATHAN
[H97]  COOKE                    H99M  MARY
     Caleb Cooke H28E           H99N  HEZEKIAH
     Deliverance Crowell H28Ea         ======
     ------                  [H100]  COOKE
                                   Benjamin Cooke H28H
H97A  ELIZABETH                     Mercy Paine    H28Ha
H97B  ABIGAIL                       ------
H97C  EXPERIENCE
H97D  CORNELIUS                H100A  SHUBAEL
H97E  MARY                     H100B  JOSEPH
H97F  EPHRAIM                  H100C  NATHANIEL
     ======                    H100D  RICHARD
[H98]  GODFREY                        ======
     Moses Godfrey H28Fa    [H101]  HOPKINS
     Deborah Cooke H28F             Caleb Hopkins H29A
     ------                         Mercy Freeman H29Aa
                                    ------
H98A  JONATHAN
H98B  SAMUEL                   H101A  CONSTANT
H98C  MOSES                    H101B  MARY
H98D  DAVID                    H101C  THANKFUL
H98E  GEORGE                   H101D  CALEB
H98F  DESIRE                   H101E  JONATHAN
H98G  MARY                     H101F  SIMEON
H98H  DEBORAH                  H101G  MERCY
H98I  ELIZABETH                H101H  JAMES
                               H101I  JOSHUA
                               H101J  ABIEL
```

[H102] HOPKINS
    Nathaniel Hopkins H29B
    Lydia -- H29Ba
    Sarah Higgins   H29Bb

H102A MARY
H102B SARAH
H102C ISAAC
H102D LYDIA
H102E PHEBE
H102F JOHN
H102G ELISHA
    a Elizabeth Snow
    f Joshua Snow
    m Hannah Paine
H102H PRISCILLA
H102I ELIZABETH
    ======

[H103] HOPKINS
    Thomas Hopkins H29C
    Deborah Bickford H29Ca

H103A SAMUEL
H103B HANNAH
    a John Lewis
H103C THOMAS
H103D REBECCA
H103E DEBORAH #1
H103F APHIA
H103G DEBORAH #2
H103H MICHAEL
H103I CALEB #1
H103J CALEB #2
H103K MARY
H103L SARAH
H103M JEREMIAH
    ======

[H104] DYER
    Ambrose Dyer H29Da
    Thankful Hopkins H29D

H104A AMBROSE
H104B THANKFUL
H104C HANNAH
H104D ABIGAIL
H104E NAPHTALI
H104F MARY
H104G JERUSHA
H104H REUBEN
    ======

[H105] TAYLOR
    John Taylor H30Ba
    Abigail Hopkins H30B

H105A MARY
H105B JOHN
H105C ANNE
H105D ABIGAIL #1
H105E EDWARD
H105F ABIGAIL #2
    ======

[H106] HOPKINS
    Elisha Hopkins H30C
    Experience Scudder H30Ca

H106A ELIZABETH
    a Benjamin Godfrey
    f Moses Godfrey
    m Deborah Cooke
H106B JOHN
H106C ELISHA
H106D MARY
H106E EXPERIENCE
H106F BARZILLAI
    ======

[H107] SMITH
    Joseph Smith H30Ea
    Mary Hopkins H30E

H107A BATHSHUA #1
H107B MARY
    a James Hickman
H107C BATHSHUA #2
H107D SAMUEL
H107E HULDA
    ======

[H108] HOPKINS
    Joshua Hopkins H30F
    Priscilla Curtis H30Fa

H108A JOSHUA
H108B PRISCILLA
H108C HANNAH
    ======

[H109] PAINE
    Ebenezer Paine H30Ga
    Hannah Hopkins H30G

H109A EBENEZER
H109B ELIZABETH

H109C NATHANIEL	[H114] STANDISH
H109D ABIGAIL	Ichabod Standish H33Ca
H109E HANNAH	Phebe Ring H33C
======	------
[H110] BIXBEE	H114A MARY
Moses Bixbee H30Ha	H114B DESIRE
Phebe Hopkins H30H	H114C PHEBE
------	H114D ICHABOD
H110A JOSEPH #1	======
H110B JOSEPH #2	[H115] RING
H110C ELIZABETH	Samuel Ring H33D
H110D PHEBE	Ruth Sylvester H33Da
H110E JOHN	------
H110F MOSES	H115A GEORGE
======	H115B GRACE #1
[H111] TUCKER	H115C GRACE #2
Samuel Tucker H31Ba	H115D LYDIA
Hannah Mayo H31B	H115E MARY
------	H115F SAMUEL
H111A KEZIAH	H115G ELIZABETH
H111B JOHN	H115H FRANCIS
H111C THANKFUL	H115I LOUISA
a Nathan Hatch	H115J ELIPHAZ
f Jonathan Hatch	H115K ELEAZER
m Bethiah Nye	======
H111D ELIZABETH	[H116] RING
H111E HANNAH	Andrew Ring H33E
H111F JOHN	Zerviah Standish H33Ea
H111G SAMUEL	------
H111H EUNICE	H116A MARY
======	H116B ANDREW
[H112] HIGGINS	H116C SUSANNA
Samuel Higgins H31Ca	H116D HANNAH
Thankful Mayo H31C	H116E WILLIAM
------	H116F SARAH
H112A WILLIAM	H116G ELEAZER
H112B JOHN	H116H DEBORAH
H112C SIMEON	======
======	[H117] FULLER
[H113] PEIRCE	John Fuller H33Fa
Joseph Peirce H32Da	Deborah Ring H33F
Elizabeth Ring H32D	------
------	H117A ELEAZER #1
H113A HANNAH	H117B ISSACHER
H113B JOSEPH	H117C JOHN
H113C ESTHER	H117D DEBORAH
H113D ELIZABETH	H117E SUSANNA
======	H117F NOAH

H117G	EZRA	H122B	LYDIA
H117H	CONSIDER	H122C	JOSEPH
H117I	ELEAZER #2	H122D	JOHN
H117J	HANNAH	H122E	DAVID
	======	H122F	ISAAC
[H118]	SAMPSON	H122G	HANNAH
	Peleg Sampson H33Ga	H122H	JAMES
	Mary Ring H33G	H122I	JANE
	------		======
H118A	MARY	[H123]	TOMSON
H118B	PELEG		Thomas Tomson H34Aa
H118C	MERCY		Mary Morton H34A
H118D	JONATHAN		------
H118E	SIMEON	H123A	REUBEN
H118F	PRISCILLA	H123B	MARY
H118G	EPHRAIM	H123C	THOMAS
	======	H123D	AMASA
[H119]	RING	H123E	ANDREW
	Jonathan Ring H33H	H123F	EBENEZER
	Sara Mitchell H33Ha	H123G	ZEBADIAH
	------		======
H119A	ANDREW	[H124]	HODGES
H119B	ELEAZER		John Hodges H34Ca
H119C	JOSEPH		Hannah Morton H34C
H119D	SARAH		------
H119E	JONATHAN	H124A	ELIZABETH
H119F	MOLLY	H124B	JOHN
H119G	ELKANAH	H124C	PETER
	======	H124D	ANDREW
[H120]	BOSWORTH		======
	Nehemiah Bosworth H33Ia	[H125]	MORTON
	Susanna Ring H33I		Ebenezer Morton H34D
	------		Mercy Foster H34Da
H120A	DEBORAH		------
H120B	SUSANNA	H125A	MERCY
	======	H125B	MARY
[H121]	CLAGHORN	H125C	JOHN
	James Claghorn H33Ka	H125D	EBENEZER
	Elizabeth Ring H33K	H125E	HANNAH
	------	H125F	DEBORAH
H121A	ELIZABETH	H125G	SETH
H121B	JAMES	H125H	SARAH
H121C	SARAH	H125I	NATHANIEL
H121D	ELEAZER	H125J	LUCIA
H121E	ELICHALETT		======
H121F	ELIZABETH		
H121G	ANDREW RING		
	======		
[H122]	STURDEVANT		
	Ephraim Sturdevant H33La		
	Lydia Ring H33L		

H122A	EPHRAIM		

[H126]   INGLEE
         Jonathan Inglee H34Ea
         Deborah Morton H34E

H126A JONATHAN
H126B JOHN
         ======
[H127]   COLE
         Israel Cole H17Ab
         Mercy Paine H17A

H127A HANNAH
H127B ISRAEL
         ======

[K10] COOKE
    unk.

K10A FRANCIS   [K11]
  a Hester Mahieu=W11Cam
  f Jenne La Mahieu
  ======
[K11] COOKE
    Francis Cooke K10A
    Hester Mahieu K10Aa

K11A JOHN   [K12]
  a Sarah Warren
  f Richard Warren
  m Elizabeth --
K11B JANE
  a Experience Mitchell [K13]
K11C JACOB   [K14]
  a Damaris Hiokins
  f Stephen Hopkins MF
  m Elizabeth --
  b Elizabeth Lettice
  f Thomas Lettice
  m Ann --
K11D HESTER   [K15]
  a Richard Wright
K11E MARY   [K16]
  a John Tomson
  ======
[K12] COOKE
    John Cooke K11A
    Sarah Warren K11Aa

K12A SARAH
  a Arthur Hathaway [K17]
K12B ELIZABETH
  a Daniel Wilcox   [K18]
  f Edward Wilcox
K12C HESTER
  a Thomas Taber   [K19]
  f Philip Taber
  m Lydia Masters
K12D MARY
  a Philip Taber   [K20]
  f Philip Taber
  m Lydia Masters
  b -- Davis
K12E MERCY
  a Stephen West   [K21]
  f Bartholomew West
  m Katherine Almy

[K13] MITCHELL
    Experience Mitchell K11Ba
    Jane Cooke   K11B

K13A ELIZABETH
  a John Washburn Jr [K22]
  f John Washburn Sr
  m Margaret Moore
K13B THOMAS   [K23]
  a unk.
  ======
[K14] COOKE
    Jacob Cooke K11C
    Damaris Hopkins K11Ca
    Elizabeth Lettice K11Cb

K14A ELIZABETH   by Damaris
  a John Doty MF   [K24]
  f Edward Doty
  m Faith Clark
K14B CALEB   [K25]
  a Jane --
K14C JACOB   [K26]
  a Lydia Miller
  f John Miller
  m Margaret Winslow
K14D MARY
  a John Rickard Jr   [K27]
  f John Rickard Sr
  m Hester Barnes
K14E MARTHA
  a Elkanah Cushman [K28]
  f Thomas Cushman
  m Mary Allerton
K14F FRANCIS   [K29]
  a Elizabeth Latham
  f Robert Latham
  m Susanna Winslow
K14G RUTH
K14H SARAH   by Elizabeth
  a Robert Bartlett [K30]
  f Joseph Bartlett
  m Hannah Pope
K14I REBECCA
  ======
[K15] WRIGHT
    Richard Wright K11Da
    Hester Cooke   K11D

K15A ADAM   [K31]
  a Sarah Soule
  f John Soule
  m Rebecca Simmons

K15A ADAM cont.
  b Mehitable Barrow
  f Robert Barrow
  m Ruth Bonum
K15B JOHN
K15C ESTHER
  a Ephraim Tinkham Jr [K32]
  f Ephraim Tinkham Sr
  m Mary Brown
K15D ISAAC
K15E SAMUEL
K15F MARY
  a Hugh Price   [K33]
  ======
[K16] TOMSON
    John Tomson K11Ea
    Mary Cooke K11E

K16A ADAM
K16B JOHN #1
K16C JOHN #2   [K34]
  a Mary Tinkham
  f Ephraim Tinkham
  m Mary Brown
K16D MARY
  a Thomas Taber   [K35]
  f Philip Taber
  m Lydia Masters
K16E ESTHER
  a William Reed Jr [K36]
  f William Reed Sr
  m Avis Chapman
K16F ELIZABETH
  a Thomas Swift Jr [K37]
  f Thomas Swift Sr
  m Elizabeth Vose
K16G SARAH
K16H LYDIA
  a James Soule   [K38]
  f John Soule
  m Rebecca Simmons
K16I JACOB   [K39]
  a Abigail Wadsworth
  f John Wadsworth
  m Abigail Andrews
K16J THOMAS   [K40]
  a Mary Morton
  f John Morton
  m Mary Ring
K16K PETER   [K41]
  a Sarah --
K16L MERCY
  ======

[K17] HATHAWAY
    Arthur Hathaway K12Aa
    Sarah Cooke   K12A

K17A JOHN   [K42]
  a Joanna Pope
  f Thomas Pope
  m Sarah Jenny
  b Patience Hunnewell
  f Richard Hunnewell
  m Elizabeth Stover
K17B SARAH
K17C HANNAH
  a George Cadman [K43]
  f William Cadman
  m Elizabeth --
K17D LYDIA
  a James Sisson   [K44]
  f Richard Sisson
  m Mary --
K17E MARY
  a Samuel Hammond [K45]
  f Benjamin Hammond
  m Mary Vincent
K17F THOMAS   [K46]
  a Hepsibah Starbuck
  f Nathaniel Starbuck
  m Mary Coffin
K17G JONATHAN   [K47]
  a Susannah Pope
  f Seth Pope
  m Deborah Perry
  ======
[K18] WILCOX
    Daniel Wilcox K12Ba
    Elizabeth Cooke K12B

K18A MARY
  a John Earle   [K48]
  f Ralph Earle
  m Dorcas Sprague
K18B SARAH
  a Edward Briggs [K49]
  f John Briggs
  m Hannah Fisher
K18C STEPHEN   [K50]
  a Susannah Briggs
  f Thomas Briggs
  m Mary Fisher
  b Judith Coffin
  f Stephen Coffin
  m Mary Bunker

K18D JOHN   [K51]
  a Rebecca --
K18E EDWARD   [K52]
  a Sarah Manchester
  f William Manchester
  m Mary Cook
K18F THOMAS
K18G LYDIA
  a Thomas Sherman   [K53]
  f Peleg Sherman
  m Elizabeth Lawton
  b Thomas Potter   [K54]
  f Ichabod Potter
  m Martha Hazard
K18H SUSANNA
  a Jonathan Head   [K55]
  f Henry Head
  m Elizabeth --
  ======
[K19] TABER
    Thomas Taber K12Ca
    Hester Cocke K12C

K19A THOMAS   [K56]
  a Rebecca Harlow
  f Samuel Harlow
  m Priscilla --
K19B ESTHER
  a Samuel Perry   [K57]
  f Ezra Perry
  m Elizabeth Burgess
  ======
[K20] TABER
    Philip Taber K12Da
    Mary Cooke   K12D

K20A MARY
  a Thomas Earle   [K58]
  f William Earle
  m Mary Walker
K20B SARAH
  a Thomas Cory   [K59]
  f William Cory
  m Mary Earle
K20C LYDIA
  a Joseph Mosher   [K60]
  f Hugh Mosher
  m Rebecca Maxson
K20D PHILIP   [K61]
  a Margaret Wood
  f William Wood
  m Martha Earle

K20E ABIGAIL
K20F ESTHER
  a Thomas Brownell [K62]
  f William Brownell
  m Sarah Smiton
K20G JOHN   [K63]
  a Susanna Manchester
  f William Manchester
  m Mary Cook
K20H BETHIA
  a John Macomber   [K64]
  f William Macomber
  m Mary --
  ======
[K21] WEST
    Stephen West K12Ea
    Mercy Cooke   K12E

K21A KATHERINE
  a Christopher Turner [K65]
K21B SARAH
K21C ANN
K21D BARTHOLOMEW   [K66]
  a Ann Eldredge
K21E AMY
  a William Peckham [K67]
  f Stephen Peckham
  m Mary --
K21F STEPHEN   [K68]
  a Susannah Jenney
  f Samuell Jenney
  m Hannah --
K21G JOHN   [K69]
  a Rebecca Sisson
  f James Sisson
  m Lydia Hathaway
K21H EUNICE
  a Beriah Goddard
K21I LOIS
  a Jonathan Taber   [K70]
  f Thomas Taber
  m Rebecca Harlow
  ======
[K22] WASHBURN
    John Washburn   K13Aa
    Elizabeth Mitchell K13A

K22A JOHN   [K71]
  a Rebecca Lapham
  f Thomas Lapham
  m Lydia Tilden

K22B THOMAS   [K72]
  a Deliverance Packard
  f Samuel Packard
  m Elizabeth --
  b Sarah --
  c Agigail Atkins
  f Thomas Atkins
  m Elizabeth --
K22C SAMUEL   [K73]
  a Deborah Packard
  f Samuel Packard
  m Elizabeth --
K22D JOSEPH   [K74]
  a Hannah Latham
  f Robert Latham
  m Susanna Winslow
K22E JONATHAN   [K75]
  a Mary Vaughan
  f George Vaughan
  m Elizabeth Hinksman
K22F BENJAMIN
K22G MARY
  a Samuel Kingsley Jr [K76]
  f Samuel Kingsley Sr
  m Hannah Brackett
K22H ELIZABETH
  a James Hayward   [K77]
  f John Howard
  m Martha Hayward
  b Edward Sale'   [K78]
K22I JANE
  a William Orcutt Jr [K79]
  f William Orcutt Sr
  m Martha Lane
K22J JAMES   [K80]
  a Mary Bowden
K22K SARAH
  a John Ames Jr   [K81]
  f John Ames Sr
  m Sarah Willis
  ======

[K23] MITCHELL
    Thomas Mitchell K13B
  -- --

K23A THOMAS   [K82]
  a Margaret Rathbone
  f John Rathbone
  m Margaret --
K23B JOHN   [K83]
  a Sarah Rathbone
  f John Rathbone
  m Margaret --

K23C JOSEPH   [K84]
  a Mary George
  f Samuel George
  m Sarah Rathbone
  ======
[K24]   DOTY
    John Doty   K14Aa
    Elizabeth Cooke K14A

K24A JOHN
K24B EDWARD
K24C JACOB
K24D ELIZABETH
K24E ISAAC
K24F SAMUEL
K24G ELISHA
K24H JOSIAH
K24I MARTHA
  ======
[K25]   COOKE
    Caleb Cooke   K14B
    Jane --   K14Ba

K25A JOHN   [K85]
  a Elizabeth Sears
  f Silas Sears
  m Anna --
K25B MARCY
K25C ANNE
  a James Johnson   [K86]
K25D JANE
  a Isaac Harris Jr [K87]
  f Isaac Harris Sr
  m Mercy Latham
K25E ELIZABETH
  a Robert Johnson   [K88]
K25F MARY
  a Robert Carver   [K89]
  f John Carver
  m Mary Barnes
K25G CALEB
  a Abigail Howland
  f James Howland
  m Mary Lothrop
H25H JAMES   [K90]
  a Abigail Hodges
  f William Hodges
  m Hannah Tisdale
H25I JOSEPH   [K91]
  a Experience Hodges
  f Samuel Hodges
  m Experience Leonard
  ======

[K26] COOKE
    Jacob Cooke K14C
    Lydia Miller K14Ca

K26A WILLIAM   [K92]
    a Tabitha Hall
    f Elisha Hall
    m Lydia --
K26B LYDIA
    a John Faunce   [K93]
    f Joseph Faunce
    m Judith Rickard
K26C REBECCA
    a Benjamin Samson [K94]
    f Stephen Samson
    m Elizabeth --
K26D JACOB   [K95]
    a Phebe Hall
    f Elisha Hall
    m Lydia --
    b Mary Tirrell
    f William Tirrell
    m Abigail Pratt
    c Rebecca --
K26E MARGARET
    a Simon Lazell   [K96]
    f Joshua Lazell
    m Mary --
K26F JOSIAH   [K97]
    a Zibiah Cushman
    f Thomas Cushman
    m Sarah Strong
K26G JOHN   [K98]
    a Phebe Crossman
    f Nathaniel Crossman
    m Sarah Merrick
K26H DAMARIS
    ======

[K27] RICKARD
    John Rickard K14Da
    Mary Cooke   K14D

K27A JOHN #1
K27B MERCY
    a Ignatius Cushing   [K99]
    f Jeremiah Cushing
    m Hannah Loring
K27C JOHN #2   [K100]
    a Sarah --
K27D MARY
K27E ESTHER

K27F ELIZABETH
    a Ebenezer Doggett [K101]
    f Samuel Doggett
    m Bathsheba Holmes
K27G JAMES   [K102]
    a Hannah Howland
    f James Howland
    m Mary Lothrop
    ======

[K28] CUSHMAN
    Elkanah Cushman K14Ea
    Martha Cooke   K14E

K28A ALLERTON
K28B ELIZABETH
K28C JOSIAH
K28D MARTHA
K28E MEHITABLE
    ======

[K29] COOKE
    Francis Cooke   K14F
    Elizabeth Latham K14Fa

K29A SUSANNA
    a James Sturtevant [K103]
    f Samuel Sturtevant
    m Mercy Cornish
K29B ROBERT   [K104]
    a Abigail Harlow
    f Nathaniel Harlow
    m Abigail Church
    b Lydia Tilden
    f Samuel Tilden
    m Sarah Curtice
K29C CALEB   [K105]
    a Hannah Shurtleff
    f Abiel Shurtleff
    m Lydia Barnes
K29D FRANCIS   [K106]
    a Ruth Silvester
    f Israel Silvester
    m Ruth Prince
K29E SARAH
    a Ephraim Cole Jr   [K107]
    f Ephraim Cole Sr
    m Rebecca Grey
K29F ELIZABETH
    a David Leach Jr   [K108]
    f David Leach Sr
    m Hannah Whitman
    ======

[K30] BARTLETT
    Robert Bartlett K14Ha
    Sarah Cooke   K14H

K30A HANNAH
    a Eleazer Churchill [K109]
    f Eleazer Churchill Sr
    m Mary --
K30B THOMAS
    a Abigail Finney
    f Jeremiah Finney
    m Esther Lewis
K30C JOHN   [K110]
    a Sarah Cobb
    f Ebenezer Cobb
    m Mercy Holmes
    b Sarah Lewis
    f Nathan Lewis
    m Sarah Arey
    c Sarah Seabury
    f Samuel Seabury
    m Deborah Wiswell
K30D SARAH
    a John Finney   [K111]
    f Josiah Finney
    m Elizabeth Warren
K30E JAMES
K30F JOSEPH   [K112]
    a Sarah Morton
    f Thomas Morton
    m Martha Doty
K30G ELIZABETH
    a Thomas Sears   [K113]
    f Paul Sears
    m Mercy Freeman
K30H WILLIAM
K30I EBENEZER   [K114]
    a Rebecca Dimmon
    f Thomas Dimmon
    m Hannah Finney
    b Abigail Finney
K30J ROBERT   [K115]
    a Rebecca Wood
    f Ephraim Wood
    m Susanna Howland
    b Jane Spooner
    f Thomas Spooner
    m Sarah --
    c Hopestill Seabury
    f Samuel Seabury
    m Deborah Wiswell

K30K LEMUEL   [K116]
    a Mary Doty
    f Isaac Doty
    m Martha Faunce

[K31] WRIGHT
    Adam Wright K15A
    Sarah Soule K15Aa
    Mehitable Barrow K15Ab

K31A ESTHER   by Sarah
    a Daniel Pratt   [K117]
    f Benajah Pratt
    m Persis Dunham
K31B JOHN   [K118]
    a Mary Lucas
    f Benoni Lucas
    m Repentance Harlow
K31C MARY
    a Jeremiah Gifford [K119]
    f Robert Gifford
    m Sarah Wing
K31D ISAAC   [K120]
    a Mary Cole
    f John Cole
    m Susanna Grey
K31E RACHEL
    a Ebenezer Barlow [K121]
    f Moses Barlow
    m Mary Dexter
K31F SARAH
    a Seth Fuller   [K122]
    f Samuel Fuller
    m Mercy Eaton
K31G SAMUEL by Mehitable [K123]
    a Anna Tilson
    f Edmund Tilson
    m Elizabeth Waterman
K31H MOSES   [K124]
    a Thankful Boles
K31I JAMES
    a Elizabeth Waterman
    f Samuel Waterman
    m Bethiah --
K31J NATHAN   [K125]
    a Hannah Cooke
    f William Cooke
    m Tabitha Hall
    ======

[K32] TINKHAM
    Ephraim Tinkham K15Ca
    Esther Wright   K15C

K32A MARTHA
K32B JOHN
K32C EPHRAIM
K32D ISAAC
K32E SAMUEL
K32F MARY
    ======

[K33] PRICE
    Hugh Price K15Fa
    Mary Wright K15F

K33A MARY
  a Samuel Sturtevant [K126]
  f Samuel Strutevant Sr
  m Mercy Cornish
K33B JOHN
    ======

[K34] TOMSON
    John Tomson K16C
    Mary Tinkham K16Ca

K34A MARY
K34B JOHN   [K127]
  a Elizabeth Thomas
  f Jeremiah Thomas
  m Lydia Howland
K34C EPHRAIM   [K128]
  a Joanna Thomas
  f Jonathan Thomas
  m Mary Steward
K34D SHUBAEL   [K129]
  a Susanna Parlour
  f THomas Parlour
  m Elizabeth Liscomb
K34E THOMAS   [K130]
  a Martha Soule
  f John Soule
  m Martha Tinkham
K34F MARTHA
K34G SARAH
K34H PETER
K34I ISAAC
K34J EBENEZER
K34K FRANCIS
K34L JACOB   [K131]
  a Mary Hayward
  f Joseph Hayward
  m Sarah Crossman

[K35] TABER
    Thomas Taber K16Da
    Mary Tomson K16D

K35A LYDIA
  a John Kenny Jr [K132]
  f John Kenny Sr
K35B SARAH
  a William Hart   [K133]
  f Richard Hart
  m Hannah --
K35C MARY   [K134]
  a Manasseh Morton
  f George Morton
  m Joanna Kempton
K35D JOSEPH   [K135]
  a Elizabeth Spooner
  f John Spooner
  m Rebecca Peckham
  b Lydia Abbott
K35E JOHN   [K136]
  a Phebe Spooner
  f John Spooner
  m Elizabeth Peckham
K35F JACOB   [K137]
  a Sarah West
  f Stephen West
  m Mercy Cooke
K35G JONATHAN
K35H BETHIAH
  a Caleb Blackwell [K138]
  f John Blackwell
  m Sarah Warren
K35I PHILIP   [K139]
  a Susannah Tucker
K35J ABIGAIL
  a Ebenezer Taber   [K140]
  f Joseph Taber
  m Mary Gladden
    ======

[K36] REED
    William Reed K16Ea
    Esther Tomson K16E

K36A BATHSHEBA
  a Nicholas Porter   [K141]
  f John Porter
  m Deliverance Byram
K36B MERCY
  a Nicholas Whitmarsh [K142]
  f Nicholas Whitmarsh Sr
  m Hannah Reed

K36B MERCY cont.
  b Andrew Ford Jr [K143]
  f Andrew Ford Sr
  ■ Abiah --
K36C JOHN #1
K36D WILLIAM [K144]
  a Alice Nash
  f Jacob Nash
  ■ Abigail Dyer
K36E MARY
K36F HESTER
K36G JOHN #2 [K145]
  a Sarah Hersey
  b Mary Wheeler
K36H JACOB [K146]
  a Sarah Hersey
  f William Hersey
  ■ Sarah Langler
  b Hannah Noyes
  f Nicholas Noyes
  ■ Sarah Lunt
K36I SARAH
  a Hezekiah King [K147]
  f Samuel King
  ■ Experience Phillips
  ======
[K37] SWIFT
  Thomas Swift K16Fa
  Elizabeth Tomson K16F

K37A THOMAS [K148]
  a Rachel Stockbridge
  f Charles Stockbridge
  ■ Abigail --
  ======
[K38] SOULE
  James Soule K16Ha
  Lydia Tomson K16H

K38A MARY
K38B MARTHA
K38C ISAAC
K38D REBECCA
K38E JACOB
  ======
[K39] TOMSON
  Jacob Tomson K16I
  Abigail Wadsworth K16Ia

K39A JACOB [K149]
  a Elizabeth Tilson
  f Edmund Tilson
  ■ Elizabeth Waterman

K39B ABIGAIL
  a Jonathan Packard [K150]
  f Zaccheus Packard
  ■ Sarah Howard
K39C MERCY
  a Nehemiah Bennett [K151]
  f John Bennett
  ■ Deborah Grover
K39D JOHN [K152]
  a Joanna Adams
  f Joseph Adams
  ■ Alice --
K39E LYDIA
  a John Packard [K153]
  f Zaccheus Packard
  ■ Sarah Howard
K39F BARNABAS [K154]
  a Hannah Porter
  f Samuel Porter
  ■ Mary Nash
K39G ESTHER
  a Ebenezer Bennett [K155]
  f John Bennett
  ■ Deborah Grover
K39H HANNAH
  a Ebenezer Reed [K156]
  f William Reed
  ■ Alice Nash
K39I MARY
K39J CALEB [K157]
  a Abigail Crossman
  f Nathaniel Crossman
  ■ Sarah Merrick
  ======
[K40] TOMSON
  Thomas Tomson K16J
  Mary Morton K16Ja

K40A REUBEN [K158]
  a Mary Tomson
  f Jacob Tomson
  ■ Abigail Wadsworth
  b Sarah Bryant
  f George Bryant
  ■ Sarah Ripley
K40B MARY
  a Samuel Waterman [K159]
  f Robert Waterman
  ■ Mary Cushman
K40C THOMAS [K160]
  a Mary Loring
  f Ignatius Loring
  ■ Sarah Shurtleff

K40D AMASA   [K161]
  a Lydia Cobb
  f John Cobb
  m Joanna Thomas
K40E ANDREW
K40F EBENEZER   [K162]
  a Mary Wright
  f Isaac Wright
  m Mary Cole
K40G ZEBADIAH   [K163]
  a Zerviah Standish
  f Moses Standish
  m Rachel Cobt
  ======

[K41] TOMSON
    Peter Tomson K16K
    Sarah --   K16Ka

K41A SARAH
  a Nehemiah Bozworth [K164]
  f David Bozworth
  m Mercy Sturtevant
K41B PETER   [K165]
  a Hannah Bolton
  f John Bolton
  m Ruth Hooper
  b Lydia Cowing
  f Israel Cowing
K41C JAMES
K41D JOSEPH   [K166]
  a Elizabeth Bolton
  f John Bolton Jr
  m Ruth Hooper
  ======

[K42] HATHAWAY
    John Hathaway K17A
    Joanna Pope   K17Aa
    Patience Hunnewell K17Ab

K42A SARAH   by Joanna
K42B JOANNA
K42C JOHN
K42D ARTHUR
K42E HANNAH
K42F MARY
K42G JONATHAN   by Patience
K42H RICHARD
K42I THOMAS
K42J HUNNEWELL
K42K ABIAL
K42L ELIZABETH
K42M PATIENCE

K42N BENJAMIN
K42O JAMES
K42P EBENEZER
  ======

[K43] CADMAN
    George Cadman K17Ca
    Hannah Hathaway K17C

K43A ELIZABETH
  ======

[K44] SISSON
    James Sisson K17Da
    Lydia Hathaway K17D

K44A RICHARD
K44B MARY
K44C JAMES
K44D JONATHAN
K44E PHILIP
K44F THOMAS
K44G CONTENT
K44H HANNAH
K44I SARAH
K44J REBECCA
  ======

[K45] HAMMOND
    Samuel Hammond K17Ea
    Mary Hathaway K17E

K45A BENJAMIN
K45B SETH
K45C ROSAMOND
K45D SAMUEL
K45E THOMAS
K45F JEDIDIAH
K45G JOSIAH
K45H BARNABAS
K45I MARIA
K45J JOHN
K45K JEDIDAH
  ======

[K46] HATHAWAY
    Thomas Hathaway K17F
    Hepsibah Starbuck K17Fa

K46A ANTIPAS
K46B APPHIAH
K46C PARNAL
K46D ELIZABETH
K46E MARY
K46F THOMAS
K46G NATHANIEL

K46H HEPZIBAH
K46I JETHRO
======

[K47] HATHAWAY
    Jonathan Hathaway K17G
    Susannah Pope   K17Ga

K47A ELIZABETH
K47B ABIGAIL
K47C GAMALIEL
K47D HANNAH
K47E SETH
K47F DEBORAH
K47G JONATHAN
K47H SILAS
K47I ELNATHAN
K47J PAUL
======

[K48] EARLE
    John Earle K18Aa
    Mary Wilcox K18A

K48A JOHN
K48B DANIEL
K48C BENJAMIN
K48D MARY
K48E REBECCA
K48F ELIZABETH
======

[K49] BRIGGS
    Edward Briggs   K18Ba
    Sarah Wilcox   K18B

K49A DEBORAH
K49B HANNAH
K49C WALTER
K49D JOSIAH
K49E CHARLES
======

[K50] WILCOX
    Stephen Wilcox K18C
    Susannah Briggs K18Ca
    Judith Coffin   K18Cb

K50A SUSANNAH by Susannah
K50B DANIEL
K50C THOMAS
K50D ELEZEBETH
K50E STEPHEN
K50F JOHN   by Judith
======

[K51] WILCOX
    John Wilcox K18D
    Rebecca -- K18Da

K51A JACOB
K51B DANIEL
K51C ELIZABETH
K51D JOHN
K51E JABEZ
K51F BARJONA
K51G REBECCA
K51H THOMAS
======

[K52] WILCOX
    Edward Wilcox K18E
    Sarah Manchester K18Ea

K52A JOSIAH
K52B EPHRAIM
K52C WILLIAM
K52D FREELOVE
======

[K53] SHERMAN
    Thomas Sherman K18Ga
    Lydia Wilcox   K18G

K53A JOSIAH
K53B DANIEL
K53C RUTH
K53D GEORGE
K53E BENJAMIN
K53F SUSANNAH
======

[K54] POTTER
    Thomas Potter K18Gb
    Lydia Wilcox K18G

K54A MARTHA
======

[K55] HEAD
    Jonathan Head K18Ha
    Susanna Wilcox K18H

K55A JOSEPH
======

[K56] TABER
    Thomas Taber K19A
    Rebecca Harlow K19Aa

K56A PRISCILLA
K56B JONATHAN

K56 cont'd		K60E	JAMES
K56C	AMAZIAH	K60F	RUTHS
K56D	ESTHER	K60G	BENJAMIN
K56E	MARY	K60H	WILLIAMN
K56F	SAMUEL	K60I	LYDIA
K56G	SETH		======

======

[K57]   PERRY   [K61]   TABER
    Samuel Perry K19Ba   Philip Taber K20D
    Esther Taber K19B   Margaret Wood K20Da

------   ------

K57A	ELIZABETH	K61A	MARTHA
K57B	DEBORAH	K61B	PHILIP
		a	Ruth Shaw
K57C	THOMAS	K61C	WILLIAM
K57D	SARAH	K61D	COMFORT
K57E	REBECCA	K61E	MARY
K57F	NATHAN	K61F	JONATHAN
K57G	MARY	K61G	JOSIAH
K57H	EBENEZER	K61H	REBECCA
K57I	SETH	K61I	JOHN
K57J	MERCY	K61J	MARGARET

======   ======

[K58]   EARLE   [K62]   BROWNELL
    Thomas Earle K20Aa   Thomas Brownell K20Fa
    Mary Taber   K20A   Esther Taber   K20F

------   ------

K58A	WILLIAM	K62A	JOSEPH
K58B	THOMAS	K62B	ELIZABETH
K58C	MARY	K62C	THOMAS
K58D	OLIVER	K62D	SARAH
K58E	SARAH	K62E	ESTHER
K58F	LYDIA	K62F	CONTENT
K58G	REBECCA	K62G	REBECCA

======   ======

[K59]   CORY   [K63]   TABER
    Thomas Cory K20Ba   John Taber   K20G
    Sarah Taber K20B   Susanna Manchester K20Ga

------   ------

K59A	WILLIAM	K63A	MARY
K59B	THOMAS	K63B	PHILIP
K59C	PHILIP	K63C	WILLIAM
K59D	PATIENCE	K63D	SARAH
K59E	MARY	K63E	THOMAS
K59F	SARAH	K63F	JOHN
		K63G	JOSEPH

======   K63H | LYDIA

[K60]   MOSHER   ======
    Joseph Mosher K20Ca
    Lydia Taber   K20C   [K64]   MACOMBER
        John Macomber K20Ha
------   Bethia Taber K20H

K60A	REBECCA	------	
K60B	PHILIP		
K60C	JONATHAN	K64A	PHILIP
K60D	JOSEPH	K64B	MARCY

```
K64C  MARY                              [K70]  TABER
K64D  ABIAL                                    Jonathan Taber K21Ia
K64E  JOHN                                     Lois West      K21I
K64F  WILLIAM                                  ------
K64G  JOB                               K70A  MARY
      ======                            K70B  MERCY
[K65]  TURNER                           K70C  REBECCA
      Christopher Turner K21Aa          K70D  LOIS
      Katharine West     K21A           K70E  THOMAS
      ------                            K70F  JONATHAN
                                        K70G  STEPHEN
K65A  MARY                                    ======
K65B  CATHERINE                         [K71]  WASHBURN
      ======                                  John Washburn   K22A
[K66]  WEST                                   Rebecca Laphaa  K22Aa
      Bartholomew West K21D                   ------
      Ann Eldredge     K21Da            K71A  JOSIAH
      ------                            K71B  JOHN
K66A  AUDRIA                            K71C  JOSEPH
K66B  WILLIAM                           K71D  WILLIAM
K66C  BARTHOLOMEW #1                    K71E  ABIGAIL
K66D  BARTHOLOMEW #2                    K71F  REBECCA
K66E  EDWARD                                  ======
K66F  THOMAS                            [K72]  WASHBURN
K66G  MERCY                                   Thomas Washburn     K22B
      ======                                  Deliverance Packard K22Ba
[K67]  PECKHAM                                Sarah --            K22Bb
      William Peckhaa K21Ea                   Abigail Atkins      K22Bc
      Amy West        K21E                    ------
      ------                            K72A  ELIZABETH  by Deliverance
K67A  SARAH                             K72B  NATHANIEL
K67B  ALMY                              K72C  HEPZIBAH
      ======                            K72D  THOMAS
[K68]  WEST                             K72E  PATIENCE
      Stephen West    K21F              K72F  TIMOTHY
      Susannah Jenney K21Fa             K72G  DELIVERANCE
      ------                                  ======
K68A  HANNAH                            [K73]  WASHBURN
K68B  MARCY                                   Samuel Washburn K22C
K68C  SAMUELL                                 Deborah Packard K22Ca
K68D  ANNE                                    ------
K68E  ALMY                              K73A  SAMUEL
K68F  STEPHEN                           K73B  NOAH
K68G  BARTHOLOMEW                       K73C  ISRAEL
K68H  SUSANNAH                          K73D  NEHEMIAH
      ======                            K73E  BENJAMIN
[K69]  WEST                             K73F  HANNAH
      John West     K21G                      ======
      Rebecca Sisson K21Ga              [K74]  WASHBURN
      ------                                  Joseph Washburn K22D
K69A  KATHRINE                                Hannah Lathaa   K22Da
K69B  MARCY                                   ------
K69C  JOHN
      ======
```

```
K74A  MILES                          [K79]  ORCUTT
K74B  EDWARD                                William Orcutt  K22Ia
K74C  JONATHAN                              Jane Washburn   K22I
K74D  JOSEPH                                ------
K74E  EBENEZER                       K79A  JOANNA
K74F  HANNAH                         K79B  ELIZABETH
K74G  BENJAMIN                              ======
K74H  EPHRAIM                        [K80]  WASHBURN
      ======                                James Washburn  K22J
[K75]  WASHBURN                              Mary Bowden     K22Ja
      Jonathan Washburn   K22E             ------
      Mary Vaughan        K22Ea   K80A  MARY
      ------                      K80B  ANNA
K75A  ELISABETH                     K80C  JAMES
K75B  JOSIAH                        K80D  EDWARD
K75C  BENJAMIN                      K80E  MOSES
K75D  EBENEZER                      K80F  GIDEON
K75E  MARTHA                        K80G  SARAH
K75F  JOANNA                        K80H  MARTHA
K75G  NATHAN                        K80I  ELISABETH
K75H  CORNELIUS                           ======
      ======                       [K81]  AMES
[K76]  KINSLEY                              John Ames       K22Ka
      Samuel Kingsley K22Ga               Sarah Washburn  K22K
      Mary Washburn   K22G                ------
      ------                      K81A  ELIZABETH
K76A  SAMUEL                        K81B  JOHN
K76B  SARAH                         K81C  SARAH
K76C  HANNAE                        K81D  ABIGAIL
K76D  MARY                          K81E  JONATHAN
K76E  BENJAMIN                      K81F  DEBORAH
K76F  SUSANNA                       K81G  DANIEL
K76G  ABIGAIL                       K81H  BENJAMIN
K76H  BETHIAH                       K81I  JOSHUA
      ======                              ======
[K77]  HAYWARD                       [K82]  MITCHELL
      James Hayward        K22Ha           Thomas Mitchell   K23A
      Elizabeth Washburn K22H             Margaret Rathbone K23Aa
      ------                      K82A  THOMAS
K77A  ELISABETH                     K82B  GEORGE
K77B  MERCY                         K82C  JOSEPH
K77C  JAMES                         K82D  MARGARET
      ======                      K82E  BENJAMIN
[K78]  SALE                               ======
      Edward Sale       K22Hb       [K83]  MITCHELL
      Elizabeth Washburn K22H             John Mitchell   K23B
      ------                              Sarah Rathbone K23Ba
K78A  BENJAMIN                            ------
K78B  JOHN                          K83A  JOHN
      ======                              ======
```

[K84]   MITCHELL
     Joseph Mitchell K23C
     Mary George   K23Ca

K84A JONATHAN
K84B JOHN
K84C JEREMIAH
K84D THOMAS
K84E MARY

  ======

[K85]   COOKE
     John Cooke K25A
     Elizabeth Sears K25Aa
     Hannah Faunce K25Ab

K85A SILAS by Elizabeth
K85B PAUL
K85C ROBERT
K85D MERCY

  ======

[K86]   JOHNSON
     James Johnson K25Ca
     Anne Cooke   K25C

K86A JOHN
K86B JAMES
K86C CALEB
K86D ANN
K86E ELIZABETH
K86F JOSEPH

  ======

[K87]   HARRIS
     Isaac Harris Jr K25Da
     Jane Cooke   K25D

K87A ARTHUR
K87B ABNER
K87C ANNE
K87D ELIZABETH
K87E JANE

  ======

[K88]   JOHNSON
     Robert Johnson   K25Ea
     Elizabeth Cooke K25E

K88A JANE
K88B JOSEPH
K88C SARAH
K88D CALEB
K88E MERCY
K88F CONTENT
K88G ANN

K88H ELIZABETH
K88I DANIEL
K88J JACOB

  ======

[K89]   CARVER
     Robert Carver K25Fa
     Mary Cooke   K25F

K89A ELIZABETH
K89B MARY
K89C ROBERT

  ======

[K90]   COOKE
     James Cooke   K25H
     Abigail Hodges K25Ha

K90A HANNAH
K90B LUCY
K90C SUSANNA #1
K90D ELIJAH
K90E SUSANNA #2
K90F MARIA
K90G BETHIA
K90H JAMES #1
K90I JAMES #2
K90J ZENAS

  ======

[K91]   COOKE
     Joseph Cooke   K25I
     Experience Hodges K25Ia

K91A ANN
K91B JOSEPH
K91C CALEB
K91D MARY
K91E SUSANNA

  ======

[K92]   COOKE
     William Cooke K26A
     Tabitha Hall   K26Aa

K92A HANNAH
K92B LYDIA
K92C HULDA
K92D WILLIAM
K92E ELISHA
K92F TABITHA
K92G PRISCILLA

  ======

[K93]   FAUNCE
     John Faunce   K26Ba
     Lydia Cooke   K26B

K93A JUDITH	K97A SARAH
K93B LYDIA	K97B LYDIA
K93C JOHN	K97C SUBMIT
K93D HANNAH	K97D ZIBIAH
K93E MARY	K97E JOSIAH
K93F MEHITABLE	K97F RUTH
K93G REBECCA	======
======	[K98]　COOKE
[K94]　SAMPSON	John Cooke　　K26G
Benjamin Sampson K26Ca	Phebe Crossman K26Ga
Rebecca Cooke　　K26C	------
------	K98A LYDIA
K94A MICAH	K98B SARAH
K94B DEBORAH	K98C LYDIA
K94C CORNELIUS	K98D SYLVANUS
K94D REBECCA	K98E MARGARET
K94E BENJAMIN	K98F MOLLY
K94F JOSIAH	======
======	[K99]　CUSHING
[K95]　COOKE	Ignatius Cushing K27Ba
Jacob Cooke　K26D	Mercy Rickard　　K27B
Phebe Hall　　K26Da	------
Mary Tirrell K26Db	K99A HANNAH
Rebecca --　　K26Dc	K99B IGNATIUS
------	K99C HANNAH
K95A JESSE　by Phebe	======
K95B ASA	[K100]　RICKARD
K95C PHEBE	John Rickard K27C
K95D JACOB	Sarah --　　K27Ca
K95E STEPHEN by Mary	------
K95F MARY	K100A JAMES
K95G JOHN　by Rebecca	K100B MARGARET
K95H JOSEPH	K100C MARY
K95I DANIEL	K100D MARIAH
======	======
[K96]　LAZELL	[K101]　DOGGETT
Simon Lazell　K26Ea	Ebenezer Doggett K27Fa
Margaret Cooke K26E	Elizabeth Rickard K27F
------	------
K96A JOSHUA #1	K101A EBENEZER #1
K96B JOSHUA #2	K101B JOHN
K96C LYDIA	K101C EBENEZER #2
K96D MARY	K101D SAMUEL
K96E JACOB	======
K96F WILLIAM twin	[K102]　RICKARD
K96G SARAH twin	James Rickard　K27G
K96H ABNER	Hannah Howland K27Ga
======	------
[K97]　COOKE	K102A JAMES
Josiah Cooke　K26F	K102B JOHN
Zibiah Cushman K26Fa	K102C BENJAMIN
------	K102D LOTHROP

K102E WILLIAM
K102F HANNAH
======

[K103]   STURTEVANT
          James Sturtevant K29Aa
          Susanna Cooke   K29A

K103A FRANCIS
K103B CALEB
K103C JAMES
K103D SUSANNA
K103E LYDIA
K103F MARY
K103G SARAH
K103H ELIZABETH
======

[K104]   COOKE
          Robert Cooke   K29E
          Abigail Harlow K29Ba
          Lydia Tilden   K29Bb

K104A CHARLES by Abigail
K104B NATHANIEL
K104C ROBERT
K104D SARAH
K104E FRANCIS
K104F SAMUEL   by Lydia
K104G SIMEON
======

[K105]   COOKE
          Caleb Cooke   K29C
          Hannah Shurtleff K29Ca

K105A CALEB
K105B BENJAMIN
K105C LYDIA
K105D ISAAC
K105E ELKNAH
K105F EPHRAIM
K105G HANNAH
K105H REBECKAH
K105I LYDIAH
K105J SARAH
K105K FEAR
K105L AMOS
======

[K106]   COOKE
          Francis Cooke K29D
          Ruth Silvester K29Da

K106A RUTH
K106B SUSANAH
======

[K107]   COLE
          Ephraim Cole K29Ea
          Sarah Cooke K29E

K107A EPHRAIM
K107B SARAH #1
K107C REBECCA
K107D SARAH #2
======

[K108]   LEACH
          David Leach   K29Fa
          Elizabeth Cooke K29F

K108A JAMES
K108B ELIZABETH
K108C MERCY
K108D SARAH
K108E SUSANNAH
======

[K109]   CHURCHILL
          Eleazer Churchill K30Aa
          Hannah Bartlett   K30A

K109A ELEAZER
K109B JOSIAH
K109C JONATHAN
======

[K110]   BARTLETT
          John Bartlett   K30C
          Sarah Cobb   K30Ca
          Sarah Lewis   K30Cb
          Sarah Seabury   K30Cc

K110A JERUSHA   by Cobb
K110B SARAH
K110C HANNAH
K110D MARY
K110E JERUSHA   by Lewis
K110F JOHN
K110G JENNY
K110H LEWIS
K110I ABIGAIL
K110J MARIA
K110K MICHAEL
K110L GEORGE
K110M CHARLES
K110N PRISCILLA
======

[K111]   FINNEY
          John Finney   K30Da
          Sarah Bartlett K30D

K111A SARAH

K111B PHEBE
K111C JOSIAH
K111D RUTH
K111E JOHN
======
[K112] BARTLETT
    Joseph Bartlett   K30F
    Sarah Morton   K30Fa

K112A SARAH
K112B JOSEPH
K112C THOMAS
K112D JOSIAH
K112E MARTHA
K112F HANNAH
======
[K113] SEARS
    Thomas Sears   K30Ga
    Elizabeth Bartlett K30G

K113A BETTY
K113B REBECCA
K113C CHLOE
K113D SARAH
K113E THOMAS
K113F WILLARD
======
[K114] BARTLETT
    Ebenezer Bartlett K30I
    Rebecca Dimmon   K30Ia
    Abigail Finney   K30Ib

K114A JAMES   by Rebecca
K114B CHLOE #1
K114C THOMAS #1
K114D REBECCA
K114E PHEBE
K114F CHLOE #2
K114G REBECCA
K114H ABIGAIL #1 by Abigail
K114I EBENEZER
K114J DIAMOND #1
K114K THOMAS #2
K114L DIAMOND #2
K114M ABIGAIL #2
======
[K115] BARTLETT
    Robert Bartlett   K30J
    Rebecca Wood   K30Ja
    Jane Spooner   K30Jb
    Hopestill Seabury K30Jc

K115A ROBERT by Rebecca
K115B EPHRAIM
K115C REBECCA
K115D ISAAC
K115E LAZARUS
K115F JOSHUA
K115G JAMES
K115H SUSANNAH
K115I JOSIAH
K115J CALEB
K115K MALACHI
======
[K116] BARTLETT
    Lemuel Bartlett K30K
    Mary Doty   K30Ka

K116A LEMUEL
K116B WILLIAM
K116C MARY
K116D JEAN #1
K116E JEAN #2
K116F STEPHEN
K116G REBECCA
K116H RUFUS
======
[K117] PRATT
    Daniel Pratt K31Aa
    Esther Wright K31A

K117A JOSHUA
K117B SARAH
======
[K118] WRIGHT
    John Wright   K31B
    Mary Lucas   K31Ba

K118A EASTER
K118B JOHN
K118C REPENTANCE
K118D BENJAMIN
K118E SARAH
K118F ADAM
======
[K119] GIFFORD
    Jeremiah Gifford K31Ca
    Mary Wright   K31C

K119A JONATHAN
K119B GIDEON
K119C JOHN
K119D SARAH
K119E ELIZABETH

```
K119F  JOSEPH                    K124B  EBENEZER
K119G  WILLIAM                   K124C  MOSES
K119H  BENJAMIN                         ======
K119I  ISAAC                     [K125]    WRIGHT
K119J  PELEG                            Nathan Wright K31J
K119K  MARGARET                         Hannah Cooke  K31Ja
K119L  ADAM                             ------
K119M  DAVID                     K125A  NATHAN
       ======                    K125B  ZADOCK
[K120]    WRIGHT                 K125C  TABITHA
       Isaac Wright K31D         K125D  HANNAH
       Mary Cole    K31Da        K125E  PRISCILLA
       ------                    K125F  LYDIA
K120A  SUSANNAH                         ======
K120B  JOSEPH                    [K126]    STURTEVANT
K120C  MARY                             Samuel Sturtevant K33Aa
K120D  RACHEL                           Mary Price       K33A
K120E  ISAAC                            ------
       ======                    K126A  DESIRE
[K121]    BARLOW                 K126B  LEMUEL
       Ebenezer Barlow K31Ea     K126C  SAMUEL
       Rachel Wright   K31E             ======
       ------                    [K127]    TOMSON
K121A  MOSES #1                         John Tomson      K34B
K121B  MOSES #2                         Elizabeth Thomas K34Ba
K121C  SETH                             ------
K121D  SARAH                     K127A  JOHN
K121E  MARY                      K127B  ELISABETH
       ======                    K127C  LYDIA
[K122]    FULLER                        ======
       Seth Fuller  K31Fa        [K128]    TOMSON
       Sarah Wright K31F                Ephraim Tomson   K34C
       ------                           Joanna Thomas    K34Ca
K122A  ARCHIPPUS                        ------
       ======                    K128A  JOANNA
[K123]    WRIGHT                 K128B  EPHRAIM #1
       Samuel Wright K31G        K128C  EPHRAIM #2
       Anna Tilson   K31Ga              ======
       ------                    [K129]    TOMSON
K123A  RUTH #1                          Shubael Tomson   K34D
K123B  RUTH #2                          Susanna Barlour  K34Da
K123C  SARAH                            ------
K123D  SAMUEL                    K129A  ISAAC
K123E  EDMUND                    K129B  SHUBAEL
K123F  JACOB                     K129C  JOHN
K123G  LYDIA                     K129D  MARY
       ======                    K129E  THOMAS
[K124]    WRIGHT                        ======
       Moses Wright   K31H       [K130]    TOMSON
       Thankful Boles K31Ha             Thomas Tomson    K34E
       ------                           Martha Soule     K34Ea
K124A  HANNAH                           ------
```

K130A	PETER		[K135]	TABER	
K130B	FRANCIS			Joseph Taber	K35D
K130C	NATHAN			Elizabeth Spooner	K35Da
K130D	JAMES			Lydia Abbott	K35Db
K130E	THOMAS			------	
	======		K135A	AMOS by Elizabeth	
[K131]	TOMSON		K135B	SARAH	
	Jacob Tomson	K34L	K135C	BENJAMIN	
	Mary Hayward	K34La	K135D	MARY	
	------		K135E	JOSEPH	
K131A	JACOB		K135F	REBECKAH	
K131B	EBENEZER		K135G	ELEANOR	
K131C	NATHANIEL		K135H	JOHN	
K131D	MARY		K135I	THOMAS	
K131E	MARTHA		K135J	ELEZEBETH	
K131F	EPHRAIM		K135K	PETER	
K131G	DANIEL		K135L	WILLIAM	
	======		K135M	ABIGAIL	
[K132]	KENNY			======	
	John Kenny	K35Aa	[K136]	TABER	
	Lydia Taber	K35A		John Taber	K35E
	------			Phebe Spooner	K35Ea
K132A	RUTH			------	
K132B	THOMAS		K136A	THOMAS	
K132C	JONATHAN		K136B	DEBORAH #1	
K132D	MARY		K136C	REBECCA	
K132E	ABIGAIL		K136D	MARY	
K132F	HANNAH		K136E	ELNATHAN	
K132G	NATHANIEL		K136F	PHEBE	
	======		K136G	AMAZIAH	
[K133]	HART		K136H	JABEZ	
	William Hart	K35Ba	K136I	DEBORAH #2	
	Sarah Taber	K35B		======	
	------		[K137]	TABER	
K133A	ARCHIPPUS			Jacob Taber	K35F
K133B	THOMAS			Sarah West	K35Fa
K133C	LUKE			------	
K133D	WILLIAM		K137A	EUNICE	
K133E	HANNAH		K137B	STEPHEN	
K133F	MARY		K137C	JERUSHA	
	======		K137D	BARTHOLOMEW	
[K134]	MORTON		K137E	LOIS	
	Manasseh Morton	K35Ca	K137F	SARAH	
	Mary Taber	K35C	K137G	JACOB	
	------		K137H	JOHN	
K134A	ELIZABETH			======	
K134B	ZEPPANIAH		[K138]	BLACKWELL	
K134C	TABER			Caleb Blackwell	K35Ha
K134D	RUTH			Bethiah Taber	K35H
K134E	SETH			------	
K134F	JOANNA		K138A	JANE	
K134G	MARY		K138B	SARAH	
	======		K138C	JOHN	

387

```
K138D  MARY                        [K142]   WHITMARSH
K138E  BETHIA                               Nicholas Whitmarsh K36Ba
K138F  ALICE                                Mercy Reed         K36B
K138G  SETH                                 ------
       ======               K142A  NICHOLAS
[K139]   TABER                               ======
         Philip Taber    K35I    [K143]   FORD
         Susannah Tucker K35Ia             Andrew Ford K36Bb
         ------                            Mercy Reed  K36B
K139A  RICHARD                              ------
K139B  THOMAS               K143A  MARCY
K139C  ZEPHANIAH            K143B  JACOB
K139D  TUCKER               K143C  HESTER
K139E  JESSE                K143D  MARY
K139F  PEACE                K143E  ANDREW
K139G  HULDAH                       ======
K139H  NOAH                 [K144]   REED
K139I  PHILIP                       William Reed  K36D
K139J  DANIEL                       Alice Nash    K36Da
K139K  AMY                          ------
       ======               K144A  ALICE #1
[K140]   TABER              K144B  WILLIAM
         Ebenezer Taber K35Ja  K144C  OBADIAH
         Abigail Taber  K35J   K144D  EBENEZER
         ------               K144E  ALICE #2
K140A  PAUL                 K144F  DANIEL
K140B  THOMAS               K144G  JAMES
K140C  MARY                 K144H  SOLOMON
K140D  JOSEPH               K144I  MOSES
K140E  HANNAH               K144J  ALICE #3
K140F  WATER #1                     ======
K140G  LYDIA                [K145]   REED
K140H  WATER #2                     John Reed     K36G
K140I  JACOB                        Sarah Hersey  K36Ga
       ======                       Mary Wheeler  K36Gb
[K141]   PORTER                     ------
         Nicholas Porter K36Aa  K145A  JOHN  by Sarah
         Bathsheba Reed  K36A   K145B  JAMES by Mary
         ------               K145C  JOSEPH
K141A  BATHSHEBA #1         K145D  MARY
K141B  NICHOLAS #1          K145E  EZEKIEL
K141C  NICHOLAS #2          K145F  PETER
K141D  WILLIAM              K145G  SQUIRE
K141E  BATHSHEBE #2         K145H  SILENCE
K141F  DANIEL               K145I  BENJAMIN
K141G  SUSANNA              K145J  SAMUEL
K141H  JOB                          ======
K141I  ESTHER               [K146]   REED
K141J  ABNER                        Jacob Reed    K36H
K141K  SARAH                        Sarah Hersey  K36Ha
       ======                       Hannah Noyes  K36Hb
                                    ------
```

```
K146A  SARAH                        [K151]  BENNETT
K146B  JACOB                                Nehemiah Bennett  K39Ca
K146C  HANNAH                               Mercy Tomson      K39C
K146D  WILLIAM                              ------
K146E  ELIJAH                       K151A  ABIGAIL
K146F  BETTY #1                     K151B  JACOB
K146G  BETTY #2                     K151C  WILLIAM
       ======                       K151D  PATIENCE
[K147]  KING                        K151E  MARTHA
        Hezekiah King   K3Cla       K151F  HANNAH
        Sarah Reed      K36I               ======
        ------                       [K152]  TOMSON
K147A  HEZEKIAH                             John Tomson      K39D
K147B  SARAH                                Joanna Adams     K39Da
K147C  SAMUEL                               ------
K147D  ESTHER                       K152A  ZACCHEUS
K147E  MARY                         K152B  JOANNA
K147F  MARCY                               ======
K147G  BARSHABA                     [K153]  PACKARD
K147H  WILLIAM                              John Packard     K39Ea
K147I  JOHN                                 Lydia Tomson     K39E
K147J  MARCY                                ------
K147K  ALICE                        K153A  LYDIA
       ======                       K153B  ABEL
[K148]  SWIFT                       K153C  ABIAH
        Thomas Swift       K37A     K153D  ABIGAIL
        Rachel Stockbridge K37Aa    K153E  JOHN
        ------                       K153F  BARNABAS
K148A  THOMAS                              ======
K148B  RUTH                         [K154]  TOMSON
K148C  JOHN                                 Barnabas Tomson  K39F
K148D  ELIZABETH                            Hannah Porter    K39Fa
K148E  ABIGAIL                              ------
K148F  RACHEL                       K154A  ABIGAIL
       ======                       K154B  BARNABAS
[K149]  TOMSON                      K154C  SAMUEL  twin
        Jacob Tomson     K39A       K154D  JACOB   twin
        Elizabeth Tilson K39Aa      K154E  JABEZ
        ------                       K154F  ASA
K149A  ABIGAIL                      K154G  NOAH
K149B  JACOB                        K154H  HANNAH
K149C  ELISABETH                    K154I  ISAAC
       ======                       K154J  DAVID
[K150]  PACKARD                     K154K  ABEL   twin
        Jonathan Packard K39Ba      K154L  OLIVE  twin
        Abigail Tomson   K39B       K154M  ADAM
        ------                       K154N  ICHABOD
K150A  JONATHAN                            ======
K150B  SUSANNA                      [K155]  BENNETT
K150C  JACOB                                Ebenezer Bennett K39Ga
K150D  JONATHAN                             Esther Tomson    K39G
K150E  ABIGAIL                              ------
       ======
```

DIVISION S
K155–K163

K155A PATIENCE
K155B JOHN
K155C ESTHER
K155D LYDIA
K155E EBENEZER
======
[K156]   REED
         Ebenezer Reed   K39Ha
         Hannah Tomson   K39H

K156A EBENEZER #1
K156B WILLIAM
K156C ICHABOD
K156D DAVID twin
K156E JONATHAN twin
K156F PAUL twin
K156G SILAS twin
K156H ABIGAIL
K156I BARNABAS
K156J EBENEZER #2
======
[K157]   TOMSON
         Caleb Tomson   K39J
         Abigail Crossman K39Ja

K157A HANNAH
K157B SARAH
K157C LUCIA
K157D HANNAH
K157E MARY
K157F WILLIAM
K157G NATHANIEL
K157H CALEB
K157I ABIGAIL
K157J SYLVIA
======
[K158]   TOMSON
         Reuben Tomson K40A
         Mary Tomson   K40Aa
         Sarah Bryant   K40Ab

K158A DEBORAH
K158B ANDREW
K158C MERCY
K158D ABIGAIL
K158E LUCY
K158F JOANNA
======
[K159]   WATERMAN
         Samuel Waterman K40Ba
         Mary Tomson   K40B

K159A EBENEZER
K159B ZEBEDIAH
K159C SETH
K159D SAMUEL
K159E THOMAS
K159F NATHANIEL #1
K159G BENJAMIN
K159H MARY
K159I NATHANIEL #2
K159J ROBERT
======
[K160]   TOMSON
         Thomas Tomson K40C
         Mary Loring   K40Ca

K160A JOSHUA
K160B ASA
K160C IGNATIUS
K160D SARAH
K160E MARY
K160F LORING
K160G LOIS
K160H SETH
K160I THOMAS
K160J BEZER
K160K CALEB
K160L SARAH
======
[K161]   TOMSON
         Amasa Tomson K40D
         Lydia Cobb   K40Da

K161A RUTH
K161B ZADOCK
K161C LYDIA
K161D MOLLY
======
[K162]   TOMSON
         Ebenezer Tomson K40F
         Mary Wright   K40Fa

K162A SUSANNA
K162B JOSIAH
K162C EBENEZER
K162D MARY
K162E EUNICE
======
[K163]   TOMSON
         Zebadiah Tomson K40G
         Zerviah Standish K40Ga

K163A REBECCA

```
K163B  RACHEL                          [K165]   TOMSON
K163C  ZERVIAH                                  Peter Tomson   K41B
K163D  ZEBADIAH #1                              Hannah Bolton  K41Ba
K163E  THOMAS                                   Lydia Cowing   K41Bb
K163F  MERCY                                    ------
K163G  ZEBADIAH #2              K165A  HANNAH
K163H  MOSES                    K165B  PETER
K163I  RACHEL                           ======
        ======                 [K166]   TOMSON
[K164]   BOZWORTH                        Joseph Tomson      K41D
        Nehemiah Bozworth  K41Aa         Elisabeth Bolton  K41Da
        Sarah Tomson       K41A          ------
        ------                 K166A  BETTY
K164A  JOHN                     K166B  JOSEPH
K164B  NEHEMIAH                 K166C  JOHN
K164C  PETER                    K166D  SARAH
K164D  DAVID                    K166E  HANNAH
K164E  SARAH                            ======
K164F  SUSANNA
```

[L10]   WINSLOW
    Edward Winslow   L9A
    Magdalene Oliver   L9Aa

L10A EDWARD   [L11]
  a Elizabeth Barker
  b Mrs Susanna White
    ======

[L11]   WINSLOW
    Edward Winslow L10A
  Mrs Susanna White L10Aa

L11A EDWARD
L11B JOHN
L11C JOSIAH   [L12]
  a Penelope Pelham
  f Herbert Pelham
  m Jemima Waldegrave
L11D ELIZABETH
  a Robert Brooks Jr
  f Robert Brooks Sr
  b George Corwin [L13]

    ======
[L12]   WINSLOW
    Josiah Winslow L11C
    Penelope Pelham L11Ca

L12A ELIZABETH
  a Stephen BurtonJr [L14]
  f Stephen BurtonSr
L12B EDWARD
L12C ISAAC   [L15]
  a Sarah Wensley
  f John Wensley
  m Elizabeth Paddy
    ======
[L13]   CORWIN
    George Corwin   L11Db
    Elizabeth Winslow L11D

L13A PENELOPE
  a Josiah Walcott [L16]
L13B SUSANNAH
  a Edward Lyde

[L14]   BURTON
    Stephen Burton   L12Aa
    Elizabeth Winslow L12A

L14A PENELOPE
L14B CHILD
L14C ELIZABETH
L14D THOMAS   [L17]
  a Alice Wadsworth
  f Elisha Wadsworth
  m Elizabeth Wiswall
    ======

[L15]   WINSLOW
    Isaac Winslow L12C
    Sarah Wensley L12Ca

L15A JOSIAH
L15B JOHN   [L18]
  a Mary Little
  f Isaac Little
  m Mary Otis
  b Bethiah Barker
  f Thomas Barker
  m Bethia Little
L15C PENELOPE
  a James Warren Jr [L19]
  f James Warren Sr
  m Sarah Doty
L15D ELIZABETH
  a Benjamin Marston [L20]
  f Benjamin Marston
  m Patience Rogers
L15E ANNA
L15F EDWARD   [L21]
  a Hannah Howland
  f Thomas Howland
  m Joanne Cole
    ======

[L16]   WALCOTT
    Josiah Walcott L13Aa
    Penelope Corwin L13A

L16A ELIZABETH
L16B JOSIAH
    ======

[L17]   BURTON
    Thomas Burton   L14D
    Alice Wadsworth L14Da

L17A MARTHA
L17B PENELOPE
  a Seth Jacob   [L22]
  f Samuel Jacob
  m Susanna Howard

L17C ELEANOR
  a Nathaniel Bishop   [L23]
  f Hudson Bishop
  m Abigail Keene
L17D ELIZABETH
  a Daniel Bonney   [L24]
  f Elisha Bonney
  m Elizabeth Lincoln
    ======

[L18]   WINSLOW
    John Winslow L15B
    Mary Little L15Ba

L18A JOSIAH
L18B PELHAM   [L25]
  a Joanna White
  f Gideon White
  m Joanna Howland
L18C ISAAC   [L26]
  a Elizabeth Stockbridge
  f Benjamin Stockbridge
  m Ruth Otis
    ======

[L19]   WARREN
    James Warren   L15Ca
    Penelope Winslow L15C

L19A JAMES   [L27]
  a Mercy Otis
  f James Otis
  m Mary Allyn
L19B ANN
L19C SARAH
  a William Sever   [L28]
  f Nichloas Sever
  m Sarah Warren
L19D WINSLOW
L19E JOSIAH
    ======

[L20]   MARSTON
    Benjamin Marston L15Da
    Elizabeth Winslow L15D

L20A BENJAMIN
  a Sarah Swett
  f Joseph Swett
  m Hannah Negus
L20B ELIZABETH
  a William Watson   [L29]
  f John Watson
  m Priscilla Thomas

L20C PATIENCE
  a Elkanah Watson [L30]
  f John Watson
  m Priscilla Thomas
L20D SARAH
L20E PENELOPE
L20F JOHN
L20G PENELOPE
L20H LUCY
L20I LUCY
  a John Watson   [L31]
  f John Watson
  m Elizabeth Reynolds
    ======

[L21]   WINSLOW
    Edward Winslow L15F
    Hannah Howland L15Fa

L21A JOHN
L21B PENELOPE
L21C SARAH
L21D EDWARD   [L32]
  a Mary Symonds
L21E child
    ======

[L22]   JACOB
    Seth Jacob   L17Ba
    Penelope Burton L17B

L22A SAMUEL
L22B PENELOPE
    ======

[L23]   BISHOP
    Nathaniel Bishop L17Ca
    Eleanor Burton L17C

L23A NATHANIEL
L23B ELIPHALET
    ======

[L24]   BONNEY
    Daniel Bonney   L17Da
    Elizabeth Burton L17D

L24A JONATHAN
    ======

[L25]   WINSLOW
    Pelham Winslow L18B
    Joanna White   L18Ba

L25A MARY

```
L25B  JOANNA                          [L30]   WATSON
L25C  child                                   Elkanah Watson    L20Ca
L25D  PENELOPE PELHAM                         Patience Marston L20C
      ======                          ------
[L26]   WINSLOW                       L30A  MARSTON
        Isaac Winslow    L18C         L30B  ELKANAH
        Eliz. Stockbridge L18Ca       L30C  PRISCILLA
      ------                          L30D  PATTY
L26A  ELIZABETH                       L30E  LUCIA
L26B  RUTH STOCKBRIDGE                      ======
L26C  JOHN                            [L31]   WATSON
L26D  SARAH                                   John Watson    L20Ia
L26E  ISAAC                                   Lucy Marston L20I
      ======                          ------
[L27]   WARREN                        L31A  JOHN
        James Warren L19A             L31B  GEORGE
        Mercy Otis    L19Aa           L31C  SARA MARSTON
      ------                          L31D  BENJAMIN MARSTON
L27A  JAMES                           L31E  LUCIA
L27B  WINSLOW                         L31F  DANIEL
L27C  CHARLES                         L31G  WILLIAM
L27D  HENRY                           L31H  WILLIAM
L27E  GEORGE                          L31I  WINSLOW
      ======                          L31J  BROCKE
[L28]   SEVER                               ======
        William Sever L19Ca          [L32]   WINSLOW
        Sarah Warren  L19C                   Edward Winslow L21D
      ------                                  Mary Symonds   L21Da
L28A  SARAH                           ------
L28B  WILLIAM                         L32A  DANIEL MURRAY
L28C  JAMES                           L32B  MARY
L28D  ANN WARREN                      L32C  THOMAS ASTOR COFFIN
L28E  JOHN                            L32D  WARD CHIPMAN
      ======                          L32E  PENELOPE
[L29]   WATSON                        L32F  EDWARD
        William Watson    L20Ba       L32G  HANNAH
        Elizabeth Marston L20B        L32H  SARAH ANN
      ------                          L32I  CHRISTIANA BANNISTER
L29A  WILLIAM                         L32J  JOHN FRANCIS WENTWORTH
L29B  ELIZABETH                       L32K  ELIZA CHIPMAN
L29C  BENJAMIN                        L32L  CATHERINE WELTDEN
L29D  ELLEN                           L32M  BROOKE WATSON
      ======                                ======
```

```
======
[N10]    NOBLE
         unk
         unk
------
N10A  THOMAS Sr        [N11]
   a  Hannah Warriner
   f  William Warriner
======
[N11]    NOBLE
         Thomas Noble Sr N10A
         Hannah Warriner N10Aa
------
N11A  JOHN
   a  A. Sacket
   b  M. Goodman
N11B  HANNAH
   a  J. Goodman
   b  N. Edwards
   c  S. Partridge
N11C  THOMAS Jr
   a  Elizabeth Dewey
N11D  MATTHEW
   a  Hannah Dewey
N11E  MARK
   a  Mary Marshall
N11F  ELIZABETH
   a  R. Church
   b  S. Loomis
N11G  LUKE
   a  Hannah Stebbins
N11H  JAMES Sr         [N12]
   a  Ruth --
   b  Catherine Higley
   f  John Higley
   m  Hannah Drake
N11I  MARY
   a  Ephraim Colton
N11J  REBECCA
   a  Samuel Loomis
======
[N12]    NOBLE
         James Noble Sr N11H
         Ruth -          N1Ha
         Catherine Higley N11Hb
------
by Ruth
N12A  JAMES Jr  (d.yng)
N12B  DANIEL
   a  R. Stebbins
   b  R. Crow
```

```
         by Catherine
N12C  LYDIA
   a  Stephen Kelsey
N12D  JAMES Jr
N12E  DAVID               [N13]
   a  Abigail Loomis
   f  Philip Loomis
   m  Hannah --
======
[N13]    NOBLE
         David Noble     N12E
         Abigail Loomis N12Ea
------
N13A  DAVID               [N14]
   a  Ruth Noble
N13B  OLIVER
   a  Lucy Weld
N13C  JAMES
   a  A. Caldwell
   b  A. Smith
   c  E. Crouch
   d  P. Branch
N13D  KATHERINE
   a  Alexander Ingham
N13E  THIRZA
   a  Jonathan Booth
N13F  ENOCH  (d.yng)
N13G  ABIGAIL
   a  Coffil Wood
N13H  AARON
   a  Eunice Bagg
N13I  LYDIA
   a  I. J. Fox
   b  S. Martin
N13J  HANNAH
   a  King Strong
N13K  JOHN  (d.yng)
======
[N14]    NOBLE
         David Noble   N13A
         Ruth --       N13Aa
------
N14A  RUTH
   a  Calvin Dunham
N14B  DAVID Jr      [N15]
   a  Sarah Taylor
   f  Asabel Taylor
N14C  REBECCA
N14D  ENOCH
   a  S. Ames
   b  C. Adams
   c  D. Adams
```

N14E EZEKIEL
  a H. Gates
  b S. Sears
N14F DANIEL
  a Lydia --
N14G THIRZA (d.yng)
N14H POLLY
  a Simon Wheeler
N14I LUCY
  a Moses Daniels
  ======
[N15]   NOBLE
      David Noble N14B
      Sarah Taylor N14Ba

N15A SALLIE
  a Leonard Ashley
N15B DAVID
  a Sarah Grummond
N15C THIRZA
  a Joseph Skidmore
N15D MARY
  a Martin Day
N15E ASIEL
  a Eliza Harberger
N15F ESTHER
  a Jesse Hoyt
N15G JAMES
N15H ROSWELL
N15I ELECTA
  a Nathan Keeler
  b Mott Hall
N15J WILLIAM TAYLOR [N16]
  a Christiana Brewer
  f William B Brewer
N15K MIRANDA
  a J. Bush
  b D. Phelps
N15L SOPHIA
  a Thomas M Weeks
N15M JAMES
  a Grace Hegeman
N15N CLARISSA
  a George Eldridge
  ======
[N16]   NOBLE
      William Taylor Noble N15J
      Christina Brewer   N15Ja

N16A DAVID WILLIAM
  a Esther A Bortree

N16B ALBERT JACKSON   [N17]
  a Helen H Wheeler
  f Heman Wheeler
N16C SARAH
N16D CARLTON MONROE
  a Mary B Churchill
N16E WASHINGTON ALPHONZO
  a Sarah J Williams
N16F SARAH MARIA
  a J.E.R. Patton
N16G CATHERINE SOPHIA
N16H ENOCH GEORGE
  a Clara J Warfield
N16I JAMES TAYLOR
N16J CHARLES HARRIS
  ======
[N17]   NOBLE
      Albert J Noble   N16B
      Helen H Wheeler N16Ba

N17A CHARLES ALBERT
N17B TRUMAN WILGUS
N17C HELEN GRACE
N17D ERNEST WHEELER
N17E HENRY O   [N18]
  a Lulia E Maynard
  f A.K. Maynard
  ======
[N18]   NOBLE
      Henry O Noble   N17E
      Lulie E Maynard N17Ea

N18A ORVILLE M
N18B HELEN L
  a C. Perry Burgess
N18C OLIVE BLANCH
N18D NORMAN W
  a Ethel Valentine
  ======

```
      ======
[P10]    PRIEST
         unk
         unk
      ------
P10A  DEGORY        [P11]
   a  Sarah Allerton
      ======
[P11]    PRIEST
         Degory Priest  P10A
         Sarah Allerton P10Aa
      ------
P11A  MARY
   a  Phineas Pratt     [P12]
   B  SARAH
   a  John Coombs       [P13]
      ======
[P12]    PRATT
         Phineas Pratt  P11Aa
         Mary Priest    P11A
      ------
P12A  JOHN             [P14]
   a  Ann Barker
   f  John Barker
   m  Ann Williams
P12B  MARY
   a  John Swan        [P15]
P12C  SAMUEL           [P16]
   a  Mary Barker
   f  John Barker
   m  Anna Williams
P12D  DANIEL           [P17]
   a  Anna --
P12E  MERCY
   a  Jeremiah Holman  [P18]
   f  William Holman
   m  Winifred --
P12F  JOSEPH           [P19]
   a  Dorcas Folger
   f  Peter Folger
   m  Mary Morrill
P12G  PETER            [P20]
   a  Elizabeth Griswold
   f  Matthew Vriswold
   m  Anna Wolcott
P12H  AARON            [P21]
   a  Sarah Pratt
   f  Joseph Pratt
   m  Sarah Judkins
      ======
[P13]    COOMBS
         John Coombs   P11Ba
         Sarah Priest  P11B
```

```
P13A  JOHN             [P22]
   a  Elizabeth --
P13B  FRANCIS= F16Faf [P23]
   a  Deborah Morton= F16Fam
   f  John Morton
   m  Lettice --
   b  Mary Barker
   f  John Barker
   m  Anna Williams
      ======
[P14]    PRATT
         John Pratt P12A
         Ann Barker P12Aa
P14A  DELIVERED
   a  James Townsend [P24]
   f  John Townsend
   m  Elizabeth Montgomery
P14B  MARY
P14C  JOHN             [P25]
   a  unk
P14D  EBENEZER         [P26]
   a  Mehitable Mudge
P14E  PHINEAS
P14F  JOSHUA
P14G  JEREMIAH
   a  Rose --
P14H  MERCY
      ======
[P15]    SWAN
         John Swan  P12Ba
         Mary Pratt P12B
      ------
P15A  SAMUEL
P15B  MARY
P15C  ELIZABETH
   a  Ezekiel Richardson [P27]
   f  Theophilus Richardso
   m  Mary Chapney
P15D  LYDIA
P15E  JOHN             [P28]
   a  Sarah Thompson
   f  Jonathan Thompson
   m  Susannah Blodgett
P15F  HANNAH
P15G  MERCY
   a  John Perry   Jr [P29]
   f  John Perry   Sr
   m  Sarah Clary
P15H  EBENEZER         [P30]
   a  Elizabeth Bruce
   f  George Bruce
   m  Elizabeth Clark
```

[P16]   PRATT
          Samuel Pratt P12C
          Mary Barker P12Ca

P16A SARAH
      a William Thomas [P31]
      f David Thomas
P16B SAMUEL   [P32]
      a Hannah Miller
      f John Miller
      ======
[P17]   PRATT
          Daniel Pratt P12D
          Anne   --   P12Da

P17A RACHAEL
      a Benjamin Beere [P33]
      f Robert Beere
      m Elizabeth Billington
      ======
[P18] HOLMAN
          Jeremiah Holman P12Ea
          Mercy Pratt   P12E

P18A ISAAC
P18B DEBORAH
      a John Garfield
      f Samuel Garfield
      m Mary Benfield
P18C NEHITABEL
P18D JEREMIAH   [P34]
      a Abigail --
P18E ABRAHAM   [P35]
      a Susannah --
P18F SARAH
      ======
[P19]   PRATT
          Joseph Pratt P12F
          Dorcas Folger P12Fa

P19A MARY
      a Joseph Edmunds [P36]
      f John Edmunds
      m Mary --
P19B JOSEPH
P19C BETHIA
      a Sampson Cartwright [P37]
      f Edward Cartwright
      m Mary --
P19D BENJAMIN
P19E DORCAS
P19F PHINEAS

P19G JOSHUA   [P38]
      a Mary Buckley
P19H LYDIA
P19I SARAH
      a Jeremiah Coleman [P39]
      f John Coleman
      m Joanna Folger
      ======
[P20]   PRATT
          Peter Pratt Sr   P12G
          Elizabeth Griswold P12Ga

P20A PETER Jr   [P40]
      a Mehitable Watrous(Waters)
      f Isaac Watrous
      m Sarah Pratt
      ======
[P21]   PRATT
          Aaron Pratt P11H
          Sarah Pratt P11Ha

P21A HENRY   [P41]
      a Hannah --
P21B DANIEL Sr   [P42]
      a Hannah Lombard
      b Elizabeth --
      c Deborah Haws
      f Joseph Haws
P21C AARON
      a Mary Whitcomb
      f Israel Whitcomb
      m Mary Stodder
P21D JONATHAN
      a Hannah Whitcomb
      f Israel Whitcomb
      m Mary Stoddard
P21E JOHN
      a Priscilla Thurber
      f James Thurber
      m Elizabeth Bliss
P21F SARAH
      a Christopher Webb
      f Peter Webb
      m Ruth Bass
P21G ELIZABETH
      a Nehemiah Hobart
      f David Hobart
      m Sarah Cleverly
P21H MOSES
      a Jane Orcutt
      f Thomas Orcutt
      m Jane Emerson

P21I MARY
P21J MERCY
    a Samuel Orcutt
    f John Orcutt
P21K HANNAH
    a Amos Hovey
    f Joseph Hovey
    m Mary Merrett
P21L ABIGAIL
    a Jonathan Neal
    f Benjamin Neal
    m Lydia Paine
P21M PHINEAS Sr
    a Sarah Lincoln
    f Thomas Lincoln
    m Mehitable Frost
P21N BENJAMIN
    a Isabelle Auchmuty
    f Robert Auchmuty
P21O NATHANIEL
    a Rachel MacVarlo
    f James MacVarlo
    m SDarah Lane
    ======
[P22] COOMBS
    John Coombs   P13A
    Elizabeth -- P13Aa

P22A ELIZABETH =A8/101
    a Eleazer Cushman =A8/100
    f Thomas Cushman
    m Mary Allerton
P22B JOHN
    a Elizabeth Ballentine
    f William Ballentine
    m Hannah Holland
P22C MARY
    a Benjamin Eaton Jr
    f Benjamin Eaton Sr
    m Sarah Hoskins
    ======
[P23] COOMBS
    Francis Coombs P13B
    Deborah Morton P13Ba

P23A DEBORAH   =F16Fa
    a Ralph Jones Jr=F16F
    f Ralph Jones Sr
    m Mary Fuller
F23B MERCY
    a Samuel Barrows

P23Baf Robert Barrows
    m Ruth Bonum
P23C LYDIA
    a John Miller Jr
    f John Miller Sr
P23D RUTH
    a Ebenezer Bennett
    f John Bennett
    m Deborah Grover
P23E FRANCES
    a Nathan Howland
    f Isaac Howland
    m Elizabeth Vaughan
    ======
[P24] TOWNSEND
    James Townsend P14Aa
    Delivered Pratt P14A

P24A JOSEPH
P24B PATIENCE
P24C JOSHUA
P24D DEBORAH
P24E RUEMOURN
    ======
[P25] PRATT
    John Pratt P14C
    unk   P14Ca

P25A JONATHAN
P25B ANN
P25C MERCY
P25D SARAH
P25E HANNAH
    ======
[P26] PRATT
    Ebenezer Pratt P14D
    Mehitable Mudge P14Da

P26A OLIVER
P26B ANNE
    ======
[P27] RICHARDSON
    Ezekial Richardson P15Ca
    Elizabeth Swan   P15C

P27A THEOPHILUS #1
P27B ELIZABETH
P27C THEOPHILUS #2
P27D EZEKIAL
P27E ABIGAIL
P27F AARON

```
======                          ======
[P28]   SWAN                     [P33]   BEERE
        John Swan      P15E              Benjamin Beere  P17Aa
        Sarah Thompson P15Ea             Rachel Pratt    P17A
        ------                          ------
P28A  JOHN #1                    P33A  CHARLES
P28B  SARAH                      P33B  JOB
P28C  JOHN #2                    P33C  RACHEL
P28D  HANNAH                           ======
        ======                   [P34]   HOLMAN
[P29]   PERRY                            Jeremiah Holman P18D
        John Perry P15Ga                 Abigail --      P18Da
        Mercy Swan P15G
        ------                   P34A  MARY
P29A  EBENEZER                   P34B  ABIGAIL
P29B  MERCY                      P34C  JEREMIAH
P29C  JAMES                      P34D  NATHANIEL
        ======                           ======
[P30]   SWAN                     [P35]   HOLMAN
        Ebenezer Swan   P15H             Abraham Holman  P18E
        Elizabeth Bruce P15Ha            Susannah --     P18Ea
        ------                          ------
P30A  ELIZABETH                  P35A  ABRAHAM
P30B  SARAH                      P35B  NATHANIEL
P30C  EBENEZER                   P35C  SUSANNA
P30D  MARY                             ======
P30E  SAMUEL                     [P36]   EDMUNDS
P30F  WILLIAM                            Joseph Edmunds P19Aa
        ======                           Mary Pratt     P19A
[P31]   THOMAS                          ------
        William Thomas P16Aa     P36A  HANNAH
        Sarah Pratt    P16A      P36B  JOHN
        ------                   P36C  JOSEPH
P31A  JOANNA                     P36D  WILLIAM
P31B  SUSANNA                    P36E  MARY
P31C  SARAH                      P36F  SARAH
P31D  ELIZABETH                  P36G  BENJAMIN
P31E  WILLIAM                          ======
P31F  MARY                       [P37]   CARTWRIGHT
        ======                           Sampson Cartwright P19Ca
[P32]   PRATT                            Bethia Pratt       P19C
        Samuel Pratt   P16B             ------
        Hannah Miller  P16Ba      P37A  ALICE
        ------                    P37B  DORCAS
P32A  SAMUEL                      P37C  PHINEAS
P32B  JOHN                        P37D  HAZADIAH
P32C  NATHAN                            ======
P32D  SARAH
P32E  HANNAH
P32F  PHINEAS
P32G  MARY
        ======
```

```
======
[P38]    PRATT                      [P42]    PRATT
         Joshua Pratt P19G                   Daniel Pratt Sr P21B
         Mary Buckley P19Ga                  Deborah Haws    P21Ba
         ------                              ------
P38A  JOSHUA                         P42A  DEORAH
         ======                      P42B  ELIZABETH
[P39]    COLEMAN                     P42C  CHARITY
         Jeremiah Coleman  P19Ia     P42D  DANIEL Jr
         Sarah Pratt       P19I      P42E  ANNA
         ------                      P42F  MARY   twin
P39A  PETER                          P42G  MARTHA twin
P39B  LYDIA                          P42H  LYDIA
P39C  SILVANUS                          ======
P39D  JOHANNAE                       [P43]    PRATT
P39E  ENOCH                                   Aaron Pratt    P21C
P39F  JEREMIAH                                Mary Whitcomb P21Aa
         ======                              ------
[P40]    PRATT                       P43A  JOHN
         Peter Pratt      P21B       P43B  MARY
         Mehitable Waters P21Ba      P43C  SARAH
         ------                      P43D  AARON Jr
P40A  ELIZABETH                      P43E  THOMAS
P40B  MEHITABEL                      P43F  JOSEPH
P40C  SARAH                             ======
P40D  PETER                          [P44]    PRATT
P40E  MARY                                    Jonathan Pratt P21D
P40F  PHINEAS                                 Hannah Whitcomb P21Da
P40G  DANIEL                                 ------
P40H  TEMPERANCE                     P44A  HANNAH
         ======                      P44B  JONATHAN
[P41]    PRATT                       P44C  LEAH
         Henry Pratt  P21A           P44D  RACHEL
         Hannah --    P21Aa          P44E  RHODA
         ------                      P44F  ELIZABETH
P41A  OLIVER                         P44G  LUCY
P41B  ZEBEDIAH                          ======
P41C  HANNAH                         [P45]    PRATT
P41D  NOAH                                    John Pratt  P21E
P41E  HENRY                                   (unk-P21Ea or P21Eb)
P41F  LEMUEL                                 ------
41G   SARAH                          P45A  JOHN
P41H  SYBIL                          P45B  AARON
P41I  EBENEZER                       P45C  PRISCILLA
P41J  JEREMIAH                       P45D  MARY
P41K  SILAS                             ======
P41L  MOSES                          [P46]    WEBB
P41M  MERCY                                   Christopher Webb P21Fa
         ======                               Sarah Pratt      P21F
                                             ------

                                     P46A  AARON
                                        ======
```

```
    ======                          P52D  MOSES
[P47]   PRATT                       P52E  ELEAZER
        Moses Pratt   P21H          P52F  WILLIAM
        Jane Orcutt   P12Ha           ======
        ------                      [P53]    COOMBS
P47A  MOSES                                John Coombs      P22B
P47B  JANE                                 Elizabeth Ballentine P22Ba
        ======                               ------
[P48]    ORCUTT                     P53A  THOMAS
         Samuel Orcutt  P21Ja       P53B  PETER
         Mercy Pratt    P21J        P53C  MARY
         ------                     P53D  JOHN
P48A  HULDAH                          ======
P48B  SYBIL                        [P54]    EATON
P48C  IGNATIUS                            Benjamin Eaton P22Ca
        ======                            Mary Coombs    P22C
[P49]    NEAL                              ------
         Jonathan Neal  P21La       P54A  WILLIAM
         Abigail Pratt  P21L        P54B  HANNAH
         ------                     P54C  JABEZ
P49A  SARAH                         P54D  SARAH
P49B  JERUSHA                       P54E  JOHN
P49C  ALICE                         P54F  BENJAMIN
P49D  JOSEPH                        P54G  MARY
        ======                      P54H  FRANCIS
[P50]    PRATT                      P54I  ELISHA
         Phineas Pratt Sr P21M      P54J  ELIZABETH
         Sarah Lincold    P21Ma     P54K  DAVID
         ------                       ======
P50A  BERNARD                       [P55]    JONES
P50B  CONSTANTINE                          Ralph Jones    P23Aa
P50C  RHODA                                Deborah Coombs P23A
P50D  JARED                                ------
P50E  OLIVE                         P55A  DEBORAH
P50F  PHINEAS Jr                    P55B  ELIZABETH
        ======                      P55C  THANKFUL
[P51]    PRATT                      P55D  BETHIA
         Benjamin Pratt   P21N      P55E  CORNALIUS
         Isabelle Auchmuty P21Na    P55F  SILVANUS
         ------                       ======
P51A  ISABELLA                      [P56]    BARROWS
P51B  BENJAMIN                            Samuel Barrows P23Ba
P51C  GEORGE                             Mercy Coombs   P23B
P51D  FREDERICK                            ------
        ======                      P56A  EBENEZER
[P52]    PRATT                      P56B  COOMBS
         Eleazer Cushman  P22Aa     P56C  ROBERT
         Elizabeth Coombs P22A        ======
         ------
P52A  LYDIA
P52B  JOHN
P52C  JAMES
```

```
   ======
[P57]   MILLER
        John Miller Sr P23C&
        Lydia Coombs   P23C
   ------
P57A  FRANCIS
P57B  JOHN Jr
P57C  DAVID
P57D  ELIAS
P57E  HANNAH
   ======
[P58]   BENNETT
        Ebenezer Bennett  P23Da
        Ruth Coombs       P23D
   ------
P58A  CORNELIUS
P58B  SARAH
   ======
[P59]   HOWLAND
        Nathan Howland  P23Ea
        Frances Coombs  P23E
   ------
P59A  SETH
P59B  CALEB
P59C  PRISCILLA
P59D  GEORGE
P59E  RUTH
   ======
```

```
    ======
[Q10]    BROWN
         unk
         unk
    ------
Q10A PETER MF      [Q11]
  a Martha --
  b Mary --
    ======
[Q11]    BROWN
         Peter Brown Q10A
         Martha --   Q10Aa
         Mary --     Q10Ab
    ------
by Martha
Q11A MARY
  a Ephraim Tinkham  [Q12]
Q11B PRISCILLA
  a William Allen
  f George Allen
  m Catherine --
by Mary
Q11C REBECCA
  a William Snow Sr    [Q13]
    ======
[Q12]    TINKHAM
         Ephraim Tinkham Q11Aa
         Mary Brown      Q11A
    ------
Q12A EPHRAIM          [Q14]
  a Esther Wright
  f Richard Wright
  m Hester Cooke
Q12B EBENEZER         [Q15]
  a Elizabeth Burrowes
  f Jeremiah Burrowes
  m -- Hewes
Q12C PETER            [Q16]
  a Mercy Mendall
  f John Mendall
Q12D HELKIAH Sr       [Q17]
  a Ruth --
Q12E MARY =D10a24     [Q18]
  a John Tomson Jr
  f John Tomson Sr
  m Mary Cooke
Q12F JOHN             [Q19]
  a Sarah --
Q12G ISAAC
  a Sarah King
    ======
```

```
    ======
[Q13]    SNOW
         William Snow Sr  Q11C
         Rebecca Brown    Q11Ca
    ------
Q13A MARY
Q13B LYDIA
Q13C WILLIAM Jr       [Q20]
  a Naomi Whitman
  f Thomas Whitman
  m Abigail Byram
Q13D JOSEPH           [Q21]
  a Hopestill Alden
  f Joseph Alden
  m Mary Simmons
Q13E HANNAH
  a Giles Rickard Jr
  f Giles Rickard Sr
Q13F BENJAMIN         [Q22]
  a Elizabeth Alden
  f Joseph Allen
  b Sarah Allen
Q13G REBECCA
  a Samuel Rickard   [Q23]
  f Giles Rickard
  m Hannah Dunham
Q13H JAMES
    ======
[Q14]    TINKHAM
         Ephraim Tinkham Q12A
         Esther Wright   Q12Aa
    ------
Q14A MARTHA
  a John Soule Jr    [Q24]
  f John Soule Sr  =T12Faf
  m Rebecca Simmons=T12Fam
Q14B JOHN             [Q25]
  a Hannah Howland
  f Isaac Howland
  m Elizabeth Vaughn
Q14C EPHRAIM          [Q26]
  a Martha Cobb
  f John Cobb    =T20Baf
  m Rachel Soule=T20Bam
Q14D ISAAC            [Q27]
  a Abijah Wood
  f Abiel Wood
  m Abiah Bowen
Q14E SAMUEL           [Q28]
  a Patience Cobb
  f John Cobb =T20Baf
  m Rachel Soule
```

404

Tinkham
Q14F MARY
  a Henry Wood [Q29]
  f Samuel Wood
  m Rebecca Tupper

======

[Q15] TINKHAM
  Ebenezer Tinkham Q12B
  Elizabeth Burrowes Q12Ba

Q15A EBENEZER [Q30]
  a Patience Pratt
  b Hannah Hatch
  f Samuel Hatch
  m Mary Doty
Q15B JEREMIAH [Q31]
  a Joanna Parlow
  f Thomas Parlow
  m Elizabeth Gibbs
Q15C PETER
Q15D JOANNA
  a Thomas Macomber Jr [Q32]
  f Thomas Macomber Sr
  m Sarah Crooker
Q15E ELIZABETH
Q15F PRISCILLA
Q15G SHUBALL [Q33]
  a Priscilla Childs
  f Joseph Childs
  m Elizabeth Seabury

======

[Q16] TINKHAM
  Peter Tinkham Q12C
  Mercy Mendall Q12Ca

Q16A MERCY
  a James Raymond [Q34]
  f John Raymond
  m Martha Woodin
Q16B JOANNA
  a Joseph Bates [Q35]
  f Edward Bates
  m Elizabeth --
Q16C SAMUEL [Q36]
  a Mary Staples
  f Benjamin Staples
  m Mary Cox
Q16D SETH [Q37]
  a Mary --

[Q17] TINKHAM
  Helkiah Tinkham Sr Q12D
  Ruth -- Q12Da

Q17A HELKIAH Jr [Q38]
  a Elizabeth Heister(Heyter)
Q17B MARY
  a Ebenezer Curtis [Q39]
  f Francis Curtis
  m Hannah Smith
Q17C JOHN [Q40]
  a Ann Gray
  f John Gray
  m Joanna Morton
Q17D JACOB [Q41]
  a Hannah Cobb
  f Ebenezer Cobb
  b Judeth Hunt
Q17E CALEB Sr [Q42]
  a Mercy Holmes
  f Nathaniel Holmes
  m Eleanor Baker
Q17F SARAH
Q17G EBENEZER [Q43]
  a Mary Bonney
  f William Bonney
  b Jane Pratt
Q17H RUTH
  a Ebenezer Cobb Jr [Q44]
  f Ebenezer Cobb Sr
  m Mercy Holmes
Q17I PETER [Q45]
  a Mary Bennett
  f Joseph Bennett
  m Joanna Perry

======

[Q18] TOMSON
  John Tomson Q12Ea
  Mary Tinkham Q12E

Q18A JOHN [Q46]
  a Elizabeth Thomas
  f Jeremiah Thomas
  m Lydia Howland
Q18B EPHRAIM
  a Joanna Thomas
  f Jonathan Thomas
  m Mary Steward

Tomson

Q18C SHUBAEL   [Q47]
   a Susanna Parlour
   f Thomas Parlour
   m Elizabeth Liscomb
Q18D THOMAS   [Q48]
   a Martha Soule
   f John Soule
   m Martha Tinkham
Q18E MARTHA
Q18F SARAH
Q18G PETER
Q18H ISAAC
Q18I EBENEZER
Q18J FRANCIS
Q18K JACOB   [Q49]
   a Mary Hayward
[Q19]   TINKHAM
        John Tinkam   Q12F
        Sarah --   Q12Fa

Q19A JOHN   [Q50]
   a Mary Allen
   f William Allen
Q19B MARY
   a Joseph Taber Jr [Q51]
   f Joseph Taber Sr
   m Elizabeth Spooner
Q19C MARTHA
   a Joseph Ellis   [Q52]
   f John Ellis
   m Martha Severence
Q19D PETER   [Q53]
   a Eunice Clark
Q19E HEZEKIAH   [Q54]
   a Grizzell West
   ======
[Q20]   SNOW
        William Snow   Q13C
        Naomi Whitman Q13Ca

Q20A BETHIA
   a Elisha Hayward [Q55]
   f Nathaniel Hayward
   m Hannah Willis
Q20B JAMES
   a Mehitable King
   f Joseph King
   m Mercy Dunham
Q20C SUSANNA
   a Israel Alger Jr [Q56]
   f Israel Alger Sr
   m Patience Hayward

Q20D WILLIAM   [Q57]
   a Mary Washburn
   f James Washburn
   m Mary Bowden
Q20E ELEAZER   [Q58]
   a Mercy King
   f Joseph King
   m Mercy Dunham
Q20F JOHN   [Q59]
   a Hannah Hayward
   f Elisha Hayward
   m Experience Harvey
   ======
[Q21]   SNOW
        Joseph Snow Sr   Q13D
        Hopestill Alden Q13Da

Q21A JOSEPH   [Q60]
   a Elizabeth Field
   f John Field
   m Elizabeth Ames
   b Marcy Smith
   f John Smith
   m Hannah --
Q21B MARY
Q21C JAMES   [Q61]
   a Ruth Shaw
   f Joseph Shaw
   m Judith Whitmarsh
   b Hannah Hovey
   f Ebenezer Hovey
   m Joanna Benson
Q21D REBECKAH
   a Thomas Wade Jr [Q62]
   f Thomas Wade Sr
   m Elizabeth Curtis
Q21E ISAAC   [Q63]
   a Hannah Shaw
   f Joseph Shaw
   m Judith Whitmarsh
Q21F JONATHAN   [Q64]
   a Sarah Soule
   f John Soule
   m Martha Tinkham
Q21G DAVID   [Q65]
   a Joanna Hayward
   f Joseph Hayward
   m Mehitabel Dunham

```
    ======
[Q22]   SNOW
    Benjamin Snow    Q13F
    Elizabeth Alden  Q13Fa
    Sarah Allen      Q13Fb
    ------
by #1
Q22A  REBECKAH
    a  Ebenezer Campbell  Jr
    f  Ebenezer Campbell  Sr
    m  Hannah Pratt
Q22B  BENJAMIN        [Q66]
    a  Jemima Snell
    f  Amos Snell
    m  Mary Packard
Q22C  SOLOMON         [Q67]
    a  Bathsheba Mahurin
Q22D  EBERNEZER       [Q68]
    a  Sarah Pratt
    f  Joseph Pratt
    m  Sarah Benson
Q22E  ELIZABETH
    a  Joseph Carver  [Q69]
    f  Eleazer Carver
    m  Experience Blake
by #2
Q22F  SARAH
    a  Nathaniel Pratt [Q70]
    f  Joseph Pratt
    m  Sarah Benson
    ======
[Q23]   RICKARD
    Samuel Rickard   Q13Ga
    Rebecca Snow     Q13G
    ------
Q23A  REBECKAH
Q23B  HANNAH
    a  Josiah Byram   [Q71]
    f  Nicholas Byram
    m  Mary Edson
Q23C  SAMUEL          [Q72]
    a  Rachel Whiton
    f  Thomas Whiton
    m  Joanna May
Q23D  BETHIAH
    a  John Chandler  [Q73]
    f  Edmund Chandler
Q23E  HENRY           [Q74]
    a  Alica Oldham
    f  Isaac Oldham
    m  Hannah Keen
Q23F  MARY
```

```
Q23G  ELKANAH         [Q75]
    a  Keturah Bishop
    f  John Bishop
    m  Elizabeth Keen
    b  Bethiah Conant
Q23H  MEHITABLE
    a  Arthur Harris  [Q76]
    f  Isaac Harris
    m  Jane Cooke
Q23I  ELEAZER         [Q77]
    a  Mary Churchill
    f  Benjamin Churchiil
    m  Mary Shaw
    ======
[Q24]   SOULE
    John Soule       Q14A
    Martha Tinkham   Q14Aa
    ------
Q24A  MARTHA
Q24B  SARAH
Q24C  JOHN
Q24D  ESTHER
Q24E  MARY
Q24F  JAMES
Q24G  REBECCA
Q24H  NATHAN
Q24I  RACHEL
    ======
[Q25]   TINKHAM
    John Tinkham     Q14B
    Hannah Howland   Q14Ba
    ------
Q25A  CORNELIUS
Q25B  JOHN
Q25C  ESTHER
Q25D  HANNAH
Q25E  SUSANNAH
Q25F  ABAISHA
Q25G  AMOS
Q25H  MARY
Q25I  SETH
Q25J  ZILPAH
    ======
[Q26]   TINKHAM
    Ephraim Tinkham  Q14C
    Martha Cobb      Q14Ca
    ------
Q26A  MOSES
Q26B  EPHRAIM
    ======
```

[Q27]   TINKHAM
          Isaac Tinkham Q14D
          Abijah Wood   Q14Da

Q27A   EPHRAIM
Q27B   ISAAC
Q27C   NOAH
Q27D   NATHAN
Q27E   ABIJAH
Q27F   MOSES
======

[Q28]   TINKHAM
          Samuel Tinkham   Q14E
          Patience Cobb   Q14Ea

Q28A   EPHRAIM
Q28B   PATIENCE
Q28C   SAMUEL
Q28D   SILAS
Q28E   FEAR
Q28F   MARTHA
Q28G   LOID
Q28H   SARAH
======

[Q29]   WOOD
          Henry Wood   Q14Fa
          Mary Tinkham Q14F

Q29A   SAMUEL
Q29B   JOANNA
Q29C   SUSANNA
Q29D   HENRY
Q29E   MOSES
=======

[Q30]   TINKHAM
          Ebenezer Tinkham Q15A
          Patience Pratt   Q15Aa

Q30A   ELIZABETH
Q30B   MARYR
Q39C   PETER
Q30D   JABEZ
Q30E   PATIENCE
Q30F   PRISCILLA
======

[Q31]   TINKHAM
          Jeremiah Tinkham Q15B
          Joanna Parlow   Q15Ba

Q31A   JOANNA
Q31B   JEREMIAH
Q31C   EBENEZER

[Q32]   MACOMBER
          Thomas Macomber   Q15Da
          Joanna Tinkham   Q15D

Q32A   THOMAS
Q32B   URSULA
Q32C   SARAH
Q32D   ELIZABETH
Q32E   ONESIMUS
Q32F   JOANNA
======

[Q33]   TINKHAM
          Shuball Tinkham Q15G
          Priscilla Childs Q15Ga

Q33A   ELIZABETH
Q33B   JOSEPH
Q33C   SARAH
Q33D   PRISCILLA
Q33E   EBENEZER
Q33F   PEREZ
======

[Q34]   RAYMOND
          James Raymond Q16Aa
          Mercy Tinkham Q16A

Q34A   PETER
Q34B   MERCY
======

[Q35]   BATES
          Joseph Bates Sr Q16Ba
          Joanna Tinkham Q16B

Q35A   JOANNA
Q35B   MERCY
Q35C   JOSEPH Jr
Q35D   ELIZABETH
Q35E   THOMAS
Q35F   PRISCILLA
======

[Q36]   TINKHAM
          Samuel Tinkham Q16C
          Mary Staples   Q16Ca

Q36A   MARTHA
Q36B   PETER
Q36C   SAMUEL Jr
Q36D   MERCY
Q36E   DEBORAH
Q36F   GIDEON
Q36G   JOANNA
Q36H   KEZIA

```
      ======                      by Hannah
[Q37]   TINKHAM                 Q41A  JACOB
      Seth Tinkham  Q16D        by Judeth
      Mary --       Q16Da       Q41B  HANNAH
      ------                    Q41C  LYDIA
Q37A  BATHSHEBA                     ======
Q37B  MERCY                     [Q42]   TINKHAM
Q37C  SETH Jr                       Caleb Tinkham  Q17E
Q37D  ELIZABETH                     Mercy Holmes   Q17Ea
Q37E  JOANNA                        ------
      ======                    Q42A  MARCY
[Q38]   TINKHAM                 Q42B  PATIENCE
      Helkiah Tinkham  Q17A     Q42C  FEAR
      Elizabeth Heister Q17Aa   Q42D  SARAH
      ------                    Q42E  NATHANIEL
Q38A  HANNAH                    Q42F  CALEB Jr
Q38B  ELIZABETH                 Q42G  ELEANOR(Nelle)
Q38C  ISAAC                         ======
Q38D  SARAH                     [Q43]   TINKHAM
Q38E  ZEDEKIAH                      Ebenezer Tinkham  Q17G
Q38F  MARY                          Jane Pratt        Q17Ga
Q38G  MARTHA                        ------
Q38H  RUTH                      Q43A  MARY
Q38I  EBENEZER                  Q43B  EBENEZER
Q38J  LYDIA                     Q43C  JAMES
      ======                    Q43D  PHEBE
[Q39]   CURTIS                  Q43E  SUSANNAH
      Ebenezer Curtis Q17Ba     Q43F  PRISCILLA
      Mary Tinkham    Q17B          ======
      ------                    [Q44]   COBB
Q39A  JACOB                         Ebenezer Cobb Q17Ha
Q39B  CALEB                         Ruth Tinkham  Q17H
Q39C  MARY                          ------
Q39D  SARAH                     Q44A  EBENEZER
      ======                        ======
[Q40]   TINKHAM                 [Q45]   TINKHAM
      John Tinkham  Q17C            Peter Tinkham  Q17I
      Ann Gray      Q16Ca          Mary Bennett   Q17Ia
      ------                        ------
Q40A  MARY                      Q45A  JACOB
Q40B  EDWARD                    Q45B  ARTHUR
Q40C  JOHN                      Q45C  HILKIAH
Q40D  EPHRAIM
Q40E  ANN                       [Q46]   TOMSON
Q40F  JOSEPH                        John Tomson    Q18A
      ======                        Elizabeth Thomas Q18Aa
[Q41]   TINKHAM                      ------
      Jacob Tinkham  Q17D       Q46A  JOHN
      Hannah Cobb    Q17Da      Q46B  ELIZABETH
      Judeth Hunt    Q17Db      Q46C  LYDIA
      ------                        ======
```

```
    ======
[Q47]    TOMSON                       Q51C  EUBE
         Shubael Tomson   Q18C        Q51D  HANNAH
         Susanna Parlour  Q18Ca       Q51E  JEMIMA
    ------                                ======
Q47A  ISAAC                           [Q52]    ELLIS
Q47B  SHUBAEL                                  Joseph Ellis    Q19Ca
Q47C  JOHN                                     Martha Tinkham  Q19C
Q47D  MARY                                ------
Q47E  THOMAS                           Q52A  SETH
    ======                             Q52B  LUKE
[Q48]    TOMSON                        Q52C  JOHN
         Thomas Tomson    Q18D         Q52D  ELIJAH
         Martha Soule     Q18Da           ======
    ------                             [Q53]    TINKHAM
Q48A  PETER                                    Peter Tinkham   Q19D
Q48B  FRANCIS                                  Eunice Clark    Q19Da
Q48C  NATHAN                                ------
Q48D  JAMES                             Q53A  CHARLES
    ======                             Q53B  CLARK
[Q49]    TOMSON                        Q53C  EPHRAIM
         Jacob Tomson     Q18K         Q53D  SARAH
         Mary Hayward     Q18Ka        Q53E  ELIZABETH
    ------                             Q53F  HEZEKIAH
Q49A  JACOB                                ======
Q49B  EBENEZER                         [Q54]    TINKHAM
Q49C  NATHANIEL                                 Hezekiah Tinkham  Q19E
Q49D  EPHRAIM                                   Grizzell West     Q19Ea
Q49E  DANIEL                                ------
    ======                             Q54A  ELIZABETH
[Q50]    TINKHAM                       Q54B  JOANNA
         John Tinkham     Q19A         Q54C  RENEW
         Mary Allen       Q19Aa        Q54D  JOHN
    ------                             Q54E  SARAH
Q50A  ELIZABETH                        Q54F  PETER
Q50B  JOHN                             Q54G  GRIZZELL
Q50C  AMY                              Q54H  NEHEMIAH
Q50D  MARY                             Q54I  DANIEL
Q50E  BARBARA                          Q54J  SAMUEL
Q50F  DEBORAH                          Q54K  PHILIP
Q50G  ABIGAIL                             ======
Q50H  HANNAH                           [Q55]    HAYWARD
Q50I  MARMADUKE                                 Elisha Hayward  Q20Aa
Q50J  HULDAH                                    Bethia Snow     Q20A
Q50K  SUSANNA                             ------
    ======                             Q55A  BETHIA
[Q51]    TABER                         Q55B  NAOMI
         Joseph Taber     Q19Ba        Q55C  EZRA
         Mary Tinkham     Q19B            ======
    ======
Q51A  WILLIAM
Q51B  ELIZABETH
```

======

[Q56]   ALGER
    Israel Alger   Q20Ca
    Susanna Snow   Q20C

Q56A ISRAEL
Q56B DANIEL
Q56C JAMES

======

[Q57]   SNOW
    William Snow   Q20D
    Mary Washburn Q20Da

Q57A WILLIAM
Q57B SETH
Q57C JAMES
Q57D MARY
Q57E SUSANNA

======

[Q58]   SNOW
    Eleazer Snow   Q20E
    Mercy King   Q20Ea

Q58A BETTY
Q58B REUBEN
Q58C ELEAZER Jr
Q58D MERCY
Q58E DANIEL

======

[Q59]   SNOW
    John Snow   Q20F
    Hannah Harlow Q20Fa

Q59A SARAH
Q59B JOHN

======

[Q60]   SNOW
    Joseph Snow   Q21A
    Elizabeth Field Q21Aa

Q60A JOSEPH
Q60B JOHN
Q60C ELIZABETH
Q60D SUSANNA
Q60E SARAH
Q60F DANIEL
Q60G JAMES
Q60H MARY

======

[Q61]   SNOW
    James Snow   Q21C
    Ruth Shaw   Q21Ca
    Hannah Hovey   Q21Cb
------

by Ruth
Q61A RUTH
Q61B ABIJAH
Q61C MARY
Q61D NATHAN
Q61E ABIGAIL
Q61F SUSANNA
Q61G JEDEDIAH
Q61H SARAH
by Hannah
Q61I JOHN

======

[Q62]   WADE
    Thomas Wade   Q21Da
    Rebeckah Snow Q21D

Q62A HOPESTILL
Q62B MARY
Q62C KEZIAH
Q62D DAVID
Q62E REBECCA

======

[Q63]   SNOW
    Isaac Snow   Q21E
    Hannah Shaw   Q21Ea

Q63A HANNAH
Q63B ISAAC
Q63C MARTHA
Q63D PETER
Q63E JOSEPH
Q63F JUDITH

======

[Q64]   SNOW
    Jonathan Snow Q21F
    Sarah Soule   Q21Fa
    Ruth Bennet   Q21Fb
------

by Sarah
Q64A SAMUEL
Q64B JESSE
Q64C SARAH
Q64D REBECCA
Q64E JONATHAN
Q64F MOSES
by Bennett
Q64G RUTH

[Q65]   SNOW
          David Snow   Q21G
          Joanna Hayward Q21Ga

Q65A DAVID
Q65B JOSEPH
Q65C JOANNA
Q65D MEHITABEL
Q65E LYDIA
Q65F RHODA
          ======
[Q66]   SNOW
          Benjamin Snow   Q22B
          Jemima Snell   Q22Ba

Q66A JEMIMA
Q66B BENJAMIN Jr
Q66C DANIEL
Q66D ELIJAH
Q66E ELIZABETH
Q66F LUCY
          ======
[Q67]   SNOW
          Solomon Snow   Q22C
          Bathsheba Mahurin Q22Ca

Q67A LEMUEL
Q67B BATHSHEBA
          ======
[Q68]   SNOW
          Ebenezer Snow   Q22D
          Sarah Pratt   Q22Da
          Sarah Hooper   Q22Db
          ------
by Pratt
Q68A EBENEZER
Q68B NATHANIEL
Q68C SARAH
Q68D CALEB
by Hooper
Q68E FRANCIS
Q68F SOLOMON
Q68G REBECCA
Q68H ZEBEDEE
          ======
[Q69]   CARVER
          Joseph Carver   Q22Ea
          Elizabeth Snow Q22E

Q69A JOSEPH
Q69B BENJAMIN
Q69C ELIZABETH

Q69D ABIEZER
Q69E SARAH
Q69F EXPERIENCE
Q69G ROBERT
Q69H REBECCA
          ======
[Q70]   PRATT
          Nathaniel Pratt Q22Fa
          Sarah Snow   Q22F

Q70A SETH
Q70B ANNA
          ======
[Q71]   BYRAM
          Josiah Byram   Q23Ba
          Hannah Rickard Q23B

Q71A SUSANNA
Q71B THEOPHILUS
Q71C MEHETABEL
Q71D REBECCA
          ======
[Q72]   RICKARD
          Samuel Rickard Q23C
          Rachel Whiton Q23Ca

Q72A LEMUEL
Q72B THEOPHILUS
Q72C SAMUEL
Q72D LAZARIS
Q72E ELIZABETH
Q72F RACHEL
Q72G REBECCA
          ======
[Q73]   CHANDLER
          John Chandler   Q23Da
          Bethiah Rickard Q23D

Q73A REUBEN
Q73B JONATHAN
Q73C JUDITH
Q73D ELIZABETH
Q73E MARY
Q73F DOROTHY
          ======
[Q74]   RICKARD
          Henry Rickard   Q23E
          Alice Oldham   Q23Ea

Q74A SAMUEL
Q74B JUDAH
Q74C ISAAC

412

```
      ======                          ======
[Q75]   RICKARD
        Elkanah Rickard    Q23G
        Keturah Bishop     Q23Ga
        Bethiah Conant     Q23Gb
      ------
by Bishop
Q75A  NATHANIEL
Q75B  ELKANAH Jr
by Conant
Q75C  SETH
Q75D  AMASA
Q75E  URIAH
Q75F  KETURAH
      ======
[Q76]   HARRIS
        Arthur Harris      Q23Ha
        Mehitable Rickard  Q23H
      ------
Q76A  BENJAMIN
Q76B  SILAS
Q76C  ARTHUR Jr
Q76D  LUCY
      ======
[Q77]   RICKARD
        Eleazer Rickard    Q23I
        Mary Churchill     Q23Ia
      ------
Q77A  MARCY
Q77B  ELEAZER
Q77C  ABNER
Q77D  MARY
Q77E  SARAH
Q77F  KEZIAH
Q77G  ELIJAH
Q77H  DEBORAH
      ======
```

413

```
-------------------------------------------------------------
[R10]   BRADFORD                 R12E  MERCY
        William Bradford Sr R9A    a  Samuel Steele    [R18]
        Alice Hanson      R9Aa     f  John Steele
        ------                     m  Mary Warner
R10A  WILLIAM BRADFORD MF [R11]  R12F  HANNAH
   a  Dorothy May                  a  Joshua Ripley    [R19]
   f  Henry May                    f  John Ripley
   b  Alice Carpenter              m  Elizabeth Hobart
   f  Alexander Carpenter        R12G  MELATIAH
      ======                       a  John Steele      [R20]
[R11]   BRADFORD                   f  James Steele
        William Bradford Jr R10A   b  Samuel Stevens  [R118]
        Alice Carpenter   R10Ab  R12H  SAMUEL          [R21]
        ------                     a  Hannah Rogers
R11A  JOHN                         f  John Rogers
   a  Martha Bourne                m  Elizabeth Pabodie
   f  Thomas Bourne              R12I  MARY
   m  Elizabeth --                 a  William Hunt     [R22]
R11B  WILLIAM II      [R12]        f  Ephraim Hunt
   a  Alice Richards               m  Ebbet Brimsmead
   f  Thomas Richards            R12J  SARAH
   m  Welthean Loring              a  Kenelm Baker     [R23]
   b  -- Fitch                     f  Samuel Baker
   c  Mary Wood                    m  Eleanor Winslow
R11C  MERCY                      R12K  JOSEPH           [R24]
   a  Benjamin Vermayes            a  Anna Fitch
R11D  JOSEPH          [R13]        f  James Fitch
   a  Jael Hobart                  m  Pricilla Mason
   f  Peter Hobart                 b  Mary Sherwood
   m  Elizabeth Ilbrook            f  Matthew Sherwood
      ======                       m  Mary Fitch
[R12]   BRADFORD                 R12L  ISREAL           [R25]
        William Bradford II R11B   a  Sarah Bartlett
        Alice Richards   R11Ba     f  Benjamin Bartlett
        ------                     m  Ruth Pabodie
R12A  JOHN            [R14]      R12M  EPHRAIM          [R26]
   a  Mercy Warren                 a  Elizabeth Brewster
   f  Joseph Warren                f  Wrestling Brewster
   m  Priscilla Faunce             m  Mary --
R12B  WILLIAM         [R15]      R12N  DAVID            [R27]
   a  Rebecca Bartlett             a  Elizabeth Phinney
   f  Benjamin Bartlett            f  Jonathan Phinney
   m  Sarah Brewster               m  Joanna Kinnicut
R12C  THOMAS          [R16]      R12O  HEZEKIAH
   a  Anne Raymond                 a  Mary Chandler
   f  Joshua Raymond               f  Joseph Chandler
   m  Elizbeth Smith                  ======
   b  Katherine --             [R13]   BRADFORD
R12D  ALICE           [R17]             Joseph Bradford R11D
   a  William Adams Jr                  Jael Hobart     R11Da
   f  William Adams Sr                  ------
   b  James Fitch Jr  [R117]  R13A  JOSEPH
   f  James Fitch Sr
   m  Abagail Whitfield
```

R13B ELISHA   [R28]
  a Hannah Cole
  f James Cole
  m Abigail Davenport
  b Bathsheba Brock
  f Francis Brock
  m Sarah Hobart
R13C PETER
  ======

[R14]   BRADFORD
   John Bradford   R12A
   Mercy Warren   R12Aa

R14A JOHN   [R29]
  a Rebecca Bartlett
  f Benjamin Bartlett
  m Ruth Pabodie
R14B ALICE   [R30]
  a Edward Mitchell
  f Experience Mitchell
  m Mary --
  b Joshua Hersey   [R119]
  f William Hersey
  m Rebecca Chubbuck
R14C ABIGAIL
R14D MERCY   [R31]
  a Jonathan Freeman
  f Thomas Freeman
  m Rebecca Sparrow
  b Isaac Cushman Jr   [R120]
  f Isaac Cushman Sr
  m Rebecca Rickard
R14E SAMUEL   [R32]
  a Sarah Gray
  f Edward Gray
  m Mary Smith
R14F PRISCILLA   [R33]
  a Seth Chipman
  f Samuel Chipman
  m Sarah Cobb
R14G WILLIAM   [R34]
  a Hannah Foster
  f John Foster
  m Hannah Stetson
  ======

[R15]   BRADFORD
   William Bradford R12B
   Rebecca Bartlett R12Ba

R15A ALICE
  a William Barnes   [R35]
  f Jonathan Barnes
  m Elizabeth Hedge

R15B WILLIAM   [R36]
  a Elizabeth Finney
  f Josiah Finney
  m Elizabeth Warren
R15C SARAH   [R37]
  a Jonathan Barnes Jr
  f Jonathan Barnes Sr
  m Elizabeth Hedge
  ======

[R16]   BRADFORD
   Thomas Bradford R12C
   Anne Raymond   R12Ca

R16A JOSHUA   [R38]
  a Mary Brooks
  f Henry Brooks
  m Mary Graves
R16B JAMES   [R39]
  a Edith Adams
  f Peletiah Adams
  m Ruth --
  b Susannah Adams
  f Samuel Adams
  m Mary Meeker
R16C JERUSHA
  a Hezekiah Newcomb [R40]
  f Simeon Newcomb
  m Deborah --
R16D WILLIAM
R16E SUSANNA
  ======

[R17]   ADAMS
   William Adams R12Da
   Alice Bradford R12D

R17A ELIZABETH
  a Samuel Whiting   [R41]
  f John Whiting
  m Sybil Collins
  b Samuel Niles
  f Nathaniel Niles
  m Sarah Sand
R17B ALICE
  a Nathaniel Collins [R42]
  f Nathaniel Collins Sr
  m Mary Whiting
R17C WILLIAM
R17D ABIEL
  a Joseph Metcalf   [R43]
  f Jonathan Metcalf
  m Hannah Kenric

[R18]   STEELE
  Samuel Steele R12Ea
  Mercy Bradford R12E

R18A THOMAS   [R51]
 a Susanna Webster
 f Jonathan Webster
 m Dorcas Hopkins
R18B ELIZABETH
R18C SAMUEL
R18D JERUSHA
R18E WILLIAM
R18F ABIEL
 a John Webster Jr [R52]
 f John Webster Sr
 m Sarah Myatt
 b Stephen Hopkins
 f John Hopkins
 m Hannah Strong
R18G DANIEL   [R53]
 a Mary Hopkins
 f Ebenezer Hopkins
 m Mary Butler
R18H ELIPHALET   [R54]
 a Katharine Marshfield
 f Josiah Marshfield
 m Rachel Gilbert
  ======

[R19]   RIPLEY
  Joshua Ripley   R12Fa
  Hannah Bradford R12F

R19A ALICE
 a Samuel Edgerton [R55]
 f Richard Edgerton
 m Mary Sylvester
R19B HANNAH
 a Samuel Webb Jr   [R56]
 f Samuel Webb Sr
 m Mary Adams
R19C FAITH
 a Samuel Bingham   [R57]
 f Thomas Bingham
 m Mary Rudd
R19D JOSHUA   [R58]
 a Mary Backus
 f John Backus
 m Mary Bingham
R19E MARGARET
 a Benjamin Seabury [R59]
 f Samuel Seabury
 m Abigail Allen

R19F RACHEL
 a Winslow Tracy   [R60]
 f John Tracy
 m Mary Winslow
R19G LEAH
 a Samuel Cook   [R61]
 f Stephen Cook
 m Rebecca Flagg
 b James Bradford
 f Thomas Bradford
 m Anna Raymond
R19H HEZEKIAH   [R62]
 a Miriam Fitch
 f John Fitch
 m Elizabeth Waterman
 b Mary Skinner
R19I DAVID   [R63]
 a Lydia Cary
 f Eleazer Cary
 m Lydia Throope
R19J IRENA
 a Samuel Manning Jr [R64]
 f Samuel Manning Sr
 m Deborah Spaulding
R19K JERUSHA
 a Edward Brown   [R65]
R19L ANNA
 a Solomon Wheat   [R66]
 f Samuel Wheat
 m Lydia --
  ======

[R20]   STEELE
  John Steele   R12Ga
  Melatiah Bradford R12G

R20A BETHIA
 a Samuel Sheperd   [R67]
 f John Sheperd
 m Hannah Peck
R20B JOHN
R20C EBENEZER   [R68]
 a Susannah Merrill
 f Daniel Merrill
 m Susanna Pratt
  ======

[R21]   BRADFORD
  Samuel Bradford R12H
  Hannah Rogers   R12Ha

R21A HANNAH
 a Nathaniel Gilbert [R71]
 f Thomas Gilbert
 m Hannah Blake

R21B GERSHOM   [R72]
  a Priscilla Wiswall
  f Ichobod Wiswall
  m Priscilla Pabodie
R21C PEREZ   [R73]
  a Abigail Belcher
  f Joseph Belcher
  m Abigail Thompson
R21D ELIZABETH
  a Charles Whiting   [R74]
  f William Whiting
  m Mary Allyn
  b John Noyes
  f James Noyes
  m Dorothy Stanton
R21E JERUSHA
  a Ebenezer Gay   [R75]
  f Nathaniel Gay
  m Lydia Lusher
R21F WELTHEA
  a Peter Lane   [R76]
  f Ebenezer Lane
  m Hannah Hersey
R21G GAMALIEL   [R77]
  a Abigail Bartlett
  f Benjamin Bartlett
  m Ruth Pabodie
        ======
[R22] HUNT
        William Hunt R12Ia
        Mary Bradford R12I

R22A MARY
  a Nathaniel Knowles   [R78]
  f Samuel Knowles
  m Mercy Freeman
R22B WILLIAM   [R79]
  a Jane Tilton
  f William Tilton
  m Abiah Mayhew
  b Sarah Gray
  f Edward Gray
  m Mary Smith
        ======
[R23] BAKER
        Kenelm Baker R12Ja
        Sarah Bradford R12J

R23A SARAH
  a John Sherman Jr   [R80]
  f John Sherman Sr
  m Jane Hatch

R23B ALICE
  a Nathan Thomas
  f Samuel Thomas
  m Mercy Ford
R23C ELEANOR
  a Benjamin Phillips [R81]
  f Benjamin Phillips Sr
  m Sarah Thomas
R23D ABIGAIL
  a Gideon Thomas   [R82]
  f Samuel Thomas
  m Mercy Ford
R23E KENELM   [R83]
  a Patience Doty
  f John Doty
  m Sarah Jones
R23F BETHIAH
  a James Scolley
R23G KEZIAH
R23H SAMUEL   [R84]
  a Hannah Ford
  f James Ford
  m Hannah Dingley
R23I WILLIAM   [R85]
  a Sarah Hurd
  f Jacob Hurd
  m Elizabeth Tufts
R23J EDWARD   [R86]
  a Mehetable Blanchard
  b Hannah Gibbon
        ======
[R24] BRADFORD
        Joseph Bradford R12K
        Anna Fitch   R12Ka

R24A ANN
  a Thimothy Dimmick   [R87]
  f John Dimmick
  m Elizabeth Lumbert
R24B JOSEPH   [R88]
  a Henrietta Swift
R24C PRISCILLA
  a Samuel Hyde Jr   [R89]
  f Samuel Hyde Sr
  m Elizabeth Caulkins
R24D ALTHEA
R24E IRENE
R24F SARAH
  a Daniel Tuttle   [R90]
  b Israel Lathrop Jr [R121]
  f Israel Lathrop Sr
  m Rebecca Bliss

R24G HANNAH
  a Timothy Buell   [R91]
  f William Buell
  ■ Elizabeth Collins
R24H ELIZABETH
  a Andrew Lisk   [R92]
R24I ALTHEA
  a David Hyde   [R93]
  f Samuel Hyde
  ■ Elizabeth Caulkins
R24J IRENA
  a Jonathan Janes   [R94]
  f William Janes
  ■ Abigail Loomis
R24K JOHN   [R95]
  a Esther Sherwood
  f Samuel Sherwood
  ■ Rebecca Burr
  ======

[R25] BRADFORD
  Esrail Bradford R12L
  Sarah Barlett R12La

R25A RUTH
R25B BATHSHEBE
  a Thomas Adams   [R96]
  f Francis Adams
  ■ Mary Buck
R25C BENJAMIN   [R97]
  a Zeresh Stetson
  f ELisha Stetson
  ■ Abigail Brewster
  b Mercy Chipman
  f Seth Chipman
  ■ Priscilla Bradford
R25D ABNER   [R98]
  a Susannah Potter
  f Hopestill Potter
  ■ Lydia --
R25E JOSHUA   [R99]
  a Hannah Bradford
  f ELisha Bradford
  ■ Bathshebe Brock
R25F ICHABOD   [R100]
  a Mary Johnson
  b Mary Samson
  f Peleg Samson
  ■ Mary Ring
R25G ELISHA
  a Mary Sturtevant
  f James Sturtevant
  ■ Susanna Cooke
  ======

[R26] BRADFORD
  Ephraim Bradford R12M
  Elizabeth Brewster R12Ma

R26A DEBORAH
R26B SON
R26C ANNA
  a Ebenezer Chandler [R101]
  f Joseph Chandler
  ■ Martha Hunt
R26D DAUGHTER
R26E ELIZABETH
  a Azariah Whiting   [R102]
  f John Whiting
  ■ Bethia Crocker
R26F EPHRAIM
R26G ABIGAIL
  a Peleg Holmes   [R103]
  f John Holmes
  ■ Mercy Ford
R26H LUSANNA
  a Seth Everson   [R104]
R26I ELIJAH
R26J son
R26K RUTH
  a Nathan Chandler [R105]
  f Philip Chandler
  ■ Rebecca Phillips
R26L EZEKIEL   [R106]
  a Betty Chandler
  f Philip Chandler
  ■ Rebecca Phillips
R26M SIMEON   [R107]
  a Phebe Whiton
  f Azariah Whiton
  ■ Elizabeth Barrows
R26N WAIT   [R108]
  a Welthea Bassett
  f Moses Bassett
  ■ Lydia Cooke
  ======

[R27] BRADFORD
  David Bradford R12N
  Elizabeth Phinney R12Na

R27A NATHANIEL   [R109]
  a Sarah Spooner
  f Thomas Spooner
  ■ Sarah Nelson
R27B JONATHAN

R27C LYDIA
  a Elkanah Cushman Jr [R110]
    f Elkanah Cushman Sr
    m Hester Barnes
  b Lazarus Le Baron [R122]
    f Francis Le Baron
    m Mary Wilder
R27D NATHAN [R111]
  a Elizabeth Groce
    f Isaac Groce
    m Dorothy Cobb
  b Sarah Sturtevant
    f David Sturtevant
    m Sarah Holmes
    ======

[R28] BRADFORD
    Elisha Bradford R13B
    Hannah Cole   R13Ba
    Bathshebe Brock R13Bb

R28A HANNAH   by Cole
  a Joshua Bradford
R28B JOSEPH
R28C SYLVANUS
R28D NEHEMIAH
R28E LAURANNA
  a Elijah McFarlin [R112]
    f Solomon McFarlin
    m Susanna Huet
R28F MARY
R28G ELISHA
R28H LOIS
R28I DEBORAH
  a Jonathan Sampson Jr [R113]
    f Jonathan Sampson Sr
    m Joanna Lucas
R28J ALICE
  a Zebulon Waters   [R114]
    f Samuel Waters
    m Bethia Thayer
R28K AZENATH
  a Nathan Estey
    f Benjamin Estey
    m Sarah Chandler
  b Daniel Waters   [R115]
    f Samuel Waters
    m Bethia Thayer
  c Benjamin Packard [R123]
    f Joseph Packard
    m Hannah Manley

R28L CARPENTER   [R116]
  a Mary Gay
    f David Gay
    m Hannah Tabor
R28M ABIGAIL
R28N CHLOE
R28O CONTENT
    ======

[R29] BRADFORD
    John Bradford   R14A
    Rebecca Bartlett R14Aa

R29A ROBERT
R29B REBECCA
    ======

[R30] MITCHELL
    Edward Mitchell R14Ba
    Alice Bradford R14B

R30A MARY
R30B ALICE
R30C EDWARD
    ======

[R31] FREEMAN
    Jonathan Freeman R14Da
    Mercy Bradford   R14D

R31A JONATHAN
R31B MERCY
R31C BRADFORD
R31D ICHABOD
    ======

[R32] BRADFORD
    Samuel Bradford R14E
    Sarah Gray   R14Ea

R32A JOHN
R32B GIDEON
R32C WILLIAM
R32D MARY
R32E SARAH
R32F WILLIAM
R32G MERCY
R32H ABIGAIL
R32I PHEBE
R32J SAMUEL
    ======

[R33] CHIPMAN
    Seth Chipman   R14Fa
    Priscilla Bradford R14F

R33A CHILD
R33B SETH
R33C MERCY
R33D BENJAMIN
    ======
[R34] BRADFORD
    William Bradford R14G
    Hannah Foster   R14Ga

R34A JAMES
R34B ZADOCK
R34C SAMUEL
R34D ELIPHALET
R34E HANNAH
R34F WILLIAM
    ======
[R35] BARNES
    William Barnes R15Aa
    Alice Bradford F15A

R35A WILLIAM
R35B LEMUEL
R35C MERCY
R35D BENJAMIN #1
R35E BENJAMIN #2
    ======
[R36] BRADFORD
    William Bradford R15B
    Elizabeth Finney R15Ba

R36A ELIZABETH
R36B CHARLES
R36C SARAH
R36D JERUSHA
R36E JOSIAH
R36F WILLIAM
R36G MERCY
R36H ELIZABETH
    ======
[R37] BARNES
    Jonathan Barnes Jr R15Ca
    Sarah Bradford   R15C

R37A SARAH
R37B REBECCA
R37C LYDIA
R37D HANNAH
    ======

[R38] BRADFORD
    Joshua Bradford R16A
    Mary Brooks   R16Aa

R38A SYLVANUS
R38B ELIZABETH
    ======
[R39] BRADFORD
    James Bradford R16B
    Edith Adams   R16Ba
    Susanna Adams R16Bb
    Leah Ripley   R16Bc

R39A THOMAS   by Edith
R39B JOHN
R39C JERUSHA
R39D WILLIAM
R39E SARAH
R39F ANN   by Susanna
R39G MARY
R39H JAMES
    ======
[R40] NEWCOMB
    Hezekiah Newcomb R16Ca
    Jerusha Bradford R16C

R40A SILAS
R40B PETER
R40C ANNE
R40D HEZEKIAH
R40E THOMAS
R40F JERUSHA
R40G ELIZABETH
R40H SAMUEL
R40I JEMIMA
R40J JAMES
    ======
[R41] WHITING
    Samuel Whiting   R17Aa
    Elizabeth Adams R17A

R41A ANNE
R41B SAMUEL
R41C ELIZABETH
R41D WILLIAM
R41E JOSEPH
R41F JOHN
R41G SYBIL
R41H MARTHA
R41I MARY
R41J ELIPHALET
R41K ELISHA

R41L SAMUEL
R41M JOSEPH
R41N NATHAN
　　　======
[R42]　COLLINS
　　　Nathaniel Collins R17Ba
　　　Alice Adams　　R17B

R42A MARY
R42B ANN
R42C JOHN
R42D ALICE
R42E NATHANIEL
R42F WILLIAM
R42G EDWARD
R42H ALICE
　　　======
[R43]　METCALF
　　　Joseph Metcalf R17Da
　　　Abiel Adams　　R17D

R43A ABIGAIL
R43B ABIJAH　twin
R43C ABIEL　twin
R43D ALICE　twin
R43E HANNAH　twin
R43F MARY
R43G ELIZABETH
R43H DELIGHT
R43I SARAH
R43J SYBIL
R43K AZUBA
　　　======
[R44]　DYER
　　　John Dyer　　R117Ea
　　　Abigail Fitch R117A

R44A SYBIL
R44B ELIJAH
R44C ABIGAIL
R44D JAMES
R44E JOHN
R44F JOSEPH
R44G SARAH
R44H EBENEZER
　　　======
[R45]　FITCH
　　　Ebenezer Fitch R117B
　　　Bridget Brown　R117Ba

R45A ALICE
R45B JAMES
R45C ELIJAH
R45D ELEAZER

R45E MEDINA
R45F EBENEZER
　　　======
[R46]　FITCH
　　　Daniel Fitch　R117C
　　　Anna Cook　　R117Ca

R46A WILLIAM
R46B JAMES
R46C EBENEZER
R46D JOHN
R46E DANIEL
R46F THEOPHILUS
　　　======
[R47]　BISSELL
　　　Daniel Bissell R117Da
　　　Jerusha Fitch　R117D

R47A JABEZ
R47B JERUSHA
R47C MARGARET
R47D DANIEL
R47E EBENEZER
　　　======
[R48]　CLEVELAND
　　　Henry Cleveland R117Ea
　　　Lucy Fitch　　R117E

R48A WILLIAM
R48B NEHEMIAH
R48C LUCY
R48D JABEZ #1
R48E JABEZ #2
　　　======
[R49]　FITCH
　　　Theophilus Fitch R117F
　　　Mary Huntington R117Fa

R49A SAMUEL
R49B THEOPHILUS
R49C PHINEAS
R49D JAMES
R49E DANIEL
R49F MARY
R49G SARAH
　　　======
[R50]　FITCH
　　　Jabez Fitch　　R117G
　　　Lydia Gale　　R117Ga
　　　Elizabeth Darbe R117Gb
　　　Rebecca --　　R117Gc

R50A JERUSHA
R50B ALICE

```
R50C  PEREZ                      R54D  MERCY
R50D  JABEZ                      R54E  THEOPHILUS
R50E  LYDIA                      R54F  ELIPHAZ
R50F  LUCY                       R54G  ELIJAH
R50G  ASHAEL                     R54H  RACHEL
R50H  ABIGAIL                    R54I  KATHERINE
      ======                     R54J  ELIPHALET #2
[R51]   STEELE                   R54K  JERUSHA
      Thomas Steele  R18A              ======
      Susanna Webster R18Aa     [R55]   EDGERTON
      ------                           Samuel Edgerton R19Aa
R51A  JERUSHA                          Alice Ripley    R19A
R51B  SAMUEL                           ------
R51C  WILLIAM
R51D  SUSANNA                    R55A  SAMUEL
R51E  THOMAS                     R55B  PETER
R51F  JAMES                      R55C  JOSHUA
R51G  NATHANIEL                  R55D  WILLIAM
R51H  JOHN                       R55E  JOHN
      ======                     R55F  MARY
[R52]   WEBSTER                  R55G  ELIJAH
      John Webster R18Fa         R55H  DAVID
      Abiel Steele R18F          R55I  ALICE
      ------                     R55J  DANIEL
R52A  ELISHA                           ======
R52B  JERUSHA                   [R56]   WEBB
R52C  AARON                            Samuel Webb Jr R19Ba
R52D  ABIEL                            Hannah Ripley  R19B
R52E  MARY                             ------
R52F  SARAH
R52G  ANN                        R56A  EBENEZER #1
R52H  SUSANNAH                   R56B  HANNAH
R52I  JOHN                       R56C  EBENEZER #2
      ======                     R56D  JOSHUA
[R53]   STEELE                         ======
      Daniel Steele  R18G       [R57]   BINGHAM
      Mary Hopkins   R18Ga            Samuel Bingham R19Ca
      ------                          Faith Ripley   R19C
R53A  DANIEL                           ------
R53B  MARY                       R57A  JERUSHA
R53C  WELTHIA                    R57B  ABISHA
R53D  TIMOTHY                    R57C  LEMUEL
R53E  ROSWELL                    R57D  ANNE
R53F  THOMAS                     R57E  MARAH
R53G  LEMUEL                           ======
R53H  SUBMIT                    [R58]   RIPLEY
      ======                           Joshua Ripley  R19D
[R54]   STEELE                         Mary Backus    R19Da
      Eliphalet Steele R18H            ------
      Katherine Marshfield       R58A  MARY
      ------           R18Ha     R58B  PHINEAS
                                 R58C  HANNAH
                                 R58D  NATHANIEL
R54A  ELIPHALET                  R58E  ELIZABETH
R54B  JOSIAH                     R58F  JOSHUA
R54C  KATHERINE                  R58G  EBENEZER
```

```
R58H  WILLIAM                      R63F  WILLIAM
R58I  JOHN                         R63G  GAMALIEL #1
      ======                       R63H  ALETHEA
[R59]  SEABURY                     R63I  GAMALIEL #2
       Benjamin Seabury R19Ea      R63J  HEZEKIAH
       Margaret Ripley  R19E       R63K  BRADFORD
       ------                      F63L  HANNAH
R59A  ABIGAIL                            ======
R59B  ELISHA                       [R64]  MANNING
R59C  SARAH                               Samuel Manning Jr R19Ja
      ======                              Irena Ripley       R19J
[R60]  TRACY                              ------
       Winslow Tracy   R19Fa       R64A  JOSIAH
       Rachel Ripley   R19F        R64B  HEZEKIAH
       ------                      R64C  ABIGAIL
R60A  JOSHUA                       R64D  SARAY
R60B  PEREZ                        R64E  SAMUEL
R60C  JOSIAH                       R64F  DAVID
R60D  ELIPHALET                          ======
R60E  NEHEMIAH                     [R65]  BROWN
R60F  SAMUEL                              Edward Brown    R19Ka
R60G  SOLOMON                             Jerusha Ripley  R19K
      ======                              ------
[R61]  COOK                        R65A  HUBBARD
       Samuel Cook   R19Ga               ======
       Leah Ripley   R19G          [R66]  WHEAT
       ------                             Solomon Wheat   R19La
R61A  PHINEAS                            Anna Ripley     R19L
R61B  REBECCA                             ------
R61C  JERUSHA                      R66A  SARAH
R61D  MARY                         R66B  SOLOMON
R61E  WELTHEAN                     R66C  MARY
R61F  MARY                         R66D  ANNA
R61G  DANIEL                       R66E  HANNAH
R61H  SAMUEL                       R66F  JEMIMA
R61I  PHINEAS                            ======
      ======                       [R67]  SHEPARD
[R62]  RIPLEY                             Samuel Shepard   R20Aa
       Hezekiah Ripley R19H              Behtia Steele    R20A
       Miriam Fitch    R19Ha              ------
       Mary Skinner    R19Hb       R67A  JOHN
       ------                      R67B  JAMES
R62A  HEZEKIAH  by Mary            R67C  BETHIA
      ======                             ======
[R63]  RIPLEY                       [R68]  STEELE
       David Ripley   R19I               Ebenezer Steele   R20C
       Lydia Cary     R19Ia             Susannah Merrill  R20Ca
       ------                             ------
R63A  FAITH                        R68A  JOHN
R63B  LYDIA                        R68B  SUSANNA
R63C  ANN                          R68C  MARY
R63D  IRENE                        R68D  DANIEL
R63E  DAVID                        R68E  HULDAH
```

423

R68F MELETIAH	[R73] BRADFORD
R68G BRADFORD	Perez Bradford R21C
R68H ELISHA	Aabigail Belcher R21Ca
======	------
[R69] HUBBARD	R73A ABIGAIL
John Hubbard R118Aa	R73B HANNAH
Elizabeth Stevens R118A	R73C ELIZABETH
------	R73D PEREZ
R69A LEVERRETT	R73E JOEL
R69B JOHN	R73F GEORGE
R69C DANIEL	R73G JOHN
R69D ELIZABETH	R73H JOSEPH
R69E WILLIAM	R73I MARY
R69F WILLIAM ABDIEL	======
R69G NATHANIEL	[R74] WHITING
R69H AMELIA	Charles Whiting R21Da
======	Elizabeth Bradford R21D
[R70] STEVENS	------
William Stevens R118B	R74A MARY
Ruhamah Earl R118Ba	R74B JOHN
------	R74C SYBIL
R70A RUHAMAH	R74D CHARLES twin
R70B WILLIAM	R74E ELIZABETH twin
R70C CHRISTOPHER	R74F GAMALIEL
R70D JOHN	R74G WILLIAM BRADFORD
R70E LEVERETT	R74H BERNICE
R70F MOSES	R74I EBENEZER
======	======
[R71] GILBERT	[R75] GAY
Nathaniel Gilbert R21Aa	Ebenezer Gay R21Ea
Hannah Bradford R21A	Jerusha Bradford R21E
------	------
R71A NATHANIEL	R75A SAMUEL
R71B HANNAH	R75B ABIGAIL
R71C THOMAS	R75C CALVIN
R71D MARY	R75D MARTIN
R71E SAMUEL	R75E ABIGAIL
R71F WELTHIA	R75F CELIA
R71G DAUGHTER	R75G JOTHAM
R71H ABIGAIL	R75H JERUSHA
======	R75I EBENEZER
[R72] BRADFORD	R75J PERSIS
Gershom Bradford R21B	R75K JOANNA
Priscilla Wiswall R21Ba	======
------	[R76] LANE
R72A SOLOMON	Peter Lane R21Fa
R72B ALEXANDER	Welthea Bradford R21F
R72C PRISCILLA	------
R72D DANIEL	R76A HANNAH
R72E HOPESTILL	R76B IRENE
R72F NOAH	R76C LUCY
R72G RACHEL	R76D GEORGE
R72H JOB	R76E LUCY
R72I JEREMIAH	R76G SYBIL
R72J ELIPHALET	R76H SARAH

[R77] BRADFORD
    Gamaliel Bradford R21G
    Abigail Bartlett R21Ga

R77A ABIGAIL
R77B SAMUEL
R77C GAMANIEL
R77D SETH
R77E PEABODY
R77F DEBORAH
R77G HANNAH
R77H RUTH
R77I PETER   twin
R77J ANDREW   twin
    ======

[R78] KNOWLES
    Nathaniel Knowles R22Aa
    Mary Hunt   R22A

R78A REBECCA
R78B MARY
R78C MALITHIAH
    ======

[R79] HUNT
    William Hunt R22B
    Jane Tilton   R22Ba
    Sarah Gray   R22Bb

R79A ABIA   by Jane
R79B MARY
R79C JANE
R79D HANNAH
R79E SARAH
R79F SAMUEL
    ======

[R80] SHERMAN
    John Sherman R23Aa
    Sarah Baker   R23A

R80A SARAH
R80B JANE
R80C ALICE
R80D JOHN
R80E ABIGAIL
R80F BETHIAH
R80G WILLIAM
R80H KEZIAH
R80I SAMUEL
    ======

[R81] PHILLIPS
    Benjamin Phillips Jr R23Ca
    Eleanor Baker   R23C

R81A JEREMIAH
R81B BENJAMIN

[R82] THOMAS
    Gideon Thomas R23Da
    Abigail Baker R23D

R82A ABIGAIL
R82B MERCY
R82C ANNA
R82D ELIZABETH
R82E SARAH   TWIN
R82F ELEANOR   TWIN
    ======

[R83] BAKER
    Kenelm Baker   R23E
    Pathience Doty R23Ea

R83A JOHN
R83B ALICE
R83C KENELM #1
R83D SARAH
R83E KENELM #2
R83F ELIZABETH
R83G WILLIAM
R83H LUCY
    ======

[R84] BAKER
    Samuel Baker R23H
    Hannah Ford   R23Ha

R84A ELEANOR
R84B HANNAH
R84C BETHIAH
R84D SAMUEL
R84E JAMES
R84F THOMAS
R84G CHARLES
R84H ELIJAH
R84I ABIGAIL
    ======

[R85] BAKER
    William Baker R23I
    Sarah Hurd   R23Ia

R85A WILLIAM
R85B SARAH
R85C BETHIAH
    ======

[R86] BAKER
    Edward Baker   R23J
    Mehetable Blanchard R23Ja
    Hannah Gibbon   R23Jb

R86A EDWARD
R86B MEHITABLE
R86C HANNAH
R86D SHUTE

[R87]   DIMMICK
        Timothy Dimmick R24Aa
        Ann Bradford   R24A

R87A ANN
R87B TIMOTHY
R87C JOHN
R87D JOHANNA
R87E JOSIAH
R87F SIMEON
R87G SYLVANUS
R87H OLIVER
R87I DAN
      ======
[R88]   BRADFORD
        Joseph Bradford   R24B
        Henrietta Swift   R24Ba

R88A ELIZABETH
R88B ANNA
R88C WILLIAM
R88D HENRY SWIFT
R88E ROBERT
R88F HANNAH
R88G JOSEPH
      ======
[R89]   HYDE
        Samuel Hyde   R24Ca
        Priscilla Bradford
        ------   R24C
R89A SAMUEL
R89B ANNE
R89C SYBIL
R89D PRISCILLA
R89E DAN
R89F PRISCILLA
R89G HANNAH
R89H ZERVIAH
R89I ABIGAIL
      ======
[R90]   TUTTLE
        Daniel Tuttle R24Fa
        Sarah Bradford R24F

R90A JOHN
      ======
[R91]   BUELL
        Timothy Buell   R24Ga
        Hannah Bradford R24G

R91A TIMOTHY
R91B ELIJAH
R91C HANNAH

R91D DEBORAH
R91E ICHABOD
R91F OLIVER
R91G JOSEPHAM
      ======
[R92]   LISK
        Andrew Lisk   R24Ha
        Elizabeth Bradford
        ------   R24H
R92A WILLIAM
R92B ANNE
R92C MARTHA
R92D ANDREW
R92E BETTY
R92F SARAH
R92G AMY
R92H HULDAH
      ======
[R93]   HYDE
        David Hyde   R24Ia
        Althea Bradford R24I

R93A DAVID
R93B SIMEON
R93C AVIS
R93D ANNA
R93E ZEBULON
R93F ELIZABETH
R93G ELEANOR
R93H JOEL
      ======
[R94]   JANES
        Jonathan Janes R24Ja
        Irena Bradford R24J

R94A DAVID
R94B JONATHAN
R94C IRENE
R94D ELIPHALET
R94E IRENE
R94F SOLOMON
R94G DANIEL
R94H MARY
R94I JONATHAN
R94J ABIGAIL
R94K ANN
      ======
[R95]   BRADFORD
        John Bradford   R24K
        Esther Sherwood R24Ka

R95A SAMUEL
R95B JOHN
R95C JOSEPH

R95D SARAH
R95E PEREZ
R95F BENJAMIN
R95G ELEANOR
R95H REBECCA
R95I MARY
======

[R96]   ADAMS
        Thomas Adams R25Ba
        Bathsheba Bradford
        ------   R25B

R96A SARAH
R96B JOSHUA
R96C BARTLETT
R96D NATHANIEL
R96E MARY
R96F DEBORAH
======

[R97]   BRADFORD
        Benjamin Bradford R25C
        Zeresh Stetson   R25Ca
        Mercy Chipman   R25Cb

R97A THOMAS by Zeresh
R97B MICHAEL
R97C PEREZ
R97D LYDIA
R97E BENJAMIN
R97F MARCY
R97G LEMUEL
R97H LYDIA
======

[R98]   BRADFORD
        Abner Bradford R25D
        Susannah Potter R25Da

R98A ELIJAH
R98B LEVI #1
R98C ZENAS
R98D MARY
R98E ABIGAIL
R98F ISRAEL
R98G LYDIA
R98H HANNAH
R98I ELISHA
R98J LUCY
R98K PEGGY
R98L LEVI #2
======

[R99]   BRADFORD
        Joshua Bradford R25E
        Hannah Bradford R25Ea

R99A CORNELIUS
R99B SARAH
R99C RACHEL
R99D MARY twin
R99E MELATIAH twin
R99F JOSHUA
R99G HANNAH
R99H JOSEPH
R99I BENJAMIN
R99J ELISHA
R99K WINSLOW
======

[R100] BRADFORD
        Ichabod Bradford R25F
        Mary Johnson   R25Fa
        Mary Samson   R25Fb

R100A ICHABOD by Johnson
R100B ELIZABETH
R100C RHODA
R100D LEMUEL
R100E ANNE
R100F ISRAEL
======

[R101] CHANDLER
        Ebenezer Chandler R26Ca
        Anna Bradford   R26C

R101A LYDIA
R101B ZILPAH
R101C SIMEON
R101D ANNA
R101E NATHANIEL
R101F JUDAH
R101G SCEVA
======

[R102] WHITING
        Azariah Whiting   R26Ea
        Elizabeth Bradford R26E

R102A JOHN
R102B EPHRAIM
R102C PATIENCE
R102D ELIZABETH
======

[R103] HOLMES
        Peleg Holmes   R26Ga
        Abigail Bradford   R26G

R103A ABIGAIL #1
R102B DEBORAH
R103C ABIGAIL #2
R103D PELEG

427

R103E ELIZABETH	R107F RUTH
R103F LYDIA	R107G DEBORAH
R103G NATHANIEL	R107H JOEL
R103H MARY	R107I EPHRAIM
R103I SARAH	R107J REBECCA
======	R107K CYNTHIA
[R104] EVERSON	======
Seth Everson R26Ha	[R108] BRADFORD
Lusanna Bradford R26H	Wait Bradford R26N
------	Welthea Bassett R26Na
R104A HANNAH	------
R104B JAMES	R108A SARAH
R104C OLIVER	R108B SIMEON
R104D LYDIA	R108C DEBORAH
R104E SETH	R108D EPHRAIM
======	======
[R105] CHANDLER	[R109] BRADFORD
Nathan Chandler R26Ka	Nathaniel Bradford R27A
Ruth Bradford R26K	Sarah Spooner R27Aa
------	------
R105A EPHRAIM	R109A NATHANIEL
R105B SELAH	R109B LEMUEL
R105C LUCY	======
R105D HANNAH	[R110] CUSHMAN
R105E CHILD	Elkanah Cushman R27Ca
R105F RUTH	Lydia Bradford R27C
R105G SARAH	------
R105H DEBORAH	R110A ELKANAH
======	======
[R106] BRADFORD	[R111] BRADFORD
Ezekiel Bradford R26L	Nathan Bradford R27D
Betty Chandler R26La	Elizabeth Groce R27Da
------	Sarah Sturtevant R27Db
R106A EPHRAIM	------
R106B DEBORAH	R111A LYDIA by Elizabeth
R106C WILLIAM	R111B JONATHAN
R106D REBECCA	R111C ELIZABETH
R106E JESSE	R111D THOMAS
R106F EZEKIEL	R111E DAVID
R106G CHANDLER	======
R106H MARTIN	[R112] McFARLIN
R106I PHILIP	Elijah McFarlin R28Ea
R106J BETTY	Lauranna Bradford R28E
======	------
[R107] BRADFORD	R112A MARY
Simeon Bradford R26M	R112B ELIJAH
Phebe Whiton R26Ma	R112C HANNAH
------	R112D JOSEPH
R107A ASA	R112E LAURANNA
R107B SIMEON	R112F ABIGAIL
R107C LUCY	R112G SABA
R107D HOSEA	R112H DAVID
R107E ABIGAIL	======

```
[R113]   SAMPSON                    R117B  EBENEZER          [R45]
    Jonathan Sampson Jr R28Ia          a Bridget Brown
    Deborah Bradford   R28I            f Eleazor Brown
    ------                             m Dinah Spaulding
R113A  JONATHAN                   R117C  DANIEL            [R46]
R113B  ELISHA                         a Anna Cook
R113C  HANNAH                     R117D  JERUSHA
R113D  EPHRAIM                        a Daniel Bissell  [R47]
R113E  DEBORAH                        f Daniel Bissell Sr
R113F  NEHEMIAH                       m Margaret Dewey
R113G  SYLVIA                     R117E  LUCY
    ======                             a Henry Cleveland [R48]
[R114]   WATERS                        f Josiah Cleveland
    Zebulon Waters R28Ja               m Mary Bates
    Alice Bradford R28J        R117F  THEOPHILUS        [R49]
    ------                             a Mary Huntington
R114A  NEHEMIAH                       f Joseph Huntington
R114B  ASA                            m Rebecca Adgate
R114C  MATILDA                        b Grace Prentice
R114D  REBECCA                        f Samuel Prentice
R114E  DANIEL                         m Esther Hammond
R114F  HANNAH                     R117G  JABEZ             [R50]
R114G  ZEBULON                        a Lydia Gale
R114H  SAMUEL                         f Abraham Gale
R114I  MOLEY                          m Sarah Fiske
R114J  CHLOE                          b Elizabeth Darbe
    ======                             c Rebecca
[R115]   WATERS                        ======
    Daniel Waters    R28Kb    [R118]   STEVENS
    Azenath Bradford R28K          Samuel Stevens    R12Gb
    ------                         Melatiah Bradford R12G
R115A  BETHIA                         ------
R115B  LUCEE                     R118A  ELIZABETH
R115C  SAMUEL                         a John Hubbard  Jr [R69]
    ======                             f John Hubbard Sr
[R116]   BRADFORD                      m Mable Russel
    Carpenter Bradford R28L   R118B  WILLIAM           [R70]
    Mary Gay          R28La        a Rumaha Earl
    ------                         ======
R116A  CHLOE                     [R119]   HERSHEY
R116B  AZUBAH                         Joshua Hershey   R14Bb
R116C  HANNAH                         Alice Bradford   R14B
R116D  WILLIAM                        ------
R116E  MARY GAY                  R119A  SARAH
R116F  CHLOE                          ======
R116G  EMILY                     [R120]   CUSHMAN
    ======                             Isaac Cushman   R14Db
[R117]   FITCH                         Mercy Bradford  R14D
    James Fitch    R12Db           ------
    Alice Bradford R12D        R120A  FEAR
    ------                     R120B  PRISCILLA
R117A  ABIGAIL        [R44]     R120C  ISAAC
    a John Dyer               R120D  ABIGAIL
    f Joseph Dyer                 ======
    m Hannah Baxter
```

[R121]   LATHROP
    Isreal Lathrop   R24Fb
    Sarah Bradford   R24F

R121A   PRUDENCE
======

[R122]   LeBARON
    Lazarus LeBaron   R27Cb
    Lydia Bradford   R27C

R122A   ISAAC
R122B   ELIZABETH
R122C   LEMUEL
R122D   FRANCIS
R122E   WILLIAM
R122F   PRISCILLA
R122G   MARGARET
======

[R123]   PACKARD
    Benjamin Packard   R28Kc
    Azenath Bradford   R28K

R123A   JOHN
R123B   LOIS
R123C   JEDEDIAH
R123D   MELATIAH
======

```
[T10]    STANDISH              T12E  MYLES              [T18]
         Unknown                    a Experience Sherman
         Unknown                    f William Sherman
         ------                     n Desire Doty
T10A  MYLES          [T11]     T12F  SARAH              [T19]
      a Barbara --                  a Benjamin Soule
      ======                        f John Soule
[T11]    STANDISH                   n Rebecca Simmons
         Myles Standish T10A   T12G  EBENEZER           [T20]
         Barbara --     T10Aa       a Hannah Sturtevant
         ------                     f Samuel Sturtevant
T11A  CHARLES                       n Mercy --
T11B  ALEXANDER      [T12]     T12H  DAVID
      a Sarah Alden           T12I  DESIRE             [T21]
      f John Alden                  a Nathan Weston
      n Priscilla Mullins           f Edmund Weston
      b Desire Doty                 n Rebecca Soule
      f Edward Doty            T12J  THOMAS             [T22]
      n Faith Clark                 a Mary Carver
T11C  JOHN                          f William Carver
T11D  MYLES                         n Elizabeth Foster
      a Sarah Winslow         T12K  ICHABOD            [T23]
      f John Winslow                a Phebe Ring
      n Mary Chilton                f Eleazer Ring
T11E  LORA                          n Mary Shaw
T11F  JOSIAH         [T13]          ======
      a Mary Dingley          [T13]    STANDISH
      f John Dingley                   Josiah Standish T11F
      n Sarah --                       Mary Dingley    T11Fa
      b Sarah Allen                    ------
      f Samuel Allen          T13A  MARY               [T24]
      n Ann --                      a James Cary
T11G  CHARLES                       f John Cary
      ======                        n Elizabeth Godfrey
[T12]    STANDISH              T13B  MARTHA
         Alexander Standish T11B  T13C  MYLES
         Sarah Alden     T11Ba       a Mehitable Cary
         ------                      f John Cary
T12A  LORA           [T14]          n Elizabeth Godfrey
      a Abraham Samson Jr           b Elizabeth Thatcher
      f Abraham Samson Sr     T13D  JOSIAH             [T25]
T12B  LYDIA          [T15]          a Sarah --
      a Isaac Samson          T13E  SAMUEL             [T26]
      f Abraham Samson              a Deborah Gates
T12C  ELIZABETH      [T16]          f Thomas Gates
      a Samuel Delano               n Elizabeth Freeman
      f Philip Delano               b Hannah --
      n Mary Pontus           T13F  ISRAEL             [T27]
T12D  MERCY          [T17]          a Elizabeth Richards
      a Caleb Samson                f William Richards
      f Henry Samson                n Mary Williams
      n Ann Plummer
```

T13G LOIS
  a Hugh Calkins
  f John Calkins
  m Sarah Royce
  b John Sprague Jr
  f John Sprague Sr
  m Ruth Bassett
T13H MERCY
  a Ralph Wheelock [T28]
  f Eleazer Wheelock
  m Elizabeth Fuller
  ======
[T14] SAMSON
    Abraham Samson T12Aa
    Lora Standish T12A

T14A NATHANIEL [T29]
  a Keturah Chandler
  f Benjamin Chandler
  m Elizabeth Buck
T14B ABRAHAM [T30]
  a Penelope Samson
  f James Samson
  m Hannah --
  b Mary --
T14C MILES SAMSON [T31]
  a Sarah Studley
T14D REBECCA
T14E EBENEZER [T32]
  a Zerviah Soule
  f Joshua Soule
  m Joanna Studley
T14F SARAH [T33]
  a Joseph Samson
  f James Samson
  m Hannah --
  b John Rouse
  f Simon Rouse
  m Christianna --
T14G GRACE
  ======
[T15] SAMSON
    Isaac Samson T12Ba
    Lydia Standish T12B

T15A ISAAC [T34]
  a Sarah Barlow
  f John Barlow
  m Elizabeth Dillingham
  b Elizabeth Hodges
  f Henry Hodges
  m Esther Gallop

T15B JONATHAN [T35]
  a Joanna Lucas
  f Benoni Lucas
  m Repentance Harlow
T15C JOSIAH
T15D LYDIA
T15E EPHRAIM [F36]
  a Abigail Horrel
  f Humphery Horrel
  m Elizabeth Smith
T15F PELEG [T37]
  a Mary Ring
  f Eleazer Ring
  m Mary Shaw
T15G PRISCILLA [F38]
  a Jabez Fuller
  f John Fuller
  m Mercy Nelson
T15H BARNABAS [F39]
  a Experience Atkins
  ======
[T16] DELANO
    Samuel Delano T12Ca
    Elizabeth Standish T12C

T16A REBECCA [T40]
  a Benjamin Southworth
  f Edward Southworth
  m Mary Pabodie
T16B PRISCILLA [T41]
  a Benjamin Simmons
  f John Simmons
  m Mercy Pabodie
T16C JANE
T16D SAMUEL [T42]
  a Elizabeth Bonney
  f John Bonney
  m Elizabeth Bishop
T16E HAZADIAH [T43]
  a Mary Taylor
  f Joseph Taylor
  m Experience Williamson
T16F MARY
T16G ELIZABETH [T44]
  a Joseph Chandler
  f Benjamin Chandler
  m Elizabeth Buck
T16H JESSE
T16I SARAH
  a Joshua Simmons
  f Aaron Simmons
  m Mary Woodworth

432

[T17] SAMSON
    Caleb Samson T12Da
    Mercy Standish T12D

T17A DAVID
T17B LORA
T17C RACHEL
T17D PRISCILLA
T17E CALEB
T17F JOSHUA
T17G RUTH
T17H JERUSHA
T17I SARAH
    ======

[T18] STANDISH
    Myles Standish   T12E
    Experience Sherman T12Ea

T18A SARAH   T[45]
    a Abner Weston
    f John Weston
    m Deborah Delano
T18B PATIENCE   [T46]
    a Caleb Jenny
    f Lettice Jenny
    m Desire Blackwell
T18C PRISCILLA
    a Elisha Bisbee
T18D MILES   [T47]
    a Mehitabel Robbins
    f Jeduthan Robbins
    m Hannah Pratt
T18E PENELOPE
    ======

[T19] SOULE
    Benjamin Soule T12Ea
    Sarah Standish T12F

T19A ZACHARIAH
T19B HANNAH
T19C SARAH
T19D DEBORAH
T19E BENJAMIN
T19F EBENEZER
    ======

[T20] STANDISH
    Ebenezer Standish T12G
    Hannah Sturtevant T12Ga

T20A ZACAEIAH   [T48]
    a Abigail Whitman
    f Ebenezer Whitman
    m Abigail Burnam
T20B MOSES   [T49]
    a Rachel Cobb
    f John Cobb
    m Rachel Soule
T20C HANNAH   [T50]
    a Seth Staples
    f John Staples
    m Hannah --
T20D ZERVIAH   [T51]
    a Andrew Ring
    f Eleazer Ring
    m Mary Shaw
    b Andrew Gray
    f John Gray
    m Susanna Clarke
T20E SARAH
    a Jabez Newland
    f Jeremiah Newland
    m Susanna Harris
T20F MERCY
    a Ebenezer Lobdell
    f Isaac Lobdell
    m Sarah Bryant
    b Benjamin Weston
    f Edmund Weston
    m Rebecca Soule
    ======

[T21] WESTON
    Nathan Weston T12Ia
    Desire Standish T12I

T21A NATHAN   [T52]
    a Hannah Everson
    f John Everson
    m Silence Staples

T21B ISAAC   [T53]
    a Mary Ripley
    f John Ripley
    m Deborah Washburn
T21C JACOB
T21D DESIRE   [T54]
    a Edmund Wright
    f Samuel Wright
    m Anna Tilson
    ======
[T22]   STANDISH
    Thomas Standish T12J
    Mary Carver   T12Ja

T22A AMOS
T22B DESIRE
T22C DAVID   [T55]
    a Hannah Magoun
    f David Magoun
    m Rachel Soule
T22D THOMAS   [T56]
    a Martha Bisbee
    f Elisha Bisbee
    m Patience Soanes
T22E MARY   [T57]
    a Joshua Witherell
    f Joseph Witherell
    m Elizabeth Sherman
T22F WILLIAM   [T58]
    a Abigail Stetson
    f John Stetson
    m Abigail Crooker
T22G BETTY
    ======
[T23]   STANDISH
    Ichabod Standish T12K
    Phebe Ring   T12Ka

T23A MARY
T23B DESIRE   [T59]
    a David Hatch Jr
    f David Hatch Sr
    m Elizabeth Chittenden
T23C PHEBE
T23D ICHABOD
    ======
[T24]   CARY
    James Cary T13Aa
    Mary Standish T13A

T24A daughter
T24B son

T24C MERCY   [T60]
    a David Thurston
    f John Thurston
    m Hannah Cary
T24D MARY
T24E JAMES   [T61]
    a Sarah Shaw
    f Joseph Shaw
    m Judith Whitmarsh
T24F HANNAH
T24G ELIZABETH   [T62]
    a John Whitman
    f Nicholas Whitman
    m Sarah Vining
    ======
[T25]   STANDISH
    Josiah Standish T13D
    Sarah --   T13Da

T25A ELEAZER
T25B JEHODEN
T25C MEHITABEL   [T63]
    a Jabez Rood
    f Samuel Rood
    m Mary Mariner
T25D SARAH   [T64]
    a Thomas Howard
    f Benjamin Howard
    m Mary Amos
T25E HANNAH   [T65]
    a Nathan Foster
    f Abraham Foster
    m Mary --
T25F MARY   [T66]
    a Thomas Perkins
    f Thomas Perkins
    m Sarah Richard
T25G JOSIAH
    ======
[T26]   STANDISH
    Samuel Standish T13E
    Deborah Gates   T13Ea

T26A DEBORAH
T26B SAMUEL   [T67]
    a Abigail Brown
    f John Brown
    m Abigail --
T26C LOIS
T26D ABIGAIL   [T68]
    a Rufus Rood
    f Jabez Rood
    m Mehitable Standish

```
T26E  SARAH                        [T30]   SAMSON
T26F  ISRAEL          [T69]                Abraham Samson  T14B
      a Content Ellis                      Penelope Samson T14Ba
      f Richard Ellis              ------
      m Mary Jelson                T30A  RUTH
      b Dorcas Bellows             T30B  HANNAH
      f Nathaniel Bellows          T30C  REBECCA
      m Dorcas Rose                T30D  JAMES
T26G  THOMAS          [T70]        T30E  ABRAHAM
      a Sarah Williams             T30F  STEPHEN
      f Joseph Williams            T30G  HENRY
      m Mary --                    T30H  PENELOPE
      ======                       ======
[T27]   STANDISH                   [T31]   SAMSON
        Israel Standish T13F               Miles Samson  T14C
        Elizabeth Richards T13Fa           Sarah Studley T14Ca
      ------                       ------
T27A  ELIZABETH                    T31A  ANDREW
T27B  MILES           [T71]        T31B  ALICE
      a Jerusha Fuller             T31C  JOSEPH
      f Matthew Fuller             T31D  SARAH
      m Elizabeth Broughton        T31E  DEBORAH
      b Hannah --                  T31F  BERIAH
      c Mehetabel --               T31G  MILES
T27C  AMY             [T72]        T31H  JUDAH
      a Simon Huntington                  ======
      f Thomas Huntington          [T32]   SAMSON
      m Elizabeth Backus                   Ebenezer Samson T14E
T27D  PRUDENCE        [T73]                Zerviah Soule   T14Ea
      a Jacob Sawyer               ------
      f Ephraim Sawyer             T32A  RACHEL
      m Elizabeth George           T32B  JOANNA
      b John Bond                  T32C  EBENEZER
      ======                       T32D  ZERVIAH
[T28]   WHEELOCK                   T32E  ABIGAIL
        Ralph Wheelock T13Ha       T32F  EUNICE
        Mercy Standish T13H        T32G  NATHAN
      ------                       T32H  ANNA
T28A  MARY            [T74]               ======
      a Jabez Bingham              [T33]   SAMSON
      f Jabez Bingham                      Joseph Samson T14Fa
      m Bethia Wood                        Sarah Samson  T14F
      ======                       ------
[T29]   SAMSON                     T33A  JOHN
        Nathaniel Samson T14A      T33B  JOSEPH
        Keturah Chandler T14Aa     T33C  BENJAMIN
      ------                       T33D  LOIS
T29A  NOAH                         T33E  SARAH
T29B  PEREZ                        T33F  RUHAMAH
T29C  FEAR                         T33G  JOHN
T29D  ROBERT                       T33H  MARGARET
T29E  NATHANIEL
T29F  KETURAH
T29G  ANNA
T29H  ABNER
```

[T34]	**SAMSON**	
	Isaac Samson	T15A
	Sarah Barlow	T15Aa
	Elizabeth Hodges	T15Ab

T34A	HANNAH by Barlow	
T34B	URIAH	
T34C	SARAH	
T34D	JOHN	
T34E	MARGARET	
T34F	ANNA by Shaw	
T34G	JACOB	
T34H	ISAAC	
T34I	HANNAH	
T34J	ELIZABETH	
T34K	LYDIA	
T34L	PHEBE	
	======	
[T35]	**SAMSON**	
	Jonathan Samson	T15B
	Joanna Lucas	T15Ba

T35A	MARY	
T35B	JOANNA	
T35C	PRISCILLA	
T35D	ABIGAIL	
T35E	JONATHAN	
T35F	BETHIAH	
T35G	JOSIAH	
	======	
[T36]	**SAMSON**	
	Ephraim Samson	T15E
	Abigail Horrel	T15Ea

T36A	ABIGAIL	
T36B	ELIZABETH	
T36C	LUSANNA	
T36D	EUNICE	
T36E	SARAH	
T36F	MARY twin	
T36G	PRISCILLA twin	
	======	
[T37]	**SAMSON**	
	Peleg Samson	T15F
	Mary Ring	T15Fa

T37A	MARY	
T37B	PELEG	
T37C	MARCY	
T37D	JONATHAN	
T37E	SIMEON	
T37F	PRISCILLA	
	======	

[T38]	**FULLER**	
	Jabes Fuller	T15Ga
	Priscilla Samson	T15G

T38A	DEBORAH	
	======	
[T39]	**SAMSON**	
	Barnabas Samson	T15H
	Experience Atkins	T15Ha

T39A	BARNABAS	
T39B	EXPERIENCE	
T39C	ELIZABETH	
	======	
[T40]	**SOUTHWORTH**	
	Benjamin Southworth	T16Aa
	Rebecca Delano	T16A

T40A	HANNAH	
T40B	EDWARD	
T40C	ELIZABETH	
T40D	THOMAS	
T40E	SARAH	
T40F	REBEKAH	
T40G	CONSTANT	
T40H	DEBORAH	
T40I	OBED	
T40J	JOSHER	
	======	
[T41]	**SIMMONS**	
	Benjamin Simmons	T16Ba
	Priscilla Delano	T16B

T41A	HANNAH	
T41B	BETTY	
T41C	AARON	
T41D	PRISCILLA	
T41E	ABIAH	
	======	
[T42]	**DELANO**	
	Samuel Delano	T16D
	Elizabeth Bonney	T16Da

T42A	RUTH	
T42B	ELISHA	
T42C	PRINCE	
T42D	ICHABOD	
T42E	BETTY	
T42F	ABIGAIL	
	======	

[T43] DELANO
    Hazadiah Delano T16E
    Mary Taylor   T16Ea

T43A JOSEPH
    ======
[T44] CHANDLER
    Joseph Chandler T16Ga
    Elizabeth Delano T16G

T44A JOHN
T44B SIMEON
T44C BENJAMIN
    ======
[T45] WESTON
    Abner Weston T18Aa
    Sarah Standish T18A

T45A MICAH
T45B SETH
T45C HANNAH
T45D DEBORAH
    ======
[T46] JENNY
    Caleb Jenny   T18Ba
    Patience Standish T18B

T46A RUBEN
T46B DESIRE
    ======
[T47] STANDISH
    Miles Standish   T18D
    Mehitabel Robbins T18Da

T47A MILES
T47B PENELOPE
T47C LYDIA
T47D EXPERIENCE
T47E HANNAH
T47F SARAH
T47G PRISCILLA
    ======
[T48] STANDISH
    Zachariah Standish T20A
    Abigail Whitman   T20Aa

T48A EBENEZER
T48B HANNAH
T48C SARAH
T48D ABIGAIL
T48E PELEG
T48F ZACHARIAH
    ======

[T49] STANDISH
    Moses Standish T20B
    Rachel Cobb   T20Ba

T49A ABIGAIL
T49B PACHEL
T49C ZERVIAH
T49D REBECCA
T49E MOSES
T49F SARAH
T49G JOHN
    ======
[T50] STAPLES
    Seth Staples   T20Ca
    Hannah Standish T20C

T50A HANNAH
T50B SARAH
T50C SUSANNA
T50D ANNE
T50E MARY
T50F ZERVIAH
T50G JOHN
T50H RUTH
    ======
[T51] RING
    Andrew Ring   T20Da
    Zerviah Standish T20D

T51A MARY
T51B ANDREW
T51C SUSANAH
T51D HANNAH
T51E WILLIAM
T51F SARAH
T51G ELEAZER
T51H DEBORAH
    ======
[T52] WESTON
    Nathan Weston T21E
    Hannah Everson T21Ea
T52A DESIRE
T52B NATHAN
T52C BENJAMIN
T52D ZABOC
T52E JOSEPH
T52F HANNAH
T52G ABRAHAM
T52H MARY
    ======

DIVISION S
T53-T63

[T53]   WESTON
    Isaac Weston T21B
    Mary Ripley   T21Ba

T53A PATIENCE
T53B MARY
T53C ISAAC
T53D JACOB
T53E ANNA
    ======

[T54]   WRIGHT
    Edmund Wright T21Da
    Desire Weston T21D

T54A LYDIA
T54B ELIZABETH
T54C ENOCH
T54D EDMUND
T54E SAMUEL
    ======

[T55]   STANDISH
    David Standish T22C
    Hannah Magoun T22Ca

T55A LEMUEL
T55B OLIVE
T55C HANNAH
T55D LUCY
T55E PRISCILLA
T55F DAVID
T55G JAMES
T55H JAMES
T55I LUCY
T55J MARY
    ======

[T56]   STANDISH
    Thomas Standish T22D
    Martha Bisbee T22Da

T56A AMOS
T56B BETTY BISBE
T56C SARAH
T56D THOMAS
T56E HADLEY
    ======

[T57]   WITHERELL
    Joshua Witherell T22Ea
    Mary Standish   T22E

T57A JOSHUA
T57B THOMAS
T57C MARY
T57D JOSEPH
    ======

[T58]   STANDISH
    William Standish T22F
    Abigail Stetson T22Fa

T58A JUDITH
T58B WILLIAM
T58C MOLLY
T58D MYLES
T58E JOB
T58F ABIGAIL
    ======

[T59]   HATCH
    David Hatch T23Ba
    Desire Standish T23B

T59A LYDIA
T59B PHEBE
T59C GAMALIEL
T59D JABEZ
T59E ICHABOD
    ======

[T60]   THURSTON
    David Thurston T24Ca
    Mercy Cary T24C

T60A JOHN
T60B ABIGAIL
T60C JAMES
T60D DAVID
T60E MARY
    ======

[T61]   CARY
    James Cary T24E
    Sarah Shaw T24Ea

T61A SARAH
T61B JOSHUA
    ======

[T62]   WHITMAN
    John Whitman T24Ga
    Elizabeth Cary T24G

T62A SAMUEL
T62B ELIZABETH
T62C JOHN
T62D JAMES
    ======

[T63]   ROOD
    Jabez Rood T25Ca
    Mehitabel Standish T25C

T63A ASA
T63B RUFUS
T63C MEHITABLE

T63D	JABEZ		T67C	ABIGAIL
T63E	JOSIAH STANDISH		T67D	ASA
T63F	JEREMIAH			======
T63G	LYDIA		[T68]	ROOD
T63H	EUNICE			Rufus Rood T26Da
	======			Abigail Standish T26D
[T64]	HOWARD			------
	Thomas Howard T25Da			
	Sarah Standish T25D		T68A	ASA
	------		T68B	ABIGAIL
				======
T64A	SARAH		[T69]	STANDISH
T64B	BENJAMIN			Israel Standish T26F
T64C	THOMAS			Content Ellis T26Fa
T64D	JOSEPH			Dorcas Bellows T26Fb
T64E	EUNICE			
T64F	MARTHA		T69A	HANNAH by Ellis
T64G	MARY		T69B	ISRAEL
T64H	ELEAZER		T69C	ELISHA
T64I	NATHAN		T69D	JONAS
T64J	JOHADDEN		T69E	NATHAN
T64K	WILLIAM		T69F	AMASA
	======		T69G	SILAS by Bellows
[T65]	FOSTER		T69H	LEVI
	Nathan Foster T25Ea		T69I	SARAH
	Hannah Standish T25E		T69J	DORCAS
	------			======
T65A	MARY		[T70]	STANDISH
T65B	NATHAN			Thomas Standish T26G
T65C	HANNAH			Sarah Tracy T26Ga
T65D	LOIS			------
T65E	EUNICE		T70A	LUCY
T65F	MEHITABLE		T70B	LYDIA
T65G	PHEBE		T70C	ASA
T65H	SARAH		T70D	LEMUEL
T65I	DANIEL		T70E	MOSES
T65J	ASA			======
T65K	STANDISH		[T71]	STANDISH
	======			Miles Standish T27B
[T66]	PERKINS			Jerusha Fuller T27Ba
	Thomas Perkins T25Fa			Hannah -- T27Bb
	Mary Standish T25F			Mehetabel Orcutt T27Bc

T66A	HANNAH		T71A	ISRAEL
T66B	JOSEPH		T71B	JOSIAH
T66C	TRYPHENA		T71C	ELIZABETH
T66D	EZRA			======
	======		[T72]	HUNTINGTON
[T67]	STANDISH			Simon Huntington T27Ca
	Samuel Standish T26B			Amy Standish T27C
	Abigail Brown T26Ba			------
	------		T72A	ELIZABETH
T67A	SAMUEL		T72B	RUTH
T67B	LOIS		T72C	SIMON
			T72D	ELIZABETH
				======

DIVISION S
T73-T74

[T73] SAWYER
    Jacob Sawyer   T27Da
    Prudence Standish T27E

[T74] BINGHAM
    Jabez Bingham T28Aa
    Mary Wheelock T28A

T73A	JEMIMA	T74A	JABEZ
T73B	ELIZABETH	T74B	RALPH WHEELOCK
T73C	EUNICE	T74C	MARY
T73D	PRUDENCE	T74D	ALVAN
T73E	EPHRAIM	T74E	SILAS
T73F	ABIGAIL	T74F	ACHSAH
T73G	DINAH	T74G	LOIS
T73H	JEREMIAH	T74H	MERCY
T73I	JEMIMA		======
T73J	CORNELIUS		
T73K	JACOB STANDISH		

======

```
[W10]   WARREN                      W12F   ELIZABETH
        unk                                a  Anthony Spragur    [W24]
        unk                         W12G   LYDIA
        ------                             a  James Barnaby      [W25]
W10A   RICHARD           [W11]             b  John Nelson       [W25]
       a  Elizabeth (Jewett ?)      W12H   MERCY
       ======                             a  John Joy           [W26]
[W11]   WARREN                             ======
        Richard      W10A           [W13]    LITTLE
        Elizabeth -- W10Aa                   Thomas Little   W11Ba
                                             Anna Warren     W11B
W11A   MARY                                ------
       a  Robert Bartlett Sr [W12]  W13A   ABIGAIL
       f  Robert Bartlett Jr               a  Josiah Keene
W11B   ANNA                                f  John Keene
       a  Thomas Little     [W13]   W13B   RUTH
W11C   SARAH                        W13C   HANNAH
       a  John Cooke(Mayfl) [W14]          a  Stephen Tilden    [W28]
       f  Francis Cooke (MF)               f  Nathaniel Tilden
       m  Hester Mahieu                    m  Lydia Huckstep
W11D   ELIZABETH                    W13D   PATIENCE
       a  Richard Church    [W15]          a  Joseph Jones      [W29]
W11E   ABIGAIL                             f  Robert Jones
       a  Anthony Snow      [W16]   W13E   MERCY
W11F   NATHANIEL           [W17]          a  John Sawyer        [W30]
       a  Sarah Walker              W13F   ISAAC               [W31]
       f  William Walker                   a  Bethiah Thomas
W11G   JOSEPH              [W18]          f  Nathaniel Thomas
       a  Priscilla Faunce          W13G   EPHRAIM             [W32]
       f  John Faunce                      a  Mary Sturtevant
       m  Patience Morton                  f  Samuel Sturtevant
       ======                       W13H   THOMAS
[W12]    BARTLETT                    W13I   SAMUEL              [W33]
         Robert Bartlett W11Aa             a  Sarah Gray
         Mary Warren     W11A             f  Edward Gray
         ------                            m  Mary Winslow
W12A   BENJAMIN           [W19]            ======
       a  Susannah Jenney           [W14]    COOKE
       f  John Jenney                       John Cooke   W11Ca
       m  Sarah Carey                       Sarah Warren W11C
W12B   REBECCA                             ------
       a  William Harlow    [W20]   W14A   SARAH
W12C   MARY                                a  Arthur Hathaway
       a  Richard Foster\_  [W21]   W14B   ELIZABETH
       b  Jonathan Morey/   [W21]   W14C   HESTER
W12D   SARAH                               a  Thomas Taber
       a  Samuel Rider Jr   [W22]   W14D   MARY
       f  Samuel Rider Sr           W14E   MERCY
       m  Anne Gamlett                     ======
W12E   JOSEPH              [W23]
       a  Hannah Pope
       f  Thomas Pope
       m  Ann Fallowell
```

[W15] CHURCH
    Richard Church W11Da
    Elizabeth Warren W11D

W15A ELIZABETH
  a Caleb Hobart [W34]
  f Thomas Hobart
W15B JOSEPH   [W35]
  a Mary Tucker
  f John Tucker
W15C BENJAMIN   [W36]
  a Alice Southworth
  f Constant Southworth
  m Elizabeth Collier
W15D NATHANIEL   [W37]
  a Sarah Barstow
W15E son
W15F CHARLES
W15G CALEB   [W38]
  a Joanna Sprague
  f William Sprague
  b Deborah --
W15H ABIGAIL
  a Samuel Thaxter [W39]
  f Thomas Thaxter
W15I SARAH
  a James Burroughs [W40]
W15J MARY
W15K DEBORAH
    ======
[W16] SNOW
    Anthony Snow W11Ea
    Abigail Warren W11E

W16A LYDIA
  a Stephen Skeffe [W41]
  f James Skeffe
W16B JOSIAH   [W42]
  a Rebecca Barker
W16C ABIGAIL
  a Michael Ford [W43]
  f William Ford
W16D SARAH
  a Joseph Waterman [W44]
  f Robert Waterman
W16E son
W16F ALICE
  a Robert Barker [W45]
    ======
[W17] WARREN
    Nathaniel Warren W11F
    Sarah Walker   W11Fa

W17A RICHARD 2nd   [W46]
  a Sarah Torrey
  f James Torrey
  m Ann Hatch
W17B SARAH
  a John Blackwell [W47]
W17C HOPE
W17D JANE
  a Benjamin Lombard [W48]
  f Thomas Lombard
W17E ELIZABETH
  a William Green [W49]
W17F ALICE
  a Thomas Gibbs [W50]
W17G MERCY
  a Jonathan Delano [W51]
W17H MARY
W17I NATHANIEL 2nd
  a Phebe Murdock
W17J JOHN
W17K JAMES   [W52]
  a Sarah Doty
  f Edward Doty 2nd
  m Sarah Faunce
W17L JABEZ
    ======
[W18] WARREN
    Joseph Warren W11G
    Priscilla Faunce W11Ga

W18A MERCY
  a John Bradford [W53]
  f William Bradford
  m Alice Richards
W18B ABIGAIL
W18C JOSEPH   [W54]
  a Mehitable Wilder
  f Edward Wilder
  m Elizabeth Eames
W18D PATIENCE
  a Samuel Lucas [W55]
  f Thomas Lucas
W18E ELIZABETH
  a Josiah Finney [W56]
  f John Finney
  m Elizabeth Bailey
W18F BENJAMIN   [W57]
  a Hannah Morton
  f Ephraim Morton
  m Hannah Finney
  b Esther Barnes
  f Jonathan Barnes
    ======

[W19] BARTLETT
    Benjamin Bartlett W12A
    Samuel Jenney   W12Aa

W19A BENJAMIN   [W58]
    a Ruth Pabodie
    f William Pabodie
    m Elizabeth Alden
W19B REBECCA
    a William Bradford
    f William Bradford
    m Alice Richard
W19C SAMUEL
    a Hannah Pabodie
    f William Pabodie
    m Elizabeth Alden
W19D EBENEZER
    a Hannah --
W19E SARAH
    a Robert Bartlett
    f Joseph Bartlett
    m Hannah Pope
W19F ICHABOD
    a Elizabeth Waterman
    f Joseph Waterman
    m Sarah Snow
    ======
[W20]   HARLOW
    William Harlow   W12Ba
    Rebecca Bartlett W12B

W20A WILLIAM
W20B SAMUEL
    a Priscilla --
    b Hannah --
W20C REBECCA
W20D WILLIAM
    a Lydia Cushman
    f Thomas Cushman
    m Mary Allerton
    ======
[W21]   FOSTER/MOREY
    Richard Foster   W12Ca
    2. Jonathan Morey W12Cb
    Mary Bartlett   W12C
    ------
by Foster:
W21A MARY FOSTER
W21B BENJAMIN FOSTER
by Morey:
W21C JONATHAN MOREY
    a Hannah Bourne
    f Job Bourne
    m Ruhamah Hallett

W21D JOHN MOREY
W21E HANNAH MOREY
    a John Bumpas Jr
    f John Bumpas Sr
    ======
[W22]   RIDER
    Samuel Rider   W12Da
    Sarah Bartlett W12D

W22A SAMUEL
W22B JOHN
    a Hannah Barnes
    f Jonathan Barnes
    b Mary --
W22C MERCY
    ======
[W23]   BARTLETT
    Joseph Bartlett W12E
    Hannah Pope   W12Ea

W23A ROBERT
    a Sarah Bartlett
    b Sarah Cooke
W23B JOSEPH
    a Lydia Griswold
    f Francis Griswold
    m Mary Tracy
W23C ELNATHAN
    a Hannah Mansfield
W23D HANNAH
    a Joseph Sylvester Jr
    f Joseph Sylvester Sr
    m Mary Barstow
W23E MARY
    a John Barnes
    f Jonathan Barnes
    m Elizabeth Hedge
W23F SARAH
    a Elisha Holmes
    f Nathaniel Holmes
    m Mercy Faunce
W23G BENJAMIN
    a Sarah Barnes
    f Jonathan Barnes
    m Elizabeth Hedge
    ======
[W24]   SPRAGUE
    Anthony Sprague   W12Fa
    Elizabeth Bartlett W12F

W24A ANTHONY
    a Mary Tilden
    f Thomas Tilden
    m Mary Holmes

W24B BENJAMIN
W24C JOHN
W24D ELIZABETH
W24E SAMUEL
  a Elizabeth Huet
  f Timothy Huet
W24F SARAH
  a Caleb Bates
  f Joseph Bates
  m Esther Hilliard
W24G JAMES
  a Elizabeth Fearing
  f Isreal Fearing
  m Elizabeth Wilder
W24H JOSIAH
  a Elizabeth Wilder
  f John Wilder
  m Rebecca Doggett
W24I JEREMIAH
  a Priscilla Knight
W24J RICHARD
  a Mary ---
W24K MATTHEW
  a Sarah Fearing
  f Isreal Fearing
  m Elizabeth Wilder
  ======
[W25] BARNABY/NELSON
  James Barnaby W12Ga
  (2)John Nelson W12Gb
  Lydia Bartlett W12C
  ------
by James Barnaby
W25A JAMES BARNABY
  a Joanna Harlow
  f William Harlow
  m Mary Shelley
W25B STEPHEN BARNABY
  a Ruth Morton
  f George Morton
  m Joanna Kempton
by John Nelson
W25C SAMUEL NELSON
  a Hannah Ford
  f Michael Ford
  m Abigail Snow
 D JOANNA
  ======
[W26] JOY
  John Joy W12Ha
  Mercy Bartlett W12H

W26A JOHN
  ======

[W27] KEENE
  Josiah Keene W13Aa
  Abigail Little W13A

W27A JOSIAH
  a Lydia Baker
  f Samuel Baker
  m Eleanor Winslow
  ======
[W28] TILDEN
  Stephen Tilden W13Ca
  Hannah Little W13C

W28A HANNAH
W28B STEPHEN
  a Mary Powell
  f Roland Powell
W28C ABIGAIL
  a Charles Stockbridge Jr
  f Charles Stockbridge Sr
W28D MARY
  a James Thomas
  f John Thomas
  m Sarah Pitney
W28E JUDITH
  a William Pabodie Jr
  f William Pabodie
  m Elizabeth Alden
W28F JOSEPH
  a Joanna Bouls
  f Samuel Bolles sic
  m Mary Dyer
W28G MERCY
  a Benjamin Stockbridge
W28H RUTH
  a Nathaniel Tilden
  b Ebenezer Pierce
W28I ISAAC
  a Martha Mudge
  f Micah Mudge
  m Mary Alexander
  b Rebecca Mann
  f Richard Mann
  m Elizabeth Sutton
W28J EPHRAIM
W28K EBENEZER
  a Mary Vinall
  f Stephen Vinall
  m Mary Baker
W28L DAVID
  a Abigail Pitcher
  f Nathaniel Pitcher
  m Mary Clap
  ======

DIVISION S
W29-W32

```
      ======                    ======
[W29]  JONES              [W31]  LITTLE
       Joseph Jones  W13Da        Isaac Little    W13F
       Patience Little W13D        Bethiah Thomas  W13Fa
      ------                    ------
W29A  JOHN                 W31A  THOMAS
   a  Elinor Winslow          a  Mary Hayhew
   f  Nathaniel Winslow       f  Matthew Mayhew
   m  Faith Miller            m  Mary Skiffe
W29B  JOSEPH               W31B  DOROTHY
   a  Sarah Ford           W31C  ISAAC =L15Baf
   f  William Ford            a  Mary Otis
   m  Sarah Dingley           f  John Otis
W29C  BENJAMIN               m  Mercy Bacon
   a  Susanna Beal            b  Abigail Cushing
   f  Nathaniel Beal          f  Joshua Cushing
W29D  PATIENCE                m  Mary Bacon
W29E  ANNA                 W31D  BETHIAH
   a  Joseph Sturtevant    W31E  CHARLES
   f  Samuel Sturtevant       a  Sarah Warren
W29F  RUTH                    f  James Warren
W29G  SARAH                   m  Sarah Doty
   a  John Doty            W31F  ABIGAIL
   f  Edward Doty          W31G  BETHIAH
   m  Faith Clark          W31H  NATHANIEL
   b  Joseph Peterson      W31I  WILLIAM
W29H  EPHRAIM                 a  Hannah Willard
   a  Margaret Fearing        f  Samuel Willard
   f  Israel Fearing          m  Eunice Tyng
   m  Elizabeth Wilder     W31J  BETHIAH
W29I  MARY                    a  Thomas Barker
W29J  THOMAS                  f  Francis Barker
   a  Catherine Caswell       m  Mary Lincoln
   f  William Caswell      W31K  LEMUEL
   m  Mercy Lincoln           a  Jane Sarson
                              f  Samuel Sarson
      ======                  m  Ann Platts
[W30]  SAWYER                ======
       John Sawyer  W13Ea [W32]  LITTLE
       Mercy Little W13E          Ephraim Little  W13G
      ------                      Mary Sturtevant W13Ga
W30A  MERCY                 ------
   a  Anthony Eames      W32A  ANNA
   f  Mark Eames            a  Thomas Gray
W30B  SUSANNA                f  Edward Gray
W30C  THOMAS                 m  Dorothy Lettice
   a  Mary --            W32B  EPHRAIM
W30D  JOSIAS                 a  Sarah Clark
   a  Martha Seabury         f  William Clark
   f  Samuel Seabury         m  Hannah Griswold
   m  Martha Pabodie     W32C  MERCY
W30E  MARY                   a  Job Otis
W30F  ANNE                   f  John Otis
      ======                 m  Mary Jacob
```

W32D DAVID
  a Elizabeth Southworth
  f William Southworth
  m Rebecca Pabodie
W32E JOHN
  a Constant Fobes
  f William Fobes
  m Martha Pabodie
W32F MARY
W32G RUTH
  a John Avery
  f Robert Avery
  m Elizabeth Lane
W32H BARNABAS
======
[W33] LITTLE
  Samuel Little W13I
  Sarah Gray   W13Ia

W33A THOMAS
W33B SARAH
  a Richard Billings
  f Ebenezer Billings
  m Hannah Wales
W33C SAMUEL
  a Mary Briggs
  b Hannah ---
W33D EDWARD
  a Mary Walker
  f Thomas Walker
  m Elizabeth Parris
======
[W34] HOBART
  Caleb Hobart   W15Aa
  Elizabeth Church W15A

W34A JONATHON
======
[W35] CHURCH
  Joseph Church W15B
  Mary Tucker   W15Ba

W35A JOSEPH
  a Grace Shaw
  f Anthony Shaw
  m Alice Stonard
W35B ELIZABETH
  a Joseph Blackman
  f John Blackman
W35C MARY
  a John Wood Jr
  f John Wood Sr
  m Mary Peabody

W35D JOHN
  a Rebecca Blackman
W35E ALICE
W35F BENJAMIN
W35G SARAH
W35H WILLIAM
W35I DEBORAH
  a Samuel Gray
  f Edward Gray
  m Dorothy Lettice
W35J ABIGAIL
  a William Simmons
  f John Simmons
  m Mercy Pabodie
======
[W36] CHURCH
  Benjamin Church W15C
  Alice Southworth W15Ca

W36A THOMAS
  a Sarah Hayman
  f Nathaniel Hayman
  m Elizabeth Allen
W36B CONSTANT
  a Patience Cook
  f John Cook
  m Mary Havens
W36C ALICE
  a Ephraim Thomas
  f John Thomas
  m Sarah Pitney
W36D EDWARD
  a Martha Burton
  f Stephen Burton
  m Abigail Brenton
W36E CHARLES
  a Hannah Paine
  f Nathaniel Paine
  m Dorothy Rainsford
W36F ELIZABETH
  a Joseph Rothbotham
  b John Sampson
  c Samuel Woodbury
W36G NATHANIEL
======
[W37] CHURCH
  Nathaniel Church W15D
  Sarah Barstow   W15Da

W37A ABIGAIL
  a James Buck
  f Isaac Buck
  b Nathaniel Harlow
  f William Harlow
  m Mary Faunce

W37B RICHARD
  a Hannah Stover
W37C NATHANIEL
  a Judith Bosworth
  f Benjamin Bosworth
  m Hannah Morton
W37D ALICE
W37E JOSEPH
  a Judith Harlow
  f William Harlow
  m Mary Shelley
W37F CHARLES
  a Mary Pope
  f Seth Pope
  m Deborah Perry
W37G SARAH
  a John Holmes
  ======
[W38] CHURCH
  Caleb Church W15G
  Joanna Sprague W15Ga

W38A HANNAH
  a Matthew Boomer
W38B RUTH
  a John Haddocks
  f Henry Haddocks
  m Mary Wellington
  b Joseph Child Jr
  f Joseph Child Sr
  m Sarah Platt
  c Thomas Ingersole
  f John Ingersole
  m Mary Hunt
W38C LYDIA
  a Samuel Hastings
  f Thomas Hastings
  m Margaret Cheney
W38D CALEB
W38E JOSHUA
W38F ABIGAIL
W38G ISAAC
  a Mary Hutchins
  f Nicholas Hutchins
  m Elizabeth Farr
W38H REBECCA
  a Joshua Warren
  f Daniel Warren
  m Mary Barron
  ======
[W39] THAXTER
  Samuel Thaxter W15Aa
  Sarah Church W15A

W39A ABIGAIL
W39B SARAH
  a Peter Dunbar
  f Robert Dunbar
W39C ABIGAIL 2
W39D DAVID
  a Alice Chubbuck
  f John Chubbuck
  m Martha Beal
W39E MARY
W39F JOHN
W39G SAMUEL
  ======
[W40] BURROUGHS
  James Burrows W15Ia
  Sarah Church W15I

W40A JAMES
W40B MARY
W40C ELIZABETH
W40D THOMAS
  a Abigail --
  ======
[W41] SKEFFE
  Stephen Skeffe W16Aa
  Lydia Snow W16A

W41A ABIGAIL
  a Shubal Smith
  f John Smith
W41B DEBORAH
  a Stephen Presbury
W41C MARCY
  a John Chipman Jr
  f John Chipman Sr
  m Hope Howland
W41D LYDIA
  a John Blackwell Jr
  f John Blackwell Sr
  m Sarah Warren
W41E STEPHEN
  a Sarah Lathrop
  f Barnabas Lathrop
  m Susanna Clark
  b Thankful Gorham
  f James Gorham
  m Mary Joyce
  ======

447

```
    ======
[W42] SNOW
     Josiah Snow      W16B
     Rebecca Barker W16Ba
     ------
W42A  ABIGAIL
W42B  LYDIA
     a  Nathaniel Winslow  Jr
     f  Nathaniel Winslow  Sr
W42C  MERCY
     a  Gilbert Winslow
     f  Nathaniel Winslow
     m  Faith Miller
W42D  DEBORAH
W42E  SARAH
     a  Samuel Baker  Jr
     f  Samuel Baker  Sr
     m  Patience Barstow
W42F  BETHIAH
     a  John Sprague
     f  Samuel Sprague
     m  Sarah Chillingworth
W42G  LUSANNAH
     a  Joseph Waterman  Jr
     f  Joseph Waterman  Sr
     m  Sarah Snow
W42H  REBECCA
W42I  ABIAH
     a  Nathan Thomas
     f  Samuel Thomas
     m  Mercy Ford
     ======
[W43] FORD
     Michael Ford  W16Ca
     Abigail Snow  W16C
     ------
W43A  LYDIA
     a  Experience Branch
     f  John Branch
     m  Mary Speed
W43B  HANNAH
     a  Samuel Nelson
     f  John Nelson
     m  Lydia Bartlett
W43C  WILLIAM
     a  Elizabeth --
     b  Patience Dilly
W43D  JAMES
     a  Hannah Dingley
     f  Jacob Dingley
     m  Elizabeth Newton
W43E  BATHSHEBA
W43F  ABIGAIL
W43G  PATIENCE
     ======
```

```
    ======
[W44] WATERMAN
     Joseph Waterman W16Da
     Sarah Snow      W16D
     ------
W44A  SARAH
     a  Solomon Hewett
     f  John Hewett
     m  Martha Winter
W44B  JOSEPH
     a  Lusanna Snow
     f  Josiah Snow
     m  Rebecca Barker
W44C  ELIZABETH
     a  Ichabod Bartlett
     f  Benjamin Bartlett
W44D  ABIGAIL
     a  Kenelm Winslow
     f  Nathaniel Winslow
     m  Faith Miller
W44E  ANTHONY
     a  Elizabeth Arnold
     f  Seth Arnold
     m  Elizabeth Gray
W44F  BETHIAH
     a  Samuel Doggett  Jr
     f  Samuel Doggett  Sr
     m  Mary Rogers
W44G  LYDIA
     a  John Thomas
     f  Samuel Thomas
     m  Mercy Ford
     ======
[W45] BARKER
     Robert Barker    W16Fa
     Alice Snow       W16F
     ------
W45A  ABIGAIL
     b  Michael Wanton
     f  Edward Wanton
W45B  JAMES
     a  Hannah Allen
     f  Daniel Allen
     m  Bathshua Hoxie
W45C  CALEB
     a  Anne Carr
     f  John Carr
     m  Waite Easton
W45D  DEBORAH
     a  Prince Howland
     f  Arthur Howland
     m  Elizabeth Prence
     b  Benjamin Keen
     f  Josiah Keen
     m  Lydia Baker
     ======
```

```
W45E  LUCEANNA                        W47D  ALICE
W45F  ROBERT                              a  William Spooner
    a  Lydia Booth                        f  John Spooner
    f  John Booth                         m  Rebecca Peckham
    m  Mary Dodson                  W47E  JANE
W45G  ALICE                               a  Philip Peckham
    a  Matthew Estes                      f  Thomas Peckham
    f  Richard Estes                W47F  CALEB
W45H  LYDIA                               a  Bethia Taber
    a  Ebenezer Stetson                   f  Thomas Taber
    f  Thomas Stetson                     m  Mary Tomson
    m  Sarah Dodson                 W47G  NATHANIEL
      ======                             a  Joanna Hathaway
[W46] WARREN                             f  John Hathaway
    Richard Warren 2nd  W17A            m  Joanna Pope
    Sarah Torrey        W17Aa             ======
      ------                        [W48] LOMBARD
W46A  JAMES                              Benjamin Lombard Sr  W17Da
W46B  SAMUEL                             Jane Warren          W17D
    a  Eleanor Billington                ------
    f  Isaac Billington
    m  Hannah Glass                 W48A  MERCY
W46C  HOPE                               a  Ebenezer Burgess
    a  David Torrey                      f  Jacob Burgess
    f  James Torrey                      m  Mary Nye
    m  Edith Rawlins                W48B  BENJAMIN Jr
W46D  ANNE                               a  Hannah Treddeway
    a  John May                          f  Jonathan Treddeway
W46E  JOHN                               m  Judith Thurston
    a  Naomi Bates                       b  Sarah Crocker(Ear.No.X31G)
    b  Anne Reed                         f  Job Crocker(Early No.X30F)
    f  James Reed                        m  Hannah Taylor
    m  Susanna Richmond             W48C  HOPE
W46F  JOANNA                             a  Benjamin Goodspeed
    a  Samuel Bumpas                     f  Ebenezer Goodspeed
    f  Thomas Bumpas                     m  Lydia Crowel
    m  Phebe Lovel                        ======
      ======                        [W49]   GREEN
[W47] BLACKWELL                            William Green    W17Ea
    John Blackwell  W17Ba                  Elizabeth Warren W17E
    Sarah Warren    W17B                   ------
      ------                        W49A  WILLIAM
W47A  JOHN                               a  Desire Bacon
    a  Lydia Skeffe                      f  John Bacon
    f  Stephen Skeffe                    m  Mary Hawes
    m  Lydia Snow                        b  Mary Fuller
W47B  MICHAEL                            f  Thomas Fuller
W47C  DESIRE                             m  Elizabeth Lothrop
    a  Lettice Jenney                     ======
    f  Samuel Jenney                [W50]   GIBBS
                                          Thomas Gibbs  W17Fa
                                          Alice Warren  W17F
                                          ------
```

W50A BETHIAH
W50B ABIGAIL(Early Mo.W32A)
   a Jireh Swift
   f William Swift
   m Elizabeth--
W50C THOMAS
   a Joanna Swift
   f William Swift
W50D SARAH
   a Isaac Cushman Jr
   f Isaac Cushman Sr
   m Rebecca--
W50E WARREN
   a Abigail Hilliard
   f William Hilliard
   m Deborah Warren
W50F EBENEZER
W50G JABEZ
W50H CORNELIUS
   a Meribah Perry
   f Benjamin Perry
   m Dinah Swift
   ======
[W51] DELANO
   Jonathan Delano W17Ga
   Mercy Warren W17G

W51A JONATHAN
   a Amy Hatch
   f Joseph Hatch
   m Amy Allen
W51B JABEZ
   a Mary(Mercy)Delano
   b Hannah Peckham
   f Stephen Peckham
   m Mary --
W51C SARAH
W51D MERCY
   a Joseph Hatch Jr
   f Joseph Hatch Sr
   m Amey Allen
W51E NATHAN
   a Elizabeth Miller
   f John Miller
   m Mercy
W51F BETHIAH
W51G SUSANNA
   a Ebenezer Nye
   f Caleb Nye
   m Elizabeth--
W51H son
W51I NATHANIEL
   a Elizabeth Durfee

W51Iaf Robert Durfee
   m Mary Sanford
W51J ESTHER
W51K JETHRO
   a Elizabeth Pope
   f John Pope
   m Elizabeth Bourne
W51L THOMAS
   a Jane Peckham
   f Stephen Peckham
   m Mary--
   ======
[W52] WARREN
   James Warren W17K
   Sarah Doty W17Ka

W52A JOHN
W52B EDWARD
W52C SARAH
   a Charles Little
   f Isaac Little
   m Bethia Thomas
W52D ALICE
   a Peleg Ford
   f John Ford
   m Hannah--
W52E PATIENCE
   a Joseph Stacey
   f Thomas Stacey
   m Hannah Hicks
W52F JAMES
   a Penelope Winslow
   f Isaac Winslow
   m Sarah Wensley
W52G HOPE
   a Nathaniel Thomas Jr
   f Nathaniel Thomas Sr
W52H MARCY
W52I MARY
W52J ELIZABETH
   ======
[W53] BRADFORD
   John Bradford W18Aa
   Mercy Warren W18A

W53A JOHN
W53B ALICE
W53C ABIGAIL
W53D MERCY
W53E SAMUEL
W53F PRISCILLA
W53G WILLIAM

[W54] WARREN
    Joseph Warren   W18C
    Mehitable Wilder W18Ca

W54A JOSEPH d.yg.
W54B JOSEPH
    a Alathea Chittenden
    f Joseph Chittenden
W54C PRISCILLA
    ======
[W55] LUCAS
    Samuel Lucas   W18Da
    Patience Warren W18D

W55A JOHN
W55B JOSEPH
    a Persis Shaw
    f Jonathan Shaw
    m Mehitable Pratt
W55C WILLIAM
    a Mehitable Doty
    f John Doty
    m Mehitable Nelson
W55D PATIENCE
    a Nathaniel Harlow Jr
    f Nathaniel Harlow Sr
    m Abigail Church
    ======
[W56] FINNEY
    Josiah Finney W18Ea
    Elizabeth Warren W18E

W56A JOSIAH
W56B ELIZABETH
    a William Bradford Jr
    f William Bradford Sr
W56C ROBERT
    a Ann Morton
    f Eleazer Morton
    m Rebecca Marshall
W56D PRISCILLA
    a Samuel Marshall Jr
    f Samuel Marshall Sr
    m Sarah --
W56E JOSIAH
    a Abigail Bryant
    f Samuel Bryant
    m Joanna --
W56F JOHN
    a Sarah Bartlett
    f Robert Bartlett
    m Sarah Cooke

W56G PHEBE
    a Jonathan Barnes
    f John Barnes
    m Mary Bartlett
W56H JOSHUA
    a Hannah Curtis
    f Francis Curtis Jr
    m Hannah Bosworth
    ======
[W57] WARREN
    Benjamin Warren W18F
    Hannah Morton   W18Fa

W57A BENJMIN d.yg.
W57B ABIGAIL
    a Joseph Rider
    f Samuel Rider
    m Lydia Tilden
W57C HANNAH
    a Eleazer Faunce
    f Joseph Faunce
    m Judith Rickard
W57D NATHANIEL
    a Sarah Morton
    f Ephraim Morton
    m Susanna Morton
W57E BENJAMIN
    a Rebecca Doty
    f Isaac Doty
    m Martha Faunce
W57F PRISCILLA
W57G PATIENCE
W57H JOSEPH
W57I MERCY
    a Sylvanus Bramhall
    f Joshua Bramhall
    m Sarah Rider
    ======
[W58] BARTLETT
    Benjamin Bartlett W19A
    Ruth Pabodie   W19Aa

W58A ROBERT
W58B SARAH
W58C REBECCA
W58D RUTH
W58E MERCY
W58F WILLIAM
W58G PRISCILLA
W58H DEBORAH
W58I ABIGAIL

DIVISION S
X10-X14

[X10] ROGERS
    unk
    unk

X10A THOMAS MF [X11]
    a Elizabeth --
    ======
[X11] ROGERS
    Thomas Rogers X10A
    Elizabeth -- X10Aa

X11A JOSEPH MF [X12]
    a Hannah --
X11B JOHN [X13]
    a Anna Churchman
    ======
[X12] ROGERS
    Joseph Rogers X11A
    Hannah -- X11Aa

X12A SARAH
X12B JOSEPH
X12C THOMAS [X14]
    a Elizabeth Snow =H12G
    f Nicholas Snow
    m Constance Hopkins MF
X12D ELIZABETH =H17Gam
    a Jonathan Higgins [X15]
    f Richard Higgins
    m Lydia Chandler
X12E JOHN [X16]
    a Elizabeth Twining
    f William Twining
    m Elizabeth Dean
X12F MARY
    a John Phinney Jr [X17]
    f John Phinney Sr
X12G JAMES [X18]
    a Mary Paine
    f Thomas Paine
    m Mary Snow
X12H HANNAH
    a Jonathan Higgins [X19]
    f Richard Higgins
    m Lydia Chandler
    ======
[X13] ROGERS
    John Rogers X11B
    Anna Churchman X11Ba

X13A JOHN [X20]
    a Elizabeth Pabodie
    f William Pabodie
    m Elizabeth Alden
    b Hannah Hobart
    f Peter Hobart
    c Marah Cobham
    f Josiah Cobham
    m Mary Haffield
X13B ANNA or (Hannah)
    a John Tisdale Jr [X21]
    f John Tisdale Sr
    m Sarah Walker
    b Thomas Terry [X22]
    c Samuel Williams
    f Richard Williams
    m Frances Dighton
X13C ABIGAIL
    a John Richmond Jr [X23]
    f John Richmond Sr
X13D ELIZABETH
    a Nathaniel Williams [X24]
    ======
[X14] ROGERS
    Thomas Rogers X12C
    Elizabeth Snow X12Ca

X14A ELIZABETH
X14B JOSEPH [X25]
    a Prudence --
X14C HANNAH
    a Maziah Harding [X26]
    f Joseph Harding
    m Bethia Cooke
X14D THOMAS [X27]
    a Sarah Treat
    f Samuel Treat
    m Elizabeth Mayo
    b Rebecca Sparrow
    f John Sparrow
    m Aphiah Tracey
X14E ELEAZER [X28]
    a Ruhamah Willis
    f Richard Willis
    m Patience Bonum
X14F NATHANIEL
    ======

452

[X15] HIGGINS
   Jonathan Higgins X12Da
   Elizabeth Rogers X12D

X15A BERIAH   [X29]
  a unk --
X15B JONATHAN   [X30]
  a Lydia Sparrow
  f Jonathan Sparrow
  m Rebecca Bangs
X15C JOSEPH   [X31]
  a Ruth --
X15D JEMIMA
  a John Mulford
  f Thomas Mulford
  m Elizabeth Barnes
X15E HANNAH
  a Nicholas Paine   [X32]
  f Thomas Paine
  m Mary Snow
X15F ELISHA   [X33]
  a Jane Collins
  b Elizabeth --
  c Rachel Lincoln
  ======
[X16] ROGERS
   John Rogers   X12E
   Elizabeth Twining X12Ea

X16A SAMUEL
X16B JOHN   [X34]
  a Priscilla Hamblin
  f John Hamblin
  m Sarah Bearse
  b Sarah Williams
  f Thomas Williams
  m Elizabeth Tart
X16C JUDAH   [X35]
  a Patience Lumbard
  f Thomas Lumbard
  m Elizabeth Derby
X16D JOSEPH   [X36]
  a Mercy Crisp
  f George Crisp
  m Hepsibah Cole
  b Sarah Hamilton
  f Daniel Hamilton
  m Sarah Smith
X16E ELIZABETH
X16F ELEAZER   [X37]
  a Martha Young
  f Henry Young
  m Sarah Snow

X16G MEHITABLE
  a Nathaniel Mayo   [X38]
  f Nathaniel Mayo Sr
  m ELizabeth Wixon
X16H HANNAH
  a James Smith   [X39]
  f Daniel Smith
  m Mary Young
X16I NATHANIEL   [X40]
  a Elizabeth Crosby
  f Simon Crosby
  m Mary Nickerson
  b Silence Dimmock
  ======
[X17] PHINNEY
   John Phinney   X12Fa
   Mary Rogers   X12F

X17A JOHN   [X41]
  a Sarah Lumbart
  f Thomas Lumbart
  m Elizabeth Derby
X17B JOSEPH   [X42]
  a Mercy Bryant
  b Esther West
  f Peter West
  m Patience --
X17C THOMAS   [X43]
  a Sarah --
X17D EBENEZER   [X44]
  a Susanna Linnell
  f David Linnell
  m Hannah Shelby
X17E SAMUEL   [X45]
  a Bethya Smith
X17F MARY
  a John Eastland   [X46]
  b Jonathan Bryant
  f John Bryant
  m Abigail Bryant
X17G MERCY
  a Eleazer Crocker   [X47]
  f William Crocker
  m Alice --
X17H RELIANCE
  a John Morton   [X48]
  f Ephraim Morton
  m Hannah Finney
X17I BENJAMIN   [X49]
  a Martha Crocker
  f Joseph Crocker
  m Temperance Bursley

```
X17I  BENJAMIN cont.              X19E  SARAH
   b Elizabeth Young                 a William Mitchell  [X58]
   f Henry Young                     f William Mitchell Sr
   m Sarah --                        m Mercy Nickerson
X17J  JONATHAN         [X50]         ======
   a Elizabeth --                 [X20]  ROGERS
   b Deborah Wade                     John Rogers         X13A
   f Thomas Wade                      Elizabeth Pabodie  X13Aa
   m Elizabeth Curtis                ------
X17K  HANNAH                       X20A  HANNAH
   ======                            a Samuel Bradford    [X59]
[X18]  ROGERS                         f William Bradford
   James Rogers    X12G               m Alice Richard
   Mary Paine      X12Ga           X20B  JOHN
   ------                         X20C  ELIZABETH
X18A  JAMES           [X51]          a Silvester Richmond [X60]
   a Susanna Tracy                   f Edward Richmond
   f John Tracy                      m Abigail Davis
   m Mary Prence                  X20D  RUTH
X18B  MARY                        X20E  SARAH
   a John Cole Jr    [X52]           a Nathaniel Searle  [X61]
   f John Cole Sr                    f Robert Searle
   m Ruth Snow                       m Deborah Salter
X18C  ABIGAIL                         ======
   a John Yates Jr   [X53]      [X21]  TISDALE
   f John Yates Sr                    John Tisdale Jr   X13Ba
   ======                            Anna Rogers        X13B
[X19]  HIGGINS                         ------
   Jonathan Higgins X12Ha      X21A  ABIGAIL
   Hannah Rogers    X12H           a William Makepeace  [X62]
   ------                            f William Makepeace
X19A  ELIZABETH                       m Ann Johnson
   a Thomas Mayo Jr  [X54]      X21B  JOHN              [X63]
   f Thomas Mayo Sr                  a Deborah Deane
   m Barbara Knowles                 f Thomas Deane
X19B  MARY                            m Katharine Stephens
   a James Young     [X55]           b Abigail Burt
   f Joseph Young                    f Richard Burt
   m Sarah Davis                     m Charity Hill
X19C  REBECCA                     X21C  ANNA
   a Jacob Hurd      [X56]           a George Leonard    [X64]
   f John Hurd                       f Thomas Leonard
X19D  JAMES           [X57]           m Mary Watson
   a Sarah Mayo                      b Nathaniel Thomas Jr
   f Samuel Mayo                     f Nathaniel Thomas Sr
   m Ruth Hopkins                    m Deborah Jacobs
   b Sarah Bixbie               X21D  REMEMBER
   f Joseph Bixbie                   a Nicholas Stephens [X65]
   m Sarah Gould                     f Richard Stephens
                                     m Mary Lincoln
```

454

[X22]   TERRY
    Thomas Terry   X13Bb
    Anna Rogers   X13B

X22A THOMAS   [X66]
  a Abigail Dean
  f Isaac Dean
  m Hannah Leonard
X22B JOHN   [X67]
  a Remember Farrow
  f John Farrow
  m Mary Hilliard
X22C BENJAMIN   [X68]
  a Joanna Spur
  f John Spur
  m Mercy --
  b Margaret Holloway
  f Nathaniel Holloway
  m Deliverance Bobet
  ======
[X23]   RICHMOND
    John Richmond X13Ca
    Abigail Rogers X13C

X23A JOSEPH   [X69]
  a Mary Andrews
  f Henry Andrews
  m Mary Wadsworth
X23B EDWARD   [X70]
  a Mary --
X23C SAMUEL   [X71]
  a Mehitable Andrews
  f Henry Andrews
  m Mary Wadsworth
  b Elizabeth King
  f Philip King
  m Judith Whitman
X23D SARAH
  a James Walker Jr [X72]
  f James Walker Sr
  m Bathsheba Brooks
X23E JOHN   [X73]
  a Hannah Otis
  f Stephen Otis
  m Hannah Ensign
X23F EBENEZER   [X74]
  a Anna Sproat
  f Robert Sproat
  m Elizabeth Samson

X23G ABIGAIL
  a Nathan Walker [X75]
  f James Walker
  m Bathsheba Brooks
  ======
[X24]   WILLIAMS
    Nathaniel Williams X13Da
    Elizabeth Rogers X13D

X24A JOHN   [X76]
  a Hannah Robinson
  f Increase Robinson
  m Sarah Penniman
X24B NATHANIEL   [X77]
  a Lydia King
  f Philip King
  m Judith Whitman
X24C ELIZABETH
  a John Macomber [X78]
  f John Macomber
  m Ann Evans
  ======
[X25]   ROGERS
    Joseph Rogers X14B
    Prudence --   X14Ba

X25A SARAH
X25B ELIZABETH
X25C JOSEPH
  ======
[X26]   HARDING
    Maziah Harding X14Ca
    Hannah Rogers X14C

X26A HANNAH
  a Bartholomew Fish [X79]
  f Nathan Fish
  m Deborah Barnes
X26B JOHN   [X80]
  a Elizabeth Young
  f Elisha Young
  m Elizabeth Merrick
X26C JAMES   [X81]
  a Mary Nickerson
  f William Nickerson
  m Mary Snow
X26D JAMES
X26E MARY
  a Launcelot Clark [X82]
  f John Clark
  m Mary Benjamin

```
X26F  ELIZABETH
      a Rowland Fish      [X83]
      f Nathan Fish
      m Hannah West
X26G  PHEBE
      a Benjamin Rogers
X26H  NATHAN              [X84]
      a Abigail West
      f Benjamin West
      m Hannah West
X26I  CORNELIUS           [X85]
      a Priscilla Curtis
      ======
[X27]  ROGERS
       Thomas Rogers X14D
       Sarah Treat   X14Da
      ------
X27A  SARAH
X27B  PHEBE
X27C  ELIZABETH
X27D  LUCY
      a Nehemiah Somes    [X86]
      f Timothy Somes
      m Elizabeth Robinson
      b Elisha Smalley
X27E  HANNAH
      a Joshua Cooke
X27F  THOMAS              [X87]
      a Ann Bartlett
      f Daniel Bartlett
X27G  HULDAH
      ======
[X28]  ROGERS
       Eleazer Rogers  X14E
       Ruhamah Willis  X14Ea
      ------
X28A  ELIZABETH
X28B  THOMAS              [X88]
      a Priscilla Churchill
      f John Churchill
      m Desire Holmes
X28C  HANNAH
      a Joseph Lewin      [X89]
X28D  EXPERIENCE
      a Samuel Totman     [X90]
      f Stephen Totman
X28E  ELEAZER
X28F  WILLIS
X28G  ABIJAH
      a Thomas Wright     [X91]
X28H  MORIAH
X28I  RUTH
      ======
```

```
[X29]  HIGGINS
       Beriah Higgins  X15A
       unk --
      ------
X29A  JOSEPH
      ======
[X30]  HIGGINS
       Jonathan Higgins X15B
       Lydia Sparrow    X15Ba
      ------
X30A  THANKFUL
X30B  SAMUEL              [X92]
      a Mehitable Phinney
      f Ebenezer Phinney
      m Susannah Linnell
X30C  HANNAH
X30D  JONATHAN
X30E  EXPERIENCE
      ======
[X31]  HIGGINS
       Joseph Higgins  X15C
       Ruth --         X15Ca
      ------
X31A  JOSEPH
X31B  BERIAH
X31C  RUTH
      ======
[X32]  PAINE
       Nicholas Paine  X15Ea
       Hannah Higgins  X15E
      ------
X32A  THANKFUL
X32B  PRISCILLA
X32C  PHILIP
X32D  LOIS
X32E  ABIGAIL
X32F  HANNAH
X32G  LYDIA
      ======
[X33]  HIGGINS
       Elisha Higgins  X15F
       Jane Collins    X15Fa
      ------
X33A  ELISHA
X33B  MARTHA
X33C  BERIAH
X33D  ALICE
X33E  APPHIA
X33F  JONATHAN
X33G  ELIZABETH
X33H  JOSEPH
X33I  RUTH
X33J  BARNABUS
X33K  PHILIP
```

[X34] ROGERS
    John Rogers   X16B
    Priscilla Hamblin X16Ba

X34A EBENEZER
X34B THANKFUL
X34C JOHN
X34D JONATHAN
X34E BENJAMIN
X34F SARAH
X34G JOSEPH
X34H PRISCILLA
    ======

[X35] ROGERS
    Judah Rogers   X16C
    Patience Lumbard X16Ca

X35A JUDAH
X35B MARY
X35C PATIENCE
X35D HANNAH
    ======

[X36] ROGERS
    Joseph Rogers   X16D
    Mercy Crisp   X16Da

X36A CRISP
X36B ELKANAH
X36C MARTHA
    ======

[X37] ROGERS
    Eleazer Rogers   X16F
    Martha Young   X16Fa

X37A HENRY
X37B ELIZABETH
X37C MERCY
X37D MOSES
X37E MARTHA
X37F ELEAZER
X37G ENSIGN
X37H DANIEL
    ======

[X38] MAYO
    Nathaniel Mayo   X16Ga
    Mehitable Rogers X16G

X38A JOHN #1
X38B JOHN #2
X38C ABIGAIL
X38D MEHITABLE
X38E RUTH
    ======

[X39] SMITH
    James Smith   X16Ha
    Hannah Rogers X16H

X39A LEVI
X39B SOLOMON
X39C JAMES
X39D JOSHUA
X39E GRACE
X39F BENJAMIN
    ======

[X40] ROGERS
    Nathaniel Rogers X16I
    Elizabeth Crosby X16Ia
    Silence Dimmock X16Ib

X40A SARAH by Elizabeth
X40B ELIZABETH
X40C NEHEMIAH by Silence
X40D RUTH
X40E JABEZ
X40F TEMPERANCE
X40G MEHITABLE
X40H SARAH
X40I NATHANIEL
X40J JOHN
    ======

[X41] PHINNEY
    John Phinney   X17A
    Sarah Lumbart X17Aa

X41A ELIZABETH
X41B JOHN
X41C THOMAS
X41D HANNAH
X41E SARAH
X41F PATIENCE
X41G MARTHA
X41H JABEZ
    ======

[X42] PHINNEY
    Joseph Phinney X17B
    Mercy Bryant   X17Ba
    Esther West   X17Bb

X42A ALICE by Mercy
X42B JOHN
X42C MARY
X42D MARCY by Esther
X42E JOSEPH
X42F PELATIAH
X42G PATIENCE
X42H EXPERIENCE
X42I HANNAH

[X43] PHINNEY
    Thomas Phinney X17C
    Sarah --   X17Ca

X43A GERSHOM
X43B THOMAS
X43C ABIGAIL
X43D JAMES
X43E MERCY
======

[X44] PHINNEY
    Ebenezer Phinney X17D
    Susanna Linnell X17Da

X44A MEHITABLE
X44B MARY
X44C MARTHA
X44D SAMUEL
X44E REBECCA
X44F EBENEZER
X44G DAVID
======

[X45] PHINNEY
    Samuel Phinney X17E
    Bethya Smith   X17Ea

X45A BETHIAH
X45B THANKFUL
X45C RHODA
X45D MARY
======

[X46] EASTLAND
    John Eastland X17Fa
    Mary Phinney   X17F

X46A ZERUIAH
X46B JOSEPH
X46C ELIZABETH
X46D MAREY
X46E HANNAH
X46F JEAN
X46G JOSHUA
X46H MARY
======

[X47] CROCKER
    Eleazer Crocker X17Ga
    Mercy Phinney   X17G

X47A MERCY
======

[X48] MORTON
    John Morton   X17Ha
    Reliance Phinney X17H

X48A JOHN
X48B JONATHAN
X48C JOSIAH
X48D JAMES
X48E DAVID
======

[X49] PHINNEY
    Benjamin Phinney X17I
    Martha Crocker   X17Ia

X49A TEMPERANCE
X49B MELATIAH
X49C BARNABAS
X49D ZACCHEUS
X49E SETH
X49F LUSANNA
======

[X50] PHINNEY
    Joseph Phinney X17J
    Elizabeth --   X17Ja

X50A THANKFUL
X50B JOSEPH
X50C JONATHAN
X50D MEHITABLE
X50E TIMOTHY
X50F JOSHUA
X50G ELIZABETH
  a John Macomber
======

[X51] ROGERS
    James Rogers   X18A
    Susanna Tracy X18Aa

X51A MARY
X51B ISAAC
X51C SUSANNAH
  a Judah Rogers
X51D JAMES
X51E ABIGAIL
X51F THOMAS
======

[X52] COLE
    John Cole   X18Ba
    Mary Rogers X18B

X52A JONATHAN
X52B JOHN

```
X52C  MARY
X52D  JAMES
X52E  NATHAN
X52F  JOSHUA
X52G  MOSES
X52H  PHEBE
X52I  JOSEPH
X52J  THANKFUL
      ======
[X53]  YATES
       John Yates      X18Ca
       Abigail Rogers  X18C
       ------

X53A  MARY
      a Crisp Rogers
X53B  RELIANCE
      a Elkanah Rogers
X53C  EXPERIENCE
X53D  DEBORAH
X53E  JOHN
X53F  MERCY
X53G  HANNAH
      ======
[X54]  MAYO
       Thomas Mayo X19Aa
       Elizabeth Higgins  X19A
       ------

X54A  ELIZABETH
X54B  THANKFUL
X54C  BATHSHEBA
X54D  ELIAKIM
X54E  JOSHUA
X54F  MERCY
      ======
[X55]  YOUNG
       James Young   X19Ba
       Mary Higgins  X19B
       ------

X55A  PHEBE
X55B  SARAH
X55C  SAMUEL
X55D  MARY
X55E  LYDIA #1
X55F  LYDIA #2
X55G  HANNAH
X55H  ELIZABETH
X55I  JAMES
      ======
```

```
[X56]  HURD
       Jacob Hurd      X19Ca
       Rebecca Higgins X19C
       ------
X56A  REBECCA
X56B  JACOB
X56C  ELIZABETH
      ======
[X57]  HIGGINS
       James Higgins  X19D
       Sarah Mayo     X19Da
       Sarah Pixbie   X19Db
       ------
X57A  REBECCA  by Sarah M
X57B  JAMES
X57C  HANNAH
X57D  DORCAS   by Sarah B
      ======
[X58]  MITCHELL
       William Mitchell X19Ea
       Sarah Higgins   X19E
       ------
X58A  JAMES
X58B  TABITHA
X58C  MERCY
X58D  WILLIAM
X58E  SETH
X58F  BETTY
      ======
[X59]  BRADFORD
       Samuel Bradford  X20Aa
       Hannah Rogers    X20A
       ------
X59A  HANNAH
X59B  GERSHOM
X59C  PEREZ
X59D  ELIZABETH
X59E  JERUSHA
X59F  WELTHEA
X59G  GAMALIEL
      ======
[X60]  RICHMOND
       Silvester Richmond X20Ca
       ELizabeth Rogers   X20C
       ------
X60A  WILLIAM
X60B  ELIZABETH
X60C  SILVESTER
X60D  PELEG
X60E  PEREZ
```

```
X60F  ICHABOD                      X64C  NATHANIEL
X60G  RUTH                         X64D  ANNA
X60H  HANNAH                       X64E  ABIGAIL
X60I  SARAH                        X64F  EPHRAIM
X60J  MARY                         X64G  MARCY
X60K  ROGERS                       X64H  MARY
      ======                       X64I  ABIEL
[X61]   SEARLE                           ======
        Nathaniel Searle  X20Ea  [X65]   STEPHENS
        Sarah Rogers      X20E            Nicholas Stephens  X21Da
        ------                            Remember Tisdale    X21D
X61A  DEBORAH                            ------
X61B  JOHN                         X65A  RICHARD
X61C  SARAH                        X65B  NICHOLAS
X61D  NATHANIEL                    X65C  JOSEPH
      ======                       X65D  ISAAC
[X62]   MAKEPEACE                  X65E  JOSIAH
        William Makepeace  X21Aa   X65F  HANNAH
        Abigail Tisdale    X21A          ======
        ------                     [X66]   TERRY
X62A  ABIGAIL                              Thomas Terry    X22A
X62B  ANNA                                 Abigail Dean    X22Aa
X62C  MARY                                ------
X62D  SUSANNA                      X66A  LYDIA
X62E  LYDIA                        X66B  THOMAS
X62F  DEBORAH                      X66C  ABIEL
X62G  SETH                               ======
X62H  WILLIAM                      [X67]   TERRY
X62I  REMEMBER                             John Terry      X22B
X62J  PRISCILLA                            Remember Farrow X22Ba
X62K  THOMAS                              ------
      ======                       X67A  SILAS
[X63]   TISDALE                    X67B  JOHN
        John Tisdale    X21B             ======
        Deborah Deane   X21Ba      [X68]   TERRY
        Abigail Burt    X21Bb             Benjamin Terry    X22C
        ------                            Joanna Spur       X22Ca
X63A  JOHN  by Deborah                    Margaret Holloway X22Cb
X63B  ABRAHAM  by Abigail                 ------
X63C  ISRAEL                       X68A  MARY    by Joanna
X63D  DEBORAH                      X68B  ROBERT
X63E  ABIGAIL                      X68C  BENJAMIN
X63F  EPHRAIM                      X68D  JOHN
X63G  JEDEDIAH                     X68E  GEORGE  by Margaret
X63H  ANNA                         X68F  JOANNA
      ======                       X68G  LYDIA
[X64]   LEONARD                    X68H  PHEBE
        George Leonard  X21Ca      X68I  WILLIAM
        Anna Tisdale    X21C       X68J  MARGARET
        ------                     X68K  SOLOMON
X64A  PHEBE                        X68L  MIRIAM
X64B  GEORGE                       X68M  SARAH
                                   X68N  DINAH
```

```
[X69]  RICHMOND                      [X73]  RICHMOND
       Joseph Richmond  X23A                John Richmond   X23E
       Mary Andrews     X23Aa               Hannah Otis     X23Ea
       ------                               ------
X69A  JOSEPH                         X73A  JOHN
X69B  CHRISTOPHER                    X73B  MARY
X69C  HENRY                          X73C  STEPHEN
X69D  JOHN                                 ======
X69E  ABIGAIL                        [X74]  RICHMOND
X69F  MARY                                 Ebenezer Richmond  X23F
X69G  WILLIAM                              Anna Sproat        X23Fa
X69H  JOSIAH                               ------
X69I  MARGARET                       X74A  EBENEZER
      ======                         X74B  ROBERT
[X70]  RICHMOND                      X74C  ANNA
       Edward Richmond  X23B         X74D  RACHEL
       Mary --          X23Ba        X74E  ELIZABETH
       ------                        X74F  SYLVESTER
X70A  MERCY                                ======
X70B  EDWARD                         [X75]  WALKER
X70C  JOSIAH                                Nathan Walker     X23Ga
X70D  NATHANIEL                             Abigail Richmond  X23G
X70E  SETH                                  ------
X70F  ELIZABETH                      X75A  NATHAN
X70G  PHEBE                          X75B  ABIGAIL
X70H  SARAH                          X75C  PHEBE
X70I  MARY                           X75D  WILLIAM
X70J  PRISCILLA                      X75E  LYDIA
      ======                         X75F  DEBORAH
[X71]  RICHMOND                            ======
       Samuel Richmond     X23C      [X76]  WILLIAMS
       Mehitable Andrews   X23Ca            John Williams    X24A
       Elizabeth King      X23Cb           Hannah Robinson  X24Aa
       ------                               ------
X71A  SAMUEL by Mehit.               X76A  NATHANIEL
X71B  OLIVER                         X76B  EXPERIENCE
X71C  THOMAS                         X76C  SILAS
X71D  HANNAH                         X76D  JOHN
X71E  LYDIA                          X76E  TIMOTHY
X71F  SILAS  by Eliz.                X76F  SIMEON
X71G  MEHITABLE                            ======
      ======                         [X77]  WILLIAMS
[X72]  WALKER                               Nathaniel Williams X24B
       James Walker    X23Da               Lydia King         X24Ba
       Sarah Richmond  X23D                 ------
       ------                        X77A  EDMUND
X72A  SARAH                          X77B  NATHANIEL
X72B  JAMES                          X77C  LYDIA
X72C  ELIAKIM                        X77D  BETHIA
X72D  ELNATHAN                       X77E  JUDITH
X72E  PETER                          X77F  ELIZABETH
      ======                               ======
```

461

```
[X78]  MACOMBER                          [X83]   FISH
        John Macomber    X24Ca                  Rowland Fish      X26Fa
        Elizabeth Williams X24C                 Elizabeth Harding X26F
        ------                                  ------
X78A  NATHANIEL                          X83A  NATHAN
X78B  JOSIAH                             X83B  EBENEZER
X78C  JOHN                               X83C  RUFUS
X78D  ELIZABETH                          X83D  CORNELIUS
X78E  JAMES                              X83E  JAMES #1
X78F  ELIJAH                             X83F  JAMES #2
X78G  MARY                               X83G  JAMES #3
X78H  ABIAH                              X83H  LOT
X78I  ANNA                               X83I  PRINCE
X78J  JOSEPH                                   ======
      ======                             [X84]   HARDING
[X79]  FISH                                      Nathan Harding  X26H
        Bartholomew Fish X26Aa                   Anna Brown      X26Ha
        Hannah Harding    X26A                   Abigail West    X26Hb
        ------                                   ------
X79A  LEMUEL                             X84A  EBENEZER  by Anna
X79B  JEDIDIAH                           X84B  LYDIA
      ======                             X84C  ELEAZER
[X80]  HARDING                           X84D  TABITHA
        John Harding    X26B             X84E  ANNA
        Elizabeth Young X26Ba            X84F  NATHAN
                                         X84G  EPHRAIM  by Abigail
X80A  MARY                               X84H  BENJAMIN
X80B  JOHN                               X84I  ABIGAIL
X80C  HANNAH                                   ======
X80D  ARCHELAS                           [X85]   HARDING
X80E  JOSHUA                                      Cornelius Harding  X26I
X80F  NATHANIEL                                   Priscilla Curtis   X26Ia
X80G  EBENEZER                                    ------
X80H  HANNAH                             X85A  PHEBE
      ======                             X85B  JOSEPH
[X81]  HARDING                           X85C  PRISCILLA
        James Harding   X26C             X85D  LUCIA
        Mary Nickerson  X26Ca            X85E  NATHAN
        ------                           X85F  CORNELIUS
X81A  THOMAS                             X85G  SETH
X81B  JAMES                                    ======
      ======                             [X86]   SOMES
[X82]  CLARK                                      Nehemiah Somes  X27D
        Launcelot Clark  X26Ea                   Lucy Rogers     X27Da
        Mary Harding     X26E                     ------
        ------                           X86A  LUCY
X82A  MARY                               X86B  NEHEMIAH
X82B  ELIZABETH                                ======
      ======
```

DIVISION S
X87-X92

[X87] ROGERS
    Thomas Rogers X27F
    Ann Bartlett X27Fa

X87A ANN
    ======
[X88] ROGERS
    Thomas Rogers X28B
    Priscilla Churchill X28Ba

X88A RUTH
X88B DESIRE
X88C SAMUEL
X88D THOMAS
X88E HANNAH
X88F ELEAZER
X88G JOHN
    ======
[X89] LEWIN
    Joseph Lewin X28Ca
    Hannah Rogers X28C

X89A JOHN
X89B MERIAH
    ======
[X90] TOTMAN
    Samuel Totman X28Da
    Experience Rogers X28D

X90A SAMUEL
X90B DEBORAH
X90C HANNAH
X90D JOSHUA
X90E EXPERIENCE
    ======

[X91] WRIGHT
    Thomas Wright X28Ga
    Abijah Rogers X28G

X91A ELIZABETH
X91B WILLIAM
X91C SARAH
X91D HANNAH
X91E PRISCILLA
    ======
[X92] HIGGINS
    Samuel Higgins X30B
    Mehitable Phinney X30Ba

X92A HANNAH
X92B EBENEZER
X92C MARTHA
X92D SUSANNA
X92E JONATHAN
X92F SAMUEL
X92G ELIAKIM
X92H SILVANUS
X92I PRINCE
    ======

```
------------------------------------------------------------
                    D1/25 HENRY HOWLAND
          D1               :              D2
------------------------------------------------------------

D1/24   John Howland Sr. MF      D1/24   John Howland Sr
D1a24   :Elizabeth Tilley MF             :Elizabeth Tilley
D1af24  :  John Tilley  MF               :

D1/23   John Howland Jr          D2/24   Hope Howland
D1a23   Mary Lee                 D2a24   John Chipman Sr
D1af23  :  Robert Lee                    :
9       :                        D2/23   Hope Chipman
D1/22   Hannah Howland           D2a23   John Huckins
D1a22   Jonathan Crocker                 :
D1af22  :  John Crocker          D2/22   Hope Huckins
D1aff/22:  William Crocker       D2a22   Thomas Nelson
        :                                :
D1/21   James Crocker=G28Aaf     D2/21   Hannah Nelson
D1a21   :Alice Swift  =G28Aam    D2a21   Jabez Wood Sr

D1/20   Lydia Crocker            D2/20   Jabez Wood Jr=A1/382
D1a20   Gates Levi               D2a20   :Joanna Short
                                          :
                                 D2/19   Joanne Wood
              D3                 D2a19   Comfort Horton
W10A    Richard Warren MF                :
        :                        D2/18   Sarah Horton
W11F    Nathaniel Warren Sr      D2a18   Jarvis Wheeler
                                          :
W17F    Alice Warren             D2/17   Betsey Wheeler
     a  Thomas Gibbs             D2a17   Levi Pierce=A1/46

W50B    Abigail Gibbs            D2/16   Elizabeth Pierce
     a  Jireh Swift              D2a16   Courtland Butler

D3/21 Alice Swift  =G28Aam       D2/15   Mary Butler
D3a21 James Crocker=G28Aaf       D2a15   Robert Sheldon

                                 D2/14   Flora Sheldon
                                 D2a14   Samuel Bush
                                          :
                                 D2/13   Prescott Bush
                                 D2a13   Dorothy Walker
                                          :
                                 D2/12   George Bush=A01/1
                                         41st U.S. Pres.
                                 D2a12   Barbara Pierce
```

```
                    D4                              D6
D1/25     John Howland Sr        D6/25   Edward Fuller MF=F11A

D4/24     Joseph Howland         D6/24   Samuel Fuller MF=F12B
D4a24     :Elizabeth Southworth
D4af24    : Thomas Southworth     D6/23   John Fuller      =F14H
D4am24    : Elizabeth Raynor
D4amf24   :  Edward Raynor        D6/22   Shubael Fuller  =F22C
D4amm24   :  Alice Carpenter      D6a22   Hannah Crocker
                                  D6af22   Jonathan Crocker D1a22
D4/23     Nathaniel Howland Sr
D4a23     :Martha Cole=A08/89             D7
D4af23    :  James Cole           D7/25   Adrain Van Schaick
D4am23    :  Mary Tilson
                                  D7/24   Cornelise Aertsen
D4/22     Nathaniel Howland Jr            Van Schaick
D4a22     :Abigail Burt
D4af22    :  John Burt            D7/23   Arie Cornelise
D4am22    :  Abigail Cheever              Van Schaick

D4/21     Joseph Howland         D7/22   Iden Van Schaick
D4a21     :Lydia Bill
D4af21    :  Ephraim Bill        D7/21   Francis Sedan
                                          Van Schaick
D4/20     Susan Howland
D4a20     John Aspinwall   Jr    D7/20   John Hampton Van Schaick
D4af20    : John Aspinwall Sr
D4am20    : Rebecca Smith         D7/19   Janet Van Schaick
D4aff20   : Joseph Aspinwall      D7a19   John Tone Jr =G50E

D4/19     Mary Rebecca Aspinwall           D8
D4a19     Isaac Roosevelt        D7/24 Cornelis Aertsen Van Shaick

D4/18     James Roosevelt=A08/2  D8/23   Henrikje Van Schaick
D4a18     :Sara Delano
                                  D8/22   Belitje Van Schaick
D4/17     Franklin D. Roosevelt  D8a22   Claes Jensen Bogaert
D4a17     Anna Eleanor Roosevelt
                                  D8/21   Jan (John) Bogaert
                    D5
D5/25     Stephen Hopkins MF=H10A D8/20  Annatze Bogaert
                                  D8a20   Jacobus (James) Roosevelt
D5/24     Damaris Hopkins
D5a24     Jacob Cooke= H11Ga     D8/19   Jacobus Roosevelt Jr
D5af24    :Francis Cooke MF=H11Gaf
                                  D8/18   Cornelius Van Schaick
D5/23     Elizabeth Cooke                Roosevelt
D5a23     John Doty
D5af23    Edward Doty MF         D8/17   Theordore Roosevelt Sr

                                  D8/16   Theordore Roosevelt Jr
                                          U.S. President
                                  D8a16   Lee Alice Hathaway
```

465

D9

D9/25 William Bradford Sr
:
D9/24 William Bradford Jr
:
D9/23 John Bradford
D9a23 :Mercy Warren
D9af23:Joseph Warren=W11G
D9am23:Priscilla Faunce

D10

D5af24 Francis Cooke MF
:
D10/25 Mary Cooke
D10a25 John Tompkins Sr
:
D10/24 John Tompkins Jr
D10a24 Mary Tinkham
D10af24 Ephraim Tinkham
D10am24 Mary Brown=Q11A
D10amf24 Peter Brown MF Q10A

D11

D11/25 Henry Spencer
D11a25 :Isabella Lincoln
:
D11/24 Thomas Spencer
D11a24 :Margaret Smith
:
D11/23 William Spencer
D11a23 :Agnes Heritage
:
D11/22 Julian Spencer
D11a22 William Wilmer
:
D11/21 Ane Wilmer
D11a21 Henry Thorton
:
D11/20 Anne Thorton=A10/71
D11a20 William Dickens=A10/70
(See A10 to George Washington
A10/1)

D12

D11/23 William Spencer
D11a23 :Agnes Heritage
:
D12/22 Thomas Spencer
D12a22 :Dorothy Spencer
:
D12/21 Susan Spencer
D12a21 John Temple
:
D12/20 Sir Thomas Temple
D12a20 :Hester Sandys
:
D12/19 Sir John Temple II
D12a19 :Dorothy Lee
:
D12/18 Mary Temple
D12a18 Robert Nelson
:
D12/17 John Nelson=A8/174
D12a17 Elizabeth Taylor
(See A08 to Franklin D Roosevelt
A08/1

D13

D13/25 Edward Gilman
:
D13/24 Bridget Gilman
D13a24 Edward Lincoln=A13/128
(See A13 to Abraham Lincoln=A13/1)

D14

D13/25 Edward Gilman
:
D14/24 Mary Gilman
D14a24 Nicholas Jacob
:
D14/23 Deborah Jacob
D14a23 Nathanial Thomas Jr
:
D14/22 William Thomas
D14a22 :Abigail Rick
:
D14/21 Margaret Thomas=A1/303
(See A1 to George Bush A1/1
U.S. President

D15
W19A Richard Warren

W11? Nathaniel Warren

D15/25 Alice Warren=W17F
D15a25 Thomas Gibbs=W17Fa
        :
D15/24 Abigail Gibbs=W50B
D15a24 Jireh Swift =W50Ba

D15/23 Alice Swift= G28Aam

D16
D1/25 Henry Howland Sr.
        :
D16/25 John Howland Sr=D1/24
D16a25 :Elizabeth Tilley
        :
D16/24 Joseph Howland=A08/176
(See A08 to Franklin D
Roosevelt A08/1 U.S. Pres.

D17
D1/25 Henry Howland Sr
        :
D17/25 Henry Howland Jr
D17a25 :Mary --
        :
D17/24 Elizabeth Howland=A03/459
(See A03 to Ricjard Nixon=A03/1

D18
D1/25 Henry Howland Sr
        :
D17/25 Henry Howland Jr
        :
D18/25 Zoeth Howland
D18a25 Abigail --
        :
D18/24 Benjamin Howland
D18a24 :Judith Sampson
        :
D18/23 Abigail Howland
D18a23 Jonathan Ricketson Sr
        :
D18/22 Jonathan Ricketson Jr
        =A04/238
(See A04 to Gerald Ford
=A04/1 U.S. President

D19
D19/25 Benjamin Carpenter=A06/120
        :
D19/24 Jotham Carpenter=A06/60
 (See A06 to James Abram Garfield
 A06/1 U.S. President

D20
D19/25 Benjamin Carpenter=A06/120
        :
D20/25 Keziah Carpenter
D20a25 Thomas Horton =A01/378
(See A01 to George S Bush A01/1)
         U.S. President

D21
D21/25 Thomas Morse Sr
        :
D21/24 Thomas Morse Jr
D21a24 :Margaret King
        :
D21/23 Samuel Morse
D21a23 :Elizabeth Jasper
        :
D21/22 Elizabeth Morse
D21a22 Robert Daniel
        :
D21/21 Joseph Daniel=A02/216
D21a21 :Mary Fairbanks
  (See A02 to William Howard
  Taft A02/1)

D22
D21/25 Thomas Morse Sr
        :
D22/25 Richard Morse
        :
D22/24 Joseph Morse Sr
D22a24 :Dorothy --
        :
D22/23 Joseph Morse Jr
D22a23 :Hester Pierce
        :
D22/22 John Morse
D22a22 :Abigail Stearns
        :
D22/21 Joseph Morse II=A03/483
D22a21 :Elizabeth Sawtelle
(See A03 to Richard Nixon A03/1)

467

```
                    D23/25 Rowland Cotymore
                    D23a25 : Katherine Miles
--------------------------------:-------------------------------
              D23
D23/24 Elizabeth Cotymore
       =A11/119
D23a24 William Tying
       :                              D24
D23/23 Anna Tying         =    D23/23 Anna Tying
D23a23 Thomas Shepard Jr  =    D23a23 Thomas Shepard, Jr
       =A11/58                        :
(See A11 to John Adams Jr)     D24/25 Thomas Shepard III
2nd U.S. President, and                =A08/170
John Quincy Adams 6th          (See A08 to Franklin D
U.S. Pres.)                      Roosevelt 32nd U.S.)
                                 President


              D25                           D26
D25/25 Warren Richard=W10A     D26/26 Isaac Sheldon=A08/232
       : =D5af23=A05/148       D26a26 :Mary Woodford=A08/233
(See A05 148 to 1, to                 :
Ulysses Simpson Grant          D26/25 Ruth Sheldon
18th U.S. President)           D26a25 Joseph Wright
                                      :
              D27              D26/24 Ruth Wright
D27/25 William Bradford MF     D26a24 Luke Noble
D27a25 :Dorothy May                   :
D27b25 Alice Carpenter         D26/23 Asa Noble
       :                       D26a23 :Bethia Noble
D27/24 William Bradford Jr            :
        W18Aaf, R11B           D26/22 Ruth Noble
D27a24 Alice Richards W18Aam   D26a22 Ezekiel Root
                                      :
                               D26/21 George Bridges Root
                               D26a21 :Honor Robbins
                                      :
                               D26/20 Elizabeth R Root
                               D26a20 Manning Francis
                                      :
                               D26/19 Frederick A Francis
                               D26a19 :Jessie Ann Stevens
                                      :
                               D26/18 Anne A Francis
                               D26a18 John Newell Robbins
                                      :
                               D26/17 Kenneth S Robbins
                               D26a17 :Loyal E Davis
                                      :
                               D26/16 Anne Francis Robbins
                               (Name change to Nancy Davis)
                               D26a16 Ronald W Reagan=A09/1
```

D28	D29
D28/25 Augustine Warner	D29/25 King Edward I of Eng.
:=A10/10	:
D28a25 :Mildred Reade	D29/24 Plantagenet Joan
:	D29a24 :Gilbert de Clare
D28/24 Mary Warner	:
D28a24 John Smith Jr	D29/23 Eleanor de Clare
:	D29a23 Hugh le Despencer
D28/23 Mildred Smith	:
D28a23 Robert Porteus Sr	D29/22 Edward Despencer Sir
:	D29a22 :Ann Ferrers
D28/22 Robert Porteus Jr	:
D28a22 :Judith Cockayne	D29/21 Edward Despencer Jr
:	D29a21 :Elizabeth Burghersh
D28/21 Mildred Porteus	:
D28a21 Robert Hodgson Sr	D29/20 Elizabeth Despencer
:	D29a20 John FitzAlan
D28/20 Robert Hodgson Jr	:
D28a20 :Mary Tucker	D29/19 Margaret FitzAlan
:	D29a19 William de Ros
D28/19 Henrietta M Hodgson	:
D28a19 Oswald Smith	D29/18 Margaret de Ros
:	D29a18 James Touchet
D28/18 Frances D Smith	:
D28a18 Claude Bowes-Lyon Sr	D29/17 Anne Touchet
:	D29a17 Thomas Sutton Sir
D28/17 Claude Bowes-Loyon Jr	:
D28a17 :Nina Cavendish-Bentinck	D29/16 Isabel Sutton
:	D29a16 Christopher SouthworthSir
D28/16 Queen Elizabeth I	:
D28a16 George VI	D29/15 John Southworth Sir
:	D29a15 :Helen Langton
D28/15 Queen Elizabeth II	:
D28a15 Prince Philip	D29/14 Thomas Southworth Sir
:	D29a14 :Margery Boteler
D28/14 Prince Charles	:
D28a14 Diana Frances Spencer	D29/13 John Southworth II Sir
	D29a13 :Mary Ashton
	:
	D29/12 Thomas Southworth
	D29a12 :Rosamond Lister
	:
	D29/11 Edward Southworth
	D29a11 :Alice Carperter
	:
	D29/10 Thomas Southworth II
	D29a10 :Elizabeth Reynor
	:
	D29/9 Eliz. Southworth=A8/177
	D29a9 Joseph Howland=A8/176
	D29af9 John Howland Sr MF=D1/24

```
        D30                              D30
D30/40  Capet Hugh King France   D30/23  Richard Prowse
                                 D30a23  :Margaret Norton
D30/39  Edith of France
D30a39  Rainiar IV of Hainault   D30/22  John Prowse
                                 D30/22  :Joan Orchard
D30/38  Beatrix of Hainault
D30a38  Ebles I Count of Roucy   D30/21  Robert Prowse

D30/37  Alice of Roucy           D30/20  John Prowse II
D30a37  Hildouin IV Count Montdidier  D30a20  :Alice White

D30/36  Margaret of Montdidier   D30/19  John Prowse III
D30a36  Hugh I Count Clermont    D30a19  :Elizabeth Collack

D30/35  Adeliza of Clarmont      D30/18  Agnes Prowse
D30a35  Gilbert de Claire        D30a18  John Trowbridge

D30/34  Richard De Claire        D30/17  Thomas Trowbridge
D30a34  :Adeliza de Meschines            =A12/152
                                 D30a17  Elizabeth Marshall
D30/33  Roger De Claire                  =A12/153
D30a33  :Maud de St.Hilaire
                                         D31
D30/32  Aveline De Claire        D31/25  Samuel Smith    =A12/160
D30a32  Goffrey FitzPiers        D31a25  :Elizabeth Smith=A12/161

D30/31  Hawise FitzGoeffrey      D31/24  Philip Smith
D30a31  Reynold  De Mohun        D31a24  :Rebecca Foote

D30/30  Alice De Mohun           D31/23  Rebecca Smith =A1/271
D30a30  Robert De Beauchamp      D31a23  George Stilman=A1/270

D30/29  Humphrey De Beauchamp
D30a29  :Sybil Oliver                    D32
                                 D32/25  William Girton
D30/28  Eleanor De Beauchamp     D32a25  :Martha Kinney
D30a28  John Bampfield Sr
                                 D32/24  John K Girton
D30/27  John Bampfield Jr        D32a24  :Margaret Shoemaker
D30a27  :Isabel Cobham
                                 D32/23  Wm.G.Girton
D30/26  John Bampfield II        D32a23  :Eliz.Kline
D30a26  :Joan Gilbert
                                 D32/22  Alfred Girton
D30/25  Thomas Bampfield         D32a22  :Emma Fisher
D30a25  :Agnes Coplestone
                                 D32/21  Jessie Girton
D30/24  Agnes Bampfield          D32a21  Daniel Hartman
D30a24  John Prowse
                                 D32/20  Helen Hartman=G54Ea
                                 D32a20  Roy Burgess  =G54E
```

```
           D33
D33/25 Philip Taber=K61B
D33a25 Ruth Shaw  =K61Ba
       :
D33/24 Pardon Taber
D33a24 :Mary Taber
       :
D33/23 Philip Taber
D33a23 :Biggs Sarah
       :
D33/22 Peleg Taber
D33a22 :Mary Lamoreaux
D33af22: Daniel Lamoreaux
D33am22: Charity Wetmore
       :
D33/21 Cordelia Taber
D33a21 Henry Smith
       :
D33/20 Lola Joseph Smith
D33a20 Robert Furneaux White
       :
D33/19 Harold Leslie White Sr
D33a19 :Margaret Appell
       :
D33/18 H Leslie White Jr
D33a18 Ruth Virginia Garrison
       :
D33/17/1 H Leslie White 3rd
D33/17/2 Virginia Loiuse White
D33/17a2 Craig Edward Jacob
D33/17/3 Barbara Elin White
D33/17a3 Joseph Thomas D Carr
D33b18  Barbara Eagleson
       :
D33/17/4 Timothy Joshua White
```

471

A1/   GEORGE HERBERT WALKER BUSH U.S. President

1 GEORGE H.W.BUSH

1a Barbara Pierce	51 Rebecca Davis	116 Jechonias Yancey
2 Prescott S.Bush	52 Joseph Beaky	117 Mildred Wood
3 Dorothy Walker	53 Catharine Shriner	118 John Field
4 Samuel P Bush	54 Elijah K Bangs	119 Sally Wood
5 Flora Sheldon	55 Esther Stackhouse	120 William Holliday
6 George H Walker	56 James H Wear	
7 Lucretia Wear	57 Elizabeth Gault	126 Samuel Dawson
8 James Smith Bush	58 David Yancey	
9 Harriett E Fay	59 Mildred Field	130 John House
10 Robert E Sheldon	60 Joseph Holliday	131 Deborah Guile
11 Mary E. Butler	61 Nancy R McCune	132 Obadiah Newcomb
12 David D Walker	62 Peter Foree	
13 Martha A Beaky	63 Eliza Dawson	134 Hezkiah May
14 James H Wear	64 Timothy Bush	135 Anna Stillman
15 Nannie E Holliday	65 Deborah House	136 John Smith
16 ODabish N Bush	66 Daniel Newcomb	
17 Harriet Smith	67 Elizabeth May	138 Henry Stevens Jr
18 Samuel H Fay	68 Ephraim Smith	139 Elizabeth Fellows
19 Susan Shellman	69 Lucy Stevens	
20 Thomas H Sheldon		144 Jonathan Fay
21 Martha Uncles	72 Jonathan Fay	145 Joanna Phillips
22 Courtland P Butler	73 Lucy Prescott	146 Abel Prescott
23 Elizabeth S Pierce	74 Samuel Howard	147 Abigail Brigham
24 George E Walker	75 Anna Lillie	148 Ebenezer Howard
25 Harriet Mercer	76 John Shellman	149 Martha Goffe
26 Joseph A Beakly	77 Maria Margareth	150 John Lillie
27 Mary A Bangs	78 Robert Monford	151 Abigail Breck
28 William G Wear	79 Anne Brodnax	
29 Sarah A Yancey		154 Baltis Fout
30 John J Holliday	88 Nathaniel Butler	155 Susanna Bocher
31 Lucretia G Foree	89 Sarah Herrick	156 James Munford
32 Timothy Bush	90 Gilbert Livingston	157 Elizabeth Bolling
33 Lydia Newcomb	91 Susannah Lewis	158 Edward Brodnax
34 Sanford Smith	92 Isaac Pierce	159 Mary Brown
35 Priscilla Whippo	93 Anna Fitch	
36 Samuel P Fay	94 Jarvis Wheeler	176 Benjamin Butler
37 Harriet Howard	95 Sarah Horton	177 Susanna Whiting
38 John Shellman Jr		178 Samuel Herrick
39 Clarissa Montfort	100 Robert Mercer	179 Silence Kingsley
40 Michael Sheldon		180 James Livingston
	102 Richard Davis	181 Judith Newcomb
42 James Uncles		182 Richard Lewis
43 Eliz. Criswell	104 Victor E Bechi	183 Susanna Vanderburgh
44 Samuel H Butler		184 Nathan Pierce
45 Judith Livingston	108 Lemuel Bangs	185 Lydia Martin
46 Levi Pierce	109 Rebecca Keeler	186 William Fitch
47 Betsey S Wheeler	110 Aos Stackhouse	187 Hannah Bourn
48 Thomas Walker	111 Mary Powell	188 Jeremiah Wheeler
49 Cath. McLelland	112 Jonathan Wear	189 Submit Hoton
50 John Mercer	114 Jonathan Gault	190 Comfort Horton

A01/
191 Joanna Wood

200 Robert Mercer
201 Ann Mounce

204 Thomas Davis
205 Rebecca Gregory

216 Joseph Bangs
217 Thankful Hamblen
218 Elijah Keeler

220 James Stackhouse
221 Martha Hastings
222 John Powell
223 Susanna Bryan

232 Jeremiah Yancey

234 William Wood

236 Robert Field

238 Jesse Wood Sr

240 Samuel Holliday
241 Janet Adair

252 Henry Dawson

260 Nathaniel House
261 Hannah Davenport
262 Israel Guild
263 Sarah George
264 Simon Newcomb

268 John May Jr
269 Prudence Bridge
270 George Stillman
271 Rebecca Smith
272 Daniel Smith Jr
273 Mary Grant

276 Henry Stevens
277 Elizabeth Gallup
278 Ephraim Fellows
279 Anne Cross

288 John Fay
289 Hannah Child
290 Ebenezer Phillips
291 Mary Smith
292 Jonathan Prescott
293 Rebecca Bulkeley
294 John Brigham Jr

296 Amos Howard
297 Judith Wallingford

300 Theophilus Lillie
301 Hannah Ruck
302 John Breck
303 Margaret Thomas

310 George Bocher

312 Robert Munford
313 Martha Kennon
314 Robert Bolling Jr
315 Anna Cocke
316 William Brodnax
317 Rebacca Champion

352 Israel Butler
353 Elizabeth Blossom
354 Ephraim Whiting
355 Abigail Mason
356 Daniel Herrick
357 Elizabeth Rust
358 Samuel Kingsley

362 Thomas Newcomb
363 Judith Woodworth

366 Henry Vanderburgh
367 Magdelena Knight
368 Mial Pierce
369 Judith Round
370 Ephraim Martin
371 Thankful Bullock

374 William Bourn Jr
375 Mary Sheffield
376 James Wheeler Jr
377 Elizabeth West
378 Thomas Horton=A19/226

379 Keziah Carpenter
380 Jonathan Horton
381 Ann Millard
382 Jabez Wood Jr
383 Joanna Short

400 Thomas Mercer

402 Christopher Mounce

408 William Davis

432 Samuel Bangs
433 Mary Hinchley
434 Ebenezer Hamblen
435 Thankful Hamblen
436 Joseph Keeler
437 Elizabeth Whitney

440 Robert Stackhouse
441 Margaret Stone
442 Samuel Hastings
443 Mary Hill
444 Isaac Powell
445 Elizabeth Perdue

480 Adam Holliday
481 Jane Macomson

536 John May Sr.
537 Sarah Brewer

1074 Daniel Brewer=A17/108
1075 Joanna --

DIVISION A
A2/1-A2/162

A02/   WILLIAM HOWARD TAFT U.S. President
1 TAFT HOWARD WILLIAM

1a Helen Herron	51 Hopestill Read	106 Daniel Holbrook
2 Alphonso Taft	52 Samuel Davenport	107 Abigail Crafts
3 Louisa Maria Torrey	53 Rebecca Holbrook	108 Eleazer Daniel
4 Peter Rawson Taft	54 David Daniel	109 Mary Holbrook
5 Sylvia Howard	55 Huldah Taft	110 Isreal Taft
6 Samuel D. Torrey	56 Jonathan Waters	111 Mercy Aldrich
7 Susan Holman Waters	57 Mehitable Giles	112 Nath. Waters
8 Aaron Taft	58 Samuel Goodale	113 Elizabeth King
9 Rhoda Rawson	59 Silence Holbrook	114 John Giles
10 Levi Howard	60 Solomon Holman Jr	115 Ann Andrews
11 Bethiah Chapin	61 Mercy Waters	116 Samuel Goodale
12 William Torrey	62 Samuel Trask	117 Mary Buxton
13 Anna Davenport	63 Anna Bond	118 John Holbrook
14 Asa Waters, Jr.	64 Robert Taft	119 Ruth Hill
15 Susan Trask Holman	65 Sarah --	120 Solomon Holman
16 Peter Taft	66 James Emerson	121 Mary Barton
17 Elizabeth Cheney	67 Sarah --	122 Richard Waters
18 Abner Rawson	68 Joseph Cheney	123 Martha Reed
19 Mary Allen	69 Hannah Thurston	124 John Trask
20 Benjamin Hayward		125 Hannah Osborn
21 Mary Wheaton	72 Grindall Rawson	126 Josiah Bond
22 John Chapin Jr.	73 Susanna Wilson	127 Eliz. Fuller
23 Rhoda Albee	74 John Hayward	
24 Joseph Torrey	75 Sarah Mitchell	132 Joseph Emerson
25 Deborah Holbrook	76 Nathaniel Allen	133 Elizabeth
26 Seth Davenport	77 Mary Frizzell	Woodmansey
27 Chloe Daniel	78 Samuel Hill	136 William Cheney
28 Asa Waters	79 Hannah Twitchell	137 Margaret --
29 Sarah Goodale	80 Samuel Hayward	138 John Thurston
30 Jonathan Holman	81 Mehitable Thompson	139 Margaret --
31 Susanna Trask		
32 Joseph Taft	84 Benjamin Wheaton	144 Edward Rawson
33 Elizabeth Emerson	85 Margaret --	145 Rachel Perne
34 Josiah Cheney	86 Joseph Rockwood	146 John Wilson Jr.
35 Hannah --	87 Mary Hayward	147 Sarah Hooker
36 Edmund Rawson	88 Seth Chapin	148 Thomas Hayward
37 Elizabeth Hayward	89 Bethiah Thurston	149 Susannah --
38 Ebenezer Allen		150 Exper. Mitchell
39 Mary Hill	92 Benjamin Albee	151 Mary --
40 Benjamin Hayward	93 Abiel --	152 James Allen
41 Hannah --		153 Anne Guild
42 Samuel Wheaton	96 Angel Torrey	154 James Frizzell
43 Mary Rockwood	97 Hannah --	155 Sarah Busketh
44 John Chapin	98 Joseph Giddings	156 John Hill
45 Dorcas --	99 Grace Wardwell	157 Hannah --
46 Obadiah Albee	100 Peter Holbrook	158 Ben. Twitchell
47 Jane --	101 Alice Godfrey	159 Mary Riggs
48 William Torrey	102 Samuel Read Jr	160 William Hayward
49 Susanna Gidding	103 Deborah Chapin	161 Margery --
50 William Holbrook	104 Johun Davenport	162 John Thompson

A02/

168 Robert Wheaton
169 Alice Bowen

172 John Rockwood
173 Joanna Ford
174 Samuel Hayward
175 Mehitable Thompson
176 Josiah Chapin
177 Mary King
178 John Thurston Jr.
179 Mary Wood
184 James Albee
185 Hannah Cooke

192 William Torrey
193 Elizabeth Frye

196 Joseph Giddings
197 Susanna Rindge
198 Uzal Wardwell

200 Thomas Holbrook
201 Joan Kingman
202 Richard Godfrey

204 Samuel Read
205 Hopestill Holbrook
206 Josiah Chapin
207 Mary King
208 Thomas Davenport

212 John Holbrook
213 Elizabeth Hemingway
214 Samuel Crafts
215 Elizabeth Seaver
216 Joseph Daniel
217 Mary Fairbanks
218 Samuel Holbrook
219 Mary Pierce
220 Robert Taft Jr
221 Elizabeth Woodward
222 Jacob Aldrich
223 Margery Hayward
224 John Waters
225 Sarah Tompkins
226 John King
227 Elizabeth Goldthwaite

228 Eleazer Giles
229 Elizabeth Bishop
230 John Andrews
231 Ann Jocobs
232 Zachariah Goodale
234 John Buxton
235 Mary Small
236 John Holbrook
237 Silence Wood
238 Eleazer Hill
239 Sarah Breck

242 William Barton
243 Anne Greene
244 John Waters
245 Sarah Tompkins

248 William Trask, Jr

250 William Osborn
251 Hannah Burton
252 Jonas Bond
253 Grace Coolidge
254 Joseph Fuller
255 Lydia Jackson

A03/   RICHARD M NIXON U.S. President
  1 RICHARD M NIXON
  1a Thelma C. Ryan
  2 Francis A. Nixon
  3 Hannah Milhous
  4 Samuel B. Nixon
  5 Sarah Wadsworth
  6 Franklin Milhous
  7 Almira Park Burdg
  8 George Nixon III
  9 Margaret Trimmer
 10 Thomas Wadsworth
 11 Mary Louise Moore
 12 Joshua Milhous
 13 Eliz. Griffith
 14 Oliver Burdg
 15 Jane M. Hemingway
 16 George Nixon, Jr.
 17 Hannah Wilson
 18 Anthony Trimmer
 19 Margaret Hunt
 20 Robert Wadsworth
 21 Elizabeth Lytle
 22 Joseph Moore
 23 Jane Brown
 24 William Milhous
 25 Martha Vickers
 26 Amos Griffith
 27 Edith Price
 28 Jacob Burdg Jr.
 29 Miriam Matthews
 30 James Hemingway
 31 Hope Malmsgury
 32 George Nixon
 33 Sarah Seeds
 34 William Wilson
 35 Elenor Scothorn
 36 Paul Trimmer
 37 Jane McElwain
 38 William Hunt
 39 Margaret Andover
 40 Thomas Wadsworth
 41 Mary Wiley
 42 George Lytle
 43 Eliz. McComas
 44 Joseph Moore
 45 Mary Clemson
 46 Isaac Brown
 47 Mary Clayton
 49 Hannah Baldwin
 50 Thomas Vickers

 51 Jemima Mendenhall
 52 Jacob Griffith
 53 Lydia Hussey
 54 Daniel Price
 55 Elizabeth Hussey
 56 Jacob Burdg
 57 Judith Smith
 58 William Matthews
 59 Ann Griffith
 60 James Hemingway
 61 Elizabeth Armstrong
 62 Benjamin Malmsbury
 63 Jane Cantell
 64 James Nixon
 65 Mary --

 70 Nathan Scothorn Jr
 71 Hannah Twiggs
 72 Anthony Trimmer
 73 Elizabeth --
 74 Moses McElwain
 75 Agnes Miller

 78 Christopher Andover
 79 Margaret --
 80 Thomas Wadsworth
 81 Rebecca Passmore

 84 Guy Lytle
 85 Elizabeth Webster
 86 Alexander McComas
 87 Deborah Hartley
 88 James Moore
 89 Eliz. Dickinson
 90 Thomas Clemson
 91 Elizabeth Strode
 92 Alexander Brown
 93 Mary Bradford
 94 Thomas Clayton Jr
 95 Mary --
 96 Thomas Milhous
 97 Sarah Miller
 98 Joshua Baldwin
 99 Mercy Brown
100 Thomas Vickers
101 Rebecca Dillon
102 Joshua Mendenhall

103 Lydia Mendenhall
104 William Griffith
105 Esther Davis
106 Recond Hussey
107 Miriam Harry
108 Samuel Price
109 Ann Moore
110 John Hussey III
111 Elizabeth --
112 Joseph Burdg
113 Sarah Morris
114 Anthony Smith
115 Lydia Willets
116 Oliver Matthews
117 Hannah Johns
118 Isaac Griffith
119 Ann Burson
120 Isaac Hemingway
121 Elizabeth Haven
122 Ephraim Armstrong
123 Eliz. McCulley
124 John Malmsbury
125 Rebecca Doane
126 James Cattell Jr
127 Hope Gaskill

140 Nathan Scothorn
141 Mary --
142 John Twiggs
143 Eleanor Thomasson
144 John Trimmer
145 Mary --

148 Robert McElwain
149 Isabel --
150 James Miller

156 Joseph Andover
157 Mary Reames

164 Luke Wiley
165 Kezia --

168 George Lytle

170 Michael Webster
171 Elizabeth Giles

A03/

172 Alexander McComas	230 Timothy Willets	
173 Elizabeth Day	231 Judith --	
	232 Thomas Matthews	364 George Strode
176 James Moore	233 Sarah Thomas	365 Margaret --
177 Susanna Forster		366 Morgan James
178 Joseph Dickinson	236 Abraham Griffith	367 Elizabeth Prothero
179 Elizabeth Miller	237 Hannah Lester	
180 James Clemson	238 Joseph Burson	376 Zebulon Clayton
181 Sarah --	239 Rachel Potts	
182 John Strode	240 Joshua Hemingway	
183 Magdalen James	241 Abigail Morse	384 Thomas Milhous
	242 James Haven	385 Elizabeth --
	243 Sarah --	386 Robert Mickle
		387 Mary --
	246 John McCulley	388 Robert Miller
192 John Milhous		389 Elizabeth --
193 Sarah Mickle	248 John Malmsbury	390 Thomas Lightfoot
194 James Miller	249 Mary Bowker	391 Mary --
195 Cath. Lightfoot	250 John Doane	392 John Baldwin Jr
196 John Baldwin	251 Hannah Wilson	393 Catharine Carter
197 Hannah Johnson	252 James Cattell	394 Joshua Johnson
198 Samuel Brown	253 Ann Rogers	395 Mary --
199 Ann Clark	254 Jonathan Gaskill	396 George Brown
200 Abraham Vickers	255 Jane Shinn	397 Mercy --
201 Mary France		398 John Clark
202 Nicholas Dillon		399 Martha Wheeler
203 Mary --		400 Thomas Vickers
204 Benj. Mendenhall		401 Esther --
205 Lydia Roberts	280 Robert Scothorn	
206 Aaron Mendenhall	281 Mary Gibbons	408 Benjamin Mendenhall
207 Rose Fierson		409 Ann Pennell
208 William Griffith		410 Owen Roberts
		411 Mary --
212 John Hursey	286 Paul Thomasson	412 John Mendenhall
213 Margaret Record	287 Felicia --	413 Elizabeth Maris
214 John Harry		414 Thomas Pierson
215 Frabces --	340 John Webster	415 Rose Dixon
216 Mordecai Price	341 Hannah Butterworth	
217 Elizabeth White	342 Nathaniel Giles	424 John Hussey Jr
218 Walter Price		425 Ann Inskeep
219 Ann --	344 Daniel McComas	
220 John Hussey Jr		428 Hugh Harry
221 Ann Inskeep	346 Nicholas Day	429 Elizabeth Erinton
	347 Sarah --	
224 Jonathan Burdg		432 Mordecai Price
		433 Mary Parsons
226 Richard Morris		434 Guy White Jr
	356 Daniel Dickinson	435 Elizabeth Griffith
228 Thomas Smith	357 Elizabeth Scott	
229 Mary Allen	358 Gayen Miller	440 John Hussey

A03/
441 Rebecca Perkins
442 John Inskeep

448 David Burdg

450 Richard Ellison Jr
451 Elsa --
452 Lewis Morris
453 Elizabeth Almy

456 Abraham Smith Jr
457 Margery --
458 Jedediah Allen
459 Elizabeth Howland
460 Hope Willets
461 Mercy Langdon

464 Oliver Matthews

472 Howell Griffith

474 Peter Lester
475 Mary Duncalf
476 George Burson
477 Hannah --
478 Jonas Potts
479 Mary
480 Joshua Hemingway Jr
481 Rebecca Stanhope
482 Joseph Morse
483 Elizabeth Sawtelle
484 Nathaniel Haven
485 Elizabeth Travers

498 William Bowker
499 Hannah Slade
500 Eleazer Doane
501 Susanna --
504 Jonas Cattell
505 Mary Pearce

508 Josiah Gaskill
509 Rebecca Lippincott
510 John Shinn Jr
511 Mary --

DIVISION A
A4/1−A4/511

A4/   GERALD RUDOLPH FORD U.S. President
1 GERALD RUDOLPH FORD Jr.(Original name Leslie King,Jr)
  1a Elizabeth Ann   119 Rhoda Ricketson 460 Edward Gove
     Bloomer   122 Anselm Comstock 461 Bethiah Clark
  2 Leslie Lynch King 123 Elizabeth Jewett 462 Moses Stickney
  3 Dorothy Ayer Gardner124 Jonathan Gridley 463 Sarah Wardwell
  4 Charles Henry King 125 Martha Adams   464 Jean Magny
  5 Martha Alice Porter 126 Wells Ely   465 Jeanne Machet
  6 Levi Addison Gardner127 Rebecca Selden
  7 Adele Agusta Ayer   468 Henry Vanderburgh
  8 Lynch King   202 William Orr   469 Magdalena Knight
  9 Rebecca Shephard   470 Johannes Van Kleeck
              224 William Ayer 471 Aeltje Terbosch
 12 Alexander Gardner 225 Sarah Little   472 John Collins Jr
 13 Sally Miller   226 William Adams 473 Susanna Daggett
 14 George Manney Ayer 227 Elizabeth Noyes 474 Jabez Gifford
 15 Amy Gridley Butler 228 Ezra Chase   475 Dinah Sheldon
              229 Judith Davis 476 Jonathan Ricketson
 24 Alexander Gardner 230 Nathaniel Gove 477 Abigail Howland
 25 Mary Brodie   231 Susanna Stickney 478 Benjamin Wilbur
              232 John Manney   479 Elizabeth Head
 28 John Varnum Ayer 233 Ann Wines
 29 Elida V Manney   234 Henry Venderburgh488 John Comstock Jr
 30 George S. Butler 235 Sarah Van Kleeck 489 Mary Colt
 31 Elizabeth E.Gridley 236 Hezekiah Collins 490 Samuel Goodspeed
              237 Catherine Gifford
 48 John Gardner   238 Jonathan Ricketson 492 Nathan Jewett
 49 Janet Hartidge   239 Meribah Wilbur 493 Deborah Lord
 50 Robert Brodie   494 Samuel Selden
 51 Margaret Burns   244 Abner Comstock 495 Deborah Dudley
              245 Eunice Goodspeed 496 Thomas Gridley
 56 Samuel Ayer   246 David Jewett 497 Elizabeth Clark
 57 Polly Chase   247 Sarah Selden 498 Isaac Pinney
 58 John Manney   248 Jonathan Gridley 499 Sarah Clark
 59 Elizabeth Collins 249 Mary Pinney
 60 Daniel Butler   504 William Ely
 61 Betsy Comstock 252 Daniel Ely   505 Elizabeth Smith
 62 Theodore Gridley 253 Ruth Wells   506 Samuel Welles
 63 Amy Ely   254 Samuel Selden 507 Ruth Judson
              255 Deborah Dudley 508 Joseph Selden
 98 Alexander Hartridge   509 Rebecca Church
 99 Margaret Scott 448 James Ayer   510 Joseph Dudley
100 William Brodie   449 Mary White   511 Sarah Pratt
101 Janet Orr   450 Daniel White
102 John Burns   451 Abiah Clement
              452 Abraham Adams Jr
112 Daniel Ayer   453 Anne Longfollow
113 Sarah Adams   454 John Noyes Jr
114 William Chase 455 Mary Thurlo
115 Abigail Gove   456 Jacob Chase
116 Wines Manney   457 Joanna Davis
117 Aeltje Vanderburg 458 William Davis
118 Hezekiah Collins 459 Mary Kelly

479

A5/   ULYSSES SIMPSON GRANT U.S. President
1 ULYSSES SIMPSON GRANT

1a Julia Boggs	77 Sarah Rowley
2 Jesse Root Grant	78 James Allen
3 Hannah Simpson	79 Elizabeth Partridge
4 Noah Grant III	
5 Rachel Kelley	128 Matthew Grant
6 John Simpson Jr	129 Priscilla --
7 Rebecca Weir	130 John Porter
8 Noah Grant Jr.	131 Ann White
9 Susanna Delano	132 Thomas Miner
	133 Grace Palmer
12 John Simpson	134 Richard Booth
13 Hannah Roberts	135 Elizabeth Hawley
14 Samuel Weir	136 Simon Huntington
15 Mary --	137 Margaret Barrett
16 Noah Grant	138 William Rockwell
17 Martha Huntington	139 Susanna Capen
18 Jonathan Delano	140 John Lathrop
19 Amy Hatch	141 Hannah House
24 William Simpson	144 Jean de Lannoy
25 Jane Hines	145 Marie Le Mahieu
26 Lewis Roberts	
27 Mary --	148 Richard Warren MF
	149 Elizabeth--
32 Samuel Grant Jr	150 William Walker
33 Grace Miner	
34 John Huntington	152 Thomas Hatch
35 Abigail Lathrop	153 Grace --
36 Jonathan Delano	154 Henry Rowley
37 Mercy Warren	
38 Joseph Hatch	156 Samuel Allen
39 Amy Allen	157 Ann --
	158 George Partridge
48 Thomas Simpson	159 Sarah Tracy

64 Samuel Grant
65 Mary Porter
66 John Miner
67 Elizabeth Booth
68 Christopher Huntington
69 Ruth Rockwell
70 Samuel Lathrop
71 Elizabeth Scudder
72 Philip Delano
73 Hester Dewsbury
74 Nathaniel Warren
75 Sarah Walker
76 Jonathan Hatch

A6/ JAMES ABRAM GARFIELD U.S. President

1 JAMES ABRAM GARFIELD		232 Henry Wheeler
1a Lucretia Rudolph		233 Abigail Allen
2 Abram Garfield	96 Maturin Ballou	234 Philip Squire
3 Eliza Ballou	97 Hannah Pike	235 Rachel Ruggles
4 Thomas Garfield	98 Valentine Whitman	
5 Asenath Hill	99 Mary --	240 Joseph Carpenter
6 James Ballou IV		241 Margaret Sutton
7 Mehitable Ingalls	104 Walter Cooke	242 William Weeks
8 Solomon Garfield	105 Catharine --	243 Elizabeth --
9 Sarah Bryant	106 John Rockwood	244 Richard Martin
	107 Joanna Ford	245 Elizabeth Salter
12 James Ballou III!		246 Francis Billington
13 Tamasin Cook	112 John Ingalls	247 Christian Penn
14 Henry Ingalls	113 Elizabeth Barrett	
15 Sybil Carpenter	114 Benjamin Ludden	
16 Thomas Garfield Jr	115 Eunice Holbrook	
17 Rebecca Johnson	116 James Wheeler	
	117 Grizell Squire	
24 James Ballou Jr	118 John West	
25 Catherine Arnold	119 Mehitable	
26 Daniel Cook	120 Benjamin Carpenter	
27 Susannah --	121 Renew Weeks	
28 Ebenezer Ingalls	122 John Martin	
29 Elizabeth Wheeler	123 Mercy Billington	
30 Jotham Carpenter Jr	124 George Thompson	
31 Mehitable Thompson	125 Sarah --	
32 Thomas Garfield		
33 Mercy Bigelow	128 Edward Garfield	
34 Samuel Johnson	129 Rebecca --	
35 Rebecca --	130 Matthew Bridge	
	131 Anna Danforth	
48 James Ballou	132 John Bigelow	
49 Susanna Whitman	133 Mary Warren	
	134 Thomas Flagg	
52 Nicholas Cook	135 Mary --	
53 Joanna Rockwood		
	194 Robert Pike	
56 Edmund Ingalls	195 Catharine --	
57 Eunice Ludden		
58 James Wheeler Jr	212 Richard Rockwood	
59 Elizabeth West	213 Agnes --	
60 Jotham Carpenter		
61 Disire Martin	224 Edmund Ingalls	
62 John Thompson	224 Ann --	
63 Elizabeth		
64 Benjamin Garfield	228 James Luddin	
65 Elizabeth Bridge	229 Mary Johnson	
66 Joshua Bigelow	230 John Holbrook	
67 Elizabeth Flagg	231 Elizabeth Stream	

A7/   THEODORE ROOSEVELT JR.   U.S. President
1 THEODORE ROOSEVELT JR

1a Alice Hathaway Lee	48 James Bulloch	108 John Baillie
2 Theodore Roosevelt	49 Jean Stobo	109 Jean Baillie
3 Martha Bulloch	50 James De Veaux	
4 Cornelius Van Schaick	51 Anne Fairchild	128 Claes Martensen
Roosevelt	52 Charles Irvine	Van Roosevelt
5 Margaret Barnhill	53 Euphemia Douglas	129 Jannetje Tomas
6 James Stphn. Bulloch	54 Kenneth Baillie	130 Jan B.Kunst
7 Martha Stewart	55 Elizabeth Mackay	131 Jannetje Adriaens
8 James J Roosevelt	56 John Stewart	132 Sicert Olfertsen
9 Maria Van Schaick	57 Hannah --	133 Itie Roelofs
10 Robert Barnhill		134 Cornelius Jansen
11 Elizabeth Potts	64 Nicholas Roosevelt	Clopper
12 James Bulloch	65 Heyltje Jans Kunst	135 Heyltje Pieters
13 Anne Irvine	66 Olfert Sioerts	136 Jan Louwe Bogaert
14 Daniel Stewart	67 Margaret Clopper	137 Cornelia Everetse
15 Susannah Oswald	68 Claes Bogaert	138 Hendrick Cornelis
16 Jacobus Roosevelt	69 Belitje Van Schaick	Van Schaick
17 Annetje Bogaert	70 Johannes Peeck	139 Neeltje C. Stille
		Stilles
18 Cornelius Van Schaick	71 Eliz. Van Imbroch	140 Jan Peeck
19 Angeltje Yates	72 Eman. Van Schaick	141 Maria Du Trieux
20 John Barnhill	73 Maria Wyngaart	142 Gysbert
21 Sarah Craig	74 Hendrick Van Dyck	Van Imbroch
22 Thomas Potts	75 Maria Schuyler	143 Rachel de La
23 Elizabeth Lukens	76 Christoffel Yates	Montagne
24 Archibald Bulloch	77 Catelyntje Winne	144 Claas Gerritse Van
25 Mary De Veaux	78 Pieter Waldron	Schaick
26 John Irvine	79 Tryntje Cornelis	
27 Ann Elizabeth Baillie	Van Den Bergh	146 Luykas Gerritse
28 John Stewart Jr		Wyngaart
29 Susannah Bacon	88 David Potts	147 Anna J.Van Hoesen
30 Joseph Olwald	89 Alice Croasdale	148 Cornelis Van Dyck
31 Ann --	90 Edmond McVeagh	149 Elizabeth Laeckens
32 Johannes Roosevelt	91 Alice Dickinson	150 David Pietersz
33 Heyltje Sioerts	92 Johann Lucken	Schuyler
34 John Bogaert	93 Merken Gastes	151 Catalyn Ver Planck
35 Hannah Peeck	94 Rynear Tyson	152 Joseph Yates
36 Cornelius Van Schaick	95 Margaret Streypers	153 Huybertsie Marselis
37 Lydia Van Dyck		Van Bommel
38 Johannes G Yates	98 Archibald Stobo	
39 Rebecca Waldron	99 Elizabeth Park	156 Willem Waldron
40 Robert Barnhill	100 Andre De Veaux	157 Engeltie Van
41 Sarah --		Stoutenburg
42 Daniel Craig	102 Richard Fairchild	158 Cornelis Gysbertse
43 Margaret --	103 Ann Bellinger	Van Den Bergh
44 John Potts	104 Robert Irvine	159 Cornelia Wynantse
45 Elizabeth McVeagh	105 Margaret Coutts	Van Der Poel
46 William Lukens	106 John Douglas	
47 Elizabeth Tyson	107 Agnes Horn	178 Thomas Croasdale

A7/
179 Agnes Hathornwaite

184 Wilhelm Lucken

188 Theis Doors

198 James Park
199 Jean Scott

206 Edmund Bellinger
207 Sarah Cartwright
208 John Irvine

212 John Douglas
213 Grizel Forbes
214 James Horn
215 Isabel Leslie

A8/   FRANKLIN DELANO ROOSEVELT U.S. President
1 FRANKLIN D ROOSEVELT

1a Eleanor Roosevelt	49 Jean Peckham	100 Eleazer Cushman
2 James Roosevelt	50 James Cushman	101 Elizabeth Coombs
3 Sara Delano	51 Sarah Hatch	
4 Isaac Roosevelt	52 Caleb Church	104 Nathaniel Church
5 Mary Aspinwall	53 Mercy Pope	105 Innocent Head
6 Warren Delano Jr	54 Samuel Perry	106 Lemuel Pope
7 Catherine R Lyman	55 Susannah Swift	107 Elizabeth Hunt
8 James Roosevelt	56 Joseph Lyman	108 Ebenezer Perry
9 Maria Eliza Walton	57 Abigail Lewis	109 Abigail Presbury
10 John Aspinwall Jr	58 Benjamin Sheldon	110 Jireh Swift
11 Susan Howland	59 Mary Strong	111 Deborah Hathaway
12 Warren Delano Sr	60 Nathaniel Robbins	112 Benjamin Lyman
13 Deborah Church	61 Eliz Hutchinson	113 Thankful Pomeroy
14 Joseph Lyman III	62 James Murray	114 Nathaniel Lewis
15 Anne Jean Robbins	63 Barbara Bennet	115 Abigail Ashley
16 Isaac Roosevelt	64 Nicholas Roosevelt	116 Thomas Sheldon
17 Cornelia Hoffman	65 Heyltje Jans Kunst	117 Mary Hinsdale
18 Abraham Walton	66 Johannes Hardenbroeck	118 Ebenezer Strong
19 Grace Williams	67 Sara Van Laer	119 Mary Holton
20 John Aspinwall	68 Nicholas Hoffman	120 Thomas Robbins
21 Rebecca Smith	69 Jannetje Crispel	121 Ruth Johnson
22 Joseph Howland	70 Robert Benson	122 Edward Hutchinson
23 Lydia Bill	71 Cornelia Roos	123 Lydia Foster
24 Ephraim Delano	72 William Walton	124 John Murray
25 Elizabeth Cushman	73 Mary Santvoort	125 Ann Bennet
26 Joseph Church	74 Gerardus Beekman	126 Andrew Bennet
27 Deborah Perry	75 Magdalena Abeel	127 Drthy. Collingwood
28 Joseph Lyman Jr		128 Claes VanRosenvelt
29 Mary Sheldon	80 Peter Aspinwall	129 Jannetje Tomas
30 Edward H Robbins	81 Remembrance Palfrey	130 Jan Barentsen Kunst
31 Elizabeth Murray	82 Christopher Dean	131 Jannetje Adriaens
32 James Roosevelt		132 Andries Hardenbroeck
33 Catharina Hardenbrock	84 Henry Smith	133 Aeffe Sijbrantsz
34 Martin Hoffman	85 Anna Shepard	134 Stoffel Van Laer
35 Tryntje Benson	86 Henry Lloyd	135 Catharina Jans
36 Jacob Walton	87 Rebecca Nelson	136 Martin H Hoffman
37 Maria Beekman	88 Nathaniel Howland	137 Emmerentje DeWitte
38 Charles Williams	89 Martha Cole	138 Antoine Crispel
39 Sarah Elizabeth --	90 John Burt	139 Petronella DuMond
40 Joseph Aspinwall	91 Abigail Cheever	140 Samson Benson
41 Hannah Dean	92 Samuel Bill Jr	141 Tryntje VanDeursen
42 William H Smith	93 Hannah --	142 Johannes Roos
43 Margaret LLoyd	94 Joshua Huntington	143 Cornelia
44 Nathaniel Howland	95 Hannah Perkins	144 Thomas Walton
45 Abigail Burt	96 Jonathan Delano	145 Mary Lawrence
46 Ephraim Bill	97 Mercy Warren	146 Jacob A Santvoort
47 Lydia Huntington	98 Stephen Peckham	147 Magdaleentje
48 Thomas Delano		Van Vleck

----

148 Wilhelmus Hendrickse
    Beekman
149 Catalina de Boogh
150 Stoffel Janse Abeel
151 Neeltje Janse Croom

162 Peter Palfrey
163 Edith --

168 William Smith
169 Martha Tunstall
170 Thomas Shepard III
171 Mary Anderson
172 James Lloyd
173 Grizzell Sylvester
174 John Nelson
175 Elizabeth Tailer
176 Joseph Howland
177 Elizabeth Southworth
178 James Cole Jr
179 Mary Tilson
180 William Burt
181 Elizabeth --
182 Thomas Cheever
183 Sarah Bill
184 Samuel Bill
185 Mercy Haughton

188 Simon Huntington
189 Lydia Gager
190 Jabez Perkins
191 Hannah Lathrop
192 Philip Delano
193 Hester Dewsbury
194 Nathaniel Warren
195 Sarah Walker
196 John Peckham
196 Eleanor --

200 Thomas Cushman
201 Mary Allerton
202 John Coombs Jr
203 Elizabeth Royall

208 Joseph Church Jr
209 Grace Shaw
210 Henry Head
211 Elizabeth --
212 Seth Pope
213 Deborah Perry

214 Ephraim Hunt Jr
215 Joanna Alcock
216 Samuel Perry
217 Esther Taber
218 Stephen Presbury
219 Deborah Skiffe
220 Jireh Swift
221 Abigail Gibbs
222 Jonathan Hathaway
223 Susannah Pope
224 John Lyman
225 Dorcas Plum
226 Medad Pomeroy
227 Experience Woodward
228 William Lewis Jr
229 Mary Cheever
230 David Ashley
231 Hannah Glover
232 Isaac Sheldon
233 Mary Woodford
234 Samuel Hinsdale
235 Mehitable Johnson
236 Ebenezer Strong
237 Hannah Clapp
238 William Holton Jr
239 Sarah Marshfield
240 Nathaniel Robbins Jr
241 Hannah Chandler
242 William Johnson Jr
243 Esther Gardner
244 Elisha Hutchinson
245 Elizabeth Clarke
246 John Foster
247 Lydia Turell
248 John Murray
249 Margaret Scott
250 Archibald Bennet
251 Barbara Rutherford
252 Archibald Bennet
253 Barbara Rutherford
254 Alexander Collingwood
255 Dorothy Lawson

340 Thomas Shepard Jr= A11/58
341 Anna Tyng   = A11/59

A9/   RONALD WILSON REAGAN U.S. President
 1 RONALD WILSON REAGAN
 1a Folks Sarah Jane
 1b Robbins Anne Frances("Nancy Davis")
 2 John Edward Reagan
 3 Nelle Clyde Wilson
 4 John Michael Reagan
 5 Jennie Cusick
 6 Thomas Wilson
 7 Mary Ann Elsey
 8 Michael Reagan
 9 Catherine Mulcahey
10 Patrick Cusick
11 Sarah Higgins
12 John Wilson
13 Jane Blue
14 Robert Elsey
15 Mary Baker
16 Thomas Reagan

18 Patrick Mulcahey

26 Donald Blue
27 Catharine McFarlain
28 Henry Elsey
29 Susannah --
30 John Baker

DIVISION A
A10/1-A10/91

A10/   GEORGE WASHINGTON   U.S. President
 1 GEORGE WASHINGTON
 1a Dandridge Martha(Mrs Custis) 42 Lawrence Townely
 2 Augustine Washington   43 Jennet Halstead
 3 Mary Ball   44 Robert Reade
 4 Lawrence Washington   45 Mildred Windebank
 5 Mildred Warner   46 Nicholas Martiau
 6 Joseph Ball
 7 Mary --   64 Robert Washington
 8 John Washington   65 Elizabeth Light (Lyte)
 9 Anne Pope   66 William Butler
10 Augustine Warner Jr   67 Margaret Greeke
11 Mildred Reade   68 Thomas Twigden
12 William Ball
13 Hannah Atherold   70 William Dickens
                                 71 Anne Thornton
16 Lawrence Washington
17 Amphyllis Twigden   84 Lawrence Towneley
18 Nathaniel Pope   85 Margaret Hartley
                                 86 John Halstead
20 Augustine Warner
21 Mary Towneley   88 Andrew Reade
22 George Reade   89 Alice Cooke
23 Elizabeth Martiau   90 Thomas Windebank Sir
                                 91 Frances Dymoke
32 Lawrence Washington
33 Margaret Butler
34 John Twigden
35 Anne Dickens

487

DIVISION A
A11/1-A11/188

A11/ JOHN ADAMS JR. & JOHN QUINCY ADAMS U.S. Presidents
1 JOHN QUINCY ADAMS

1a Louisa C. Johnson	52 George Fowle	126 Nicholas Parker
2 JOHN ADAMS JR.	53 Mary --	127 Ann --
3 Abagail Smith	54 Henry Bright	128 Henry Adams
4 John Adams II	55 Anna Goldstone	
5 Susanna Boylston	56 Edmund Quincy	160 Henry Boylson
6 William Smith Jr	57 Joanna Hoar	
7 Elizabeth Quincy	58 Thomas Shepard	162 Thomas Bastian
8 Joseph Adams Jr.	59 Anna Tyng=A8/340	163 Sara Wright
9 Hannah Bass	60 William Norton	
10 Peter Boylston	61 Lucy Downing	184 Edward Cogswell
11 Ann White	62 Arthur Mason	185 Alice --
12 William Smith	63 Joanna Parker	186 William Thompson
13 Abigail Fowle	64 John Adams	187 Phyllis --
14 John Quincy II	65 Agnes --	188 John Hawke
15 Elizabeth Norton	66 Henry Squire	
16 Joseph Adams		
17 Abigail Baxter	74 William Savil	
18 John Bass		
19 Ruth Alden	78 William Mullins MF	
20 Thomas Boylston	79 Alice #2 --	
21 Mary Gardner	80 Edward Boylston	
22 Benjamin White	81 Anne Bastian	
23 Susanna Cogswell		
24 Thomas Smith	84 Thomas Gardner	
25 Sarah Boylston		
26 Isaac Fowle	92 John Cogswell =A19/3002	
27 Beriah Bright	93 Elizabeth Thompson=A19/3003	
28 Daniel Quincy	94 Adam Hawkes	
29 Anna Shepard	95 Ann --	
30 John Norton		
31 Mary Mason	100 Edward Boylston	
32 Henry Adams	101 Anne Bastian	
33 Edith Squire		
34 Gregory Baxter	108 Henry Bright	
35 Margaret Paddy	109 Mary --	
36 Samuel Bass=A19/1466	110 Heny Goldstone	
37 Ann Savell =A19/1467	111 Anne--	
38 John Alden MF	112 Edmund Quincy	
39 Priscilla Mullins MF	113 Judith Pares	
40 Thomas Boylston	114 Charles Hoar	
41 Sarah --	115 Joanna Hincksman	
42 Thomas Gardner	116 Thomas Shepard	
43 Lucy Smith	117 Margaret Touteville	
44 John White	118 William Tyng	
45 Frances Jackson	119 Elizabeth Coytmore	
46 William Cogswell	120 William Norton	
47 Susanna Hawkes	121 Alice Bownest	
	122 Emanuel Downing	
50 Thomas Boylston	123 Lucy Winthrop	
51 Sarah --		

A12/   RUTHERFORD BIRCHARD HAYES U.S. President
1 RUTHERFORD B HAYES
1a Luce Ware
2 Rutherford Hayes Jr
3 Sophia Birchard
4 Rutherford Hayes
5 Chloe Smith
6 Roger Cornwall
7 Drusilla Austin
8 Ezekiel Hayes
9 Rebecca Russell
10 Israel Smith
11 Abigail Chandler

14 Daniel Austin
15 Abigail Phelps
16 Daniel Hayes
17 Sarah Lee
18 John Russell
19 Sarah Trowbridge
20 John Smith III
21 Elizabeth Smith
22 Isaac Chandler
23 Abigail Hale
26 Joseph Jacob Jr
27 Mary Storrs
28 Nathaniel Austin
29 Abigail Hovey
30 Timothy Phelps
31 Abigail Merrick
32 George Hayes
33 Abigail Dibble
34 John Lee
35 Elizabeth Crampton
36 Samuel Russell
37 Abigail Whiting
38 Thomas Trowbridge
39 Mary Winston
40 John Smith Jr
41 Mary Root
42 Benjamin Smith
43 Ruth Buck
44 Henry Chandler
45 Lydia Abbott
46 John Hale
47 Abigail Gleason

52 Joseph Jacob
53 Sarah Lindsey
54 Samuel Storrs Jr
55 Martha Burgess

56 Anthony Austin
57 Esther Huggins
58 Thomas Hovey
59 Sarah Cooke
60 Nathaniel Phelps
61 Grace Martin
62 John Merrick
63 Mary Day

66 Samuel Dibble

68 Walter Lee
69 Mary --
70 Dennis Crampton
71 Mary Parmelee
72 John Russell
73 Rebecca Newberry
74 John Whiting
75 Sybil Collins
76 Thomas Trowbridge
77 Sarah Rutherford
78 John Winston
79 Elizabeth --
80 John Smith
81 Mary Partridge
82 John Root Jr
83 Mary Ashley
84 John Smith
85 Mary Partridge
86 Henry Buck
87 Eliz. Churchill
88 Thomas Chandler
89 Hannah Brewer
90 George Abbott Jr
91 Sarah Farnum
92 Thomas Hale Jr
93 Priscilla Markham
94 Isaac Gleason
95 Hester Eggleston

106 John Lindsey
107 Mary Alley
108 Samuel Storrs
109 Mary Huckins
110 John Burgess
111 Mary Worden
112 Richard Austin

114 John Huggins
115 Bridget --

116 Daniel Hovey
117 Abigail Andrew
118 Aaron Cooke3rd=A20/138
119 Sarah Westwood=A20/139
120 Nathaniel Phelps
121 Elizabeth Copley
122 William Martin
123 Lydia Marsh
124 Thomas Merrick
125 Elizabeth Tilley
126 Thomas Day
127 Sarah Cooper

132 Thomas Dibble

134 William Graves

142 John Parmelee

144 John Russell
145 Phebe Collins
146 Thomas Newberry
147 Jane --
148 William Whiting
149 Susannah --
150 Edward Collins
151 Martha --
152 Thomas Trowbride
153 Elizabeth Marshall
154 Henry Rutherford
155 Sarah --
160 Samuel Smith
161 Elizabeth Smith
162 William Partridge
163 Mary Smith
164 John Root
165 Mary Kilbourn
166 Robert Ashley

168 Samuel Smith
169 Elizabeth Smith
170 William Partridge
171 Mary Smith

174 Josiah Churchill
175 Elizabeth Foote
176 William Chandler
177 Annis Bayford

180 George Abbott

---

182 Ralph Farnum	234 Robert Andrews
183 Alice --	235 Elizabeth --
184 Thomas Hale	236 Aaron Cooke Jr
185 Jane Lord	237 Mary Cooke
186 William Markham	238 William Westwood
187 Priscilla Graves	239 Bridget Kerrington
188 Thomas Gleason	240 William Phelps
189 Susanna Page	241 Elizabeth --
190 James Eggleston	246 John Marsh
191 Esther (Hester)	247 Grace Baldwin
212 Christopher Lindsey	
213 Margaret --	252 Robert Day
214 Hugh Alley	253 Editha Stebbing
215 Mary --	254 Thomas Cooper
216 Thomas Storrs	255 Sarah --
217 Mary --	
218 Thomas Huckins	
219 Mary Wells	
220 Thomas Burgess	
221 Dorothy --	
222 Peter Worden	
223 Mary --	
232 Richard Hovey	

DIVISION A
A13/1—A13/143

A13/   ABRAHAM LINCOLN U.S. President
1 ABRAHAM LINCOLN
1a Mary Ann Todd   64 Samuel Lincoln
2 Thomas Lincoln   65 Martha Lyford
3 Nancy Hanks   66 Abraham Jones
4 Abraham Lincoln   67 Sarah Whitman
5 Bathsheba --
6 James Hanks   70 John Bowne
7 Lucy Shipley   71 Lydia Holmes
8 John Lincoln
9 Rebecca Flowers   78 Richard Lambe
                             79 Lucy Baillie

14 Robert Shipley Jr.
15 Sarah --   128 Edward Lincoln
16 Mordecai Lincoln Jr.   129 Bridget Gilman
17 Hannah Salter   130 John Lyford
18 Enoch Flowers
19 Rebecca Barnard   132 Thomas Jones
                             133 Ann --
32 Mordecai Lincoln   134 John Whitman
33 Sarah Jones   135 Ruth --
34 Richard Salter   140 William Bowne
35 Sarah Bowne   141 Ann --
36 William Flower   142 Obadiah Holmes
37 Elizabeth Moris   143 Katherine Hyde
38 Richard Barnard
39 Frances Lambe

A14/ BENJAMIN HARRISON & WILLIAM HENRY HARRISON U.S. Presidents

1 BENJAMIN HARRISON

1a Caroline L Scott
2 John Scott Harrison
3 Elizabeth Ramsey Irwin
4 WILLIAM HENRY HARRISON
5 Anna Tuthill Symmes
6 Archibald Irwin III
7 Mary Ramsey
8 Benjamin Harrison V
9 Elizabeth Bassett
10 John Cleves Symmes
11 Anna Tuthill
12 Archibald Irwin Jr.
13 Jane McDowell
14 James Ramsey Jr.
15 Elizabeth Porter
16 Benjamin Harrison IV
17 Anne Carter
18 William Bassett IV
19 Elizabeth Churchill
20 Timothy Symmes Jr.
21 Mary Cleves
22 Henry Tuthill III
23 Phoebe Horton
24 Archibald Irwin

26 William McDowell
27 Mary --
28 James Ramsey

32 Benjamin Harrison III
33 Elizabeth Burwell
34 Robert King Carter
35 Elizabeth Landon
36 William Bassett III
37 Joanna Burwell
38 William Churchill
39 Elizabeth Armistead
40 Timothy Symmes
41 Elizabeth Collamore
42 John Cleves Jr.

44 Henry Tuthill Jr.
45 Hannah --
46 Caleb Horton
47 Phebe Terry

64 Benjamin Harrison Jr
65 Hannah --
66 Lewis Burwell Jr.
67 Abigail Smith

68 John Carter
69 Sarah Ludlow
70 Thomas Landon
71 Mary --
72 William Bassett
73 Bridget Cary
74 Lewis Burwell Jr
75 Abigail Smith
76 John Churchill
77 Dorothy --
78 John Armistead
79 Judith --
80 William Symmes
81 Mary Chickering
82 Anthony Collamore
83 Sarah Chittenden

88 Henry Tuthill
89 Bethia Horton

92 Barnabas Horton
93 Sarah Wines
94 Nathaniel Terry
95 Mary Horton

128 Benjamin Harrison
129 Mary --
132 Lewis Burwell
133 Lucy Higginson
134 Anthony Smith
135 Martha Bacon

138 Gabriel Ludlow
139 Phyllis --
140 Sylvanus Landon
141 Anne --
144 William Bassett
145 Anne --
146 Miles Cary
147 Anne Taylor

148 Lewis Burwell
149 Lucy Higginson
150 Anthony Smith
151 Martha Bacon
152 Henry Churchill
153 Bridget --
156 Willilam Armistead
157 Ann Ellis=A15/157

160 Zachariah Symmes

161 Sarah Baker
162 Francis Chickering
163 Anne Fiske

166 Isaac Chittenden
167 Martha Vinal

176 John Tuthill
177 Deliverance King
178 Jonathan Horton
179 Bethia Wells

184 Caleb Horton
185 Abigail Hallock
186 Barnabas Wines
187 Mary --
188 Richard Terry
189 Abigail --
190 Caleb Horton
191 Abigail Hallock

264 Edward Burwell
265 Dorothy Bedell
266 Robert Higginson
267 Joanna Tokesy

270 James Bacon
271 Martha Woodward

276 Thomas Ludlow
277 Jane Pyle

292 John Cary
293 Alice Hobson
294 Thomas Taylor

296 Edward Burwell
297 Dorothy Bedell
298 Robert Higginson
299 Joanna Tokesy
302 Bacon James
303 Martha Woodwardll
304 Richard Churchill
312 Anthony Armistead
313 Frances Thompson

```
A15/          JOHN TYLER   U.S. President
 1 JOHN TYLER IV        50 Robert Booth Jr
  a  Letitia Christian  51 Ann Bray
 2 John Tyler III
 3 Mary M. Armistead
 4 John Tyler Jr.       68 Walter Chiles
 5 Anne Contesse
 6 Robert B Armistead   70 John Page
 7 Anne Shields         71 Alice Lukin
 8 John Tyler           96 William Armistead=A14/156
 9 Elizabeth Jarrett    97 Ann Ellis=A14/157
10 Louis Contesse       98 Robert Ellyson
11 Mary Morris
12 Ellyson Armistead   100 Robert Booth

14 James Shields Jr    102 James Bray
15 Anne Marot
16 Henry Tyler Jr
17 ELizabeth Chiles
18 John Jarrett
19 Joanna Lowe

24 Robert Armistead

28 James Shields

30 Jean Marot

32 Henry Tyler

34 Walter Chiles Jr
35 Mary Page

38 Michael Lowe

48 Anthony Armistead
49 Hannah Ellyson
```

DIVISION A
A16/1—A16/239

```
---------------------------------------------------------------
```

A16/   MILLARD FILLMORE U.S. President

1 MILLARD FILLMORE		
1a Abigail Powers	53 Deliverance Owen	118 Nicholas Olmstead
2 Nathaniel Fillmore		119 Sarah Loomis=G10Aam
3 Phoebe Millard	56 Stephen Hopkins	120 Andrew Messenger
4 Nathaniel Fillmore	57 Dorcas Bronson	
5 Hepzibah Wood	58 Samuel Butler	124 Robert Royce
6 Abiathar Millard	59 Elizabeth Olmstead	
7 Tabitha Hopkins	60 Samuel Messenger	126 James Morgan
8 John Fillmore Jr		127 Margery Hill
9 Dorcas Day	62 Nehemiah Royce	
10 Ebenezer Wood Jr	63 Hannah Morgan	140 Edmund Littlefield
11 Philippa Story		141 Agnes (Anna) Austen
12 Robert Millard	68 William Tilton	156 Roger Langton
13 Hannah Eddy		
14 Ebenezer Hopkins	70 Fran. Littlefield	160 Edward Wood
15 Susannah Messenger		161 Ruth Lee
16 John Fillmore	76 John Rowe	
17 Abigail Tilton		164 Thomas Hassen
18 Nathaniel Day	78 Joseph Langton	
19 Ruth Rowe	79 Rachel Parsons	166 Thomas Grant
20 Ebenezer Wood	80 Thomas Wood	167 Jane Haborne
21 Mary Rudd		
22 Stephen Story	82 Edward Hazen	172 Stephen Post
23 Mary Emerson	83 Hannah Grant	173 Elinor Panton
24 Nehemiah Millard	84 Jonathan Ruud	174 William Hyde
25 Phoebe Shore		
26 Eleazer Eddy	86 John Post	178 Renald Foster
27 Elizabeth Randall	87 Hester Hyde	179 Judith Wignol
28 Ebenezer Hopkins	88 William Story	
29 Mary Butler=R18Gam	89 Sarah Foster	184 Thomas Emerson
30 Daniel Messenger		185 Elizabeth Brewster
31 Lydia Royce	92 Nathaniel Emerson	
		188 John Perkins Jr
34 Abraham Tilton	94 Jacob Perkins	
35 Deliv. Littlefield	95 Sarah Wainwright	190 Frances Wainwright
36 Anthony Day	96 John Millard	191 Philippa Sewell
37 Susannah Matchett		
38 Hugh Rowe	98 William Sabin	198 Richard Wright
39 Rachel Langton	99 -- Wright	
40 John Wook	100 Sampson Shore	202 Aquila Purchase
41 Isabel Hazen	101 Abigail Purchase	203 Ann Squire
42 Nathaniel Rudd	102 John Hathorne	204 William Hawthorne
43 Mary Post		
44 Samuel Story	106 William Owen	228 Roger Brownson
	107 Elizabeth Davis	229 Mary Underwood
46 Thomas Emerson		
47 Philippa Perkins	112 John Hopkins	236 James Olmstead
48 Robert Millard		237 Joyce Cornish
49 Elizabeth Sabin	114 John Bronson	238 Joseph Loomis
50 Jonathan Shore	115 Frances Hills	239 Mary White
51 Priscilla Hathorne	116 Richard Butler	
52 John Eddy		

DIVISION A
A17/1-A17/231

A17/   FRANKLIN PIERCE U.S. President

1 FRANKLIN PIERCE	53 Elizabeth Johnson	223 John Johnson
1aJane M Appleton	54 Daniel Brewer	224 William Harris
2 Benjamin Pierce	55 Hannah Morrill	225 Agnes Mason
3 Anna Kendrick	56 John Harris	
4 Benjamin Pierce	57 Bridget Angier	228 William Angier
5 Elizabeth Merrill	58 John Pearson	
6 Benjamin Kendrick		230 John Rogers
7 Sarah Harris	64 Thomas Pierce	231 Bridget Ray
8 Stephen Pierce Jr		
9 Esther Fletcher	66 Rice Cole	
10 Abel Merrill		
11 Sarah Bodwell	72 Robert Fletcher	
12 Caleb Kendrick		
13 Abigail Bowen	76 Ezekiel Richardson	
14 Stephen Harris		
	78 William Underwood	
16 Stephen Pierce		
17 Tabitha Parker	80 Nathaniel Merrill	
18 William Fletcher		
19 Sarah Richardson	84 John Webster	
20 John Merrill	85 Mary Shatswell	
21 Lucy Webster	86 Nicholas Batt	
22 Henry Bodwell		
23 Bethia Emery	92 John Emery	
24 John Kendrick		
25 Esther Green	104 Griffith Bowen	
26 John Bowen	105 Margaret Fleming	
27 Hannah Brewer	106 Isaac Johnson	
28 Timothy Harris	107 Elizabeth Porter	
29 Phebe Pearson	108 Daniel Brewer =A1/1074	
32 Thomas Pierce Jr	110 Isaac Morrill	
33 Elizabeth Cole		
34 Jacob Parker		
36 William Fletcher	114 Edmund Angier	
	115 Bridget Rogers	
38 Josiah Richardson		
39 Rememberance Underwood	152 Thomas Richardson	
40 Nathaniel Merrill	153 Katherine Duxford	
41 Joanna Ninian		
42 John Webster Jr	160 Nathaniel Merrill	
43 Ann Batt	161 Mary Blacksoll	
46 John Emery Jr	172 Richard Batt	
48 John Kendrick	208 Francis Bowen	
49 Anna Smith	209 Ellen Franklyn	
50 John Green	210 Henry Fleming	
	211 Alice Dawkins	
52 Henry Bowen		

495

```
A18/        ZACHARY TAYLOR II  U.S. PRESIDENT
1  ZACHARY TYALOY II           51 Alice Savage
1a Margaret Mackall Smith      82 Edward Hancock
2  Richard Taylor=A84D         83 Alice Jeffreys
3  Sarah D Strother
4  Zachary Taylor              90 William Brewster MF=A10Abf
5  Elizabeth Lee               91 Mary --
6  William Strother
7  Sarah Bayly                100 William Thornton
8  James Taylor               102 Anthony Savage
9  Martha Thompson
10 Hancock Lee
11 Sarah Allerton
12 Francis Strother
13 Susannah Dabney

16 James Taylor
17 Frances --

20 Richard Lee
21 Anne Constable
22 Isaac Allerton Jr
23 Elizabeth Willoughby
24 William Strother
25 Margaret Thorton

40 John Lee
41 Jane Hancock

44 Isaac Allerton MF =A10A
45 Fear Brewster    =A10Ab
46 Thomas Willoughby
47 Alice --
48 William Strother
49 Dorothy --
50 Francis Thornton
```

A19/   (JOHN) CALVIN COOLIDGE JR. U.S. President

1 CALVIN COOLIDGE	56 Aaron Franklin	124 Stephen Grover
1a Grace A. Goodhue	58 Comfort Starr III	125 Elizabeth Bateman
2 John C. Coolidge	59 Judith Cooper	
3 Victoria J. Moor		128 Obadiah Coolidge
4 Calvin G. Coolidge	62 Eleazer Grover	129 Elizabeth Rose
5 Sarah Almeda Brewer		130 Josiah Goddard
6 Hiram D. Moor	64 Obadiah Coolidge	131 Rachel Davis
7 Abigail Franklin	65 Rachel Goddard	
8 Calvin Coolidge		136 Joseph Priest
9 Sarah Thompson	68 Joseph Priest Jr	137 Hannah Hagar
10 Esrael C. Brewer	69 Margaret Childs	138 Richard Child
11 Sally Brown	70 Jonathan Lawrence	139 Hannah Train
12 John Moor	71 Joanna Phillips	140 Nath. Lawrence
13 Mary Davis	72 James Thompson	141 Anna Fiske
14 Luther Franklin	73 Abigail Hamlet	142 Andrew Phillips
15 Priscilla Pinney	74 Ebenezer Jones	143 Sarah Smith
16 John Coolidge	75 Elizabeth Dale	144 James Thompson
17 Hannah Priest	76 John Eaton	145 Hannah Walker
18 William Thompson	77 Abigail Roberts	146 Jacob Hamlet
19 Dorcas Eaton	78 John Boutwell Jr	147 Mary Adford
20 Eliab Brewer	79 Elizabeth Parker	148 Samuel Jones
21 Sally Rice	80 Jonathan Brewer	149 Abigail Snow
22 Israel Putnam Brown	81 Arabella Goulding	150 Robert Dale
23 Sally Briggs	82 John Bent III	151 Joanna Farrar
	83 Hannah Rice	152 Jonathan Eaton
26 Nathaniel Davis Jr		
27 Lydia Harwood	88 Adam Brown	154 Abraham Roberts
28 Jabez Franklin	89 Esther Parkman	155 Susanna Thompson
29 Sarah Starr	90 Tarrant Putnam	156 John Boutwell
30 Jonathan Pinney	91 Priscilla Baker	157 Grace Eaton
31 Priscilla Grover	92 Silas Briggs	158 John Parker Jr
32 Josiah Coolidge	93 Esther Soper	159 Elizabeth Goodwin
33 Mary Jones	94 James Paul	160 John Brewer Jr
34 James Priest	95 Sarah White	161 Elizabeth Rice
35 Hannah Lawrence		162 Peter Goulding
36 William Thompson	104 Daniel Davis	
37 Abigail Jones	105 Mary Hubbard	164 John Bent Jr
38 Thomas Eaton	106 John Lane Jr	165 Martha Rice
39 Betsey Boutwell	107 Katherine Whiting	166 David Rice
40 Samuel Brewer	108 John Harwood	167 Hannah Walker
41 Martha Bent		
	110 David Pulsipher	176 Jacob Brown
44 Adam Brown Jr	111 Elizabeth Stowell	177 Sarah Burnham
45 Priscilla Putnam	112 Philip Franklin	178 John Parkman
46 Asa Briggs	113 Rachel Horton	179 Abigail Fairfield
47 Elizabeth Paul		180 Tarrant Putnam
	116 Comfort Starr Jr	181 Elizabeth Bacon
52 Nathaniel Davis	117 Elizabeth Perley	182 Thomas Baker Jr
53 Susanna Lane	118 Timothy Cooper	183 Mary Capen
54 John Harwood	119 Sarah Guile	184 Seth Briggs
55 Mary Pulsipher		185 Ann Whitmarsh
		186 Samuel Soper Jr

----

187 Esther Littlefield
188 William Paul
189 Mary Whitmarsh
190 John White
191 Elizabeth Hathaway

208 Samuel Davis
209 Mary Meddowes
210 Jonathan Hubbard
211 Hannah Rice
212 John Lane
213 Susannah Whipple
214 Samuel Whiting III
215 Elizabeth Read
216 James Harwood
217 Lydia Barrett

220 David Pulsipher

222 David Stowell J
223 Patience Herrington
224 James Franklin Jr
225 Martha Ormsby
226 Thomas Horton Jr
227 Hannah Garnsey

232 Comfort Starr
233 Mary Stone
234 Isaac Perley

236 John Cooper
237 Elizabeth Winter
238 Ephraim Guile
239 Martha Bradley

248 Stephen Grover

250 Eleazer Bateman
251 Elizabeth Wright

366 Joseph Capen
367 Patricia Appleton

374 Edmund Littlefield Jr
375 Bethia Waldo

732 John Capen
733 Mary Bass

750 Daniel Waldo
751 Susanna Adams

1466 Samuel Bass=A11/36
1467 Anna Savell=A11/37

1500 Cornelius Waldo
1501 Hannah Cogswell
1502 Samuel Adams
1503 Rebecca Graves

3002 John Cogswell   = A11/92
3003 Elizabeth Thompson =A11/93

3006 Thomas Graves
3007 Katherine Gray

6014 Thomas Gray

BIOGRAPHIES

Biographies of some of the persons of note, who are listed in the INDEX.

ADAMS JOHN: (A11/2) (1735-1826) 2nd U.S. President. Wife, Abigail Smith. Vice President 1788-1792. He died on the same day that Thomas Jefferson died; the 50th anniversary of the Declaration of Independence.

ADAMS JOHN QUINCY:(A11/1) (1767-1848). 6th President of the U.S., son of John Adams. Wife, Louise Johnson. Served as American minister to various European capitals. U.S. Senator 1803-08. Sec- retary of State 1817. Helped formulate the Monroe Doctrine. Served 17 years in Congress. Helped establish the Smithsonian Institution. Died in Speakers Room from a stroke.

ALDEN JOHN:(D13af24) Mayflower Passenger. Married Priscilla Mulllins, also a Mayflower Passenger. Assistant Governor of the Plymouth Colony. His marriage to Priscilla gave rise to the romantic legend made familiar by Longfellows poem, The "Courtship of Miles Standish".

BROWN PETER (Q10A) Mayflower Passenger

BUSH, GEORGE HERBERT:(A1/1)(1924-). 41st U.S. President. Wife, Barbara Pierce. Distinguished Flying Cross, U.S. Navy, World War II. House of Representatives 1966 and 1968 terms. Ambassadore to the United Nations. Director C.I.A. Engaged U.S. forces in Panama to oust Noriega. Engaged forces to defeat Iraq's invasion of Kuwait.

CAPET, HUGH: King of France (D30/40) Son of Hugh the Great REIGN [987-996] Nobles chose Hugh Capet as King over the rightful heir, Charles of Lorraine.

COOKE,FRANCIS: (D6/25) Mayflower Passenger

DAWES, CHARLES GATES: (G22A) 30th U.S. Vice President under Calvin Coolidge. Practiced law in Lincoln, Nebr. Comptroller of the Currency under McKinley. Organized Central Trust Co. of Ill. Volunteer in World War I. Brigadier General. Director of Budget under Harding. Author of the "Dawes Plan" His successful career includes the following professions: engineer, lawyer, politician, banker, philanthropist, soldier, ambassadore, and Vice President of the U.S..

DOTY EDWARD (D7af25) Mayflower Passenger.

FORD, GERALD RUDOLPH: (A4/1) (1913-). 38th U.S. President. Name changed from Gerald King. Wife: Elizabeth Ann Blocmer. Lt. Commander in the Navy during World War II. Served 23 years in the House. Vice President under Nixon.

FULLER EDWARD: (F11A) (1575-1621) Mayflower Passenger.21st signer of the Mayflower Compact

BIOGRAPHIES

FULLER SAMUEL: (D16/25) Mayflower passenger. 8th signer of the the Mayflower Compact. Deacon of the Church of Leyden and Plymouth. First physician among the pilgrims. Married 1st Alice Glascock, who died before Samuel left Leyden. 2nd marriage ended before 1613, 3rd Bridget Lee. Died 1633.

GARFIELD, JAMES A: (A6/1) (1831-1881) 20th U.S. President. Wife, Lucretia Rudolph. Ohio Senate 1859. Major General in the Civil War. Shot and died of wounds by an office seeker, Charles Guiteau in 1881.

GRANT ULYSSES SIMPSON: (A5/1) (1822-1885) 18th President of the U.S. Original name, Hiram Ulysses Grant. Married Julia T. Dent, 1848. Commander in Chief of the Union Army in the Civil War. Made full General in 1866.

HAYES RUTHERFORD B: (A12/10) (1822-1893). 19th U.S. President. Wife, Lucy Ware Webb. Major of the 23rd Ohio Volunteers in the Civil War. Rose to Major General. Congress 1864-1867. Governor of Ohio. Election as President disputed, due to submission of two different sets of electorial votes. Elected by an electorial commission, by one vote.

HOPKINS STEPHEN: (D5/25) Mayflower Passenger. (1595abt-1644)

HOWLAND JOHN SR.: (D1/24) (1593ca-1673) Mayflower Passenger. Married Elizabeth Tilley (MF). A near tragedy came to John when the Mayflower had completed about one half the journey. During a heavy storm, he stepped out on the deck and was swept overboard. He grabbed a rope for hoisting the top sail that was dangling over the side. Several men saw him and pulled him up with the assistance of one man with a boathook. He was on two of the first expeditions ashore when the ship landed at Plymouth. He served as Assistant Governor of the colony from 1629 to 1635.

KING EDWARD 1 : King of England (D29/25) Son of Henry III.
    Longshanks. b.1239   REIGN: [1272-1307]

KING GEORGE VI:(D28a16) King of England b.1904 REIGN: [1936-1962]
    Second son of George V

LINCOLN, ABRAHAM: (A13/1) (1809-1865). 16th U.S. President. Wife, Mary Ann Todd. Congress (1847-1849). President during the Civil War.Remembered by his elequent Gettysburg and Inaugural speeches. Assassinated by John Wilkes Booth in 1865.

NIXON RICHARD MILHOUS:(A3/1) (1913-). 37th U.S. President. Wife, Thelma Catherine (Pat) Ryan. House of Representatives 1946 and 1948 terms. Vice President under Eisenhower.

QUENN ELIZABETH II: (D38/15)Queen of England. Daughter of
                George VI   [REIGN 1952-   ]

BIOGRAPHIES

REAGAN, RONALD WILSON: (A9/1) (1911-   ) 49th U.S. President.
Wife,(1) Sarah Jane Folks (Jane Wyman). Sports announcer for 5
years. Successful career as film actor. Captain in the Army Air
Force during World War II. Governor of California.

ROGERS, THOMAS (X10A) Mayflower Passenger

ROOSEVELT FRANKLIN DELANO: (A8/1, D4/17) (1882-1945) 32rd U.S.
President. Married Anna Eleanor Roosevelt. a niece of Theodore
Roosevelt. He was Asst.Secretary of the Navy under Wilson; served
two terms in the New York Senate;Governor of New York, two terms.
He died during his fourth term as U.S. President. He was the
first president to break the "no third term" tradition.

ROOSEVELT THEODORE Jr.(A7/1,D10/16): (1858-1919) 26th President
of the U.S.(1901-1909). Wife Alice Hathaway Lee. Rancher in North
Dakota, an explorer, hunter, and writer. He won the Noble Peace
Prize in 1905 for successfully organizing a peace arbitration
between Russia and Japan. Writer of some 40 books: his "Winning
of the West" was his best known. He organized the "Rough Riders",
and led his volunteers in a famous charge up Kettle Hill in the
war with Spain. Governor New York.

STANDISH MILES: (D13/25) (1584-1656) Mayflower passenger.
Military leader of the Plymouth Colony. Founder of Duxbury, Mass.

TAFT, WILLIAM HOWARD:(A2/1) 27th U.S. President (1857-1930. Wife,
Helen Herron. Father was Secretary of War, and Attorney General
under Grant. He was minister to Russia and Austria. First civil
governor to the Philippines. Professor of constitutional law at
Yale. Chief Justice of the U.S.

WARREN, RICHARD: (W10A) Mayflower passenger. 12th signer of the
Mayflower Compact.

WASHINGTON,GEORGE:(A10/1)(1732-1799) First U.S. President, inaug-
urated in 1789. Married Martha Custis,1759. Commander-In-Chief in
the Revolutionary War.

WILLIAMS ROGER: (C74B) (1599-1683). Married Mary Barnard.
Minister of the Church of England. Came to Boston from England
on the "Lyon" in 1631. He was banished from the colony for his
stand on separation of church and state, and freedom of religion.
He founded Rhode Island, and secured a charter for the colony.
He was governor of the Providence Plantations.

WINSLOW, EDWARD: (D12/25) (1595-1655) Mayflower passenger. 3rd
signer of the Mayflower Compact. Son of Edward Sr born 1560,
Droitwich, Eng. 3rd governor of the colony. Commander of United
Colonies. m 1st Elizabeth Barker at Leyden Holland, 2nd to
Susanna Fuller.

BIBLIOGRAPHIES

American History Co.: Colonial and Revolutionary Lineages.
  American History Co. of America,1939
Andrews,H. Franklin:The Hamlin Family of Barnstable, Mass. 1639-
  1902. 1894. Pub. by author.
Austin, John:Stephen Hopkins of the Mayflower. Gen.Soc.
  Mayflower Descendants 1989
Banks,Charles Edward:The English Ancestry and Homes of
  The Pilgram Fathers. The Gen. Publishing Co., Baltimore Md.1984.
Bloodgood, George M.: Ancestors and Descendants of Captain Franse
  Bloetgoet. Pub. by author, 1980
Brayton, I.:The Story of Hartford, N.Y.
Burgess, Roy: Early Missourians and Kin. The Heritage Books, Inc.
  Bowie, Md. 1984.
Browning, Charles H.:Americans of Royal Descent. A collection of
  genealogies of American Families. J.B. Lippincott Co. Phila-
  delphia, Pa. 1894.
Bryan W.S. and Rose Robert:Pioneering Families of Missouri 1876.
Caffrey,Kate: The Mayflower. Stein and Day, NY
Churchill,Allen:The Roosevelts. American Aristocrats. Harper and
  Row, New York, London.
Clemens Wm. M.:American Marriage Records. Biblio Co., Pompton
  Lakes,N.J. 1926
Colonial Dames, Nat. Society, XVII Century. Members' lineages.
Connecticut Historical Society:Collections of the Society,
  Vol. XII 1909.
Cutter, William Richard: New England Families.
Daniell/Sawtele:Thomas Rogers, Pilgrim and Descendants 1980
  Gateway Press Baltimore
Daughters of American Revolution, Missouri.The Cross Roads State
  1964.
Daughters of American Revolution:Service Index, National Society
  Daughters of Am. Rev. 1966.
De Young, Dirk P.:The Ancestry of the Van Schaicks of Manhattan
  and Elsewhere. By author, Avenal N.J. 1938.
Dwight, B.W.:History of Descendants of John Strong
Farmer,John: Genealogical Register of the First Settlers of
  New England. Genealogical Pub. Co., Baltimore Md. 1983
Ferris, Mary Walton: Dawes-Gates Ancestral Lines,Vol.II. 1931.
Holmes,Frank R.Directory of the Ancestral Heads of New England
  Families, 1620-1700. Gen. Pub. Co. Baltimore Md. 1964
Hotten, John Camden: List of Emigrants to America: Genealogical
  Pub. Co. Baltimore, Md. 1974
Kellogg, Lucy Mary:Mayflower Families Through Five Generations
  Vol.1 Published by General Society of Mayflower Descendants
  1975.
King, Everett Marshall: History of Maries Co. Mo. Ramfre Press,
  Cape Girardeau, Mo. 1963
Loomis,Elias and Elisha:Descendants of Joseph Loomis 1875
MacGunnigle:Edward Fuller of the Mayflower Gen.Soc.Mayflower
Mayflower Descendants 1987
Manwaring:Early Probate Records of Connecticut.
Mass. Society of Mayflower Descendants:The Mayflower Descendant.
  Pilgrims Gen. and History, 1900
McGuyre Ruth:Edward Winslow of the Mayflower.Gen. Soc. of
  Mayflower Descendants 1988

502

Miller,Nathan: The Roosevelt Chronicles, Doubleday & Co., Garden
City, NY 1979

Mormon Gen. Society: International Genealogical Index, Salt
Lake City, Utah.

Morningside Cemetery, Hartford N.Y. Tombstone Records.

McCullough,David:Mornings on Horseback. The Roosevelts
Simon & Schuster New York.

Neff, Lewis Edwin:Mayflower Index, The Gen. Society of Mayflower
Descendants. Pub. by The Gen. Soc. of Mayflower Descendants
1960.

New England Hist. and Genealogical Register:Children of Robert
White. Jan.1901.

Olmsted H.K. and C.K. Ward:Olmsted Family in America. 1912.

Otis,Amos: Otis Papers.

Patterson.D. Wm.:George Gates of Haddan,Ct.1865.
Plymouth Colony Records.

Roberts,Gary Boyd:Ancestors of American Presidents. Pub. by the
New England Historic Genealogy Society. Boston, Mass.1989

Daniel/Sawtelle:Thomas Rogers Pilgram.Gateway Press Baltimore1980

Shaw,Hubert Kinney and Eugene Stratton: Families of the Pilgrims.
RICHARD WARREN. Mass. Soc. of Mayflower Descendants. Boston,
Mass. 1981.

Shurtleff,Nathaniel B.:Records of The Colony of New Plymouth, in
New England, 1633-1689. By Legislature of the Commonwealth of
Mass. 1857

Snow,Corine and Frank:Snow Genealogy, Descendants of Nicholas
Snow and Constance Hopkins 1979. Owned by Wallace Snow,
Bradenton, Fl. 1979.

Swift,C.F.: The Amos Otis Papers. Genealogical Notes of Barnstable Families. Pub. by The Barnstable Patriot Press, Barnstable, Mass. 1888

Terry/Harding: Mayflower Ancestral Index. Gen.Soc.Mayflower
Descendants 1981

Tone,Dr, Frank Jerome:History of the Tone Family. Compiled by
Dr. Tone, Niagara Falls, NY 1944.

Townsend/Wakefield/Stover: Degory Priest of the Mayflower
Gen. Soc. Mayflower Descendants 1989

U.S. Census Reports 1790-1900

Van Scoyoc, Melwood:Descendants of Cornelis Aertsen Van Schaick,
Published by author,Sarasota Florida, 1982.

Virkus, Frederick Adams:The Compendium of American Genealogy.
Volumes IV,V,VI,VII. By The Institute of American Genealogy
Chicago., Ill. 1942

Wakefield,Van Wood: Francis Cooke of the Mayflower. Gen.Soc.
Mayflower Descendants. 1987

Wakefield Robt. Isaac Allerton of the Mayflower. Gen.Soc.
Mayflower Descendants 1990

Wakefield Robt.:William Bradford of the Mayflower. Gen.Soc.
Mayflower Decsendants. 1988

Van Antwerp/Radasch/Sherman: Mayflower Families Gen. Soc
Mayflower Descendants. 1975

Wakefield Robt.:Richard Warren of the Mayflower. Pub by The
General Society of Mayflower Descendants 1989

Warner Russell:Miles Standish of the Mayflower. Gen.Soc.Mayflower
Descendants 1988